ELEMENTARY CURRICULUM

A Book of Readings

EDITED BY ROBERT E. CHASNOFF

Professor of Education, Newark State College, Union, N. J.

PITMAN PUBLISHING CORPORATION

NEW YORK • TORONTO • LONDON

PITMAN EDUCATION SERIES

Rychard Fink, General Editor

Foreword

TWO CENTRAL CONVICTIONS dominate *Elementary Curriculum*. First and perhaps most important is the conviction that teachers have classroom decisions to make, and the way the choices are made and what choices are made constitute the difference between effective and ineffective educational programs. In school systems where many requirements are passed down to teachers by their administrative superiors, the teachers sometimes feel that they have no chance to choose anything. But every teacher in every classroom has some margin of freedom. Few or many, there are real decisions to be made: What should I recommend for extra reading? How shall I handle current events? Can I get the children to build their own science material? What is the best way to correct mistakes in writing? The real limitation to educational decision making in the classroom is that many teachers do not know enough about curriculum. A modest revolution may be in the making if this book can persuade those who are teaching and those who are preparing to teach that they have endless choices to make about their programs.

Second, Dr. Chasnoff is convinced of the importance of research findings. The sad truth about educators is that we know far more about teaching and learning that we bother to apply. If those who use this book come to understand this, then perhaps in time we will abandon guess work and rely on solidly proven facts and sound judgment.

This book never overlooks the ultimate educational objective: Our schools must help each young person find his special vision of himself. Dr. Chasnoff is no mere sentimentalist. He simply offers ideas that reflect a wide-ranging concern for the potentialities of the young.

A text with such perspectives should help a great many teachers accomplis a great deal.

RYCHARD FINK

iii

Preface

THIS BOOK about elementary curriculum was prepared with two groups of readers in mind: first, college and university students who are learning about planning the curriculum in elementary schools, and second, beginning in-service teachers.

The definition of the term "curriculum" has changed over the centuries. Until our time, curriculum generally stood for the course of study: the prearrangement of the subjects learners had to encounter. In the Middle Ages, for example, books were not plentiful and each course was generally compressed into a single book. The teacher frequently read the book to his students, and this reading was called a lecture. Thus, the book, the prearranged ideas in it, and the lecture were viewed as the real curriculum.

In this century, curriculum has been given a different meaning. Today, more interest is directed to the learner, to his perceptions, and to his behavior in his social setting. For example, a teacher may wish to teach democracy by ordering his pupils to recite the Gettysburg Address. He may be satisfied that this teaching material contains many ideas about democracy. But if his teaching methods are dictatorial and harsh, his attitudes may be remembered more clearly than his lesson about democracy. Again, suppose a teacher invites pupils to ask questions and to formulate hypotheses about a story they have read. Suppose there is utter chaos in the classroom; then scholarship flies out the window and the result is chaos. Hence, modern educators define curriculum as the pupils' cognitive, affective, social experiences. These experiences, it is believed, are influenced by teachers' methods.

Planning the curriculum, then, means making professional decisions about the experiences that teachers hope pupils will have in school. There are many ways to make these decisions for and sometimes with a group of elementary pupils, because curriculum planning is a creative act and teachers vary in the ways they plan. However, all teachers must make decisions about such questions as:

I. What *objectives* does society expect my pupils and me to achieve?

II. What *ways of teaching* shall I use in my classroom?

III. What *subjects and topics* should my pupils learn?

IV. What means of *evaluation* shall I employ?

V. What are my views on important *issues* being debated by members of my profession?

The five main sections of this book discuss these questions. Part One deals with some aspects of our culture which influence educational objectives. Part Two is concerned with ways of teaching, that is, the methods and materials used in classrooms. Part Three is devoted to some of the subjects and topics commonly taught by teachers and, it is ardently hoped, learned by pupils in elementary schools. Part Four discusses methods of evaluating a wide range of goals, positive uses of tests, and ways of reporting to parents. Part Five contains articles about some important unresolved educational issues. This final part is included because these issues require important curriculum decisions. No doubt these issues will continue to be significant long after readers of this book have gained positions of leadership in education and in society.

Some selections in this book describe typical curriculum approaches in schools, while others describe more advanced educational concepts. Many articles present and interpret research findings. Several articles give special attention to "culturally deprived" or "socially disadvantaged" children. Some articles stress the theoretical. Others describe outstanding school programs. Most articles combine the theoretical and the practical.

This volume was prepared with the belief that teaching is a vocation, an intellectual challenge, a creative act, and a public trust. The tremendous knowledge explosion of the past few decades makes it imperative that teachers not seek pat answers or ultimate solutions to how and what to teach. Teachers need rather to gain the know-how and the will to scholarship which will prepare them to keep abreast of new theories and discoveries about teaching. Thus, the decision-making process for teachers becomes that of deciding what to do with this year's class while keeping a professional eye open to new developments.

Readers of this book must recognize that, in addition to being educators, they are an important segment of the body politic of their immediate communities and of their nation. It is interesting to note that an increasing number of men are finding careers in elementary education stimulating, fulfilling, and significant. Improved financial rewards increasingly make these careers possible. The men and their communities gain. Many women look forward to "split careers." They plan to teach for a few years after completing their higher education, then marry and raise a family, and return to teaching some years later. These women must clarify their thoughts about their several roles, first as young teachers, then as citizen-mothers, and later as mature members of their profession and of their communities. They constitute a significant segment of our population, potentially a knowledgeable and able group. Well-read, intellectually mature, and philosophically sound individuals can exert profound influence upon decisions about professional and social issues. How helpful they can be in aiding others to discriminate between sound educational policy and the recommendations of educational opportunists!

I hope that this book will contribute to the consideration of broad social views as well as to the vocational aspects of education. I hope, also, that teachers will make it a practice to keep informed after their formal education is completed. Reading professional literature is one way to keep in touch. This book will perhaps serve as a formal introduction to many outstanding journals and books in education.

This book does not contain all the answers to all questions about teaching; no single volume can accomplish that. But the book does permit the reader to delve deeply into selected questions rather than to read superficially about many. A bibliography is given at the end of the book for those who will investigate specific topics more fully. This is not a book of recipes. No expert can really tell us what to do if he does not know our particular class. But the selections do contain many practical, realistic suggestions. An expert *can* clarify goals. He *can* point out good practices. He *can* interpret research findings. He *can* excite us with enthusiasm for teaching. In these ways, the authors of these selections can help us make our curriculum decisions.

This book does not provide sections specifically labeled psychology, philosophy, child development, or theories of learning. Nor does the book attempt to teach students the subject matter they must teach. I expect that you have already studied these fields, currently are studying them, and will continue to study them.

Many additional factors enter into becoming an able teacher: reading adult literature, theater and concert going, museum attendance, and travel. Living a life that is fulfilling in a personal and social way also helps a mature adult make appropriate curriculum decisions. These decisions, in turn, may add to a teacher's personal growth.

This book reflects the efforts of many people whose help I would like to acknowledge. Authors and publishers were most gracious in giving permission to reprint the articles herein. My friend and colleague Rychard Fink was as always a constant source of encouragement and intellectual stimulation. Paul Levesque of Pitman Publishing Corporation contributed liberal amounts of patience, scholarship, and skill. For their advice about the conceptual design of the book I would like to thank Patricia Dolan, Maurice Eash, Anna Jane Leinbach, and Jane Morrell. For their many hours of assistance and for their comments on the materials, I wish to thank these teachers-to-be: Jeanne Berard, Joyce Janoff, Carol Lesser, and Felix Schwartz. Special thanks go to Gail Chasnoff for helping in so many ways during the preparation of this book.

ROBERT E. CHASNOFF

Contents

ix

Part Three

THE SUBJECTS WE TEACH   215

Part Four

THE SCOPE OF EVALUATION

Part Five

SOME CURRICULUM ISSUES

Part One

❧

EDUCATIONAL OBJECTIVES

WHAT SHOULD BE the results of our professional efforts in the classroom? We want pupils to learn. What should they learn, we ask, and how do we decide what they should learn? Here we are face to face with a basic curriculum decision. Toward what educational objectives shall we strive?

Part One consists of four chapters designed to help you in your study of the objectives of elementary education. In my introduction to each chapter, I suggest some possible educational objectives. The current social scene as a source of educational objectives is described by selections in Chapter 1. Chapter 2 suggests the kinds of thinking we hope pupils will learn in a nation dedicated to democracy. In Chapter 3 educational objectives are discussed in relation to the efforts of individuals and classroom groups. Chapter 4 concludes this section with articles on classroom discipline—not discipline and order appropriate to a police state, but discipline congruent with a democratic society.

CHAPTER I

Values in Our Society

THE SELECTIONS in this chapter present some of the factors which influence educational objectives. The first selection points up the rapidity of change in "the social sea around us." The second discusses the widespread interest in science and technology. Next, some hard social facts of life are brought to our attention. The final selection outlines beliefs held by the American people about education. In this last selection we read, "The American people have traditionally regarded education as a means of improving themselves and their society."

What broad objectives does society wish our elementary schools to contribute to? I suggest that society wants to produce people with the following qualities:

1. individuals whose healthy sense of personal autonomy and social empathy are reflected in mature personal, social, and political behavior;
2. innovators ready to use their knowledge to devise ways to help rather than exploit others;
3. citizens creative enough to invent, support, and insure peaceful political methods and productive, satisfying lives for all people.

These goals may be attained only by healthy and mature people. This view is supported by a psychiatrist who writes, "I think that what we need to add to the goal of education is something that can be called emotional maturation, ... the harmonious coordination and integration of conscious and unconscious levels of personality."[1]

1. Lawrence Kubie. The psychiatrist considers curriculum development. *Teachers College Record*, 50:246, January, 1949.

The social sea around us

J O H N   R .   S E E L E Y

The "social sea around us" surges with excitement, turbulence, and change. Social values once considered irrevocable certainties have disappeared or have been greatly altered by new ideas. Newly acquired knowledge changes before it is fully comprehended, and educational objectives become more difficult to define, more arduous to fulfill.

IT IS TRUE only in a loose and dangerous way of talking that the school is a reflection of society. If the school is only a reflection of something, it is pointless for educators or parents to get together to talk about school.

But if it is not true that the school is merely a reflection, neither is it true that the school is wholly independent. The school, like other institutions, has the rest of the world for its setting, and from time to time the setting needs to be re-examined.

The educator must be especially concerned with the world in which he lives. For as the world changes, the limitations within which and the opportunities on which the school acts also change. Then, too, the world is part of the subject matter of the educator—the very subject he is supposed to be describing to his students. Finally, only an examination of the world as it now is will give any clues to the world as it will be when the students come into the management of it. It is for this task that school is their preparation. The only sound foundation for that preparation is a realistic appreciation of how things are and some best guess as to how they will be.

The educator who is pressed to look out, clear-eyed, on the world for the sake of his students runs a considerable risk in doing so. He may be so appalled at what he sees, so frightened by the chaos and uncertainty, that he may lose whatever capacity he has to act from day to day on small problems. Every educator must decide for himself whether he will run this risk and whether he can, in conscience, encourage his students to do so if he himself is not willing. For those who care to go forward, I have sketched a view of how the world now presents itself to the educator, together with some reflection on the lines of action still open to him.

.   .   .   .

Ours is a world not only of change but of a transience so rapid that

Reprinted from *The School Review*, 67:422-23, 428-34, Winter, 1959, by permission of The University of Chicago Press. Copyright 1959 by the University of Chicago.

phenomena are—not merely in the long cast of philosophic thought, under the canopy of eternity, but immediately, here and now, in the everyday givenness of life—ephemeral, evanescent. Even in material things—in so-called durable goods—duration is unendurable, and we now have obsolescence planned and built in. In ideas, today's discovery is tomorrow's cliché, and an insatiable press uses every innovation it can make comprehensible to sensation-loving readers, who have been made sensation-loving, even as they are numbed, in the swirl of that tireless output. In values . . . But this is the problem with which we began.

Man, the individual, stands thus at mid-century looking one way to a series of monoliths, the other to an infinitude of unrelated fragments. As he seeks to act on the world, the monoliths—giant state, business monopoly, gigantic union—confront and prevent his effectiveness. As he seeks to gather meaning, organization, value, or strength out of his experience, he encounters a sea of meaningless, disjointed pieces. Small wonder then if, doubting his potency, he lends increased facility and necessity to the very processes that render him without power!

Against these telling, tolling signs, what has modern man to set? Material abundance for all? On the horizon, certainly, if we can limit the blind multiplication of the species. Material power? Yes: power now reaching out beyond the globe to tap on the very firmament itself. Swiftly multiplying knowledge? Quite surely. Possible permanent relief from drudgery both physical and intellectual by way of automation and the automated production of automation? Yes, that too. Almost everything that man has dreamed of lies in his hand or just outside his grasp. Only the want of answers to two related questions threatens to snatch defeat from the very arms of victory: What of man himself? What for? His ultimate nature and his purpose—these still escape man's understanding, and the deficiency renders his triumphs empty and his victories pyrrhic.

And what, in such a world, can the educator do? The least he can do is try to see the world clearly. If he has the courage, he can let the child see something of how the world is, not in a children's version, but as he sees it. He can point to the search. He can even exemplify it. But he cannot lead the child into the promised land, for the dawn is not yet nor the sign of it nor even the direction known from which it is to come. So much at least he might communicate to his students.

A great deal of what has been said so far may seem a counsel of despair. It is just as foolish to despair prematurely as it is to hope inanely. Can we, without inanity, take more hopeful ground?

Curiously, one rational ground of hope—or at least one reason for refusing full access to despair—lies in our knowledge of our ignorance. We now know with certainty, or so it seems, that we live only in a world of probabilities, that determinism in the nineteenth-century sense is an exploded myth. Even in physics, the seemingly safe domain of cause and effect, we now talk of probability distributions, one such distribution being succeeded by another—a very different picture from the neat "A causes B" science on which we grew up. In the social sciences, we have never got beyond dealing with probabilities and have not, hence, had the jolt of the physicists in renouncing comfortable certainty. Even in mathematics—the queen of sciences and the heartland of certainty—we may have to content ourselves with mere probabilistic statements. In at least one of its domains, number theory, where little progress has been made for a long time, some advance now seems possible if the demand for certainty is relaxed to a demand for a probability statement similar to those that we make in the concrete sciences.

Why should one say that such knowledge—knowledge which, if true, means that man is permanently condemned to lack of certainty and therefore, ultimately, ignorance—is ground for hope? I am not sure that one can really go so far. But one can surely argue without excessive optimism that a merely probabilistic universe, whatever emotions it may arouse as to its present state, does not justify despair as to its future. Despair requires certainty: certainty that hope is doomed to defeat. If certainty cannot be had—and it seems that even if we had full knowledge it cannot—then the future cannot be foreclosed on the basis of any knowledge of the present. Sobered we may be or worried or anxious: probability statements are, after all, statements of certainty on the average. But that final qualification should rule out hopelessness in its full impact.

It must be some such argument that justifies so clear-eyed, hard-headed, and knowledgeable a man as J. Robert Oppenheimer in a sort of limited optimism, even in the area immediately surrounding his specialty: international control of atomic energy. Only so can he, presumably, justify his logic in falling back, in the face of utter defeat in the present, on the age-old sustaining view that something must be left to time and nature. See, for example, his famous essay, "The Open Mind."[1] Something must so be left indeed; but only because time and nature embody the very principle of the permanently uncertain future, which is, it now seems "certain," part of the ineluctable condition of man in nature.

When we say that something must be left to time and nature, we are referring clearly to the settlement of our state of hope, not to a principle of

1. *The Open Mind,* New York: Simon and Schuster, 1955, chap. 3.

action. It is not, I take it, being suggested that men should abandon effort or their sense of agency and urgency simply because they recognize that the outcome of action cannot be fully foretold. At least, I hope that no such inference is being drawn. What, then, does this escape hatch from despair imply if it does not permit rest in faith?

It implies, I think, no more than a permissible escape into activity, secure that it is not patently pointless (though it may turn out to be so) nor inescapably futile (though it may turn out to be that). In the face of our circumstances, what activities might we think least surely foredoomed?

The first to come to mind—it goes back to the beginning of this article—is the philosophical or religious quest. The more obvious it becomes that every philosophy now extant, when driven to its logical conclusion, becomes either trivial or contradictory of what is solid in human experience, the more desperate becomes the need for a new philosophy. The more it becomes evident that no existing religion—or combination of them or variation on them—is even remotely likely to command universal assent or even to unify more than it divides mankind, the more urgent does the need of just such a religion become. But neither philosophies nor religions, if the lessons of history mean anything, can be ordered up at will. They cannot be constructed; they occur —like biological mutations in one terminology or the bestowal of grace in another. The most that can be done, if even so much can be done, is to provide the conditions under which such occurrences seem likely. We shall speak further of these later.

The second activity to come to mind is the political quest, a quest that in this generation can hardly mean anything but the quest of peace. The power of modern weapons means that, failing peace, there will be no politics at all. There are no issues in graveyards. It goes without saying that the peace sought must indeed be peace with justice, for if nonpeace implies death, peace without justice implies life not worth living. So we stand. I think we can count on it that the image of peace with justice wakes a responsive thrill in nearly every human breast. But we must also recognize that hardly anyone in power or in prospect of getting power sees a road to peace except through war or by means that almost certainly will bring about what they are designed to avoid.

Only as we are assured that every ounce of available energy is devoted to, and distributed between, these quests, the political and the religious, do other quests and searches make sense. The search for knowledge is idle if we do not know what to do with knowledge or if we can be confident that our civilization will be destroyed before we can use our knowledge. The amassing of more material goods has the same futility: all it can provide is an escape from living into a new sort of galloping consumption, consumption for the sake of consuming, consumption in which what is ultimately consumed is the zest of life itself.

Can educators as educators further these quests or educate persons for them? Even if they can, is it proper for them to do so? While I hold firmly to the view that the school is no place for propaganda, I also think it inevitable that the school in its every activity and in its totality implicitly answers the child's question: What in life is important? The child may refuse the answers the school gives, but he can scarcely fail to note them, inferring them, of course, less from what the school says than from what it is and does. This is, in fact, a propaganda of the act, but it cannot be avoided, nor should it.

If the most vital quests open to the child center on peace and purpose, what can the school do to prepare him? Certainly nothing by adding more functions to an already overloaded institution, nor by adding more courses to an overdiversified and underorganized curriculum. We shall neither make nor encourage philosophers and politicians by adding lessons in philosophy or politics to the curriculum. But just as there is hardly a school subject that does not profitably lend itself to expanding the child's understanding of men and their motives, so also there is hardly a subject that does not raise or lead into philosophical or political questions or both. Whether we seek to convey insight into motives or to stimulate philosophical or political awareness, it is less a matter of adding subjects to be taught than one of enriching their contexts, so that lessons may be learned in their vital bearings. If this is not a program for all students, is it not part of the answer to that cry of despair: What shall we do with the gifted child? If he cannot or should not be pushed too far ahead of his contemporaries in subject matter, could he not, at least, be taught the same subjects in their bearing on the most urgent of contemporary problems?

But an address to the gifted alone is insufficient. What they can do, at best, in our kind of society is conditional upon, and limited by, what the less gifted (or otherwise gifted) will encourage, respond to, or permit. This brings us back to the question left unanswered earlier: What circumstances or conditions might reasonably be expected to encourage or further these quests? We cannot, I feel sure, produce leaders as many a textbook on leadership now recommends. But certain climates of feeling, valuation, and opinion seem to call out leaders. Is it not in such a climate that there arises a sense of vocation? When the sense of being lost is widespread and vivid, when the memory of what has been lost or what is yet to find lies close to every heart, when those who seek are respected and heard because they seek even when they do not find, when the sense of urgency is combined with the sense of imminence, when minds and hearts are open to hope but hardly dare, the climate is perhaps ripe for innovation and hence for at least one more chance for life. Can we encourage such a view? Should we? What other ground for hope can we point to? What other promise worth pursuing can we hold out?

◦◦◦

2   *Science and society: integration through education*

ALAN T. WATERMAN

Our society has always valued technological achievement. In our early days we built canals and bridges, railroads, clipper ships, and steamships. Now we delight in the products of mass production and are excited by the idea of sending rockets far into space. From many corners we hear cries of "More science!"

The author points out the differences between science and technology and defines the following educational objective: "We have an obligation not only to train the scientists that our society requires but to make sure that the entire school population is at least literate in science and has some appreciation of the forces that are shaping our world."

THE WISDOM WITH WHICH we use the new forces of science and technology may well be the deciding factor for our future. Because the rapid advance of technology is now so closely tied to political developments throughout the world, society must not only be aware of the potentialities of science, but nations must learn to cooperate in their constructive use if society as we know it is to survive.

As we develop this theme, we should bear in mind that science and technology should be carefully distinguished. Science generally develops with motivations altogether different from those of technology, and the confusion of the two in the public mind is a common error that leads to widespread misunderstanding. By itself, science seeks only to make new discoveries about

Reprinted from *Teachers College Record,* 64:151-58, November, 1962.

nature and its laws. Pure science demands the utmost in creative imagination, as music, poetry, and art do. Bertrand de Jouvenel observes that,

> No one can become a scientist who is not driven by a primary urge for discovery, who is not the ardent suitor of a hidden beauty. Somewhat romantically, scientists can be likened to a company of knights dispersed in search of Sleeping Princesses, all of whom are more or less distantly related. The spirit of the quest is essential to the making of a scientist and forms a fundamental bond between scientists.[1]

In his book *The Two Cultures* C. P. Snow[2] has advanced the thesis, which has been widely discussed, that there is a deep gulf between the scientist and the humanist, across which there is little or no communication. I do not wholly share Sir Charles's view; I believe there is much closer affinity between the arts and sciences than he avers. Certainly science is an integral part of the cultural milieu and ought to be recognized as such.

SOCIETY'S DECISIONS

Science, in its pure form, is not concerned with where discoveries may lead; its disciples are interested only in discovering the truth. Development, on the other hand, takes the discoveries of science and applies them to a wide variety of human wants and needs, ranging all the way from intercontinental ballistic missiles to the desalination of sea water. Technology encompasses the entire spectrum, beginning with the practical aspects of science and running through development, production, sales, and distribution. It is society that makes the ultimate decision as to the uses to which new discoveries shall be put. Because of the heavy emphasis that has been placed on the role of science and technology in relation to defense and security, we have tended to underappreciate the positive role that scientists are playing and are potentially capable of playing in relation to many other problems that plague the world today.

The pure scientist, working in his laboratory, usually cannot foresee or predict the uses to which his work may eventually be put. Indeed, such is not his aim. Society, therefore, has a double obligation: to support and encourage basic research in all fields, since there is no way of predicting in advance those fields in which important breakthroughs or discoveries may occur; and, as new forces are discovered, to apply them usefully for the betterment of mankind.

History has demonstrated that most capital discoveries have potentialities

1. Bertrand de Jouvenel. The republic of science. *The Logic of Personal Knowledge*, E. Shils (ed.), Glencoe, Ill.: Free Press, 1961.
2. C. P. Snow. *The Two Cultures,* New York: Cambridge University Press, 1959.

for both good or evil. Now that these potentialities have become global, and even extraterrestrial in scope, they have become the concern of all nations. With the first release of nuclear energy, it was clear that international safeguards and controls would ultimately be necessary for the safety of mankind. Progress toward this goal has been disappointingly slow, however. The long stalemate over the nuclear test ban and the limitation on the use of nuclear weapons is one of the frustrations of our time. But there are a few bright spots. One is the Antarctic Treaty, under which twelve nations have agreed to set aside the continent of Antarctica for purely scientific purposes. Another, in the closing days of 1961, was the action of the 103-member Political Committee of the General Assembly of the United Nations in unanimously approving "a resolution calling for the internationalization of space and world cooperation in the use of space satellites for the development of weather forecasting and communication." You will recall that this matter, too, was stalemated for a few years through the Soviet Union's boycott of the meetings of the U.N. Committee on the Peaceful Uses of Outer Space. The reason for the Soviet Union's unexpected action is not known. William L. Laurence, of the *New York Times,* has speculated that the Soviet action may reflect pressure from within its own scientific ranks. If so, it would be a fresh reminder of the proven ability of scientists to cooperate effectively despite national and political differences, and therein lies one of the great hopes for the future.

PACE OF TECHNOLOGY

One of the distinguishing features of the technological revolution is the rapidity with which it moves. Until recent years, the time lag between a basic discovery and its eventual application might be as much as several decades. Now the lead time is shortening considerably. In fact, the technological revolution appears to be proceeding at an accelerating rate. The hypothesis of nuclear fission was put forth at a conference on theoretical physics in Washington, D.C., in January of 1939. The first atomic bomb was dropped at Alamogordo on July 16, 1945, and since that time we have witnessed the rapid development not only of nuclear weapons but of the application of nuclear energy for power, for propulsion, and a host of beneficent uses in medicine and research. It is true, of course, that the development of nuclear energy was achieved in a phenomenally short time because of the war, but in the postwar years, technological progress has continued at an accelerated pace in practically every field. Thus, we have witnessed a revolution in communications and transportation through rapid developments in radio, television, transoceanic telephones and Telstar, and jet air travel.

Chemistry has produced countless new industries based on the discovery and development of plastics. It has also created whole families of synthetic fibers, which after seriously challenging the natural fiber industries, stimulated these to numerous improvements resulting from research. The growth of the synthetic rubber industry has relieved us of dependence upon sources of natural rubber far removed from our own shores. Entire industries are being automated, and we have turned over to the electronic computer a wide variety of industrial and commercial problems that formerly required armies of clerical workers.

Progress in the agricultural sciences has enabled a rapidly diminishing number of agricultural workers to feed an expanding population, with enormous surpluses left over. During the decades of the 1950's, for example, farm output in the United States increased by slightly more than 25 per cent, while the farm population decreased by a little less than 25 per cent.

And finally, the application of science to nutrition, medicine, sanitation, and public health has added years to our lives. The average life expectancy of Americans at birth is now more than twenty years longer than it was at the turn of the century. During the same period, the crude mortality rate dropped 46 per cent, from seventeen deaths per thousand of population in 1900 to nine in the middle 50's. It has been estimated that the number of people now living is between 5 and 7 per cent of the total number of people born during the entire Christian Era.

We cannot take full satisfaction in the high standards of living and the good life which science and technology have produced, however, because these benefits are enjoyed by so relatively small a proportion of the world's population. It is possible, in a few hours of air travel, to go into regions where economic and social conditions are still completely primitive.

Despite the growth of life expectancy from about twenty-five years in the Greco-Roman world to about seventy years in the United States at present, in some areas it is no higher now than it was at the time of Christ. In a recent article on UNICEF, the United Nations organization for the relief of children, the following statement appeared:

> There are estimated to be a billion or more children on earth, and about six hundred million of them live in areas where the average individual income is less than a hundred dollars a year, where most babies in the vulnerable period after weaning receive only protein-deficient, starchy foods, and where malaria, tuberculosis, yaws, trachoma, and leprosy—

any of them or all of them—are widespread. Next year, a hundred million babies will be born, and in the economically underdeveloped countries three out of ten will die before they reach the age of six. Some of the rest—no one knows exactly how many—will be disabled for life by disease and malnutrition.[3]

In the midst of our own teeming surpluses and those of other nations, we are troubled and frustrated by our inability to achieve an equitable distribution. A distinguished member of our National Science Board, Dr. Lee A. DuBridge, who is also president of the California Institute of Technology, has recently observed that from a purely technical standpoint we now know enough to,

> Produce enough food to feed every hungry mouth on earth—and to do this even though the population should double or treble.
> Make fresh water out of sea water and thus irrigate all the world's arid regions.
> Produce enough energy from uranium to light and heat our homes and offices, electrify our railroads, and run all our factories and mills.
> Build houses, buildings, and indeed whole cities, which are essentially weatherproof, heatproof, coldproof, and stormproof—and make every city as nice as California![4]

"But," Dr. DuBridge goes on to point out, "a host of techniques capable of solving mankind's problems and easing his burdens cannot be used because we do not know how to bring adequate resources of money, labor, and materials, and most of all management, to bear on the problems—or bring them to bear in such a way that the results achieved would, in a monetary sense, justify the costs."

EDUCATIONAL LABOR AHEAD

Ultimate solutions to the world's inequalities depend upon the development or capacity on the part of nations with substandard economies to solve their own problems in a way that will enable them to occupy a responsible place in terms of the world economy. Education, of course, is a necessary part of the process. This implies sound education at all levels because it is not possible to create out of an educational vacuum the numbers of trained scientists, engineers, economists, and other specialists to enable a backward nation to compete with its more sophisticated neighbors. To bridge the gap, such spe-

3. J. Wechsberg. At the heart of UNICEF. *The New Yorker, 37*:69-112, December 2, 1961.
4. L. A. DuBridge. How things could be. *Vogue, 139*:72ff., January, 1962.

cialists can be trained and are being trained in other countries. For the long range, however, each nation must, as a practical matter as well as a matter of national self-respect, develop its own system of education and research. To achieve these goals, much work remains to be done. According to UNESCO estimates, about 45 per cent of the world's population is illiterate, and there are some countries where the percentage of illiteracy among the adult population is 80 per cent or higher.

The reduction of poverty, disease, malnutrition, and illiteracy requires the combined intellectual resources of the physical sciences, the life sciences, and the social sciences, as well as the humanities. We need the humanities to help us to see and feel these problems, and the sciences to help us solve them. Fortunately, all these great areas are finding it increasingly possible to share techniques and processes and to work together for the solution of common problems.

There is an ascending order of difficulty in the sciences, and this appears to be linked to the ability to describe a process in exact, quantitative terms. As Lord Kelvin once said:

> When you can measure what you are speaking about and express it in numbers, you know something about it, and when you cannot measure it, when you cannot express it in numbers, your knowledge is of a meagre and unsatisfactory kind.

The physical sciences have made the greatest progress to date because the problems can be expressed in quantitative terms and are susceptible to experimentation. The life sciences are more difficult, dealing as they do with living matter, but the development of new instruments and techniques and the application of some of the methods of the physical sciences have made it possible to deal with life at the molecular level, and progress is increasingly rapid.

The social sciences, which deal not only with the integrated being but with man in society, are understandably most difficult of all. Even here, however, it is gradually becoming possible to adapt some of the approaches of mathematics and the physical sciences. The computer, for example, now makes possible, through the construction of much more complex models than have hitherto been available, an approach to the permutations and combinations that abound in social situations. By a combination of survey techniques and computer simulation of social processes, scientists can, in effect, perform experiments in such complex fields as economics, sociology, and human problem solving.

We should do all that we can to stimulate and encourage the growth of the social sciences as the last and perhaps the most formidable of the research frontiers. In the present world crisis, however, time will not permit us to wait upon research for the solution of the most pressing problems. This does not mean that we should not take advantage of all the sciences can do to help. At a Conference of the Planned Parenthood Association in 1959, Sir Julian Huxley observed,

> What has been called the Revolution of Expectation has begun and will certainly continue. The hungry believe that they could and ought to be fed, the sick that they could and ought to be healthy, the illiterate and ignorant that they could and ought to receive a decent education.[5]

And Sir Winston Churchill, at the Mid-Century Convocation at the Massachusetts Institute of Technology in 1949, commented with characteristic directness that,

> If, with all the resources of modern science, we find ourselves unable to avert world famine, we shall all be to blame, but a peculiar responsibility would rest upon the scientists. I do not believe they will fail, but if they do, or perhaps were not allowed to succeed, the consequences would be very unpleasant because it is quite certain that mankind would not agree to starve equally, and there might be some very sharp disagreements about how the last crust was to be shared. As our greatest intellectual authorities here will readily admit, that would simplify our problem in an unduly primordial manner.

There are two important areas that afford special opportunities for effective cooperation among the natural sciences: They can collaborate, as they have so fruitfully done in the past, in the attack on large-scale scientific problems whose solution requires massive cooperative effort; and they can bring assistance to underdeveloped areas in ways that will help the people to acquire the capacity to solve their own problems.

COOPERATION AND DEVELOPMENT

Let us consider these separately. The long tradition of international cooperation among scientists was brilliantly illustrated in the highly successful International Geophysical Year of 1957-58. You will recall that during that eighteen-month period, the scientists of some sixty-six nations collaborated in intensive exploration of the earth and its environment. The Antarctic program, which received its impetus during the IGY, has developed into a continuing program. The space research program, which began with the earth

5. Reported in the *New York Times* for November 29, 1959.

satellites, also had its inception in the IGY. A feature of all these programs is the interdisciplinary approach that brings to bear on a given problem the specialized knowledge of a number of traditional fields. Thus the IGY and the Antarctic programs employed meteorologists, oceanographers, geologists, and physicists, to name but a few. The space program requires a host of skills, including those of the most theoretical physicists as well as those of the most practical engineers.

The success of such broad undertakings has led scientists to consider other critical areas of science that would lend themselves to large-scale attack by the scientists of many nations and a variety of disciplines. Such a field is oceanography, which has been neglected in the past and which promises rich returns in increased scientific knowledge of a largely unexplored area of the earth's surface as well as information of great economic value about the oceans as a major source of food supply.

In the United States, a major program in oceanography has been recommended by the National Academy of Sciences, projected over a ten-year period. In addition, there is the more recently suggested International Expedition to the Indian Ocean, a scientific project of extraordinary scope and magnitude in which this country is participating. Biologists, chemists, geologists, meteorologists, and other scientists are taking part in this effort which began late in 1960 and will extend through 1964. The program is expected to increase greatly man's knowledge of the Indian Ocean's 28 million square miles, which cover 14 per cent of the earth's surface about which relatively little is known or understood. Under the nongovernmental sponsorship of the International Council of Scientific Unions and its Special Committee on Oceanic Research, the expedition consists of vessels provided by marine laboratories of nations experienced in oceanographic research. A special effort has been made to obtain participation by each nation bordering the Indian Ocean. The biology and meteorology programs of the U.S. effort are being organized in such a way that scientists from nations that are not planning to man research vessels may apply for U.S. support if they wish.

At the Seventh Conference on Science and World Affairs, an international group of scientists, meeting together as private citizens rather than as representatives of their respective governments, worked out and proposed a detailed program for international cooperation in science.[6] The program calls for international cooperation in such fields as exploration of the oceans and of the earth's crust and mantle; cooperation in space research, in the preservation and promotion of health, in studies of the effects of pollution on the

6. Conferences on science and world affairs. *Science,* 134:984-99, 1961.

earth's atmosphere and water, and cooperation in fields requiring such large-scale facilities as high-energy physics, controlled thermonuclear and plasma research, ultra-heavy-element chemistry, and large-scale computers. Such a program, if adopted by the nations, would result in important increments of scientific knowledge and would give scientists a positive role to play to balance somewhat the magnitude of the scientific effort that is presently going into military research and development.

THE PROMISE

The challenges and the promise of science—particularly in such large-scale programs as space research—could readily absorb both the money and the energies that nations have in the past devoted to far less fruitful occupations, such as the harassment of their neighbors. Science and technology are now a matter of keen rivalry among nations, but such rivalry could be directed into more constructive channels. Perhaps it is not too much to say that in the present state of affairs, science, especially in its more fundamental aspects, is one of the few subjects on which nations can agree.

Assistance to developing countries, the second great area in which the scientists of the world can fruitfully cooperate, must be undertaken as far as possible on a partnership basis between the scientists representing technologically sophisticated nations and those of nations that are seeking to develop their intellectual and physical resources. It is not surprising that the scientists themselves are already thinking along these lines. An International Conference on Science in the Advancement of New States was held in Rehovoth, Israel, in 1960. A similar conference on the application of science and technology to the problems of new nations was held in August, 1961 in Geneva under the sponsorship of the United Nations.

The problems are complex because the newer nations are naturally eager to superimpose the fruits of technological progress on an economy and an educational system which are not yet equal to the strains of the new technology. As noted by the Seventh Conference on Science and World Affairs, assistance to developing nations must be closely linked to problems of education in all its aspects. There are some problems for which immediate assistance is required, while others will require steady and long-range planning.

Still another fruitful area of cooperation, which can also be related to assistance to developing nations, is the exchange of scientists. From time immemorial, scientists and other scholars have traveled from country to country, enriching themselves and their colleagues as they went through the sharing of knowledge. Their contribution to international understanding and to the progress of science would be greatly enhanced by the provision of financial support and government backing to make such exchanges possible on a much larger scale.

I do not mean to imply in these remarks that science possesses some special formula with which it could successfully solve all the world's problems if it were given sufficient funds and a free hand. I do hope I have emphasized, however, that there are a number of important areas in which the scientists of many nations might usefully work together. Some of these are intellectual, the marshaling of the world's scientific resources for concentrated attack on the unknown; others are practical, in the form of assistance—in an atmosphere of minimum political consideration—toward removing the blights of poverty, malnutrition, and disease that continue to spawn trouble and unrest.

POLITICAL QUESTIONS

Whether the scientists are given the opportunity to collaborate in both these areas is dependent in considerable measure upon the understanding and backing of their governments. James Reston, the *New York Times*'s competent observer of the Washington scene, observed in a recent column,

> In one field after another, the nations of the West have discovered since the war that they cannot solve an increasing number of major problems by themselves. First, it became evident that the poverty of Europe immediately after the war affected the political security of the whole free world: hence the Marshall Plan. Then it was seen that the separate national armies of the Atlantic could not withstand the pressures of the Soviet Union: hence the North Atlantic Treaty Organization.
>
> Now this principle of common action on common problems is spreading to economic and monetary problems, and in due course will no doubt spread even beyond Britain to the United States in an effort to find new partners of trade, a coordinated lowering of tariffs, a common means of dealing with agricultural surpluses and a joint program for stabilizing commodity prices and helping underdeveloped nations.[7]

Mr. Reston might also have included science as another and already proven area to which the principle of common action on common problems could be applied.

In closing, I should like to sound one note of warning. The pursuit and exploitation of science impose profound responsibilities. Capital discoveries are only just beginning, and continued progress will inevitably raise issues of the deepest social significance. Whether future developments take the form of stupendous power over nature's resources, of influence and control over

7. From Mr. Reston's column in the *New York Times* on December 13, 1961.

life or over men's minds, or of traffic with our sister planets, they will certainly create problems of such concern to the human race that mankind will have no choice but to cooperate in their solution.

Outstanding breakthroughs should not be permitted to become the subject of hostile competition or to be exploited without adequate study of the possible consequences. The emphasis that has been given to nuclear development foreshadows potentialities of other possible developments, such as the ability to alter climate materially or to apply genetic research findings without proper safeguards and control. Although these developments have not yet been realized, they are well within the realm of possibility. This nation and all nations have a solemn obligation to maintain an awareness of such possibilities and to make certain that new developments are used constructively and in the interests of mankind.

It follows, too, that a public awareness of science and its implications is of the utmost importance. We have an obligation not only to train the scientists that our society requires but to make sure that the entire school population is at least literate in science and has some appreciation of the forces that are shaping our world. The establishment of scientific literacy must begin in the earliest grades and continue through the highest levels of education. The scientific revolution has overtaken the present generation of adults—taken it by surprise, as it were—but much can be accomplished through vigorous and imaginative programs. Tomorrow morning, pick up your newspapers and note how many headlines relate in some way to the impact of science and technology upon our lives. Can we afford to ignore or fail to understand the forces that are doing so much to shape our future and the future of our children?

3   *Sociological perspective on the education of culturally deprived children*

ELEANOR P. WOLF

LEO WOLF

This article shows us that our country's magnificent ideals are marred by the stark reality of poverty and social disintegration and by our frequent failure to face them. "Culturally deprived" may not be the most adequate term to describe vast numbers of people, but there are youngsters who are cold and underfed, who grow up with a feeling that the majority in our society do not like them and will not help them. Their deprivation—and society's—is real.

We have a tendency to think of the city as the sole stage on which the massive drama of deprivation is being played. We must remember that this is also a rural phenomenon.

DURING THE PAST FEW years there has been an increasing recognition of the importance of social class as a variable that affects the processes of learning and teaching in the public schools. Not only have a great many educators in administrative, training, and supervisory positions learned the language of sociology, but many classroom teachers as well as students in colleges of education have become more aware of pertinent sociological research and have been alerted to the implications of these findings. After years during which many school people considered the term "social class" part of the vocabulary of a snob rather than a concept useful in understanding behavior, interest in social stratification has assumed almost the proportions of a fad in some school systems. Undergraduates in training speak knowingly (and disapprovingly!) of the middle-class biases of teachers, and in classroom discussions they remind one another that many behavior patterns of lower-class children (sexual precocity, physical aggression, profane language) are likely to disturb teachers and create barriers between them and the children they are trying to teach.

At the same time, a number of the school systems in our great metropolitan centers are attempting to launch attacks on the deficiencies in the education of the so-called culturally deprived or culturally disadvantaged children. There has never been greater interest or more discussion of sociocultural variables in personality development and educational growth. In-service training programs, workshops, conferences, and committees are grappling with the special problems of such children, and there is much talk of stimulus-deprivation, urban-assimilation, middle-class values, and negative self-images. Sociologists cannot but be gratified at this recognition of the tremendous importance of sociocultural factors. Increased sensitivity to social factors in learning and a deepened knowledge of the consequences of class position are immensely valuable, and the spread of this information throughout the teaching profession represents a great step forward. Even more encouraging is the determination of many dedicated persons on all levels of the school system to develop programs designed to improve the education of those children who seem to be in greatest need of such assistance.

Because these efforts are important and because they have engaged the energies and stirred the hopes of many of the most valuable members of the teaching profession, it is necessary to maintain proper perspective. Exaggerated claims and expectations only contribute to a sense of frustration and failure when unrealistic goals prove unattainable. Closely related to this danger is the problem of the distortion of knowledge as it is transferred and incorporated from the parent discipline to the applied field. Thus, the educational philosophy associated with John Dewey became at times almost unrecognizable by the time it was articulated at the level of certain practitioners. The observations that follow are made in the hope of avoiding these pitfalls.

1. *There is sometimes a tendency to overgeneralize and oversimplify the problems of minorities by focusing mainly on the similarities between groups while neglecting crucial differences.* A recent call to an excellent "education for opportunity" conference illustrates this orientation very well:

> The newcomer into the Northern, urban industrial social milieu generally encounters subjective and objective problems, and we believe that *these problems are similar for those from predominantly white Southern hill sections, the Negro from Southern rural areas, the new in-migrant to the United States, as well as for local citizens of lower socio-economic groups* [italics ours].[1]

There are certainly some points of similarity, but there are even more striking crucial differences that are of considerable importance to the schools. Teachers who have recently encountered "new in-migrants to the United States" from Europe, for example, have typically found such children to be suffering mainly from language difficulties and the sense of strangeness and dislocation that is the lot of all newcomers. (Many have had more rigorous training in some subjects than most American children.) It would puzzle a teacher to suggest that the educational problems he confronts with such children are similar to those he faces with a group of poverty-stricken Negro children whose whole life and background represent deprivation and subordination. It is true that present-day European newcomers are in many respects an unusual group. But more than twenty years ago John Dollard, to

1. *Conference Call,* Michigan Fair Employment Practices Commission, February 9, 1961.

mention but one example, called our attention to the significant differences between immigrants and Negroes in American society. Speaking of European immigrants he said:

> They came here under the spur of ambition and with the intention to take every advantage of American opportunities. . . . They know America as the "land of opportunity"—the land of rapid rise in economic position and social status and their anticipations are organized around this conception. Once here there are no categorical barriers put in their way and they are able to continue their determined fight for social advancement.[2]

Gunnar Myrdal documents this thesis in many sections of *An American Dilemma*.[3] The authors of *Who Shall Be Educated?* noted in 1944 that "the theory of the melting pot does not work for the Negro. . . . The school cannot help him as it has the immigrant, *for his problem is different* [our emphasis]. If American education could have functioned for the Negro as it did for our ethnic groups, the Negroes as variant people would have long since disappeared from American life." Warner, Havighurst, and Loeb do not suggest that the schools cannot help the Negro child in his struggle for advancement —indeed they indicate how this can be done—but they do point out that they cannot help in the same way, because the problems are vastly different.[4]

We have so little European immigration now that this is a relatively minor phase of our problem. The few who do come to our shores are usually urbanized, many are prepared to work at a trade or profession, and they have some resources, either personal or organizational assistance. There seems no point in including this small and strikingly different group in the umbrella concept of "newcomers to the city." Mexicans and Puerto Ricans (if they can escape the designation *Negro*) have problems somewhat more like those of the masses of low-status European immigrants of the past, made more acute by the declining need for unskilled labor and other changes in the American economy. The special case of the Southern white in-migrant has been described by William Simon as "standing . . . on the very borders of ethnicity . . . they are characterizable by three factors that tend to facilitate access to desirable status positions. They are white, Anglo-Saxon, and Prot-

2.   John Dollard. *Caste and Class in a Southern Town*, New Haven, Connecticut: Yale University Press, 1937, pp. 428-29.
3.   Gunnar Myrdal. *An American Dilemma*, New York: Harper and Brothers, 1944, especially chap. 3, sects. 1 and 2. See also chaps. 1 and 2 of James B. Conant's *Slums and Suburbs*, New York: McGraw-Hill Book Company, 1961, which appeared some months after the Wolfs had completed their manuscript.
4.   W. Lloyd Warner, Robert J. Havighurst, and Martin B. Loeb. *Who Shall Be Educated?* New York: Harper and Brothers, 1944, especially p. 139.

estant . . ."[5] After discussing some of the problems now faced by these people in our big cities, Simon goes on to predict for them a probable course of development different at once from both the Negro and the foreign-born:

> Mobility will tend to be an individual occurrence within a context that provides little necessity for continued group identification or participation. It is almost a matter of definition; with upward mobility one merely ceases to be a hillbilly and becomes a southerner—the two are not the same.[6]

The assertion by sociologist Nathan Glazer that "there is no natural history of migration" may seem to some an overstatement.[7] But there is no doubt that the combination of visibility—the physical marks of race—and the history of slavery, later transformed into a castelike system of social relations, is unique in American society. No other minority group in our nation has problems comparable in severity to those of the Negro. Even when economic status is held relatively constant, the inferior social status of the Negro appears to have a depressing effect on educational achievement.[8] These uncomfortable truths ought not to be obscured by euphemistic references to newcomers and minority groups.

2. *There is a tendency to exaggerate the nature and scope of the influence that schools can wield.* It has often been pointed out that the public schools are peculiarly vulnerable to attack. Certain structural features of the institution make the system accessible; at the same time there are widely shared beliefs within American culture that attribute great power to the educative process. Thus, the anxiety of the public over communism found some segments of society fearfully scrutinizing the schools for evidence of subversion, while other groups insisted that the school play a more active role in immunizing against the infection. Shock at sputnik was instantly translated into a widespread attack on school failure and efforts to greatly increase school emphasis on the physical sciences. Racial tensions during World War II were largely responsible for the development of widespread programs of intercultural education in the schools, designed to promote intergroup understanding.

5.   William R. Simon. Southern white migrants: ethnicity and pseudoethnicity. *Human Development,* 1:20-24, Summer, 1960 student publication, Committee on Human Development, University of Chicago.
6.   *Ibid.,* p. 22.
7.   Nathan Glazer (in book review of Oscar Handlin's *The Newcomers*). *Commentary,* 29:266, March, 1960.
8.   Martin Deutsch. *Minority Group and Class Status as Related to Social and Personality Factors in Scholastic Achievement,* Ithaca, New York: Society for Applied Anthropology, Cornell University, 1960.

Periodic concern over the alleged increase in mental illness often results in the focusing of attention on the psychological traits of teachers and provokes demands that they assume certain quasi-therapeutic or diagnostic functions.

It is worth noting, at least, that some scholars believe that we cherish excessive expectations of what schools can accomplish. For example, in a recent discussion of the effectiveness of school programs designed to improve intergroup relations, H. D. Schmidt, of the Institute for Advanced Study, reminded us that these programs are based on the assumption "that it is primarily the schools which transmit the heritage of the past to the young, and that the schoolroom is therefore the place where group antagonism can most effectively be rooted out." He goes on to say:

> But these beliefs are based on an exaggerated estimate of the influence of teachers and preachers in Western society generally, and in particular of their influence on the minds of the young. . . . Evidence both of a sociological and psychological character now exists, in fact, which strongly suggests that the school plays only a minor role in the development of basic social attitudes among children, and that the *teacher is almost powerless in this area unless his work is visibly substantiated and backed up by the society in whose midst he operates* [italics ours].[9]

In the present movement the schools are being asked to solve many problems that American society has failed to solve. (This is perhaps epitomized by the "bus-ing" of school children in New York City to achieve racial integration, an effort made necessary by the failure of our cities to substantially alter segregated patterns in housing.) Generally, the schools are being asked to improve the economic and social position of deprived children through education, to break through the vicious circle of low education—low socioeconomic status that now exists. Specifically, the schools are being asked to compensate for the massive deprivations from which these children have suffered and to stimulate and motivate them to learn and achieve. Such a program, it seems to us, can be of tremendous significance if careful distinctions are made between what the schools can and cannot do.

We might consider some of the limitations that must be faced in developing a workable program for the schools.

First, the schools cannot create aspirations on the part of the overwhelming majority of deprived and apathetic children if the surrounding society gives the lie to such hopes. In his study of today's urban poverty Michael Harrington observes:

> The decline of aspiration among slum dwellers partly reflects a sophisti-

9. H. D. Schmidt. Bigotry in schoolchildren. *Commentary*, 29:253-57, March, 1960.

cated analysis of society: for the colored minorities there *is* less opportunity today than there existed for the white population of the older ethnic slums, and the new slum people know this. *The poverty of their myths reflects the poverty of their reality* [italics ours].[10]

Many educators are not aware of the extent to which marked differentials between income of Negroes and whites persist at varying levels of education.[11] For example, if we compare all families where the family head has completed only eight years of schooling, the median family income is $4,487 for whites, $3,167 for nonwhites. Nonwhite median family income is thus seen to be approximately 70 per cent of white family income. If we compare only families where the head has completed high school, the gap still remains: median family income for whites is $5,742, for nonwhites it is $3,929, about 68 per cent of white family income. Current unemployment statistics show a similar disproportion. A recent study prepared for the National Urban League summarizes this problem: "Unemployment rates for nonwhite males since 1951 usually have been twice as high as rates for white males, and frequently two and one half times as high."[12]

Parenthetically, it is ironic that even in some school systems that are much involved in programs to increase aspiration levels of culturally deprived children one can find evidence of discrimination against Negroes. The presence of Negro teachers in all-white schools and their employment, when qualified applicants are available, as administrators and supervisors of white subordinates might be more effective as spurs to lagging ambition than many other methods being discussed.

Second, there is little the schools can do to compensate for the fact that the new slum dwellers are often fatherless families, in contrast to the immigrant families of the past, which, though under stress, were usually intact. Further, in a great many cases, problems of family instability are compounded by the effects of residential mobility. This movement (which often, though not always, involves school changes) is at present being intensified in many areas by displacement because of urban renewal programs. Some of the talk heard at conferences and meetings is a bit glib and overly optimistic. Father images are not supplied by contacts with men teachers; self-conceptions are not re-formed by words of praise, nor is a sense of emotional security restored by a friendly smile. All these are desirable in and of themselves, but the school

10.   Michael Harrington. Slums, old and new. *Commentary*, 30:119-24, especially 120-21. August, 1960.
11.   This information and the data that follow are taken from Table 13, P-60 Series, Bureau of Census, United States Department of Commerce, 1958.
12.   Mollie Orshansky and Thomas Karter. Economic and social status of the Negro in the United States, 1961. New York: National Urban League, 1961, p. 20.

is not a primary group, and thus far there is little evidence that teachers can, in a school setting, restructure basic personality.[13]

Third, how many social-welfare functions can the school assume? There is a tendency to take other aspects of our social structure as given and concentrate our fire on the most vulnerable institution—the public school. Thus we note the many suggestions that the local elementary school in the slum or multiproblem area become the focal point of neighborhood organization, the instrument for adult education, the recreation center for adults as well as children, and the coordinating agency for all children's social services. It has been suggested that teachers visit the homes of all pupils regularly and participate in local neighborhood affairs and action programs. Yet research indicates that pupils in such schools already suffer from inadequate time devoted to teaching; the actual number of minutes of instruction is startlingly low in some classrooms.[14] Teachers are already burdened with a number of seemingly unavoidable tasks such as saving-stamp sales; sale and distribution of milk; collection of lunch money; vision checks; hall, playground, and lunch duties; and general record-keeping. All these tasks drain time and energy.

There is undoubtedly merit in some of the plans for the use of the school as the coordinating center of a many-faceted program for children, but these functions cannot be piled on the duties of the present staff. The problem of staffing the difficult school has already begun to assume serious proportions. It must be made clear that such proposals would require considerable reorganization as well as additional staff trained in these fields. However, the use of other facilities ought to be seriously considered. It might well be that aggressive programs in family casework, for example, could be conducted much more effectively by augmented and expanded social-work agencies quite apart from the school system.

3. *We must guard against a tendency to scapegoat the individual classroom teacher. Teachers are often confronted by contradictory admonitions.* For example, those who work with deprived children are frequently criticized for expecting too much of them:

> We know that by and large teachers are middle class in value orientation and tend to treat all children "alike" or to assume they are "normal."

13. In this connection see *Husbands and Wives* by Robert Blood and Donald Wolfe, Chicago: Free Press, 1960, chap. 2, for suggestive evidence that even the intimate relations of family life do not offset the powerful impact of societal status on the role of the husband in marriage. Regardless of the presumably endless variations in family climate and wife's personality, low-status husbands in this study tend to be weak in their decision-making power in the home.
14. Deutsch, *op. cit.,* p. 23.

. . . The demands of the traditional middle-class-value geared and middle-class socially functioning school are unrealistic and punitive for too many of the disadvantaged children.[15]

In his distinguished monograph, Martin Deutsch, discussing the poor test performance of lower-class Negro children, notes that such children do not expect "future rewards for present activity" and goes on to say:

This inconsistency between the lack of internalized reward anticipations on the part of the Negro child and *his teacher's expectations that he does have such anticipations* reflect the disharmony between the social environment of the home and the middle-class oriented demands of the school [emphasis ours].[16]

However, another observation frequently encountered is that expressed by Eleanor Leacock, in her commentary in the same monograph: "teachers' *low expectations* for these children are reflected by the children's lack of expectations for themselves" (emphasis ours).[17]

Obviously, if teachers' expectations are high, they are unrealistic and may be punitive. But if expectations are low, they reinforce the child's low esteem and reflect what is sometimes (not, we hasten to add, in the materials quoted) alleged to be teacher prejudice. This dilemma is reflected in the plaint frequently heard from teachers who work in schools in changing neighborhoods. They often report that if they adhere to the same grading standards they used with previous (more privileged) populations they may be accused of prejudice, or at least harshness, as demonstrated by a large number of failures and poor grades. But if they alter their grading system, they may be accused of relaxing standards to the detriment of their new pupils.

Another example of the damned-if-you-do, damned-if-you-don't dilemma is the contention that the middle-class background of teachers, with their ingrained propriety and respectability, seriously hampers their effectiveness with deprived children. But some (often within the same speech or article) assert that even worse is the teacher from a lower-class background, anxious to establish social distance between himself and his lower-class pupils. Similarly, it is stated that the lower-class child is handicapped in school and underachieves academically because he lacks middle-class work habits and values that stress order, neatness, and punctuality. Yet the presentations of these values, their

15. August Kerber. An experimental project to improve the school experiences of culturally deprived children and the in-service education of their teachers. Mimeographed memorandum, Detroit: College of Education, Wayne State University, no date.

16. Deutsch, *op. cit.,* p. 23.

17. *Ibid.,* p. 31.

display and demonstration by teachers, are often held to be a handicap in the educational process and an occasion for reproaches to be hurled against them. Just how important are these behavioral factors in their effect on the role of the school as an instrument for social mobility?

We are in no position to answer the question we have raised. But it may be an aid to better perspective to recall that although some observers have attributed much importance to the role of the schools in assimilation of European immigrants, their success could hardly be traced to the desirable behavior of the teachers of that era:

> From the desk the teacher looked down, a challenge they dared not meet. . . . What an arsenal was at her command to destroy them! The steel-edged ruler across the knuckles was the least of her weapons. Casually she could twist the knife of ridicule in the soreness of their sensibilities; there was so much in their accent, appearance, and manners that was open to mockery. . . . As she snapped shut the closet upon the symbols of her ladyhood within—the white gloves, the rolled-up umbrella, and the sedate hat—she indicated at once the superiority of her own status. There was visible evidence of her correctness in her speech and in her bearing, in her dress, and in the frequent intimations of the quality of her upbringing. Perhaps a few were touched with sympathy at the condition of their charges. But what these offered was pity, nobler than contempt, but to the children no more acceptable. It was rare indeed to find the dedicated woman whose understanding of her students brought a touch of love into her work. After all, it was not this they had dreamed of in normal school . . . that they would devote the rest of their lives to the surveillance of a pack of unwashed ruffians. Mostly the teachers kept their distance, kept flickering the hope that a transfer might take them to a nicer district with nicer pupils from nicer homes. When that hope died, bitterness was born; and there was thereafter more savagery than love in their instruction.[18]

In this vivid passage the historian Oscar Handlin re-creates for us the public school in the era of great immigration. Yet apparently it did function fairly effectively as an instrument of acculturation for the immigrant pupil:

> If it did nothing else to the child, the school introduced into his life a rival source of authority. The day the little boy hesitantly made his way into the classroom, the image of the teacher began to compete with that of the father. The one like the other laid down a rigid code of behavior, demanded absolute obedience, and stood ready to punish infractions with swift severity. The day the youngster came back to criticize his

18. Oscar Handlin. *The Uprooted*, Boston: Little, Brown and Company, 1951, pp. 247-48.

home (*They say in school that . . .*) his parents knew they would have to struggle for his loyalty.[19]

What enabled the schools to exert influence, if the teacher's attitude toward the pupils was often as unsympathetic as the quoted passage suggests?[20] The key can be found, we believe, in the fact that the child was surrounded by enough examples of success, enough instances of upward movement, to really believe in these possibilities. Herein lies an all-important difference. As Schmidt has pointed out, "the teacher is almost powerless . . . unless his work is visibly substantiated . . . by the society in whose midst he operates."[21] The school that taught the immigrant's children reflected the basic approach of American society toward the European immigrant. This approach encouraged assimilation and amalgamation; it was the theory of the melting pot. The prevailing American attitude toward the Negro, by contrast, as Myrdal and others have pointed out, is still one of anti-amalgamation and social segregation. In addition, a decreased demand for unskilled labor has made it much more difficult for disadvantaged groups to get an initial foothold on the economic escalator. These factors, rather than the shortcomings of individual teachers, appear to be of considerably greater importance in explaining our difficulties in the education of lower-class Negro children.

The literature is replete with exhortations to teachers in today's slums to try to overcome the apathy and listlessness of their disadvantaged pupils. Yet there is ample evidence that such children typically come to school (or stay home from school) undernourished, inadequately clothed, without sufficient sleep (partly because of severe overcrowding of their dwellings), and with untreated physical ills, sometimes of an acute nature—such as toothaches. A dramatic illustration of the significance of these conditions was recently seen in the Detroit area when a thousand low-income Negro pupils from the Carver school district were placed under the jurisdiction (after considerable controversy too lengthy to be reported here) of a middle-class, all-white suburb, Oak Park. Little notice had been taken of the conditions under which these children were trying to learn until they became the responsibility of the Oak Park system. Then, in the words of J. N. Pepper, superintendent of schools: "It looks as if we'll have to begin at the beginning. In this case the beginning

19.   *Ibid.,* p. 244.

20.   An abundance of anecdotal material indicates that the educational methods and teacher attitudes of the old-country Jewish *cheder,* for example, would scandalize modern educators. Yet it would be hard to exaggerate the high regard in which learning and scholarship were held by the over-all community, and these factors were apparently far more influential than teacher behavior in developing children's attitudes toward education. See Mark Zborowski and Elizabeth Herzog, *Life Is with People,* New York: International Universities Press, Inc., 1962.

21.   Schmidt, *op. cit.,* p. 253.

is to get these children healthy enough to learn."[22] The school officials went on to call attention to "nonexistent health records," to the fact that only a few of these children had been inoculated against serious contagious disease, and to evidence of malnutrition. These conditions had long existed in the Carver school district, and they are common in slum schools in our great cities. But one rarely hears any demands that the medical or dental profession do something about the health needs of these children. Ordinarily it is teachers who hold meetings and conferences where they wonder rather hopelessly what they can do to teach these children who come to them hardly fit to learn.

One cannot help noting that the practice of focusing attention on the shortcomings of teachers and on educational materials and techniques serves to distract attention from more basic (and less easily attacked) problems. For example, a subject currently much discussed at teachers' conferences on under-privileged children is the extent to which illustrations and story content of textbooks should reflect middle-class life. We noted earlier that we tend to attribute exaggerated powers to the educational system, partly, at least, because it seems more accessible to our intervention rather than because it truly plays the role we ascribe to it. Similarly, in considering the ways in which our educational system itself meets the learning problems of deprived children, there is a tendency to concentrate on the variables that are most readily manipulated. Especially attractive are the programs (like those designed to change teachers' attitudes) that do not require substantial expenditures. Unfortunately, these are not necessarily the programs that will be most effective.

It is far from our purpose to provide any kind of rationale for a do-nothing policy or a defeatist attitude toward the problems of disadvantaged children. Their special needs confront us with all the unsolved problems in American education, problems that have begun to bore us with their wearisome recalcitrance, their stubborn refusal to go away: not enough good teachers, too-large classes, not enough facilities for emotionally disturbed or mentally retarded children, not enough money for trips, equipment, remedial teaching, and other enrichment programs—and all the rest. Children who have been deprived at home and in the community need more of all these aids to learning, but they usually get less.[23] Even more disturbing is the way these children accuse us of our continued failure to solve basic problems of American society —inadequate health care, slum housing, prolonged unemployment, segregation, and discrimination.

---

22. *Detroit News,* December 4, 1960, p. 23A.
23. For impressive evidence of inequalities in the educational facilities provided for lower-class children in a large school system see Patricia C. Sexton, *Education and Income,* New York: Viking Press, 1961.

Despite all this, much can be done, and is being done every day, by gifted and compassionate teachers, working against great odds. The present pioneering efforts of the Higher Horizons programs and the Great Cities project will provide invaluable information for future planning. There has long been a tendency for many gifted and sensitive teachers to avoid the slum school, not because they are lazy or indifferent, but because they feel inadequate and helpless in the face of overwhelming odds. We need to remember the magnitude of problems they face and not add to these burdens by excessive expectations. Rather, as educators who can also act vigorously as citizens, we must redouble our efforts to improve the social and economic conditions under which slum children live and which so profoundly affect their learning.

❧

4   Education in the American society

EDUCATIONAL POLICIES COMMISSION

From time to time, various professional organizations ask groups of educators, other distinguished scholars, and prominent citizens to formulate broad educational policy statements. Reprinted below is Part I of a statement by the Educational Policy Commission, written at the invitation of the National Education Association and the American Association of School Administrators.

The commission describes rational powers as "central to all other qualities of the human spirit" and defines these powers as fundamental educational objectives. How are rational powers related to the emotional aspects of human experience?

IN ANY DEMOCRACY education is closely bound to the wishes of the people, but the strength of this bond in America has been unique. The American people have traditionally regarded education as a means for improving them-

Reprinted from *The Central Purpose of American Education*, National Education Association and American Association of School Administrators, Washington, D.C., 1961, pp. 1-12.

selves and their society. Whenever an objective has been judged desirable for the individual or the society, it has tended to be accepted as a valid concern of the school. The American commitment to the free society—to individual dignity, to personal liberty, to equality of opportunity—has set the frame in which the American school grew. The basic American value, respect for the individual, has led to one of the major charges which the American people have placed on their schools: to foster that development of individual capacities which will enable each human being to become the best person he is capable of becoming.

The schools have been designed also to serve society's needs. The political order depends on responsible participation of individual citizens; hence the schools have been concerned with good citizenship. The economic order depends on ability and willingness to work; hence the schools have taught vocational skills. The general morality depends on choices made by individuals; hence the schools have cultivated moral habits and upright character.

Educational authorities have tended to share and support these broad concepts of educational purposes. Two of the best-known definitions of purposes were formulated by educators in 1918 and 1938. The first definition, by the Commission on the Reorganization of Secondary Education, proposed for the school a set of seven cardinal objectives: health, command of fundamental processes, worthy home membership, vocational competence, effective citizenship, worthy use of leisure, and ethical character. The second definition, by the Educational Policies Commission, developed a number of objectives under four headings: self-realization, human relationship, economic efficiency, and civic responsibility.

The American school must be concerned with all these objectives if it is to serve all of American life. That these are desirable objectives is clear. Yet they place before the school a problem of immense scope, for neither the schools nor the pupils have the time or energy to engage in all the activities which will fully achieve all these goals. Choices among possible activities are inevitable and are constantly being made in and for every school. But there is no consensus regarding a basis for making these choices. The need, therefore, is for a principle which will enable the school to identify its necessary and appropriate contributions to individual development and the needs of society.

Furthermore, education does not cease when the pupil leaves the school. No school fully achieves any pupil's goals in the relatively short time he spends in the classroom. The school seeks rather to equip the pupil to achieve them for himself. Thus the search for a definition of the school's necessary contribution entails an understanding of the ways individuals and societies choose and achieve their goals. Because the school must serve both individuals and the society at large in achieving their goals, and because the principal goal of the American society remains freedom, the requirements of freedom set the frame within which the school can discover the central focus of its own efforts.

The freedom which exalts the individual, and by which the worth of the society is judged, has many dimensions. It means freedom from undue governmental restraints; it means equality in political participation. It means the right to earn and own property and decide its disposition. It means equal access to just processes of law. It means the right to worship according to one's conscience.

Institutional safeguards are a necessary condition for freedom. They are not, however, sufficient to make men free. Freedom requires that citizens act responsibly in all ways. It cannot be preserved in a society whose citizens do not value freedom. Thus, belief in freedom is essential to maintenance of freedom. The basis of this belief cannot be laid by mere indoctrination in principles of freedom. The ability to recite the values of a free society does not guarantee commitment to those values. Active belief in those values depends on awareness of them and of their role in life. The person who best supports these values is one who has examined them, who understands their function in his life and in the society at large, and who accepts them as worthy of his own support. For such a person these values are consciously held and consciously approved.

The conditions necessary for freedom include the social institutions which protect freedom and the personal commitment which gives it force. Both of these conditions rest on one condition within the individuals who compose a free society. This is freedom of the mind.

Freedom of the mind is a condition which each individual must develop for himself. In this sense, no man is born free. A free society has the obligation to create circumstances in which all individuals may have opportunity and encouragement to attain freedom of the mind. If this goal is to be achieved, its requirements must be specified.

To be free, a man must be capable of basing his choices and actions on understandings which he himself achieves and on values which he examines for himself. He must be aware of the bases on which he accepts propositions as true. He must understand the values by which he lives, the assumptions on which they rest, and the consequences to which they lead. He must recognize that others may have different values. He must be capable of analyzing the situation in which he finds himself and of developing solutions to the problems before him. He must be able to perceive and understand the events of his life and time and the forces that influence and shape those events. He must recognize and accept the practical limitations which time and circumstance place on his choices. The free man, in short, has a rational grasp of himself, his surroundings, and the relation between them.

He has the freedom to think and choose, and that freedom must have its roots in conditions both within and around the individual. Society's dual role is to guarantee the necessary environment and to develop the necessary individual strength. That individual strength springs from a thinking, aware mind, a mind that possesses the capacity to achieve aesthetic sensitivity and moral responsibility, an enlightened mind. These qualities occur in a wide diversity of patterns in different individuals. It is the contention of this essay that central to all of them, nurturing them and being nurtured by them, are the rational powers of man.

THE CENTRAL ROLE OF THE RATIONAL POWERS

The cultivated powers of the free mind have always been basic in achieving freedom. The powers of the free mind are many. In addition to the rational powers, there are those which relate to the aesthetic, the moral, and the religious. There is a unique, central role for the rational powers of an individual, however, for upon them depends his ability to achieve his personal goals and to fulfill his obligations to society.

These powers involve the processes of recalling and imagining, classifying and generalizing, comparing and evaluating, analyzing and synthesizing, and deducing and inferring. These processes enable one to apply logic and the available evidence to his ideas, attitudes, and actions, and to pursue better whatever goals he may have.

This is not to say that the rational powers are all of life or all of the mind, but they are the essence of the ability to think. A thinking person is aware that all persons, himself included, are both rational and nonrational, that each person perceives events through the screen of his own personality, and that he must take account of his personality in evaluating his perceptions. The rational processes, moreover, make intelligent choices possible. Through them a person can become aware of the bases of choice in his values and of the circumstances of choice in his environment. Thus they are broadly applicable in life, and they provide a solid basis for competence in all the areas with which the school has traditionally been concerned.

The traditionally accepted obligation of the school to teach the fundamental processes—an obligation stressed in the 1918 and 1938 statements of educational purposes—is obviously directed toward the development of the ability to think. Each of the school's other traditional objectives can be better achieved as pupils develop this ability and learn to apply it to all the problems that face them.

Health, for example, depends upon a reasoned awareness of the value of mental and physical fitness and of the means by which it may be developed and maintained. Fitness is not merely a function of living and acting; it requires that the individual understand the connection among health, nutrition, activity, and environment, and that he take action to improve his mental and physical condition.

Worthy home membership in the modern age demands substantial knowledge of the role that the home and community play in human development. The person who understands the bases of his own judgments recognizes the home as the source from which most individuals develop most of the standards and values they apply in their lives. He is intelligently aware of the role of emotion in his own life and in the lives of others. His knowledge of the importance of the home environment in the formation of personality enables him to make reasoned judgments about his domestic behavior.

More than ever before, and for an ever-increasing proportion of the population, vocational competence requires developed rational capacities. The march of technology and science in the modern society progressively eliminates the positions open to low-level talents. The man able to use only his hands is at a growing disadvantage as compared with the man who can also use his head. Today even the simplest use of hands is coming to require the simultaneous employment of the mind.

Effective citizenship is impossible without the ability to think. The good citizen, the one who contributes effectively and responsibly to the management of the public business in a free society, can fill his role only if he is aware of the values of his society. Moreover, the course of events in modern life is such that many of the factors which influence an individual's civic life are increasingly remote from him. His own firsthand experience is no longer an adequate basis for judgment. He must have in addition the intellectual means to study events, to relate his values to them, and to make wise decisions as to his own actions. He must also be skilled in the processes of communication and must understand both the potentialities and the limitations of communication among individuals and groups.

The worthy use of leisure is related to an individual's knowledge, understanding, and capacity to choose, from among all the activities to which his time can be devoted, those which contribute to the achievement of his purposes and to the satisfaction of his needs. On these bases, the individual can become aware of the external pressures which compete for his attention, moderate the influence of these pressures, and make wise choices for himself.

His recreation, ranging from hobbies to sports to intellectual activity pursued for its own sake, can conform to his own concepts of constructive use of time.

The development of ethical character depends upon commitment to values; it depends also upon the ability to reason sensitively and responsibly with respect to those values in specific situations. Character is misunderstood if thought of as mere conformity to standards imposed by external authority. In a free society, ethics, morality, and character have meaning to the extent that they represent affirmative, thoughtful choices by individuals. The ability to make these choices depends on awareness of values and of their role in life. The home and the church begin to shape the child's values long before he goes to school. And a person who grows up in the American society inevitably acquires many values from his daily pattern of living. American children at the age of six, for example, usually have a firm commitment to the concept of fair play. This is a value which relates directly to such broad democratic concepts as justice and human worth and dignity. But the extension of this commitment to these broader democratic values will not occur unless the child becomes aware of its implications for his own behavior, and this awareness demands the ability to think.

A person who understands and appreciates his own values is most likely to act on them. He learns that his values are of great moment for himself, and he can look objectively and sympathetically at the values held by others. Thus, by critical thinking, he can deepen his respect for the importance of values and strengthen his sense of responsibility.

The man who seeks to understand himself understands also that other human beings have much in common with him. His understanding of the possibilities which exist within a human being strengthens his concept of the respect due every man. He recognizes the web which relates him to other men and perceives the necessity for responsible behavior. The person whose rational powers are not well developed can, at best, learn habitual responses and ways of conforming which may ensure that he is not a detriment to his society. But, lacking the insight that he might have achieved, his capacity to contribute will inevitably be less than it might have become.

Development of the ability to reason can lead also to dedication to the values which inhere in rationality: commitment to honesty, accuracy, and personal reliability; respect for the intellect and for the intellectual life; devotion to the expansion of knowledge. A man who thinks can understand the importance of his ability. He is likely to value the rational potentials of mankind as essential to a worthy life.

Thus the rational powers are central to all the other qualities of the human spirit. These powers flourish in a humane and morally responsible context and contribute to the entire personality. The rational powers are to the entire human spirit as the hub is to the wheel.

These powers are indispensable to a full and worthy life. The person in whom—for whatever reason—they are not well developed is increasingly handicapped in modern society. He may be able to satisfy minimal social standards, but he will inevitably lack his full measure of dignity because his incapacity limits his stature to less than he might otherwise attain. Only to the extent that an individual can realize his potentials, especially the development of his ability to think, can he fully achieve for himself the dignity that goes with freedom.

A person with developed rational powers has the means to be aware of all facets of his existence. In this sense he can live to the fullest. He can escape captivity to his emotions and irrational states. He can enrich his emotional life and direct it toward ever higher standards of taste and enjoyment. He can enjoy the political and economic freedoms of the democratic society. He can free himself from the bondage of ignorance and unawareness. He can make of himself a free man.

THE CHANGES IN MAN'S UNDERSTANDING AND POWER

The foregoing analysis of human freedom and review of the central role of the rational powers in enabling a person to achieve his own goals demonstrate the critical importance of developing those powers. Their importance is also demonstrated by an analysis of the great changes in the world.

Many profound changes are occurring in the world today, but there is a fundamental force contributing to all of them. That force is the expanding role accorded in modern life to the rational powers of man. By using these powers to increase his knowledge, man is attempting to solve the riddles of life, space, and time which have long intrigued him. By using these powers to develop sources of new energy and means of communication, he is moving into interplanetary space. By using these powers to make a smaller world and larger weapons, he is creating new needs for international organization and understanding. By using these powers to alleviate disease and poverty, he is lowering death rates and expanding populations. By using these powers to create and use a new technology, he is achieving undreamed affluence, so that in some societies distribution has become a greater problem than production.

While man is using the powers of his mind to solve old riddles, he is creating new ones. Basic assumptions upon which mankind has long operated are being challenged or demolished. The age-old resignation to poverty and inferior status for the masses of humanity is being replaced by a drive for a life of dignity for all. Yet, just as man achieves a higher hope for all mankind, he sees also the opening of a grim age in which expansion of the power to create is matched by a perhaps greater enlargement of the power to destroy.

As man sees his power expand, he is coming to realize that the common sense which he accumulates from his own experience is not a sufficient guide to the understanding of the events in his own life or of the nature of the physical world. And, with combined uneasiness and exultation, he senses that his whole way of looking at life may be challenged in a time when men are returning from space.

Through the ages, man has accepted many kinds of propositions as truth, or at least as bases sufficient for action. Some propositions have been accepted on grounds of superstition; some on grounds of decree, dogma, or custom; some on humanistic, aesthetic, or religious grounds; some on common sense. Today, the role of knowledge derived from rational inquiry is growing. For this there are several reasons.

In the first place, knowledge so derived has proved to be man's most efficient weapon for achieving power over his environment. It prevails because it works.

More than effectiveness, however, is involved. There is high credibility in a proposition which can be arrived at or tested by persons other than those who advance it. Modesty, too, is inherent in rational inquiry, for it is an attempt to free explanations of phenomena and events from subjective preference and human authority, and to subject such explanation to validation through experience. Einstein's concept of the curvature of space cannot be demonstrated to the naked eye and may offend common sense; but persons who cannot apply the mathematics necessary to comprehend the concept can still accept it. They do this, not on Einstein's authority, but on their awareness that he used rational methods to achieve it and that those who possess the ability and facilities have tested its rational consistency and empirical validity.

In recent decades, man has greatly accelerated his systematic efforts to gain insight through rational inquiry. In the physical and biological sciences and in mathematics, where he has most successfully applied these methods, he has in a short time accumulated a vast fund of knowledge so reliable as to give him power he has never before had to understand, to predict, and to act. That is why attempts are constantly being made to apply these methods to additional areas of learning and human behavior.

The rapid increase in man's ability to understand and change the world and himself has resulted from increased application of his powers of thought. These powers have proved to be his most potent resource, and, as such, the likely key to his future.

THE CENTRAL PURPOSE OF THE SCHOOL

The rational powers of the human mind have always been basic in establishing and preserving freedom. In furthering personal and social effectiveness they are becoming more important than ever. They are central to individual dignity, human progress, and national survival.

The individual with developed rational powers can share deeply in the freedoms his society offers and can contribute most to the preservation of those freedoms. At the same time, he will have the best chance of understanding and contributing to the great events of his time. And the society which best develops the rational potentials of its people, along with their intuitive and aesthetic capabilities, will have the best chance of flourishing in the future. To help every person develop those powers is therefore a profoundly important objective and one which increases in importance with the passage of time. By pursuing this objective, the school can enhance spiritual and aesthetic values and the other cardinal purposes which it has traditionally served and must continue to serve.

The purpose which runs through and strengthens all other educational purposes—the common thread of education—is the development of the ability to think. This is the central purpose to which the school must be oriented if it is to accomplish either its traditional tasks or those newly accentuated by recent changes in the world. To say that it is central is not to say that it is the sole purpose or in all circumstances the most important purpose, but that it must be a pervasive concern in the work of the school. Many agencies contribute to achieving educational objectives, but this particular objective will not be generally attained unless the school focuses on it. In this context, therefore, the development of every student's rational powers must be recognized as centrally important.

CHAPTER 2

Children's Thinking

THIS CHAPTER and the two that follow present a framework for understanding how the elementary school and the teacher can contribute to the objectives suggested in Chapter 1. This chapter deals with children's thinking. Thinking has been described as follows:

> Thinking is a process rather than a fixed state. It involves a sequence of ideas moving from some beginning, through some sort of pattern of relationships, to some goal or conclusion.[1]

This statement raises the following questions: Which thinking processes are congruent with the values associated with a democratic society? Which are most helpful for the attainment of personal goals? A well-known senator observes:

> Our constant objective in education must be the cultivation of the free mind—the mind which is free of dogma, cant, and superstition, free to fulfill the highest measure of its capacity, free to explore the limitless realm of ideas and values.[2]

An educator asserts:

> To tell an American child—the inheritor of Thomas Paine, Thomas Jefferson, Walt Whitman, and Abraham Lincoln—*what he must think* is to deny him his inheritance.[3]

This chapter views some kinds of thinking that I believe are appropriate and useful for free men and women—sequential and interrelated thought, creative thought, problem solving.

1. David Russell. *Children's Thinking,* Boston: Ginn and Company, 1956, p. 27.
2. J. W. Fulbright. The American agenda: evaluation of our society. *Vital Speeches of the Day,* 29:523-24, June 15, 1963.
3. V. M. Rogers. Textbooks under fire. *The Atlantic,* 195:48, February, 1955.

5 Not so fast

NORMAN COUSINS

A former teacher who is a well-known commentator on the social and political scene writes about sequential thought, fragmentation, effective thinking, and "speed-up."

THE ULTIMATE TEST of education is represented by the ability to think. We are not talking about casual or random thought. We are talking about sequential thought, that is, the process by which one frame of ideas is attached to another in workable order so that they fit together without rattling or falling apart the moment they come in contact with a logical objection or query.

Sequential thought is the most difficult work in the entire range of human effort. Even when undertaken by a highly trained intelligence, it can be enormously fatiguing. When attempted by untrained minds, it can produce total exhaustion within a matter of minutes, sometimes seconds. For it requires an almost limitless number of mental operations. The route must be anticipated between the present location of an idea and where it is supposed to go. Memory must be raked for relevant material. Facts or notions must be sorted out, put in their proper places, then supplied with connective tissue. Then comes the problem of weighting and emphasis.

Sequential thought, like any other advanced form of human activity, is the result of systematic training. Just sitting in front of television screens watching baseball games for a dozen years or more doesn't automatically qualify a man to throw strikes with blazing speed. Either he has the educated muscles to pitch or he hasn't. The same is true of thought. A man who doesn't know how to use the muscles of his intelligence can hardly be expected to cope with a problem requiring concentration and the ability to think abstractly.

How, then, can a person be taught to think sequentially? It isn't necessary to devise special courses of study for this purpose. All that is necessary is for existing courses to foster those conditions that promote proper habits of thought.

Fragmentation is the enemy of sequential thought. Yet there is a large degree of fragmentation in the way a youngster is called upon to meet his educational obligations. He may have four or five different courses of study. In the space of a few hours he has to shift his focus of attention drastically several times, resulting often in a blurring of the significance of what he is being

Reprinted from *The Saturday Review*, 46:14, July 6, 1963.

taught. Each class or course tends to be something of a universe in itself. This may provide welcome relief in some cases but it also violates many of the basic laws of concentration as they apply to intellectual absorption and retention. This is hardly reassuring at a time when the relationships among the various fields of learning have become a prime need in education.

Homework assignments are only rarely correlated. On some nights a student may have three or four major assignments, making it virtually impossible to do them all adequately. We have never been able to understand why a homework paper in history, say, and an assignment in English composition cannot be combined. Far better to give a youngster a chance to put his history paper into decent English than to require him to go racing through separate assignments in both subjects. More basic still: why shouldn't the school attempt some measure of coordination in homework assignments, with each course having at least one night a week in which genuine concentration and sustained work would be expected and made possible?

H. L. F. Helmholtz, the noted German physicist who died thirty years ago, described three principal stages in effective thinking. In the first stage, a problem is carefully examined in all its aspects and all directions. In the second stage, ample time is allowed for a problem or an idea to get through to the subconscious in order that the mind may work on it and develop it even when not specifically focused on it. The third stage involves the conditions or circumstances under which an idea is brought to full term and makes its appearance. Helmholtz's analysis may not hold for all people—nothing is more individualistic than a man's thoughts—but at least he emphasizes the need for thought about thinking. Most of our confusion, James Harvey Robinson once wrote, comes from this failure to give thought to thought.

If we are to help Johnny to think—which is to say, if we are to help him become truly educated—it becomes necessary to respect the natural requirements of thought. Somewhere along the line in recent years, a speed-up has taken place in large areas of education. Johnny is expected to read faster, study faster, write faster, and think faster. No doubt, this is less the fault of educators than of the world itself. But the problems posed by an Age of Speed are not met by snap judgments, one-page memos on complex subjects, lightning-fast reading techniques, or rapid writing. We meet our problems only as we comprehend them and give them sustained and sequential thought. The quickest way to compound these problems is to put them in a pressure cooker.

6   How children build meanings

LOUIS RATHS

"Our own actions in a situation are steppingstones to meaning."
How does Louis Raths' statement relate to our definition of cur-
riculum?

THE WORLD STARTS its work of impressing meanings upon us as soon as we
are born. The first and probably the most persistent meanings come to us in
these early years. We are participants in situations which involve love and
hate and indifference; intense activity and quiet; excitement and monotony;
laughter and grief; accomplishment and failure; pride and guilt; poise and
anxiety; and a thousand-and-one others.

These meanings are not thrust upon us without our involvement. Very
early we must venture to think or to guess the character of a situation and as
we act we find our judgment confirmed, rejected, or neglected. It is through
this continuing testing of our opinions that we build meanings.

We learn thus to listen for the feelings that are behind the words. We find
cues relating to rewards or deprivations for us, and these cues help us to identify the meaning of each new situation. We use past experience to find new
meanings in the present but it is in the "here and now" that they are tested.

Our own actions in a situation are steppingstones to meaning. If we act
aggressively and it leads to success for us, we more readily recognize the cue
for the expression of aggression. And so with other kinds of responses, we
learn through the consequences of our doing, and slowly and steadily we
build our meanings and make them a part of the world in which we live.

The learning of new meanings is probably best achieved where this
learning is a shared experience—if others, near and dear to us, are also concerned. Out of this sharing we can assert or deny; exchange opinions or be
quiet; we can test ourselves in shared action, and this is probably mankind's
greatest good.

We build meanings also in spontaneous and imaginative play and in rev-
erie. As children we try out hundreds of the ideas suggested to us by things
and fantasy, by songs and dreams, and by people in our environment. We need
freedom to dream, to imagine, and to try; through the use of that freedom we
venture to build meanings.

Reprinted by permission of the Association for Childhood Education International,
3615 Wisconsin Avenue, N.W., Washington 16, D.C. "How children build meanings,"
by Louis Raths. From *Childhood Education,* December, 1954, Vol. 31, No. 4, pp.
159-60.

Sometimes the meanings which we have built become stumbling blocks. Usually these meanings are rigid: the "never, never change" kind. Probably the context in which we acquire meanings has the greatest influence upon flexibility or rigidity. If the reward or deprivation was for us very intense, if those whom we love and respect were rigid or flexible, our own meaning will be considerably influenced.

As we grow older we become involved with more social institutions all of which have their patterns of action. These institutions tend to impose requirements upon us and they reward and penalize our conduct. Through our participation we learn the cues for action; we watch others, we imitate, and we experience the consequences of our behavior. In this context the school begins to have certain larger meanings for us; so does the church, industry, government, communications, and the others.

And as we learn to read, new areas of experience are opened to us and to the extent that we can identify cues, generate opinions of our own, try them out, or share them in a "testing" manner with others, we continue the task of building meanings. As with reading, so with the arts and music and play and work. We need almost boundless opportunities for exploring the world and as the range increases, and opportunity to share increases, we more richly and more securely build meanings.

Inevitably it happens that some of our meanings conflict with each other. Our attempts to resolve these differences are the central character of child development. We *develop* as we integrate the meanings we have experienced. We do this through puzzling over the conflict; through reflecting upon it. We try sometimes to choose one or the other. On other occasions we see a middle ground or a synthesis. On still other occasions we go forward, confused and uncertain. We build meanings as we tackle the never-ending job of reducing these conflicts born of our own experience.

If *our* meanings are so greatly influenced by those whom we love, cherish, and respect, and who hold us dear, it probably follows that if we as a group have very different home-and-experience backgrounds, that our meanings also will differ significantly. How these differences are handled by the adults around us and by our peers are also strong determinants of meaning. If *our* meanings gained from *our* experiences are frowned upon—are devalued—it constitutes a rejection of *our* life, and that is intolerable to every one of us so treated.

There are two major reasons for the pride in and defense of our own experience. Meanings tend to persist and to have a large share in guiding our lives. Meanings which we hold uniquely identify us as individuals. We are what we believe; at least we act so, and hence we want respect for what life has meant to us and our development.

In the second place, we have come to learn that there is no single "right" meaning for everybody. Just as we respect the meanings of others and share in testing them, so do we expect an initial acceptance and further testing of the meanings which we bring to a situation. If those around us have genuine respect for us, they will not want to remake us into images of themselves. They will respect what is unique in our own living and so will encourage us to share with them the aim of being ourselves. Under these circumstances we, too, can contribute to a world which expects so much from us and yet seems to have so little time to listen or to share.

7   *The taxonomy: guide to differentiated instruction*

JOHN JAROLIMEK

Educators must translate theory about thinking into usable terms. Such a task was attempted by a distinguished group of educators and psychologists, whose first report, Taxonomy of Educational Objectives, Handbook I: Cognitive Domain (1956) *is viewed as a basic statement in education. It must be carefully studied by all students of education. A second volume* (Handbook II), *dealing with the affective domain, appeared in 1964.*

In this article, the author uses the six categories of educational objectives proposed in Handbook I *and brings them closer to the actual job of planning for teaching. Jarolimek, a social studies specialist, uses his field to illustrate the taxonomy.*

DISCUSSIONS OF differentiated instruction in the social studies ordinarily focus upon variations to be made in learning activities which the pupil is expected to perform. Most frequently the recommendations have to do with variations in reading requirements or variations in work-study activities. The teacher is advised to use more difficult reading material with the more capable pupil than with the less able one. Similarly in the case of work-study activities, the

Reprinted from *Social Education,* 26:445-47, December, 1962.

suggestion is made that the able pupil be directed toward activities which involve more independent research, more reading and elaborative thinking than his slower-learning classmate. In general, these recommendations are sound ones; but they are apt to be something less than adequate unless, in addition, careful consideration is given to the complexity of the intellectual tasks with which each of the pupils is going to concern himself.

Varying the difficulty of intellectual tasks relating to a social studies unit is a procedure which seems to have received less attention from teachers than it deserves. The hope is that if pupils are placed in reading materials of varying difficulty and are involved in varying types of instructional activities, this will, in itself, result in some differentiation of instruction with respect to complexity of learnings. No doubt this occurs to some extent. However, variations in complexity should be a deliberate and planned part of the teaching plan rather than be allowed to come about by a happy accident. In order to build such diversity in conceptual complexity into the program, one needs to begin with instructional objectives. The procedure under consideration here would hold general objectives constant, but would vary specific objectives in terms of the capabilities of individual pupils.

In an effort to plan deliberately for differentiated instruction in terms of the complexity of intellectual operations, the teacher may find Bloom's *Taxonomy of Educational Objectives, Handbook I: Cognitive Domain*[1] to be a helpful model. The *Taxonomy* classifies various types of educational objectives into six groups or categories as follows:

1. Knowledge	4. Analysis
2. Comprehension	5. Synthesis
3. Application	6. Evaluation

These are ordered in terms of a hierarchy representing an increasingly complex set of cognitive relationships as one moves from category one to category six. Behaviors in each succeeding category are to some extent dependent upon an understanding of related objectives in a prior category. Subheads of each of the six categories indicate that they, too, are ordered from simple relationships to complex ones. Hence, children in the primary grades need not concern themselves solely with objectives in the knowledge category but may make applications, analyses, and evaluations providing these are kept simple and clearly within the realm of direct experience.

It is perhaps true that the bulk of elementary social studies instruction concerns itself with objectives represented in category one—*Knowledge*. This

1. Benjamin S. Bloom *et al. Taxonomy of Educational Objectives, Handbook I: Cognitive Domain,* New York: Longmans, Green & Company, 1956.

includes knowledge of specifics, facts, terminology, events, etc. To a degree, an emphasis on knowledge is inevitable at early levels since pupils are rapidly building their cognitive structure. However, the knowledge category is itself spread along a continuum ranging from a knowledge of specifics to a knowledge of universals and abstractions in a field. Pupils of varying abilities might be expected to deal with different specific objectives in the knowledge category. Instruction is limiting and narrow when all pupils deal with knowledge objectives pertaining only to specifics, facts, terminology, and events.

The teacher must, of course, be concerned with objectives in category one—*Knowledge*—because it is fundamental to all of the others. Particularly important would be the development of a knowledge of the terminology of the social studies. Without a grasp of the vocabulary, the pupil is unable to consider problems in social studies thoughtfully. Knowledge of specific facts is important, too, not as an end in itself but because such specifics are prerequisite to the achievement of more complex intellectual objectives. Objectives in this category are relatively easy to teach and evaluate because they depend almost entirely upon recall of information. They have traditionally been a part of the social studies curriculum in most schools and consequently are familiar to teachers. While they are important, at the same time this does not give the teacher license to teach them in ways which are educationally and psychologically unsound.

In addition to knowledge of specifics, one finds in this category two other types of knowledge objectives. The first of these—"knowledge of ways and means of dealing with specifics"—would seem to have especial significance for the social studies. Included would be such knowledge of conventions as might be called for in the understanding of procedures in various affairs of citizenship—how a bill becomes a law, how government officials are elected, how laws are enforced, and so on. It deals, too, with trends and sequences such as knowledge of events which led up to more important events, steps in the production of goods, or the chronology associated with historical developments. The third large subhead entitled "knowledge of the universals and abstractions in a field" constitutes the highest order of the knowledge category. In the social studies it would call for a knowledge of major generalizations relating to the social sciences as these are forged out of the varied experiences of pupils. An example of such a generalization would be "Man's utilization of natural resources is related to his desires and his level of technology."

The second large category—*Comprehension*—requires somewhat more complex intellectual activity than recall, as is the case in the knowledge category. "Translation" and "Interpretation" are the two facets of comprehension most appropriate for elementary social studies. Data gathering brings the pupil into contact with a great variety of source materials. He uses maps, charts, graphs, encyclopedias, atlases, and others. Data so abstracted must be translated into usable form for the purpose of problem solving. Literary material, when used, requires both translation and interpretation. Much of the social studies reading material is presented in highly condensed form and has within it many possibilities for interpretation and extrapolation. If pupils are to avoid making "bookish" reports, for example, they need to be able to make a translation of the material into their own everyday language. Social studies programs could be greatly enriched, especially for the capable pupil, by directing greater attention to objectives which fall into this category—translation, interpretation, and extrapolation.

The third category is called *Application*. It means essentially that the pupil is able to use what he learns; that he can bring his knowledge to bear upon the solution of problems. Numerous authors have called attention to the need for pupils to apply what they learn. Many interesting and stimulating experiences for children have resulted in situations where imaginative teachers have provided opportunities for children to apply what they have learned to life about them. Applications of learning may be represented by some classroom activity such as dramatic play, a construction, or a report given to the class; or they may include a service project in conservation, school government, or community service. Applications need not manifest themselves in overt behavior; applications may be made wholly at the intellectual level. The pupil may, for example, apply and use knowledge previously gained in thinking creatively about new problems or situations. Perhaps most of the applications which are made are of the intellectual type.

Categories four and five—*Analysis* and *Synthesis*—represent high-order intellectual processes. In the case of analysis, the pupil must delve into the subject to a sufficient depth to perceive its component elements, relationships, or organizational principles. Such procedure enhances the development of concepts in depth, for the pupil is led to ever finer discriminations in what is relevant and what is irrelevant with reference to topics under study. Problems in the social studies oftentimes seem deceptively simple because an inadequate analysis is made of factors relating to them. It is only when one explores a problem in depth and makes a careful analysis of fundamental elements, relationships, or organizational principles that he appreciates the complexity of it. Many elementary pupils are ready for the stimulation which such analyses could provide.

While analysis calls for the isolation of relevant data, synthesis requires the bringing together of related elements and reorganizing them into new cognitive structures. In the *Taxonomy*, synthesis is further described as "the production of a plan or proposed set of operations," or the "derivation of a set of abstract relations." For elementary social studies, synthesis can be represented by the reporting of research which a pupil has conducted over a period of time. The reporting of work done on "Pupil Specialties" would be a case in point. Bright pupils find this to be an especially challenging and interesting learning experience. A capable fifth- or sixth-grade child can, through accumulated research, present an amazingly well-prepared synthesis if he has proper guidance from his teacher.

The final category—*Evaluation*—concerns itself with judgments. It assumes a considerable knowledge of the topic on the part of the pupil in order to make such judgments. To some extent it demands the use of learnings which are represented in all of the other categories. Judgments, according to the *Taxonomy*, are of two types—those based on internal evidence and those based on external criteria. Internal evidence would constitute evaluation made on the basis of clearly recognized standards with respect to internal consistency, organization, or structure. For example, a pupil looks at a map and must decide whether or not it is a correct and honest representation—rivers cannot be shown to run toward higher elevations; cities cannot be placed across rivers; colors used on the map must be consistent with those in the key, and so on. Charts, graphic material, or written reports should not contain conflicting data. A mural showing the life of the Woodland Indians should not show an Indian weaving a Navajo blanket. Judgments of this type are not especially difficult to make when one is thoroughly familiar with the material and knows what standards to apply. Judgments in terms of external criteria probably involve a level of criticism too complex and much too involved to be handled by elementary-school-age children.

It is apparent that the *Taxonomy* has much to recommend its use as a model in planning for differentiated instruction in elementary social studies. The teacher would have to become thoroughly familiar with it and with the types of objectives which might be placed in each of the categories. Perhaps the teacher would find it helpful to prepare the various categories in chart form, and in planning a unit, list possible objectives in the various categories. Use of the *Taxonomy* may also result in objectives stated more clearly in behavioral terms, as has been suggested by some authors.[2] Thus, with a knowl-

2.   Dale P. Scannell and Walter R. Stellwagen. Teaching and testing for degrees of understanding. *California Journal for Instructional Improvement,* 3:1, 13, March, 1960.

edge of the capabilities of individual members of his class, the teacher could move pupils in the direction of those objectives which are best suited to their abilities. This would ensure that all categories had been considered and that ideas would be dealt with at varying levels of difficulty.

Thus, as the teacher plans his unit, he makes a careful analysis of the topic to be studied. Then he identifies specific, attainable objectives which could be classified in several categories included in the *Taxonomy*. In accordance with this knowledge and a knowledge of the pupils he teaches, he plans appropriate learning activities which make the attainment of those objectives possible. Combining this procedure with other generally accepted practices for individualizing instruction, the teacher would present his class with a highly diversified and stimulating attack on the study of problems in the elementary social studies. Certainly the *Taxonomy* deserves further investigation not only in terms of its usefulness in curriculum improvement but also as a guide to the teacher in differentiating instruction.

8 *Creativity and the gifted child*

PAUL R. GIVENS

The author documents the need for a more professional definition of a much-abused term, "the gifted." He also describes some of the ingredients of creative thinking, another generally misunderstood concept. Be sure to notice that thinking is not divorced from the unconscious: "Nonconscious processes are extremely important in creative intelligence."

THE WORD "UNDERSTANDING" has been identified with the gifted child for so many years that psychologists and others often lose sight of the fact that "creativity" is also an important aspect of human cognition. In our enthusiastic support of the high I.Q. child, clinicians and researchers alike often feel that the intelligence quotient is a God-given formula which is descriptive of the total range of possible cognitive functions. Getzels and Jackson in their

Reprinted from *Educational Theory*, 13:128-31, April, 1963.

engaging research report remark, "On the contrary, the items on the typical intelligence test seemed to us to represent a rather narrow band of intellectual tasks. . . . To do well on the typical intelligence test, the subject must be able to recall and to recognize, perhaps even to solve; he need not necessarily be able to invent or innovate."[1]

This introduction is to emphasize that the word "gifted" is in need of a new definition. For too long we have made distributions of I.Q.'s, determined the cut-off point, and labeled the top group "gifted." The dimension of creativity has been ignored, minimized, or allocated to the arts and given the highly enigmatic label, "talent."

Guilford, who instigated the present scholarly enthusiasm for the systematic study of creativeness in his 1950 APA presidential address, said, "If the correlations between intelligence test scores and many types of creative performance are only moderate or low, and I predict that such correlations will be found, it is because the primary mental abilities represented in those tests are not all important for creative behavior."[2]

Since this insightful guess, there are research hints that this is the case. Guilford himself has developed tests of "convergent" thinking and "divergent" thinking which seem to measure distinctly different aspects of cognition. The first category includes those who tend to "play it safe"; persons for whom risk is too uncertain. The divergent thinker will, as Gardner Murphy suggests, "let the mind leave harbor and travel fearlessly over an ocean of new experiences."

Maslow submits that there is evidence of two kinds of creativity, primary and secondary. Primary creativeness includes, "the source of new discovery, of real novelty, of ideas that part from what exists at this point." He suggests that this type of creativity draws primarily from the unconscious. Secondary creativity is more a rational productivity which requires the patience of a deliberate analytical-minded scientist.[3] Perhaps presently we measure secondary creativity and call it "intelligence" but have yet to discover the secrets of primary creativeness.

The notion that the creative behavior of children is often ignored or even punished is supported in the research findings of Torrance and his associates at the University of Minnesota.[4] These investigators find that elemen-

1. J. W. Getzels and P. W. Jackson. *Creativity and Intelligence,* New York: John Wiley & Sons, 1962, p. 2.
2. J. P. Guilford. Creativity, *American Psychologist,* 5:445, 1950.
3. A. Maslow. Emotional blocks to creativity. *Humanist, 18:*239, 1958.
4. P. Torrance *et al. The Minnesota Studies of Creative Thinking in the Early School Years: Research Memo,* Minneapolis: Bureau of Educational Research—60—1, 1960.

tary-school teachers exercise sanctions against creative children. In one school, for example, the highly creative children (as compared with the high I.Q. children) were considered less desirable as pupils by teachers, were rated as less well known, less ambitious, and less hard working. The creative children, furthermore, received fewer nominations from their schoolmates as "best friend." These findings are also consistent with those of Getzels and Jackson who found that teachers favor high achievers in school who have high I.Q.'s but *not high achievers who are highly creative.*[5]

ADAPTIVE AND CREATIVE INTELLIGENCE

The present concern about the relationship of creativity and intelligence calls for a re-evaluation of the concept of intelligence. The traditional concept of intelligence usually involves the idea of ability to deal with abstract concepts and *adapt* to new situations. Adaptive ability and intellectual status are nearly synonymous terms in the thinking of many individuals, and this reflects a narrow estimate of the total cognitive potential of man. In view of this it is proposed here that perhaps educators and others should speak of two kinds of intelligence—*adaptive* and *creative.*

Adaptive intelligence, which corresponds to our present notions of intelligence as measured by I.Q. tests, is analytical and thus involved in problem-solving activities of man. It is the instrumental behavior of man which is directed toward the modification of man's surroundings primarily for the purpose of human survival, comfort, and enhancement. This kind of intelligent behavior is rewarded in our culture as we seek to develop individuals who show a high degree of analytical and critical behavior. Such individuals are labeled "the gifted."

Creative intelligence is the important aspect of the human cognitive structure with which we should become better acquainted. It is the category of behavior which emphasizes spontaneous expression without regard to the instrumental values of the behavior. Synthesis, originality, and "divergent thinking" are characteristic of this kind of intellectual effort.

It becomes evident, as we view the attitudes toward the gifted child, that adaptive intelligence is given high priority in our thinking regarding the kind of behavior we seek to reward. The school, home, and society, in the main, encourage habits of scrutiny but often ignore habits of originality and synthesis. In fact, in our efforts to develop highly evaluative attitudes of scrutiny

5. Getzels and Jackson, *op. cit.,* p. 31.

and analysis, critical thinking is given such high rewards that the total effect is the *inhibition* or *extinction* of creative effort. Some of our educational programs seem particularly designed to thwart creative expression. Rather than encourage the individual showing a yen to ask the unusual or suggest the unorthodox, schools often insist that the ideas be discarded simply because they do not stand the immediate scrutiny of presently accepted standards and principles. Many creative thought sequences are aborted because of this immediate insistence upon critical analysis; and this arises because of the narrow concept of adaptive intelligence.

CREATIVITY AND THE UNCONSCIOUS

Several theorists have speculated regarding the role of conscious, preconscious, and unconscious functions in the development of creative behavior. Although it is not the intention of the writer to elaborate on this aspect of creativeness, it seems that nonconscious processes are extremely important in creative intelligence and especially those functionings which make up the preconscious. It seems reasonable that the unconscious may produce psychotic distortions while creativity derives more directly from preconscious processes which include a blend of nonconscious spontaneity and conscious control. The term "preconscious" is used here to describe those response tendencies which are not part of our awareness, but are easily brought to awareness. Kubie describes the role of preconscious processes in creativity as follows:

> Preconscious processes are assailed from both sides. From one side they are nagged and prodded into rigid and distorted symbols by which unconscious drives are oriented away from reality and which consist of rigid compromise formulations, lacking in fluid inventiveness. From the other side they are driven by literal conscious purpose, checked and corrected by conscious retrospective critique. The uniqueness of creativity, i.e., its capacity to find and put together something new, depends on the extent to which preconscious functions can operate freely between these two ubiquitous, concurrent and oppressive prison wardens.[6]

While Kubie's concept that creative processes can only be realized when freed from some of the unconscious and conscious persuasions is a very tentative one, it seems that some such relationships will possibly account for much creative behavior.

Hersch has conducted some interesting research with the Rorschach Test which relates to Kubie's notion that the real center of creativeness is in the

6.   Lawrence Kubie. *Neurotic Distortion of the Creative Process*, Lawrence: University of Kansas Press, 1958, p. 45.

preconscious processes.[7] Hersch compared the cognitive functions of schizophrenes, normals, and artists as they are reflected in Rorschach responses. He found that while the schizophrenes and artists both show primitive responses, the artists seem to have controls more readily available to them and so they shift frequently from operations of conscious control to primitive modes. It would seem then that the creative person, assuming he is represented by the artist, maintains a balance between free, spontaneous engagement in nonconscious exploration on the one hand, and rational control on the other. He therefore sacrifices neither flexibility for control nor control for flexibility. It would seem that these findings might be interpreted as supporting Kubie's idea in that preconscious cognition allows neither the abandonment of the unconscious nor the rigid literality of the conscious.

In present-day America the gifted child—in fact most children—is often not encouraged to engage in free expression of nonconscious thought patterns. The busyness which characterizes the schedule of the American child is not conducive to the kind of self-exploration and expression which draws from the resources of the nonconscious. Maslow has noted this in saying that, "The lack of meditativeness and inwardness, of real conscience and real values, is a standard American personality defect; a shallowness, a superficial living on the surface of life, a living by other peoples' opinions rather than by one's own native inner voice."[8] The gifted youngster (the highly creative child is included here in this term) must find the opportunity for meditation or deliberation. In modern America he is often caught up in the frenzy of overt activity (usually organized) so that there is little time or opportunity to quietly reflect the meaning of his experience to him.

This "standard American personality defect" results in the thwarting of free, spontaneous expression. Again, the emphasis is on socially-approved analytical problem-solving efforts, and creative intellectual expression is given second status.

A RE-DEFINITION

This paper opened with a plea for a re-definition of the gifted based on the belief that only a portion—and perhaps a small one at that—of human cognition is included in the criteria we use for defining the gifted person. To

7. C. Hersch. The cognitive functioning of the creative person: a developmental analysis by means of the Rorschach Test. Doctoral dissertation, Clark University, 1958.
8. A. Maslow. Personality problems and personality growth. *The Self*, C. E. Moustakes (ed.), New York: Harper and Brothers, 1956.

indicate an I.Q. of 137 or the top 2 or 3 per cent of the school population is not sufficient definition of such a highly significant group of individuals. Spontaneous creative pursuits must be given more precise definition, and more status among the criteria for giftedness. While we should not disparage the utilitarian value of adaptive intelligence, to ignore or minimize creative intelligence is to fail a large group of children in our schools who deserve to be recognized and encouraged. It seems highly possible that new strides in human development will be made when this recognition and encouragement is given.

9   *Problem solving*

L A V O N E   A.   H A N N A

G L A D Y S   L.   P O T T E R

N E V A   H A G A M A N

Are citizens capable of the rational "strategy of inquiry" called problem solving, which is essential to modern democratic society? Can the experiences of pupils in elementary school contribute to this "strategy"? The authors base their formulation on John Dewey's philosophy, which is permeated with such questions.

CHARACTERISTICS OF A PROBLEM

Sometimes teachers confuse simple questions and problems. Doing research to find the answer to one's questions is not problem solving; it is only one step in the process. Who made the first glider? is a question the answer to which can be found in books. How can we make gliders that will fly? is a problem that requires scientific thinking to solve.

To be worthy of classroom consideration, problems must be real and meaningful to children and must be problems that have created a tension in children, have made them feel frustrated, confused, perplexed, or blocked. There must be more than one possible solution so that a choice must be made after all possible solutions have been considered and evaluated. These are the two essential characteristics of any problem: first, there must be concern about it, some tension that can only be resolved by the solution of the problem; and second, there must be more than one possible solution so that a choice is involved.

Problem solving in the classroom as a technique in teaching is simply the application of John Dewey's definition of reflective thinking to group thinking and action.[1] In order to think, Dewey says, one must (1) feel confused, perplexed, or blocked; (2) intellectualize the difficulty or perplexity by defining and stating the problem to be solved; (3) test one hypothesis after another by gathering factual data in an effort to find a solution to the problem so that the tension or perplexity will be resolved; (4) develop by reasoning the idea that offers the best solution; and (5) accept the conclusion that has been proved valid by known facts and experimental evidence and reject those that the data do not support.

The learner with past experiences	faces a situation new to him resulting in	a block, a tension, a disturbance
out of which emerges a *purpose* or *need*	to solve a *problem* and resolve the tension; he	uses past experiences and knowledge to formulate hypotheses;
tests hypotheses by experimenting, reading, asking questions, listening, observing, constructing;	organizes and verifies facts by discussing, writing, rechecking;	draws conclusions which give satisfaction and resolve tension and disturbance and leave the learner ready to face a new situation with increased power.

Adapted from Paul R. Hanna, "Flow Chart' of a Complete Living Experience" (Stanford University, n.d., mimeographed).

STEPS IN PROBLEM SOLVING

When a group attempts to solve a problem as a group activity, it must proceed in much this same way. The steps in problem solving—

recognizing and defining the problem

1. John Dewey. *How We Think,* Boston: D. C. Heath & Co., 1933, pp. 106-18.

analyzing the problem into its basic elements and forming tentative hypotheses
gathering pertinent data
organizing, verifying, and interpreting data
forming conclusions
applying conclusions

—sound formidable, but are not. It is not expected that the steps will be taken in a one, two, three order. Many activities will be going on simultaneously. Yet even the simplest problem is solved by this formula whether one recognizes it or not. Children certainly should not be made aware of the steps of problem solving as specific steps when they decide how to get the news for their newspaper, how to make a glider, how to make a model of the civic center, or how to solve the problem of the lunchroom. However, the rudiments of this analysis are found in their thinking and acting. Many experiences with problem solving will give them control over the processes of their thinking, and these skills will be implicit in their behavior. It is through this process of thinking individually and in groups that they will grow into the kind of maturity that will equip them to handle the problems of a complex world.

CHAPTER 3

Classroom Groups

IN MOST ELEMENTARY SCHOOLS the basic organizational unit is the classroom group. The average number of pupils in public elementary schools is about thirty, although classes sometimes vary in number from about twenty to over forty. Teachers are expected by society to wield "bits of sovereign power" over groups of students who are required to be in school,[1] and they are expected to work with these groups for nearly ten months. Unlike groups that constantly deal with the same product, the materials, foci of attention, and forms of evaluation in classroom groups alter in the course of these months. There are many population changes because of our highly mobile society.

Experienced teachers observe that "no two classes react in the same way," and that the same class reacts differently from one occasion to another. These teachers notice that on certain days a group will work productively, yet on other days the pupils "can't settle down." The pupils become upset when a particular child "acts up" but appear to accept the same behavior from another child. A group will work productively with one teacher but not with another.

Although for more than a generation elementary-school teachers have been helped to understand individual children, formal study of groups by teachers has been limited. Assuming that readers of this book already have studied the psychology of individual behavior, we present here some selections about the behavior of groups. The main purpose of these selections is to help readers clarify their understanding and con-

1. See Edward T. Ladd. The perplexities of keeping order. *Harvard Educational Review, 28*:19-28, Winter, 1958.

struct theories about the dynamics of the behavior of people in groups.

A fundamental question in the study of learners in school groups is this: How can a group work productively to accomplish the school's objectives and at the same time how can the group experience provide individuals a sense of participation, "belonging," and gratification?

What then might a teacher's educational objectives be with respect to the over-all functioning of his classroom group? This statement by a pair of researchers appears to summarize these objectives:

> The first problem of all organizational life is how to take an aggregate of individual people with varied capabilities and predispositions and get them involved in a cooperative activity which adds up to success for the organization and satisfaction for the individual concerned.[2]

How may children learn to work productively and engage in cooperative activity? Do we just trust to luck? Do we lecture them about being cooperative? Do we reject this goal as "just theory" with no practical application and forget it? No responsible educator will say that such a goal is easy to attain. Yet, supported by research evidence on the productivity of democratic groups, some educators contend that reaching for it is worth a try. One way to help pupils learn to work productively is by teacher-pupil planning. When a teacher and his pupils have learned how to plan their work together, when the teacher's goals and the pupils' personal goals appear to be satisfied, then the teacher knows that he and his pupils have learned a fundamental skill: how to work together as a group.

The first article in this chapter discusses one of the classic researches on the behavior of groups. The second selection suggests a way to study group functioning. An additional selection in this chapter suggests ways to help pupils gain personal satisfaction and contribute to group productivity. A final article, about dropouts, shows how school experiences and social conditions may impede satisfying individual participation and feelings of belonging, thus reducing group productivity.

2. E. Wight Bakke and Cris Argyris. *Organizational Structure and Dynamics: A Framework for Theory,* New Haven, Conn.: Yale Labor and Management Center, 1954, p. 4.

What are the effects of a democratic atmosphere on children?

GOODWIN   WATSON

This article describes a research approach to the understanding of groups. The author presents some of the research findings reported by Kurt Lewin and his associates at the University of Iowa. These famous researchers were basically concerned with the overt behavior and the reports of perceptions of children under the influence of three kinds of leadership: autocratic, democratic, and laissez faire.

Watson interprets the vocational-political-social-ethical implications of the data derived from these studies. Notice that this essay was written in 1940. Does this essay give you any ideas for formulating your own theory about groups?

Articles written by Lewin, Lippitt, and White appeared in several journals in 1939. You may want to look into these important articles, which have caused and continue to cause much discussion.

WHAT DIFFERENCE does it make whether the teacher is a dictator, a democrat, or only an ornament? Amid the volumes of discussion there have been very few actual investigations. Recently a brilliant series of experiments has been undertaken at the University of Iowa under the direction of Professor Kurt Lewin and Dr. Ronald Lippitt. Clubs of boys and girls have been scientifically observed, sometimes under democratic control, sometimes under autocratic control, sometimes with the leader playing so little part that the arrangement might be called "laissez faire" or "anarchy."

The same children and the same leaders, the same equipment and projects were used, now in one "social climate" and now in another. Under the "autocratic" pattern, the leader was not unfriendly, but he definitely organized the work of the club. He decided what would be done at each meeting. He assigned the groups of boys to work together. The steps of the total curriculum were organized in his own mind, but he revealed them only one at a time, when the group was to execute them. His attitude placed him definitely *above* the members of the club. They came to him for direction and help. Until he told them what to do, they could not get started. He distributed praise and blame for good or poor work.

Reprinted from *Progressive Education,* 17:336-43, May, 1940.

The "democratic" leader was *in* the group. He worked alongside the other members. He had more experience than they had, so he could tell them what other groups had done, but he left it to them to decide what they would do. They discussed plans together and voted on crucial decisions. The leader led in making suggestions, but his suggestions were sometimes accepted and sometimes turned down. The group as a whole had the entire project in mind, and work could go forward, whether the leader was present or not. The pupils made their own assignments as to how they would work, and with whom they would work. They treated the leader as an equal on a friendly basis, and sometimes made comments in which they told him what to do or not to do. More of the comments from leader to group or group to leader were objective or matter of fact. He did not praise or blame on a personal basis but pointed out specifically what needed to be done in any particular piece of work to improve it.

The "laissez faire" leader was *apart from* the group. He stood at one side and let the pupils do as they pleased. If they came to him for help he gave it, but he volunteered no suggestions.

Some comments from the children about the leaders may be helpful in understanding the three types. About the autocrat they said:

> We just had to do things. He wanted us to get it done in a hurry. The other two guys suggested and we could do it or not, but not with him.

The comments on the democratic leader were:

> He was a good sport, worked along with us, and thought of things just like we did. He never did try to be the boss, but we always had plenty to do. Just the right combination.

The anarchic leader drew such remarks as:

> He was too easygoing. He had too few things for us to do.

The same individuals served sometimes as autocratic, sometimes as democratic, and sometimes as anarchic leader, drawing different comments from the boys they led in each role. Indeed, unusual precautions were taken to be sure that the observed differences could not have been due to the group members, the personality of the leaders, the equipment, or the content of the work.

A group of observers, separated from the club group and unknown to them, recorded stenographically all conversation, and kept a complete account, minute by minute, of what each of the group members was doing. Some moving pictures were taken from time to time to supplement the record.

Analysis of the records showed that both democratic and autocratic leaders took the initiative more than did the average group member. The democratic leaders made 41 per cent more suggestions than did the average pupil, while the autocratic leaders made 118 per cent more suggestions than did the average pupil. Still more significant is the fact that as time went on the autocratic leader had to carry more and more responsibility, while the difference between the democratic leader and the members of his group decreased with time.

DIFFERENCES IN ATTITUDE

A big difference appeared in the attitude of group members toward one another. While under democratic leadership the children were friendly, co-operative, talkative about things in general. They had more constructive suggestions to offer. They were more objective in their comments. They more often praised one another. There was, as a matter of count, three times as much conversation about matters outside the immediate club project in the democratic as in the autocratic atmosphere. The autocratic atmosphere seemed to show much more tension. This was revealed in two contrasting ways. Some children were subdued and repressed. Others were aggressive and defiant. Usually they were submissive toward the leader but aggressive toward one another. The biggest difference in the first experiment was in the number of expressions of hostility, unfriendliness, resentment, negative criticism, and competition, made by one boy toward another in the group. Such expressions numbered 185 in the autocratic group to only 5 in the democratic group! These expressions were seldom directed at the leader, although it was the leader who exerted the autocratic control. The record showed twice as much submission to the leader, in the autocratic groups, but then, perhaps in compensation, more dominance by pupils of one another. The groups during autocratic control showed less smiling, joking, and freedom of movement. They were not unkindly treated and were not acutely uncomfortable, but just seemed restrained and rather lifeless. Lewin describes one transition in these words. "There have been few experiences as impressive for me as seeing the expression in children's faces change during the first day of autocracy.[1] The friendly, open, and cooperative group, full of life, became within a short half-hour a rather apathetic-looking gathering without initiative."

Some parents and teachers may find too familiar one of the patterns that developed. In the authoritarian group the children developed the habit of ignoring the suggestions and directions of the leader. This occurred three times as often in the authoritarian as it did in the democratic atmosphere.

1. These were children who had been under a democratic regime and were being transferred, without their awareness, to an autocratic leader.

Another big difference occurred in the practice of cooperation. Study of the conversation showed twice as much use of "we," "our," and "us," in the democratic as in the autocratic régimes. Under autocracy the club members were more self-centered, more attention-demanding, and more inclined to try to exalt their own ideas and to belittle other people. The difference could be found in their behavior as clearly as in their conversation. Under democratic leadership, the members were never assigned to work together, but they voluntarily formed subcommittees and worked in cooperation a large share of the time. The authoritarian leader tried to assign group work, but the groups disintegrated almost as fast as he formed them. It should be remembered that the same children, under democratic leadership, showed cooperative behavior, but under authoritarian behavior showed individualism and dependence on the adult. Apparently their capacity to work together depended not so much on their inner character as upon the situation in which they were placed. Under a leader who directed them in what to do and how to do it, they were all for the big "I." Under a leader who said, "Now how shall we go about this?" they showed a strong development of "we" feeling.

One observation of the psychologists is very illuminating. Lewin says, "In our experiment, every individual in the democracy showed a relatively greater individuality, having some field of his own in spite of the greater 'we' feeling among them, or perhaps because of it. In the autocratic group, on the contrary, the children all had a low status without much individuality." Apparently cooperation and individuality went together. They were not in contrast to one another. Isn't it true that when one feels at home, most accepted by the group, then one is most free to be different?

RISING IN STATUS

In the groups under different leadership there seemed to be different ways in which individuals sought to rise to superior status. In the autocratic groups, some sought status by being very submissive and, like the perfect teacher's pet, doing whatever the leader said. Others in the autocratic group followed a different plan and tried to boost themselves by kicking the other fellow down.

One incident in one of the authoritarian groups may illustrate the persecution of racial minorities in totalitarian states. One group of boys, apparently feeling the repression and tension of being under the leader's personal control, began to pick on Tom, who had been originally a fairly popular member of the club. Only one hostile remark had been directed at Tom during the first meeting, but in the fifth meeting, 31 antagonistic comments were made to and about him, and in the next meeting there were 13. Then he left the group, explaining that the doctor thought it would be better for his eyes if he played outdoors during the club time! At the next meeting of this same club the boys turned upon Joe, who had hitherto never been attacked by more than 8 hostile remarks during a single session, and he received 15. The following session there were 26 attacks on Joe, at the next session there were 40, and then Joe quit the club. No such pattern of venting feelings on a scapegoat ever developed in any of the groups under democratic leadership.

The effect of the change from one atmosphere to another is well illustrated by two girls. Near the end of the period, Sarah and Sue, who had been alike in friendly responses and in dominating responses at the beginning of the experiment, were compared. Sarah had been put in an autocratic group and had developed a pattern of dominating others. Sue had been put in a democratic group and had developed pronounced friendly and objective responses, with little tendency toward personal dominance. As an experiment they were placed in exchanged groups. At the very first session in the new groups each took on the pattern of the group into which she went. Friendly Sue became aggressive and egocentric. High-handed Sarah became cooperative and matter of fact.

More striking were the changes when whole groups shifted from democratic to authoritarian or laissez faire control. The first few days were not always a fair indication of what to expect. Clubs which had been under close direction of an autocratic leader often over-reacted to a chance for freedom. Thus in one case where under autocracy there had been an average of 3 aggressive acts per meeting, on the first day of democracy there were 40. This soon settled down, however, to about 15, which was normal for those youngsters. In another group which had shown only 2 aggressive acts per meeting, the first day of laissez faire leadership brought a reaction of 63 acts of aggression, and thereafter, with no special leadership, this group maintained an average of 42 per meeting. It is this initial period of reaction from the strain of long repression which has so often dismayed teachers in their first ventures with democratic control. They grow alarmed and decide, "This will never do!" The old controls are clamped down before the group really adjusts to its new freedom.

LAISSEZ FAIRE VS. DEMOCRACY

Lewin explains that the tension the children experienced under laissez faire was actually more like autocracy than it was like the freedom of democracy. Pupils were not really free to do things, because they had nothing to do. They had no forward perspective to live by. Their life-space was cramped. Since there was no cooperation, they interfered with one another, and they had less space of free movement than they had under democratic control. What is sometimes called "license" is not excess of freedom, as the psychologist sees it, but is really a kind of restraint. The discomfort of the children showed itself in squabbling and joking hostility. The averages show more aggressive actions per meeting under laissez faire than under any other type of social control. Here are the figures: For laissez faire, 38; for aggressive autocracy, 30; for democracy, 20; for autocracy which creates submission and apathy, 2. The strain beneath this apathy is suggested by the fact that when the leader left the room the number of aggressive acts quickly rose to ten times its former level.

Because one common charge against democratic procedure is "inefficiency" it is interesting that in these clubs which were making theatrical masks, model airplanes, soap carvings, oil paintings on glass, and many other projects, there was no inferiority of product in the democratic groups. Actually the quality was better, because the children were more careful; they offered more suggestions for improving the work; and fewer of them left their part unfinished. In the moving picture of the boys in several of the clubs, an observer can see a real difference in the spirit with which the boys clean up the clubroom when the end of the period arrives. Under autocratic leadership the boys get out of as much work as possible. This spirit does not make for excellence of quality. In one experiment when boys had been making theatrical masks, the question arose as to what should be done with the products. The boys in the democratic group voted to give theirs to the leader as an expression of appreciation. The boys in the autocratic group announced that each was going to keep his own. Then, the report relates, "Jack immediately begins to throw his around violently, pretending to jump on it. He throws it down again and again, laughing. Ray wants to know if it won't break, then starts to throw his down too."

The sense of dissatisfaction which the boys experienced under autocratic control expressed itself in resentment at the masks they had been making, and also in other ways. In one club a minor "strike" arose. A number of the boys signed a paper "resigning," but then did not quite have the courage to give it to the leader. Instead they sabotaged in sly ways by breaking rules, injuring property, leaving early, and pretending not to hear when spoken to.

DEMOCRATIC LEADERS FAVORED

The boys and girls in the various experiments knew they had been given various leaders, but they did not know the principles upon which the leaders had operated. When the children were later interviewed, there was little doubt about their preference. Ninety-five per cent preferred whichever leader had, in their club, been following democratic procedures. As second choice there was some doubt, but 70 per cent preferred laissez faire to autocracy.

What happened in a series of club meetings in Iowa is not very important, but running through those experiments are some general truths which apply to all groups. Democratic procedure is not a "fad" of progressive educators; it is the psychological environment which best develops friendliness, cooperation, initiative, responsibility, objective attitudes, and the essential skills upon which democratic government must depend. Autocracy may look like the simple way of "getting results" at the moment, but the evidence is indisputable that it sets up tensions which find expression in either submission or attempts at domination, in acts of subservience or aggression, and self-centered efforts to get attention. The teacher who uses autocratic control for the sake of temporary gains runs the risk of setting up barriers which make cooperation difficult not only between himself and youth, but between one child and another. In the light of this evidence it is inconceivable that any teacher or parent, or youth leader, or government official who genuinely seeks democratic goals, will find it "too much trouble" to use the instrument of democratic, cooperative planning.

HOW TO SAVE DEMOCRACY

There is only one way in which democracy is to be saved. That is not the flinging of a challenge into the teeth of the armies of the world. It is the less dramatic but more effective procedure of adoption of day-by-day methods of democratic work. We are to learn to plan together so the resulting plan is better than any one of us or any small group of us could have done alone. We are to learn to work together so that everyone develops a sense of belonging, and is the more free to be himself because he is more truly accepted by the group. We are to evaluate results cooperatively, so that together we may find out how to do better next time. The worth of democracy is not demonstrated only by appeal to the Founding Fathers. The merit of democratic human relations in our classrooms may be discovered anew each day.

II   *The sociopsychological structure of the*
      instructional group

GALE JENSEN

The National Society for the Study of Education publishes yearly
volumes for which distinguished authorities are invited to write on
a central topic. This is an excerpt from a chapter in the 1960 N.S.S.E.
Yearbook, which was devoted to the dynamics of instructional
groups. Here Jensen presents his conception of the nature of
groups. He notes six dimensions or possible types of relationships
existing in groups. Test this formulation by observing a group of
children; test it on a college class also. See if you can observe the
dimensions that Jensen suggests.

DIMENSIONS OR POSSIBLE TYPES OF SOCIOPSYCHOLOGICAL RELATIONSHIP AMONG CLASS MEMBERS

Problem-solving and work relationships

THERE ARE A number of possible sociopsychological relationships which members of an instructional group can establish as a means of providing for their personal needs and of meeting the requirements of group solidarity. An example of such coordination of functions can be designated as the problem-solving and work-relationship roles. It is this relationship which is closely identified with the progress the group will make toward its learning objectives and the extent to which individual group members will experience the growth they desire. Each time a member of an instructional group attempts to participate in the planned learning activities of the group, he performs some kind of problem-solving function which may either facilitate or impede the work of the group.[1] Each time the group launches a new project or phase of its work, it is necessary to determine the kind of work roles which need to be created in order to implement the various parts of the project.

The connections which members of an instructional group establish among themselves to perform the problem-solving functions and work roles necessary for achieving the learning goals of the group represent one type

Reprinted from *The Instructional Dynamics of Groups,* Chicago: The National Society for the Study of Education, 1960, pp. 92-95.
1. Gale E. Jensen, *Socio-Psychological Analysis of Educational Problems,* Ann Arbor, Michigan: Ann Arbor Publishers, 1957, pp. 33-35.

of the possible kinds of sociopsychological relationship they can form with one another. This type of relationship might be designated as one dimension of the social structure of instructional groups.

Authority relationships for decision making

A second type of sociopsychological relationship which develops within instructional groups has to do with decision making. With each meeting or session, numerous decisions have to be made about such things as the best procedures to follow, length of time for assignments, policies relating to examinations, and bases for giving grades. The way in which these decisions are made and the fixing of responsibility for making certain they are made affect both the degree of group integration or cohesion and the progress that the group and its individual members will make toward accomplishing the learning objectives. Instructional groups are likely to establish different patterns of authority for decision making, depending on the extent to which the teacher desires to exercise his authority over decisions. The thing to be stressed at this point, however, is that this type of relationship between instructional group members can be designated as another dimension of group structure.

Social influence or power relationships

A third type of relationship develops because of the differences between members or subgroups with respect to the resources and skills they possess for gratifying the needs of others or for depriving them of gratifications they anticipated. Stated otherwise, class members have different ability and potentiality for rewarding and punishing one another. The teacher, for example, by virtue of the authority vested in him by the school system, has a great deal of power to influence the behavior of student group members. The teacher may also have a great deal of knowledge which students wish to possess and which might be withheld unless the students behave in certain specified ways. Students may hold the power to reward or coerce one another, depending upon their ability to frustrate or to gratify one another's needs.[2] This matrix of social influence which develops in an instructional group provides another dimension of group structure which is relevant to problems of achievement and satisfaction with classroom experience.

Social acceptance relationships

Another type of relationship which can develop between instructional group members is based on their personal evaluations of one another. Each

2. Cf.: Alvin Zander and A. R. Cohen. Attributed social power and group acceptance: a classroom experimental demonstration. *Journal of Abnormal and Social Psychology,* 51:490-92, November, 1955.

member will portray certain emotional behaviors, evidence of social position, customs, skills, and value attitudes. Judgments will be made by group members about the worth and appropriateness of these behaviors and social characteristics as manifested by other members. On the basis of these judgments, some group members will be recognized as socially acceptable and some will not. The degree to which a person will wish to be identified with a group is dependent upon the extent to which the group is comprised of persons who manifest the social characteristics, behavioral norms, customs, and skills he values. It is this relationship which can account for the fact that some students remain silent and withdrawn from participation in the activities of an instructional group. As such, it constitutes another dimension of group structure which is relevant to individual achievement and satisfaction in classrooms.

Sex relationships

The sex composition of an instructional group provides the basis of another type of relationship which develops between members. This dimension of group structure is complicated by the fact that this type of relationship has sociological, psychological, and biological aspects.[3] Sociologically, certain behaviors are prescribed for both males and females. That is, society defines how members of either sex should act toward their own sex as well as how they should act toward members of the opposite sex. Psychologically, both men and women will develop both attraction and repulsion to one another sexually. The kind of pattern which develops between members of an instructional group with respect to this type of relationship is likely to influence strongly the group progress, individual achievement, and emotional atmosphere of the group.

Informal, private, or friendship relationships

The need to share personal or private perceptions and feelings leads to the development of another type of relationship in the instructional group. Group situations, both within and outside the instructional group, often produce strong reactions on the part of the participating members. The experiences which produce these reactions need to be examined and assessed by the individuals involved. In most instances, individual students will find within the instructional group other persons with whom they can privately and intimately discuss these experiences and their personal reactions to them. Stu-

3.   Gale E. Jensen. The social structure of the classroom group: an observational framework. *Journal of Educational Psychology*, 46: 362-74, October, 1955.

dents have strong urges to establish these friendship or informal relationships among members of student groups. The desires of the teacher for a productive and orderly group often come in conflict with these desires of the students. The nature of the association which develops between this type of interstudent relationship and the problem-solving pattern of the instructional group is closely related to the so-called disciplinary problems a teacher experiences. At any rate, this informal or friendship type of relationship which develops among students constitutes a dimension of the sociopsychological structure of the instructional group.

12   *Ways of providing for individual differences*

J . CECIL PARKER

DAVID H . RUSSELL

One of the ways of assuring both group productivity and individual gratification is to provide learning experiences that each individual can handle. There is no greater deterrent to adequate functioning of a group than work that is far too easy or far too hard. These excerpts from a longer article offer a few recommendations for providing activities suited to differences. There will be more recommendations in later articles.

SUBGROUPING WITHIN THE CLASS

THE DIVISION OF a class group into smaller groups for instructional purposes has become a widely accepted practice in recent years, especially in the elementary school. For reading, spelling, arithmetic, and other individual skills, teachers find some advantage in working with six or eight or ten pupils instead of thirty or thirty-five. Instruction can be adapted more nearly to the

Reprinted from *Educational Leadership, 11*:170-71, 173, December, 1953. Copyright 1953 by the Association for Supervision and Curriculum Development.

needs of pupils, and the social advantages of the smaller group for children of elementary-school age and even in adolescence seem to be considerable. There is little research proof, however, that grouping adds to the effectiveness of instruction. Stendler, for example, has pointed out that the rigid division of a class into three groups has no advantage over a fixed full-class grouping.

The present-day approach to grouping suggests that it should be kept as flexible as possible and that children should work in a number of different groups during the school day. The child may work in one reading group and then shift to work with a partner and later work in a different social-studies group preparing a report. The principle of flexibility is illustrated in a recent curriculum guide of the Oakland Public Schools, which suggests that the elementary-school teacher may employ at least six types of grouping: (1) *interest grouping*—children who are interested in a particular topic such as "butterflies" in science will pool the information they have gained from reading different science books and other materials; (2) *special needs grouping*—certain children from other reading groups may be called together to form a special group for learning a particular technique they need, such as help with vowel sounds in phonetic analysis of words; (3) *team grouping*—here two children are working together as a team on a specific problem common to both; (4) *tutorial grouping*—this refers to a group formed for direct instruction by the teacher or sometimes by a more advanced child who needs help from the teacher in planning what he will do with the small group which he is leading; (5) *research grouping*—this is a useful device when two or more children work together on a particular topic to prepare a report for the class or other rooms in the school; (6) *full class grouping*—there are a number of activities which are best introduced to a total class in the sense that they are common or core learnings. For example, no matter what the different reading levels of a fourth grade may be, all of the children will need some help in learning how to use a dictionary effectively. There seems to be little reason why the teacher cannot teach the total group for this and other common topics. Choral reading, dramatization, reporting, and listening to records are other examples of total class activities.

.   .   .   .

INDIVIDUAL ATTENTION

In a class of thirty-five children or a school of five hundred students, it is difficult to give each child the help in a face-to-face situation which he sometimes needs. The teacher's questions, tone of voice, gestures, praise, blame, and ignoring may all be interpersonal reactions. Such individual attention should not be reserved for the troublesome or retarded pupil. Many teachers plan their school day or periods so that part of the time they are free to walk around a room and talk to individuals. Others plan systems of "pupil partners" where the child is working as an individual with one other individual. Even a large school attempts some individual attention through its counseling services. All of these are attempts to treat the child as an individual in his own right. In the widest sense, his learning and his development are his own. He can be helped most when he is considered as an individual or an individual in a small group. There is probably no substitute for the direct personal attention which a teacher can give by snatching a few moments from the busy school day. Such individual attention becomes more effective as class size is reduced.

13   *Key to the dropout problem: the elementary school*

A . HUGH LIVINGSTON

Why do some pupils meet with failure, feel that they don't belong, and drop out of school early? What are the social-intellectual-academic characteristics of these youngsters? This research report gives evidence about a topic of profound significance not only to the pupils but also to our entire nation. What can elementary-school teachers do to help pupils "belong" and be productive members of their classroom groups?

IN RECENT YEARS, concern for the sizable proportion of American youths who fail to complete high school has increased significantly. This concern has prompted many studies of high-school graduates and dropouts and many work conferences and seminars. Although much effort has been invested in the search for a satisfactory solution, the problem of the early school-leaver is still a major one in many schools across the nation.

Reprinted from *The Elementary School Journal*, 59:267-70, February, 1959 by permission of The University of Chicago Press. Copyright 1959 by the University of Chicago.

Thus far, much attention has focused on the high school. Various aspects of the high-school program have been examined in connection with early withdrawal. But till now, only limited attention has been given to the question of identifying potential dropouts early enough to permit the development of sound remedial programs.

The importance of the elementary school in early identification of potential dropouts is paramount. The fact is, many pupils withdraw before they ever enter high school. According to a recent study,[1] more than 21 per cent of the total dropout in the schools of one city occurred before ninth grade, and an additional 16 per cent occurred during ninth grade.

It is probable that many forces that contribute to the withdrawal of students in later grades are first felt during the elementary-school years. It is clearly evident that any effort to keep these pupils in school should be started as early as possible in their elementary-school career.

WHO ARE THE DROPOUTS?

Research has fairly well established the fact that, on the average, the early school-leaver is less talented academically than his contemporaries who graduate from high school. His performance in academic areas of the school program rates below that of his classmates who win high-school diplomas.

We are discovering something else about the potential dropout. Apparently his achievement in the nonacademic prestige-bearing facets of the school program does not measure up to the achievement of the students who graduate. Unable to see how school experiences tie up with his goals; unable, for one reason or another, to find success in the activities provided by the school, the student decides to withdraw before graduation. Undoubtedly we have here major reasons that contribute to early withdrawal.

No formula for detection

Still we have not developed indices that would allow the school to identify the potential dropout. Multiple correlation analyses have failed to identify patterns of information that accounted statistically for more than half the difference between groups of graduates and dropouts.[2]

The unilluminating results may be due in part to the fact that, in the typical study, the dropout group includes only those who withdrew after

1. A. Hugh Livingston. High-school graduates and dropouts—a new look at a persistent problem. *School Review,* 66: 195-203, Summer, 1958.
2. *Ibid.*

they entered high school. Actually, there may be as much difference between the students who leave school in eighth grade and the students who leave school in twelfth grade as there is between the total group of dropouts and the graduate group. Consequently, when dropouts at all levels are studied as a single group, significant differences may be obscured. In recognition of this possibility, our study focused on a group of dropouts who did not enter high school. By limiting our study to this group, it was possible to examine the role of the elementary school in the development of remedial programs.

The study reported here was part of the larger study mentioned earlier. The subjects were drawn from a group of entering first-graders in an Illinois city that had a population of 45,000. The children—who should have graduated in June, 1956—started school in this city in the 1944-45 school year and remained until they left voluntarily for a variety of stated reasons.

The most significant fact about the pupils who withdrew before they entered ninth grade is that each child was retarded at least one grade. Eighty-four per cent were retarded at least two grades. On the other hand, only about 1 per cent of those who graduated were retarded one grade, and none was retarded more than one grade.

Retardation, in itself, may not be the significant factor. The effect of retardation on peer relations and classroom activities would seem to be important. We are not suggesting that the practice of holding a pupil "in grade" should be abolished. Rather, a special effort should be made to provide learning activities that reach the retarded pupil.

Elementary-school teachers may resent grade failures in their class and all but ignore them. However, the very fact that a child was not promoted should immediately alert the entire elementary-school staff to the fact that here is a pupil who requires special help and individualized activities if he is to develop his full intellectual and social potential.

Aloof from school life

A second noteworthy fact about pupils who failed to enter high school appeared in the record of their participation in both the formal activities of the school and in the day-to-day informal activities of the classroom and the playground.

More than three-fourths of these pupils did not participate in any formal school activity in their entire elementary-school career. More than 85 per cent were regarded as less than average in their participation in the informal life of classroom and playground, while 60 per cent were classed by their teachers as nonparticipants or isolates.

The overly quiet

Here is strong evidence of the danger of overlooking the introverted and submissive pupils who are often passed by because they are not aggressive enough to attract the attention of teachers or classmates.

The academic performance of these pupils was not particularly successful in the elementary grades. Almost 85 per cent of the group were below average in scholarship; a third of the pupils ranked in the lower 10 per cent of their class. At the beginning of seventh grade, 36 per cent were reading at a level two grades or more below their placement. From these findings, it seems obvious that these pupils did not achieve success in these facets of the school program.

In mental ability, as measured by a standardized intelligence test, the dropouts ranged from a high intelligence quotient of 114 to a low of 67. This fact along with the other findings suggests that the activities available to these pupils did not meet their needs and abilities. Since all but two of the pupils withdrew when they reached their sixteenth birthday, the compulsory attendance limit in Illinois, we suspect that for many pupils genuine participation in school life may have ceased much earlier. The implications of the findings are too serious to be ignored.

The dropouts were nearly equally divided between boys and girls. In general, racial background was typical of the total dropout group and of the total student population.

The home environment of many pupils left much to be desired. Fifty-two per cent of the group came from homes broken by death or divorce. Only 40 per cent lived with both parents.

Information on the formal education of the parents was available for 68 per cent of the group. The parents of only 12 per cent of the dropouts had gone beyond tenth grade, and none had finished high school. The parents of 20 per cent had not completed eighth grade. The low level of educational achievement coupled with the instability of a majority of the homes would seem to support the idea that the children received little encouragement for educational achievement.

Only 8 per cent of the parents held jobs that were not semiskilled or unskilled. The majority of the pupils lived in the less desirable residential areas of the community. For many children, school may have been the only source of stimulation and encouragement. When they failed to find activities in school related to their needs and abilities, it is not difficult to see why withdrawal seemed desirable.

It is apparent that a complex pattern of factors underlies a pupil's decision to withdraw from school before he graduates. Many forces that contribute to early withdrawal presumably are first felt during the elementary-school years, although they may not be clearly perceived there. It is of utmost importance to realize that early withdrawal is not exclusively a high-school problem. Preventive programs must begin in the elementary school as early as danger signs are perceptible.

The high association between grade failures in the elementary school and later withdrawal indicates that the failure of a grade may be an immediately recognizable sign of the dropout. The elementary-school faculty that is seriously concerned about this problem may well take a serious look at its promotion policy. The staff may well ask not only how many pupils are failed and why, but also what kind of pupils are failed and what happens to them in school in later years.

Attempts to design an elementary-school program that meets the special needs of such pupils may go a long way to counteract the adverse effects of grade failure. Teachers who fail pupils should recognize that the problems of these pupils demand the same special consideration as the "gifted" or the mentally and physically handicapped.

The task is not simple and can be achieved only by the creative effort of the entire school staff. To ignore these pupils is, in effect, to speed them on their way to early withdrawal.

The high relation between early withdrawal and aloofness from school activities indicates the danger of allowing the meek, submissive, or disinterested pupil to drift through elementary school. For many pupils, the elementary school may be the only source of a feeling of achievement and personal worth. Many pupils who need this type of experience most are also the least aggressive in seeking it. Merely to provide meaningful experiences without concerted effort to guide each child in finding his place in school will not result in individual involvement for these children.

Programs set up to overcome the problem of early withdrawal should not set these children and young people apart from other pupils. Rather, the individualized instruction and the attention to special needs should guard against the waste of valuable human resources. Here are problems that are within the scope of the proper responsibility of the school.

CHAPTER 4

Discipline

STUDENTS PREPARING to become teachers say that classroom discipline is their major concern, and they are right—classroom discipline is extremely important.

Some people think immediately of punishment when the topic of classroom discipline is raised, arguing that discipline means the immediate suppression of the evil spirits in each pupil. Then again, some teachers-to-be delude themselves by harking back to their own early school memories. "I was no problem to my teachers," these optimists muse. "I liked them and they liked me. So why worry? I'll just get the kids to like me and I'll smile and be friendly all day." What a lovely dream!

Teachers and other adults in our society have the responsibility of helping pupils learn appropriate social behavior. I suggest that teachers must plan to teach classroom discipline as deliberately as they might plan to teach anything else. This planning to teach discipline should be based upon a professional understanding of how groups function. Also involved are the teachers' assessment of their own feelings about themselves, about authority figures, and about the pupils they teach.

What are the objectives of discipline? What do you think of the following?

1. Pupils follow orderly procedures because they know what to expect and what is expected of them.
2. Pupils operate in a classroom climate conducive to permitting everyone to give attention to the educational program.
3. Pupils learn that their right to free education will be protected.

4. Pupils know that infringements of other pupils' rights to free education cannot be tolerated.
5. Pupils gain a feeling of satisfaction in being significant members of a vital social enterprise.
6. Pupils learn the appropriate times to control their responses and the appropriate times to react more freely.
7. Pupils know that school and personal property must be respected.
8. Pupils develop self-discipline.

In Chapter 2 independent thinking and creative thinking are presented as appropriate objectives for democratic living. Yet in this chapter the emphasis is upon the need for orderly classrooms and disciplined children. This is not a paradox, for social discipline is needed in classrooms to achieve the kinds of thinking discussed in Chapter 2.

14 *Group psychological elements in discipline problems*

FRITZ REDL

In the previous chapter, the need for theoretical knowledge about group behavior was stressed. Redl, re-asserting this need, directs our attention to the "disturbances of group climate" which can produce discipline problems. He says that "about 90 percent of the discipline problems teachers deal with" are caused by the "group climate." He maintains: "The handling of individual cases of discipline disturbers for their own good is one matter; the handling of the group, so the problem-producing factors are taken care of, is an entirely different thing."

CONFUSION around the concept of discipline is so great that even a short presentation cannot afford a start without a few terminological clarifications. For the word discipline is widely used in three entirely different meanings.

1. *Discipline as synonymous with "order."* Thus we say that one class shows "less" or "more" discipline than another, or we state that our colleague's classroom obviously betrays a "lack of discipline."

Using the term in this meaning, we really refer to something we want to establish and maintain in a group of children. Discipline in this respect is a *partial goal* of the educator.

2. *Discipline as a means of education.* Thus we hear people ask just "what kind of discipline" a teacher uses, really meaning just what she does to get her children to behave. Using the term thus, we refer to techniques, means, tools used in the process of establishing or maintaining the state of order meant under the previous point. Practically, this means we use the same word for *statue* and *chisel*. No wonder we rarely get anywhere in our discussions about the item.

3. The verb "to discipline" is used with still another connotation. People invariably say "I had to discipline him" when they mean punish. Thus, the words "to discipline" become a euphemism for punishment, not infrequently for corporal punishment. This use is obviously fallacious, for it presupposes the validity of the theory that punishment is the best or even only means to establish order in a group of children.

In this study, however, we deal with another variation of the discipline

Reprinted from *American Journal of Orthopsychiatry,* 13:77-81, January, 1943. Copyright, the American Orthopsychiatry Association, Inc. Reproduced with permission.

concept; the words "discipline problems" do not so much refer to the order the educator wants to establish, or to the techniques by which he does so, but to the resistance he meets in the pursuit of his duties. We shall refer, when using this term, to the situation when *something in the attitude or behavior of the members of a group tends to block or disturb the leader in his attempts to establish or maintain order.* This definition is not the only possible one, but it is the one to which, for reasons of practicability, we shall adhere in the following presentation.

This discussion, however, does not plan to deal with the whole question of discipline problems. All we can aim at is to throw two points out and encourage further study of these in more detail.

Thesis No. 1. Even those discipline problems which are clearly centered around the conspicuous problem behavior of one individual cannot be sufficiently understood or handled through just an individual study and treatment of the main actors involved. Even they require some *group psychological analysis* and handling.

It is painful to have to make such an emphatic and sweeping statement without adequate time to describe the observations on the basis of which it was made. Two types of cases seem to corroborate these suggestions most vitally:

1. The source for the problematic behavior of the main hero of an outspoken discipline problem does really lie in trends toward disturbed behavior which this youngster shows. Let us assume the child is referred to a psychiatric counselor and is studied and treated by him. Even then, so far as the teacher is concerned, the problem is not over, for the problem behavior of the youngster may have left its traces in an aftereffect on the group spirit of the whole classroom. And as soon as the teacher receives suggestions for the handling of this child by the psychiatric adviser, she had better realize one fundamental law of group life—that everything done to one may color the emotional reactions of the others. Many a rightly planned suggestion as to what should be done for the treatment of Johnny ended in failure because it had not been translated into group psychological terms before it was applied in class.

2. In many cases it is easy to observe that the hero of a discipline problem is not identical with its source. Quite frequently the actions of the main person on the stage of disciplinary resistance are actually an expression of the problem trends of other members of the group. Thus we may often find a relatively unaggressive boy spurred into mischievious action by the lure of "tough guy" prestige offered to him by more aggressive but less audacious friends. Or we may remember the cases in which a gang of children, badly

frustrated in their most vital sex curiosities, seduce their somewhat more developed pal to become their seducer and then play the central role in a subsequent disciplinary scandal. In short, the classroom behavior of some children seems odd and out of focus when held together with their own case histories, while it suddenly makes sense when viewed as a part of a group pattern.

In all previous examples the discipline problems were visibly, though not always correctly, focused on the problematic behavior of one individual. We go a step further and recall those cases where the teacher feels a clear increase in the difficulty of keeping discipline, but where the source of this difficulty does not culminate in outstanding problem acts of individual children. Rather, the resistance manifests itself in a diffuse way, distributed all over the group, though hardly noticeable in each individual member. Or, where an outburst of wrong behavior in one individual does occur, but where it is obvious that this individual only acts out what is really "floating in the air," that he lends himself as an expression of group feeling. These cases are well known to every group worker, and can be summarized in the following.

Thesis No. 2. A group of normal children may suddenly produce problem behavior, whenever disturbances of the existing "group climate" occur. The question as to who will be the actor in these cases of problem behavior depends on the individual case history of the children. The fact, however, that some form of problem act will be performed by someone in the group *is a group psychological necessity* and highly independent of personnel. *In short, a certain amount of readiness on the side of individuals given, disturbances of group climate in themselves can produce discipline problems.*

Since we believe that about 90 per cent of the discipline problems teachers must deal with are of this nature rather than of the one discussed under *Thesis 1,* the problem obviously hinges on the question: *Just what are the main sources of disturbance of group emotional climate?*

Concepts like "group emotional climate" are artificially constructed concepts and there is no excuse for not defining them precisely and beyond doubt. I think I can clearly differentiate between at least ten types of group emotional climate.[1] It may be sufficient here to name some of the main factors which constitute what we called group emotional climate.

1. Emotional interrelationships between group members.
2. The degree of identification of group members with the total group purpose and the symbols and persons representing it.

---

1. A presentation of these materials appears in *Psychiatry,* November, 1942, under the title, The psychoanalysis of group emotion and leadership.

3. The basis on which this identification occurs (love, fear, guilt avoidance, etc. For details see footnote 1).
4. Emotional relationships of group members to, and their demands upon, the leader.
5. The leader's identification with the group purpose and the basis of this identification.
6. Emotional relationship of the leader to group members.
7. The private gains the leader derives from his group activity for his own mental hygiene (expression of surplus needs for domination, narcissistic satisfaction, etc.).
8. The nature of leadership techniques and controls applied and their relationship to the drive-superego constellation within the group members. (Kurt Lewin and Ronald Lippitt have made extensive studies along this line.)
9. The mental hygiene index of the activities which make up the group program and the degree to which it fits the intra-psychological constellation within the group members (aid in drive expression or drive control, sublimation level of activity as compared with sublimation level of group members).
10. Degree of mixture of incompatibles contained in one and the same group unit (homogeneity, as to what?—subgroup formations, etc.).
11. Conformity and discord between leader standard, cultural level of group goal, and private behavior code of group members, etc.

To discuss just which of these factors constitute which type of group emotional climate would be of the greatest interest. For this short presentation it may be more satisfactory, though, to point out only five of the most frequent factors which have been observed to disturb group climate in classroom work.

1. *One individual, or several, insist on group-conflicting satisfactions.* Sometimes it is the satisfaction itself which is group-conflicting, as in the case of a youngster who aims at sadistic satisfactions in a group of nonmasochists. Sometimes, however, it is more the form of satisfaction the youngster insists on that produces conflict. For instance, some types of clowning are acceptable or highly flattering to the group, the "seeking for personal attention" the youngster expresses in his activity may be freely granted him as a reward for the pleasure he grants them. And yet, sometimes a clown loses his audience quite suddenly, and indignant rejection takes the place of laughter and applause. This is usually the case when the clown betrays too much narcissistic pride along with his skill, or when he frightens the group by too open

an appeal to urges which are all too contradictory to their own wish for leader-identification.

2. *The group leader insists on group-conflicting satisfactions.* Most groups permit a leader much personal gratification even at their own expense. But when the pleasure-gain from suppressive commands becomes so obviously topheavy compared with the lack of need for such, or when his satisfaction out of hyperorganization and compulsive neatness begins to hamper all normal pleasure from everyday group interplay, then we find quantities of intensive dissatisfaction undermine the morale of an otherwise quite willing group.

(Items 1 and 2 are more often than not unconscious to one or both parts, and even if conscious are rarely clearly verbalizable.)

3. *The group, or considerable parts of it, is exposed to events producing emotional strain, conflict, or insecurity.*

    (a) Many subgroup formations on a highly competitive or aggressive basis.

    (b) Personal conflict between subgroup leaders.

    (c) Exposure to intensive waves of affect, like fury, fear, hatred, enthusiasm, depression, hilarity.

    (d) Exposure to the constant pressure of boredom and fatigue, fear of the future, or guilt about the past.

    (e) Exposure to sudden changes, unexpected substitution for customary leader, switch in program, in surroundings (museum trip instead of classroom), etc.

4. *Mistakes are made in leadership techniques.*

    (a) Too much adult interference, so group is doomed to passivity.

    (b) Too little adult interference, so they are left to their own drive-superego conflicts without any ego support.

    (c) Choice of group-conscience too high above, too low below, or too much out of focus with class or family code children bring with them.

    (d) Inequalities in emotional proximity and emotional distance between leader and individual group members.

    (e) Forced group unity, attained through scapegoat production, etc.

5. *Mistakes are made in the construction of the group pattern.*

    (a) Too much heterogeneity in the activity-relevant characteristics.

(b) Mixtures of too incompatible growth phases.

(c) Placement of problem individuals in group pattern which necessarily stirs up their own problem background (sibling rivalry in strongly autocratic group consisting of much younger or care-needing children), etc.

Summarizing, we say that: (1) Any one of these factors, or any combination of them, may disturb the existing group emotional climate so much that discipline problems will result even where no strong problem behavior trends were existent among the group members before. (2) The handling of individual cases of discipline disturbers for their own good is one matter; the handling of the group so the problem-producing factors are taken care of, is an entirely different thing. (3) Preventive planning against discipline problems must focus its attention on the group psychological elements in the picture and requires skillful "group situational analysis."

Application to the Problems of School Guidance and Teacher Training

If even only part of the points raised before are true, then the following generalizations seem to suggest themselves:

1. Some of the problems teachers must face are clearly of a group psychological nature. These cannot be met by "more knowledge about the individual child," however desirable such knowledge may be on other counts. They require skill and training in *group situational analysis*.

2. Some resentment of teachers and their distrust against the psychology, mental hygiene, and psychiatry of the individual should not be called "just that much resistance" and does not flow from a lack of good will or understanding on the teacher's side. It corresponds rather to a real lack of help and should be faced squarely. We should stop trying to sell teachers on the idea that their problems will disappear to the degree to which they know more about the individual. We should start giving them more help on their group psychological problems.

3. The slogan "A school psychiatrist for every disturbed child" would not meet the full problem of the teacher, even if it were realizable within the near future. For some of her tasks and problem situations the guidance service of a school will be more helpful if it provides for group situational analysis besides.

We know surprisingly little in concrete terms about these group psychological phenomena, and about the way in which they cooperate with the individual's case history in order to produce problem action. Yet these phenomena lie more openly before us than many of the subtle processes within the individual which we have studied. More effort and money must be spent in the detailed and concrete study of group psychological elements in school life.

15   *Discipline and preventive techniques*

LESLIE J. CHAMBERLIN

Student teachers and beginning teachers should consider the advice given in this article. Would you call Chamberlin's preventive techniques autocratic? Or do they sound democratic? They certainly are not laissez faire.

Viewing this article with Jensen's in mind, where do you think the teacher should stand with regard to the friendship dimension? The power dimension?

THE TEACHER WHO LEARNS to avoid, prevent, or control classroom situations which lead to disorder, discourtesy, or inactivity not only improves his effectiveness as a teacher but also his job security and chances for future progress.

Good teachers realize that modern discipline, which emphasizes self-control and self-direction, is one of the most difficult things a child must master in our rapidly changing, complex social framework. These teachers realize that any contribution they may make toward students' development of character, good citizenship, and self-control depends largely on their skill in managing pupils in a manner which conforms to a psychology of self-direction.

Adequate classroom control involves:

1. providing a learning situation that is free from serious distractions;
2. establishing and maintaining respect for authority in the classroom of the school;
3. attempting to develop student ideals, interests, and skills which contribute to self-control and good citizenship;
4. presenting a dynamic, but not dominating, sympathetic, and pleasing teacher personality to the pupils.

Reprinted from *School and Community,* 48:24, 38, October, 1961.

What can the teacher do to provide a learning situation free from serious distractions which maintains respect for authority and contributes to self-control and good citizenship?

The teacher must realize that problems will not occur if they are not allowed to develop. Establishing mutually meaningful standards is the foundation of good discipline.

Therefore, early in the school term the teacher and the students should discuss the standards which the group will accept. This prevents many problems resulting from ignorance of what is acceptable, from carelessness, or from just seeing how far a student can go.

An effective teacher must:

1. be free from any driving need to be liked by all of the students;
2. accept the role of the parent figure;
3. realize that boys and girls do not want to be given absolute freedom to do whatever they please;
4. be consistent in upholding the adopted standards.

Specific routines will help students take care of many recurring classroom situations. The teacher must accept and perform his part in these routines.

For example, it is a good idea for the teacher to meet his classes at the door of the room every day and each new class period. This permits him to supervise his corridor and to greet his pupils as they come into the room. To be effective, however, the teacher must be at his post regularly.

Routines dealing with book and paper distribution, making assignments or giving directions, student seating, and forgotten articles must be worked out. In fact, all small details must receive careful consideration.

Often teachers use student monitors in connection with these various routines. This practice is educationally sound, but a teacher should exercise care since the efficiency of the monitor program depends on the selection of reliable children.

The monitor's function should be carefully defined as assisting the teacher and nothing more. Until controls are established, it is well for the teacher to limit the number of simultaneous classroom activities and to handle most of the details himself.

An inexperienced teacher may want to avoid certain teaching procedures, such as group work and other activities which require a good deal of self-control on the part of students, until he becomes more skillful in maintaining good control.

Keeping a class constructively busy has much to recommend it as a policy of maintaining satisfactory classroom discipline. A five- or ten-minute assignment written on the board each morning encourages classes to enter the room promptly and to get to work quickly. Such morning work also enables the teacher to attend to the latecomers individually, to make last plans for the day and to complete many other daily duties.

This policy of keeping students busy with interesting, well-planned assignments applies to the last few minutes of the school day, also.

Often teachers talk too loudly, on too high a pitch, or simply too much. Good teachers learn to listen to themselves, stop talking, and then to continue in a more conversational tone that is free from anger, annoyance, or anxiety.

Children resent being yelled at or screamed at and often will be hostile as a result. Many successful teachers use signals such as the classroom lights, a small bell, or putting a finger to the mouth to request silently that everyone lower his voice.

Teachers need to remember that children's attention spans are short. Often when children work on an activity too long, restlessness and noise seem to grow spontaneously. This should be considered when planning lessons, but should it happen during a lesson, the farsighted teacher should start a new activity before the noise gets out of hand.

Since many discipline problems arise when a student or a few students cannot do an assigned task, the teacher should try to individualize instruction whenever possible. It is better for the less capable student to complete a modified version of the general assignment than for him to drift into a disciplinary situation.

In the classroom, easily recognizable rewards should follow approved behavior without delay. The wise teacher gives recognition to his students whenever possible for their superior work or behavior.

A child who is hungry or tired is apt to become a discipline problem. The teacher should analyze his class periodically as to proper rest and diet.

Being aware of certain physical and/or mental defects can help a teacher avoid many difficult classroom situations. The school's cumulative records help a teacher learn about a child's physical and mental status.

All teachers sincerely interested in providing a good teaching-learning situation should welcome constructive supervision.

Supervision encourages the teacher to try for better classroom control. It sometimes calls attention to previously unnoticed or flippant or sarcastic remarks or unfriendly looks on the part of the teacher.

Supervisors may notice antagonistic or rebellious pupil attitudes as a result of teaching techniques which invite disorder. If this information is presented to the teacher in a professional manner, he then has an opportunity to take corrective action before serious situations develop.

In summary, proper classroom organization improves the teaching-learning situation by saving time and energy, helping preserve order, and contributing to character development. Good teachers devise definite modes of seating pupils, recording attendance, directing traffic, distributing and collecting materials, arranging and caring for equipment, regulating light, heat, and ventilation, and for seeing that desks and floors are kept neat.

Preventive measures help keep problems from occurring, but when serious discipline problems do develop they should be dealt with objectively and firmly without rejecting the misbehaving child as a person.

16   *Teaching classroom routines*

ROBERT E. CHASNOFF

This brief essay proposes that classroom routines must be taught as carefully and as deliberately as anything else a teacher would teach his pupils. I believe that at the beginning of the school year a teacher must break down a school day into specific episodes and plan the routines as carefully as a choreographer would plan a dance.

THIS ARTICLE PRESENTS a positive approach to teaching routines in elementary-school classrooms. Basic to this approach is the premise that a teacher should make plans, in advance, deliberately to teach disciplined ways of working in the classroom.

How does a teacher make such plans so that pupils work and learn in an atmosphere of decorum? Four important steps are suggested for teachers to follow at the beginning of the school year. These steps, I believe, lead to a more productive classroom setting and eventually to greater freedom.

1. The teacher first analyzes the school day into a number of specific episodes. One example of a specific episode is "opening exercises." Another episode is the first formal lesson of the day. Still another episode is one in

This essay was prepared for this volume.

which the class leaves the room and goes down four flights of stairs to the school auditorium.

2. The teacher determines the kind of experiences he hopes his pupils will have during each of these episodes. Although teachers of varying persuasions differ with regard to the degree of freedom and the opportunities for self-expression that pupils should have, teachers do agree that pupils should experience a feeling of order.

3. The teacher plans the "choreography" of each episode. Choreography is used here in the way that the term is used in the dance. That is, the teacher plans in detail the design of the episode. For each episode the teacher decides the sequence of the instructions he will give. He decides the kinds of behavior which would be appropriate for the pupils. He decides where he, himself, will stand or walk. He anticipates the difficult areas which may need particular attention. In short, he creates a plan for the episode in as much detail as a choreographer would for a scene in dance.

4. The teacher plans the transitions between episodes. These transitions, themselves, are considered as specific episodes. They, too, are planned in the ways noted above.

Having (1) analyzed the episodes, (2) determined the appropriate experiences, (3) constructed the choreography, and (4) planned transitions, the teacher may begin each episode of school day with a clear idea of how that episode may look. The teacher is able to teach directly and clearly. If, for example, a teacher is planning to lead his class down several flights of steps, he walks the route *in advance*. He carefully plans numerous places where he will stop . . . turn . . . look at and settle his group . . . before moving to the next stopping place. In this way he is able to plan to communicate kinesthetically, as well as vocally and visually, his ideas of how he would like his group to move. He plans places to stop to say something to the group if saying something is necessary. He certainly plans such stopping places to be those where he can see all his pupils, and his pupils can see him.

And when a teacher plans to hand out books for the first time, he plans in advance where the books will be at the beginning of the episode. He plans who will hand out the books. He plans what each recipient of his book will do. While some teachers might plan merely to instruct pupils what to do with the books, other teachers might plan to conduct a discussion to determine what pupils should do with the books when the books are received. Whether a teacher chooses one of these methods or another, the teacher does plan what the choreography will be.

In conclusion, this article has been delimited to deal with the need to plan in advance for carrying out the so-called routines of classroom living. Other equally important aspects of good discipline have not been discussed. Such considerations include the following: the need for an interesting academic program that makes sense to the teacher and to the pupils; the significance of the teacher's feelings about himself and about his pupils; the fact that not all classes can be handled in the same way; the better methods of teaching toward self-direction and self-discipline; and the ways in which preplanning actually helps the teacher to cope with the many unexpected events which cannot be anticipated in any classroom. All these considerations contribute to a teacher's effective leadership. However, it has been stressed here that the first step to a positive approach to classroom routines is to plan the choreography of the specific episodes within the school day. Finally, I suggest that by planning a possible choreography a teacher will find he need not be as rigid as he might be in a planless situation.

17   *Characteristics of leadership*

DAVID H. JENKINS

Questions about the leadership role of classroom teachers are most important to new teachers. How can a teacher be a leader yet remain sensitive to his pupils' needs and feelings?

IT MUST BE UNDERSTOOD that the best kind of working relationship is built over a period of time as the teacher and class work together. It is not established full grown on the first day of school. (Of course, the fact that the teacher has a reputation around school for being worthy of trust will aid the adjustment of a new class.)

Effective leadership behavior can be developed if the teacher works intelligently to develop it.

1. He does not attempt to divest himself of his power and authority.

Reprinted from *The Dynamics of Instructional Groups,* Chicago: The National Society for the Study of Education, 1960, pp. 183-84.

He cannot do so, even if he wishes, and students are realistic enough to know that he should not. He must accept the fact that he has authority and power in the class. Once he has accepted this fact, he will have the assurance needed to work with the students. He will not have to use his authority excessively in order to prove to himself he has it.

2. He comes to a working understanding with his class about the areas of authority which he retains and the areas of decision making which he delegates to the class. Once the matter of authority is clarified, he consistently behaves in accordance with the understanding reached. He does not invade the decision responsibility he has given the class, nor does he permit them to usurp the decision he has to make.

3. He clarifies for himself and with the class what behavioral limits he intends to establish and to enforce with his power, what freedoms they have as a group to establish limits on their own behavior. He is consistent in maintaining and enforcing his limits; he does not narrow these limits arbitrarily and without warning.

4. In areas in which he permits the students to have the freedom to make decisions, he permits them to suffer the consequences of their decisions. If it is necessary on rare occasions for him to interfere, he does so with a full and frank explanation to the class why this is necessary and shows that it does not violate their basic working agreements.

5. He works within the context of stated educational purposes which he has explained to the students as fully as possible. He also aids the students, both individually and as a group, to set up purposes and goals for themselves. He is active in evaluating in terms of established goals the amount of progress being made.

6. He respects the aspirations, wishes, and needs of the students and expects them to respect his aspirations and needs. He is scrupulous to avoid using his authority or power unnecessarily to limit the need satisfaction of the students. He is able to demonstrate to the students that, when he demands that they perform certain learning activities, they will find, upon completion, that these activities will be beneficial and satisfying to them. They will be able to recognize their own progress.

7. He is willing to be influenced by the students in the same manner he expects them to be influenced by him. He is willing, in fact, to consider their point of view and their concerns so that he may deal realistically with the actual conditions in the classroom. If he does not do so, he risks making decisions and plans which are out of line with the existing conditions in the group.

As the teacher behaves consistently in the manner indicated, the students come to learn that he can be trusted. If he makes a request or demand they come to feel that "it must not be so bad or he wouldn't ask it of us," or "we can trust his judgment that it will be worth our doing."

In an atmosphere of trust, the student is able to accept influence from the teacher and looks for it. He recognizes the leadership being shown by the teacher to be purposeful, relevant, objective, and realistic. There is a minimum of fear or threat in the situation and a maximum of work and productivity. The teacher, under these conditions, is free to lead.

❧

18   *Four schools of school discipline—a synthesis*

NORMA E. CUTTS

NICHOLAS MOSELEY

This article contains descriptions of four views on discipline. Do you now subscribe to any of these views?

THE "PROBLEM OF DISCIPLINE" ranks near the top in all surveys of teachers' difficulties. It is not a chimera of the critics of modern education; it is a hard fact. But the professional literature on the topic is rather meager. In general, writers and theorists are enrolled in one of four schools.

The first refuses to recognize discipline as a problem—or even to use the word. Unfortunately, the authors of some of the most popular textbooks on curriculum and methods belong to this group. They may speak of "classroom control," or "classroom management," or even "the so-called problem of discipline." But they imply that the teacher who practices what they preach will always have the full cooperation of all of his pupils. Teacher and class will always plan and work together happily and purposefully. Perhaps these writers never have had to teach an over-aggressive child whose main purposes seem to be to hurt other pupils, avoid work, and irritate the teacher.

In contrast, the second, or "traditional," school believes that the only way to maintain good order is to punish all transgressors promptly and, if

Reprinted from *School and Society*, 87:87, February 28, 1959.

necessary, severely and that, if this were done, there would be little disorder in school and little delinquency out of school. The trouble, the traditionalists say, is that a combination of parental permissiveness and progressive education has produced a generation that does not know the meaning of discipline.

The adherents of the third school grant that children do on occasion behave disruptively, and they may grant that a measure of control is necessary for the sake of other children. But, they say, problems disappear if the teacher can accept the child's behavior as a method of releasing tensions. The principal cause of disorder, according to this school, is teacher domination, which piles frustration on frustration and results in rebellion.

The fourth school maintains the principle of mental hygiene that all misbehavior is a symptom and that, if the teacher can find the cause and correct it, the child will reform. Common causes are said to be ill health, a curriculum that is too easy or too hard for the individual, and a cracked or broken home.

The classroom teacher can profit from looking at discipline from each of these points of view. If he is skillful enough to inspire the majority of his pupils with a desire to learn, he will have little if any trouble with group disorder. Confident in the cooperation of his class as a whole, he will be able to deal with the individual offender calmly. The teacher who firmly and consistently maintains good order is regarded by the children as a good friend; the majority feel secure and are actually encouraged to undertake adventures in growth because they know they will not be allowed to go too far; and the troubled child welcomes a restraint which strengthens his efforts to control himself. The secure teacher who likes children does not need to dominate his class; he laughs at the occasional aberration; he does not regard the chronic offender as a personal opponent, but as a child to be helped. The teacher who views the chronic offender from the standpoint of mental hygiene recognizes that the child, if he is to achieve permanent good adjustment, will need help in solving his difficulties or in gaining the strength to overcome them.

Part Two

❧

WAYS OF TEACHING

HAVING READ about some elementary-school objectives, we turn now to the task of attempting to attain them. Here, immediately, we see that some curriculum decisions are required. What kind of curriculum pattern should you choose? What materials should you employ? Until you know exactly which group of pupils you will be teaching, you cannot make a definite decision. However, to delay pondering these questions until the day you actually begin teaching is to venture forth intellectually unprepared. This part presents some answers to these questions by a discussion of curriculum patterns, methods, and materials.

Chapter 5 discusses the various objectives, learning experiences, and curriculum patterns planned and followed by teachers. Chapter 6 deals with the planning of lessons and units of work. (See Chapter 28 for a sample lesson plan.) Chapter 7 contains practical suggestions for devising ways of teaching that will stimulate children's thinking.

Pupil's responses to ways of teaching are also influenced by teaching materials and resources. Uses of materials and resources are considered in Chapters 8 and 9.

I would suggest the following as your professional goals with regard to resources:

1. become acquainted with some teaching materials—send away for some and study others in the curriculum materials center at your college;
2. decide upon which among a multitude of possibilities would be appropriate for certain classes you know;
3. hypothesize upon the possible reactions to certain films, particular trips, or other teaching resources;
4. develop a theory on the use of resources.

CHAPTER 5

Patterns of Curriculum Programs

THIS CHAPTER AFFORDS an opportunity to study several patterns of curriculum organization. More variations exist than are mentioned here, but these will do for a start. The first article shows how curriculum thinking, once teacher-oriented, has become learner-oriented. The second article discusses three kinds of curriculum pattern.

R A L P H   W .   T Y L E R

After reviewing the changes that have occurred in educational ob-
jectives since the beginning of this century the author turns to the
question of the selection of learning experiences. Notice that edu-
cators now use the term "learning experiences" instead of older
terms such as assignments, recitations, and examples. Tyler describes
learning experiences in terms of the learner's perception of and
interaction with all aspects of the learning situation. Finally, Tyler
discusses three criteria commonly considered essential for a well-
organized program.

ANY EFFORT to review the past half-century's development of the school
curriculum in the United States encounters a confusing complexity. To
bring my task into manageable size, I have chosen to focus attention on the
development of curriculum theory, with occasional comments on the ways
in which courses of study and curriculum guides diverge from the accepted
rationale and with still fewer comments on the discrepancies between teaching practices and curriculum theory. To simplify this complex review still
further, I shall examine each of three major aspects of the curriculum in
turn: the formulation of educational objectives, the selection of learning experiences, and the organization of learning experiences. Although evaluation
of the effectiveness of the curriculum is commonly included as an aspect of
the curriculum itself, I shall not discuss it here.

THE FORMULATION OF EDUCATIONAL OBJECTIVES

A major step in most theories of curriculum development is the formulation of the educational objectives of the school, that is, the goals to be attained by its educational program. Since the turn of the century there have
been several marked changes connected with the formulation of objectives.

Change in conception of nature of objectives

One of the most obvious of these changes has been the changed con-

Reprinted from *The Elementary School Journal,* 57:364-74, April, 1957, by permission of The University of Chicago Press. Copyright 1957 by the University of
Chicago.

ception of the nature of educational objectives. The dominant educational psychology in 1900 was based on the theory of formal discipline and was expressed in terms of "faculty psychology." The mind was thought to have certain faculties, such as memory and reason, which could be trained or disciplined by proper exercise. The objectives of the school were stated in terms of the faculties to be trained, and the learning experiences were exercises in which these faculties were engaged on content particularly rich in opportunities for memorization, reasoning, and the like. Certain subjects, by the very nature of their form and content, were superior means for cultivation of these faculties. A foreign language, for example, particularly Latin, was a superior subject because learning it required the exercise of memory, while its grammatical structure provided exercise in orderly reasoning.

With the decreasing acceptance of faculty psychology and of the theory of formal discipline, the prevailing view became increasingly behavioral. Learning was then conceived of as the acquisition of patterns of behavior which the student had not previously followed. Human behavior was defined quite generally to include all the reactions of an individual—his thinking, feeling, acting.

Educational objectives are now couched in behavioral terms. An "objective" is a statement of a kind of behavior pattern which the school seeks to have the student develop. In the first flush of behavioral concepts, roughly from 1918 to 1925, the objectives were commonly stated in highly specific terms, such as ability to add 2 and 3, ability to use the indefinite article *an*, ability to spell *believe*, ability to recall the atomic weight of sulphur. This was a natural corollary to the prevailing associationist theory in the psychology of learning. Every number combination, for example, was viewed as a different stimulus to which the pupil was to learn an appropriate response. This extreme view led to the listing of nearly three thousand specific objectives for arithmetic, nearly two thousand for English. A pupil had attained the goals of the curriculum when he had learned to make the appropriate responses to all the specific stimuli, that is, when all of this vast array of "objectives" had been reached.

By 1925, this view of objectives had largely fallen of its own weight. On the side of the teacher, it required keeping in mind far too many goals, and, on the side of the pupil, it denied the development of generalized behavior patterns which quite obviously were developing. The formulation of other theories of learning, which took into account the phenomenon of generalized behavior, provided terms in which educational objectives have commonly been stated since 1930. For example, in 1936 the Department of Superintendence of the National Education Association published a yearbook on *The Social Studies Curriculum*. Among the objectives suggested were:

1. Acquisition of important information
2. Familiarity with technical vocabulary
3. Familiarity with dependable sources of information on current social issues
4. Immunity to malicious propaganda
5. Facility in interpreting social-science data
6. Facility in applying significant facts and principles to social problems of daily life
7. Skill in investigating social-science problems
8. Interest in reading about social problems and in discussing them
9. Sensitivity to current social problems
10. Interest in human welfare
11. The habit of working cooperatively with others
12. The habit of collecting and considering appropriate evidence before making important social decisions
13. Attitudes favorable to social improvement[1]

These obviously present a conception of generalized behavior. They avoid the piecemeal aims of highly specific objectives, but they may be as limited in their value for guiding teaching as were the earlier statements of faculties to be developed unless each of these thirteen objectives is clearly enough defined to have meaning for the teacher so that he can easily think of concrete illustrations of the general aims.

The developments since 1935 in the conception of the nature of educational objectives have largely focused on defining, in concrete terms, aims which are expressed at a similar level of generality as those above. These efforts have been directed toward defining the kind of behavior implied by such general terms as "understanding," "applying principles to concrete problems," and "ability to interpret reading material," and toward indicating the range of content to which each kind of behavior is to be applied. Thus the objective "to develop understanding of the basic concepts of physiology" has been defined from the standpoint of behavior and of content. The behavior "understanding" is defined as "the ability to recall the concepts, to state them in one's own words, to give illustrations of them, to recognize illustrations given by others, and to compare and contrast related concepts." The content termed "the basic concepts of physiology" is defined by listing some twoscore concepts which curriculum makers have selected as basic to this science. This kind of definition helps greatly to clarify the aims of the

1. *The Social Studies Curriculum*, Fourteenth Yearbook of the Department of Superintendence. Washington: Department of Superintendence of the National Education Association, 1936, pp. 320-40.

curriculum so that they can actually be utilized in planning and conducting an educational program in terms of the prevailing conception of the psychology of learning.

Change in sources of objectives

A second marked change in the formulation of the objectives of the American school curriculum has occurred in the sources used to derive the aims. To some extent, all the five major sources have been used in every period of American history, but at a given time certain sources are dominant in their influence while others are given only minor attention.

Between 1900 and 1918, the judgments of subject specialists and the prevailing conception of the psychology of learning were dominant in formulating objectives. At the high-school level the Committee of Ten used subcommittees of mathematicians, historians, language scholars, and the like, to outline the objectives of secondary-school instruction in these fields. Although the prevailing educational philosophy had already emphasized knowledge and skill for the layman as a major aim of the American high school, this was given little attention in deciding on objectives. No studies were made of the needs of society or of the needs of students to help in identifying appropriate objectives.

As a result of the success of job analysis in building vocational curriculums during World War I, the process of formulating objectives from 1918 to 1933 leaned heavily upon job analyses, activity analyses, word counts, and other techniques for identifying the demands made on the individual by contemporary social life. At that time, curriculum makers also gave attention to the educational psychologists' notions of what behaviors could be taught. However, during this period little attention was given to the prevailing social and educational philosophy regarding the characteristics of the good man and the good society. The opinions of subject specialists were given much less weight than in the previous period.

From 1933 to 1945, with the emphasis upon the responsibility of the school for meeting the needs of children and youth, data from child and youth studies served as a major source of suggestions for objectives. This largely coincided with the prevailing emphasis of educational philosophy, and to some extent the work of educational psychologists was used. But the use of studies of social demands was notably less than in the previous decade, while the opinions of subject specialists played a very minor role.

Since the Second World War, the shift in emphasis among the five kinds of sources has been marked. Primary attention is currently given to the opinions of subject specialists, particularly in mathematics and science.

Little weight is currently given to studies of the learner, but the specialists are asked to outline what they believe to be important potential contributions of their fields which will be of value to laymen as well as persons planning to specialize in the area. In this respect the emphasis is different from that in 1900. Today some attention is also being given to an examination of social demands and, to a lesser extent, to the current conception of the psychology of learning. Much less use is made today of studies of the learner than was true fifteen years ago. In general, the shifts which have taken place in the primary sources used to derive educational objectives parallel closely the changes which can easily be seen in the statements of objectives appearing in courses of study and in curriculum guides. Because the actual teaching in classrooms depends so largely on the habits and outlooks of thousands of teachers, the shifts in practice are not so easily discerned.

Increase in range of objectives

A third marked change has been the expansion in the range of objectives which the American school not only has accepted for itself but has actively championed. At the turn of the century the claims made regarding the school's general contribution in promoting citizenship and character were not reflected in the working objectives of the curriculum, which were focused on knowledge and skills and intellectual disciplines. The development of many basic attitudes, values, interests, and habits was considered to be a primary function of the home and the church. In the case of those habits, attitudes, and skills relevant to work, the employer was expected to play a strong role. The school today commonly lists as educational objectives the whole range of goals required for the induction of young people into effective adulthood. It includes objectives relating to home life, personal-social relations, civic life, occupations, and so on. It includes not only knowledge and intellectual abilities but interests, attitudes, and social and recreational skills. Frequently, too, there is no indication of relative weighting. Developing social skills and a cooperative attitude appears to be viewed as a job that is as important for the school as developing understanding of basic concepts of science and the social studies or as teaching the skills involved in reading.

Discrimination in selection of objectives

Since a high level of learning is required of people today, a major problem in education is to select wisely, from all the possible goals, the important tasks which the school can do well and to concentrate its energies effectively. Since the total educational job is very great, the home, the church, the employer, and the other potential educative agencies of the community need to be encouraged and strengthened to do their share, while the school concentrates on the things it can do best and on those things that only the school can do. Hence the present shift in school objectives is toward a more discriminating selection—selection of the kinds of learning which involve intellectual skills, which require sequential experiences to reach the necessary level of competence, and which involve concepts and principles that are not apparent on the surface and for this reason are not likely to be learned through the guidance of laymen. This shift is likely to reduce the range of objectives and to diminish the emphasis upon social adjustment and similar goals which fail to recognize the importance of individuality and individual creativity in responding to experience and in solving problems. The increasing emphasis upon understanding and thinking as kinds of objectives, with lessened stress upon attitudes and habits as primary goals, may help to revive the conception of the educated man as a person who controls his feelings and actions in terms of his knowledge and thought rather than one who simply seeks to express "acceptable" attitudes and feelings and to do the "proper" thing. This is a shift in objectives which will be interesting to observe.

THE SELECTION OF LEARNING EXPERIENCES

Among the changes taking place in the learning experiences provided by the American schools, changes in the prevailing notions of the nature of learning experiences are particularly significant. At the beginning of this century the term "learning experiences" was not used. "Exercises," "assignments," "examples," "problems" were the words commonly employed to designate the learning tasks set for the pupil to do outside the class session, while the term "recitation" referred to the oral responses expected of the pupil in the class. No mention was made of the pupil's mental reactions in the class, although it was clear that he was expected to pay attention, that is, to watch and listen to the teacher's presentations. When I began to teach, more than thirty-five years ago, we had to file lesson plans for each week in advance. These plans outlined the content to be covered, the methods that the teacher expected to use, and the out-of-class assignments to be made. The focus of planning was on the teacher.

Consideration of the activity of the learner

Later, attention was placed upon the activity of the learner as the basic factor in attaining educational goals. John Dewey and other educational leaders gave wide publicity to the increasing psychological evidence that learning can be most readily interpreted in terms of what the learner does; that it is his reactions that he learns, not the teacher's; that the teacher's role is to stimulate, guide, and reward the learner as he carries on the behavior which the school seeks to teach him. By 1925, both writings of theorists and curriculum guides were commonly using the term "learning activities" to refer to the basic elements of the teaching-learning situation. Courses of study were listing reading activities, listening activities, study activities, and laboratory activities in outlining the day-by-day program of the school.

By 1935, writers about the curriculum were pointing out certain limitations in the concept of learning activity. For example, two students might both be reading a historic account of the California Gold Rush, yet each might be carrying on quite different mental reactions and making different emotional responses. One might be thinking of the excitement and challenge involved in the pioneers' long wagon haul across the country, thrilling as he imagined the Indian encounters. The other student might be thinking of the rough, lawless life of the early mining community, wondering why people would leave the comforts of civilization to live in such trying conditions. In terms of the course of study, both students were engaged in the same learning activity, but both were having different experiences and to that extent were learning something different. This kind of analysis led to the adoption of the term "learning experience" to refer to the reactions of the student in the situation. In 1936, Dewey's book on *Experience and Education* clarified this concept further by emphasizing the notion that "experience" involves the interaction of the individual with the situation. This interaction involves some mutual effects: the individual modifies his reactions in terms of the demands of the situation, and he also modifies the situation through his reaction to it. Today, almost all writers on the curriculum use the term "learning experience," and they seek to plan the learning situation so as to give direction to the experience the student has, that is, to his internal perception of the situation and his own interaction with it. This requires consideration of what the learner brings to the situation, what it will mean to him, and how he is likely to respond to it mentally, emotionally, and in action.

Beginning with James and Thorndike and exercising increasing influence in recent years is the conception that the learning situation should provide for certain essential conditions of learning. Thorndike's earlier work emphasized two conditions: exercise and affect. Current curriculum guides mention such conditions as motivation, opportunity for practice, guidance of desired behavior, provision of satisfaction when desired behavior is elicited, and the like. Hence some of the current courses of study are pointing out the need to consider these conditions in selecting the learning experiences for a particular class group.

Increase in range of experiences

A second marked change in learning experiences can be found in their range. Although the sloyd movement had influenced some forward-looking American schools in the late 1800's to introduce manual training, not as vocational training, but as a means of "learning through the hands," most of the learning exercises employed at the turn of the century were verbal. The "academic subjects" were learned through listening and reciting, reading and writing, except for the laboratory periods in high-school science. Even the laboratory exercises were heavily verbal, detailed instructions and a formal plan for writing up each "experiment" being given in the manual. Map work in geography and field work in biology were strongly recommended by the writers of the period from 1905 to 1915. Most courses of study advised having children make maps and locate points of geographic interest on them. At this time, too, high-school botany courses typically required the student to collect and identify fifty or more plants.

By 1910, high-school agriculture was widely offered in rural areas. These were the first courses to introduce the *project*, or "student-initiated" enterprise, which, it was hoped, would help him to understand and to apply the knowledge he was gaining in the course. The use of projects spread to other fields and to the elementary school, thus providing a much wider range of learning experiences than schools had commonly used. The writers who urged the introduction of projects conceived of them as involving a range of experiences as broad as life itself, but, in the actual use of projects in the schools, activities involving the construction of objects have been predominant. Many teachers think of a project as making, growing, or producing some physical object. The extended inquiry which Dewey thought had largest potentialities as an educational project is rarely found. The intellectual learning experiences are frequently subordinate to the physical manipulations required to complete a "construction project."

During the Depression, with its great reduction in opportunities for remunerative work for youth, many secondary-school leaders recommended the addition of work experience to the high-school program. Although only a small minority of high schools introduced work experience as part of the curriculum, some developed well-planned programs which involved using a wide variety of work activities as means for attaining educational objectives related to science, social studies, mathematics, and English, as well as vocational fields.

The greatest impetus to extending the range of learning experiences has been the technological developments in communication. Lantern slides were in use at the turn of the century but were not found in many schools. At best they served only to extend the number of pictures which could be employed, to add concreteness, or to give variety to the teacher's presentation. The perfection of the motion picture, however, made it possible to analyze movements, to show time and space relationships much more graphically, and to increase the sense of reality in dealing with many subjects which require vicarious treatment. The addition of the sound track heightened the sense of reality and added another dimension of analysis. The sound filmslide gave some of the features of the sound motion picture in a more economical form, but it lacked the distinctive asset provided by motion. Television made possible the instantaneous viewing of events in a fashion much like the motion picture but with a further sense of the reality of the event because the viewer realizes that it is taking place at the same time he is seeing it. These technological developments have gone far to remove the physical limitations to providing in the school a range of learning experiences as wide as those of life outside. But much of the comprehensive, effective development of these potentialities lies ahead. They still represent a small per cent of the learning experiences provided by American schools.

Provision for individual differences

The selection of learning experiences so as to provide for individual differences among pupils is another respect in which changes have taken place in the last fifty years. Attention to individual differences has been accentuated by two factors: the psychological studies which have identified the extent of differences among schools, among classes, and among pupils in the same class; and the increased visibility of individual differences brought about by the enrollment in the school of children from heterogeneous ethnic groups and social classes. There are few teachers now who fail to recognize a variety of differences among the children in their classes—differences which affect interests, meanings, efforts, and outcomes in school work.

Typical devices to provide for differences among pupils have involved adaptations in the time given for completing learning exercises, or variations in the exercises themselves, or both. The first type of adaptation requires a plan for pupils to work at varying rates. Among the early developments were the San Francisco, Dalton, and Winnetka plans, all of which involved organizing the school day into two parts, one for group activity and the other for individual work. These plans also required the development on paper of a series of assignments with full directions, so that the pupils could work as individuals on different assignments at the same time. As a pupil took an assignment, it became his "contract," which he undertook to finish before he went on with another assignment in the same field. He might, therefore, complete his assignment much earlier or much later than the average pupil.

Adaptations of the learning experiences themselves were first found in courses of study which included some exercises to be required of all students and others that were optional for the better students. By 1915, such courses were common among American schools. By 1925, a number of cities had introduced "ability grouping," in which the course of study was differentiated in such fields as reading and arithmetic into three levels: the superior, the average, and the slow sections. These three courses of study differed in the time provided for learning exercises and, to a lesser extent, in the nature of the exercises. In reading, the amount of material dealing with personal and social activities of children was greater in the slow sections, while the more adult material was greater in the superior sections. In arithmetic, more concrete objects were counted and compared in the slow sections than in the others.

The use of individual projects was also a means of adapting to differences in interest and ability. This was recommended in courses of study as early as 1915. Learning exercises carried out by small groups (from two to ten pupils) were first employed in the late 1800's to compensate for inadequate laboratory equipment. By 1930, small-group projects were being used by many schools as a manageable means of providing for individual differences. The projects themselves could differ in the rigor of their intellectual demands, and the division of labor among the members in the small group could adapt further to the abilities and interests of the individual pupils. Unfortunately, all too often the slowest learner was given some handwork which involved little, if any, new learning. By 1950, with the publication of research on the psychology of small groups, educational writers were recommending the use of small-group projects as a means of heightening motivation and increasing the amount of meaningful learning activity.

Since 1948, the attention of educational leaders has focused increasingly on the "education of the gifted student." This has led to emphasizing learning experiences which require greater understanding or skill or effort than those usually provided in the course of study. It has also stimulated some schools to develop learning experiences that can be carried on as independent work.

In the past twenty years the most typical development found in courses of study to provide for individual differences has been the listing of a large number of suggested learning experiences, from which a teacher may select those particularly appropriate for his class as a whole or for groups or individuals within the class. The uniform lesson plan so common when I started to teach is almost unknown now. Most curriculum guides include a discussion of how to select, from among the large number of learning experiences suggested in the course of study, those which are likely to be most effective for pupils with varying backgrounds and abilities.

THE ORGANIZATION OF LEARNING EXPERIENCES

Important educational objectives involve patterns of behavior of such complexity that they can be developed only gradually over considerable periods of time. For example, the ability to read critically and to make comprehensive interpretations of what one reads is not acquired in a few brief lessons. To understand the basic principles of science and to use these principles in explaining the biological and physical phenomena around us require a variety of related experiences extending over many hours. If the development of such complex behavior patterns is left to isolated or unrelated periods of learning, adequate achievement is impossible. Hence a major phase in building a curriculum is to work out an organization of the many, many learning experiences required so that the student develops these complex behavior patterns gradually, day by day, and relates them to others so as to have an increasingly unified understanding of essential knowledge and a well-integrated command of essential skills.

The purpose of organizing learning experiences is to maximize the cumulative effect of the large number of learning experiences required to develop complex behavior patterns. Three criteria are commonly considered necessary for a well-organized curriculum, namely, continuity, sequence, and integration. *Continuity* refers to the reiteration of the desired behavior through the many learning experiences used. *Sequence* refers to the gradation of the learning so that each experience not only builds on, but goes beyond, previous experiences in order to require a higher level of skill or a broader or deeper degree of understanding. *Integration* refers to the practice of relating what the student is learning in one field to what he is learning at about the same time in other fields. A broader and deeper understanding is facilitated by comprehending the relation among the various concepts, facts, and principles being studied, and a more adequate command of basic skills is achieved as the relation of these skills to one another is seen.

Continuity and sequence of learning experiences

One surprising fact about curriculum development in the last fifty years has been the limited attention given to the theory of curriculum organization. Other than the commonsense notions of the three criteria mentioned above and of such rule-of-thumb principles as "learning experiences should proceed from that which is known to that which is unknown, from the simple to the complex, from the easy to the difficult," no new formulations have been made since the time of Herbart and of James. This is an area crying for substantial theory to be tested in practice and to provide a guide for practice.

At the more specific level, developments in reading and in the foreign languages have been most marked. In reading, continuity and sequence are commonly achieved through carefully controlled vocabulary development, new words being added gradually and systematically, and through the control of sentence structure in the reading materials, beginning with simple declarative sentences and moving gradually to compound and complex ones. Integration is sought both by relating the reading material to the common activities of the children and by introducing work-type reading in the other subjects on a gradual basis. A similar scheme of organization is commonly followed in the teaching of foreign languages.

In arithmetic the development of skills is usually facilitated through an organization which begins with learning experiences involving addition and subtraction, then multiplication and division, then common fractions and decimal fractions. No explicit scheme of organization for concept development in arithmetic can be found in current courses of study. The content of arithmetic problems has changed greatly since 1900. Beginning about 1920, studies were made of the kinds of problems commonly encountered by children and adults. Typically, arithmetic courses now order the problem content in terms of frequency of occurrence of the problems outside of school and in terms of the age level at which problems of various kinds are commonly encountered by children.

The typical high-school curriculum in mathematics has changed little in the past fifty years so far as organization is concerned. Tenth-grade geometry builds little, if at all, upon algebra. Advanced algebra and solid geometry in the eleventh grade have little sequential relation to tenth-grade geometry, and trigonometry in the twelfth grade does not provide a clear sequence for the eleventh-grade work. The so-called modern mathematics program, which is now getting under way with the sponsorship of the mathematical organizations, should provide a better-organized curriculum for high-school mathematics.

In organizing the so-called content fields, like the sciences and the social studies, major attention has been given to the ordering of content rather than behavior. At the beginning of this century, science was not commonly taught in the elementary school. In the high school, botany was more frequently offered in the tenth grade; physics, in the eleventh; and chemistry, in the twelfth. By 1920, general science was offered as the introductory science course in more than one-fourth of the high schools, and now it is taught in almost all schools in the eighth or ninth grade. Biology is offered in the tenth grade, and physics and chemistry, where offered, are placed in the eleventh or twelfth grade.

The content of general science is usually selected to relate to the scientific phenomena most commonly observed by children. The content of biology is usually chosen to explain the human body, the maintenance of health, and the conservation of natural resources. The organizing notion here is to begin with phenomena which are common in the student's environment and in which he is likely to be interested. The advanced science courses, physics and chemistry, deal with the more abstract principles, which are thought to be less common and more difficult. The organization of these two courses has not greatly changed in the past fifty years. These illustrations in the field of science indicate the attention given to organizing the content dealt with in the learning experiences, but no similar effort has been made to organize the behavior, that is, the skills and abilities to be developed.

This is also true for the social studies. The changes taking place in their organization have been changes in the ordering of content. The most common sequence of content in the social studies is to begin with the community, then to study the state, then the union, and finally the world. There is little evidence to indicate that this is sequential in terms of difficulty in learning.

Integration of learning experiences

Thus far we have been reviewing the continuity and sequence of learning experiences in the content fields. The problem of integration, that is, how to relate learning experiences to enable the student to see the connection between what he is learning in one field and what he is learning in another, has been attacked most frequently through changes in the structure of the curriculum. In 1900, the elementary-school curriculum was composed of ten or more specific subjects like reading, writing, spelling, arithmetic, geography, history, nature study, hygiene, music, drawing. Now, the typical course of study includes reading and the language arts, arithmetic, science, fine arts, health. This reduction in the number of subjects has been accomplished by building a closely related series of learning experiences in language, in which reading, writing, and spelling are involved; in social studies, where geography and history are interrelated; and in the fine arts, where music, drawing, and painting are brought together.

In the high school the broad fields of English, mathematics, science, social studies, foreign language, and fine arts have frequently replaced more specific subjects. Some schools have developed the core curriculum, which provides a large structure for learning experiences that occupy from one-third to one-half of the student's day. Since these larger structures are usually planned as courses rather than several separate subcourses, there is opportunity for better integration. Typically, however, the only principle of integration which has been explored is to bring together the content and the skills needed to deal with each of the student "problems" which provide basic units of the course. This principle does not always provide for the necessary continuity and sequence nor for all of the more helpful relationships among the fields which are involved. In many cases, a particular problem involves knowledge or skills from certain fields in only a minor degree and does not suggest the more significant ways in which these fields are related.

Reading the works of curriculum theorists and examining courses of study make it clear that the past fifty years have not seen great development in the organization of learning experiences. In this respect, curriculum changes have been relatively few. The careful, systematic work done in the field of reading is a shining exception. The arousal of interest and the stimulation of thought among secondary-school teachers who have worked on the construction of core curriculums suggest the great intellectual resources available, under effective leadership, for attacking fundamentally and systematically the problem of developing a better-organized curriculum.

SUMMARY

This review of changes in the curriculum of the American schools during the past fifty years has touched several high spots, but it has not presented possible explanations for the kinds of changes noted. It is probable that many of these developments can be understood in terms of the tasks which the American schools were facing at these different periods and in terms of the prevailing psychological ideas which school leaders found when they sought from scholars assistance in attacking critical school problems.

Throughout the fifty years the schools have been pressed by continuing conditions which create critical problems that cannot be solved without further curriculum developments. The first of these is the rapid change in technological development and social life, which requires a continually increasing level of education on the part of our people. The second is the increasing proportion of children and youth who are sent to the schools for education. The third is the dislocation in other educational institutions—the home, the church, the neighborhood—which rapid social change has engendered. The educational needs of today and the immediate future are greater than ever before. American education has done an amazing job in getting almost all children and youth into school and providing schools for this immense number. The schools have been astoundingly successful in building confidence on the part of the public in the capabilities of education in building our civilization. The time has come, however, to recognize realistically the magnitude of the job; to identify the objectives which the schools can best attain; to encourage the home, the church, and other institutions to undertake the tasks appropriate to them; to devise learning experiences clearly relevant to the school's proper objectives; and to work out an organization of the curriculum which aids the students in attaining a high level of educational competence. These steps still lie ahead of us.

20   *Patterns of textbook use—key to curriculum development*

HERBERT C. RUDMAN

The purpose of this article is to examine the influence of textbooks on curriculum plans. The first pattern the author describes is one in which the textbook determines all aspects of the course of study. In the second pattern the textbook determines only the skills to be learned and the sequence in which these skills might be learned. The third pattern uses teaching materials other than textbooks.

IN ONE popularly-held analysis of curriculum types, curriculums are divided into three categories: those curriculums that are based solely upon organized bodies of knowledge (subject-centered); those based upon, and circumscribed by the interests of children (child-centered); those based upon the everyday aspects of living (society-centered). If this analysis is valid, it

Reprinted from *The Elementary School Journal,* 58:401-407, April, 1958, by permission of The University of Chicago Press. Copyright 1958 by the University of Chicago.

would appear that the overwhelming majority of curriculums in the United States are of the subject-centered variety. One author has estimated that 96 per cent of all curriculums are of this type.[1] Timmerman concluded, after investigating the curriculums of state-approved secondary schools of a southern state, that 74 per cent of these schools selected learning experiences from organized bodies of knowledge. Although his study also pointed out that 48 per cent of these schools were investigating possible alternatives, the significant point here is the high average of subject-oriented schools.[2]

And this situation is a national one. This is a disturbing fact. Why are subject-centered curriculums so prevalent? Is our analysis of curriculum types in error? Do administrators and teachers fail to see the significance of curriculums based on experiences other than formal academic subjects? An answer to this enigma lies in the approach we have taken to the description and analysis of existing practices. Our approach is hypothetical; our descriptions and analyses are based upon hypothetical curriculum models.

Researchers attempting to locate these hypothetical curriculum models have had difficulty because these models do not exist in actual practice. Actual practice finds teachers using textbooks in arithmetic, textbooks in social studies, textbooks in a multitude of content areas. Small wonder, then, that investigators searching for hypothetical curriculum models can find only the subject-centered curriculum. The prevalent basic instructional material is the textbook, and the textbook is organized around formal subjects.

PATTERNS OF TEXTBOOK USE

Textbooks have been designed to perform one function—supplying a course of study. The textbook is most effective when used for this purpose. In a recent publication of the American Textbook Publishers Institute, the role of the textbook as a course of study is clearly defined:

> Development of a course of study and the selection of textbooks should go hand in hand. It is an unwise and wasteful procedure to attempt to develop a course of study without regard to instructional materials available. One sure way to have a course of study which will *actually* function in the classroom is to (a) define the broad objectives of the program, (b) prepare a tentative draft of the course of study, (c) select the teaching materials that come closest to meeting the broad objectives in the tentative draft, (d) *after textbooks are selected revise the tentative draft in*

1. Lee J. Cronbach (ed.). *Text Materials in Modern Education*, Champaign, Ill.: University of Illinois Press, 1955, p. 207.
2. Gene W. Timmerman. Differentiated curriculum designs, especially with reference to curriculum practices in the high schools of South Carolina. Unpublished doctoral dissertation, University of South Carolina, 1956.

terms of the materials [*texts*] *adapted* [italics and parenthetical insertion are those of this author].[3]

Since the textbook is clearly the course of study in a classroom, the text, to be used most efficiently, must be utilized to its fullest extent. This would mean that the textbook is responsible for three essential elements of any curriculum: (1) the content of the curriculum, (2) the skills to be learned, and (3) the sequence in which these skills are to be learned.

The way we use textbooks determines, to a large extent, the actual curriculum of a school and of a classroom unit. It would seem that the way to discuss, to analyze, and to evaluate curriculums would be to make a careful analysis of how textbooks are used. An analysis of the patterns of textbook use yields at least three major emphases: (1) using the textbook as the determiner of content, skills, and the sequence in which skills are to be learned; (2) using the textbook as the determiner of skills to be learned and the sequence in which they are to be learned; (3) using no texts but employing "trade" books and other instructional materials.

Pattern 1. The textbook as a determiner of content, skills, and sequence. Children can profit greatly when a teacher uses a textbook as it was designed to be used. The text gives teachers and pupils ample opportunity to use other instructional materials, such as field trips, movies, filmstrips, recordings, and the like, and it encourages pupils and teachers to seek elsewhere further detailed information not to be found in the textbook being used.

A casual observer in a classroom which utilized the text to its fullest extent would be unable to distinguish the learning activities in this classroom from the learning activities of any other classroom using a different basis for the determination of the curriculum being explored. Children might well be engaged in committee work, individual library research, devising skits, painting murals, and a host of other activities which we have come to associate with good learning.

The distinguishing feature here lies in the source of these activities, the content studied, the skills practiced, and the like. The interests of children supplement the content areas to be explored, but it is the textbook itself which determines what the children will study. The use of the textbook in this manner presents the pupils with the kinds of skills that they will practice at this stage of their intellectual development. It also determines the sequence in which these skills will be studied. As an example, the prime reason for having children study percentages in Grade 7 rather than in Grade 4 is

3. *Textbooks Are Indispensable!* New York: American Textbook Publishers Institute, 1956, p. 70.

the fact that arithmetic textbooks do not introduce percentages until approximately the seventh-grade level. It is not that youngsters have no interest in the use of percentages before they reach Grade 7; fourth-grade boys are discussing batting averages of baseball players long before they have a clear concept of what these batting averages actually represent.

The use of the textbook as a determiner of content, skills, and sequence has several distinct advantages. If used to its fullest extent, the textbook supplies both teachers and pupils with a complete course of study. It gives both teachers and pupils great leeway in the use of many of the educational inventions of the past several decades, such as committee organization, audio-visual aids, use of resource people. It also presents teachers and pupils with a logical development of skills and gives a total over-all development through the twelve years of public education.

The basic disadvantage of this use of the textbook is that it limits the intellectual development of children by predetermining the content to be studied. It does not take into account the differences in the communities in which children live. It fails to consider the dynamic nature of the world we live in and thus sets the boundaries of children's intellectual horizons and forces them to follow the paths drawn for them by textbook authors.

Pattern 2. Using the textbook as a determiner of skills to be learned and the sequence in which they will be learned. A second approach to the use of the textbook, and a modification of the preceding approach, is to use the textbook only to determine the skills to be practiced and the sequence in which they will be practiced. The content itself is derived from the interests of the children, the nature of the community in which they reside, and the demands of the society in which they live. By studying the contents of texts in language, reading, and arithmetic, the teacher can determine the skills called for at a particular grade level. These skills are listed, and the teacher's responsibility is to see that these skills are used during the course of the academic year. The content in which these skills are practiced is determined by the interests held by the children in a particular classroom, by the nature of the community in which they live, and by the demands made upon individuals by the larger community in which they live—the world.

As pointed out by various authors in the 1956-57 issues of the *National Elementary Principal*,[4] the dynamic nature of the world in which we live has posed new problems for mankind and has emphasized certain of the old

4. H. J. McNally. What shall we teach and how? *National Elementary Principal*, 36:6-11, May, 1957.

problems. The concerns of the adult population cannot be totally ignored in developing a set of learning experiences for children, for these concerns affect the nature of the smaller communities in which children reside and these, in turn, have a direct positive relationship to the immediate interests of children.

Using the complex of these three factors—total social conditions, the nature of the local community, and children's concerns—the teacher determines the content to be studied at a particular grade level. The complexity of the skills to be practiced, the nature of the skills to be practiced, and the total sequential development of skills are determined by the textbooks. In schools following this pattern, only the teacher uses a textbook. The children use other printed materials—trade books, pamphlets, brochures, and many materials of instruction of a nonverbal nature.

One advantage of this pattern of textbook use is that it gears the curriculum to the needs of the children and to the needs of their community. By retaining the use of the text as determiner of skills, the sequential development of skills through the twelve years of public school will be retained; yet the content which children will study will be related more closely to the interests of children and less to the predetermined content of textbook authors. It is conceivable that, within a given community, two schools would have curriculums that would differ greatly, although the skills to be learned and to be practiced would remain constant throughout the school system. It would thus be possible to develop a curriculum that would adhere more closely to the psychological advantages of deriving content from the needs of the pupils and still retain the logical development of skill subjects.

One disadvantage of this type of use of a textbook is the danger that children's interests may become the major basis for determining the curriculum. Since interests are learned, we are interested in those things with which we are most familiar. If we circumscribe the entire curriculum by the familiar, we leave little room for the unfamiliar. Unless, therefore, a balance is maintained between the three sources of content to be studied—interests, the local community, and the total society—the curriculum might well be as limiting as if the content were derived solely from the textbook.

Another disadvantage lies in the demands made upon a teacher. This pattern of textbook use assumes a relatively high order of sophistication on the part of the teacher. It calls for a teacher who is familiar with the nature of the society in which he lives; it calls for a teacher who is aware of the environmental backgrounds of his pupils; and it calls for a teacher who possesses the necessary insights and sensitivities for understanding the needs and the interests of the children in his class.

Pattern 3. Using trade books[5] and other instructional materials in the place of textbooks. This pattern represents an extreme departure from the use of text materials. The content, the skills to be practiced, and the sequence in which they are to be practiced would be determined solely by the interests of children, the nature of the community, and societal demands.

Although there would be no textbooks, a vast amount of printed material would be used: free and inexpensive materials published by major industries and businesses, chambers of commerce, and trade unions; pamphlets published by various governmental agencies; and trade books. Schools utilizing this pattern would devote the money normally allotted to the purchase of textbooks to the purchase of trade books and other instructional materials.

Of necessity, a description of this pattern of use of materials must be couched in normative terms. The available research data give little evidence that many schools are at present engaged in using materials of instruction in this manner. The uniqueness in this approach lies in the fact that there is almost no predetermining of the content, skills, or sequence in which skills and content are to be learned. Patterns 1 and 2 predetermined one or more of these factors for the learner. Pattern 3 does not.

An advantage of this pattern of use of textbooks stems from the psychological concept that children learn most effectively those things which hold the greatest meaning to them. The content to be studied and the various skills to be practiced are determined solely on the basis of the needs and interests of the pupils and upon the environmental demands made upon the children. The sequential development of these skills would be closely related to the demands made upon children. Referring back to the example dealing with the batting averages of famous baseball players, it is quite conceivable that fractions and percentages could be taught much earlier in the elementary school than they are now taught and could be taught with a great deal of meaning. On the other hand, it is equally conceivable that some other concepts, for example, the concepts of profit and loss or of compound interest, could be delayed until they became meaningful to the learner.

Teachers employing this pattern of textbook use would have great opportunities to develop the skills closely associated with the understanding of man's physical and natural environment. The skills associated with social education could be more meaningfully brought into play. All in all, this

---

5. Publishing companies have come to apply the term "trade books" to printed materials of a topical nature, such as books about stars, birds, famous people, and so on. Trade books are available at all reading levels on a wide variety of topics. They have found their way into public and school libraries and from there to classrooms.

pattern would give the pupil the greatest opportunity to explore meaningfully his environment and to broaden his intellectual horizons.

This third pattern of textbook use has some serious inherent disadvantages. It takes a secure, confident, skillful teacher to work with boys and girls in this manner. This pattern calls for a widely read teacher, a person who has more than a nodding acquaintance with contemporary affairs. It demands a teacher who can foresee the consequences of the activities undertaken by his pupils. The only guide for the teacher in this situation is his best professional judgment concerning the content to be studied. Unless the teacher has great skill, this situation might be as limiting upon the development of new interests as Pattern 1 would be. Care would need to be exercised to see that children did not study and restudy only those topics which were familiar to them.

Another disadvantage is derived from the present organization of school systems. This pattern demands a high degree of coordination between the supervisory staff, the administrative staff, and teachers. As administrators and teachers report the demands made upon them and the time consumed in meeting these demands, it appears that few schools are now organized so that administrators, supervisors, and teachers would be free to implement such a pattern.

CURRICULUM CHANGE THROUGH THE USE OF TEXTBOOKS

Implied in the normative discussions of curriculum theorists has been the notion that present curricular experiences can be described, analyzed, and evaluated by employing hypothetical curriculum models. These models carry many labels, but all center on one or more of three major themes: subject-centered, child-centered, and society-centered curriculums. Yet, when existing practices are surveyed, it becomes difficult to locate any but the subject-centered curriculum model. Although these curriculum models are convenient vehicles for the normative projections of what theorists would like to see, they are hardly accurate yardsticks by which to measure existing curriculums.

As has been pointed out, the textbook as the basic instructional material is subject-oriented and is designed to be the basic course of study. Since this is the case, a more fruitful approach to analyzing and modifying curriculums lies in modifying the use of the textbook. Although this writer holds value judgments concerning the relative worth of each of the three patterns of textbook use described, these value judgments are subject to scrutiny by research and need not be aired at this point.

Nevertheless the basis for any curriculum modification is a dissatisfaction with existing practice. When change is considered, it is invariably held that there is something better than that which presently exists. This applies with equal validity to textbook use. The important concept central to change in this case, however, is the relationship between a pattern of textbook use and its effect upon the complex experiences in which the learner is engaged—the curriculum.

Literally thousands of man-hours are expended annually by teachers and administrators who, in good faith, work together in committees to modify or change existing curriculums. But so long as these committees develop curriculums without relating them to the manner in which textbooks will be used, so long will they run the risk of engaging in fruitless endeavor.

IN SUMMARY

Pattern 1 is a reflection of the majority of existing curriculums. It determines most of the learning experiences in which children are engaged. Pattern 2 suggests that the textbook is a guide for a sequential development of the twelve-year program but that it is limited exclusively to that use. Pattern 3 is a modification of Pattern 2, for it implies not only that children will abandon the use of textbooks but that teachers will do so as well. It implies that the basis for the sequential development of the twelve-year program lies less in an arbitrarily determined organization than it does in the complex of interests, community, and societal demands.

The major purpose of this article has been to trace the relationship that exists between textbook use and curriculum development. Like other analyses, this one is subject to criticism. It may be construed as an oversimplification of a complex problem. Perhaps it is. But the point to underscore is that the key to effective curriculum change lies less in the hypothetical logic of curriculum theorists than in the practice of those who must use existing instructional materials.

Practitioners interested in modifying curriculums cannot wait for the publishing companies to provide other types of textbooks—textbooks that are not organized as basic courses of study. They need a blueprint that is geared to the realities of school situations. The textbook and its use supplies a key to a realistic appraisal and modification of existing educational practices.

CHAPTER 6

Lessons and Units of Work

IN MANY WAYS this is quite a practical chapter. However, do not be misled into thinking that these selections lack theoretical bases. The first two articles contain helpful suggestions about planning lessons and larger units in any school. The next six selections deal directly with the tasks involved in planning units of work. Remember that, while these articles refer to specific subject matter areas and grade levels, the authors' recommendations can be applied to other areas and levels as well.

21   *Ninety suggestions on the teaching of mathematics in the junior high school*

E D W I N   J .   S W I N E F O R D

The ninety suggestions in this article may be used in many subject-matter areas, not in mathematics alone. Swineford tells us things to do before teaching a class: become steeped in the subject matter, plan for pupil interest, and make sure to plan to use a variety of teaching materials. He offers next thirty-eight practical recommendations about the lesson itself, including six on assignments and homework. The article ends with six more suggestions for providing for individual differences during a lesson.

THE FOLLOWING ITEMS indicate specific things to do in the teaching of mathematics. These suggestions come from many sources. You may review them for your own purposes or have an observer use them as a check list for reactions to your teaching. Feel free to agree or disagree with these suggestions, or to extend and modify them for your use.

ON PREPARING TO TEACH MATHEMATICS

1. Secure a copy of the state curriculum guide and study the section on mathematics.
2. Study several courses of study on mathematics from other school systems. Examine Resource Units and Teaching Units on mathematics.
3. Examine several textbooks on the teaching of mathematics and several used by students in the schools.
4. Analyze your own mathematical strengths and weaknesses as you review the content of junior and senior high-school mathematics courses. Remove your own deficiencies before you start to teach.
5. Visit as many classes in mathematics as possible. In addition to observing mathematics teaching on the secondary level, visit classes on the elementary level.
6. Talk with an experienced teacher and make notes on his suggestions.
7. Compare your number symbols with the recommended form shown on a standard chart. Practice writing the correct form of numerals on the chalkboard.

Reprinted from *The Mathematics Teacher, 54:*145-48, March, 1961.

8. Start collecting, classifying, and filing pictures, puzzles, games, and exhibits that relate to the units or topics you may teach.

9. Preplan the semester's work so that proper time allotments may be made for each unit or topic.

10. Read, and if possible, subscribe to such professional journals as the *Clearinghouse, The Mathematics Teacher, The Arithmetic Teacher.*

11. Review the yearbooks of The National Council of Teachers of Mathematics.

TO HELP YOU CHART A STRAIGHT COURSE

12. Read the preface or introductory statements in the textbook. Determine the author's viewpoint.

13. Familiarize yourself with the teacher's manual for the textbook.

14. Look upon the textbook as one resource. Avail yourself of others.

15. Remind yourself that it is not the purpose of the mathematics teacher to make mathematicians of all students.

16. Do not limit the mathematics you teach to the immediate demands of the average person.

17. Keep your eye on the distinct purposes of mathematics instruction for the junior high school.

18. Aim for the achievement of a simple, definite, sequential mathematical objective in each lesson.

19. Let the students know what your objectives are for each lesson.

20. Teach students mathematics; do not just teach mathematics.

21. Point out for some students the "bread-and-butter" value of mathematics.

22. Think through and be prepared to answer the students' question, "Why study mathematics?"

23. Crystallize clearly what you believe about transfer of learning as it relates to mathematics.

TO MOTIVATE OR INTEREST STUDENTS IN MATHEMATICS

24. Appraise the total classroom atmosphere and quality of human relationships. Study the group rapport.

25. Engender readiness for instruction in each new concept before it is taught.

26. Inventory students' mathematical abilities and skills. They cannot learn something they already know.

27. Take advantage of the wonder motive and the systematizing motive for the learning of mathematics.
28. Preview the lesson for your class. Summarize at the end.
29. Lecture sparingly. Demonstrate copiously.
30. Tap the multitude of number problems suggested by a student's visit to the supermarket.
31. Use intrinsic motivation rather than grades, fear, punishment, or sarcasm.
32. Encourage the enjoyment and thrill of reading about our number system and its development.
33. Refer the students to the daily newspaper for challenging problems in computation.
34. Utilize mail-order catalogues for additional problems.
35. Provide opportunity for gifted students to demonstrate before the class their competence in working with numbers.
36. Cause the students to face and live with unsolved problems. Do not undermine their learning by giving them help too soon, or too late.
37. Prove to the students that you want them to grow in mathematical insights and understandings.
38. Move toward laboratory teaching in mathematics—an emerging concept.
39. Stimulate interest in mathematics by bulletin board displays and pictures of famous mathematicians.

ON MATERIALS AND OTHER RESOURCES

40. Take advantage of a variety of audio-visual resources.
41. Demonstrate with such resource materials as flannel boards with fractional parts, place-value charts for decimals, and hundred boards for per cent.
42. Construct, with your students, an arithmetic kit with fractional cut-outs, squared and rectangular strips, compass, ruler, and protractor.
43. Equip your classroom as a laboratory for teaching mathematics; include exploratory, symbolic, and visual materials.
44. See the *22nd Yearbook* of The National Council of Teachers of Mathematics for a list of materials and facilities needed for laboratory teaching in mathematics.
45. Utilize the chalkboard in drills or student demonstrations.
46. Chalk as you talk.

ON TEACHING THE LESSON

47. Treat the textbook kindly. It is your best friend, but not your master.
48. Calculate the answers. Do not vote or accept majority opinion on problems.
49. Teach in order to achieve pupil participation and discovery.
50. Change the pace in your lessons. Monotony thrives in abstractions.
51. Require an understanding of the process instead of just a correct numerical answer.
52. Leave the "I want" out of your assignments and discussion.
53. Require mathematical effort from all students—gifted, average, and slow.
54. Set high standards of neatness and in the systematic setting down of mathematical computations.
55. Involve students in the core of mathematical learning experiences.
56. Promulgate the correct reading of mathematical symbols.
57. Harmonize orderly and systematic class procedures with the orderliness and exactness of numbers.
58. Realize that teaching pure mathematics to youth may be too rich for consumption for some of them. If you cannot handle an experience unit, try a subject-matter unit.
59. Think in terms of informational mathematics as well as computational mathematics.
60. Find a basis in the previous experience of the student that will involve the problem to be presented.
61. Be cautious concerning student verbalizations. They may not know as much as you think they do.
62. Emphasize the development of the ability to grasp ideas, processes, and principles in the solution of concrete problems, rather than just skill in manipulation.
63. Help the students to develop methods of attack on problems and the ability to see relationships.
64. Guide students in successful procedures for attacking thought problems involving mathematical calculations.
65. Spend precious class time building meanings in number relationships. Collect and record grades and other clerical details before or after class.
66. Supervise your students in the mathematics study period in order to give them individual help.

67. Administer frequent short tests to keep contact with the student's understandings.
68. Test—teach—retest—reteach.
69. Consider as possible causes of student failure: physical defects, poor attitude, and lack of understanding of basic concepts.
70. Diagnose student errors by means of homework, class responses, and diagnostic tests.
71. Be familiar with the school-wide testing program participated in by your students. Chart or graph pertinent mathematical test data about them.
72. Help students develop a recognition of reasonable answers.
73. Admit your mathematical errors. Work toward eliminating them.
74. Build understanding before you drill.
75. Vary drill procedures. Vary the doses, time, content, and participants.
76. Introduce novelty in your drill by the use of such devices as "magic squares" and "lattice" work.
77. Be familiar with and use at different times all of the seven different types of lessons in mathematics: inductive development, drill, deductive development, review, examination, appreciation, and conversational.
78. Try the review lesson which summarizes the main features of the work but in a manner different from that previously used.

ON THE ASSIGNMENT AND HOMEWORK

79. Assist students in their assignments by systematic procedures and individual help.
80. Do not use homework assignments as punishment.
81. Follow up class corrections of homework with a discussion of errors and their causes.
82. Assume that the students will learn their mathematics in class. Homework provides practice.
83. Be informed of the school policy regarding homework.
84. Practice differentiation in making assignments.

TO HELP MEET INDIVIDUAL DIFFERENCES

85. Try three levels of work in your class: an enriched program for the accelerated group; a core program for the average or normal group; a minimum program for the slow-moving group.

86. Determine the level at which each student is functioning in each of the seven different areas of arithmetic.
87. Provide for individual differences, since good teaching separates individuals.
88. Practice student grouping in mathematics.
89. Accept the student on the level at which he can perform.
90. Remember that you teach and that they learn—in their own way and at their own rate.

22 *Using curriculum guides*

KOPPLE C. FRIEDMAN

Friedman outlines ways to use curriculum guides and points out that "the curriculum is not so much what is found in the printed guide as what the teacher actually makes of it in the classroom." Be sure to investigate some curriculum guides.

EDUCATORS probably will not agree on a common interpretation for the proper use of the curriculum guide by teachers. This may often be perplexing to beginning teachers, let alone experienced ones. The purpose of this manuscript is to state a point of view about the role of the curriculum guide, and to concede that there may be opinions that differ from it.

Just what is a curriculum guide? Basically, it sets forth a framework which furnishes guideposts to the teacher for the development of learning experiences. It does not prescribe a particular method of instruction nor does it outline a detailed pattern of content which must be followed rigidly. It is a document which should give the teacher the security of knowing definitely what is to be taught, and yet leave him with a feeling of independence on how to approach the job.

A guide may consist of an outline of objectives, content, understandings, skills, and attitudes. It may further include sections on such topics as the characteristics of children at various age levels, the nature of the learning proc-

Reprinted from the December, 1961 issue of *Education*. Copyright 1961 by the Bobbs-Merrill Co., Inc., Indianapolis, Indiana.

ess, modern methodology, the selection and utilization of various instructional resources, suggested teaching and learning activities, reference lists, and illustrative teaching units.

Although the outline of content need not be followed rigidly, there are certain major areas that must be included in the year's study. The curriculum guide is not just an optional document on a take-it-or-leave-it basis. It should be understood that it is to be followed.

There is a difference between a curriculum guide and a resource unit. A resource unit is suggestive; it indicates many ideas for the organization of content, activities, and resources. There is a difference, also, between a resource unit and a teaching unit. Usually a teaching unit is only provided for illustrative purposes. It is the blueprint of what one teacher has planned and carried on for a particular class. In this sense it is more specific than a resource unit. Other teachers may use it for whatever good it does them.

. . . .

PITFALLS AND THEIR AVOIDANCE

It is in the utilization of the curriculum guide that pitfalls confront the teacher. Too frequently the teacher plans daily lessons without thinking in terms of "wholes" or units spread over a block of time during which a "bundle" of content and classroom activity is handled. Too frequently the teacher may get bogged down in a mass of detail and lose sight of major and underlying purposes.

In handling a larger unit of work the teacher must take the needed time to motivate and to initiate. The class must study the unit as far as it can in depth during the period allotted and then move on to another "whole."

During the course of the year a limited number of these "wholes" or units is selected for intensive study. This saves the teacher from spreading his instruction thinly over "everything" and then becoming frantic when he is not able to cover all of the desired content. By selecting and planning a limited number of studies in depth, the teacher can maintain a balanced program for the year.

A pitfall that the beginning teacher, in particular, often meets is to start teaching the way he has been taught in college, namely, through the lecture method. Too many teachers plan to use their college class notes as the basis for their instruction. They would be far better advised to throw away these old notes and start from the first day of school by getting to understand their students and learning how their interests, needs, and abilities can shape what ought to be taught. They will soon find that many of their students don't share their enthusiasm for learning or their love of subject matter.

Another pitfall is to confuse the textbook with the curriculum. The basis for determining the learning activities is the curriculum guide. The textbook, in whole or in part, is used only as it fits the framework for the year. Pity the poor class that has to plod through the textbook chapter by chapter, paragraph by paragraph, line by line, getting bogged down in details instead of focusing on understandings. Pity all the more when the class wearily outlines the chapter or writes answers to the questions at the end of the chapter as the chief basis for a so-called instructional program during the whole year.

TEACHING BY UNITS

It has already been stated that the selection of a limited number of units for study in depth is preferable to trying to "cover" everything. This selection, based on the framework of the curriculum guide, should provide a good balance in the year's work. It has also been stated that the unit is a bundle of content together with the activities that are used to develop that content.

It is frequently desirable for the teacher to let the students participate in planning the general organization of the learning activities for the unit. Unfortunately, too many teachers hesitate to do this because they associate it with the "Now, class, what shall we study?" school of thought. By all means the pupil-teacher planning situation should not be conducted until the teacher has adequately warmed the class up to the importance and scope of the unit.

This is in contrast to the teacher-dominated situation where there is mostly "telling" going on by teachers. Here the students do not get enough chance to be active learners. The teacher is doing too much talking and the students are not doing enough learning.

In a pupil-teacher planning situation, it can be determined just what everyone is going to study in common and what everyone, individually or in groups, is going to work on in specialization. This specialization is important, because it must be recognized that every student does not come to school each day expecting or needing to learn things in exactly the same way as every other student.

Failure to provide for such individualization, whether it be for the able, the average, or the slow learner, is indicative of failure to take account of what is known about child growth and development and the psychology of learning.

THE TEACHER AND THE GUIDE

In conclusion, it might be said that the curriculum is not so much what is found in the printed guide as what the teacher actually makes of it in the classroom. It is his adaptation of it to meaningful learning experiences that really counts. The teacher should use the guide as a framework and must feel free to express his teaching methods in the way that can best help make him a success in the classroom.

The teacher must not be kept from being resourceful and inventive. By all means he should not permit the textbook to determine the curriculum. He should only use the textbook or parts of it in such ways as to achieve the major objectives of the unit and of education in general.

23 *The teaching unit; what makes it tick?*

WALTER E. MCPHIE

The author defines the teaching unit and presents four basic steps to be used in planning a unit. While you read the article, ask yourself what curriculum decisions must be made with regard to each step.

ANYONE WHO HAS COMPLETED a teacher-preparation program at some university or teachers college has heard the word "unit"—and heard it often. It may be a teaching technique or method to some, a part of curriculum structure to others, or a combination of both to still others, but one thing is clear: the word itself is no stranger in the teaching profession.

Most of the literature on units in teaching is supportive. It is a rare methods text for either secondary or elementary-school teachers that does not promote, either openly or by implication, teaching with units. It is championed as the "modern" way of teaching, the most effective method of curriculum arrangement.

Occasionally in the professional literature a questioning voice is heard which suggests that another look at the basic assumptions about unit teaching is needed. Criticism, however, is more often heard from practitioners in the field, new and experienced teachers who honestly and sincerely prefer to teach on a day-to-day basis. To some of the critics, developing units of study is "busy work," a nonsensical submission to the whimsical desires of people in

Reprinted from *The Clearing House, 38*: 70-73, October, 1963.

ivory towers who are too far removed from reality. To others, unit teaching is still a hazy concept; these people are not really sure what a teaching unit is. In their eyes the literature seems to be contradictory, professors of education do not appear to be in full accord on the matter, and discussions with colleagues shed little additional light. For this group of teachers, unit teaching is not clearly enough defined to be seriously considered as an alternative to already established daily routine.

What is a *"unit"?* Perhaps the easiest way to define a unit of teaching is to draw back and look at the word in other contexts. For example, a busy mother, while shopping in a local department store, sees a skirt-blouse combination on sale which would just fit her daughter. She really likes the skirt but does not care for the blouse.

"How much would it cost if I just bought the skirt?" she inquires.

"I'm sorry," replies the clerk, "but we must sell this set as a unit."

Some people who become a little panic-stricken at the thought of being forced into using teaching units would not give a second thought to the explanation given by the clerk. They would immediately understand that for some reason the composite parts of the skirt-blouse set belong together as a whole entity and that to use them otherwise would be disadvantageous.

Other examples of the word "unit" could be given which would demonstrate the general use of the term (automobile mechanics speak of the various units in the complex make-up of their machines; refrigerator and radio repairmen often refer to units in their work; and so on). Certain common elements emerge from these examples, which should help to clarify the meaning of the term "unit" as it applies to teaching. First, there is a single mass or entity characteristic which is often composed of minor parts. Second, there appears to be some logical reason for the kind and/or size of the mass or entity and this reason most often is based on function or purpose. Therefore, a unit of teaching would be a single mass or quantity of subject matter (concepts, skills, symbols, and so forth) which for some logical reason appears to belong together or to form some reasonable single entity. Units of teaching involving the American Revolutionary Period, Punctuation, or the Backstroke in Swimming serve as good examples. In each case smaller bits and pieces of information are grouped together into a larger, meaningful mass of subject matter which can be identified easily as an entity and which can be referred to logically as a "unit." Such a process is no more complex or confusing than seeing a skirt and blouse kept together for a given reason.

Why teach with units? Having established that the word "unit" is neither awesome nor difficult to understand in teaching or any other context, there still remains the task of demonstrating the advisability of using such an approach. Once again, it may prove helpful if activities in life other than teaching are examined first.

For example, consider the businessman who must drive from Salt Lake City to attend a conference in San Francisco. If asked where he is going he will respond unhesitatingly, "San Francisco." This response indicates an awareness of the *ultimate* goal—just as a teacher if asked what he is teaching might respond, "United States history," "home economics," or "algebra." If it were possible, however, for the questioner to look secretly inside the businessman's mind and just as secretly accompany him on his trip, he would discover that he does not *actually* drive from Salt Lake City to San Francisco, but that he drives from Salt Lake City to Grantsville, from Grantsville to Wendover, from Wendover to Wells, from Wells to Elko, from Elko to Carlin, and so on until he reaches his ultimate goal, San Francisco. The eight-hundred-mile trip is too distant, too remote, and too time-consuming to represent a realistic, workable goal. Therefore, the traveler breaks the trip into smaller, identifiable goals which are more satisfying because progress is more easily seen and because achievement is in the immediate foreseeable future. It is significant to note, however, that he does not carry the breakdown of the utimate goal to the extreme. For example, he does not attempt to drive from tar-strip to tar-strip on the highway, from telephone pole to telephone pole, or from mile to mile as indicated on his speedometer. Such short, unchallenging goals would be too small, too insignificant, and too unrelated to the ultimate goal for the traveler to find them useful.

Once home from his trip, the businessman notes that he has a backlog of unfinished tasks. As he starts to take care of the unattended chores, he once again demonstrates the natural tendency to approach major tasks in terms of *units.*

While mowing his lawn he finds himself cutting a swath across the middle of a particularly large section, dividing it into two or three smaller areas rather than working his way tediously toward the center of the apparently never-ending larger section. He does not, however, pluck the grass blade by blade, nor does he cut his lawn in square foot or square yard sections.

While other examples are plentiful, the foregoing clearly illustrate several obvious facts: (1) when man is faced with a large task, he naturally—almost automatically—divides the task into smaller segments which are more easily handled and are psychologically more motivating; (2) the smaller segments are not just selected at random, but represent logical, meaningful portions of the larger goal; (3) if the smaller segments of the large task become too small, they lose appeal, challenge, and identity with the larger task.

Teaching with the unit approach offers no exceptions to the generalizations given above. In teaching, the larger goal is represented by the basic knowledge which the students should acquire from a given course. Since the task of teaching is so large, it is unmanageable and too distant to be challenging. Therefore, the teacher divides the basic understandings of the course into smaller segments. These smaller segments (or units) are chosen on the basis of their logical cohesiveness and their ability to stand alone as subject-matter entities. Teaching on a day-to-day basis rather than from within the framework of a unit is the equivalent of breaking the large goal into areas that are too small to be challenging and that are not easily related to the larger task.

How is a unit planned? Once a person has convinced himself that the unit approach to teaching is not mysterious and that it is the natural way to attack any large task, he is ready to start with actual unit planning. This will involve four basic steps: (1) selection of objectives, (2) determination of teaching procedures, (3) identification of teaching materials, and (4) justification of the three previous steps.

The teacher's first step, within the confines of the unit chosen, is to *select* the basic understandings (concepts), skills, or new vocabulary which need to be developed. This suggests that the teacher will analyze the subject matter contained within the unit very carefully and will decide on certain things to be emphasized, learned, and remembered. Some authorities disagree with such a suggestion; they maintain that such an authoritarian approach kills the incentive and initiative of the students. Such opposition is based on a misunderstanding of the proposal. The suggestion that the teacher should select the fundamental objectives to be achieved in advance *does not* imply a lack of flexibility. It simply suggests that it is necessary for the teacher to be prepared to give focus and direction in his teaching. It allows for deviation from the advance plan, *but offers something from which to deviate.*

The second consideration for the teacher is the procedures necessary to achieve the objectives. Most literature on unit planning speaks of multitudinous lists of activities which could conceivably fit within the framework of a given unit, but it seems advisable to seek out methods, techniques, and procedures which apply *specifically* to the individual objectives. Whether the teacher includes many or just a few procedures for teaching each objective depends upon whether the teacher wants the unit to be a resource unit or a unit plan from which to teach directly. In either case, however, there should be a specific relationship between the stated objective and the procedures proposed. Then nothing is left to chance; each objective has its corresponding procedures which have been planned to ensure that the desired learning takes place. Again, this does not suggest rigidity. Rather, it insists on basic preparation with the clear understanding that the teacher has the right and obligation to deviate and make adjustments whenever the current situation demands.

Identifying materials which will aid in the achievement of the objectives is in reality part of the responsibility in determining procedures. It is given separate space here since many teachers feel that it is important to list the materials in a special place on the unit plan where the list can be quickly checked prior to commencing a lesson. This helps to prevent an often-heard statement: "I had meant to bring such-and-such today to demonstrate this point, but I seem to have forgotten." The advisability of using materials such as films, slides, realia, charts, graphs, pictures, the chalkboard, and other audio-visual aids is generally conceded by most teachers. The most important thing to be remembered is that these materials are only *means*—not ends.

The fourth task in unit planning is one which rightfully encompasses the other three. What is the justification for the objectives selected? For the procedures chosen? For the materials to be used? The teacher should ask: "Am I attempting to teach this basic concept because I have thought it over carefully and believe it is important for the students to understand *in the light of some purpose*—or am I attempting to teach something simply because it is today and I taught something yesterday which seemed to precede this? Am I going to show this film because it will really help to clarify a justifiable concept or skill—or is it because film-showing takes up most of the period and requires relatively little of me?" Unit planning which is scrutinized with such introspection cannot help but yield superior results.

In summary, the unit approach to teaching is a simple, natural one. It has been demonstrated that man uses this approach in nearly every large task. Unit planning involves the segmenting of large teaching goals into smaller, cohesive, and meaningful entities of subject matter. It also involves the selection of basic objectives within the smaller segments (units) which are important for the students to learn and retain. Once the latter has been done, it is then necessary for the teacher to determine the proper procedures to be employed in achieving the objectives, to identify appropriate materials to be used in the learning process, and to justify the objectives, procedures, and materials. With all of this clearly in mind, and with a determination to teach well, teachers should be able to look forward to the security and satisfaction which comes from knowing what needs to be done and how to do it.

24   Stating goals

R . M U R R A Y   T H O M A S

Thomas states here a view currently held by leading educators about educational goals; that is, goals are defined in terms of the students' behavior—by what they know, do, feel, and think. You will remember that goals are defined in this book in a similar manner. In his book, Thomas says:

"The most profitable way for the educator to state his objectives is by describing the type of behavior characteristics of the person who performs successfully; *that is, the person who performs successfully is the person who* has learned. *This is known as describing the objectives of the school in terms of* student behavior. *Because the student is the one who is being changed, the focus should be on his behavior, not on the teacher's nor in terms of the topic of subject matter."*

In this selection Thomas shows the relationship between goals, methods, and evaluation. A teacher named O'Brien discusses his plans with his supervisor, Mr. Harris.

MR. O'BRIEN explained his chart [shown here on pp. 132-33]:

"I put down the main methods I would use to reach those objectives. I would use all the methods under *likes* literature to reach goals 1 through 4 and all the methods under *understands* literature to reach goals 5 through 9. I mean that in this list there isn't one particular method for a particular goal. I think all the methods would help develop these kinds of behavior. I'd plan to use the methods throughout the year, since these are long-term goals and not just objectives for a particular unit. Across from each objective from 1 through 4 I listed the ways I think I could gather evidence about how well the children reached that goal. So the evaluation numbers correspond to specific objectives. That's why I have listed such things as the parent-teacher conference for more than one objective. Of course, I wouldn't have a conference for each objective. I just meant that objectives 2, 3, and 4 are kinds of behavior I could try to learn about in a conference with a child's parents. There is one more thing I might mention about the evaluation column. Some of the techniques listed there are more practical than others. For

---

From *Judging Student Progress*, by R. Murray Thomas. Second edition, 1960. Reprinted by permission of David McKay Company, Inc.

Objectives	Methods	Evaluation Techniques
Following his learning experiences, the student shows he *likes* literature because he:	(In general all the methods listed would help students pursue the goals of liking literature.)	(Numbers in front of evaluation techniques correspond with numbers in front of objectives.)
	The teacher will:	*The teacher will:*
1. Voluntarily secures books to read.	From time to time bring books to class. Give brief summaries of what stories are about. Read passages from books to class.	1. Have students keep lists of books read. Check with librarian or class-room library.
2. Discusses with others what he has read.	Give students opportunities to tell class about stories. Give them chances to draw pictures of scenes from books to show class.	2. Observe students in class. Talk with parents.
3. Suggests that others read books he has enjoyed.	Display book jackets on bulletin board. Give brief discussion of books displayed in class.	3. Observe students in class. Talk with parents. Have class book reports.
4. Voluntarily spends free time reading.	Provide time for entire class to go to library and browse and select books. Suggest particular books to individual students according to teacher's knowledge of their interest and abilities; do not force them, merely suggest.	4. Observe students in class. Talk with students and parents.

OBJECTIVES	METHODS	EVALUATION TECHNIQUES
The student shows he *understands* literature because he:	Read stories to (and with) class, and by use of leading questions show how to analyze plot, describe character traits, analyze character growth, locate story setting, give personal reaction to characters.	(All the evaluation techniques help measure growth toward all goals.) Lead class discussions. Have students give book reports directed at objectives (oral and written reports). Give written tests.
5. Relates the plot sequence in a story or play.		
6. Describes the character traits of the main characters in the story.		
7. Tells how one or two principal characters might be different at the end of the story than at the beginning.		
8. Accurately locates the locale of the story on a map, if tale involves an exact location.		
9. Tells what characters he liked best and least, and why.		

example, I probably would not be able to have a conference with each child's mother or father. Therefore, I would base my judgments more on the other devices, which are more practical for my class."

The curriculum director believed that the plan was sound and that the evaluation techniques suggested were logical ones for checking the objectives. When Mr. Harris commented upon the absence of a *matching test* among the evaluation techniques, the teacher pointed out that previously he had thought of evaluation mainly in terms of tests like the one requiring pupils to match authors with their works. However, in the present case he had begun by stating the objectives as the kinds of behavior he wished to result from his teaching. Consequently, he saw that evaluation means judging how closely a person's behavior approaches the objective. Sometimes tests are appropriate techniques for making this judgment, but many times other approaches are more appropriate or are used in combination with tests.

Before leaving, Mr. O'Brien asked two final questions:

"Earlier today I was showing this scheme of mine to one of the sixth-grade teachers. She said it looked all right, but she thought I had too much in the objectives column. She said my objectives were really just 'likes and understands literature,' so those are the only things that should appear under objectives. She said these other more specific behaviors belonged over in the evaluation column, because those were the things I was looking for when I evaluated. What do you think?"

Mr. Harris said, "I prefer the way you have done it. These behaviors you have listed are ultimately your goals in terms of the ways you will see them reached by the children. Some teachers prefer to move these specifics into the evaluation column. This is all right too, if you like. What is important is that you actually do define them down into observable or measurable specifics, despite the column you assign them to. The scheme you have outlined in literature is a good one. It should work nicely."

Mr. O'Brien's second question was:

"Now that I've broken appreciation of literature down into two categories, liking and understanding, how do I lump them together again when I have to give a student a single mark on his report card? It's quite possible a bright student meets the understanding goals but doesn't like to spend much time reading on his own, so he would rank lower on the 'liking' objectives. Maybe he prefers playing ball in his spare time."

Mr. Harris admitted, "You're right. This means we'll have to look over the report card again for the middle grades. At least in the case of your class, it will need some revision so parents and students can better understand it. Let's talk is over next time the teachers of the intermediate grades meet."

25 *The unit in modern teaching*

A . J . F O Y C R O S S

Many of the theoretical notions already discussed in this book are contained in this comprehensive plan for a unit. For example:

1. *the belief that pupils should actively build meanings;*
2. *the concentration on objectives for a total group and for individuals;*
3. *the use of cooperative planning for simultaneous satisfaction of individual and group goals;*
4. *the use of a variety of objectives, methods, and materials.*

You will find that many curriculum guides include a format similar to this one.

FEW SCHOOLS now measure the success of their instruction program solely by weighing its effectiveness in teaching the 3 R's. Today's youth must possess and be skilled in the use of the best tools of learning, and modern schools are more effective than ever in developing such skills. But schools and teachers nowadays are judged by what their students do with the tools of learning, not merely by how sharp these tools are. This means that professional teaching is much more of a job than it used to be. In fact, if it is good teaching, it is a highly complex job.

Our nation has been busy in the last half-century discovering and developing new ways of teaching. Thus an important part of American heritage today is a vastly increased body of knowledge about how people learn and about how schools and teachers can assist individuals to absorb the knowledge, skills, and behavior patterns which assure a better, happier life.

The modern teacher is one who is skilled in bringing this heritage to his students. He is one who can bring to bear on learning problems the vast resources of new knowledge in the sciences of human behavior. He has at his disposal improved ways of helping young people think and plan, and gain skill and confidence in recognizing and working individually and cooperatively on the important problem of everyday living.

Involved in the modern teacher's planning is what has been variously called a "unit plan," a "resource unit," and a "plan for a unit of instruction." While its variety of titles probably indicates a varying emphasis in purpose

Reprinted from *Audiovisual Instruction,* 3:168-69, September, 1958.

and use, the general adoption of the unit as a device for planning learning activities reflects increased attention by teachers to this complex job of directing a total learning process.

While the written form of this planning may vary from teacher to teacher, there are certain common characteristics. The following outline used in an actual school situation will serve as an illustration. (From *Integrating Unit Plan Form* by Helen Halter Long. Mamaroneck, N. Y. Mimeographed.)

I. *Integrating theme*
    A. For _____ grade pupils
    B. By _____ (teacher)

II. *Group objectives*
    A. Attitudes
        1. What specific attitude development is to be concentrated upon?
        2. How will attitude development be measured?
    B. Skills and Abilities
        1. What specific skills and abilities are to be emphasized?
        2. How will these skills and abilities be tested?
    C. Knowledges
        1. What knowledges should be acquired?
        2. How is it planned to test for these knowledges and their possible application?

III. *Individual objectives*
    (List of names of pupils and the objectives to be emphasized for each, personally, during progress of this unit.)
    (Individualized plans for assisting each student.)

IV. *Analysis of the integrating theme*
    A. How is it related to the life problems of these pupils?
    B. How can pupils participate in its selection?
    C. In what ways will pupils be provided opportunities to suggest things that they wish to find out about?
    D. What are the several phases of the integrating theme which might be explored in the progress of this unit? Which ones are likely to be most important to the pupils involved?

V. *Subject areas*
    (A detailed plan of how any or all of the following subjects areas might be used in this unit.)
    A. English (reading, oral and written communications)
        1. How may practice be provided for use of previously learned skills, attitudes, knowledges in English?
        2. What opportunities does this unit offer new learning in this subject area?
    B. Social Studies

    c. Science
    d. Mathematics
    e. Arts, Crafts, and Music

VI. *Instructional materials, equipment, and other resources*
    A. Reading Materials—Books
       1. What book references might be used by all pupils? Which are the best references for all pupils?
       2. What enrichment references are desirable?
       3. Which are likely to be the best references for extended-interest reading, committee work, etc?
       4. What book references are likely to be better for the below-average readers?
       5. Where and how are these materials made available?
    B. Reading Materials—Other Than Books
    C. Photographs, Flat Pictures
    D. Maps, Graphs, Charts, Posters
    E. Slides and Filmstrips
    F. Motion Pictures
    G. Recordings
    H. Radio Programs
    I. Telecasts
    J. Models, Specimens, Exhibits
    K. Experimental Equipment
    L. "Creative Materials" and Equipment
    (Includes materials for drawing, construction work, printing, photography, making displays, etc.)
    M. Field Trips
    (For whole class, small groups, individual pupils)
    N. Resource Persons

VII. *Activities and projects*
    A. Class Projects
       1. What are some of the possible class projects?
       2. How will pupils be given an opportunity to discuss and select one or more class projects?
       3. How will the pupils be helped to organize their planning for a class project?
    B. Committee Projects
       1. What are some of the possible small-group or committee projects?
       2. How are groups and/or committees to be formed?
       3. How will pupils be given the opportunity to discuss and select committee projects?
    C. Individual Projects
       1. What opportunities will there be for individual-interest projects?

2. Which individual projects are best suited to:
   a. Art expression
   b. Scientific investigation
   c. Mathematical interest and ability
   d. Reading interests and ability
   e. Writing interests and ability
   f. Speaking and dramatizing
   g. Organizing abilities

D. Individual Activities Which May Be Carried Out at Home or During Out-of-School Hours

E. "Administrative" Activities
   (List of pupils showing activities which might meet the particular needs of each one.)
   1. Planning Committees
   2. "Bulletin" Boards Committees
   3. Library Committees
   4. Projection Committee
   5. Typing Committee

VIII. *Provisions for drill*
(This section includes subsections for each area of drill.)
A. Who needs "drill" on what?
B. What are the probable best ways of motivating "drill" for the group or for particular members of the group?
C. What are the possible ways of varying procedure for drill?
D. What are the ways of helping students to evaluate the results and to recognize success and gain a desirable feeling of success in the objectives of the drill?
E. What are the possible "vital situations" to which the students can relate their drill?

IX. *Cooperative planning of a schedule*
A. Preliminary Schedule Planning
   1. What appears to be the amount of time it will take for *these* pupils to finish the unit?
   2. At approximately what time is this unit likely to "come up"?
   3. How much and what part of the school day will probably be devoted to this unit?
   4. What days will probably be most appropriate for introduction and culmination of work?
   5. What are probably the best ways of involving all of the students (and parents) in the scheduling?

It will be remembered that the process is the important factor in a unit such as the one illustrated here. Content, subject, problem, so long as they are interesting and vital to the learner, could be from virtually any field and still the unit experience would result in desirable learning.

After all, the prime purpose of going to school is to learn how to learn. A unit becomes important largely to the degree that it serves the purpose of helping the students gain confidence in their own ability to learn, to identify a problem, and to follow it through to a satisfying resolution. A unit becomes relatively less important to the degree that it denies the students opportuninities to grow at an optimum rate in their ability to initiate, plan, and follow through, themselves, the learning opportunities inherent in it.

No school attempts to teach a child all that he needs to learn. However, through participation in a sufficient number of such learning experiences as are provided by units taught effectively, the child can grow in the skills and attitudes that will meet his learning needs.

26 *Bridging the gap between textbook teaching and unit teaching*

RAYMOND H. MUESSIG

Students of education are often discouraged by the apparently wide gap between the theory they hear at college and their experience in the teaching situation. Unit teaching is generally considered the best way for pupils to learn, but some teachers-to-be have never experienced such teaching themselves, and although teaching right out of a textbook is often decried as ineffective, practical ways to abandon this method are not always easy to find. This article presents some matter-of-fact ways to begin to bridge the gap between familiar textbook teaching and the more favored unit teaching method. Upper-grade teachers, in particular, will find this article helpful.

ONE OF THE PERENNIAL problems in the history of mankind is the difference which has existed between the ideal and the real, the gap between theory and practice, or the dichotomy between what is said and what is done. The stereotypic view of a politician includes in it the assumption that the campaign promises made before election and the activities engaged in after the

Reprinted from *The Social Studies*, 54:43-47, February, 1963.

person has taken over the duties of the office may be widely separated or even unrelated. Kneeling before his beloved, the young suitor promises the object of his affection the moon, the stars, castles, furs, and jewels. Imagine the young lady's disillusionment a few years after their marriage when she is still cooking over a leaky gas stove, waiting for more hot water so she can finish washing the dishes, and doing the family laundry by hand in a set tub in the basement! In a more serious vein, the "Sunday Christian" may be a long way from the Sermon on the Mount when he composes an advertisement for a forthcoming "bargain" sale in a department store.

Countless articles in professional education journals have discussed the cultural lag which exists between rather widely accepted educational theories and actual practices in classrooms. Perhaps there is no more profound or troublesome breach than the one that exists between the theory of unit teaching so widely espoused in the social studies and other content areas and the highly structured, constricting, uncreative use of textbooks which one may observe in so many social studies classrooms. Almost four decades have elapsed since Professor Henry C. Morrison championed an early unit plan which was one of the forerunners of today's unit method, yet many teachers still fall short of mastery of this procedure—let alone more advanced practices like the problems approach.

Simply deploring this condition does little good. Exhorting teachers to throw down their textbook crutches and run to the unit seems to have had a negligible impact. Giving in to the dead weight and long-standing tradition of the single textbook is a solution which might appeal to a substantial number of teachers, but this is the coward's way out and would mean denying our students the best of which our profession is capable.

Just as the skillful teacher "begins where the students are" in their developmental levels and their academic mastery, it is only reasonable to assume that the teacher has to walk before he can run, master some basic methods before attempting more complex ones, and move from the approaches where he feels secure to those where he feels less secure.

The approach which I am going to outline very briefly is not a panacea. It must be considered as tentative, subject to error, open to revision and improvement. As a matter of fact it is proposed as a *temporary* measure to aid teachers in getting a feeling for unit teaching. Once this feeling has been grasped, I hope that this idea will be discarded and new operational levels sought. I worked out this procedure initially to help a group of experienced teachers, used to single textbook teaching, move into unit work. They reported that the idea "worked." Whether this suggestion is good, right, new, or old, it is at least "pragmatic."

The only task which remains before I attempt an explanation of this system for bridging the gap between textbook teaching and unit teaching is a definition of terms. What do I mean by "textbook" and "unit" teaching as I perceive them? I hope that I am not creating two "straw men" just for the sake of contrast, but I see a rather significant difference in these two methods and in their underlying philosophies.

Textbook-centered teaching has a medieval heritage. The teacher who could secure a book or commit the contents of a manuscript to memory was "in business." The text was a source of authority, often unquestioned and unchallenged. The more faithfully the learner could return its contents to his teacher, the more approbation he earned. This approach, therefore, has been with us a long time. To many it seems to have the same kind of familiarity as a well-worn smoking jacket. There are many allies in the textbook-centered camp including husky bruisers like Status Quo, Custom, Mental Discipline, and Apathy. The facts contained in the single source have some kind of magical intrinsic value—worthy in and of themselves. The assign-study-recite-test procedure is generally followed. The teacher generally originates, directs, and passes judgment upon all learning activity. Only those evaluation techniques which attempt to assess the degree to which the names, dates, places, and events have been "learned" are employed. Motivation is provided by the teacher by way of grades and other extrinsic rewards. The teacher's main aim in life seems to be "covering the text." More and more facts accumulate as research continues over the years and as man's stay on earth is extended; textbooks get larger; and it gets harder and harder for the teacher to reach first page 523, then page 678, and later page 751 by the end of the year. A teacher's life is further complicated by parents who can conceive of no other approach and who believe in "fundamental" learning void of "fads and frills," by administrators who insist that various kinds of standardized tests be given to all groups as a means of comparing teachers or schools, by students who either cannot read the text or are bored by it, and by the fact that his courses seem to be more dull and drab each year they are repeated.

This is not to say that the use of a textbook is wrong. That assumption would be absurd. The textbook can be one of the finest resources available to a class and a teacher. Textbooks are often written by persons who are well qualified both as scholars and teachers. Texts may be well documented and illustrated and may even be graded in an endeavor to meet some of the reading problems. They may even contain suggestions for meaningful activities which can enhance learning. The problem is, however, that too many teachers rely exclusively upon the text and never move out to other green pastures like additional books containing related but varied material and written at different reading levels, pamphlets and booklets, newspapers and magazines, films and filmstrips, recordings, field trips, resource persons, community studies, independent research, ad infinitum.

Unit teaching in a more simplified form is not always a radical departure from the most enlightened textbook teaching, nor is it any kind of a final answer; but it does attempt to correct many of the shortcomings of narrowly conceived textbook-centered methodology. Unit teaching at its best can be a thing of beauty, however, and has some unique properties which distinguish it from its more mundane cousin, the textbook approach. Unit teaching attempts to integrate, combine, coordinate, or articulate understandings, skills, attitudes, and appreciations around large significant topics. It seeks wholeness rather than fragmentation, clusters of ideas and data rather than isolated particles, more of a montage than a series of single snapshots taken one by one. The unit approach does not avoid facts, but it does try to build facts into concepts and generalizations which may have more meaning, may be transferable in more situations, and may be more lasting. This method recognizes that any single source of information, however good it may be, imposes unnecessary limitations upon the class and the teacher. Pupil-teacher planning in the drafting of objectives, search for materials, selection of methods of study, and development of evaluative processes is more common. Actual interests, needs, aspirations, and problems of students are tapped and kept in mind, and greater student involvement and identification with objectives of learning tends to upstage intrinsic rather than extrinsic motivation. The unit may deal with material similar in content to that which the textbook approach gives its allegiance, but there is no pressure to cover any given text. Unit teaching encourages creative, independent, critical thought rather than memorization for its own sake. It relies on a variety of evaluation techniques in addition to the typical standardized and teacher-made tests. We could go on, but the basic thing, it seems to me, is that the unit teacher is after more *meaning* in what goes on in a classroom.

I believe that one of the reasons the unit approach has not found its way into more social studies classes is that the distance from basic textbook teaching to the full-blown unit teaching is too great to travel all at once. I propose that the teacher already used to the text begin there. The first step is to make the most of the textbook, to get more meaning out of it, to emphasize relatedness. Later, a few added resources may be brought in and some activities with a "unit flavor" blended in. Still later, a simple unit could be worked out with the students, and so on until a complete unit approach is attempted in the spring.

This article begins with and stops at the first stage of this process—using

the text as a more unified teaching tool. The steps for the procedure are outlined below:

1. Let us assume for the sake of this illustration that it is a few weeks
before the start of the school year. Taking the basic textbook for the course,
the teacher might begin by writing the chapter titles on separate 3 x 5 cards.
It is sometimes useful to jot down a few of the subtopics under the chapter
title just to have a reminder of some of the basic things included in the
chapter. The cards should be separated into several stacks by priority. Some
chapters which the teacher considers to be of primary importance will fall
into the "essential" pile; others of secondary importance will fall into the
"helpful" stack; and still others which may have doubtful value for a particular class would go into a "possible," "hold," or "delete" group. (Realizing that
many textbooks try to be all things to all people, the teacher is already beginning a discrimination process by seeking significant aspects of the course
for his point of focus.)

2. Next, the teacher works out a rough approximation of the number of
teaching weeks in the school year. His purpose for doing this is not to see
how much material—regardless of its importance—he can cram into the course
but to work out *areas of emphasis* or "unit" topics. Now he roughly divides
the total number of weeks into blocks of approximately five weeks. Later, as
actual "units" emerge they may vary from three to six weeks in length depending on the teacher's objectives, the interest of the class, and other factors.
In a typical school year, there would be from six to eight of these textbook
units. Glancing quickly at the 3 x 5 cards in the "helpful" stack and thumbing
more carefully through those in the "essential" pile, the teacher tries to list
from six to eight over-all problems, topics, or content areas around which the
units can be constructed.

3. The remainder of the 3 x 5 cards in the top priority group, probably
most of the cards of secondary importance, and perhaps even a few of the
cards in the third questionable pile may now be separated under the basic
unit copies. This unit distribution may or may not follow the organization of
the textbook. The important thing is whether the over-all topics make sense
to the teacher and the students. The order of the unit topics can be arranged
chronologically, logically, psychologically, or developmentally according to
the teacher's perception of the nature of the class and the content discipline.
The first unit might be so placed because it is fundamental or foundational in
its content, interest arousing, more concrete or understandable, or for some
other reason.

4. Now the teacher is ready to build the first of the units. He takes the

3 x 5 cards in the group assigned to the initial topic and notes the chapters they represent. (Each unit would include from about three to six chapters in the typical social studies text.) It is at this point that a rather tedious, but rewarding, process begins. The teacher carefully reads only those chapters which will be used for the first unit. On fresh, additional 3 x 5 cards he writes down the *crucial, basic* facts contained in each chapter, using one card for each factual statement. Just "any old facts" will not do! These must be facts with lasting importance, facts which will lead to significant understandings, attitudes, and appreciations. Altogether, though it is not possible to assign a magic number, the teacher might have from one hundred to two hundred essential facts.

5. The "fact" cards are now separated into three basic piles, "understandings," "attitudes," and "appreciations." The "understandings" pile will probably be the largest by far.

6. The cards in the "understandings" pile are again subdivided. The teacher tries to find groups of facts which support a given concept. A concept is a class of related information, a "basket" which holds a cluster of facts and gives them real meaning. A given unit might contain from ten to twenty concepts each of which would be supported by from five to ten basic facts which "add up to something." One last refinement is necessary, however, to complete the treatment of "understandings." This is the formulation of from one generalization up to five generalizations. A generalization is the interrelationship of two or more concepts and should emerge quite naturally when the teacher analyzes the concepts already developed. One of the most important goals in social studies education is the ability to generalize, to fit particulars into a configuration, to draw inferences from data, or to perceive applications. The generalization, therefore, is the cognitive capstone of the unit. It is the vein of gold which is the produce of all of the digging which the students and the teacher do throughout the unit.

7. A single unit may lead to only one or two important attitudes and appreciations. The "attitude" pile may contain only two or three concept cards and the group of fact cards which buttress the concepts, and a similar situation usually exists with the "appreciation" pile. Attitudes and appreciations are mixtures of both facts and feelings, cognitive and emotive elements. They carry the values, predispositions, and aesthetic elements of the unit.

8. The teacher is now at the "blueprint" stage of building a textbook-oriented unit. He takes a large piece of butcher paper and divides it into three columns. At the top and center of each of the three columns he prints "Content," "Activities," and "Evaluation" from left to right, respectively.

9. In the "Content" column the teacher prints a complete structural out-

line of the material he has gathered on the 3 x 5 cards. A Roman numeral is assigned to each generalization, attitude, and appreciation. Capital letters are given to supporting concepts which go under each generalization, attitude, and appreciation. Arabic numbers are assigned to the facts which undergird their respective concepts. Now the teacher can "see" what he is after, where he is going, what he wants to build. This view can be quite satisfying, for it gives a textbook teacher a sense of purpose which he may have missed before.

10. In the "Activities" column the teacher prints *over-all activities* which will serve the purposes and content of the unit like reading from the text, group discussion, etc. and *specific activities* like student panels, individual student papers, etc. which match up on a one-to-one basis with particular generalizations, attitudes, and appreciations or individual concepts which support them. Later, these more traditional activities may be augmented with procedures typical of a full-blown unit approach. The teacher could begin this expansion process on the second unit by having students write for free and inexpensive materials, by ordering several films, by forming a few research committees, by securing a resource person, etc.

11. In the "Evaluation" column the teacher would again list both general and specific procedures for assessing student growth on the unit as a whole and on given generalizations, attitudes, appreciations, or underlying concepts. During the first trial "unit" the teacher might be contented with just teacher-made essay tests, multiple-choice tests, etc. In later units, the teacher may include inventories, check lists, observation, open-ended procedures, etc.

12. The final step in the process is for the teacher to ditto copies of the "unit" for all of the students. A cover with a "catchy" title and a clever illustration can help a great deal to interest the students. The teacher should write a one paragraph over-view of the nature of the unit to secure student involvement. A group of basic unit objectives might be listed. This time they will be the teacher's, but later they will come out of class discussion. Also included would be a copy of the teacher's outline of content, activities, and evaluation so the students have a "preview of coming attractions." The first dittoed unit might contain daily assignments with some options for differences in students' interests and capacities. Students will read selectively from the text and use it as a genuine resource. Additional enrichment activities could be suggested too. Culminating, or wrap-up activities might be planned by the students themselves after they have a feeling for this approach. This would also initiate some pupil-teacher planning. Finally, if the teacher has caught the spirit by now, the unit might have a brief bibliography for the students so they could start getting in the habit of consulting other sources.

This has been an attempt to suggest a procedure by which teachers could bridge the gap between textbook-centered teaching and unit teaching. The "bridge" suggested probably bears a closer resemblance to a log dropped across a creek than a sleek, steel suspension bridge, but it is a beginning. The rest of the construction task is up to the dedicated teacher who wants to do more for the wonderful, unique, challenging young people who walk through his door.

27   *Earmarks of a functional unit*

C. C. T R I L L I N G H A M

The author defines and outlines the characteristics of a well-planned and well-administered unit. Investigate for comparison some published unit plans and visit some classrooms to see how these criteria are met.

THE UNIT as a basis for instruction and learning originated out of the necessity to break up the total world of human experience into practical subdivisions for facilitating the administration of classroom procedure. The unit may be defined as a learning experience which consists of purposeful and related activities that grow out of and fulfill the individual or social needs recognized by the pupil. Assuming this definition, a unit is not an aggregate of subject matter to be learned; subject matter, rather, is utilized only as it contributes to the meaningfulness of the total learning experience provided for in the unit.

Characteristics of a well-planned and well-administered unit:

1. It recognizes immediate needs and interests of pupils.
2. It possesses social significance.
3. It has unity, as it is organized around a central interest or problem; it is not just a hodge-podge of miscellaneous subject matter.
4. It is comprehensive, as it utilizes a desirable and natural fusion of the

Reprinted from the *NEA Journal,* 24:282, December, 1935.

various subject fields, permitting the use of pertinent content from the wealth of possibilities.

5. It has continuity in that it relates to the preceding and the following units.

6. It involves reading materials and learning activities suited to the varied maturity and capacity of pupils.

7. It makes of the classroom a laboratory for constructive work rather than a mere place to recite.

8. It stimulates progress in those phases of the tool subjects which are a natural part of it.

9. It offers opportunities for pupil participation in planning, executing, and evaluating the work of the unit.

10. It improves the pupil-teacher relationship by making the teacher a co-adventurer with the pupil.

11. It contributes to the development of wholesome social habits and attitudes on the part of the pupils.

12. It equips the pupil with concepts, generalizations, or techniques which may be applied to other situations.

28   *Eighth graders approach a world outlook*

MORTON J. SOBEL

While you are reading this article, apply Trillingham's criteria to the project Sobel describes. What conclusions do you reach? It is also useful to study this article in the light of the concepts discussed by Watson in Chapter 3 and in the articles in Chapter 2.

CONCEPTS AND TERMINOLOGY of meaningful education have been enunciated, evaluated, restated, argued, and discussed in many contradictory ways. The classroom teacher, therefore, sometimes finds himself in a state of complete confusion when he tries to set up an actual program of purposeful living with his group. Mere discussion of making education meaningful to the pupil at his own stage of development does not automatically make the theory become fact.

Often the teacher must determine within himself to begin to plan a program with his students, within the school and community situation as they actually exist at the present time. In so doing, he may find that while not all conditions are ideal, at least some of them will favor the success of the program if he and his group intelligently use what they have in their planning and doing.

The project described in this article did not develop many final answers, but did lead to the satisfaction of certain needs of the pupils and of the teacher. It was set up in accordance with actual conditions, and an attempt was made to utilize the very best available educational theories and resources.

NEED FOR A WORLD OUTLOOK

An emotional-needs test was administered to two eighth-grade groups in a school in a large Midwestern city. One surprising result of the test showed that *the need for a world outlook* was second only to the need for achievement and even superseded the need for economic security in the comparatively low-income district in which the school was located.

When the test results were revealed to the two groups, a lengthy and earnest discussion led to the decision to make up a unit on The Proper Study of Mankind. Accordingly, a list of study areas evolved. The two classes divided into ten small groups of five or six members each. Each group centered its work in one of the ten areas agreed upon.

One group concerned itself with man's religions, another with man's races, another with his governments, and others with his hopes, knowledge, beliefs, problems, organizations, recreations, and, finally, man's great benefactors. Each group met as a unit from three to five times a week, determining what it ought to do in the way of study and how to demonstrate results to others.

THREE GOALS UNDERTAKEN

In class discussions with the teacher, it was decided that each group would undertake three goals, one to be something "seeable," one "touchable," and the third the responsibility for the room bulletin board for one to two weeks. "Seeable" projects might be plays, round-table discussions, or something similar; "touchable" projects might be along the lines of scrapbooks or written stories; and the bulletin-board project would be a visual demonstration of what the group was concerned with in its study.

One period was spent on a class discussion of group organization and its mechanics, and it was decided that the group would elect a chairman and a secretary who would keep complete notes for reference and evaluation. When the project was well on its way, it became necessary, in the teacher's opinion, to hold a sort of critique and review of group procedure. A socio-drama of a democratic group in operation was the basic feature of this period. This proved helpful at a time when interest seemed to be lagging and the whole tenor of the job appeared to be bogging down. It proved to be a rather successful procedure, as the youngsters were becoming so enmeshed in the unfamiliar mechanics of group process that the entire success of the project seemed endangered.

THE GROUPS REPORT

The group on religions drew a mural denoting the three large religious groups in the United States, and also those of the Moslem, Confucian, and Hindu beliefs. Each member of the group wrote a short report on one of the religions. This group also gave a play which had been obtained from the United Nations by mail, and prepared a most interesting and informative bulletin board on the subject of religions.

The group on races drew pictures and wrote a commentary for showing through the opaque projector. Much of their information was obtained from material written by Ruth Benedict and by Eva Knox, and from a booklet called *Peoples of the Earth*. Also, they produced a book comprising five chapters written by various members of the group. The thirty pages of the book told of the adventures of two girls who won an essay contest and were awarded a trip around the world.

The group studying governments gave oral reports on the various characteristics of different systems of governments, including democracy, communism, socialism, fascism, monarchy, and feudalism. In addition, they compiled a scrapbook which showed through pictures and written commentaries some of the aspects of the different forms of government which they had studied.

The group on organizations did only one portion of the job which they had set for themselves. They spent their time in writing a play which they presented as a puppet show. They made hand puppets from scraps of material and bits of waste products. Before they had their puppet show ready for performance, most of their time was gone, and they felt that their attempt at giving oral reports was a pretty sad affair. However, there seemed little doubt that they had participated in the learning process at least to the same extent as their classmates, and perhaps more. They considered organizations in broad general groupings, such as international, fraternal, youth, charity, and a number of other classifications, each of which they illustrated with appropriate examples, such as the United Nations, Boy Scouts of America, and the like.

The recreations group, too, had difficulties. This seemed due in part to the fact that it included the fairly large number of nine pupils, and also to the fact that it was made up mostly of boys who expected only to discuss various kinds of sports. Eventually, they succeeded in working up a fairly good round-table discussion on recreation, including not only sports, but reading, movies, radio, hobbies, and music. This group required more teacher guidance than any other.

The group concerned with great men studied six men and women whose contributions to world progress had been most notable. These included people such as Pasteur, Jane Addams, Confucius, and others whose contributions lay in varied fields. In their oral reports and scrapbooks, the group attempted to link the contributions of these great people to modern life and to the progress of mankind toward better living.

The children who considered man's hopes drew a mural which depicted various aspects of health, crime, education, war, prejudice, and the like. A scrapbook which they made encompassed these subjects, with a section devoted to each. The well-organized, carefully collected pictures and commentaries illustrated high idealism.

Man's problems were defined in several areas, including atomic energy, world trade, peace, social advances, child-adult relationships, and economic security. Each pupil took one organization which specialized in the study and solution of the problems. He wrote to the organization for materials, which were compiled into written reports to be discussed and clarified in a round-table conference. An extremely lively class discussion followed this presentation.

Man's knowledge was grouped into four large areas: science, industry, agriculture, and transportation. The teacher suggested the inclusion of philosophy or ethics, but the children did not wish to go into areas which seemed rather illusory to them, and no point was made of the issue. These children drew a mural illustrating the four areas and some of the accomplishments in each, and also wrote and presented a radio script discussing not only man's knowledge, but also his use of it in ways considered constructive and destructive.

The group concerned with beliefs wrote a play on superstitions called

The Superstitious Teacher. By slightly disguising the teacher's name, they demonstrated certain incidents of daily occurrence in the classroom which would have been performed in other ways, if the actions of pupils and teacher had been guided solely by logic. The play was given as a radio script in order to do away with the necessity for scenery and props. It was performed, as were all the group projects which lent themselves to such presentation, in the school auditorium before other sections. The other project of this group involved the use of very large sheets of construction paper on which were pasted pictures illustrating some of the common beliefs of mankind. These tended to be more on the positive side, demonstrating belief in the equality of man, in freedom of speech and of worship, and concepts of this general nature.

CLASS DISCUSSIONS INVALUABLE

One of the most valuable features of the entire project was the class discussion which developed after each group presentation. Each of these discussions tended to be of a constructive nature, emphasizing not only improvement in the particular group's technical work, but also a general broadening of the concepts presented by the reporting group. Ideas and ideals which were generated not only from home influences, but also from reflective thinking and talking on the part of the child himself, became a commonly accepted part of the procedure. This seemed most worth-while.

As the project drew to a close, general discussions of the unit by the pupils took place to determine what had been learned and what benefits had been derived from the endeavors of the preceding eight weeks. Comments of a derogatory nature were few, either because of the presence of the teacher or because of a firm belief on the part of the pupils in the worth of the entire project. It is difficult to determine precisely the cause for this lack of criticism, although a knowledge of the reason for this lack might be of great value to the teacher for future reference.

THE GROUPS EVALUATE

Advantages cited by the boys and girls were: the opportunity to express themselves freely about their own feelings in regard to their neighbors; a new point of view of themselves as a part of a big, wide world; the chance to work and plan as rapidly or as slowly as they wished; the feeling of new respect for their classmates because they had worked profitably in the small groups; the opportunity for contact with some of the organizations doing constructive work in the fields which they had studied; a realization that democratic living involves many more responsibilities than they had ever known of before; and, perhaps most important of all, a realization of the true importance of team-work and what it can accomplish, either in small groups such as theirs or in the world as a whole. This concept of cooperative thinking was an unlooked for by-product of the original planning, yet certainly a very important one. The boys and girls were also encouraged to write anonymous evaluations of the project. Much evidence of original and creative thinking appeared in the oral and written evaluations.

THE TEACHER EVALUATES

Opportunities for written and oral expression were numerous, fulfilling to some extent "requirements" for English study and practice. When reports were being prepared for presentation, the children in the various groups criticized sentence structure, capitalization, punctuation, and other features of purely mechanical nature in each other's papers. On at least three occasions, English textbooks were taken down from the shelves and used for reference purposes. The ability to express oneself ably became very important to many of the youngsters.

Since much of the reading the children did for the project was motivated by personal need, it became of vital importance to them and in many cases, books were attempted which would ordinarily be considered out of the reach of these children. No complaints of reading difficulties came to the attention of the teacher, although he watched very carefully for such cases.

The amount of creative writing and speaking involved in the project made available to all pupils an opportunity for trying their own hands at literary accomplishment. Some of these efforts were highly successful. Readings outside of class in connection with the project were recorded for each of the group members.

If the aim of a general language program is understanding and knowledge of other peoples of the earth and a feeling of closer kinship with them, the teacher felt that this particular unit was quite satisfactory.

Other types of work performed by the groups included outlining of materials read, and practice in the use of dictionaries, atlases, encyclopedias, and other reference books.

One notable deficiency of the entire project was the fact that it took place primarily in one classroom of the school. Though it boiled over into the auditorium and the library, still for all practical purposes it was conceived, planned, and executed with the assistance of one teacher only, representing one specialized field and one point of view. There seems little doubt that greater success could have resulted if the project had been broader in scope.

One other result of this project was the noticeable improvement in human relationships in the classroom. Tensions were lessened, academic achievement was increased, teacher-pupil rapport was improved, and behavior was on a much higher plane than before.

CHAPTER 7

Experiences for Thinking

SOME ELEMENTARY-SCHOOL classrooms are alive with children thinking and working with all their might; others house unresponsive children who seem merely to be "putting in time." Some teachers and laymen are content to attribute these differences solely to the heredity of the pupils.

However, this explanation fails to come to grips with the question of how the school can create an environment stimulating to young minds. The selections in this chapter suggest many ways to provide a vigorous and fruitful school curriculum. Other selections throughout this book offer specific suggestions for teaching academic skills which are closely related to effective thinking. See particularly the Wilson selection in Chapter 8 and MacCarthy's article in Chapter 10.

29   *Promoting intellectual development through problem solving*

FANNIE SHAFTEL

CHARLOTTE CRABTREE

The authors present thirteen do's and don'ts for teachers who wish to provide a favorable problem-solving climate. Their approach is applicable to many subject-matter areas.

THE PROCESS OF SEARCH

WHEN TEACHERS reward mainly "right answers," children cannot afford to be wrong. They focus upon learning the answer, not on search. If such learning is the focal one, children do not (a) explore, (b) learn the zest of hypothesizing, (c) try something and back away from an ineffective hypothesis and develop another, and (d) use imaginative thinking and *create new situations*. *They are too busy finding out what the teacher wants them to learn!*

By the same token, the teacher who so values "right answers" usually hears only "right responses" and, by so doing, cuts off the wide exploration and creative questioning so basic to problem-solving thinking. This same teacher may tend to look upon the coverage of many facts as learning and is therefore so focused on covering ground that he feels that he cannot afford to take the time required for hypothesizing, searching, and testing out an idea. He thereby fails to realize that learning to think one's way through a problem is vital learning.

Teachers, then, must be convinced that this *process* of search is as important as the answers or *products*. They must so value the zest of this search that they welcome the accompanying muddling and, frequently, "busy" disorder.

A "climate," then, is not a time of day when we have a problem-solving lesson. It is a general attitude toward learning. It is a recognition that while some learnings are necessarily routine and habituated responses, *there are parallel* and *more important learnings that are problem-solving-focused.*

Reprinted from *Curriculum for Today's Boys and Girls,* Robert S. Fleming (ed.), Columbus, Ohio: Charles E. Merrill Books, Inc., 1963, pp. 293-301.

TEACHER PROCEDURES AND TECHNIQUES

Teacher behavior is crucial to the creation of the problem-solving climate. The teacher not only presents situations that stimulate problem-solving thinking and provoke exploration, experimentation, and discovery, but deliberately uses procedures and techniques that further the development of a problem-solving climate.

Some "Do's" and "Don'ts" may serve to illustrate the processes and techniques needed to realize the desired climate:

1. Always respond to children's questions. They are important and merit respect. The teacher, by responding, is demonstrating his faith in each child's ability to ask questions, define problems, and do something intelligent about them. If questions are ignored or minimized, children interpret this response as meaning that they are incapable of asking "good" questions, that their ideas are not worthy and, eventually, that they are inadequate personally. Soon, such children stop asking questions.

Occasionally the teacher may act as a source of data when judgment dictates the necessity for an immediate action, but generally the more desirable response would be to counter with a helpful question. "How do you think we can find out?" "What is your notion (hunch, or hypothesis) of what is happening?" "Do you have any idea of how we can test this out?" "Do we need more information (or facts or data) before we can answer that question?

2. Some questions deserve group attention; others are individual and should be followed through with the one child who is concerned. For example, in a study of truck farming in the local area, John asks, "What will Mr. Del Rosso do if smoke from the new factory is spoiling his tomato crop?" This thoughtful and important question deserves group attention. It may be acted upon immediately or recorded for further study.

However, Jimmy's very personal interest in the rocks of the Southwest may not be central to the class study of the Hopi culture. He can be helped to find appropriate material to answer his questions individually, and then he may share his findings with the group if he wishes.

3. Encourage children to challenge each other's ideas, and even the teacher's ideas—politely, of course. It is in considering the "pros" and "cons" of ideas that children's perceptions are refined and further delineated. "Talking back," thoughtfully, helps a child to maintain the integrity of his thinking rather than to give in or retreat when an idea he holds valuable is challenged.

One danger in this procedure, however, is the development of an attitude that one shows his brilliance by always attacking other people's ideas. The destructive use of this process results in a game in which everyone uses other classmates' ideas as a target for his own intellect. When sardonic remarks or name-calling or belittling is used on someone's contribution, the results can be destructive. Bill says, "What a crazy idea!" or, "You're not thinking very straight!" to Alec's proposal. If this is permitted, Alec is defenseless and he and others, who may fear similar treatment, learn to remain silent. Instead, what is desired is a climate in which all ideas are valued but at the same time are open to further analysis.

In such situations, we are working to encourage individual children to hold onto an idea they value *and* to give up ideas that no longer appear tenable in the light of reasoned analysis, rather than to feel personally disgraced if the idea does not stand up against the test of further inquiry.

A word of warning: this highly desirable but difficult procedure is sometimes further complicated by the power structure of the class. For example, Barbara offers a possible solution to the traffic snarl at the bicycle rack each morning. Because she is rejected by a group of girls in this sixth grade who have formed an inner clique, Mary hastens to attack Barbara's proposal, or, to offer a counterproposal, *not on the merits of the idea, but as a rejection of Barbara.* Teachers cannot achieve open problem-solving and ignore the social dynamics of the class. Challenging inquiry can best be achieved when children are helped to healthy acceptance of one another.

4. Help the children to recognize that a search involves trial-and-error behavior. When a mistake is the product of search, help the class to see that they have not failed; they have now learned that something will not work and must restate their plan (hypothesis) to further the search. For example, in the film *Learning Is Searching*,[1] members of a third grade are explaining how they would make weapons if they had no tools or special materials, but only what they could find in the woods. After trying to tie stones to branches of trees with grasses in order to make crude hammers, they face the fact that this device is ineffective. They then sit down to think through what other materials might be available and usable. They finally decide that strips of animal hide (leather) might work. They are now ready to explore the possibility and test it out.

5. Wherever possible, *emphasize the search alongside of the more routine learnings.* For example, in arithmetic, organize both individual and group

1. Vassar Institute of Child Study. *Learning Is Searching,*

work for figuring out how a problem *might* be solved. An illustration of the possibilities of this procedure is present in the following problem:

"Forty-four children were having a hot dog roast at the picnic grounds. On the way to the picnic, four children rode in each car. How many cars were needed for the children who went to the picnic?"[2]

Organize the class into groups, ask each group to think of as many different ways as possible to work this problem. Then have them decide which way (or ways) is most efficient. Finally, have them review the procedures suggested in the text. Such procedures as the above enable the teacher to give recognition to the many kinds of thinking and different ways of using arithmetic processes that might work. You may go on to show the class a most efficient way, but you have rewarded independent, exploratory approaches as well.

In social studies place the spotlight on how children *think* a social problem might have been solved, let the class hypothesize *before* they find out what actually was done and *then* explore how it might have been done better. The class that is studying truck farming can be encouraged to hypothesize about what Mr. Del Rosso may do to protect his tomato crop. They may have such ideas as "Maybe he can find a special spray to protect his tomatoes," or "Maybe he can cover them with some material." A study can then be instituted to find out what is done. The children may find out that this is as yet an unresolved problem that involves smog control, zoning for industry and green belts, and other proposals that are part of the demands of our rapidly changing society.

In the study of Early America, children may be asked to figure out what they would have done if they were faced with the task of building a house with what was available in the local environment and with limited tools and few nails. They may be asked to plan to build these frontier houses in different geographic sections of the frontier. What would they use? How would they put their local materials together? After speculating and making proposals, they are helped to do research reading and compare their ideas with the historical records of the materials and processes used in building log cabins, the sod houses, lean-tos, etc. *Finally,* they may be asked whether they think if they were pioneers or frontiersmen, they could have devised other forms than the ones used.

In such procedures children are encouraged to speculate, to make varied proposals, to relate data to the cultural and physical conditions of the problem situation, and to explore the possible consequences of each proposal.

2. *Seeing Through Arithmetic,* Chicago: Scott, Foresman and Company, 1955, p. 193.

6. Reward exploratory thinking! Whenever children hypothesize or theorize about something, give recognition to this important process. Mary says, "When they learn to control the weather, I wonder what it will be like around here." This is worth brief, sometimes lengthy, exploration, depending upon the teacher's judgment of class needs. But the important point is that imaginative thinking receives recognition and reward.

Richard Suchman, in the University of Illinois Inquiry Training Project, is proposing that we teach children to be hypothesis-makers.[3] He has set up experiments in science, in the field of physics, and presents them to elementary-school children. He finds that when children are asked to handle problems in *very concrete terms,* without technical terminology or definitions or the symbols of a formalized science, they go to work on the problems in logical and productive ways. He comments that, "Their insights are remarkably clear and penetrating and lead them to formulations that are usually quite sound." He concludes that children want to explore, manipulate, and master their environment. Such drives do not need special motivation. Children who are imagining, exploring, and discovering orderly ways of explaining their environment gain self-confidence with the power that comes from autonomous discovery.

The initial phase of such a process is that of creating opportunities for exploratory thinking. When children begin to theorize or hypothesize, they are on the road to productive thinking. Suchman and his staff take this process further by creating experimental conditions for training children in the skills needed for efficient productive thinking. They may give us much-needed guidelines to more systematic approaches than we now have. Meanwhile, we can initiate the process of being alert to children's exploratory thinking.

7. Help the class to understand the importance of delaying action whenever possible in order to think the problem through. When children make proposals for action, encourage them to ask: "Is this a decision we must make on the spot?" or "Is this a decision we can postpone while we think it through and test it out?" Ask such questions as "How do you know?" "Where can you find out for certain?" Help the class to see the feeling-doing-thinking sequence and try whenever possible to make this a feeling-*thinking*-doing sequence.

8. Establish the understanding that not all problems are immediately solvable, but that we make progress by working on them. Help children to learn to tolerate ambiguity. This is basic to the search for new answers. When the children studying truck farming cannot find a definite solution to the

3. J. Richard Suchman. Inquiry training: new roles and goals in the classroom (mimeographed). Illinois Studies in Inquiry Training, University of Illinois.

smog problem and Mr. Del Rosso's tomatoes, they can be helped to see that we make progress slowly, often with many ideas which must eventually be abandoned, before important as well as daily problems are solved.

Sometimes, in evaluating progress, we help children to conclude that they have solved one aspect of a problem but need further ideas, or data, or experimentation, before they can go on to complete the task.

9. *Make it safe to have ideas, try them on for size, and abandon them for better ones.* If children are not directed at always coming forth with the "right" answer, or on being the one who is right, but rather on doing hunch thinking, speculating, sharing of notions, we create a climate in which it is "safe" to be experimental.

Tommy is faced with the fact that tugboats are rounded at each end. He has cut his miniature boat into points fore and aft, like a whaleboat.

Asked for suggestions, the class has many ideas.

Pete says, "Why don't you start another one."

Jane says, "That would be wasting wood. Why not cut off the points, use a drill and round it out?"

When Pete can say, "Yes, I think that is a better suggestion," he has arrived at the place where he does not have to defend an idea for fear of losing status. We can help children to this kind of maturity by encouraging the free flow of ideas and then guiding children to careful evaluation without focusing on "who is right." Rather, we may say, "All these suggestions have given us many ideas. Let's sift them and decide which ones are most useful for this problem."

10. *Provide opportunity for children to experience the realization that hypotheses can be proven false as well as true.* This again is basic to the scientific method and helps children to learn to tolerate ambiguity and continue the search for solutions. In a culture that is absorbed with "happy endings" and panaceas for all ills, what could be more important than to help the young to understand and accept the need to change their hypotheses and tolerate unresolved situations as one of the challenges of life?

11. *Wait for children to think.* Teachers get anxious when an immediate response is not forthcoming. By waiting quietly *and* confidently, you are telling children that you know they can manage the search.

12. *Demonstrate your faith in problem-solving thinking by participating in it yourself.* Admit to the children when you don't know something, hypothesize with them (but don't dominate their thinking!) and thus assure the class that adults don't have all the answers but also enjoy the everlasting search.

13. Ask yourself continuously, "Does the curriculum I plan permit the emergence of problems that are real for the children or is it so preplanned that the class can only respond to teacher-given cues?" One does not learn to ask questions or pose problems when this is all done by the teacher.

SUMMARY

Underlying these suggestions for creating a "climate" for problem solving in the elementary grades lie several basic assumptions. First, there is a faith in the child's ability to face and solve problems which are real for him and appropriate to his maturity level. Second, there is conviction on the part of the teacher that problem solving is a creative process, a search, and the most "human" aspect of learning. In a good "climate" teachers help children to postpone quick answers, play with possibilities, listen to each other's ideas, seek out expertness, test out the possibilities, and exult in the search.

30   *Transforming curiosity into learning skills*

BARBARA FORD GROTHE

Questions posed by pupils are probably more important than questions asked by teachers. I feel that we teachers are often too impatient to gain closure on an idea and race on to the next one. We must learn to help pupils raise their questions about what they perceive so that they can integrate ideas, build meanings, and spark with creativity.

CURIOSITY MAY BE fatal to felines, but to man it is almost as fatal not to be curious. Without curiosity there would be no need to wonder about the

Reprinted by permission of the Association for Childhood Education International, 3615 Wisconsin Avenue, N.W., Washington 16, D.C. Transforming curiosity into learning skills, by Barbara Ford Grothe. From *Childhood Education,* May, 1963, Vol. 39, No. 9, pp. 435-37.

future of scientific development. It would remain static. If people did not express curiosity to some extent in the various fields of endeavor, we would not be living in the society of conveniences which we now enjoy.

Curiosity is a quality which is an essential part of learning for all children. Curiosity may be simply explained as the *why* behind each question.

A questioning attitude plays an important role because it leads to problem solving, use of the scientific method, critical evaluation, experimentation, logical reasoning, trial-and-error method of learning, and the development of creativity within the individual.

Learning can be defined in terms of change in behavior which produces more desirable patterns of living, acceptable to both the individual and to the society in which he resides. The individual learns because he feels a need for change—he has a personal need for learning which may take the form of reward, recognition or approval, acceptance by society, and the growth of self-esteem. Most important of all, the individual must possess a desire for change before learning can take place. Then how can curiosity be transformed into learning skills in elementary-school children?

Curiosity can be transformed into problem-solving ability. When a child asks a question, the teacher can point the way toward learning. The teacher can have a questioning attitude himself. Instead of providing pat answers for the child, he should stimulate investigation. He should encourage the child by suggestions of possible reference material, resource people, and study methods.

When Harry, a second-grader, asked how many legs a grasshopper has, his teacher suggested that they find out. She provided reading materials and also pointed out that grasshoppers were plentiful in the field adjoining the school play yard. Harry *found out* and in the process was able to compare the grasshopper with other insects he had seen in a way which was meaningful to him.

Skills involved in using the scientific method can grow out of curiosity. The child invariably expresses a desire to find out why certain things are so. The teacher can encourage him and offer assistance in defining his problem; but then the teacher must let the child take the initiative in forming hypotheses, theories and possible conclusions.

Gretchen, an eighth-grader, was enrolled in an art class for gifted children. The project assigned to the class involved writing a story and providing illustrations. Gretchen wanted to attach her pictures to the reverse side of the paper upon which the text of her story appeared. She found that when she pasted two papers together, wrinkles were inevitable. She decided that she would experiment at home to see which types of glue would be most effective in making her pages adhere smoothly to one another. After much experimentation, she discovered that a combination of adhesives—plus the use of a hot iron—produced the desired effect.

A third learning skill to be derived from curiosity is critical evaluation. One who blindly accepts all information presented to him has little or no curiosity—or the skill has atrophied through nonuse. The child can utilize his curiosity and, if properly guided, will develop the learning skill designated as critical thinking. Children should be encouraged by their teachers to make use of critical thinking.

Teachers can help by asking such questions as: "Is this statement fact or opinion?" "Is this writing shaded by prejudice?" "Is the writer qualified in the field in which he is writing?" Teachers can encourage students to compare data from different sources. In this fashion curiosity can lead to true critical thinking, a valuable learning skill.

One teacher of sixth-grade children asked her pupils to bring articles from the newspaper, discuss them with the class, and then to determine whether the items were fact or opinion. Thus she helped to establish patterns of critical thinking.

Experimentation is a fourth learning skill fostered by curiosity. Student experimentation can be utilized in any grade. Experimentation can be of short duration or may involve much research and initial planning. In either case, it is an important tool for learning.

A small child who asks, "What will float?" can find out for himself if he is encouraged to do so. The pupil in high school can carry on experimentation on a more advanced level. If he wishes to discover more about the effects of weather, he should be encouraged to work on such a project. He may discover information hitherto unexplored.

A fifth learning skill which has its basic roots in curiosity is logical reasoning. A question that asks *why* tests reasoning powers, assuming the youngster is truly searching for an adequate answer. Because the child is curious, he should be taught the value of finding the *why* in a valid thought process. To develop logical reasoning, the teacher might have the child use methods of outlining work in logical sequence or plan activities which require certain orderly procedural steps.

One teacher of high-school mathematics proposed to his students the problem of solving a geometric proposition by reversing the accepted procedure. The students realized that logical sequence was necessary, although one boy was able to unite two of the steps involved in the problem!

The trial-and-error method of learning is a valuable skill when correctly used and when stimulated by curiosity. Teachers can suggest to students, "See for yourself!" Perhaps unique methods discovered by pupils may bring about discoveries or improvements in recognized fields of endeavor. Through the trial-and-error method, many innovations of world importance have been developed. Children have the opportunity to contribute much if properly stimulated and encouraged.

Creativity is often a result of curiosity. Teachers can give much helpful assistance along this line. They can provide countless opportunities for creativity. In writing, music, art, and drama, creativity is essential. Teachers should stimulate interest by providing audiovisual experiences for children through such media as bulletin boards, realia, recorded music and stories, films, and filmstrips. The teacher can express confidence in the abilities of children to work individually to produce new ideas. Thus children are further motivated to express themselves creatively. The task of the teacher is to help the child evaluate his creative efforts in a constructive and objective fashion.

After seeing a film on butterflies, one child was able to compose his own song about the Monarch butterfly. Another youngster wrote a story about the butterfly, utilizing the butterfly's "point of view."

What skills can be developed through curiosity? There are many to be developed, depending to a large extent upon the ingenuity and interest of the teacher. Through curiosity the teacher should be able to create in children techniques of problem solving, use of the scientific method, critical evaluation, experimentation, logical reasoning, the trial-and-error method of learning, and the desire to be creative.

If the teacher can promote interest in subject matter through the direct use of the intrinsic curiosity of youngsters, a first step has been accomplished. It is the task of the teacher to discover methods of promoting interest, and he can work through curiosity—the tool which the child himself provides.

One word of warning: curiosity may be easily aroused but it can be quenched just as easily. Teachers must use care and judgment in making assignments. Meaningless detail, work without a purpose, is deadly. A teacher must consider the value of the assignment given—value with respect to the child as well as to the teacher-formulated goals. The child is usually eager to put his curiosity to work but only in a manner significant to him.

Teachers must help children to help themselves. By fashioning learning skills from curiosity, learning can be a pleasure—a more meaningful and rewarding experience.

CHAPTER 8

Using Reading Resources

IN SOME SCHOOLS you will be handed a list of teaching resources you may employ and an exact schedule for their use. Other schools will give you nearly free rein. And, of course, there are many schools whose policies fall between these two extremes. Student teachers who observe practices in several different schools are often startled by the variety of approaches to the use of resources. Yet, each teacher still has the ultimate professional responsibility for deciding how resources will be used in his own class and what the curriculum for his pupils might be.

Some educators stress the use of reading materials; others favor direct experiences with many concrete objects. Most responsible educators now recognize that a variety of resources is needed.[1] A film can be studied as seriously as can a book. A trip to a grocery store can prove as orderly and as useful as a reading lesson. A bulletin board can pulsate with invitations to learn. A lesson on television can be as serious as a laboratory session. A visitor from another country reminds children that real people live there. And a book—let us not forget—can sparkle with excitement for children whose teachers have helped them to believe that school is a great place to learn things. In this chapter some teaching materials that depend largely upon reading are discussed. Such resources are commonly called "abstract" learning materials.[2] Some materials which might provide more "concrete" experiences will be presented in Chapter 9.

1. See: Edgar Dale. The cone of experience. *Audio-Visual Methods,* New York: The Dryden Press, Inc., 1954, pp. 42-56.
R. Murray Thomas and Sherwin G. Swartout. *Integrated Teaching Materials,* New York: Longmans, Green & Company, Inc., 1960.
2. Other "abstract" reading materials—programed instructional materials—are discussed in Chap. 26.

31   *How to use multiple books*

M A R Y   C .   W I L S O N

*This selection, originally prepared for the National Council for the So-
cial Studies, has possible applications in many other areas.*

THE CONCEPT OF using many books for the teaching of social studies is more
than a half-century old. The practice of using many books for the teaching
of social studies is still in its infancy. Today the average grade level attained
by pupils is steadily increasing. For this reason the need for using multiple
reading materials in the instruction of social studies at all grade levels is increasingly more important.

WHY USE MULTIPLE BOOKS?

The reasons for using multiple reading materials in social studies classes
are varied and numerous. Textbooks introduce many different, difficult concepts and a vast assortment of strange and technical words. No single textbook can develop adequately all aspects of the various concepts that are introduced. No basal textbook can supply sufficient detail to enable all pupils
of a class to visualize the various concepts vividly, to understand them adequately, and to think about them critically. The whole range of the library
is necessary to supply reading materials which will make it possible for pupils
to gain breadth and depth of understanding.

Experience backgrounds of pupils in the elementary and secondary schools
are limited. Since one must interpret the printed page in light of his own experiential background it is desirable to supplement the brief textbook presentations by extensive reading from various types of materials. From such
reading, one may gain vicarious experiences and greater insight into complex
problems.

The range of aptitudes, interests, and reading abilities of the pupils in
every class is surprisingly great. A five-grade range in reading ability is
normal. One chief reason for recommending the use of multiple books is to
provide for the individual needs and abilities of all pupils in a class. Well-
chosen materials for each topic of study make it possible to provide for the
reading level of every pupil. A wide variety of reading materials will present

Pamphlet 16 of the How to Do It Series. Washington, D.C.: National Council for
the Social Studies. 1960.

different viewpoints, provide for different pupil and group interests, supply timely and up-to-date information, provide ample quantity for extensive reading, and present the central topic in various styles of writing. These materials make it possible for each child, whatever his reading level, to read, learn, and contribute to the class study of a problem.

WHAT TYPES OF MATERIALS TO OBTAIN

At present, publishers are producing a wide variety of materials for use in social studies classes. In every classroom abundant and varied social studies materials should be made accessible to pupils and teachers on the social studies bookshelf and reading table. Necessary and useful materials include:

Reference books—Juvenile, adult, and special encyclopedias; pictured, juvenile, and unabridged dictionaries; atlases; directories; yearbooks; almanacs; government bulletins; anthologies.

Textbooks—History; geography; fusion books; reading textbooks containing material pertinent to social studies; related science books. (Different difficulty levels of textbooks should be available. An advantage of using reading textbooks is that the approximate difficulty of the material is immediately known.)

Newspapers, magazines, and periodicals—Juvenile and adult subscriptions to periodicals; clipping files of permanent information; vertical-file materials; pictorial materials.

Source materials—Letters; diaries; sample ballots; published reports; autobiographies; speeches; logs of activities; maps; minutes of meetings; time tables; recipes; directions; songs; photographs.

Pamphlets—Unit booklets; free and inexpensive materials; local, state, and national bulletins.

Literary materials—Biographies; travel books; fiction; poetry; folklore; short stories.

Teacher-made and pupil-made materials—Charts; graphs; personal anecdotes; summaries; reports; scrapbooks; group records.

Materials for the teacher—Adult source materials; adult textbooks; authentic references. (Teachers should read critically and widely in preparation for and during the study of a unit.)

HOW TO SELECT MATERIALS

The problem of selecting reading materials for use in social studies classes is important and difficult. Limited budgets, rising costs, changing curriculums, and increasing enrollments include factors that cannot be overlooked by those who obtain reading materials. The following criteria are helpful in selecting materials:

The books should contain authentic and informative material. Materials should be rich in vivid detail.

Materials should provide for the amplification and explanation of unusual, difficult, and obscure concepts that are introduced in social studies textbooks.

The materials should present a range of difficulty commensurate with and appropriate for the reading abilities of the pupils in the class.

Abundant materials approximately one grade level lower than the average reading level of the class should be available.

The literary style, sentence structure, and vocabulary of the materials should vary and should be appropriate in difficulty for the pupils who will use them.

The materials should appear in a variety of formats, bindings, and sizes.

The content of the books and materials should vary to include those replete with pictures; those with few pictures; and those with maps, graphs, charts, diagrams, and tables.

The content of the books should vary to include source materials, authentic versions, imaginary versions, and poetry.

Most of the materials should contain tables of contents, indexes, glossaries, and appendixes in order to facilitate pupils in locating information.

HOW TO OBTAIN MULTIPLE READING MATERIALS

The supply of books in a usual classroom is inadequate and insufficient to afford the wide reading that is necessary for pupils to attain adequate understanding and to reach valid conclusions about important social concepts. In lieu of a central library, teacher initiative and ingenuity are essential. Parents and pupils will often contribute a small fee that can be invested in minimum requirements for the classroom library. A set of encyclopedias encased in a shelf on rollers can be purchased for the entire school and can be wheeled from classroom to classroom. Files containing clippings from magazines and newspapers, state and national bulletins, authentic leaflets of free and inexpensive materials can be organized by any teacher. Relevant selections from outmoded and mutilated books can be bound into folders for pupil reference. Some teachers find time to write a few authentic but extremely simple materials each year.

No teacher should overlook the service of any available library. In schools which maintain a central library, teachers can call for books that relate to the unit of study and expand their classroom collection of reading materials. Books from public libraries, church libraries, and special loan collections from state library commissions should be obtained when such services are available. City and county school systems often purchase books and send them to teachers upon call. Some school systems maintain a materials library which circulates kits of books and reading materials for units in the content fields. Traveling libraries which circulate from school to school are available in other systems. Each teacher should use to the fullest extent all available sources of reading material.

HOW TO USE MULTIPLE READING MATERIALS

Most schools of today use some modification of the unit organization and the teaching-unit procedure for social studies. For this reason the use of multiple materials will be discussed with this procedure in mind. Unit organization implies that important content is centered about a class purpose or problem. In teaching-unit procedure, four stages or steps are necessary: (1) the introduction, which uses approximately 20 per cent of the teaching time; (2) the study-work period, which uses approximately 40 per cent of the teaching time; (3) the discussion-organization period, which uses approximately 30 per cent of the teaching time; and (4) the evaluation, which uses approximately 10 per cent of the teaching time.

The introductory phase of a unit is especially important in using and in preparing for the use of many different types of reading materials. During this initial period it is desirable to stimulate interest, arouse curiosity, raise questions for study, and plan how to succeed in the study. Two ways to stimulate interest are through sharing background experiences and through exploratory reading. Various unit booklets and different textbooks of appropriate difficulty levels are desirable for this brief, initial reading to stimulate inquiry. As a result of this reading and the discussion of background knowledge, the pupils and the teacher cooperate in formulating questions to guide their study of the unit. Teachers should not hesitate to propose questions, for they have a comprehensive grasp of the entire unit which should be used in eliciting questions from pupils and in suggesting important questions that are overlooked by the pupils. These questions make up the long-range assignment which will direct the reading for the entire unit.

The success of the study-work stage of the unit depends largely upon the excellence of the questions raised for study. Pupils who share the responsibility of discovering and stating study questions are usually eager to learn and to read to obtain authentic answers and solutions. For a prolonged and extensive study, it is wise to organize the questions into major and subordinate problems. In the event of great numbers of questions, the pupils and teacher may plan together the questions of fundamental importance that all members of the class will study and those which individual volunteers or small groups may use for special study. As the study-work period of the unit proceeds, important new questions will arise. These questions should be noted and used for renewing interest and for additional study.

The study-work period follows the introductory period. Many different types of activities, such as taking excursions, viewing films, conducting experiments, and listening contribute to learning. Reading, however, is recognized as one valuable means of learning and usually it is the activity that consumes most of the study-work period.

Multiple books are particularly important for the study-work portion of the unit. For maximum value, reading must be purposeful and critical and it must be individualized. Pupils locate materials that bear on their problems. They read under the stimulation of the questions and problems they have raised. While sitting heterogeneously in the classroom, they read from different authors, from different types of materials, and from books of appropriate difficulty levels.

In order to explain how to use multiple reading materials in teaching social studies, usual questions of teachers have been stated and answered tersely in accordance with accepted research and present trends. These questions follow:

How difficult should the multiple books be? The books relating to each topic should present a wide range in difficulty. Too many books of adult difficulty will repel and discourage pupils in the elementary grades and in junior high school. The problem of study reading is closely allied to purpose and incentive for reading. Pupils who are keenly motivated and eager to learn about a particular problem can read successfully from difficult books that bear on that problem.

The majority of the materials assembled for study should be easy for the large average group of pupils. Books that are one-grade or two-grade levels lower than the grade classification in which they will be used are especially desirable. In selecting books for particular children, it is well to encourage them to read a little to determine whether the book is appropriate in difficulty. For independent reading a book is difficult for a primary child if he meets one new word in a running two hundred; the book is difficult for an intermediate child if he meets one new word in a running one hundred. With instruction and teacher guidance, the pupils can cope with more difficult materials. Pupils should be able to read the books with facility and to center on the solution of a problem rather than on the identification of numerous strange and difficult words.

Pupils with accelerated reading ability should be encouraged to read books on their reading level. These pupils should not, however, be denied the privilege of reading appealing books that are easy for them. Superior pupils enjoy reading easy books with important content on the class problem. Less proficient pupils feel encouraged when they find that they can read some of the books that the superior pupils enjoy reading.

Should one textbook or more than one textbook be used? Much controversy exists over the question of whether to use one or more textbooks. Customary procedure decrees that the same textbook be purchased for every child in the class. Advocates of several textbooks recommend purchasing social studies textbooks by different authors and of different levels in limited sets. Regardless of whether one textbook or several textbooks are the policy, extensive use should be made of other types of reading materials.

In the use of several textbooks there is no single correct procedure. Reading from different textbooks may be used to kindle interest and enthusiasm during the introduction of a unit. Similarly, reading from the different textbooks provides an effective means of summarizing or concluding a unit. Throughout the study-work phase of a unit, pupils can use different textbooks. In the class study of a specific topic, the pupils may use the index to locate information and read on the topic. If reading-study time is limited, the teacher may denote specific page references for each of the textbooks on the chalkboard. After reading from the various textbooks, pupils may locate further information and read from other books. Different textbooks are particularly suitable for small-group instruction in which pupils are grouped according to reading ability.

A desirable social atmosphere should be maintained in the class regardless of whether one textbook or several different textbooks are used. The practice of using the same book for all pupils except a few very weak ones inevitably leads to embarrassment for those weak pupils. The practice of having all pupils use the same book and follow laboriously together while paragraph after paragraph is read aloud, explained, and discussed creates an equally unwholesome situation. The practice of making a uniform assignment from the same textbook is one that fails to challenge the accelerated pupils and one that leads the less proficient pupils to discouragement and failure. Through the use of individualized assignments and textbook materials, each pupil can read from a book on his ability level and relate information on the class topic that every other pupil has not already learned.

Should all pupils read about one question at the same time? The policy of teacher-pupil selection of an important question for all members of the class to study is desirable. This selection can be made prior to the day for reading. The teacher then has an opportunity to assemble all books which contain information pertinent to this particular question.

On the day for reading, the question for study and its significance should be recalled. Vocabularly assistance with prevalent proper names, special terms, and technical words used in most of the books treating on the topic should be provided. Each pupil should receive a book which contains information on the study question. In distributing the books the teacher should bear in mind the reading abilities of the various pupils. A pupil who has acquired superior ability to read should be given a more difficult and a longer selection than a pupil who has average reading ability for his grade level. Conversely, a pupil who has deficient reading ability should be given a book that is appropriate in difficulty to his reading ability.

This procedure of having all pupils read about the same question has distinct advantages. As all pupils study and read about a common problem there is a feeling of unity and belonging which is desirable. All pupils have been provided with books which they *can* read and books which will make it possible for them to succeed in their reading and study. Entire-class study of one problem helps to break down any feeling of inferiority that may have developed during necessary ability-grouping periods within the classroom. Pupils who read independently and rapidly and who understand and remember what they read, may read a longer and more difficult article; or they may read pertinent selections from several books. If the supply of multiple materials is limited, pupils who complete books at approximately the same time may exchange materials. Some teachers encourage pupils who complete their first book to turn to textbooks or encyclopedias for further information on the class problem.

Immediately after reading about a particular problem, it is wise to arrange for a discussion period. Different books contain different details and different ideas about the common problem which make the discussion period livelier and more interesting. As pupils listen to the ideas presented by other pupils they often ask to exchange books and engage in further reading on the problem during their voluntary reading time in school or at home. Vocabulary difficulties are also lessened as key words are met and reported from books with different versions of the class problem.

Should individual study problems be used? There is need for all pupils in the class to read from a variety of different books on individual problems. Sufficient time is never available to study every aspect of content in a unit. Teachers should plan with the pupils the most crucial phases of the problem that all members of the class will study. Nevertheless, there are many significant and intriguing phases of content suggested by extensive reading that the entire class cannot study. After working as an entire class on certain aspects of the unit, it is desirable to encourage different pupils to select a subordinate phase of the unit for individual study.

There are many ways to proceed in using individual study problems when multiple books are accessible. As individual pupils discover new problems and acquire new interests they should be encouraged to explore these personal interests through wide reading and intensive study. Such study may or may not be reported in class. Another procedure is to ask each pupil to select a certain aspect of the unit that is particularly interesting to him and to obtain all possible information on this problem to report to the class. These individual-interest selections may be made early or toward the close of the study-work period of the unit. Still another practice is to excuse accelerated pupils from basic-developmental reading classes and to guide them in reading and studying about a problem of personal interest. In addition to the class study, a variety of related topics may be selected by individual members of the class for intensive study.

Should there be small-group study? Units can be introduced and completed successfully without any small-group work. Multiple books, however, provide excellent materials for small-group work.

Special-interest groups may be formed to study intensively some particular phase of the class problem and report to the entire class. Voluntary choice may be used as the basis for forming these interest groups. Within the group there may be found wide ranges in reading ability. The most superior and the least advanced pupils in reading ability may choose to work on the same topic. For this reason, the teacher must be sure that the scope and difficulty of the book collection are wide enough to provide for the various pupils in each of the special-interest groups.

Pupils within a class may be grouped according to reading ability for special study work. In this grouping policy a stimulation motivation period is provided on the class problem. After this motivation period in which purposes for study are set, each group receives materials of appropriate difficulty and reads together. Textbooks are frequently used for this type of grouping.

Limited sets of textbooks of three or more difficulty levels dealing with the class problem are obtained. Comprehension exercises should be differentiated as well as the books.

Another procedure for grouping includes a combination of class, group, and individual work. After the entire class has studied certain essential aspects of a unit, other important topics are listed for small-group or individual study which will be reported orally to the entire class. The teacher should assist in suggesting problems for group and individual study and be sure that some topics are simple while others are complex. Pupils should be guided in selecting topics that are appropriate to their ability levels. For example, after the entire class has studied essential aspects of the Civil War, topics that would be simple enough for the weakest pupils might center around a biography such as Abraham Lincoln or Robert E. Lee. A difficult topic that would challenge the ablest pupils might center around a comparison of reconstruction practices following the Civil War and World War II.

All grouping in social studies classes should be kept flexible. Undue emphasis on grouping should be avoided. Activities carried on by the entire class and individual study are equally profitable as small-group study and committee work.

How can discrepancies in facts be resolved? Frequently there is some deviation in the facts that are presented by different books. This condition cannot be altered by avoiding the use of multiple books. Situations in which the facts in different books deviate can be used to elicit critical thought.

Pupils should be guided to reconcile the discrepancies in facts through careful reasoning. Copyright dates should be checked to see whether new inventions, discoveries, or developments are accountable for the difference in facts. For variations in the pronunciations or spellings of geographical names, pupils should abide by the most reliable atlas. For slight variations in historical facts, students should turn to a standard encyclopedia. As the members of a class discuss items that differ they learn to think on their feet, to compare authors, to recall relevant data, to engage in original reasoning, and to search out the truth. For example, pupils in one fifth-grade class who read from several different books found two dates given for the invention of the cotton gin. This incident provided keen motivation for extensive reading. One date was verified by reference to three standard encyclopedias for children. Finally, the pupils resolved the problem through reasoning that one date was that of application for the patent while the other date denoted the time the patent was granted. As the pupils reasoned together they realized that several different dates could be given and that each one would have a measure of accuracy. Through this experience, the pupils were impressed with the need for precise accuracy of expression.

Is oral reading desirable? Excellent opportunities are presented through the use of multiple books for occasional oral reading. The teacher may read orally an important current article that is too difficult for the pupils to read. A poem that will provide depth of feeling or aesthetic values may be read by a pupil or the teacher. Pupils can prepare different chapters of an important biography and take turns in reading them orally to the class. Pupils can listen with profit to the oral reading of an authentic excerpt which presents vivid detail. The description by a competent writer of a jungle, of the freezing of an arctic bay, or of the interior of a coal mine will make an indelible impression upon pupils. Source materials provide another important type of material for oral reading. Excerpts read from a letter, a speech, or a diary help to impress pupils with reality. Encouragement should be given pupils to read briefly from references to prove a point when deviations in point of view occur in class discussions. Authentic stories or articles written by pupils are often worthy of sharing with the entire class.

The following principles will guide teachers in the use of oral reading:

Read silently and study a selection carefully before reading it to the class.
Read only very significant and worthy materials.
Avoid reading lengthy selections.
Avoid reading selections that have been read previously by two or more pupils.
Avoid overemphasis on oral reading.
Rotate opportunities for oral reading.
Use a variety of different types of selections for oral reading.

Should pupils be referred to specific pages? The purpose for the day and the amount of time available for reading must determine whether the teacher will specify the pages or require the pupils to locate information independently. If the chief purpose of the pupils and the teacher is to read from several references in order to obtain information on a problem, there may be insufficient time for the pupils to locate the information. Frequently during a study period there is not time for pupils to locate the information and also to read the selections.

The ability to locate information rapidly and accurately is a very important study skill for pupils to acquire. Throughout the study of a unit, time and guidance should be devoted to perfecting this skill. Multiple books provide a rich opportunity for pupils to acquire the ability to locate specific information in a natural, functional manner. As the need for greater skill in this ability is recognized by the pupils and the teacher, it is wise to spend occasional class periods in directing pupils in locating information and marking specific pages which will be read and studied at a later time.

A well-balanced combination of providing specific page references and requiring pupils to locate information independently is the best course to follow. One recommended procedure is to find specific page references for the most important books and to provide many other books in which pupils must locate information through skimming, using topical sentences, the table of contents, and the index.

How much time is needed for reading? No rule for time allotments can be made. For the social studies class, a generous block of time should be scheduled. At least an hour is needed from the primary grades through high school. Within this block of time, various activities other than reading take place. The entire hour need not and should not be used for reading. Group planning about the next question for study, locating information in the many different books, helping with strange and difficult words, locating important data on maps, distributing books, planning how to take notes, assisting pupils with keeping a list of references read, and discussing the information read are an incomplete list of necessary activities related to reading that consume some of the class period.

Pupils should not be permitted to read until they are unduly fatigued. The optimum amount of time for pupils to read will vary from grade to grade; it will vary for different pupils within a particular class; and it will vary for an individual pupil from day to day. The amount of time to spend in reading will depend upon the motivation of a class, the cruciality of the problem, the suitability of reading materials, and innumerable personal and physical factors.

How much reading should be done? Different amounts of material should be read by different pupils in the class. The amount that any pupil can read will be closely related to the purpose for which he is reading, the difficulty and nature of the reading material, and the amount of time available for reading.

How can desirable study habits be implemented? Teacher guidance during the reading of multiple materials is very important. Cooperatively the teacher and pupils should formulate specific study questions. Together they should plan how to proceed. As pupils work from day to day and from grade to grade, they should acquire knowledge about how to study as surely as they acquire knowledge about social problems. Essential information about study includes:

How to formulate a question for study
How to locate information
How to read under the stimulation of a problem
   How to weigh the value of ideas read
   How to accept and reject ideas in light of a problem
   How to obtain precise meaning
   How to question an author and compare authors
How to take notes
How to recall what has been read
   How to make an outline of essential content
   How to write a summary
How to make a second reading after a recall exercise

Should there be home study? Research indicates that the most helpful type of home study is that of a differentiated, voluntary nature. Multiple books provide an excellent opportunity for this sort of home study. For pupils of the upper elementary and secondary grades, supplementary reading in relation to social studies is particularly desirable. Multiple books provide the means for adjusting the quantity and difficulty of home reading to the abilities, needs, and peculiar environmental factors of the individual pupils.

How should appraisals be made? The surest mark of successful reading from multiple books is found through the careful observation of pupils. Children who want to read, who turn to books voluntarily to find information, who find personal satisfaction in reading, and who assume personal responsibility for obtaining accurate information and for sharing it are successful readers.

Mechanical appraisals violate the purposes that are fundamental to reading from multiple books. Routinized methods of checking reading often repel students from reading. Reading that is invariably accompanied with formal written exercises becomes associated with a difficult chore. Pupils who dislike written work and book reports may avoid reading in order to avoid the formal appraisal.

A variety of ways of evaluating reading should be used. The best appraisal is that which requires a pupil to construct his own opinions and ideas on the basis of what he has read and to make use of these ideas in some challenging situation. Oral discussions reveal the breadth and depth of a pupil's reading. Pupils should be encouraged to originate their own schemes and plans for appraising and recording their reading. Tests, written summaries, outlines, personal notes, written reports, oral reports, class discussions, and research themes are some of the forms of evaluation most often used. All of these types of appraisal have merit and can be used advantageously in a variety of different ways.

CONCLUSION

Educational progress is not made through following routines. There is no single correct technique for using multiple books. Abundant and varied reading materials rarely fail to challenge teachers to study pupil needs, to experiment, and to devise a variety of excellent classroom procedures. The idea of using multiple books in social studies is an old and a persistent one. This idea has been tested and proved successful. The fact that multiple books are not more generally used is no criticism against the concept. Lack of books and lack of teacher insight in how to use multiple books account largely for the present status of this policy.

32   *Workbooks! tool or crutch?*

RICHARD MADDEN

Workbooks have long been a topic of fierce controversy. The author asks whether workbook activity is worthwhile or merely busy work. He offers seven guidelines for constructive use of workbooks and advises that the size of one's class and amount of one's teaching experience should influence curriculum decisions regarding workbooks.

"WHY ARE TEACHERS so eager for workbooks? I have to fight against their use all the time." These words of a school administrator point up a controversy of concern to educators throughout the country today. Why do so many

Reprinted from the *NEA Journal,* 45:94-95, February, 1956.

elementary-school teachers demand workbooks, and why do so many administrators and supervisors reject the requests?

What are the arguments for and against workbooks? Are these arguments more valid in some situations than in others? How may an elementary-school teacher use workbooks in the most profitable manner? A simple resolution of the controversy is not likely to emerge immediately.

Opponents of the workbook list these objections:

The teacher comes to rely upon the workbook and ceases to do developmental teaching.

The workbook often becomes the textbook in fact, even though it may not be so designed.

School becomes monotonous and uninspiring. Pupils do the exercises with very little reflective thinking. Independence is lost.

All pupils do the same things, regardless of individual needs.

Workbook activity is piecemeal and seldom reaches the high level of creative thinking.

Workbook children are weak in writing complete sentences and are often poor in written expression in general.

In a market flooded with workbooks, teachers find it difficult to select wisely.

Teachers and school programs lack time for workbook activities to be tailored to pupils' needs.

Advocates of the workbook deny that the aforesaid evils need result, or that their occurrence is unique to the usage of workbooks. They list these reflections upon the use of workbooks:

Workbooks are but tools; misuse need not occur. Teachers who cannot use workbooks properly usually do other things no better.

Workbook exercises are usually prepared by writers much more skilled than the teacher who duplicates his own materials.

The time needed to write and duplicate materials is prohibitive.

In early school years, when pupils are beginning to write, their versatility is so limited that workbook activities help greatly. Various pencil-and-paper activities are needed to aid in the transition from concrete experiences to abstractions.

A workbook accompanying a textbook complements the learning and adds variety. Pages may be used to give parents an idea of pupil achievement.

Instruction in overcrowded classes is not going to be completely efficient; no instructional material will be completely adapted to individual needs.

Readily available materials aid class control.

Inappropriate drill leads to distaste and eventually to dislike for a subject. Copying problems is a waste of students' time.

Workbooks contain good diagnostic tests. They also provide concrete evidence of an individual's performance and needs.

Good work habits are established.

Workbooks encourage independence by setting a task, a plan, and a time to do the task.

Although the arguments for and against workbooks are confusing, an examination of the issues may aid one's judgment regarding the use of workbooks in specific situations.

Four principles of learning should be kept in mind as one makes choices as to what pupils should or should not be doing:

1. Basic to all learning is personal mental activity on the part of the learner.
2. Activity operates best when it is purposeful for the learner.
3. Learning is best when the understanding of the learner is high.
4. The teacher's primary task is to provide experiences that continuously evolve understandings at each pupil's level of development.

With these principles in mind, let us examine questions that one should answer as he decides for or against workbooks, or as he may choose a specific workbook or type of workbook.

What would pupils be doing if they were not using workbooks? Some pupils might be reading in the rich heritage of children's literature. Some might be engaged in a construction activity in order to have a wholesome experience in planning, in cooperation, in reading for information, and in the development of manual skills. Some might be doing an experiment in science. Others might be expressing ideas in writing or in art media.

Skillful and creative teachers may duplicate arithmetic exercises that are especially needed or reading exercises about pupils' activities. Countless teachers in our classrooms prove that good teaching can be done without workbooks.

Another teacher who is equally creative in his teaching may be doing these same things, but, with judicious use of a workbook, may be conserving some time. Excellent as he is, he may feel a special need for the support of a well-organized aid in arithmetic or he may not yet have mastered the finer points of word analysis.

The third teacher, representing a type considerably more numerous than the first two, is less creative or has had less experience working with children. Possibly he does not understand well the sequences of learning in arithmetic or the broader objectives of teaching reading. This teacher's control in a free activity period may result in pupil experiences which are not productive of good learning. Workbooks may bring orderliness to certain areas of instruction and save time.

One infers from the principles of learning stated above that personally organized activity, with adult help, is most productive of growth in learning. But there are enabling knowledges and skills which need to keep pace with a pupil's growth in thinking and in the expression of his thoughts. The role of the workbook must lie primarily not in the mainstream of mental growth but in the coves where the pupil develops these enabling abilities.

Is the workbook activity worthwhile, or is it busy work? Some teachers will maintain that any device which will bring stability into a classroom of thirty-five pupils is worthwhile. Values must be judged relatively. In the growth of a pupil's higher mental processes, certain knowledges and skills must be pinned down. Once achieved, these are better maintained in lifelike activities than through the practice exercise.

Workbooks least likely to be "busy work" are those designed to supplement the textbook used in the class. Their activity has meaning in reference to another portion of the work of the day. If well developed, they provide a variety of goals and of objectives. They are usually quite superior to a teacher's hurriedly duplicated efforts. Pupils accept them more naturally than they accept unrelated exercises.

What are the problems of a consumable text? One must first ask whether the consumable text is sufficiently complete in itself, or is merely supplementary.

Is it an exercise book or is it one that develops understanding?

Spelling books are the most widely used self-contained consumable textbooks. In many ways they are similar to nonconsumable spelling texts. They contain the same word lists, similar suggestions for developing insights into word structure, and a similar program for teaching the spelling of sounds and the use of the dictionary. Differences may appear, however, as one answers these questions:

Does one stimulate pupil writing more than the other?
All things considered, which is cheaper?
Will pupils keep useful notebooks with both?

How motivating is the pride of ownership of a consumable?

How helpful is the consumable's provision for identifying one's own misspelled words for systematic review?

Will the teacher permit blank-filling to supplant word study, or will he use the exercises to promote related abilities and insights?

Is the clothbound text more likely to become merely a word list?

How can teachers who are using workbooks be guided into more effective use of them? The abuse of workbooks has led some educators to conclude that workbooks should not be used at all. Others meet the issue by limiting the number that may be used. But some teachers do use them, and education will be advanced if they learn to make wiser use of them.

These guidelines are offered to teachers who are using workbooks:

1. What kind of workbook will meet your pupils' needs? Do you want a workbook that continues the learning of the text? Do you want a practice or drill book that ignores understanding? Do you want a self-contained consumable text?

2. Do the pupils of your class need workbooks of different levels of difficulty or development?

3. Are pupils aimlessly filling in blanks, or have you taught or retaught the learnings involved, so that practice always follows understanding?

4. Do you analyze pupils' work and reteach where necessary?

5. Do you use the diagnostic provisions of a workbook, or determine by your own analysis which portions are profitable to a pupil and which he should omit?

6. Are you continuing to search for alternative procedures of greater value? Pupils need to develop initiative in their own learning activities. Do you provide a library corner, interest tables, and opportunities for reference work and the writing of reports?

7. Do you avoid having pupils spend too much of their time with workbooks? Use of several workbooks is likely to interfere with pupils' growth in organizing their own expression.

The workbook is a tool in education which may be used well or may be used badly. A highly competent teacher may have greater need of it with a class of forty than with a class of twenty-five. An inexperienced teacher may have more need for its use than he will have after he gains experience. A teacher well prepared in most curriculum areas may profit by use of a workbook in his weaker areas, but he must prevent it from becoming a crutch.

33 *Library assignments: fruitful or frustrating?*

AGNES KRARUP

A director of library services offers advice about making library re-
sources more useful to teachers and students. She notes: "Whether
a library assignment will be fruitful or frustrating to the students is
determined primarily by the skill and the resourcefulness of the
teacher."

IN PLANNING to use library materials with classes, thoughtful teachers will consider the limitations of the library and of their students, tailoring their assignments accordingly. Because a library can make available only what has already
been published and then only in the quantities actually bought by the library,
many assignments are doomed to failure for sheer lack of available resources.
Teachers should know that some areas within a subject lend themselves to
supplementary reading by an entire class, but many others can be studied more
productively by committees or by individuals.

Teachers who thoroughly understand this have learned to distinguish
between general exploration of a broad phase and reading in depth about a
small rather specialized segment of their subject; between the minimum information needed by all who will pass the course and enrichment for the
above-average students; between the needs of those in the group who grasp the
daily work with ease and those who need more drill; and between subjects
for which there are ample materials in print and those for which only a few
references can be found in even large library collections.

The forethought or time required to determine in advance whether an
assignment is feasible as conceived is not great. A teacher sitting in the classroom should be able to guess that all of the libraries in Pittsburgh combined
would not be able to meet certain demands from a whole class or group of
classes. Can an *entire class* be asked to look up:

1. *A nature poem?* Yes. Any library has many anthologies of poetry, usually
   some on reserve.
   A poem about baseball? No. Suitable for one child, but the subject is too
   seldom written about in poetry to appear in many anthologies.
2. *A book about or by an immigrant to America?* Yes. Assignment permits
   use of both biographies and fiction.
   A book about or by someone from your father's background? No. There

Reprinted from *Pittsburgh Schools*, 36:11-13, September-December, 1961.

may be no book about or by someone from Luxembourg suitable for the child, or not enough books about Finland if most of the class should happen to have a Finnish background.

3. *A life of one of our nation's great men?* Yes. Many lives of men like Washington, Lincoln, Carver, and Edison are available.
   A life of a great Pittsburgher? No. Local material and state material are always in short supply. Good for one child.

4. *An English novel?* Yes. An easy request at the high-school level.
   Tale of Two Cities? No. Libraries do not buy enough copies to supply thirty students each with a copy of a single title.

5. *Hardships endured by pioneers?* Yes. Subject can be found in many books even in our smallest school library collections.
   The Donner Party? No. Too specific and even specialized.

6. *A book about a European country?* Yes. Barely. These are still scarce.
   A book about Iceland? No. A good assignment for one child.

CHECK WITH YOUR LIBRARIAN

Before students can get excited about a piece of research that they are pursuing through the library, they must have been properly motivated in the classroom and must know exactly what they are seeking and how to go about finding it.

The time spent on discussing assignments thoroughly with a class so that each student knows what to do will be made up later because they will work with greater concentration and efficiency. Avoidance by teachers of some common pitfalls may mean the difference to the students between success and frustration in completing their projects. This requires some flexibility on the part of the teacher.

Remember that children are very literal-minded. If the teacher says, "a travel book of one hundred pages," no book of ninety-six pages will do.

Accept the encyclopedia as a reference source always. It will give the best overview of any subject it covers; furthermore, it is frequently the only source left on the shelves, and with it the children can at least begin their work.

Encourage children to use what can be found in pamphlets, periodicals, or pages in books; do not insist on whole books nor on a set minimum of references.

Be flexible about the bibliographies in your textbook. They become out of date before the book is ever published. Tell the children specifically that other titles recommended by the librarian are also acceptable.

Understand that certain sophisticated titles on best-seller lists and on some college reading lists are not in the school library and possibly may not be given to minors in the public library without written permission from their parents.

Break big subjects like the cold war or the United Nations down into pieces small enough for your students to grasp and to do something with in the time allowed.

Permit students to discuss in class what they need to know.

Notify the librarians in advance whenever large numbers of students are about to descend upon them. Friendly conversations between teachers and librarians often serve within a school as well or better than more formal written notification. The public library, however, will appreciate a call or a note so that its service to children and young people can be both knowledgeable and smooth.

If teachers keep some of these basic principles in mind, students will enjoy their library research and will inspire each other to pursue information assiduously. This is one way that a teacher can motivate reading and studying in depth. When assignments are rewarding to the students, teachers will find that their teaching also becomes more rewarding. The two essentials, then, to a successful use of the library by children and young people are perfect understanding of what they are to do and materials adequate for the need. Whether a library assignment will be fruitful or frustrating to the students is determined primarily by the skill and resourcefulness of the teacher.

34   *Learn with* BOOK

R .   J .   H E A T H O R N

This article describes books and programed instructional materials in an unusual and amusing way. See Chapter 26 for a more typical discussion of programed instructional materials.

A NEW AID to rapid—almost magical—learning has made its appearance. Indications are that if it catches on, all the electronic gadgets will be so much junk. The new device is known as Built-in Orderly Organized Knowledge. The makers generally call it by its initials, BOOK.

Reprinted from *Punch*, 242:712, May 9, 1962. © *Punch*, London.

Many advantages are claimed over the old-style learning and teaching aids on which most people are brought up nowadays. It has no wires, no electrical circuits to break down. No connection is needed to an electricity power point. It is made entirely without mechanical parts to go wrong or need replacement.

Anyone can use BOOK, even children, and it fits comfortably into the hands. It can be conveniently used sitting in an armchair by the fire.

How does this revolutionary, unbelievably easy invention work? Basically BOOK consists only of a large number of paper sheets. These may run to hundreds where BOOK *covers* a lengthy program of information. Each sheet bears a number in sequence, so that the sheets cannot be used in the wrong order. To make it even easier for the user to keep the sheets in the proper order they are held firmly in place by a special locking device called a "binding."

Each sheet of paper presents the user with an information sequence in the form of symbols, which he absorbs optically for automatic registration on the brain. When one sheet has been assimilated a flick of the finger turns it over and further information is found on the other side. By using both sides of each sheet in this way a great economy is effected, thus reducing both the size and cost of BOOK. No buttons need to be pressed to move from one sheet to another, to open or close BOOK, or to start it working.

BOOK may be taken up at any time and used by merely opening it. Instantly it is ready for use. Nothing has to be connected up or switched on. The user may turn at will to any sheet, going backwards or forwards as he pleases. A sheet is provided near the beginning as a location finder for any required information sequence.

A small accessory, available at trifling extra cost, is the BOOKMARK. This enables the user to pick up his program where he left off on the previous learning session. BOOKMARK is versatile and may be used in any BOOK.

The initial cost varies with the size and subject matter. Already a vast range of BOOKS is available, covering every conceivable subject and adjusted to different levels of aptitude. One BOOK, small enough to be held in the hands, may contain an entire learning schedule. Once purchased, BOOK requires no further cost; no batteries or wires are needed, since the motive power, thanks to the ingenious device patented by the makers, is supplied by the brain of the user.

BOOKS may be stored on handy shelves and for ease of reference the program schedule is normally indicated on the back of the binding.

Altogether the Built-in Orderly Organized Knowledge seems to have great advantages with no drawbacks. We predict a big future for it.

CHAPTER 9

Using Other Resources

WHEN THE BRITISH House of Commons was being rebuilt in 1944, Winston Churchill observed: "We shape our dwellings and afterwards our dwellings shape us." So too does the classroom environment which teachers create also shape pupils' experiences. The resources we use in teaching may provide a sterile or a rich learning environment: In some classrooms, the learning environment is drab, dull, monotonous; in others, the environment seems to glow with varied, exciting invitations to learn, with eager pupils reflecting their teachers' interest and competence.

Many resources help create a classroom environment that stimulates children's thinking. Slides and movies can provide excellent opportunities for analysis, synthesis, and evaluation. Planting seeds and watching plants grow are personal experiences which words alone cannot describe. Using materials such as these, together with the symbolic materials discussed in Chapter 8, pupils are helped to learn a variety of ways of thinking.

Before we continue, however, a word of caution: As you read about these materials and think about your curriculum decisions, avoid the disastrous mistake of believing that educative materials possess educative values in and of themselves. There is value to bulletin boards, films, TV programs, trips, and books only when these materials are significant aids to learning. Unfortunately, some teachers come to grief when they copy a dazzling teaching material they have seen in another classroom without thinking through the potential experiences of the pupils in their own classrooms.

The selections in this chapter deal with pictorial and manipulative materials and with ways of teaching which take pupils and teachers out into their own communities—to places where life itself is a learning resource.

❦

35   *Let the children plan the bulletin boards!*

SISTER CHRISTINA MARIE, S.N.D.

Classroom bulletin boards can be effective teaching-learning resources. They may be used to make a clearly organized presentation of a topic of study; to display pupils' work; and to provide pleasant and attractive surroundings. The author feels that pupils can learn a great deal if they share in the actual planning and arranging of bulletin board materials.

CLASSROOM bulletin boards speak volumes, not only by conveying the message of their caption, but also by revealing the active or inactive role which the pupils are allowed to play in the classroom. How refreshing it is to enter a room that has evidences of being alive, where initiative and creative thought have left their indelible mark. Pupil-planned and produced displays are not only a positive expression of a learning environment, but function as a motivating force to further endeavors.

But the teacher will hesitate. "Pupil-planned displays are a possibility but how do you make this possibility into a reality?" The answer to this question and the secret to success lies more in developing the thought processes than in using the artistic abilities of the children. A happy combination of these factors is the ideal. Actually all that goes into a good display could never be described in one article. Thus all that will be attempted here is a structure of basic "musts" for the teacher to develop at her own discretion.

The obvious starting point is the subject matter for class discussion. Here we encounter a primary "must," namely that motivation has to be guided. It is not enough that the children be excited about a project; they have to know

Reprinted from *The Catholic School Journal*, 63:26-27, May, 1963.

something about the subject as well. This is why displays and illustrations elicited from students after well-taught lessons in social studies, science, or history make such excellent bulletin boards. Ideas are then clear as well as creative.

A second "must" is direct and simple communication. Often the choice of caption will help determine the total plan. An intriguing caption seizes on a central idea and at the same time invites further investigation of the theme. Suggestions for the content of these captions or headings will come quite spontaneously from classroom discussion. Some children have a natural sense for clinching ideas with words. Perhaps their constant televiewing has developed this ability. The caption may read in bold print or attract the eye with bright colors, but its major objective is to convey an instantaneous communication. Neat, legible, and horizontal placement of lettering hastens readability. Fancy lettering sometimes detracts from the content of the message and therefore is to be avoided. Simplicity remains the keynote in lettering as it does in the entire approach to bulletin-board display.

Arranging a preliminary layout for the desired display is the next step. "Must" number three: let the class participate in the planning. In the primary grades where it is impossible for the children to mount and display their work effectively, participation in the planning phase is of major importance. Surprisingly, too, their ideas are often very helpful. The following story may illustrate this point:

A first-grade teacher had a maritime theme in mind for a bulletin board. She imagined that an octopus would be an excellent eye-catcher, but when she asked her pupils for their ideas on this theme, one child suggested a treasure chest. The teacher could see that this had great possibilities, so the octopus idea was dropped. Acting on the child's suggestion and enlarging on the idea, the teacher placed the class papers in such a way that they gave an effect that the treasure chest was overflowing and spilling out onto the ocean floor. A few pieces of yarn pinned over the scene for an underwater impression made it effective enough for a real pirate to invade the room—all because a teacher listened to a six-year-old.

Children in the intermediate and upper grades need to gain firsthand experience in carrying their plans to completion. A thorough readiness program, giving the children some formal lessons in the principles of design is a "must" for them. Unless they know the rhythms of line, the moods of color, and the use of form and space, success will not accompany their efforts. Children have a tendency to clutter space; they can be brought to value the empty space realizing that the unfilled areas are as important as the filled ones. Diversity and harmony in composition need to be taught also. Bringing in a scrapbook with selections of good advertisements, where the principles of design are effectively illustrated, is an excellent way to inculcate these principles. Likewise, this activity teaches them to look. Many people cannot draw simply because they have not seen clearly. A follow-up assignment after the scrapbook entries would be to make their own posters selling some idea. A bulletin-board display should then be an easy matter.

Lastly, few things have greater impetus to pupils than the fact that their work is appreciated. When student papers make the headlines, instead of becoming small print beneath a neat and perfect teacher-made display, then the teacher achieves her goal. No one realizes more than the children when their work is fully appreciated.

In closing here are a few suggestions of a general nature that might be applied to the making of bulletin boards:

Use of paint. Large classes can present difficulties where all must use paint. Set up a card table as a paint station and allow children to rotate during a seatwork period. This procedure requires fewer art materials and gives the children opportunity for quiet, thoughtful creativeness.

Use of proportion. One way to get appropriate human and animal forms is to cut the paper to the desired proportion. Ask the children to make the feet touch the bottom and the head touch the top of the page. With an animal express the proportion as nose to tail.

Use of sensorial approach. Make use of all types of sensorial experiences to enrich concepts. For example, send sea shells around to be touched as well as to be seen. An increased perception of texture will be the outcome.

No matter what the precise communication of the classroom bulletin board may be, universally it will state that the class thinks, creates, and is alive to the joy of learning and living.

36   Using films for a purpose

E D G A R   D A L E

*Shortly after World War II there was a spurt of interest in the use
of motion pictures in schools, and within the past few years educational television has received a lot of attention. This article comes
from Dale's monthly newsletter, which contains a great deal of valuable information on all kinds of instructional materials.*

MILLIONS OF DOLLARS are being spent every year by schools, churches, unions,
business concerns, for motion picture projectors and films. Will this money
be spent wisely? Will the dollar spent on motion pictures return a dollar's
worth of learning? Will we teach well or badly with this newer tool of education?

We speak so easily of a revolution in methods of teaching. But old habits
persist and the new world sometimes bears an unfortunate resemblance to the
old one. We do the old things but give them a new name, thus appearing
"up-to-date" but upsetting no old routines. But do we need to change our
teaching methods when we use films? Surely no new principles of learning
are involved.

This is quite right. But old methods of teaching, learned almost uncon-
sciously as a student, are likely to persist. These mental pictures of appropriate
teaching methods may lead us astray when we use films. Let us see why this
is so.

The motion picture, properly conceived, is not another textbook. It is
not a compendium of facts, a tightly knit summary. If it is a film such as
World Without End, which deals with the UNESCO fundamental education
program in Thailand and Mexico, it does not present two countries in two
pages. Instead it is a realistic, dramatic story, with full-bodied explanatory
materials. The film has a beginning and an ending.

You can't study a film bit by bit, page by page. You take all or you take
nothing. It does not lend itself to drill, repetition, or memorization. Rich
understanding comes with a single viewing. A film may be rerun with profit,
but you get the big idea the first time and look again chiefly for points that
may have been missed.

There is little parallel between the intelligent use of a film and the reading and reciting process that too frequently accompanies the use of textbooks.

Reprinted from the *Ohio State Newsletter, 21*:1-4, October, 1947.

This reading and reciting are based upon a series of facts—parts of speech, dates, definitions, vocabulary, grammatical errors, arithmetic combinations. Emphasis is placed upon drill, review, memorization as a way to make these discrete facts stick.

Now if you understand something, you don't need to memorize or drill on it mechanically. Too often, students merely repeat words, without understanding what they mean. The high degree of forgetting which follows mere memorization is a testimony to its wastefulness. Further, to memorize is not to apply. Indeed, memorization without understanding may prevent broad application of what is learned. You cannot use with understanding what has not been learned with understanding.

Bare facts, facts not understood, are easily forgotten. They lack the connective tissue, the detail, the human interest, the concreteness which enable a learner to tie up the idea, the word, the abstraction, or the principle with his own experience.

Abstractions and generalizations are learned not by memorizing them, but by developing one's own. The student can be helped, of course, but he must make the necessary inferences from his own experiences. We don't expect him to re-invent the alphabet or the decimal system of notation. But we do expect him to see the evolutionary, man-made characteristics of such a system of generalizations.

Let's apply this to grammar. Ask students who have been studying grammar for several years just why there are eight parts of speech. Why aren't there seven or seventy? Most of them are baffled by the question. They accept the eight parts of speech as unquestionably as they accept unthinkingly a rule against splitting infinitives or ending a sentence with a preposition. They memorize the definition of a "peninsula" and never see that its Latin derivation gives its meaning away—"almost an island." Few students know that "Ecuador" means "equator" in Spanish, one clue to its location.

That our methods of teaching geography leave something to be desired was shown in a Gallup poll where individuals were asked to locate Greece, France, and Spain. Only one-third of Americans knew where Greece was on the map. Nearly one-half did not know where Spain was. One-third could not locate France. Now failure to do this is certainly not due to new methods of teaching (since these were adults who had been out of grammar school for seven to perhaps sixty years). The failure is precisely because they didn't really learn it in the first place.

You can locate Spain on the map if Spain has become related to your life. It's the country Columbus started from. It's the country that sided with Germany and Italy during the war. At its tip is located the once strategic

Gibraltar. Films such as *Spain: The Land and the People* and the recent *People of Spain* give us rich detail concerning the country today. Other films can re-create in unforgettable detail the life in ancient and present-day Spain. The point that I am making is that the average student doesn't know where Spain is because he doesn't think Spain makes any difference in his life.

The motion picture, then, in geography, in history, in mathematics can supply the concrete detail which will help ward off experiential anemia. But it can do more. The commentary and the picture make it possible to match the abstract word with the concrete image. You literally see what is being talked about.

Thus in the color film *The Monarch Butterfly* we see the growth of a butterfly from the egg to the adult. The commentator sharpens the concept of four stages of growth. But he does not do in the film what the teacher can do later in the classroom, namely, see this cycle of growth as another example of cycles which have already been studied. Previously the class may have learned the terms "egg," "larva," "pupa," and "adult." This film uses the terms "egg," "caterpillar," "cocoon," and "adult." Previous associations can be brought into play and we may discover that not all insects go through these four stages. We also discover in this film that the Monarch butterfly migrates —something that the students may have thought was characteristic only of birds.

There is yet another fundamental difference between a textbook and a film. The textbook carefully defines and limits the responses of the students. We don't have "general" textbooks. We have textbooks in various subjects. But motion pictures, partaking as they do of many of the general aspects of life, may not be so easily classified, and if the vocabulary of the commentary has been wisely prepared, the film may be used in a wide range of grades.

This being true, many varying purposes can be achieved with a single film. Too often the teacher doesn't know why she is using the film and neither do the students. If you don't know what you're looking for, you'll not find it.

The importance of the teacher in the use of films is quite clear. Every important educational experience is a bridge between one's past experience and his future life. Unless the teacher and her students see this, the film experience may not be highly educative. This does not mean that the teacher or the class must always overtly and sometimes mechanically state what is being looked for. Sometimes it is so apparent that it would be infantile to discuss it. However, the very lifelike characteristics of the motion picture make it harder to handle. Student responses are not narrowly defined. A broad experience may be reacted to mathematically, economically, politically, sociologically, geographically, historically.

Our purposes are like the strings on which beads are placed. By relating film content to purpose we string beads of experience together in a pattern. A question may help build such a pattern. If we are to see a film on a foreign country, we may ask: "How does it resemble our state, or differ from it? How advanced is the nation industrially? What are some possible handicaps to industrialization?" The right question is as important as the right answer.

Must purposes always be carefully stated before a film is shown? Not necessarily. There are certain general questions that we ought always to ask in regard to certain films. A friend of mine once thought he would teach a class of school administrators the necessity of setting up explicit questions before showing a film. Without any preliminary discussion he showed the film *And So They Live*, which depicts school and community life in the Kentucky mountains. He then gave a test, and to his amazement the administrators did unusually well.

The instructor was mechanically applying a teaching principle, but he forgot that these administrators already had consciously formulated certain key questions to use in analyzing a new school situation. They had already learned how to look.

But equally important as providing the right mental context for the showing of films is the provision of the right physical context. The setting, both physical and mental, will affect the nature and quality of student response.

Instructional films should be shown in the regular classroom. Auditorium use of films usually connotes a mental holiday, an opportunity to take one's mind off his work. Films seen as entertainment involve no obligation. Schools, therefore, should be hesitant about using the auditorium to show classroom films to large groups of students.

Yet there is a real place for film assemblies, for the auditorium use of motion pictures. We can use the auditorium to show films dealing with problems that we want to have faced by all students, problems about which we want to develop a common denominator of information.

The key word in the evaluation and use of films is purpose. Harnessed to a plan, a purpose, these films will not only give a dollar's worth of return for every dollar spent on them, but will also yield a high rate of interest.

37 *Stepping stones in learning to think*

JAMES W. HOERGER

The use of such resources as filmstrips and phonograph records to teach pupils a research approach is described here. Can you think of other ways to use resources to stimulate thinking? Remember that the term "stepping stones" was used in the Raths article in Chapter 2. In addition, see how the present article documents some of the recommendations for providing for individual differences made by Parker and Russell in Chapter 3.

FOR MANY TEACHERS in the elementary schools, reading is the main if not only resource used in teaching social studies by the research method. While reading is and will remain the backbone of this style of teaching, there is no reason why the broad spectrum of audio-visual materials cannot be brought in to help. As the communication arts develop and diversify, there is increasing need not only to give children practice in using these other channels of thought, but also to help them distinguish good from poor quality.

Let us see how the grade teacher and her pupils might use these tools in research, and as stepping stones in learning to think. We will assume that the usual overview of the new topic has been gained in class discussion and that the pupils have been organized into groups ready to investigate various problems about which they will later report to the class as a whole. We will assume too, that the textbook, supplementary classroom books, the library, and other reading materials provide much of the information the children seek.

For many teachers, the use of an audio-visual material such as a filmstrip or phonograph record automatically signifies a whole-class lesson. One key to the use of these materials in research teaching is to permit individuals and small groups to work with them largely on their own. With table viewers, individualized use of slides and filmstrips can be arranged in daylight and without disturbing classmates engaged in other activities. With earphones, records and tapes can be used in much the same way. Another device is to plan the use of sound films by small groups before or after class, or while part of the class is absent pursuing other activities. Viewing picture sets involves no complications at all.

The use of still pictures is a good place to begin a discussion of the special technique of handling AV materials in a research situation. As in the case of films and records, merely putting a picture before a child is no guarantee that

Reprinted from *Audiovisual Instruction,* 6:386-87, October, 1961.

he will learn anything from it. Some pictures in books and magazines are well chosen by intelligent editors to illustrate a point. They are captioned to drive this point home. Others are not. They are used because illustrations are customary and appealing or because they are available and cheap. They do not teach. A good caption (or good teacher) will ask questions. Better still, the caption or teacher will bring the pupil to the point where he will begin to ask questions. One might say:

"What do you see in this picture that explains why these people are so poor?"

"What evidence does this picture present that shows that Brazil is a tropical country?"

"How many kinds of transportation can you find in this picture?"

"Judging from what we have read, what do you suppose these houses are made of?"

By means of such questions, the child is led to involve himself in the picture he sees, and to use what he already knows to make the picture yield more.

A further step consists of requiring the child to find, choose, or even make pictures that illustrate a newly learned concept. Comparing, contrasting, summarizing, and proving by means of pictures is fine practice in thinking, as well as a means of learning the subject at hand. For example, if I had a committee studying ancient civilization I would put them to work comparing the buildings and roads of the Greeks, Romans, and Egyptians with those of the Aztecs, Incas, and Mayas whom they had studied the previous year. This can be done by the selection of pictures and has the virtue of integrating learning which normally takes place in one grade with that of another. The principles discussed here in viewing still pictures apply as well to single pictures seen in a filmstrip and the sequences of a movie.

Maps are a useful resource for learning, but they have one very serious pitfall. Often they are too detailed for the child's comprehension. One way out of this situation is to have the child trace or project a simple outline map and plot on it the information he has gained from a book, another map, or some other source. Thus he has made a map to suit his own purposes and has learned to read a map in very concrete fashion. An opaque projector is invaluable in this process. The overhead projector is also useful. With the proper set of transparencies it is possible to build a map progressively to make the tiniest detail visible to every pupil. A third device is a filmstrip of outline maps.

The use of resource persons is an excellent avenue of research learning and is easily adapted to individual, small-group, or whole-class situations.

Whether or not the school maintains a formal listing of resource persons, most teachers are aware of such individuals in the community. In understanding the everyday life of the recent past, for example, almost any child could profit by interviewing one of his grandparents. A little scouting around will usually produce some relative, neighbor, or local merchant who has lived part of his life in a foreign country or other interesting region. Nearby universities with foreign students are also likely possibilities. Interviews with persons who have once followed, or now follow, some interesting occupation make valuable experiences for children. They can be interviewed inside or outside of class.

In either case, before interviewing resource people, it is well to lay the groundwork in class. What do we need to know about England, about life in the 1920's, about running a ferryboat—or whatever this person is able to tell us? How old was Mr. Smith in 1925? Is a bank manager a typical Mexican? What the prospective interviewee might be expected to know must be anticipated and matched with what the class wants to find out. After the interview (or report or visit) it is also desirable to take class time to summarize and evaluate what was gained. The class should also determine if there are still things left to learn.

As a research resource, the phonograph record offers interesting possibilities. Historical events and biographies have been imaginatively transcribed and records provide a unique insight into the music and folk tales of many lands. Again the fact that a particular experience is not appropriate for a whole class should not deter the teacher from directing smaller groups to this medium, using earphones or perhaps having the record played at lunchtime, after school, or at home. A committee may also illustrate a report to the class by playing a selection or two from a record used in their research. Laying the groundwork and evaluating results are just as necessary here. The committee should know not only what the record tells, but why the class needs to know this.

The motion picture, while a tool of great power, poses special problems. Viewing a sound film is almost necessarily a whole-class activity. Most teachers, moreover, do not have film libraries at their disposal. Rentals take time and planning. So, why not involve the children in this very planning process? The films on educational subjects number in the thousands, and even those devoted to a single topic may be numerous. Children become responsible for their own education when they are required to study the catalogs, discuss the needs of their committees, read descriptions and reviews of films, ascertain the availability of funds, consider the rental cost and shipping time, and, in short, reach a real decision after taking real factors into account. Surely this sort of involvement should contribute to an interested and responsible audience when the film arrives. Previewing the film may be a committee responsibility, as may leading the discussion before and after the showing.

An opportunity to learn to think analytically lies in the effort to understand the technique and limitations of each audio-visual medium. Children can be prompted by such questions as:

"Suppose you were illustrating a book, and you could use only five pictures to show the life of people in Sweden. Where and when would you take your photos?"

"Why do you think this movie included Pablo and his grandfather instead of just showing us a Mexican village?"

"Suppose we put a play on tape to show the building of the transcontinental railroad. What real persons will we need to write speeches for? How do we get across the changes the railroad brought to the farmers, the Easterners, the Indians? How do we tell the audience that this is Leland Stanford speaking? How do we put over the idea that the construction foreman is walking toward the other men?"

Recently I explained the technique of planning a motion picture to my fifth-grade class. I discussed the use of close-ups, process shots, panoramic views, and aerial shots, and pointed out the need for some narrative thread or viewpoint to hold the movie together. My reward was that what might have been a dull report on Rio de Janeiro turned into a scenario by a bright ten-year-old girl who planned her "movie" around a honeymoon couple in Rio. All the facts she had gleaned from her reading were worked cleverly into the script.

It sometimes helps to ask children how a job, albeit done by professionals, might have been done better, or differently. Many a movie presents too much too fast. Children sense this. Why not bring it out in the open? Other films concentrate on spectacle, or the visually attractive, and fail to tell us how people live, do their work, and so on. Children could discuss whether their purpose in seeing the film was the same as that which the producers evidently had in mind.

Conflicts of authority arise, and can be grist for the teacher's mill. For example, the classroom visitor describes Brazil as a metropolitan society. The class has just seen a film on the primitive people of the Amazon Valley. The two concepts do not jibe. Which is the real Brazil? Are there two Brazils? Are there two U.S.A.'s?

Audio-visual materials, like books, yield their treasures only to trained and purposeful minds. As the newer media carry an ever larger burden of society's communication, there is a growing need for the teacher to give each pupil the skills, the experience and the desire to use them wisely.

38   *Using community resources*

ELEANOR A. JAEGER

This article describes ways in which creative teachers can use every-
day materials as instructional resources. Can you think of more such
things you might use?

THE RESOURCEFUL teacher is a scavenger. He is ever alert to discarded materials that can be utilized in the classroom. Cardboard cartons, old telephone
books, wood scraps, tin cans, plastic containers and bags, coat hangers, aluminum foil plates, and glass jars are just a few treasures he salvages from trash.
He looks at waste materials with a gleam in his eye, knowing that he can use
disposed materials in new and creative ways.

CANS AND JARS FOR SCIENCE

Have you ever made tin-can constellations? On the bottom of a can, mark
out the reverse position of each star of a constellation. Make a small nail hole
in the position of each star marked. Hold the can up to the light. As you look
into the can, the constellation is seen. A series of cans can depict many different constellations. Consider nesting cans for easier storage.

Screw-top jars lend themselves to preservation of science specimens.
Fasten a core of soft wood or styrofoam (shorter than jar) to the jar top and
pin insect specimens on this. Add moth flakes to preserve the display before
screwing on top. Screw-top jars filled with rubbing alcohol are adequate for
preserving animal specimens. Jars become insect cages with screening or net-
ting covering the jar mouth.

A wide-mouthed gallon paste jar becomes a terrarium when placed on its
side. To keep the jar from rolling, grease one side and press it into a box
cover filled with wet plaster of Paris which creates a form that fits the
terrarium and nestles it in place.

Aluminum foil plates are bountiful. They serve as fireproof material which
can be cut with scissors and twisted easily into Christmas ornaments. They
make unbreakable waterproof containers for science specimens, roofs for bird-
feeding stations, or center axes on which paper cups are stapled for homemade
anemometers.

Reprinted by permission of the Association for Childhood Education International,
3615 Wisconsin Avenue, N.W., Washington 16, D.C. Using community resources,
by Eleanor Jaeger. From *Childhood Education,* September 1960, Vol. 37, No. 1, pp.
16-18.

What about wood scraps? Lumber yards are eager to get rid of them. All children enjoy nailing odds and ends together to make toys. Young children feel immediate pleasure if they have different shapes and sizes of wood and glue them into fanciful skyscrapers or other objects. The delight of completing a task quickly is especially satisfying to the child with a short attention span.

Children need to display their work; often effective displays help interpret school programs to the public. A little ingenuity will lend interest and variety.

Folding card tables are a natural for exhibits. For flexibility add a pegboard backdrop (24″ x 30″). The pegboard is held upright by inserting it into slots cut into two 2″ x 4″ legs. Each leg is 18″ long; the slot is cut across the wood 9″ from the end. This backdrop comes apart easily and stores flat in a minimum of space.

BULLETIN BOARDS

A simple bulletin board can be made by fastening together narrow strips of wood (1″ x 2″) with a series of screw eyes and wires. Screw eyes are attached to the top and bottom of each strip a few inches from each end. Wire is strung between the top screw eye of one strip and the bottom screw eye of another on each end of the strips. The space between strips can be adjusted by lengthening or shortening wires. The number of strips joined and their length vary according to space requirements.

Commercial display racks are useful for calling attention to books, science experiments, collections, or similar items. These are often available for the asking in drug, grocery, jewelry stores, and the like. Cover the advertisting with paint or colored paper.

Suit boxes become dioramas when windows are cut into the covers and objects mounted inside. Transparent pliofilm keeps displays clean and intact inside boxes.

Old cardboard, telephone books, cellophane and newspapers afford untold advantages when put to different school uses.

A piece of cardboard (20″ x 26″) cut from the side of a box serves as a surface to which a child clips his paper for painting. Old telephone books make fine flower presses. Remove every few pages to keep the press from bulging and place a heavy rock on top for weight. Cellophane coverings from cigarette packages are good transparent envelopes for seed displays. Newspapers substitute for painting and chart paper. The print of newspapers becomes inconspicuous if writing is done with a felt nibbed pen in black or colored ink. Poster paint turns a newspaper into an attractive painting.

USE FOR PLASTICS

This is the age of plastics; use them and reuse them. To prevent plants from drying out, especially over long holidays, invert a plastic bag over each plant and its container. Prop up the bag with a stick or coat hanger frame.

Use plastic for covering kite frames. Fasten plastic with rubber cement which is made by adding benzol to small pieces of rubber bands or inner tubes.

Nozzled plastic dispensers (ketchup and mustard) make excellent rubber cement, glue, and paste dispensers for the classroom. They are easy to handle, prevent spilling, and keep the material from drying out if a nail or thumb-tack is inserted into the nozzle tip.

Plastic turns any low box into a hothouse. Line the box with foil to make it waterproof. Bend two wire coat hangers into the shape of croquet wickets and fasten to the corners to form a roof support. Split a large plastic bag (dry cleaner's) and wrap it around sides and over roof supports. Keep the plastic in place with masking tape, remembering to leave one side loose for watering.

For teachers and children, scavenger hunting is a challenge to powers of imagination. What fun it is to free our thinking from the narrow bounds of commercially prepared materials and reach out to create something different! It is also a surprise to discover how much can be done for so little in terms of the budget dollar.

39 *Outdoor education through school camping*

D O R O T H Y   H I C K S

This excerpt discusses the value of the great outdoors as a teaching resource.

Every child should have mudpies, grasshoppers, waterbugs, frogs, tad-poles, mud turtles, wild strawberries, acorns, chestnuts, trees to climb, brooks to wade in, water lilies, woodchucks, bats, bees, butterflies, various animals to pet, hay fields, pine cones, rocks to roll, sand, snakes, huckle-berries, and hornets; and any child who has been deprived of these has been deprived of the best part of his education.   —Luther Burbank

Reprinted from *School Activities*, 33:141-42, January, 1962.

A SIGNIFICANT place in the outdoor program is given to pupil adjustment, self-reliance, democratic living, moral and spiritual values, health and safety, social grace and poise, recreational skills, and creativity. But even greater emphasis throughout the entire program is on outdoor science and conservation of natural resources. This is the *heart* of the program.

The demands of a growing population upon natural resources make conservation a matter of acute importance. We must teach the wise use and management of natural resources; therefore, the whole forest, community of plants, birds, insects, animals, and reptiles (as well as water, soil, air, and minerals) receive attention. And wise and proper use of scenic, scientific, historic, and recreational resources of our land receives consideration.

At camp where pupils can see, taste, touch, hear, and smell, they readily develop appreciation of man's interdependence with nature. They also correct erroneous ideas regarding the abundance and inexhaustibility of our natural resources. Selection of craft materials, handling fires during cookouts, erosion control, trail development and maintenance, building check dams, cleaning streams, protecting scenic spots, and a host of other planned work projects are fun. But they are also conservation experiences. And through these experiences (which they enjoy) children develop respect for the land and for our national heritage. They also develop appreciation for the most valuable of all natural resources—human beings.

Outdoor science is solidly integrated into the camp program through hiking, exploring, discovering, investigating, and studying on the scene. With the help of teachers, counselors, and resource personnel, children come to understand broad concepts and relationships. Readily available are illustrations of the changing earth or the interdependence of plants and animals. Seeing these manifestations, the children also sense and come to know the place created for them in nature. Such opportunities and experiences are enjoyable teaching-learning situations.

40   *Downtown Community School on wheels*

NORMAN STUDER

Members of the faculty at Downtown Community School in New York City believe that the material their pupils study in the classroom is illuminated by class trips. Norman Studer, the director of the school, discusses the many lessons to be learned from visits to farms, villages, and homes in the rural areas near New York City. He suggests ways to prepare the pupils for these trips, ways to record the experiences of the trips, and the educational and personal benefits the children receive.

EFFECTIVE EDUCATION in the capacity to experience deeply is not present in the curriculum of many schools. Education today does very little to give children the *feel* of our complex and specialized society. Most learning goes on in the sealed box of a classroom, and the words and skills that children master are devoid of the flavor of living experiences. A century ago this was not such an urgent problem; the world was smaller, and children had other ways of finding out about their way of life. But today, if we are to reveal to children the world of productive activity, we must make a special effort.

Fortunately, the capacity for using experiences can be developed in children at any early age. We do not have to wait until a college travel year to develop an ability to get the most out of new experiences. Thoreau once said that he had traveled much in Concord. Our children can have deep and enriching experiences right in their own Concords, if we help them to take off their blinders and see the world. Our trips at Downtown Community School begin with the very youngest children—our nursery classes—to whom a walk around the block is an exciting and illuminating excursion. The program of trips runs through our whole school and culminates in a series of extended, out-of-town trips for the fifth, sixth, seventh, and eighth grades.

The director of the school is a trip specialist. He arranges the itinerary and makes many of the necessary plans, including chartering the bus that remains with a group for an entire journey. A great effort is made to keep the prices down as this is a special cost for the parents, and on occasion the group stays inexpensively at a summer camp and cooks its own meals. Three days is the standard length of an excursion.

Reprinted from *The Downtowner*, November, 1963, pp. 3-8.

THE SEVENTH-GRADE TRIP

The seventh-graders' trip is an introduction to a two-year study of American civilization. This trip is geared to life in the "Age of Homespun," to that Old America which seems so remote to them. We demonstrate that it is possible for children from the region of skyscrapers and subways to submerge themselves in the past.

Each of the three days of this trip through part of New York State has its special focus. The first day centers around Kingston and Old Hurley. The latter is a village whose main street of old stone houses suggests the life and tempo of the eighteenth century. We walk down this unusual street to the high-steepled Dutch Reformed church and chat with the pastor. One of the owners of an old stone house welcomes us and conducts us through the old building, with its steep stairways and its many fireplaces; the legends of Revolutionary days seem to haunt the upstairs rooms.

The climax of the day is a visit to another of these stone houses, the home of Sojourner Truth, a great leader in the fight for women's rights and Abolition. Here is an excellent opportunity to introduce a great but forgotten woman and to underscore the fact that minority groups share in the history of our country.

The second day of this excursion is spent at the Farmers Museum at Cooperstown. The students devote the day to wandering through the old houses of the pioneer village, riding an ox cart, and seeing women spinning, weaving, and making cheeses. The guides are excellent and the day becomes living history.

The third day is spent in the Catskills, on our way home. Here we visit Dry Brook Valley, a place where the Age of Homespun is not too far away. Here still live the Haynes, the Todds, the Fairbairns, with their family remembrances that reach back to the days of the first pioneers. We visit with John and Lena Haynes, who are deeply interested in local history and folklore. The rest of the day is spent at an old covered bridge and at the site of an old iron forge, which produced iron during the War of 1812.

THE EIGHTH-GRADE TRIP

The eighth-graders' trip centers on the problem of changes in society as the nation moved from its homespun days to the "Age of the Machine." To see at first hand the changes brought about by expanding technology, we visit what remains of an obsolete method of transportation—the old Delaware and Hudson Canal—which once linked the coal fields of Pennsylvania with the markets of New England and New York.

On our way to the canal route we cross the Shawangunk Mountains near Ellenville, and pause for a picnic lunch at Sam's Point. We view the landscape many miles in each direction from this spectacular cliff. Here, just below the jutting rock, we come upon a village of huckleberry pickers, city workers who live simply in shacks and pick berries as a vocation. We find this an excellent reminder of pioneer life. We see two men rigging up a crude pile driver for drilling the well they are excavating by hand power. They had located the water vein by a "divining rod," borrowing their folk techniques from local people. The shacks, with their crude handmade furniture and their little gardens, make an excellent introduction to our trip, with its focus on changing technology and changing ways of life.

Continuing down into Ellenville, a town which came into existence because of the Delaware and Hudson Canal, we visit a man in his late eighties, John Miller, who spent many of his best years traveling back and forth on a canal boat. We sit in his stone patio and look out across the quiet backyards, as the old man relives his days. He is happy to have an audience and to have his life assume the importance of a history lesson.

From John Miller's home we go to Port Ben, another village that was born because of the canal. When the canal went out of business in 1900 the village was threatened with decay, but it got a reprieve when the railroad came through on the canal bed. Like archaeologists, we stand in the canal bed, opposite the abandoned depot, and see written on the landscape the story of two methods of transportation that eventually became obsolete. Across the valley, on the main road, we see the buses and trucks that supplanted the railroad which had in turn taken the place of the canal.

On the second day we turn to the effect of machines and modern methods on farming. The first farm is a large one, some nine hundred acres in the valley of the Esopus River, near Old Hurley. Our bus rides out into the cornfields and we walk down the rows to meet the Spanish-speaking migratory workers who are harvesting the last of the sweet corn for the supermarkets of New York City. Jack Gill, the owner, drives up in his pickup truck. Against the background of cornfields and men he tells the story of the large, mechanized farm—the labor problems, the struggle of science against weather and insects, the ways of marketing, the vagaries of price and demand.

The second farm we visit is small and intimate. Two older people greet us warmly and invite us to sprawl out on the grass and the wide front porch. Harry Siemsen, a chicken farmer, explains about the new and highly mechanized chicken farms that will eventually make it impossible for his type of small operation to continue. Our conversation with Siemsen rounds out the central theme of the trip, but we do not confine ourselves to talking to him and his sister about chickens. Mr. Siemsen is fire warden, local historian, and folk-lorist, and he takes all his jobs seriously. He brings out the clippings, photo-graphs, mementos, and the many scrapbooks of material he has collected in his work as town historian. As an active folklorist, he is full of homespun stories. His best are about the Irish immigrants who worked in the bluestone quarries that flourished in this region.

There are several reasons for the success of these trips—and we have had none that were not successful. To begin with, we have made the regions to which we return every year an extension of the school community. We know the areas well and are familiar with all the possibilities they hold for success-ful trips. We know many people in these areas. They are alert for ways to improving the trips and give us valuable suggestions. They are in sympathy with our efforts to show city children what country life is like, and they have important contributions to make. They are a living refutation of the cliché that all Americans are alike and that our country has become standard-ized. Each of them is a product of his particular regional culture, the way of life in his particular valley or country or area.

But it is not enough to have developed interesting trips and found inter-esting people. We have learned over the years that there are important tech-niques and procedures involved in making these experiences an integral part of the lives of the children. We want these trips to develop our young people so they will be open to the testimony of their senses, sensitive to the quality of the personalities they meet. We know that it is possible for young people to be physically on a well-planned trip of this kind and yet untouched by any of the experiences unless some effort is made to help them to see what is be-fore them.

There must be adequate preparation for the trip. The students must come on the trip with some knowledge of the places and the people they are going to see, and some questions to ask of them. It is especially important that there be thorough map-study of the region, so students can readily identify the mountains, rivers, and valleys they will see.

As important as the acquisition of necessary facts relating to the places to be visited is the development of a capacity to receive sense impressions, in-formation, and ideas. Our school constantly seeks to cultivate the qualities that make for receptivity to experiences, and in preparation for the trips stu-dents limber up their capacity to take in sense impressions by writing about people and places in the city and by making sketches of city scenes. They are given instruction in sketching so they will get the knack of making quick drawings, which are a form of note-taking.

On the trip, students carry a shopping bag containing a notebook, sketchbook, pencils, erasers, and perhaps a camera. Their assignments specify the number of sketches they are expected to make and the times at which they will be expected to take notes. Every student keeps a trip diary of his own, and there is also a class diary, with members of the class in charge on one-hour shifts. During the bus travel these students sit in the front seats and take notes on the nature of the passing landscape. So, too, sketchers look out from the front windows of the bus and make drawings of the shape of the landscape. The students return with a wealth of material that is then digested and used in a number of ways—for poems, essays, paintings, murals, or other forms of self-expression.

During the current trip season we added a portable tape recorder to our ways of capturing experiences. This is not intended to take the place of the pencil and notebook but to supplement them. When we returned from this year's trips the students transcribed the material from the tapes, and we have more stories, legends, songs, and anecdotes to add to the school archives.

Major benefits of these trips are a quickened zest for learning and a sharpened capacity for taking in experiences and increased ability to relate these experiences to their studies at school.

For those who would add such trips to their curriculum I would say that trips are possible only if teachers and administrators will expend the necessary effort and thought in planning and preparation. If the trip is to be more than a superficial jaunt, much preliminary spadework must be done. Knowing the community to be visited is the first essential. Having the right attitude in approaching the people of the community is another "must." Teachers will find that a direct and friendly approach, based on a genuine regard for people, will open doors and pave the way for a successful trip. We have found that people respond in a positive way when they know that their personal experiences and information are valued. This is the foundation for successful trips.

41　Enrichment for the asking

DONALD R. PINDER

The best way for a prospective teacher to become familiar with the many sources of free or inexpensive teaching materials is to send for these materials while he is still involved in his teacher-education program. This article merely suggests many possible sources. Where the author refers to Illinois you may substitute the name of your own state, because statewide professional organizations and state education departments are frequently able to provide the same materials as those mentioned here. Remember, too, that suppliers of free or inexpensive materials are more likely to respond favorably to requests written on official school stationery.

THERE ARE MANY sources of free or inexpensive materials for curriculum enrichment, to be used in correlation with the regular curriculum offerings. Materials are available from sources at the local, state, national, and world levels and are varied enough to lend themselves to social studies, language arts, science, arithmetic, health, and physical education.

AT THE LOCAL LEVEL

The most obvious and accessible source of enrichment material at the local level is the field trip. For a field trip to be of any value, it must be preceded by study of what is to be seen on the trip. A class should not visit a firehouse if, at the time, the class is studying about hospitals. To take a field trip that doesn't supplement a particular part of the course of study at that time is almost useless. Look around. Aren't there many places that fit into your curriculum right in your town? Why not make use of them? For instance, the post office is an excellent place to go when you're learning about letter writing—and it also ties in with social studies and the history of communication. A local city council meeting offers fertile ground for supplementing a study of local government in the social studies area.

When your first-graders are talking about big stores it might be well for them to visit a large store and perhaps, with previous arrangement, the man-

Reprinted from *Illinois Education,* 49:158-60, December, 1960.

ager will talk to them and show them the store and some of its functions. The second grade studies about trains and railroads. Ask your class how many have been on a train; you may be surprised at the number who have not. Here is an excellent opportunity to work up a unit on railroads. Charts, filmstrips, and other material can be secured from the Association of American Railroads; the unit can build up to an actual short trip on a train, complete with a conducted tour of the train. After the trip pupils can write and tell stories in language arts class, figure the amount of money they spent in arithmetic, draw various pictures in art, and look at pictures of the development of trains in social studies. The cost—perhaps 75 cents in train fare (paid by the pupil) and a five-cent stamp for a letter to the Association of American Railroads.

There probably are factories and businesses in your community that will conduct tours through their plants—such as a canning factory, a pottery, etc. The field trips are available; it is up to the initiative of the teacher or principal to use them. The cost is very little, if anything.

Local experts

The use of "experts in the field" to talk with classes about something under discussion is often very helpful. A few words of caution, however. Let the guest speaker know what you have studied, and don't overwork this type of curriculum enrichment until prospective speakers are reluctant to come. A local nurse or doctor can often supply the "extra something" to stimulate a health class to remember certain needed facts. In language arts, a local lawyer can impress upon the class the importance and essence of good speech; this could be tied in with social studies if you happen to be working on government and law at the time. There are many other local "experts" who could help and would, if you think about your curriculum.

Use of maps

Arithmetic books in the elementary school are crowded with problems of addition, subtraction, division, and multiplication—especially at the beginning of the texts where there are row upon row of problems for review. You can "spice up" the review. Go to a local gasoline station and ask for some road maps of the state. Give each student a road map and have a lesson on how to read maps. Ask the class how far they are from your home town, for instance. To arrive at the answer the pupils, of course, have to use addition. This type of addition can be expanded as pupils look for the mileage to towns of friends and relatives. Next, tell them where they are going in the state and ask, if they got twenty miles to the gallon, how many gallons of gas it would take. Now they are having a review in addition and division. Ask them to find the cost of the gas at 32 cents per gallon. Now they are adding, dividing, and multiplying. Last, give them a budget for an imaginary trip of their choosing and ask them to figure their gas at twenty miles to the gallon at 35 cents per gallon. Have them tell how much money would be left for other items on the trip. In addition to practicing the fundamentals in arithmetic, pupils enjoy it and, at the same time, learn about their state and how to read road maps. The total cost of enriching the beginning of the year review in arithmetic—exactly nothing.

In one fifth and sixth grade, the class worked out a social studies project that ran all year. The fifth grade studied the Western Hemisphere in geography and the sixth grade the Eastern Hemisphere. They made a huge outline map of the world in art. As the fifth grade came to the states in the United States or other countries in this hemisphere, they would draw in the states or countries. At the same time, the sixth grade was busy doing the same thing with the countries they studied in the other hemisphere. They also were stapling to the map actual samples of the products of the countries or states and stretching strings from the state or country to the various places in the world where these products were exported. When actual products were not available, pictures were used. At the end of the year they had a complete map of world trade. Again, this project of enrichment was completely free from cost.

Other sources

Other sources of curriculum material at the local level would include holiday posters or show cards from local stores for room decoration. A great number of stores throw away the Santa Claus, Halloween, Thanksgiving, and Easter displays that often come with their advertising. Just by asking, you probably could get them for school use.

Do not throw away a *Look* or *Life* magazine. The very fine pictures offered, often in color, make an excellent source for a picture file for the various areas of study in a school program. There is a small cost involved, but if you buy the magazine anyway, nothing is lost. Perhaps you can ask class members to bring the magazines to school after parents are finished with them at home.

At the local level, there is a wealth of material that costs little or nothing: the enrichment can be yours and you don't have to go out of town to get it.

AT THE STATE LEVEL

At the state level, *Illinois Education* has a column that features the listing of free or inexpensive materials as advertised in the magazine for the month. This can be an immense help to the teachers of Illinois.

The Illinois State Library is filled with material that can be used to supplement the school material for curriculum enrichment. Upon request, teachers in Illinois can secure phonograph records for social studies, language arts, music, and just entertainment. The library's art department offers wall pictures for classroom use, packets of pictures for study of particular subjects, View-Master reels of various states and countries, filmstrips, and flan-o-grams. One can also secure supplementary books, for both library and remedial use. In addition, a school can secure sight-saving books for the pupil who has eye difficulty.

The secretary of state and state highway department add still other sources of free material related to social studies. Booklets and materials are available regarding the state's products, people, industries, climate, leading cities, etc.

The state health department has free material on the various diseases, available for classroom use. A unit of work in health could be coordinated with a unit in letter writing to obtain this information.

Another source of free material at the state level is the state university. Here is an example of what can be gained from this source. In talking with a colleague, the author learned he had a very fine rock collection in his building for use by the teachers. He had received it from the Illinois Geological Survey at the University of Illinois. A letter was sent from the author to this department requesting the rock collection; he received, in a matter of days, "35 typical rocks and minerals of Illinois." It was mounted on a large piece of plywood and the teachers used it in social studies and science. The total cost of securing this collection was 65 cents postage.

AT THE NATIONAL LEVEL

As in the state education association magazine, one can find free or inexpensive material listed in the *NEA Journal*. All you have to do is skim the listed material and write to the address indicated, submitting, when necessary, the amount of money required. Don't overlook this as a quick and valuable list of supplementary material.

Information, charts, graphs, and maps relative to various agricultural products are available by writing to the national Department of Agriculture.

Information on cotton, sugar cane, tobacco, forestry, and almost anything you wish is yours for the asking by writing to the federal government in care of the particular branch in which you are interested.

Another source of valuable free material is the United States Weather Bureau, Washington, D.C. One school recently received, for a sixth-grade study of weather, a small weather map for each student and a large one for classroom display.

The Educators Progress Service of Randolph, Wisconsin, issues annually the *Elementary Teachers Guide to Free Curriculum Materials*. The book is indexed by source, subject, and title. Nothing listed costs more than the five-cent stamp needed to mail the letter of request. There are more than twelve hundred items listed for curriculum enrichment. The cost of the book is $7.50 and worth every cent. Other books are available from the same source, listing films, filmstrips, science materials, etc. If a teacher wants supplementary material for a certain unit—in the social studies, language arts, arithmetic, health, or science—she can refer to the book, see what is available, and send for it.

Most elementary educators are familiar with the Chicago Motor Club and its school patrol program. In addition, the club has safety posters that are sent free every two months to schools upon request. Have you considered saving the posters and starting a safety file with them? In a short time you will have posters to cover many of the facets studied by the various grades in safety programs.

How many of you, when teaching about this great land of ours, would like to be able to take the boys and girls to each and every state so they could see firsthand what these states are like? It can be done, if you are willing to settle for the vicarious experience of colored pictures, charts, and maps. Many of our periodicals, particularly in the spring, carry travel advertisements relating to the different sections of the country. Generally included are forms to be filled in and mailed for free travel material. It doesn't take long to add to your curriculum file; if you paste the forms on a post card the cost is relatively small.

AT THE WORLD LEVEL

For material on the world level, the *Elementary Teachers Guide to Free Curriculum Materials* is an excellent source. For your social studies program, you can receive material on history and geography on countries in Europe, Middle East, Far East, North and South America, Central America, and Australia.

As your class studies various foreign countries, pupils can write to the embassy of each country in Washington, D.C., addressing the letter to the ambassador, requesting material about his country. You can also coordinate this with a business-letter writing project. One class which did this on an extensive scale received material from 85 per cent of the countries to which it wrote. The Chamber of Commerce in Kimberley, South Africa, sent material about diamond mining which the class requested.

This article has not included free or rental films and filmstrips—which is an article in itself. However, one should not overlook this as another valuable source of free or inexpensive material. There are other sources of materials which you undoubtedly will be able to add to this list.

If this article will lead the reader to consider some of these sources and thus enrich his class program, some young people will have a more interesting curriculum and some teacher a more interesting job.

Part Three

THE SUBJECTS WE TEACH

THE MOST commonly taught subjects in elementary schools are the three R's, a little history, less geography, and some science. Other areas of study are sometimes suffered admittance into the program, but usually only "after the pupils have finished their real work." Let us consider some of the myths associated with teaching the subjects.

1. *"One subject is more useful than all others for all students."* Some pupils become attracted to, say, science, or to a science teacher, and for these pupils science becomes the central focus of their response; other pupils fasten themselves to history, or art, or literature, and this early interest in a particular subject matter may be the beginning of a lifelong attachment to the subject. However, as needs and abilities change, so do overt responses. How often have we seen children enjoy a "kick" with one subject, then hop to another, then another, and another? And how often have we teachers imposed upon pupils our personal notions of what they should perceive about the subjects, with the result that they perceive only the restrictions of our impositions?

Our schools are often run by verbal people who emphasize verbal subjects. Some educators do not regard the visual arts, or physical activities, or music as valuable means of thinking, feeling, and express-ing. Study of topics close to pupils, such as "How my body works" or "How I feel about myself and others," often gets shoved aside. Similarly, play is misunderstood by some educators who still think that work is good and play is bad.

English grammar is still presented all carefully desiccated and pre-fabricated by some teachers who forget that children are burning inside to use language to express, to play, to relate, to communicate.

We urgently need to scrutinize the view that one subject is pre-eminent. It is one thing to communicate interest, but it is an entirely different matter for adults to impose their own needs, fascinations, and personalities upon all pupils by insisting that this or that subject is intrinsically more valuable for all.

2. *"The subjects have been and will forever be the same."* When we were youngsters in school, many of our teachers gave us the impres-sion that the explanations they purveyed about the several subjects were inherently and eternally true. But let us look at what we are finding out about the subjects. A noted historian advises us, "Our past isn't what it used to be." He writes:

> A decade or two is a brief span of time as history goes, but it can make a difference. Those who "learned" their American history be-fore World War II or in the years immediately following would be in for some surprises were they to return to the old lecture halls to-day. The same professor might be holding forth. The names and dates and "facts" might sound familiar. But the old grad would soon become aware of new meanings attached to dates, altered signifi-cance given to names and unfamiliar associations of "facts."[1]

The facts and theories of science also change. A scientist at the Cali-fornia Institute of Technology warns us about the facts that pupils learn in elementary school:

> After all, it would be 10 to 15 years before the student has an op-portunity to make use in adult life of the technological facts which he learned in the elementary grades. By this time, a large fraction

1. C. Vann Woodward. Our past isn't what it used to be. *The New York Times Book Review, The New York Times,* July 28, 1963, Sec. 7, p. 1.

of the explanations which we accept today as factual will have been grossly modified.[2]

I could go on with other examples, from language or mathematics or what have you, but these examples are sufficient to impel us to investigate the myth, supported by some, that the subjects have been and will forever be the same.

3. *"Teaching by subjects is the only possible way to teach."* Three curriculum models, subject-centered, child-centered, and society-centered, are cited in the article by Herbert Rudman, who observes that "when existing practices are surveyed, it becomes difficult to locate any but the subject-centered curriculum model."

This is an interesting statement in light of three important facts: *First*, children relate directly to intellectual problems, with little consideration for what the subject matter is. *Second*, there are no issues or problems in any society which knowledge in only one subject can resolve. Moon shots, world government, poverty—name anything—require knowledge that is derived from the scientific, social, moral, political, judicial, and language areas. Yes, the specialist may contribute specific information but the ultimate decisions rely upon multi-varied data. *Third*, results of research studies do not support the superiority of the subject-centered curriculum as a way of teaching. The literature notes that the nonsubject-matter-centered approaches in elementary schools produce knowledgeable, self-directed, experimentally minded pupils who are capable of using their knowledge, reading ability, and critical-thinking ability in practical situations.[3] These three reasons are sufficient for us to question the myth that teaching by subjects is the only possible way to teach.

2. A. R. Hibbs. Science for elementary students. *Teachers College Record, 63*: 137, November, 1961.
3. See: Arthur T. Jersild *et al.* An evaluation of aspects of the activity program in the New York City Public Elementary Schools. *Journal of Experimental Education, 8*: 166-207, December, 1939.
Arthur T. Jersild *et al.* A further comparison of pupils in activity and nonactivity schools. *Journal of Experimental Education, 9*: 303-309, June, 1941.
Frederick Pistor. Evaluating newer school practices by the observational method. *Appraising the Elementary Curriculum.* Sixteenth Yearbook of the Department of Elementary School Principals, Washington, D.C.: The Department, N.E.A., 1937, pp. 377-89.
J. W. Wrightstone. *Appraisal of Newer Elementary School Practices,* New York: Bureau of Publications, Teachers College, Columbia University, 1938.

4. *"Information is all that pupils learn in school."* There is more to a subject than the information contained in books about it. Certainly facts and information are important. So, too, are skills and attitudes and the patterns of action a person might follow as a result of studying these subjects. Science teaching that neglects scientific method and scientific attitudes is a waste of time. History that fails to stimulate learners to apply knowledge of history in trying to understand man's ways is useless. A course in health which does not cause pupils to follow certain health principles is worthless and potentially harmful.

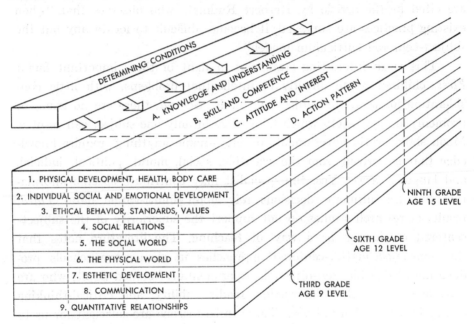

The behavioral continuum — broad curriculum areas intersecting major behavior categories.

In the chart on this page the numbers represent broad subject-matter areas and the letters refer to various categories of behavior.[4] As you review the book up to this point, what do you think should be the qualities of behavior under each of the letters? As noted in Thomas's selection in Chapter 6, modern educators state these qualities of behavior in terms of *what the learners actually do or learn or feel;* that is, in behavioral terms. Try it. It is not an easy thing to do. However, because

4. The chart is reprinted with permission of the Russell Sage Foundation from *Elementary School Objectives* by Nolan C. Kearney, p. 38. Copyright 1953 by the Russell Sage Foundation.

pupils learn skills, attitudes, and action patterns along with information, it is a useful enterprise for a teacher.

In this introduction I have discussed four current myths about the subjects we teach in schools. Keep them in mind as you prepare to read the selections in the following chapters. It is impossible to divide the subject-matter areas in a clearcut way. Language, for example, is used in all aspects of a school program. Furthermore, one cannot and should not view various aspects of communication—such as reading, listening, spelling—as separate from each other. We know that a child in school never ceases to study his social environment or react to the aesthetic world about him. Informal study of the physical world is a constant occupation for children. Children may learn aesthetics in a mathematics lesson, oral communication in science, and scientific attitude from many lessons. Adults study these subjects as discrete entities, but real curriculum for children is something else again. Thus, although for our convenience we may set down various subject areas into what may appear to be rigid compartments, we must remember that in actual school life it is impossible and inadvisable to try to separate them.

Chapters 10 through 13 are concerned with ways of helping pupils learn effective communication by means of the language arts. Chapters 14, 15, and 16 deal with some staples of elementary-school programs: mathematics, science, and the social studies. Chapter 17 is about health, physical activities, play, sex education, and family life education—those areas of concern which are close to pupils' feelings and needs. Chapter 18 presents some of the many formal ways of contributing to children's aesthetic development in elementary schools. The concentration here is upon visual arts and music.

CHAPTER 10

Reading Effectively

A TEACHER who will make decisions about teaching children to communicate must first be aware that many factors influence pupils and teachers of the language arts. The diagram on page 222 displays what one writer calls a "galaxy of factors" about the language arts. He explains the factors as they relate to the pupil and the teacher:

> Some of them exist because children are born in a social order, others because that social order has elaborate systems of communication and literary entertainment. . . .
> Teaching language arts, therefore, is a coordinating enterprise. It tries to marshal diverse forces in such a manner that they will produce literate children.[1]

On the right side of the diagram you will see many of the topics already discussed in this book; on the left side are topics not yet discussed. Starting at the top and reading counterclockwise, you can readily see that the interaction of pupil and society is stressed. Notice that the English language itself and the teacher's knowledge of it are given a significant place, and the various aspects of the language arts are interrelated.

What rich responsibility a teacher has! He must communicate to pupils in such a way that they may become effective at communicating. What a challenging job to orchestrate so many factors into a school program that is orderly and filled with meaning and adventure!

Let us turn first to a professional view of the job of helping pupils

---

1. Wilmer K. Trauger. *Language Arts in Elementary Schools.* New York: McGraw-Hill Book Company, Inc., 1963, p. 5.

learn a most important and complex means of seeking information and enjoyment—reading.

If pupils are to learn to read or learn to read better, their teachers must make some important organization decisions. Three general ways to organize are used in the teaching of reading in our elementary schools. In some classrooms, a "homogeneous" approach is used whereby all children read from the same book. In other schools, individualized reading approaches are returning to favor. A third form of organization is the division of a classroom into three subgroups according to estimates of pupils' reading ability. The most commonly used reading materials for this plan are basic readers, supposedly written in graduated levels of difficulty.

Will you want to use one of these three approaches? Or will you want to combine two of them? What kinds of reading materials will you choose? Will all your pupils read from the same book? Will you choose to have three groups? If so, how will you determine them? Or will you follow individualized reading programs, which require that a teacher be familiar with a wide range of children's literature? Will you teach reading only from books? Will you use other resources? Will you teach reading only during reading periods? Will you teach reading (and the interrelated language arts) at other times of the day too? Finally, why will you teach reading? What curriculum decisions will you make?

42   *Reading and the self-concept*

A L M A   C R O S S   H O M Z E

The author brings research to bear on the questions: What does learning to read do to a child? What effect can reading have upon his concept of himself? She suggests a possible relationship between reading and the self-concept.

Reprinted with the permission of the National Council of Teachers of English and Mrs. Alma Cross Homze from *Elementary English*, *39*:210-15, March, 1962.

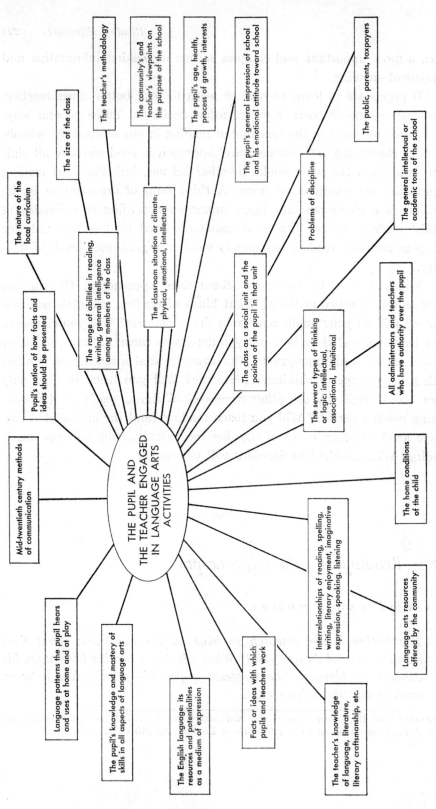

The teacher's methodology

The community's and teacher's viewpoints on the purpose of the school

The pupil's age, health, process of growth, interests

The pupil's general impression of school and his emotional attitude toward school

The size of the class

The public, parents, taxpayers

The nature of the local curriculum

The range of abilities in reading, writing, general intelligence among members of the class

The general intellectual or academic tone of the school

Pupil's notion of how facts and ideas should be presented

The classroom situation or climate: physical, emotional, intellectual

Problems of discipline

Mid-twentieth century methods of communication

The class as a social unit and the position of the pupil in that unit

The several types of thinking or logic: intellectual, associational, intuitional

All administrators and teachers who have authority over the pupil

THE PUPIL AND THE TEACHER ENGAGED IN LANGUAGE ARTS ACTIVITIES

Language patterns the pupil hears and uses at home and at play

The home conditions of the child

The pupil's knowledge and mastery of skills in all aspects of language arts

Interrelationships of reading, spelling, writing, literary enjoyment, imaginative expression, speaking, listening

Language arts resources offered by the community

The English language: its resources and potentialities as a medium of expression

Facts or ideas with which pupils and teachers work

The teacher's knowledge of language, literature, literary craftsmanship, etc.

From *Language Arts in Elementary Schools*, by Wilmer K. Trauger. Copyright 1963. McGraw-Hill Book Company, Inc. Used by permission.

READING is the school subject most discussed by educators and laymen today. It is written about in journals and books, spoken about on radio and television, and heard about in conferences and meetings. Yet reading is usually attacked from one vantage point, "How is it done?" An overabundance of new formulae for teaching reading continually appear. They are, in turn, advertised as panaceas for the problems involved in making our nation literate.

While we abound in these "how-to-do-it" books, we are oblivious of the paucity of thoughtful information emphasizing such basic questions as, "What are the effects of reading?" We develop different methodologies for different reading levels, while we often fail to consider the relationship between the child's development and his reading.

One aspect of child development, the self-concept, is being explored in terms of motivation and learning but not specifically in terms of reading. It is my purpose to describe briefly the research in the general effects of reading and the development of the self-concept, and then draw a hypothetical relationship between the two.

1. The effects of reading. In spite of the necessity of including "effects" in a consideration of reading, that aspect of interpretation of the printed page is grossly neglected. In Betts' bibliography of 8278 articles and studies, there was only a limited reference to research studies on the effects of reading.[1] The studies which did relate to the effects of reading stressed mass media. They included investigations of newspaper and magazine reading and effects of TV on reading rather than emphasizing the direct effects of reading on the child.[2] Russell clarifies the point further:

> Studies in the effects of reading are the present no man's land of this large domain in the language arts area. Since at least the 1880's starting with Janal and Cattell, the psychology of the reading act has been charted with considerable care. Beginning a little later, the problems of reading behavior and instruction have been explored and analyzed by Buswell, Dearborn, Gates, Gray, McKee, Thorndike, and by their students and other workers. It is in the third large area, the investigation of the effects of reading, that large unknown regions and unmapped territories exist today.[3]

There are, of course, valid reasons for the neglect of research in the effect of reading on the individual. The teacher places greater emphasis in her reading program on the "process" or "methodology" of reading rather than

1. Emmett Albert Betts, E. W. Dolch, Arthur Gates, and David H. Russell. Unsolved problems in reading: a symposium I. *Elementary English, 31*:335, October, 1954.
2. *Ibid.*, p. 336.
3. *Ibid.*, p. 335.

the "product" of reading. The large classes prevent her from following through the complete reading cycle so that she can observe the effects of reading on the child. The second reason for the neglect of this area is inherent in the problem: the task is a complex one. Many factors are related to changes in reading and "it is rarely possible to discover one immediate effect linked to a single cause."[4] The research that has been done concerns the effects of reading on personality, attitudes, and groups of people.

In *What Reading Does to People*, Douglas Waples reports the results of his studies of the effects of reading on groups of people. He has identified five general areas:

a. The instrumental effect: the results of reading for knowledge, information
b. The prestige effect: the results of reading for self-approval
c. The aesthetic effect: the results of reading for the beauty of expression
d. The respite effect: the results of reading that relieves tension
e. The reinforcement effect: the results of reading that enforces our attitudes[5]

Although Waples' work chiefly concerns groups, his five effects should be kept in mind as we develop a relationship between reading and the self-concept.

It has been believed for many years that reading would develop "a desirable" personality. The Colonial days fostered the reading of the Bible for this reason. While recent studies have given impetus to this theory, Louise Rosenblatt in *Literature as Exploration*[6] stresses the "value of books in terms of their effects upon the pupil's personal life and adjustment."

In the book *The Reader's Guide to Prose Fiction*, Elbert Lenrow presents a comprehensive compilation of "lists of books designed to aid pupils in understanding themselves and their personal environment, in comprehending social problems and issues, and in finding 'escape' or entertainment."[7] Evalene Jackson tried to determine the effects of reading on race prejudices. She measured racial attitudes, advised the group to read a particular book which dealt with the problem, readministered the racial attitude questionnaire and compared the "pre" and "post" measures. She found a small but significant shift from a less, to a more favorable attitude

4. *Ibid.*
5. Douglas Waples, Bernard Berelson, and Franklin R. Bradshaw. *What Reading Does to People*, Chicago, Ill.: University of Chicago Press, 1940, p. 114.
6. Paul Witty. Relationship of reading to personality development. *Supplementary Educational Monograph*, 72:173, October, 1950.
7. *Ibid.*

toward Negroes.[8] However, the effect was not a lasting one which may indicate that in order to change attitudes more than one book during one time period is necessary.

I have considered only the "book" partner of the "man-book" team necessary for reading. Perhaps the effects of books depend more on the receptivity of the individual rather than the content of the book, or perhaps the process is more one of total interaction. Certainly the predisposition of the readers must be considered. Waples lists the following factors as determinants of the response to, and the effects of literature:

a. The age of the person: We go through reading stages at particular ages. Children's interests are generally uniform because of the similarity of their experiences.

b. The sex of the person: There are differences in selections of reading material between men and women. See Douglas Waples' book, *What People Like to Read.*

c. The education of the person: The educational background determines the types of study and reading habits and the levels of vocabulary one has.

d. The occupation of the person: Various occupations encourage us to read certain types of literature.

e. The income level of the person: The income may limit the number and type of material available. (The rise of paperback books may alter this factor.)

f. The group membership of the person: The people one contacts through family, school friends, vocational associates, church, club, and sport groups may all help explain interests in types of reading material.[9]

The group membership factor may be, for a child, the most important of the six personal factors. His group determines, to a large extent, many of the actions and opinions that later become part of his self-concept. His group also determines to some extent, according to Waples, his reading choices. This too becomes part of his self-concept. How then does reading relate more specifically to the child's self-concept?

2. The child's self-concept. The self-concept is defined as the "person as known to himself, particularly stable, important and typical aspects of himself as he perceives them."[10] The social forces which act on children and help them form their self-concepts are widely varied. At first, the child's

8. Evalene P. Jackson. Effects of reading upon attitudes toward the Negro race. *Library Quarterly, 14*:53, January, 1944.
9. Waples, *op. cit.,* p. 89.
10. Ira J. Gordon and Arthur W. Combs. The learner: self and perception. *Review of Educational Research, 28*:433, December, 1958.

contact with the world is through empathy. This is the child's form of communication, and a rather nebulous one.

When language develops, the child has a more precise form with which to contact people. It is in this early language growth that the child is beginning to recognize himself. At first, his needs are all directed toward himself; they are "mine" and "me." The child is establishing his identity through bodily possessions, material possessions, and abstract possessions. First, he identifies his nose; next he can identify his shoes; finally he identifies his responsibility. All three are part of the child's self-concept.

The child continues through the "mine-me" stage until he begins to recognize and accept others around him.[11] He no longer can rely on "mine-me"; he begins to recognize the power of "his-hers" and his position with other people becomes clearer. His self-concept has evolved from the time when he was alone most of the time, to the period when he was identifying himself as a person, to his beginning socialization. This probably takes place when he reaches school age and is placed in a situation with a great number of children his own age. The development of his self-concept is now as dependent on his social contacts as on his language development.

The roles of his peers determine much of what behavior the child will assume. The roles of his peers become his life-models. He is at about the same stage of development as his playmates so he can more easily identify with his young companion than he can with an older neighbor.

This ability to *identify* with others is perhaps the most important factor in the development of his self-concept. The child selects those parts of others which he desires for himself and adapts them to himself. As the child selects actions which he wants to use as part of his self-concept he also recognizes certain patterns of action, or roles, which he may assume so that he can be effective with different people. We are all familiar with the child who has a role at home with his parents and assumes a different role when he comes to school. Different approaches are more successful with different people, and the child recognizes it.

The actions he assumes which are satisfying and socially rewarding are adopted by the child as part of his self, and as each is chosen to be part of the self, so the next choice is influenced. The process is an overlapping and a continuous one. As he grows, the more successfully the child can relate the actions of others to himself and understand how they concur with or alter his own actions, the more successful he will be in understanding his self-concept.

11. M. Sherif and H. Cantril. *The Psychology of Ego-Involvements,* New York: John Wiley and Sons, Inc., 1947, p. 179.

Although this article is primarily concerned with the relationship between reading and the self-concept, the implications of the self-concept for all of education are pointed out in the doctoral dissertation of Hugh V. Perkins.

> Specifically the self-concept can be used in education: (a) as a psychological construct which enables teachers, counselors, parents, and others to achieve with training deeper understandings and insights into the behavior and development of children, and (b) as a vital and important aspect of learning and development which the school through its educational processes seeks to promote and foster in every child.[12]

3. The hypothetical relationship. How are reading and the self-concept related? How does reading ability affect the self-concept? How does the self-concept affect reading performance?

Reading has various effects on the reader. Waples has described these effects and the personal factors of the reader which permit or prevent these effects from taking place. If we accept that some of these effects do take place to varying degrees depending on the reader, then it may be the individual's ability to *identify* that produces the greatest effects. It is that ability to identify that transmits the effects of reading to the self-concept.

Before he reads, the child identifies most readily with people. He uses people as models for his behavior or thinking. He adapts and adopts portions of their behavior for his own. He uses them to define and develop his self-concept. The child acts as a mirror to a wide variety of actions from a wide variety of people. From this image-making the child is formulating what he is as a person, and this becomes his self-concept.

As the child learns to read, he selects some of his models from the books he reads.[13] He identifies with a central character, a family, a problem, or a desire he shares with characters in the books.

A child may read of a character who ran away from home and ask himself, "Why did he do it?" "How did he feel?" "How would I feel?" or "What would I do?" He is internalizing the motives of the book character, searching his own thinking, and arriving at a better understanding of why some children do run away from home. If the child can ask himself, "Would I do that?" and arrive at an answer, then he is using reading to examine himself. He can, in this way, begin to recognize and to build on his self-concept. The child may not be aware that this is taking place, but the next

12. Hugh V. Perkins. Teachers and peers conceptions of children's self-concepts. *Child Development, 29*:204, June, 1958.
13. Ethel J. Alpenfels. All children need to identify. *Childhood Education, 25*:394, May, 1949.

time he encounters either a real or a fictitious character who ran away from home, or if he ever feels the urge himself, he will be better prepared to understand the situation. He becomes able to give a meaning to things that will happen to him and things that have happened to him.[14] He begins to build and clarify his self-concept through reading.

In her article "The personal and social values of reading," Nila Smith presents the results of a study of children in grades four through eight. She asked the children if they "remembered any book, story, or poem which had changed their thinking or attitudes in any way." Of 502 responses, 60 per cent indicated that they had experienced changes in their attitudes as a result of reading. An additional 10 per cent said that they had also felt changes in their behavior.[15] It is possible that such changes indicate changes in the basic way the children perceive themselves—in their self-concept.

However, two factors must be present for such changes, a child's receptivity to the change and the stimulus for the change. Beyond that, we really cannot be sure what character or plot will encite a change in a child's attitude or behavior. No book would produce the same effects on any two children. Good! A great part of reading is exploring; let the children ramble through many different kinds of books until each child finds the models that give him satisfaction.

In addition to considering what a child reads, we must also consider how well he reads, for this too influences his self-concept. If the child is highly proficient in extracting ideas from the printed page and he recognizes this, he will have a positive approach to reading. He is able to read, therefore his concept of himself is as a "reader." He is more apt to read widely; he will attempt more difficult material; he will have great pleasure in reading. Since his self-concept is that of a reader, so he reads more widely, and he does become more of a reader; the cycle is complete.

However, if the child has great reading problems, and he experiences little success in reading, his concept of himself will be that of a "nonreader." He has difficulty with word recognition; he struggles to glean ideas from groups of words; he may not like reading at all; a vicious cycle develops. The child experiences little success in reading and his self-concept becomes such that he feels he is not a reader. Since the conception he has of himself in reading is a negative one, he fails to make the progress necessary for him to experience success and improvement.

14. Arthur T. Jersild. *In Search of Self,* New York: Teachers College, Columbia University, 1952, p. 17.
15. Nila Banton Smith. The personal and social values of reading. *Elementary English,* 25:490, December, 1948.

It is readily understandable that the remedial work we give such children sometimes has little or no effect. A child with reading difficulties once said to me, "I can't read because I don't have a reading head." Previous attempts at remedial reading with this child had proved unsuccessful. It was not until the child was helped to succeed in simple reading experiences that she began to see herself as a reader. Consequently, succeeding attempts in building skills also included strong encouragement to help the child see herself as a reader. In this way, the child's reading skills improved as did her attitude toward herself as a reader. The gradual and slight change in the child's self-concept helped her improve the necessary reading skills; the relationship is, again, interdependent.

IMPLICATIONS FOR EDUCATION

The interdependence of reading and the self-concept has important implications for education. Educators must become more aware of the kinds of books children need. Then they must provide a wide variety of materials for all children of all ages. The children must have many different types of characters from which to select models. They must have a wide variety of story situations in which they can place themselves. Most of all, they must have freedom to select the book that best fills their immediate appetite. Then, books will help children in understanding themselves.

Educators must add a second dimension to all remedial reading programs. This would stress developing the child's attitude toward himself as a reader as well as developing reading skills. Such a program would include many successful reading experiences to help build the child's confidence. It would include discussions which would help the child relate the reading to his personal life. Only then will the "reluctant reader" find that reading is a part of himself, and only then will he improve because he does see himself as a reader.

Educators must provide *time* for every child to read. That is not the "six pages of the second story beginning on page 31" type of reading time. There must be a time in every day when a child can pull himself up in his own place and say, "Now, book, you belong to me, and I belong to you!" Let the child meet someone in that book. Let him go somewhere in that book. Let him see something in that book. He will enjoy reading just for that chance.

The pleasure will not be the same for every child: "Undoubtedly, individual children vary greatly in the amount and type of their identification ... but the possibilities exist even in later childhood. Juvenile literature must be considered as one of the more important avenues for identification from early childhood. . . ."[16] The problems involved in examining this facet of reading are fascinating ones. They are open for exploration. Well then, what does reading do to you?

〜❧〜

43   *Teaching selections in the reader*

PAUL MC KEE

McKee outlines nine kinds of activities for reading programs in second and third grades. He writes: "The teaching of the fundamentals of reading in the second and third grades consists of carrying on certain definite teaching and learning activities which, from the teacher's point of view, may be called instructional jobs. The most important of these jobs are (1) teaching selections in the reader, (2) providing for miscellaneous reading in connection with various school activities, (3) developing independence in the identification of strange printed words, (4) improving reading through skillful teaching of the content subjects, (5) developing independence in coping with meaning difficulties, (6) providing for seat work, (7) providing practice in reading for various purposes, (8) locating and removing pupils' reading deficiencies, and (9) measuring pupil achievement. All but two of these nine instructional jobs need to be carried on at both second- and third-grade levels. The fourth and fifth jobs are to be considered at only the third-grade level."[1]

The following selection elaborates upon the first job on McKee's list, teaching selections in the reader. He offers a framework for planning and conducting reading lessons with a group using a basal reader. Many teacher's manuals contain similar advice.

In The Teaching of Reading *McKee captured the imagination of*

Reprinted from *The Teaching of Reading in the Elementary School,* Boston: Houghton Mifflin Company, 1948, pp. 286-91.

16. David H. Russell. Identification through literature. *Childhood Education,* 25: 397, May, 1949.
1. McKee, *Teaching of Reading,* p. 285.

adult readers by presenting them with a difficult and new alphabet
which caused some of the same reading problems that school children
encounter. Be sure to have a look at it.

IT IS COMMON practice in most second- and third-grade classrooms for the
teacher to spend many of the reading periods in teaching selections contained
in the so-called basal reader or in one or more so-called supplementary readers.
Poor teaching of these selections can block the child's progress in reading.
Good teaching of the selections can help him learn to read with pleasure and
effectiveness.

In the judgment of the writer, certain activities should be carried out in
teaching any prose selection contained in the reader. These activities are
(1) introducing the selection to the pupils, (2) reading of the selection by
the pupils, (3) discussing ideas presented in the selection, and (4) making
further use of ideas gained from the reading.

INTRODUCING THE SELECTION

In introducing any given selection to pupils before they begin to read
that selection the teacher should seek (1) to stimulate the child to think along
the lines of the selection to be read, (2) to help the pupil to identify certain
strange words contained in the selection, (3) if necessary, to help the pupil
build certain strange concepts included in the selection, and (4) to set a
purpose for the reading.

Stimulating pupils to think along the lines of the selection to be read is
to be accomplished, not by telling the story or the information that is presented in the selection, but rather by making comments and asking questions
which will lead the pupils to think and tell of and to discuss briefly experiences
they have had which are similar to those given in the selection. It is understood,
of course, that the purpose of this activity is not that of arousing pupils'
interest in reading the selection. If a given selection has a strong interest-
pull in itself, there is no need for the teacher to spend time trying to arouse
the child's interest in reading that selection. His observing of "teasing" pictures
which the book provides for introducing the selection and his reading of the
first two paragraphs or so of the selection itself will get that job done. If the
selection is dull, there is nothing which the teacher should do to convince
the pupil that the material will be fun to read, and there is little she could
do to stimulate an interest which would stay with the pupil after he had
read the first page.

By a prereading of the selection, the teacher will have discovered the words which she thinks are strange to her pupils. Because practically all of those words, at least at the second-grade level, are within the child's listening vocabulary, each of them will be strange to him only in the sense that the form is unfamiliar. He needs merely to become acquainted with the form and to associate the familiar pronunciation and the familiar meaning with the form. With the tools of independent identification taught up to this time, he can work out some of these words readily as he reads the selection; a few he cannot attack successfully. Consequently, the teacher, choosing those few words carefully, prints each form in context on the blackboard, tells the child the pronunciation of each word, sees that he associates the familiar pronunciation and meaning with the form, and thus helps him to identify each word so that he is better prepared to read the selection. The other strange words, those which the child can attack independently with success, are ignored before the reading begins. The teacher hopes that by attacking them independently as he reads, the child will get practice in using identification tools she has taught.

Because suitable second-grade readers contain no concepts which are strange to second-grade pupils, there will be little need for the teacher at that level to help pupils construct concepts needed for reading a given selection. In general, however, most third-grade readers, particularly those which include so-called social studies content, do present concepts which are strange to many pupils for whom the books are intended. Obviously, therefore, the third-grade teacher, by her prereading of the selection to be taught, will have discovered the concepts or meanings which she thinks are strange to her pupils.[1] Because she knows that the child must construct those strange concepts in order to read the selection with adequate understanding, she then uses objects, pictures, simple explanations, and other means to help the pupil do most of that constructing before he begins to read. The few strange concepts she ignores are those which are explained adequately by pictures and verbal context in the selection itself, and which she believes the child, if he has been taught to use pictures and context to build the meaning of a strange word or group of words, can construct as he reads.

Because there is good reason to believe that the pupil reads more effectively when he reads with a definite purpose than without, the teacher should set, or lead the pupils to set, a purpose for the reading of the selection. That purpose is no trivial matter which pertains only to some

1. Finding the strange concepts in a given selection is not at all the same as finding the strange word forms. A strange concept may be represented by a single word, a group of words, or even a sentence. It may be a strange meaning that goes with a familiar word form, or a strange meaning that goes with an unfamiliar word form.

relatively unimportant detail included in the selection. It is concerned, rather, with some important understanding to be achieved by reading the entire selection and by using the details presented therein. It may be concerned with an understanding of the general situation described, with the wisdom of a series of actions related in the selection, with the motives that led to certain actions or events in the story, with the value of certain suggestions made in the selection, or with the kind of person a given character is. Usually, the purpose, set before the reading is begun, is expressed in the form of one or more questions.

READING THE SELECTION

After the introduction has been made, the pupils read the selection. Often that reading is entirely silent; sometimes it is oral, the pupils taking part when asked to do so. During the reading, the teacher gives whatever help is requested by pupils who are not able to overcome difficulties through their own efforts. In addition, she observes the children's reading closely to discover pupils with undesirable habits such as lip movement and word pointing, and to locate those individuals who need special attention or who should have practice in one or another skill.

GROUP DISCUSSION

Usually, the reading of the selection is followed by group discussion. That discussion, far from being a quizzing activity in which the teacher asks questions to check pupils' comprehension, is in reality an informal conversation about interesting items in the selection. It consists of comments that pupils wish to make about the selection, of questions they wish to raise about this or that point, and of the suggestions by the teacher designed to clear up important matters in the selection which need clarification. The length of these discussions varies with the number of reactions which pupils wish to express verbally and with the amount of clarification required.

MAKING FURTHER USE OF IDEAS READ

Following the discussion of the selection, provision is made in one or more subsequent reading periods for pupils to use in one or more ways the ideas they have gained from the reading of the selection. The following list of uses is suggestive but by no means exhaustive:

1. Working out one or more experiences, pertaining to the selection, which are contained in the workbook that accompanies the reader.

2. Working out homemade exercises covering important items given in the selection.

3. Dramatizing one or more parts of the selection.

4. Constructing an interesting object described in the selection.

5. Reading important parts of the selection aloud at a program or an assembly.

6. Collecting and reading other books and selections which pertain to the topic or to one or more parts of the selection read.

7. Making and collecting pictures to represent items contained in the selection.

8. Talking over the implications of certain statements given in the selection, such as the effect of increased use of airplanes upon the way in which people live.

9. Telling of other material read which pertains to the topic of the selection, and comparing that material with the selection read.

10. Finding and listing the main points of the selection.

MISCELLANEOUS STATEMENTS

In general, the teaching of a given selection in the reader consists of carrying out the four steps just described. However, certain adjustments are often necessary. First, two or more periods sometimes are used for the reading of the selection. When this happens, a brief time at the beginning of each of the second and later periods is spent in recalling the part or parts already read and in setting a purpose for the reading of the next part. Secondly, the pupils are sometimes led to reread the selection or some part of it a second and even a third time. Such rereading should be done in the light of a definite purpose other than that used for the first reading. Carrying out any one of the uses of ideas mentioned in the paragraph above may require at least one rereading of part or all of the selection. Thirdly, variations probably will need to be made for each group. To illustrate, for the slow and even the average group more time may be required in teaching strange words and in setting specific purposes before the reading is begun than is required for the high group. It may be necessary also for the slow group to read and discuss the material page by page, just as the primer is read in most first-grade classes, rather than to read all or several pages of the selection before the discussion is begun. In addition the degree of interpretation of what is read required of the high group should be much greater than that required of the low group.

44 *How effective are your reading lessons?*

JOSEPHINE B. WOLFE

How would you evaluate a reading lesson? What are the specific aspects of an effective reading lesson? How can a teacher find out whether these positive qualities were present?

IF YOU WERE TO ASK a group of teachers, "Why do you teach reading? What *procedure* do you use?" direct and positive replies would be received. Teachers would agree that their chief purpose in teaching reading is, of course, to raise their pupils' levels of competency in reading. Furthermore, they would concur that the most commonly used procedure for improving reading ability is, regardless of the approach (basal reader, experience, or individualized) *good reading lessons*. Yet, if you were to query, "How effective are your reading lessons?" the replies would be astonishing! Teachers would respond with broad, vague, and indirect generalizations. The reason for such uncertainty is simple! Most teachers are not equipped with a list of "specific standards" to evaluate *how effective their reading lessons really are*. Realizing the need for such an "evaluative tool" the list below has been formulated. It consists of a series of questions designed to alert teachers *what to look for* as they guide or terminate each reading lesson. It may be used with an individual, a small group, or a class group to identify specific strengths and weaknesses.

WHAT TO LOOK FOR

1. How many *concepts* and new *words* were introduced and developed?
2. Did most of the children appear to understand the *concepts* and *new words* that were introduced and developed?
3. Were the children able to formulate their own questions? to vary their kinds of questions?
4. Was the teacher able to vary her questions? Does the selection lend itself for her to do so?
5. Did the children appear to understand 75 per cent (three of every four questions) asked during the guided silent reading? Can they verify their answers?
6. Could the children anticipate the meaning of the questions asked by the teacher or the questions formulated by themselves and their classmates?

Reprinted with the permission of the National Council of Teachers of English and Dr. Josephine B. Wolfe from *Elementary English*, 40:275-76, March, 1963.

7. Did the children ask for help with more than one out of twenty running words during the silent reading? during their oral rereading?

8. Did the children appear to have head movement, finger pointing, thumbing, or other tensions during their silent or oral reading?

9. Did any child use lip movement or vocalization during his silent reading?

10. Were substitutions, repetitions, omissions, and regressions evident as the children participated in the oral rereading?

11. Did any child read word by word during his oral rereading?

12. Did all members of the reading group complete their guided silent reading at approximately the same time?

13. Were the children provided an opportunity to assess their reading needs? If so, are they able to do so?

14. What kinds of independent follow-up activities and experiences did the children appear to need? Did they do further experience with newly introduced skills or maintained skills?

15. How could the independent experiences be most effectively developed—meaningful related practice? meaning practice integrated with a content area? workbooks? research? extended reading?

WHAT TO EXPECT

As you study the above list, your reactions may produce dissatisfaction and discouraging opinions of current efforts, especially at first. While this may be true, you must be mindful that the fifteen criteria have been listed *to encourage*, not *discourage*, improvement in your reading practices. By analyzing and studying the weaknesses of your pupils, and by emphasizing the use of their strengths, you will be providing them with *good reading lessons.* You will be able to proudly and positively announce to your school community, *"my reading lessons are effective."*

Suggested week's program, three-group plan

LILLIAN LOGAN

VIRGIL J. LOGAN

Beginning teachers often have difficulty with the sheer mechanics of planning for group reading, and this difficulty reduces the effectiveness of their reading lessons. These teachers frequently forget to build gradually to the complex shiftings and movings required. Sometimes, too, they do not have a clear mental picture of how the program might be scheduled. A possible three-group plan is presented below.

DAY	MIN.	GROUP I	GROUP II	GROUP III
Monday	20	Direct teacher guidance: new material	Work on individual problems: solo, team	Free reading: individual interests
	20	Committee work: planning of book reports	Direct teacher guidance: reading from text	
	20	Free reading	Reaction to story in art, drama, or writing	Direct teacher guidance: new story, guided reading
Tuesday	20	Free reading: individual interests	Direct teacher guidance: discuss story or answer specific questions	Independent activities, work-study, games
	30	Direct teacher guidance: presentation of oral reports, dramatization	Committee work, individual work	Free reading, work on skills
	10	All-group activity: choral reading, story, dramatizations, etc.		
Wednes-day	25	Reading related to unit of work	Work on individual needs: team, solo reading related to unit of work	Direct teacher guidance: silent-oral reading, work on skills
	25	Direct guidance: new story	Reading related to unit of work	Reading related to unit of work
	10	Help to the children from different groups who have a common need to practice a specific skill; others continue their activity		

Reprinted from *Teaching the Elementary School Child,* Boston: Houghton Mifflin Company, 1961, p. 279.

DAY	MIN.	GROUP I	GROUP II	GROUP III
Thurs-day	20	Silent reading and reaction to story	Direct teacher guidance: discussion related to stories, planning of activities	Reading related to stories: help by pupil assistants
	20	Direct teacher guidance: discussion, oral-silent reading, work on skills	Developing activities related to reading (committee work, etc.)	Reading related to stories: help by pupil assistants
	20	Individual guidance on book selection for free reading, for unit reports, etc.; use of library aids		
Friday	40	Free reading	Work on individual needs: team, solo; committee work; reading related to unit, etc.	Direct teacher guidance: discussion; plans for sharing with class
	20	All-group activity: library, dramatizations, storytelling, etc.		

46   *Individualized reading: teaching skills*

L Y M A N   C.   H U N T ,   J R.

Another possible plan that teachers of reading might adopt is an individualized reading program. Hunt asserts that to follow an individualized reading program teachers must know in advance what skills the pupils are to learn. Hunt outlines some important facts about words, discusses phonics, cites ways to help pupils build a sight-recognition vocabulary, and stresses the need to keep an account of progress made. His advice applies to teachers using any kind of organizational pattern for reading programs.

Teachers who have employed an individualized reading program say that to carry out effectively this kind of program demands a great

Reprinted from the May, 1961 issue of *Education.* Copyright 1961 by the Bobbs-Merrill Co., Inc., Indianapolis, Indiana.

deal of preparation; they also report that the heightened interest in reading shown by the pupils makes the preparation worth-while. The preparation must include reading and becoming familiar with many sources of children's literature. Preparation also includes making careful plans for the organization of the program in the classroom.

THEY SAID it couldn't be done. They say it isn't being done. Yet teachers are doing it. Teachers are teaching children in the reading program as individuals, and they are teaching them needed skills. It is exciting to watch teachers who are trying to work out their own particular approach to teaching skills to individual children.

These venturesome teachers use every resource for improving skills. The textbook manual is a reference, not a heavily beaten path from which they cannot depart. While it may be true that the constant use of the manual gives greater security, it is not necessarily the best way to help each individual child learn skills. The days when the teacher, manual in her lap, herds her three ability groups through various exercises in revolving-door fashion are waning.

Many teachers say, "I want to try individualized reading, but will my children learn skills?" It is a sobering idea for the teacher to "go it alone." Undertaking an individualized program requires courage, vision and know-how.

Advocates of the basal-reader program say that teachers neglect skills if they try to individualize their reading instruction. There may be some truth in this contention. But what about controlled vocabulary? What about sacred sequences? What about organized structure? Have they been successful?

It is becoming increasingly clear to many teachers that many children do not learn reading skills according to the organized sequences and structures of the textbook manuals. The theory upon which the prescribed patterns are based may be sound; unfortunately, though, many children just don't grow according to the pattern.

Successful teachers are finding ways to identify skills needed by each individual child. Successful teachers are finding ways of developing those skills with individual children. Successful teachers are finding ways of organizing children into temporary groups for the purpose of studying skills needed by the groups and for the purpose of giving individual children help at the moment of need. Successful teachers are finding ways of showing children how to help themselves with skills. Successful teachers are accomplishing this in programs where every child is reading a book of his own choice at a pace consistent with his purpose.

FOUR MAJOR SKILL AREAS

Important skills lie in four areas: (1) sight-recognition vocabulary; (2) word study; (3) oral-reading fluency; and (4) silent-reading efficiency.

Careful study will reveal that success must be built on the first step. Without an adequate sight-recognition vocabulary and without assurance of constant accumulation of words into the sight-recognition vocabulary, the child will stumble and falter. He will not gain the foundation needed to uphold the other three skill areas.

Word study is an important skill area primarily because it enables the child to help himself. It is always subordinate to accumulating a sight-recognition vocabulary, however.

Oral-reading performance is closely linked to a sight-recognition vocabulary. We often err by expecting fluent oral reading when the child has not truly accomplished the first step; he simply does not have sufficient skill in sight recognition to read well orally.

Sight recognition is a bond between the relatively separate processes of oral and silent reading. We unrealistically expect a child to read silently when his sight-recognition vocabulary is insufficient for the vocabulary included in a particular selection.

It is evident that skill development is intricate and complex. Nevertheless, we are becoming increasingly aware of the variety of individual patterns through which children learn skills in each area. It will help to keep our focus on truly important skills and to avoid over-emphasis on lesser skills. It is easy to become lost in a maze of minor skills.

ARE THE SEQUENCES SACRED?

The advocates of the basal-reader program claim that only through a controlled-vocabulary approach can the child successfully acquire sight-recognition skills. The proponents say that the scientifically worked-out sequences and structures for related skills development are so well defined that every child can succeed.

Let's examine the theory. The basal-reader program has a dual approach to word recognition. First, and rightly so, it begins with building a sight-recognition vocabulary which rests on predetermined sequences of words, arranged story by story, book by book, grade by grade, for the total program.

Once accumulation of a sight-recognition vocabulary is off to a good start, and even though there is an increasing number of words to be accumulated with each new story, a second skill task is introduced. This new element, word study, confronts the child with structures and sequences related to phonic development, to variations in word forms, and to syllable sensitivity.

There is a dual approach, too, to the silent- and oral-reading steps. With each story, provision is made for directed silent reading of the material to realize some teacher-designated purpose.

Following silent reading comes each child's opportunity to read orally or, at least, to listen as one of his groupmates reads orally. In this sequence of silent-followed-by-oral reading, each child is given roughly equal time and consideration. In the individualized reading program, with each child reading a selection of his own choice, silent reading far exceeds oral reading in time and emphasis. Yet neither is neglected.

WHAT IS THE ISSUE?

The critical issue lies within this complex of sequences. The system which prescribes that particular words are to be learned for each particular book during each particular year by every child must be carefully considered by the teacher. Is this a sequence of controlled vocabulary or overcontrolled vocabulary? Prescribing the particular time for learning words is too brittle and too rigid a system for many children and for many teachers. This system lacks flexibility.

basal-reader

The result of over-attention to a prescribed order for learning words can be disastrous for both the able and the unable. If the child does not assimilate the designated words into his recognition vocabulary at the particular time they are introduced (with the number of allowed repetitions) then this vast, but fragile, superstructure can fall all about him. This condition of accumulating specified words at a specified time in order to be successful can serve as a handicap and a hindrance to many children even though it may be beneficial to others. The able child bursts out of the structure; the slow child struggles unsuccessfully to maintain the pace.

When teachers have realized this fact and certain other basic facts about words, they do not necessarily need to become entangled with their children in this vast system in order to help children accumulate an adequate sight-recognition vocabulary.

IMPORTANT FACTS ABOUT WORDS

Fact: A word means something. When teachers try to teach children to recognize words for which meaning is inadequate or lacking, they violate a basic principle about words and how children should learn them.

Fact: Each word looks different from every other word. With minor exceptions, no two words look alike; each word has its unique, individual appearance. While it is true that many words have brothers and sisters of close resemblance *(wake, fake)* and while there are a few identical twins, *(read, read)* these latter are the rare exceptions. Words most alike in appearance are frequently most difficult for children to learn to recognize. It is only through a slow, laborious process that some children come to respond to subtle differences in appearances. True sight recognition involves responding to differences in appearance in total word forms.

Fact: A word can have variations in form. Word appearances are modified slightly by adding common endings or common beginnings or by combining one word to form a compound word. Slight changes affect appearances markedly. Some children find it difficult to respond to these minor variations in word appearances.

Fact: A word is made of letters combined together, and the letters represent sounds. We can study word forms by examining letter-sound blends. Some people proclaim this to be the primary fact about words, but blending letter sounds is no substitute for responding to differences in appearances on sight.

When teachers know these facts about words and when teachers can base teaching practices on these facts, they can help youngsters to develop skills. Approaches to sequences and structures can be worked out in a more flexible manner. Instruction with respect to accumulating recognition vocabulary and studying words can be tailor-made to children's needs. Instruction in skills need not consume everyone's time as it often does when we try to fit groups into the previously prepared patterns.

WHAT ABOUT PHONICS?

Most teachers are not sufficiently sensitive to the most important fact about phonics. One system is based on the fact that words are composed of letters which stand for sounds and which, when combined, form words. When the letter sounds are known, word forms automatically emerge. This is an unwarranted assumption.

As stated previously, even though each word appears to be different in its total form from every other word, there are many brothers and sisters among words and many dozens of aunts, uncles, and cousins. This means that a part or parts of any particular word may be common to a part or parts of many other words. As we study these parts, we can see the relationships that exist among them.

Relationship phonics, the second system, is the study of these similar parts. A very well-defined sequence supports such study. We start with the most obvious relationship, words that rhyme. Rhyming words must be perceived prior to recognizing the second relationship, words which start with the same initial letter. We continue by developing the relationship emerging from the fact that many words end with the same letter; then we move on to the more complex relationship based on words which begin or end with double and triple consonants. Next come relationships built around vowels, both long and short, and finally the relationships built on the syllable structure of words.

This five-part sequence underlying relationship phonics is delicately balanced. We err by attempting to teach an advanced step when children are barely managing some of the preliminary steps. We err because our manuals tell us to develop a complex relationship even though the child needs to learn a more elementary step. When we attempt to teach vowel relationships while the child is still confused by changes in initial or final consonants, we are guilty of this error. Critics say we err in phonics because we do not teach letter-sound blend phonics. This is nonsense. We err by trying to teach the wrong relationship to the wrong children at the wrong time.

COMMON WAYS TO WORD RECOGNITION

Any teacher who is endeavoring to help youngsters build an adequate sight-recognition vocabulary, any teacher endeavoring to help children learn ways to help themselves study words must have instant command of the seven common ways of helping children gain acquaintance with word forms.

1. Word form with pronunciation. Ordinary consideration is given to the word form, its pronunciation, and, if needed, its meaning.

2. Visual scrutiny. The child is asked to exercise extreme effort to study word appearance visually and to construct mental images of word forms.

3. Contextual meaning. Words are recognized through their stress on meaning.

4. Word structure. Attention is paid to changes in word forms which result from adding beginnings and endings, or from combining words.

5. Configuration or outline. Notice is given to lengths, shapes, and outlines of word forms.

6. Relationship or letter-sound blend phonics.

7. Syllables. Studying syllables as subparts of word forms.

The secret of success, discovered by teachers teaching skills to individual children, can be revealed. Success comes from combining several of the seven ways of recognizing words according to the child's needs and according to his present mastery of skills. Teachers can learn to utilize proper combinations effectively.

Teachers should sense the balanced relationships within the four skill areas and the major subdivisions thereof. They should be able to detect individual patterns of accumulation of sight-recognition vocabulary, to manage the two phonic systems, and to command the seven ways of knowing words. Then skills can be taught individually.

HOW DO TEACHERS DO IT?

How do teachers detect the needs of each child when they have thirty to thirty-five children? Each teacher has her own individual approach, but a common practice is to maintain some kind of check sheet on which the basic skill areas are listed as major headings. This list may take the form of a graph or a notebook page for each child; the teacher, through individual conferences or through work in skill groups, notes the child's accomplishment and records needed work.

Sometimes teachers have children keep their own records with respect to performance in sight-recognition vocabulary, word study, oral reading, and silent reading. Children can work out word lists for self-study.

A variety of ways for independent word study exists. While most skills teaching is accomplished with the individual during conferences, many teachers form groups to work on skills, according to needs of children within the group. Sometimes teachers will announce to the class which skill element will be developed and the children themselves volunteer to participate in that group. If a child is not sufficiently aware of his need for working with the group, the teacher will counsel with him. He can learn to recognize his own need for attending the group which has been formed to work on double-consonant beginnings, if that happens to be a point of weakness for him.

Word examples taken from the reading of one child might be used to teach a particular skill to the group. Word examples taken from another child's reading might be used in teaching another skill. Many times the teacher, sufficiently skilled, can determine whether the children in this group need to work to perfect recognition of the difficult "wh" words. This can be done through a game-motivating approach.

Appraising progress again rests on the ingenuity of the teacher. While record-keeping is primarily the responsibility of the teacher, valuable assistance can come from the children. A teacher must be able to discern and record when any particular child is making great strides in accumulating a sight vocabulary; when he is barely crawling up the steep incline; when he is perhaps stalled or even gradually slipping backward.

She must be able to discern and record the approach most frequently used by the child as he tries to study out words for himself. She must teach students to look within the word, to cover up endings, to use meaning, and/or to use the seven common ways to help themselves.

She must be able to discern and record whether oral reading is becoming more fluent, more enjoyable, more presentable to herself and to the group. She must be able to discern whether silent reading is becoming truly effective. She must help children to concentrate on meanings when they read to themselves. She must constantly try to transfer to the child her know-how in all the skill areas so she can help him to help himself.

WHAT DIRECTION DO WE TAKE?

It is most important to realize that many teachers are ready, willing, and able to put the manual aside and venture forth on their own in teaching skills. There is an urgent need to stop giving teachers recipe books which prescribe steps. Rather, teachers need to have a clear command of major skill areas, and need to utilize this source.

A great deal of our present word-study program as developed in manuals of the basal-reader program is repeated and duplicated in the spelling program. We should do more reading of an individual type during so-called reading class and place more emphasis on the word-study program in connection with writing where spelling fits naturally.

We should have, above all, faith that we as teachers can learn to know important reading skills and transmit to the children the ways of mastering skills on an individual basis. The happy result will be that all children may be engaged in reading books of their own choosing at their own rate of speed during reading class.

47　*Reading readiness check list for the first-grade teacher*

LILLIAN LOGAN

VIRGIL J. LOGAN

This is a suggested check list for reading readiness to be used by first-grade teachers. If you plan to teach a grade other than first, make a check list appropriate for the grade level you plan to teach. Be sure to remember that within any grade you will find a wide range of ability.

Name of Child	*Teacher's Comments*	*Dates*
1. He enjoys picture books.		
2. He asks questions about the printing below the picture.		
3. He listens with comprehension to the story read.		
4. He can tell the story in sequence.		
5. He can "read" the titles of a number of books.		
6. He has developed motor coordination and can handle books with ease.		
7. He sees a relationship between oral and written words and can associate ideas.		
8. He shows evidence of desire to find out what the marks on the page or chalkboard mean.		
9. He has developed ability in auditory and visual discrimination.		
10. He has mastered the specific pre-reading skills required for success in beginning reading.		

Reprinted from *Teaching the Elementary School Child,* Boston: Houghton Mifflin Company, 1961, p. 259.

Name of Child		
	Teacher's Comments	*Dates*
11. He shows evidence of social, emotional, physical, and intellectual maturity and general readiness.		
12. He gives evidence of wanting to read and eagerly asks questions about reading.		
13. On the basis of teacher observation, informal tests, language facility, and records, readiness is highly probable.		
14. On the basis of any good reading-readiness test, he is in the category predicting success.		

48   *When elementary children use reference books*

J O S E P H I N E   I .   M A C C A R T H Y

How many kinds of thinking might a teacher encourage by following this author's recommendations? Also, ponder her observation that "we can count on the fact that youngsters themselves will be able to suggest techniques for doing reference work." This article elaborates on the Wilson selection in Chapter 8.

TODAY, elementary children are going far beyond the use of a single text in their quest for knowledge. They are using encyclopedias, reference books, and materials written by authorities—actually making a beginning at research reading. In doing such study, they are gaining much greater knowledge of a subject than they would gain if they used only one source. No one textbook

Reprinted with the permission of the National Council of Teachers of English and Miss Josephine I. MacCarthy from *Elementary English, 36:*240-43, April, 1959.

can give full, rich treatment to a great number of subjects. The best it can do is give limited emphasis to a number of important ones. Granted, any youngster who has studied the contents of a basic text in science or social studies may have developed an interest, and may have gained some knowledge of a field, but it is very likely that he has only "scratched the surface." By contrast, the child who has followed through with further reference reading has gone below the surface, and usually he has been able to uncover some extra "nuggets" of information and insight. Moreover, he is making a beginning at real scholarship, and is enhancing his personality. It is this extra knowledge that not only gives a person fuller background for comprehension of and evaluation of further experience, but also makes him more sure of himself, more interested in life, and more interesting to others.

Supplemental reference reading tends to make the learner a thinking person. Through such reading, he discovers that there are differing points of view on some problems, and also that some authors report facts more fully and more accurately than do others. Once a student discovers these things, he tends to reflect upon the varying points of view, to seek full and accurate data to help him make his own decisions, and to be critical of the accuracy of data presented in books, checking them before accepting them as facts.

Some children may not have the maturity, reading ability, persistence, or interest necessary to do much beyond the study of a basic text. It is hard to find reference texts to meet the needs of these children, although some steps have been taken in this direction. However, the average youngster, beginning perhaps somewhere in the latter part of fourth grade, is at a stage where he is ready for reference reading, though it might be in a limited way.

We might call such work research. But, of course, a child does not do research in the sense in which we apply the term to scholarly, scientific study—the collecting of data from a great many sources, the careful verification of facts, and so on. This requires maturity, a background of knowledge, and intensive, skilled effort over a long period. But children can at least make a start at using the study methods of the scholar.

It does not take much effort to help children see the values of reference reading. They are well able to reason for themselves in this matter. All a teacher needs to do is to ask, "What values might there be in going to more than one book (or other source) for information on a subject?" and inter-mediate-grade children at once have logical answers. They show that they recognize many of the values mentioned above.

Moreover, we can count on the fact that youngsters themselves will be able to suggest efficient techniques for doing reference work. They will make the kinds of suggestions listed below, although some of these we would expect only from the more mature pupils. And, of course, children will "learn to do by doing"—will gradually discover effective techniques as they work with their reference books.

At some point a class discussion may be held on the use of reference books, and a list of suggestions for their efficient use may be drafted and posted on a chart to furnish reminders. Suggestions might be formulated by a sixth-grade group in some such manner:

PREPARATION FOR REFERENCE WORK

1. Write a clear statement of your main problem or topic, and then outline its subdivisions. Number them.
2. Inspect each topic to look for, think about, and list words that will give you clues for finding information in reference books. (For example, in studying "industries of the Northeast," the words "industries" and "Northeast" suggest that you look up *manufacturing, mining, ship-building*, etc., of the Northeastern states. "Northeast" brings to mind that there are certain states in that region, and that information regarding their industries might be gained by looking under the names of the various states.
3. Make a list of the reference books in which you might be likely to find the information needed.

WORKING WITH REFERENCE SOURCES

1. Use the index and table of contents of your reference books.
2. Read all you can find on one subtopic. Be sure to follow up the cross-references.
3. After you finish on each subtopic, stop to make notes in outline form.
4. Use the bibliography to get the names of other books and of authorities on your subject.
5. Try to find at least one of these books.
6. Place your information on each subtopic on a separate sheet of paper, with a numbered topical heading on it. This makes it easy to assemble your information in good order later.
7. Use some kind of symbol to indicate the source of your information. This will help you to find the material later in case you have further use for it.
8. Remember that people, things, and situations can be resources. Ask questions, observe, and take notes.

Such a statement would need to be greatly modified for the use of most fourth-grade children, but in general they can work with these ideas. Moreover, these younger children, as well as some older ones, might need detailed and direct instruction in:

a. The organization of encyclopedias and other reference books.

b. The use of the index.
c. Use of topical clues.
d. Cross-referencing.
e. Skimming the introductory paragraphs on each topic to see whether they offer promise of providing needed data.
f. Using the sideheads for the same purpose.
g. Outlining.
h. Using a dictionary in conjunction with the use of reference books.

The question of *copying* comes up in connection with the gathering of data from reference books, particulary when the material is to be used for reporting to one's classmates. Children sometimes copy whole pages assiduously from an encyclopedia or other source, and later read the material to the class as a report. Maybe this is the best that can be expected from immature pupils. The fact that they even know what to select for copying might be considered a helpful sign. (But, perhaps we should not encourage children to use encyclopedias for written reporting until they are able to outline, or to write material in their own words!)

However, since we know that little intellectual gain is achieved through wholesale copying of references, a real effort must be made to encourage children to do their own organizing of materials read. For one thing, the *reading* of reports to the class should be discouraged. There is much better learning if pupils are asked to report *orally*, even if the product is not as finished as the report which is read. Oral reporting develops the power of recall, tends to fix ideas, and demands a certain amount of *independent organization of thought*.

We afford another stimulus to independent thinking when we encourage children to use more than one source to gather their information. Then it becomes necessary to combine or change statements—the student *must* organize. When only one source is used, the student finds the whole body of information handily organized for him. Some children also reason, "Why should I try to put this into my own words—the encyclopedia is accurate, and 'says it' much better than I could." And we have to admit there is some logic in this! It is a nice question how much effort children should spend in paraphrasing what they find in reference books, for this, like anything else, can be overdone.

In any case, we should help children to see that when they use materials verbatim, quotation marks should be used, and the sources credited.

The problem of how many pupils can do reference reading at any one time must be considered by teachers. One factor that is important in this connection is the availability of materials. In my experience, difficulties arose on several occasions when I, as a novice, turned about eighteen pupils loose to do reference work. I thought I had supplied enough materials, and we had broken down our main topics into a large number of subtopics. Even so, we found that too many people were heading for the "B" volume at the same time. It reminded me of situations in a college library when seventy graduate students are trying to use twenty references for the next day's assignment! If adults find it disconcerting to make changes in their study plans, and have to find something profitable to do while waiting for a book to be released, children might be expected to find it frustrating. I found that, with a well-stocked classroom library and two sets of encyclopedias, reference work could not be done effectively by more than six or eight pupils at a time without very close supervision. However, maybe we can help children to become adaptable in such a situation, to look at their outlines and think what might be done with the "W" volume while the "B" volume is in use!

There is one more consideration which deserves a teacher's attention in connection with children's use of reference books. Reference reading, by contrast with such activities as reporting and discussion, is largely an individual process. It is probably more of an individual matter than work with a basic text, which is interspersed with comment and questioning. Reference work might be group work in the sense that a child may be looking up data on a subject under consideration by a committee group, or on some aspect of a subject being studied by the whole class. But for a group of three children, say, to try to do reference work together, reading for a few seconds, then interrupting each other's "train of thought" and interfering with comprehension by interjecting comments and questions, is not fruitful. Granted, children need to learn to work together, to help each other; there are plenty of other school situations in which they can have opportunities for give and take. But it would seem desirable to afford pupils chances to do reference work uninterruptedly. It is not without reason that universities furnish "cubicles" for students. If college students need cubicles in order to concentrate, what can we expect of youngsters if we encourage them to try to study together in groups?

There is much concern today about enriching the school program, but the practical steps to achieve this sometimes fall short of the goal. Enrichment means that the teacher must have available a *variety of supplemental resource materials* for most topics studied. It seems as if the most expeditious way to do this would be on a schoolwide basis.

It would seem desirable for each school to provide a well-stocked resource center with reference books and pamphlets, pictures, maps, diagrams, slides, charts, samples of children's work, scrapbooks, back numbers of school newspapers and magazines, resource directory of the community, recordings, poetry, collections of realia, science equipment and collections, and files of science experiments, to mention some of the items. Unless and until some such step is taken, classrooms will have relatively limited resources. Most classes need to make only temporary use of such items, and these become immobilized in certain rooms unless a central depot, or at least some scheme of cataloguing and circulation is in use. Teachers must know what is available, where it is, and when it can be used.

Possibly a parent committee could help in stocking, cataloguing, and maintaining a resource collection. Or a pupil committee might well take over such a project as an all-school service activity. In some communities the public library serves such a function, though the service is usually limited to providing books, pictures, and recordings. But, particularly do communities without good public library or museum facilities need resource centers in the schools. Reference reading may help to give direction to a student who has not found himself. As he goes deeply into a number of fields, he may develop an enthusiasm that will stand him in good stead as a lifetime hobby or vocation. Such reading also gives opportunities for the average youngster to become a "special" sort of person, interesting and respected because he has accumulated knowledge beyond the ordinary on some subject, whether it is space travel, the ways of the Aztecs, prehistoric animals, or ships.

⌐ Let's work to make all these benefits of reference reading available to our elementary youngsters.

49   *A linguistic approach to reading*

CHARLES LOYD HOLT

You will be hearing a great deal about linguistics in the educational dialogue of the next few years. This article may serve as an introduction to the subject for some readers.

Reprinted from *The National Elementary Principal*, 42:6-11, February, 1963. Copyright 1963, Department of Elementary School Principals, National Education Association.

You are reading now. With an agility approaching virtuosity, you are some-how translating these comfortable orthographic symbols on the page in front of you into the noises you make when you open your mouth to order a tank of gas, propose to the girl across the street, or bid four spades vulnerable. Reading, in other words, is a kind of talking—or at least good reading is.

The bad reader is busy elsewhere. Groping feverishly among the alleged sounds of traditional orthography, he clears his throat, grimaces, and produces a series of staccato grunts intended to represent in careful order the words of language. His difficulties are several. Pronouncing sounds in blatant series is no more language than the clicking of an IBM machine is language. Sounds in morphemic, or meaningful, sequence in English are inevitably relative one to the other in pitch, loudness, and degree of separation or termination.

Moreover, the bad reader's concern with words and their "proper" oral rendition one—after—the—other has practically nothing to do with speech. We don't talk words—group of words, yes, but never "words" in splendid etymo-logical isolation. Both sounds and words in English are significant only in utterance context.

If you want to teach a child to read, teach him how sounds fall into morphemic sequence, how words fall into measurable order within the utter-ance. If you want to teach a child to read, teach him that reading in a very important sense is a way of talking to oneself.

There are some thirty-three meaningful segments or slices of sound used by English speakers, or so the descriptive linguists remind us: twenty-one consonant phonemes, or tension-restricted sounds; nine simple vowel phon-emes, or comparatively unrestricted sounds; and three semi-vowel phonemes, meaningful sound categories that in production show the characteristics of both consonants and vowels. The only significant differences between /pin/and pen/, between /sit/ and /bit/, between /slip/ and /sliyp/ are differences of single sound classes. These differences involve a meaning change and are there-fore phonemic. Simple phonic exercises based in graded drill will introduce the six-year-old native speaker to English to the curious curlicues on the printed page that regularly correspond to, say, the voice velar stop (the /g/ sound in *go*) or the voiceless alveopalatal affricate (the /č/ sounds of *church*). The irregularities of English spelling need be brought up only when the child is ready for them.

Were educators generally to fret less about the irregularities of English orthography and spend more time categorizing the broad areas of perfectly regular sound-symbol correspondence within that orthography, children would grasp at least part of the dialect of American English known as reading almost as rapidly and completely as their teachers argue confusion.

Obviously, the letters of the English alphabet do not stand for sounds; *dough, ought, enough,* and *slough* illustrate the occasional vagaries of English spelling. At the same time, one has only to be familiar with the diachronic existence of language, with the sound and spelling changes of Old through Middle through Early Modern English, with the studies of the vigorously inept folk etymologists of the English Renaissance and the so-called Enlightenment of the eighteenth century—in short, one has only to be familiar with the total English language in order to realize that English spelling is not only basically regular but also completely teachable if the teacher has the patience to categorize and to describe what is in front of him.

STRESS PHONEMES

Take a deep breath now and do something you have done perfectly well since you were about six years old—speak English. Say the name of your country. Give it the full dimensionalization of that remarkable sound that is our language. If you are an American, you probably said, "The United States of America." And if you are an American, you almost certainly said the name in a predictably complex but measurable way. In addition to the twenty-eight or more slices of sound you used to make the utterance (depending, of course, on the phonemic peculiarities of your speech community), you pronounced three of the syllables louder than the other seven syllables (although none of the three syllables was sounded with the same degree of loudness); your voice started on a normal pitch level, went up one level on the second syllable of *America* and went down two levels through the penultimate and ultimate syllables of the word; you separated slightly the words *The* and *United, United* and *States,* and *States* and *of;* and at the end of *America* your voice "trailed off" phonemically to indicate that you were finished with what you had to say.

Each of the intonational phenomena listed in the preceding paragraph is a phonemic or meaning phenomenon. Certainly, different stress patterns change meaning in English: per-VERT is identified immediately by an English speaker as a verb; PER-vert is an English noun. HE hit him (I didn't); he HIT him (he didn't pat him); he hit HIM (he doesn't strike ladies). Obviously, primary stress in an English utterance may be shifted from word to word depending on the desired emphasis. Each of these emphases is accomplished because stress in English is phonemic.

Since capitalizing syllables will not accurately differentiate among the four separate meaningful degrees of stress in our language, linguists have devised a convenient method of indicating these relative degrees of loudness: / ′ / signals the loudest sound or group of sounds in a given phonological phrase; / ˆ / is second loudest; / ˋ / is tertiary or third loudest; and / ˘ / (or nothing at all) signals the weakest stress. The utterance "elevator operator" permits us to hear the four degrees of loudness functioning within easily contained limits. Whether we say "élĕvàtŏr ôpĕràtŏr" as opposed to someone who operates a trolley car or "êlĕvàtŏr ópĕràtŏr" in contradistinction to the fellow who merely washes the thing, the four relative degrees of stress are operative within the phonological phrase and should be thoughtfully categorized as such.

In the designation "The United States of America," the second syllable of *America* usually receives primary stress in the mouth of an American, *States* regularly is secondary, and the second syllable of *United* is tertiary.

Making use now of comparatively familiar phonemic symbols to suggest the segmental phonemes (the slices of sound), I can indicate as well the stress phonemes of the utterance "The United States of America":

/ ðɨ̆ yŭwnàytɨ̆d stêyts ə̆və̆méhrɨ̆kə̆/.

(It is possible, of course, to vary the stress contour of this cluster of words according to the number of phonological phrases involved in the speaker's production. If I may, however, I shall reserve discussion of these variations to a later paragraph.)

As regards pitch (or rate of vocal-fold vibration), there are also four distinct meaning levels for the speaker of American English. How many different "melodies" can you meaningfully pattern with the following words?

What are we having for dinner, Mother?

A typical production of this sentence would probably involve first a normal pitch level, a rise to a second higher level on the first syllable of *dinner,* a single level drop on the second syllable of the same word, a slight pause, a reintroduction of the same pitch level on the first syllable of *mother,* and a full level lift on the second syllable. Suppose, however, I had dropped two full levels within the word *dinner,* let my voice fade away, and returned to a normal level of pitch for the first syllable of *mother* and made a full pitch level rise on the second syllable. You would, of course, deplore immediately my cannibalistic tendencies and realize that the only way to write the second utterance in traditional orthography would be

What are we having for dinner? Mother?

Regularly, the four levels of pitch are symbolized /4/, /3/, /2/, and /1/ (from very high through high and normal to low) or are linearly depicted on the page. I shall combine the two techniques in our incrementally patriotic repetition:

3

2/ ðɨ̆ yŭwnàytɨ̆d stêyts ə̆və̆ | méhr | ɨ̆kə̆/.

1

It is important to note that this 231 pitch contour is perhaps the most usual one in the English language. Many assertions and most questions whose answers involve more than a "yes" or a "no" arrange themselves within this contour.

SOUND JUNCTURES

If the relative pitch of sounds can have definite meaning in English, so can the separation of sounds or the terminal rendition of a sound have a distinct significance.

When I pause before the /s/ sound in /ayskriym/, I have said, "I scream." When, however, I pause gently *after* the /s/ sound, I've said "ice cream." There is no other phonemic distinction between the two utterances. The distinction is known as a plus juncture and is symbolized /+/.

For many Americans the utterances

> He said, "Mary, the girl next door."

and

> He said, "Marry the girl next door."

are precisely the same as far as sound slices, stress, and pitch go, but are obviously different in final production. A level juncture after the word *Mary* /mehriy/ in the first response signals that the remaining words are a nonrestrictive appositive of a girl's name. The absence of such a group juncture signals that the words following *marry* /mehriy/ are the object of an imperative verb. Level junctures in speech frequently correspond to commas in writing; certainly, this is the case in the contrasting of restrictive and nonrestrictive elements in the sentence. The level juncture is symbolized /→/.

Two other sound junctures / ↗ / and / ↘ /, the rising and falling terminals, occur at the end of syntactic units, whether single words, phrases, groups, clauses, or complete utterances. When I say

> one/ ↗ / two / ↗ / three/ ↗ /

and trail the sound off in an upward direction (normally not a full pitch level, but perceptibly) you recognize that I haven't finished counting as yet; but when I say

> one/ ↗ / two / ↗ / three/ ↘ /

and my voice fade-falls at the end, you know perfectly well that I have run out of things to count. Moreover, the rising terminal regularly signals a question whose answer is "yes" or "no." Compare "Are you going?" and "Where are you going?" Repeat the questions aloud. You will notice and be able to contrast immediately the two different terminal signals.

Finally, then, we are able to transcribe completely the way that most native Americans say the name of their country:

₂/ðŭ + yŭwnàytĕd + stêyts + ŏvŏ̀mérhĭkɔ̌ ↘ /.

Had I or any native speaker decided to emphasize that our union is one and indissoluble, however, the second syllable of *United* could have received a primary stress as well; but in that case we would be dealing with two phonological phrases instead of one, and a level juncture would necessarily separate *States* and *of*. Every phonological phrase in English is separated from the other by one of the terminal junctures, /→/, / ↗ /, or / ↘ /. In other words, only one primary stress is possible within a phonological phrase. Reduce the number of terminals and you reduce the number of possible primary stresses. I could, for example, say simply, "The"; the transcription would be:

/ ðíy ↘ /: one primary stress, one terminal. Or I could say, "The United"
/ ðŭ+ yŭwnáytĕd ↘ /:   still only one primary stress, one terminal juncture. Having shifted the original falling terminal to a plus juncture and having moved perforce the primary stress to another syllable, I necessarily give a weak stress to *The* and I change the phonemic shape of the word from a full glide / ðiy/ to the unstressed barred i/ ðɨ/.

Professor Donald Lloyd, Wayne State University, has suggested a kind of hierarchy of these units of sound:

> Terminals may override each other in relation to the speed of the utterance. A level or phrase-terminal replaces any lesser juncture as we speak more slowly and use more heavy stresses; a [rising] terminal can replace a level terminal or any lesser juncture; and, as we speak very deliberately, a [falling] terminal can replace any of the others. . . . The utterance divided into phonological phrases is something like a string of sausages stuffed by a careless hand—some large, some small, some long, some short, but each set off by a neat twist of the casing from the sausage before and after.[1]

In the same way that it isn't necessary to teach a third grader the complex terminology of articulatory phonetics in order to get him to hear the

1. Although I have generally avoided documentation in this paper, I ought to point out here that my obligation to Donald Lloyd does not end with this brief quotation from a paper presented originally to the International Reading Association (1962). Most of the basic concepts delineated in these paragraphs are ultimately his. I hasten to point out, however, that he is in no way responsible for strained understanding on my part or awkward application. A full treatment of *Linguistics and the Teaching of Reading* by Dr. Lloyd and Professor Carl Lefevre has recently been published. The phonemic notation system employed in these pages is that of Trager and Smith, excepting the symbolization of terminal junctures which has been promulgated by H. A. Gleason. The examples used in the final paragraphs of this essay are in part from an unpublished student paper by Hugh W. Black.

sounds he makes and to learn the orthographic symbols of those sounds, so he need not be burdened with the descriptive details of intonational phonemes.

But try him on this: write "I like girls" on the blackboard. Have him argue this friendly assertion aloud. He will undoubtedly stress the sentence "Ĩ lĭke gírls." Then in rapid succession ask him, "Who likes girls?" "How do you react to girls?" and "What is it you said you liked?" Each red-blooded American boy between San Diego and Oyster Bay who has outgrown the mud-throwing stage will inevitably stress the three words in respective and respectful order: "Ĩ lĭke gírls," Ĩ lĭke gírls," and "Ĩ lĭke gírls."

Or if your students already have some command of the written dialect of American English, ask each of them to take out a piece of paper; then you write this sentence on the board:

John went fishing.

Don't ask them to say the words aloud this time. Rather, ask them to write the sentence and to hear and mark the different stress patterns that occur in the answers to the following four questions:

1. Who went fishing?
2. Where did John go?
3. Did John go hunting?
4. When is John going to go fishing?

DEVELOPING PITCH AWARENESS

Pitch awareness (although one of the first things a language-learning baby has command of) is perhaps more difficult to teach children than stress patterns. Contrasted questions and assertions, identical assertions whose only meaning difference is in pitch—How many ways are there in which to say "yes"?—an actual attempt to "sing" the melody of a given assertion—these are possible exercises in helping a child to understand that an awareness of pitch contour is a meaningful guide to better reading.

Too, since relative pitch is finally the common denominator of all intonational phonemes, perhaps exercises leading students to a complete awareness of the stress and juncture differentiations among utterances comparable to the following examples will prove to be most valuable in the end.

FOR JUNCTURE

The sun's rays meet.	(The rays of the sun meet.)	The+sun's+rays→meet ↘
The sons raise meat.	(They're in the meat business.)	The+sons→raise+meat ↘

This bear's watching.	(A bear is watching.)	This+bear→'s+watching ↘
This bears watching.	(Keep your eye on this.)	This→bears+watching ↘

FOR STRESS AND JUNCTURE

a lighthouse keeper	(keeper of a lighthouse)	líghthouse→kêepĕr ↘
a light housekeeper	(a skinny housewife)	líght→hóusekêepĕr ↘
the green house	(a house painted green)	grêen→hóuse ↘
the Greene house	(Mr. Greene's house)	Gréene→hôuse ↘
the greenhouse	(where they grow flowers)	grêenhoùse ↘
a blackbird's nest	(nest of a blackbird)	bláckbird's→nêst ↘
a black bird's nest	(the nest is black)	bláck→bírd'snêst ↘
a black bird's nest	(the bird is black but not a blackbird	bláck+bîrd's→nést ↘

SYNTACTIC CONSTRUCTION

The remarkable complexity of an English utterance is not limited to phonemes in morphemic sequence; sounds combine, separate, and take their relative positions in larger performance as well. Words, groups, phrases, clusters, and clauses assume for the good reader immediate comparative significance one to the other within that handy-dandy meaning generator known traditionally as the sentence.

Probably the simplest approach to the syntactic mechanisms of Modern English is a historical approach, a diachronic evaluation of synchronic probabilities.

When Alfred's scribes at the end of the ninth century laboriously rendered the Latin of Boethius or Bede into the West Saxon dialect of Old English, they were translating into an English best described as synthetic and inflectional—which is to say that Old English syntax depended in great measure on inflectional additions to words in order to signal case, person, gender, number, and tense. Old English word order, like the word order of Latin, was primarily stylistic or conventionalized.

The period of Middle English (1100-1500) was a period of syncretized inflections; endings blended one into the other, and, in an effort to compensate for waning inflectional signals, English developed a much more rigid word order and gave prepositions and other structure words the task of signaling the syntactic relations formerly accomplished by inflectional affixations.

Although still an inflectional language, Modern English is much more analytic than synthetic. Word order reigns supreme. But a note of caution here. In present-day teaching, too great an emphasis has been placed on "words" in order and on their relative "part-of-speech" definition. It isn't the word that is important, really, nor its "part" of speech. What matters syntactically is the function area of the utterance in which the word occurs.

Thus, in the sentence

Gertrude, who has a gold tooth in front, loves taffy pulls.

neither the beautifying dependent clause nor its adjectival modification of the noun-subject has anything to do with the basic sentence functions of the declaration. Both Gertrude and her gold tooth serve as N-subject to the verb function in this assertion in the same way that two nouns, one modifying the other (*not* an adjective and a noun) function as N-object; the function pattern of the sentence, in other words, is N V N.

Indeed, if we were to measure out the function patterns of English declarative utterances in general, these several patterns would all be implicit in a basic pattern, A N V N N A. Obviously, N V (I gave), NVN (I gave my all), and N V N N (Mary gave mother a hotfoot) are all variations within the adverbial confines of the basic pattern. Adverbial modification of an English utterance normally precedes or follows a syntactic unit, excepting adverbs of frequency and occasional single-word adverbs which serve as a part of the verb-group function.

Given these function patterns, it is of primary importance to point out that the noun functions in any of these sequences may be fully maintained by what traditional grammarians call verbs or adjectives or adverbs as well as nouns, by a "group" of words (any one of these "parts of speech" with pre-modification), by a "cluster" of words (any of these "parts of speech" with pre- and post modification), by a prepositional phrase, or by a clause.

In the same way, the verb function can be fulfilled by a single verb, an analytic verb group, or by an adverb plus a verb or a verb group. The adverb functions are accomplished by singleword adverbs, adverbial groups, adverbial phrases, or adverbial clauses. In other words, *conversion* (the shifting of function of a "part of speech") and *reduction* (the making use of groups, phrases, clusters, and clauses as single sentence functions) characterize the English we speak today as much as does word order. Why not make these characteristics, then, at least part of the syntactic basis of our teaching of reading?

If youngsters are made aware that the long dependent clauses and the seemingly complicated noun and verb clusters that stare back at them from the printed page serve only a single sentence function and that the significant words within these complexes are carefully signalled in speech by normal intonational contours, their reading capabilities must necessarily improve.

CHAPTER 11

Listening and Speaking

PERHAPS YOU NEVER thought that listening and speaking might be skills, attitudes, and behavior patterns to be deliberately taught in elementary schools. Today, we recognize that communication is not simple. We must consider more than the words that are formed and sent through the air to the ears of potential listeners. We know that intent is important both to speaker and listener. We know that children come to school with habits of speaking and listening already set. We know that as children mature, they are able to learn more complex ways of verbal interaction: to focus their attention, to evaluate what they say and hear, and to relate what they say and hear to other ideas. In an era of mass media, one in which person-to-person and group-to-group communication are so vitally important, can teachers dare neglect direct attention to listening and speaking?

In this chapter, the first article discusses ways to concentrate attention upon listening. The second article offers ways of helping children communicate by means of creative dramatics. The third article offers suggestions for leading classroom discussions. The article deals with children who know little English when they come to school. The final article discusses another aspect of communication, learning a foreign language.

50   *Teaching children to listen*

MAURICE S. LEWIS

In this article, the author presents goals and research evidence for instruction in listening, and makes suggestions for providing an environment conducive to effective listening. Finally, he states some principles of learning which seem to apply to the teaching of listening in elementary schools.

NEVER IN THE history of our country have we had a greater need for listening skill than we have today. We desperately need citizens who can comprehend the vast amount of oral discourse which emanates daily from our radio and TV sets; citizens who withhold judgment until the facts are known; citizens who are not easily moved by emotion-laden words woven skillfully into political speeches, news reports, and commercial advertising; citizens who do not panic easily at startling emotional outbursts by those whose responsibility it is to lead us.

We have long emphasized the importance of speaking ability, and silver-tongued orators are among our list of heroes. The ability to influence listeners is cherished by all who possess it. Our schools have done a good job of teaching oral language, but they have done little to help those who are on the receiving end of communication, the listeners.

Until recently, the instructional program in listening amounted to no more than admonishing children to listen in most classrooms. Good listening was identified with sitting quietly with folded hands, good posture, and attentive eyes.

RESEARCH IN LISTENING

Listening, in the past, was assumed to be like reading. While thousands have studied the reading process, few have paid attention to this comparable assimilative skill. In recent years, however, researchers have awakened an interest in listening, and we have begun to give it its rightful place in the school curriculum.

Reprinted from the April, 1960 issue of *Education.* Copyright 1960 by the Bobbs-Merrill Co., Inc., Indianapolis, Indiana.

Studies by Rankin[1] and Wilt[2] have helped us to realize the importance of listening as a communication skill in daily life and as a tool for learning in the classroom. Nichols analyzed the factors in listening and set up a successful instructional program for teaching college freshmen.[3] Brown's study[4] resulted in the first published test of listening comprehension. Lewis studied the effect of listening upon reading and constructed tests to measure the listening ability of intermediate-grade children.[5] Pratt and Marsden evaluated the effectiveness of instructions in listening.[6] These and other studies have opened the door for further development of methods and techniques for teaching listening.

Listening is the process of attaching meaning to the spoken word. It is a complex process involving much more than the physical act of hearing or the external attitude of paying attention. Like reading, it is an assimilative communication skill which includes the understanding and interpreting of symbols and requires the development of certain skills and attitudes. It is unlike reading in that the listener has but one opportunity to comprehend, whereas, in reading, he may reread that which he does not understand.

The development of listening skill begins in the cradle as the newborn child uses his most highly developed organs, his ears, to attach meaning to the many sounds in his environment. In the process of learning to communicate, much energy is expended in imitating those sounds.

It is through this interaction with his environment that the preschool child acquires his listening and speaking vocabularies. Early studies estimated the size of these vocabularies to be relatively small. However, a more recent study by Smith[7] found that first-grade children had an average listening

1.   Paul T. Rankin. The importance of listening ability. *English Journal, 17*:623-30, October, 1928.
2.   M. E. Wilt. Study of teacher awareness of listening as a factor in elementary education. *Journal of Educational Research, 43*:626-36, April, 1950.
3.   Ralph G. Nichols. Factors in listening comprehension. *Speech Monographs,* No. 2, *15*:154-63, 1948.
4.   James I. Brown. The construction of a diagnostic test of listening comprehension. *Journal of Experimental Education, 18*:139-46, December, 1949.
5.   Maurice S. Lewis. The effect of training in listening upon reading. *Journal of Communication,* pp. 115-19, November, 1953. See also: Lewis. The construction of a diagnostic test of listening comprehension for grades four, five, and six. Unpublished doctor's field study, Colorado State College of Education, 1954.
6.   Edward Pratt. Experimental evaluation of a program for the improvement of listening. *The Elementary School Journal,* pp. 315-20, March, 1956.
     Ware W. Marsden. A study to determine the effect of training to listen upon ability to listen. Unpublished doctor's field study, Colorado State College of Education, 1952.
7.   Mary K. Smith. Measurement of the size of general vocabulary through the elementary schools and high schools. *Genetic Psychology Monographs,* Part II, *24*: 311-45, 1941.

vocabulary of 23,700 words (16,900 basic words and 6,800 derived words) with a range from 6,000 to 48,000 words. From these and other facts, we must assume that children enter school with considerable listening skill.

Research has shown that children continued to show improvement in listening until about the end of the sixth grade. Then, as they achieve a fair degree of proficiency in reading, they cease to improve in listening.

A comparison of reading and listening leads one to conclude that, with a few exceptions, the actual skills involved are identical. Both are dependent upon the same experience background of the child; both require thinking; both have an inherent developmental sequence. It would seem, then, that listening skills, because of the vocabulary advantage, should always precede comparable reading skills. Proficiency in a specific listening skill, in effect, should constitute readiness for learning the same skill in reading.

Research has shown that listening can be improved by providing definite instruction in listening. It has shown also that reading improves when children are given training in listening. On the other hand, it has been found that listening does not improve when only reading is taught.

It is the purpose of this paper to suggest: some goals for listening; some aspects of a desirable listening environment; and some principles of learning to be observed in teaching listening—all of which may be helpful in planning a program of instruction.

GOALS FOR LISTENING

Before we can make curricular revisions to include an adequate program of instruction in listening, we first must ascertain what skills, attitudes, and understandings our elementary children need to learn. This can be done best by describing some of the aspects of the behavior of a good listener and by suggesting different levels of maturity which children may attain.

A good listener does more than sit quietly and look attentive while someone is speaking.

1. He is aware of the importance of listening in the learning process. Through discussion in the classroom, the good listener becomes aware of the many sounds in his environment and what they mean. He becomes aware of the fact that he learns many things by listening. He learns that the concepts he has are a product of many types of learning, and that many concepts have been learned by listening. He uses listening as one of his most important tools for learning.

2. He understands the roles of the speaker and the listener in the communication process. The good listener plays these roles in small groups; he may act as speaker in one group and as listener in another group. As a more mature listener, he understands the responsibility that is shared by the speaker and the listener. He participates in evaluative activities to determine the effectiveness of communication in reports, storytelling, and oral reading.

3. He listens through to the end of a discourse before he attempts to draw conclusions. The good listener listens through to the end of a story read by the teacher in order to participate actively in a discussion of the ending. He withholds judgment until all the facts have been presented. He is aware of certain emotion-laden words which affect his listening. He can summarize discussions and help his group reach decisions based upon facts.

4. He can follow directions given orally. The good listener remembers the first step and, with the teacher's guidance, can complete the task. He listens to remember the first time the direction is given. He learns to keep a sequence of steps in mind.

5. He adjusts his listening to the purpose at hand. At first, all listening seems to be very general. Later, the good listener learns that one listens for several different purposes: to follow directions, to remember details, to get the general idea, to draw conclusions, and to enjoy.

6. He enjoys listening. The good listener enjoys listening to stories and music. His tastes mature as he matures. He likes to listen to increasingly difficult discourse, because it challenges his listening ability. He enjoys listening to classical music.

7. He is a critical listener. The good listener learns to discriminate between fact and fiction. He learns to question the validity of statements and to check the competence of the authority before making a final decision. He learns to check his own understandings and to modify them in light of new evidence. He learns the art of skillful questioning to make certain that he understands the speaker's viewpoint and the facts upon which the speaker bases that viewpoint.

LISTENING ENVIRONMENT

Children have the best opportunity to improve their ability to listen in a classroom environment which is conducive to good listening. It will be most helpful if:

1. The classroom environment stimulates speaking and listening. Children communicate about those things which they find in their classroom environment. The vocabulary they use and the richness of their experiences will depend upon what they and the teacher create within the four walls of that room. The room may be quite empty, with only bare walls and basic textbooks, resulting in a minimum of interaction, or it may be alive with materials and activities which stimulate communication, not only in the classroom, but in the cafeteria, on the playground, and in the home. It is this meaningful speaking and listening which affects both the quantity and quality of learning.

2. The classroom arrangement is flexible. Children learn to communicate best when they have opportunities to practice in small groups first, and, later, in increasingly larger groups. Furniture which allows freedom of movement from one type of organization to another is desirable. However, a creative teacher can find ways to group children in the most traditionally equipped classroom.

3. There are opportunities for reaction. Communication is a two-way process. It involves the transmission of ideas between individuals through speaking and listening. When the listener is active in the process, his level of personal involvement reaches its highest peak, and the quality of the experience is best. Children need opportunities to react to the ideas expressed by their peers, their teachers, and others.

The amount of reaction possible is dependent upon the group structure. A minimum of reaction is possible in a discussion involving the total class with the teacher asking the questions and the children providing the answers. A maximum amount of reaction occurs when children work in pairs in problem solving, oral reading, and other activities. We should provide opportunities for children to practice communicating in many sizes of groups and for many different purposes.

4. There is a permissive atmosphere. Children who are permitted to interact with their environment and to communicate about the things they are trying to learn will probably learn to listen better. They must learn, of course, to recognize and live within the limitations imposed by the teacher or those democratically constituted under the skillful guidance of the teacher.

Children should learn to adjust the type and amount of communication to the situation at hand. It may be loud or soft, much or little, depending on the activity. The maximum noise level is reached when children work in pairs.

PRINCIPLES OF LEARNING

There are several basic principles of learning which seem to apply to the teaching of listening in the elementary school.

1. Children learn what they practice. Unless positive steps are taken to teach listening, it is fair to assume that the learning may be negative.

2. Children need to understand what it is that they are trying to learn. Talking about listening will help them to understand that it is like reading in some ways, but unlike it in other ways.

3. Children need to become aware of their ability to listen. Listening has been taken for granted for so long that it is best to begin any program of instruction by administering a standardized test,[8] or a teacher-made test, as a means of motivating children to set up individual and group goals for the improvement of listening.

4. Children need opportunities to discover that they can improve their listening ability. It is difficult to tell children exactly what they must do to improve their listening ability. However, if they are given an adequate number of opportunities to listen for various purposes and to evaluate the results of their efforts, they will discover those things which make a real difference in their comprehension.

5. Oral reading should be taught so that it fosters good listening. When children read new material in a well-prepared manner to their classmates, they are providing good listening experiences. When these experiences are followed by discussions and other activities, they provide the listener with an opportunity to react.

6. Oral language is taught with an emphasis upon communication. Young children should have many opportunities to express ideas orally to their classmates and to be judged by what they communicate, not by how they speak. When the emphasis is upon communication of ideas, children will become concerned with what they say and whether it is understood by their listeners. As the communication process becomes understood, there will be a need to teach children to use better posture, a more pleasing voice, and accurate grammar.

7. Children have opportunities to listen to difficult material read to them by the teacher. Elementary-school children usually can comprehend materials read to them, which are one or more years above their reading level. Content materials read by the teacher, or by a child who is a good oral reader, will provide excellent listening experiences.

8. Individual differences in listening should be recognized. It is common practice for teachers to repeat directions and instructions so that the slowest child in the room will comprehend. This teaches brighter children not to listen the first time but to adjust to the pattern followed by the teacher.

---

8.   Cooperative Sequential Tests of Educational Progress, Princeton, N.J.: Cooperative Test Division, Educational Testing Service, 1957.

Children will become better listeners if instructional talking is done at a higher-than-average level to challenge all children. If a few children comprehend less well, they should be helped to improve their listening in a separate grouping.

CONCLUSION

We need more experimental research which will provide us with further data about the listening process. We need more action research in the classroom to develop methods and techniques for teaching and evaluating listening skill. We need more creative teachers of listening. Will you meet the challenge?

51   *How to conduct a class discussion*

RUTH ANNE KOREY

By means of classroom discussions, a teacher can help pupils think through meaning in all subjects. Successful discussions are those in which the teacher achieves his goals, and the pupils find intellectual satisfaction. This article offers concrete suggestions for attaining these objectives.

FOR MOST PHASES of language arts, teachers are equipped with specific techniques. For our basic program we have detailed teachers' manuals. In spelling and penmanship lessons we have definite routines. There are several excellent books to guide us in teaching composition. But good discussion techniques are harder to find. This is an important area in which we ourselves must do much of the preliminary thinking involved.

PURPOSES OF CLASS DISCUSSION

The purposes of class discussion are many. Sometimes it is an end in itself.

We want the children to learn how to carry on polite, logical, interesting discussion because they will need this ability throughout school and adult life. Our emphasis in such lessons is on skill.

At other times the discussion period is a means to an end. It may be a means of establishing rapport among the pupils, or between pupils and teacher. It may be a group guidance activity preparatory to such events as polio inoculations or taking important standardized tests. It may be used to contribute to better behavior in the auditorium or lunchroom.

Discussion may be an integral part of the curriculum area such as social studies, health or safety. In its simplest form the discussion may be a planning period to get ready for a special project such as making a diorama. In its more advanced form it may be based on extensive reading and research on such topics as How the United States became a world power, Medical discoveries of the twentieth century or Safety in the home.

HOW TO BEGIN A DISCUSSION

A short discussion may arise spontaneously from such events as a bad storm, an accident in the schoolyard or an important election. Children come to class full of things to say.

"I tumbled into a snowdrift."

"Bill fell and hurt his leg."

"I saw the parade and the governor was there!"

There is urgency in the children's need to talk on such occasions. In fact this urgency exists almost every day, and some teachers regularly begin morning and afternoon sessions with a short discussion period.

For other purposes the teacher may prepare a way of introducing the discussion. This may be an amusing or thought-provoking picture cut from a magazine, a moving picture related to social studies or other subject areas, a short story, poem or newspaper clipping, a personal experience of her own or perhaps a question or quotation written on the chalkboard.

As an example, I once saw an excellent lesson which began with the teacher's reading of a poem called "Christmas at Our House." The children enjoyed the poem, requested a second reading and then began a spirited discussion related to their own lives and homes. A good deal of wholesome family pride was generated as they told of favorite foods and customs. The problem of sibling rivalry came out into the open where children could benefit from realizing that, to some extent, it exists in all families.

In this instance the teacher's purpose was group guidance. The take-off should be carefully chosen according to the specific purpose in view.

HOW TO CONDUCT THE DISCUSSION

Much of the discussion will, and should be spontaneous. For maximum effectiveness, however, the teacher must do a certain amount of guiding. Much can be learned by listening to some of the youth forums on radio and television and taking notes on the comments of the moderator, whose role is similar to that of the teacher.

During a large portion of the time, the teacher or student chairman will merely act as traffic officer, giving the name or nodding to the person who will have the next turn to speak.

But with or without a student chairman, the teacher has several important functions:

1. To keep a few from dominating the discussion
2. To help the more retiring to speak at least once
3. To keep the discussion moving in a forward direction
4. To encourage courtesy, relevance and interest

All of this can be done without conspicuous interference. "That's an interesting suggestion," "Yes, but how about our main point?" and "Nancy, what do you think about it?" are typical teacher comments which may be needed now and then to improve the discussion.

HOW TO END THE DISCUSSION

The method of summarizing or concluding will depend on the grade level and maturity of the pupils.

In the kindergarten, individual drawings or a group project may be the concluding step in a discussion on thunder and lightning, traveling to the city, or some other familiar topic.

In the primary grades, a chart may be made, both as a summary of the discussion and as an aid to reading. Before a holiday, for example, we may have a group-constructed summary on chart or chalkboard with sentences such as:

Mary will go to a party.
Helen will go to the city.
John will go to see his grandmother.
William will go skating with Alfred.
We will all have a good time.

In the second and third grades, the slower group will work on the group chart with the teacher, while the more mature pupils may write individual summaries. Thus we give the same general activity to all the children, but provide more help for the slow, and encourage initiative and originality in the more gifted pupils.

For intermediate and upper grades, the concluding work may be done by a class secretary or reporting committee which will take notes during the discussion and then orally summarize the main points at the end.

Intermediate and upper grades should also form the habit of evaluating their more formal discussions, using criteria such as wide participation, courteous phraseology, relevant contributions, interest and sense of accomplishment.

52 *Learning through creative dramatics*

MARGARET S. WOODS

Creative dramatics is a way of stimulating verbal, creative, and social interaction among children. Too often pupils are handed scripts and told to say only what the scripts say. The teachers and the pupils are missing so much!

I have learned that the head does not hear anything until the heart has listened, and that what the heart knows today the head will understand tomorrow.[1]

REALIZATION of maximum individual potential *is* possible through one of the most natural but neglected avenues of learning. Through individual, group, and small-group experiences in creative dramatics, described by Dienesch as improvised activity in which the child creates his own forms, full self-realization develops as the child becomes involved in thinking, feeling, and experiencing.[2]

Reprinted from *Educational Leadership*, *18*:19-23, 32, October, 1960. Copyright 1960 by the Association for Supervision and Curriculum Development.

1. James Stephens. *The Crock of Gold*, New York: The Macmillan Company, 1960.
2. Marie Dienesch. Creative and formal dramatics. *World Theatre*, No. 3, 2:30, 1951.

Quality human experiences should be carefully planned by a teacher proficient in knowledge of growth and development of the individual and skilled in techniques of dramatic art. Such experiences help the child develop awareness of purposeful living and promote self-initiated activity. They also enable the child to manage the events which occur within his culture and result in his ever-increasing movement toward balanced intellectual, physical, social, emotional, and spiritual growth.

In all types of creative drama there are opportunities to experience a variety of situations and roles. Such opportunity provides constructive channeling of emotions, promotes acquisition and retention of knowledge, develops appreciation of the wonders and beauty of the world, and helps the child relate himself to the world about him through a form uniquely his. Dienesch believes that, whether the dramatic creation be spontaneous or elaborate, elementary or complex, it is by making a work of art, in his own way and according to his own capacity that the child or adolescent develops most fully and harmoniously.[3]

One aspect of creative drama included in make-believe of the child is dramatic play, which is spontaneous activity full of adventure and discovery.[4] No suggestions are needed for "trying on life" and playing out thoughts and feelings, for dramatic play is the child's means of enjoying, exploring, testing, releasing, remembering, working. The pilot flying the jet, the puppy playing with the ball, or Mother washing dishes, exists as the creation of the moment which Slade indicates is the joy of dramatic play.[5]

The oldest form of dramatic expression is pantomime, a means of communication which knows no national barriers. Through large muscle activity, rhythmically expressed through the elephant swinging his trunk, the stealthy approach of the men swinging aboard the ship during the Boston Tea Party, the delicate rhythmic movement involved in signing the Declaration of Independence, the exacting stitches taken with care in making the first flag, all communicate thought and feeling through movement, which Siks indicates is basic in the art of drama.[6]

When a group of children make a story come alive by playing it spontaneously, whether it is original or taken from literature, history, or current happening, they are having an experience in story dramatization, which differs from dramatic play because of plot.[7] Although considered by

3. *Ibid.*
4. Winifred Ward. *Playmaking with Children,* New York: Appleton-Century-Crofts, Inc., 1957, p. 10.
5. Peter Slade. *Child Drama,* London: University of London Press, Ltd., 1954, p. 45.
6. Geraldine Brain Siks. *Creative Dramatics: An Art for Children,* New York: Harper & Brothers, 1958, p. 105.

some as "drama for drama's sake," creative dramatics can be integrated with subject matter without losing the art quality since, according to Lee and Lee, stories related to topics being dealt with in other subject areas can be utilized.[8] Here the values of creative dramatics can be achieved while deeper understandings in other learnings are also being developed.

PERSONAL INVOLVEMENT

Learning experiences built around personal involvement through creative drama can enhance acquisition and retention of new facts and stimulate desire to do research. A display of china plates designed by the children decorated the chalk-lined shelves on the blackboard in one third-grade classroom. As a result of experiencing sensitivity to the beauty of china during the dramatization of "The Little Blue Dishes," children displayed the sets with great pride to teachers and children in the school. Price lists indicating cost per piece, per place setting, settings of four, six, eight, and even twelve enabled children to practice the multiplication table as children placed orders.

Probably a longing to give one's best, and to succeed, effectively communicated by one demonstrating teacher, inspired at least one child to do research and to learn to read. David knew he would have to repeat the fifth grade because he had not been interested in or able to read. However, he had a keen desire to be Tom Sawyer in the playing of the whitewashing scene from the *Adventures of Tom Sawyer*. Because he insisted, "I've *always* wanted to be Tom," the teacher finally chose David rather than another highly capable boy in the group. Throughout the play, Tom had difficulty making decisions, but he made them with all the courage he could summon.

Following the play an evaluation was made, "What did you like best about the play?" Many positive comments resulted with suggestions for improvement. Hurrying up to the teacher as the other boys and girls were leaving, David, eyes sparkling, asked, "How did I do?"

"How do you think you did, David?"

"Well, you know, if I had a chance to do it again, I could it a lot better."

"You know, David, I too did something for the first time this morning and when I repeat it, I'll do it a lot better. But tell me, what will you do to improve your playing?" The teacher then discussed with David the strong points and possibilities for improvement on a subsequent occasion.

The following day, David's mother revealed the boy's sudden renewed

7.　Ward, *op. cit.*, p. 10.
8.　J. Murray Lee and Dorris May Lee. *The Child and His Curriculum*, New York: Appleton-Century-Crofts, Inc., 1960, p. 522.

interest in reading. "Mom, could we stop and buy the book of Tom Sawyer? You know, I never have read that book all the way through. I want to see if Tom could reach the top board as easy as I could."

Through continued effort in providing opportunities for story dramatization, David was able to assume roles which helped him to build courage and confidence, a desire to do research and to understand words. Like others, David felt the satisfaction that comes when one struggles with a new idea, taking out the truth, sticking to it, being responsible for his own actions, and successfully solving a problem. Empathy with human experiences of the ages, truths inherent in great works of literature, art, music, develop understanding, as Anderson indicates:

> A child's first act of creativity is to get in relation symbolically to something or somebody outside himself. This will appear as language as soon as play, for in play the child begins the never-ending struggle to understand both his world and the world as conceived by others.[9]

It is not always necessary to dramatize a story. Through pantomimic activity, students in one Spanish class improvised situations involving specific characters of the present and past through the game, "*¿Quién soy?*" The spontaneity with which students responded brought forth a need for new word combinations, knowledge of verb tenses, ability to think on one's feet. Questions such as "*¿Esta Vd. en los Estados Unidos? . . . ¿Esta Vd. en TV? . . . ¿Vive Vd.?*" placed the entire responsibility of identifying the characterization through questions asked in Spanish. As a result, discipline problems began to disappear, for the need to know was ever present.

LIFE CYCLE

The joy of creating develops a capacity to approximate intellectual and emotional heights. As the child creates, he lives fully and richly the character which seems so real to him.

An understanding of the life cycle became most meaningful in one first-grade room in an experience with maple wings. These wings snuggle under the "dirt blanket" to rest until Spring whispers, "It's time to grow." One day Susan commented, "We're going to have a new baby at our house, and I get to name it Judy or Jim." The teacher aroused the curiosity of the group with the statement, "Isn't it nice that Susan is going to have a baby brother or sister

9. Harold H. Anderson, ed. *Creativity and Its Cultivation,* New York: Harper & Brothers, 1959, p. 185.

at her house? But you know, I have something here in this box, something for each one of you. It has a tiny baby inside. It isn't exactly like Susan's baby brother or sister will be, but it is a tiny baby." Asking the children to close eyes and hold out hands, the teacher deposited a maple wing with each child. She then suggested that they touch, feel, think, wonder about it. "How does yours feel to you?" she asked.

"Mine is soft as fur."

"Mine isn't, it's like Daddy's face when he doesn't shave."

"Mine feels scratchy like my rusty handlebar."

"Well, if there's a baby in there, he doesn't even wiggle."

"Sure, it has to rest first so it can be strong enough to move." Silent thoughts indicated wonder about the baby closed up tight inside.

"Could it move if it wanted to?"

"Can I break it open and take it out?"

"No, Johnny, it will come out when the time is right. What will help?"

Answers from the children included, "Sun . . . wind . . . rain . . . a good, warm, dirt house."

The teacher then suggested, "Let's all snuggle down in our own warm dirt house. When the music tells you it's growing time, let the sun help you push your way out of the little house."

Thirty-two children, closing in as small as possible, responded slowly, sensitively to "Morning" by Grieg, in complete rhythmic unfolding, exploring, pushing up and out, each with a rhythm all his own, struggling to go beyond but with an inner harmony that results from giving one's all.

Evaluation by the children included such comments as, "I felt the warm sun on me, when I pushed up through the ground."

"I got a drink from the sprinkler."

"I saw one plant that was growing faster and faster into a tree so it could grow more seeds."

"My seed got warm just like when I pop popcorn and away I went clear up through the ground."

"I popped back quick into the dirt because I heard thunder," exclaimed one startled child.

The teacher encouraged real thoughts and feelings by asking, "What do you feel like doing when you hear thunder?"

"It makes me feel like running and hiding in the closet."

"It makes me all hunched up, and I put my hands over my ears."

"You know, boys and girls, I used to be frightened by thunder until my daddy told me that it was just Station S. K. Y. broadcasting."

A chorus of "What's that?" from the children indicated no recognition of the word, S. K. Y. "I'm going to let you find out. I hope you do before that station broadcasts again."

The following day, Tommy, who seemed to spend almost as much time in the principal's office as he did in his classroom, arrived early and was down on the floor with five books spread out in front of him when his teacher arrived. Since there was a rule in that room that no child could enter ahead of the teacher, he again made a visit to the principal's office.

"But I was only trying to find S. K. Y.," he tearfully explained. "I looked in all my comic books at home but I couldn't find it, so I had to come early because it takes me so long to figure out words." The principal, with Tommy and five other first-graders who had been unable to locate the station that broadcast thunder, borrowed a picture dictionary and discovered for themselves, a word which expressions on their faces indicated they should have known all the time.

A CLIMATE FOR CREATION

Dramatization of worth-while material provides the child with quality human experiences and promotes capacity for coping with problems. A desire for more of the quality feeling and a willingness to struggle for it are evident when opportunity exists to feel the difference between order and chaos, love and hate, ridicule and praise, bravery and cowardice. For example, empathy with General Washington and his men at Valley Forge may bring renewed effort in coping with failure, facing a problem, finding a means for successful solution. Such understanding may set greater forces in motion in the process of striving and becoming, ultimately equipping the child with wisdom and skill as he slowly but surely acquires responsibility for behavior.

The child discovers what life appears to be through participation in worth-while experiences some of which exist only through participation in the art of creative dramatics. As Trevis indicated, "Imagination is the faculty of forming images whereby the Soul beholdeth the Likeness of Things that be Absent."[10] By tapping the individual's feelings through identification with things and people, one has reached a source of energy which can provide a most effective means for learning.

A climate conducive to constructive creative expression, whether it be in writing, painting, movement, or dramatics, challenges the teacher. Although there is no one set of techniques, results can be achieved by acting upon

10. Florence Cane. *The Artist in Each of Us*, New York: Pantheon Books, Inc., 1951, p. 124.

suggestions of a number of educators.[11] However, it would seem that a climate which houses "enemies of creativity" is easier to identify, because remarks which place courage and confidence in the deep-freeze are clearly evident. Some such remarks include:

"It doesn't look like it to me."

"When you're older you'll understand."

"Why did you have to do that?"

"How many forgot their money again?"

"It's time for the Bluebirds to read."

"Those of you who miss more than five will have to stay in during recess."

"How did you happen to spill so much?"

"You'll have that next year—if you pass."

"Let's get back to our seats. We still have to finish the next page before the bell rings." (As the children gaze with awe and wonder at the first snow-flakes of the season.)

Elimination of some of these "enemies of creativity" marks a beginning, for some teachers, of a desire to help children realize maximum potentialities by making way for constructive creative expression.

Participation in creative dramatics rewards not only the learner but the teacher as well: In reaching far below the surface for the child's best; in the struggle to provide situations which combat the stifling effects of mass culture; in removal of pressures which discourage appreciation of awareness of beauty, truth and goodness, so vital in the cultivation of taste; in the presentation of dramatic situations which build inner controls in discipline; in the joy of creating as one seeks to understand, appreciate, and respect self and all mankind. Anderson believes creativity as personality development is not only a product of openness in human relating; it is a further opening to higher levels of harmony in the universe.[12]

If one would but lend an ear to those who learn through a dramatic approach to teaching, through the art of creative dramatics, one might hear in response to the question, "Why was it fun?" such comments as these:

"Because I got to be President." (A fourth-grade boy who, as General Washington, inspected the flag.)

"Because you can do the best you know how to do and nobody grumbles." (An eighth-grade boy who had just appeared in the front of the room for the first time in six months.)

11. Bibliography at the close of the article.
12. Anderson, *op. cit.,* p. 141.

"Because I have a whole bucketful of new words." (A fifth-grade girl who enjoyed contributing "picture words" for descriptions of characters in Rachel Field's poem, "Roads.")

"Because when you use your imagination, everything comes out all right." (A fifth-grade boy who had become a pilot making a daring rescue on Mt. McKinley.)

"Because you seem to understand our needs." (A shy fifth-grade girl who felt awe in sighting the tower in "Why the Chimes Rang.")

"Because you can be mean and not hurt anybody." (A fourth-grade boy who enjoyed playing the role of the giant in "Jack and the Beanstalk," but realized that the giant does not gain the respect of the players.)

"I've learned enough to last me for three days." (An eighteen-year-old student about to receive a certificate of attendance from a special school for slow learners.)

Through the art of creative dramatics, dreams and ambitions, attitudes and values, inner controls, aesthetic appreciation, sensitivity of spirit, and a song in one's heart daily fill the learner's storehouse. Through identification with quality human experiences which help build rather than destroy, courage and confidence to go beyond that which is expected, wisdom and ability to respond effectively to change, develop on a high level through a dramatic process of thinking, feeling, experiencing, a process which affords the learner opportunity to achieve full self-realization in the world of tomorrow.

BIBLIOGRAPHY

Logan, Lillian, *Teaching the Young Child*. Boston: Houghton Mifflin Company, 1960.

Mearns, Hughes, *Creative Power*. New York: Dover Publications. 1958.

Woods, Margaret S. *Creative Dramatics*. Washington, D. C.: NEA Elementary Instructional Service. March, 1959.

Zirbes, Laura, *Spurs to Creative Teaching*. New York: George Putnam's Sons. 1958.

53 Opportunity classes help Spanish-speaking pupils

NORMA E. RODRIGUEZ

JAMES X. BOYLE

How would you like to spend from four to six hours a day confused by the newness of your surroundings, burning with ideas, wanting to communicate, hoping to belong? This article describes one way of helping young Spanish-speaking Americans become well-adjusted and productive members of society.

JUANITA SHOUTED in delight, "Teacher, can we play with the red ball?" Pleased, even secretly thrilled, the teacher tossed her a large red ball and stood smiling as a Puerto Rican game of ball-bouncing began. What caused the teacher to smile, to be elated at so simple a request? The cause was what seems to be a minor miracle each time it happens—Juanita was speaking English, and speaking it beautifully.

Juanita had arrived at the John Philip Sousa Branch of Mark Skinner School a month and a half before from Santurce, Puerto Rico, with her two sisters and brother—all elementary-school age. When they had arrived none of them had any real ability to speak English. Juanita, her sisters, and brother were placed in what are called opportunity classes. There are two such classrooms in the school: a primary class for children aged six to nine, and an advanced class for children of ten and older. On the first day, they took their seats gently and quietly and began the painful, bewildering experience of learning not only a new way of expressing themselves but a new way of living in a new land.

Children like Juanita encounter many difficulties in beginning school in the United States, difficulties over and above the obvious one of using a new language. First, they face the problem of acclimatization. They have been accustomed to life in the sunny island of Puerto Rico, *La isla del encanto*, "the island of enchantment," where the temperature constantly fluctuates between seventy and ninety degrees the year around, never, or at least rarely, surpassing these limits.

CHILDREN MUST LEARN NEW WAY OF LIFE

Secondly, they face the problem of adapting to urban living in general.

Reprinted from the February, 1962 issue of the *Chicago Schools Journal,* published at the Chicago Teachers College.

Although there are a few fairly large-sized towns in Puerto Rico, only three of the island-born children in one such opportunity class, for example, were born in towns of any considerable size or having any urban or cosmopolitan flavor. (This situation in Chicago is in direct contrast to that of New York. Many more islanders from Puerto Rico's larger communities migrate to New York than to Chicago.) Most of the Puerto Rican children, therefore, must adapt themselves to a mode of living radically different from that to which they have been accustomed. The opportunity classes make a beginning toward producing what is hoped will be eventual complete adaptation to urban ways of living.

There is a gap between the past and the new present which the Puerto Rican child who is a newcomer to Chicago must bridge. The gap is social and psychological as well as academic and linguistic. In other words, the classes are especially designed for those who have not learned our "city ways."

OPPORTUNITY CLASS TEACHERS SPEAK SPANISH, ENGLISH

In the opportunity classes, the use of the pupils' native language by the classroom teacher is always kept at a minimum; this despite the fact that teachers of both opportunity classes speak both Spanish and English. Spanish is usually reserved for those times when it is impossible to communicate with the children or their parents in English. There are those who believe that the teacher's knowledge of the native language is of most importance in establishing school and teacher rapport with parents. It is also helpful in putting new children, especially the smaller ones, who have enrolled in school for the first time, at ease. A few words of greeting and encouragement in their native language can do much to relieve the obvious anxiety with which many of these children face an almost totally new situation. When an emergency, such as an accident, arises it is also advisable to use the child's native language.

Experience has suggested that it is extremely helpful if the teacher is able to use the child's mother tongue, but the use of the language should be kept to a minimum, and the teacher should employ discretion in choosing situations in which to use it. It should never be used as a crutch on which the teacher leans when first attempts to get the child to respond to English fail. Unfortunately, there is sometimes a strong temptation to express oneself in the common language which is understood easily by all, instead of trying to use the new language which the children so sorely need. Self-discipline must be maintained and a clear view of the aims of the opportunity classes must be kept in mind to avoid the hazard of delaying adaptation by taking this easy way out of situations which are sometimes difficult.

CLASS PROVIDES PRACTICE IN USING ENGLISH

English is used, then, as much as is possible, from the very first day children enter an opportunity class. The pace of work and of speech in the class is kept slow, and the teachers make a special effort to speak with precision and clarity. Since the main objective of the opportunity class is to prepare children as soon as possible for transfer to regular classrooms appropriate to their age and amount of previous schooling, and since the children's lack of familiarity with English is the most obvious deterrent to their beginning regular schoolwork, emphasis in the daily classroom activities is primarily upon language.

A typical day in the intermediate and upper-level opportunity class, for children of ten years or older, follows a pattern of varied activities in which the concentration point is almost always English—written and spoken. The day begins with a writing exercise in both manuscript and cursive script. The children here begin to get the feel of putting on paper the correct spelling of familiar objects in the classroom, most frequently in short sentences. After twenty minutes of writing, an aural-oral lesson on the same pattern is ready on the blackboard. The teacher may write five or six sentences all using the same basic pattern and repeating a number of key words: "Show me the book," "Show me your shoes," "Show me the window," "Show me the closet." The teacher says each sentence several times. Each child then repeats the whole group of sentences. Responses to the requests embodied in the sentences are also a part of the exercise.

PHONETIC SKILLS DEVELOPED FROM KNOWN WORDS

Next, a lesson in phonetics is developed, frequently from one of the words used in the sentences. In this case, the word "show" and the special consonant symbol "sh" plus the standard vowel digraph "ow" provide the basis for developing word recognition skills in English and at the same time expanding vocabulary. Children learn to recognize the symbols in words such as "blow," "row," and "know," and in "shop," "ship," and "she." Students practice recognition of the symbols and pronunciation of the sounds.

After recess and outdoor play as a respite from the ordeal, the class works on arithmetic, particularly the English vocabulary of arithmetic. Through the use of flash cards, the students are introduced to the sounds and names of the numbers and to other mathematical vocabulary: "2 plus 2 equals what?" 2 minus 2 equals what?" "2 times 2 equals what?" This kind of practice is repeated slowly and carefully each day until children learn enough of English mathematical vocabulary to work successfully in regular classes. Following the flash-card drill, students work on actual arithmetic problems, chosen for each child on the basis of his actual grade placement in arithmetic.

FILMSTRIPS, RECORDS AID SPEECH DEVELOPMENT

The morning may end with a fifteen- or twenty-minute filmstrip accompanied by a record. The children look at vividly colored filmstrips with printed English captions which the teacher pronounces several times in a clear voice. Afternoon programs are somewhat more diversified than morning programs. Each afternoon begins with a half hour of oral reading. Students may listen as the teacher reads a short selection from a science book dealing with the natural phenomena with which all children are familiar—air, plants, animals, the food we eat. Several students may try reading the passage orally after the teacher has provided a model of pronunciation. Usually the oral reading is followed by oral and written practice in various aspects of the grammar of English, always embodied in simple sentences dealing with what are hoped to be familiar practices: "I *buy* clothes at Wieboldt's." "I *bought* clothes at Wieboldt's." "I *will buy* clothes at Wieboldt's."

Various other activities are pursued during the remainder of the afternoon. Each day the end of the afternoon is spent in free learning. The rooms are equipped with library corners with books of all levels of difficulty. There is a wide range of content. The children may read silently or orally in pairs. The teacher may use this part of the day to explain the geography of the United States, using a map. Another day the children may listen to phonograph records of folk music and marches of the United States. They may view films which are of interest to them and yet are suited to their limited understanding of English. Time is found almost every day for art and music activities, activities which transcend the language barrier.

MASTERY OF ENGLISH IS GOAL OF CLASSES

As soon as any child shows sufficient evidence of having a working knowledge of the newly-acquired language, he is transferred to a regular classroom. There are no rigid time schedules which determine the length of a child's enrollment in the opportunity class; each child is recognized as an individual and treated accordingly. By attempting to change the unknown to the known for these new arrivals in Chicago, the opportunity classes provide the key to the city and to life in the United States for each of them.

There is nothing to equal the thrill and delight the teacher of the opportunity class experiences when Juanita calls, "Teacher, can we play with the red ball?"

54 *The culturally deprived child in our verbal schools*

EUNICE SHAED NEWTON

Communication is the basic objective of language. Do you think that pupils who are not very good learners are so because they cannot communicate with the people about them? The author raises an important social issue and offers some specific professional suggestions.

IN A HIGHLY LITERATE society such as ours, the tremendous advantage of the verbally facile person over the verbally inept one may be observed in any sphere of endeavor. Within recent years, the importance of language in our culture and the role that it plays in practically all learning have been more cogently understood than formerly. It is now recognized that the child whose experience and background have provided him with good verbal development usually will exceed the verbally destitute child in almost every intellectual pursuit.

Today, it is scarcely a moot question that the foundation for the child's verbal development is laid subtly, yet inexorably, in the general cultural level of his home and through the language patterns of his parents and his immediate associates. It is recognized, too, that the nature of the community culture during the child's formative years may similarly contribute to his language growth. Abundance in educational resources in the child's external environment may enrich his learning, stimulate his interests, and extend his experience. On the other hand, paucity in intellectually stimulating activities may stultify language development and thus depress learning potential.

Of national concern in America today is the vital question of how to insure the maximum development of all persons through efficient programs of education. Of crucial importance, therefore, to all educators is the student on any level of American education who possesses inadequate language skills. Frequently his verbal ineptness is so comprehensive that it is characterized by functional inadequacy in speaking and listening as well as in reading and writing. His language problems act as a veritable barrier that thwarts his attainment of even minimal academic goals in our verbal schools. It is not unusual that the standard English usage of the teacher and the textbook is virtually an alien tongue to this student.

There is a need for many and varied explorations of the role and function of the educative process in our extremely literate society. Somehow, through

Reprinted from the *Journal of Negro Education*, 31:184-87, Spring, 1962.

such explorations newer perspectives, newer techniques, and newer approaches might be realized which may lead to more effective instruction of the verbally inept child. In this regard, the discussion that follows will: (a) present a brief synthesis of significant contemporary thinking about the effects of culture on language, (b) present a general image of the verbally destitute child, and (c) suggest an approach in language arts programs for the student of limited language skills.

CULTURE AND LANGUAGE

Language is the basis of human cooperation and interaction. Without language, human social organization as we know it would be impossible. Some authorities have proposed in unequivocal terms that the birth of language was the dawn of humanity, for language is the highest and most amazing intellectual achievement of the symbolistic human mind. Language is woven inextricably, therefore, into the woof and warp of all aspects of a culture. Human institutions, as we know them, developed through group and individual interaction as man shared his ideas, feelings, desires, imaginations, experiences, and aspirations with others. In turn, he decoded his brothers' real and symbolic concerns.

In a literate society such as America, the greatest single external influence on the normal child's intelligence during his developmental years is of necessity the verbal environment in which he lives. In a society that depends almost entirely upon vocal and visual symbols for the transmission of ideas, facility in the use of verbal symbols determines largely (if not entirely) the extent to which one can communicate ideas or can in turn be communicated with. Thus, the culturally depressed environment has a particularly deleterious effect upon the language of the developing child.

Words, it is now known, are merely the labels man gives his things, his actions, his experience, his ideas, his imaginings. If the growing child does not mature in an environment which affords both breadth and depth in educationally stimulating activities, then he will not have the background concepts to which to relate verbal symbols. When the early environment of the child is not book-centered, is bereft of the arts, and is lacking in conversation about the happenings of the world, then he is likely to enter school unmotivated, diffident, "inwardizing," unaware, and uninterested. Perceptual unreadiness is similarly a by-product of the culturally depressed community.

THE VERBALLY DESTITUTE CHILD

The socioeconomic status, personal characteristics, and language patterns have been catalogued for the child who has comprehensive problems in all aspects of standard English communication.

A synthesis of his image follows:

1. He is usually a member of a family in which there are less than two full generations of literacy.
2. He is often the product of small, substandard public school systems which are located in communities barren of cultural advantages. In urban centers, he is often from the ghetto-like areas.
3. He is frequently a member of a submerged cultural entity of our society and/or resides in a geographically isolated place—e.g., Puerto Rican, Negro, recent immigrant, very rural farm dweller, migratory worker, *et al.*
4. During his formative years, he communicated customarily through nonstandard English characterized by: (a) casual observance of standard inflections, (b) simple, monosyllabic words, (c) frequently mispronounced words, (d) rare use of descriptive or qualifying terms, and (e) the simple sentence or sentence fragment in both oral and written expression.
5. He often performs two or more years below grade expectancy on verbal tests, but frequently demonstrates adequate scholastic potential on nonverbal tests.
6. General disenchantment with all types of book-centered learning is frequently displayed by him through aggressive, defensive, or indifferent attitudes in class and throughout the school community.

When the student who possesses the personal history and verbal problems just described encounters the spoken and written language of the school, academic disaster often occurs.

AN APPROACH IN A LANGUAGE PROGRAM FOR THE CULTURALLY DEPRIVED

It may be postulated with confidence today that intellectual curiosity is fostered by variety of mental experiences and that the role of motivation is paramount in the learner's predisposition to utilize the resources available to him. It is recognized, further, that the learner of any age gains or grows in intelligence in accordance with the opportunities he finds for utilizing the abilities he possesses and that he may differ markedly from others in his recognition and use of the opportunities afforded him.

It is claimed with assurance, too, that the goals which the learner sets for himself are related to the levels of the goals of his associates and determine to a large extent the effort he will put forth to achieve. And finally, it is understood that adult-models, whether parents or teachers, may set standards for the learner through the levels of expectation. When the learner "translates" the expectations of the adult-models into self-goals, it is possible for him to derive a functional level of aspiration.

It is within the framework of these postulates that this approach to a language program for the culturally deprived child is submitted:

Climate-of-acceptance. The classroom must be free from derision and depreciation and should be literally infused with a *climate-of-acceptance* of the verbally handicapped student. Teacher rejection of this student through mockery or sarcasm may lead ultimately to rejection by his peers. This may lead to the rejection of all things educational by the student who possesses poor language skills. The teacher of this pupil, therefore, must veritably radiate optimism and belief in the attainability of reasonable goals. The teacher must be buoyant, energetic, and supportive; for only in a *climate-of-acceptance* may basic rapport be established upon which mutuality of goals be structured between teacher and student.

Many and varied experiences. Every effort should be made to provide the student who lacks language facility with great variety in real and vicarious experiences. Systematic exploration of his natural environment and his social and economic environs should be made through field trips and related readings. All types of audio-visual aids and graphic interpretations should be utilized regularly to reinforce, extend, and clarify those abstract concepts in the educational program which may be outside the student's scope. "Priming the pump" of the verbally handicapped student through building his apperceptive-mass will bring dividends in the form of increased perceptual readiness.

Teacher-model. The teacher must be himself a model of the best in standard English usage. Being exposed regularly to an unimpeachable model is considered to be one of the best ways of learning an alien tongue, for it is primarily through the ear that languages are mastered. As a model of the best in diction and rhetoric, the teacher acts as a "living level of aspiration" for the student who possesses ineffective language skills.

Functional practice. Every effort should be made to involve the student in the many opportunities for oral and written expression currently afforded in the modern school curriculum. These opportunities for practicing standard English usage under teacher guidance occur in a variety of informal activities: discussions, story-telling, reporting, dramatics, choral-reading, assembly programs, etc. It is through these functional activities that the student may become aware of standard English patterns with a minimum of insecurity.

Regular "translation." The informal language forms of the student must be "translated" regularly by the teacher into the language of the school. Specific illustrations and the use of several synonyms for the student's idiom may prove to be of value. An unfailing technique of instruction for the teacher of the verbally destitute child should be that of continually relating abstractions suspected of any degree of esotericism to the student's concrete experiences.

Awareness of levels of English usage. Quite early in his educational career the verbally destitute student must be made aware of the fact that communication may be executed in many different forms. It must be brought to his attention that some forms of usage are more precise than others and that some have greater social acceptability. In fact, the student who lacks language dexterity must learn that the quality of his language may determine to a considerable extent his levels of social aspiration and interaction.

Indeed, even in the elementary school the learner may be brought to realize that although ideas can be conveyed in slang, cant, "pidgin," and other informal forms that mankind has customarily utilized standard usage when preserving its ideas in permanent, written records. The crux of the argument for the verbally destitute student on any educational level to upgrade his language skills is this: in our culture, the educated person must have mastery of the standard usage of his mother tongue in order to be reasonably literate; functional literacy, moreover, is basic to even marginal participation in our way of life.

A FINAL WORD

The child in our schools who comes from a depressed cultural area poses many instructional problems. Of pivotal importance in his entire educative experience is his frequent lack of language fluency. Somehow our best efforts must be marshaled in the development of newer approaches in language arts instruction to the end that the verbally inept child may realize his true potential.

BIBLIOGRAPHY

Center, Stella S. The hazards of semi-literacy. *Perspectives on English.* New York: Appleton-Century-Crofts. 1960.

Conant, James B. *Slums and Suburbs.* New York: McGraw-Hill Book Company, Inc. 1961.

Golden, Ruth. *Improving Patterns of Language Usage.* Detroit: Wayne State University Press. 1960.

Hall, Robert A. *Linguistics and Your Language.* Garden City, New York: Doubleday & Company. 1960.

Langer, Susanne K. The language line. *The Meaning in Reading.* New York: Harcourt Brace Company. 1960.

National Council of Teachers of English. *The English Language Arts.* New York: Appleton-Century-Crofts. 1952.

National Society for the Study of Education. *Intelligence: Its Nature and Nurture.* Volume XXXIX, Parts I and II. Bloomington, Illinois: Public School Publishing Company. 1940.

Newton, Eunice Shaed. The non-standard student versus the standard college textbook. *Journal of Developmental Reading.* 4:239-45. Summer, 1961.

————. Verbal destitution: the pivotal barrier to learning. *The Journal of Negro Education.* 29:497-99. Fall, 1960.

Sturtevant, Edgar H. *An Introduction to Linguistic Science.* New Haven: Yale University Press. 1960.

55   *The meaning of FLES*

NELSON BROOKS

*In recent years the number of foreign-language programs in elemen-
tary schools has grown enormously. Probably fewer than five-thousand
elementary-school pupils studied a second language twenty years ago.
Now, more than a half-million pupils are involved in foreign-language
programs. What can learning a foreign language do for a child?*

THESE FOUR LETTERS—sometimes pronounced as a word, rhyming with "chess"
—stand for the term "Foreign Languages in the Elementary Schools" and refer
to a postwar phenomenon of country-wide proportions, whose existence was
officially recognized in 1952 by the Office of Education in Washington, D. C.
and by the Modern Language Association in New York.

FLES is essentially an adaptation of the supreme psychological fact of the
learning of the mother tongue: that any child can learn any language with
nothing to go on save what he was born with and the "language in action" of
those about him. We recognize of course that circumstances are not the same
as in the learning of the mother tongue. The learner already knows one language well. Rather than learning at home he is in school, and instead of being
within the limits of the culture in which the target language is in current use,
he is in another country. If so, how certain can we be that the child will learn
the new language as he did the mother tongue? It turns out that the degree
of certainty is surprisingly high, provided that right conditions are created
and the right things done. From a study of many programs that vary considerably with regard to starting point, time schedule, course content, and
continuity, there emerges a pattern that appears to typify the best both in
what may be observed and may be recommended.

There are many considerations that suggest the third grade as an optimum
starting point. On the one hand, the child of eight has already become
familiar with the school world in which he is to spend so much of his time.
He has already become literate in his mother tongue—an intellectual achievement of immense significance—and has by now a sharpened sense of awareness
of the business of learning. On the other hand, he is still young enough to
enjoy talk for its own sake, to imitate new sounds with an almost mirror-like
accuracy, and to accept and use new expressions without feeling a strong

Reprinted from *Teacher Education Quarterly, 16*:27-29, Fall, 1958.

urge to take them apart or to compare them word for word with the mother tongue. Time will bring about changes in these factors that will make the beginning of a second language markedly more difficult if he postpones his start until later years.

There is general agreement that the best time schedule is a fifteen-to twenty-minute class daily, occurring in regular school hours and as early in the day as possible. Language achievement at this level is necessarily limited in extent but is of a special quality not attainable later, and will be enhanced or negated according to the learnings that follow in subsequent years. The chief concerns with regard to continuity are that the skills of hearing and speaking must not be permitted at any point to become dormant, that the learner be given full credit for accomplishment in these skills (traditional measurement in terms of grammar and translation are wholly inadequate for this) and that these acquired skills be fully integrated with those of reading, writing, and structure control that will of course be encountered as learning proceeds. The learner's participation in the new language experience will be in terms of his involvement in the threefold interplay of hearer, speaker, and situation. By choosing situations with which he is already familiar and presenting them first in linguistic terms and eventually in cultural terms that are authentic in the area where the new language is spoken, the learner is gradually made bilingual within the limits of possibility. This is done by making only the slightest use of the mother tongue, by resolutely avoiding all conscious analysis of grammar and all translations from the target language into English, and by requiring that the skills of reading and writing be made to wait until the learner is sufficiently secure in hearing and speaking the new language; this usually means in the elementary school about two years' experience before reading and writing are begun, and then the material read and written must consist of what is thoroughly familiar to ear and tongue.

The preparation of materials to be used in FLES classes is a serious and difficult matter of great complexity. It requires the collaboration of experienced and expert teachers whose efforts must be modified and reinforced by constant references to three adjacent disciplines: descriptive linguistics (with regard to language), psychology (with regard to learning), and cultural anthropology (with regard to meaning). Of materials currently in print, only those prepared by the Modern Language Association—and these are modest enough—can presume to meet these requirements.

To qualify as a FLES teacher, an individual must of course understand and like children, and should have a sufficient degree of performance competency to "model" the learnings that are desired. He or she must also have made a special study of the discipline of second-language learning and must have an acquaintance with the American school world at the elementary school level. FLES teachers now in service are usually either specialists who have trained for teaching positions of this kind, or are high-school (occasionally, college) teachers, who can readily accept the protean transformation required by the change in level. Some are classroom teachers at the elementary level who have acquired the necessary language competency and have received training in the teaching of a second language to children.

The outcomes of FLES are of at least three kinds: language achievement, attitude shifts (toward those who speak the new language), and individual growth. The first of these is readily apparent and accessible to measurement. The second and third are no less apparent, but when we wish to measure and express changes in attitude and in personality we lack the devices and the neat symbols that seem adequate when we are dealing with language achievement. As far as attitudes and improvement of self are concerned, evaluations of FLES will for the time being probably have to be content with anecdotal records.

Important as it is for its own sake, FLES is no less so for having shed much light upon the nature of language learning at the secondary level and in college. The basic elements found in FLES coincide with those of any language course—at whatever level—that is founded upon an understanding of second-language learning in formal education. The most important of these may be briefly stated as follows:

Language is first of all something you say.
Reading and writing must wait until hearing and speaking are well established.
The learner must be involved in the threefold interplay of hearer, speaker, and situation.
Nobody talks in single words: the memorization of word lists is a waste of time.
Language learning is not problem solving but habit formation.
Language functions not by analysis but by analogy; grammar as usually presented does more harm than good.
At the start, the learning of structures must be maximized while vocabulary is minimized.
Until the learner is well along in his mastery of the new language, translation into English is not only pointless but detrimental.
No skill once developed may be allowed to fall into disuse.

Anyone with an intimate knowledge of the possibilities and achievements of the FLES programs soon realizes how thoroughly the language courses at the upper levels must be revised, not only if justice is to be done to the products of FLES, but also if these advanced courses are ever to accomplish even a modest share of what is claimed for them in every syllabus and catalogue. A wholly new understanding of the language skills and the order in which they may be mastered, of the harmful effects of the book, of grammar, and of translation when ineptly used, of the radical difference between the learning of Latin and of a contemporary language, of the importance of a model to go by, a person to talk with, and a suitable situation to talk about, of the relationship of talk to writing and of language to culture—all this is apparent or implied, vigorously, in FLES.

CHAPTER 12

Communicating by Writing

SOME TEACHERS patiently permit pupils to try out their language not in narrowly constrictive exercises, but with freedom to make creative use of words. We all know the moral of the story about the pupil who had to write "I have gone" on the chalkboard a hundred times, then scrawled this note to his teacher: "I have wrote *I have gone* 100 times and I have went home."

The first three articles in this chapter show ways to make language come alive for pupils by helping them write creatively. The fourth selection deals with some research on creative writing, and the final selection comes to grips with some knotty questions about grammar and language.

56   *Creative writing in the elementary school*

MIMI BRODSKY

The writer has captured the essence of the feeling found in some class-rooms, where there exists an affection for words and an appreciation of pupils' efforts.

Reprinted with the permission of the National Council of Teachers of English and Mrs. Mimi Brodsky from *Elementary English, 40*:189-90, February, 1963.

THE ROOM is quiet. Twenty-eight fifth-grade faces look intently at the board. The teacher waits.

"Black feels sticky. Like falling in tar," says Carol.

"Black is gloomy, thick, and heavy," says Ronnie.

"I think of black as mysterious. Shadowy. Scary," says Alan.

The teacher lists impressions on the board. A flood of reactions to the color black pours from the children.

"That was fun. Let's do more."

And so, the first "lesson" in creative writing begins. To introduce the new "activity," the teacher has discussed senses—sight, smell, sound, touch, and taste.

"What does spring smell like?"

"What do you see when you think of winter?"

"What sounds do you hear when you think of morning?"

The children meet the challenge to their senses. Perhaps, for the first time, many of them have exercised imagination and translated it into words; have tried their minds on given stimuli; have sought memory for descriptive terms. They listen to each other's responses and nod their heads, "Yes, Autumn does feel crunchy."

In a day or two, they will listen to poetry and try to picture the images presented. They will begin to view words in a new way. Some words will evoke more responses than others. Some words will move and sing. Others will stand still and do nothing.

After listening to poetry, the children themselves will want to write. To remind them, the teacher lists the five senses on the board. "Use them," she says and may give them a starter. "Write of summer or night or dawn." The room is hushed. The children write:

"Beauty is seen when rain is falling on a quiet night," writes Linda.

"Beauty is seen in the autumn, in the sun rising over the river and trees hanging over the water and the happiness of a child catching his first fish," writes Jackie.

"Beauty is seen in the weeping willows, hanging so low in the breeze, letting the wind blow their fingerlike branches through the air," writes Scott.

"Beauty is seen in the forests every morning when the doe takes her baby to eat. They are very quiet about it," writes Donna.

"Beauty is heard in a mother's soft voice singing her baby to sleep, the gurgling of a mountain stream, the purring of a cat, the singing of a bird," writes Diane.

"What is lonesome? When the sun goes down ... when you have no friends ... when you wander in the meadows ... when the flowers begin to die ... when you go to sleep. ...," writes Linda.

"... the silent flight of the owl in the darkness. The way it glides through the trees. The strangeness of its hoot. ...," writes Scott.

Patti wrote about a forest fire:

"... then there's a moan / and a groan / as if the monstrous trees were dying / and upon the ground lying / the little grasses, weeds and such / suddenly feel the lightning's touch / they grow to extra tremendous size / and throw their heads up to the skies / ..."

The children have just finished arithmetic. They have a five-minute break. Some read, whisper, draw, start their homework. One comes to the teacher's desk shyly holding sheets of paper. He wrote a story last night, a story called, "Tommy Trout." He will read it to the class and they will respond with genuine pleasure and pride. A girl approaches. She hands the teacher five pages of poems which she wrote over the weekend. The class will listen and praise them.

Soon, so many children are writing on their own that the class has enough material for a book. "What will we do with them?" someone asks. They agree that it isn't necessary to *do* anything with them after listening and enjoying them. However, they would like to share their work with others. How about a magazine? or a book to give to a hospital? They will carefully correct and rewrite their work, illustrate it neatly on the pages of a greeting card catalogue (these large, attractive books may be donated by stationery store owners, etc.) and, after circulating it to other classes, present it to the children's ward of the local hospital. The possibilities for their material are numerous.

On PTA night, some parents tell the teacher of their children's new interest: how absorbed they are in observing common sights; how much more they are reading; how interesting they have become.

And the children perhaps are the true artists and writers. With a gentle push, with the proper climate for seeing, listening, thinking provided, with a little time given them, who knows the depths and heights their minds can reach?

There are many techniques for introducing creative writing. They cannot fail if they are used by teachers who deeply believe in the values derived from developing the awareness, appreciation, and expression of children. This "activity" requires little preparation or training. It simply requires a teacher willing to spend some time in a relaxed, free atmosphere—a teacher who is willing to exercise her own imagination along with those of the young minds in her care.

In this whirlwind world of rockets and TV, rare are our opportunities to "sit and stare." Creative writing may not produce an Eliot or a Melville, but perhaps that moment of creative quiet is reason enough to justify its experimentation.

❧

57   *"Room 23 Weekly"—a creative writing experience*

PERCY KRICH

In reading this report of an actual class project, one can see the breadth of experience the weekly newspaper provided for the pupils. Many valuable educational objectives appear here. What are they? Is Krich using the word "creative" in the same sense it is used in the Givens article in Chapter 2?

TEACHERS USE many methods to encourage creative work from children. Achieving results in creative writing with third-graders can be difficult, especially if one hopes for results from all the children.

I wanted to challenge each child in my class to do creative work. At the same time I wanted to use a method that would make sentence structure and grammar meaningful and important without inhibiting creative potential. I chose story-writing as my method.

I had a class of thirty-six third-grade children, and I was sure that every one of them could be creative if encouraged and guided. My task was to furnish the encouragement and the guidance as well as the means and materials. The idea of a classroom newspaper appealed to me, for it held out not only the promise of individuality on the part of the child but the motivation for a good language-arts program as well. So I presented the idea to the class.

The children were excited at the prospect. We spent an hour talking about the newspaper and the possibilities it offered. To maintain the children's interest, I asked them to bring newspapers to school for study.

Reprinted from *The Elementary School Journal,* 63:336-41, March, 1963, by permission of The University of Chicago Press. Copyright 1963 by the University of Chicago.

We promptly realized that there was more to preparing a newspaper than met the eye. The children saw the paper, the print, and the headlines but did not understand what they saw. We proceeded to analyze the paper so that the children could recognize the various sections. The first section that they noticed without help was the comics. It took a little effort to steer them to other sections.

We discussed the headlines and decided that they are for the newspaper what titles are for stories. We soon discovered patterns in the stories. Each one told certain facts about something that had happened.

From these studies and analyses we developed six questions that any news story should answer. The questions, which I wrote on a chart, were: Why? What? Who? When? Where? How?

We noticed that the newspaper had a name. Immediately the children wanted to name their paper. The first name suggested was "Beachy Avenue Daily," after the school.

We thought over the suggestion carefully. How could we put out a daily? When the children realized what it meant to put out a newspaper every day, they considered a monthly instead.

But they soon realized that this proposal was at the other extreme. With a monthly there would not be enough issues in the semester to satisfy them. We finally settled for a weekly publication.

With that question decided, we discussed the coverage we could handle. It was obvious that we had to limit our coverage to our own room first. We felt we should choose a name that would indicate the time of publication and the scope of the news coverage. We finally settled on the name "Room 23 Weekly."

The first hurdle was over. Now we were ready to write.

I made another chart. This one listed the categories under which the stories would be written. The categories were based on those we had discovered in studying real newspapers that the children brought in. But we listed only the categories that were applicable to our room: weather, sports, news, features, and cartoons.

News and features needed clarification, but the class seemed to understand what the other categories were.

On the chart I listed story ideas the children suggested: sick and absent pupils, changes in our schedule, children's behavior, talking in class, playing games, and a series of stories based on the daily activities of the classroom.

We had selected a name, we had a list of departments, we had story ideas to write about, but we needed more information on getting out a newspaper.

I brought books from the library that described newspaper activity. The books referred to editors and reporters. They described a newspaper plant and told how a newspaper was run.

We learned that we needed editors and rewrite men. We needed a schedule for writing stories and for printing. So we chose editors and decided that every person who wrote a story would be a reporter and every reporter would be his own rewrite man.

Time for work on the paper was limited to fifteen minutes a day. We had to plan carefully to make the most of it. The children were to write their stories on Monday and complete them on Tuesday. I would correct them, and the children would rewrite on Wednesday. I would type and print the stories on Thursday, and we would distribute the newspapers on Friday. With the schedule established, we were ready for the actual writing.

The children's inexperience inhibited them on their first attempt. They wanted to know how and where to begin. Despite all our talks, some of the children still wanted to be told exactly what to write. We shared ideas, and the suggestions helped some of them to start.

Then their weakness in spelling began to interfere. They hesitated to go on with their stories as long as they were unsure of their spelling. I reminded them of the way real newspaper stories are written.

First the stories were written as rough drafts, then they were rewritten and edited. During the editing they were corrected and then rewritten for publication. The children were encouraged to write, to disregard spelling problems and simply get the story idea down on paper.

This approach took a lot of time because it went against all their previous training, but it proved to be the only way to get them started. Twenty-five children wrote stories for the first issue. Those who still could think of nothing to write were encouraged to draw cartoons for the paper.

I corrected the first set of stories myself and returned them the following day. The children were given new sheets for rewrite. Using their best handwriting, they copied their stories and submitted them for publication. They kept corrected versions of their misspelled work in their wordbooks, which became a source for correcting their spelling in later stories.

I took home the rewritten stories and typed them on a ditto carbon for duplicating. The amount of time that this part of the project took almost discouraged me. But I felt it was worth the time and decided to carry on as long as possible. I made thirty-six copies of the first newspaper, which were distributed to the children for study and discussion. In spite of our schedule it took two weeks to get the first issue out.

The children took their copies home and shared them with their families.

The reports they brought back indicated great interest in the newspaper. Many of the children were thrilled with the responses. One child brought back a letter from his mother that turned out to be the biggest boost our project received.

This mother made many valuable suggestions and volunteered to help us in any way she could. She even offered to type the paper for us and make stencils, if necessary. Her help soon proved to be necessary.

When we totaled the number of requests for additional copies, we found that we would need at least two hundred copies for our second issue. Since the order was too large for our ditto machine, we had to plan to mimeograph the newspaper.

The children were excited at this development. One of them suggested that we sell the newspaper to the people in the neighborhood. They tried to set a price but soon saw how difficult it was to set a realistic price.

I used the problem as material for several arithmetic lessons. The children were given the assignment of finding out how much material we would need down to the number of pencils. We counted the number of sheets of paper we would use. We counted all the materials we would need and worked out the cost of every item. The children then added and arrived at the cost of two hundred copies. After a little division by the teacher, we learned that the cost for each paper would be two cents.

The children wanted to sell the paper, but since we could not sell anything that was school property, we now had to furnish our own material. To get the money for the supplies, we decided, after a bit of wrangling, to set a price of five cents a copy.

The mother who had volunteered to help had had experience on school newspapers and could step right in now. She was assigned the job of typing the stencils and proofreading the copy. To facilitate the proofreading she typed a mock-up and submitted it for correction before final typing on the stencils. The completed stencils were put on a mimeograph machine, and the children ran off the necessary copies.

Issue Number 2 was an immediate success. The first to be mimeographed, it had four pages on two sheets of paper. Each page had two columns. We had major news on the front page. Page 2 had the editor's box and editorials. Pages 3 and 4 offered sports news, poetry, and short stories on minor news items.

The stories did not quite fill the space, but the children had the opportunity to see how much space they had to fill. They soon realized that they would have to write more and that their stories would have to be more interesting because strangers to our class were going to read them.

Our goal for the next issue was to fill the entire paper with interesting stories. We also had to set deadlines for the stories, for printing, and for distribution.

Every child who wrote a story and rewrote it after corrections were made had his story printed. Now the motivation was so strong that some children wrote so much that their copy filled three pages of paper on both sides.

After two or three weeks, the children no longer asked for help with spelling on their first draft. I corrected every paper and returned each one for rewrite. The children were told that the rewrite should be in their best handwriting so that the printer could read it. They worked hard on preparing clear copy. Misspelled words were listed and saved, to be used for the daily spelling lessons.

After several weeks the routine began to function smoothly. The children needed no prompting. Every event of note was listed for use in stories.

Once a week the story ideas were listed on the board, and the children chose their topics. When we ran short of topics to fill a paper, we wrote poems to take care of the space problems. Each week we had two or three poems for the newspaper.

The children's interests began to broaden, and they wanted to include news from other rooms. Reporters were selected to visit other classrooms and bring back news for the paper.

By this time we had a circulation and business manager. His job was to see that the papers were delivered to the parents and friends who had ordered copies, to collect money, and to disburse money for supplies.

Spelling was a constant concern. We tried to learn as many words as we could during our regular spelling lesson. For the most part the children's spelling improved as their stories improved. As soon as they had learned to correct their own spelling, I felt that they were ready to learn proper sentence structure.

The procedure for sentence-writing was simple. I would merely select a story that had not been edited and write it on the board. The class and I would edit it together. We developed rules for capitals and commas. We followed this procedure with several stories. I noticed results very soon.

Those who wanted to edit their own stories were allowed to do so. Soon most of the children were doing just this. They were concentrating on correct sentence structure and punctuation. Whenever possible they were using their wordbooks as reference for the correct spelling of their words.

When they seemed to have an understanding of sentence structure, we went into paragraphing. They found it difficult to understand the paragraph and did not really master it.

Quantities involved in printing and distributing the newspaper each week gave the children arithmetic work to do. Each week we tabulated the number of orders we had and the number of copies that had to be printed. We estimated the quantity of materials needed and the amount our circulation manager would have to pay out for supplies. We totaled our income and learned how much regular income we needed to continue to operate in the black. As it happened, we came out with a profit. We even had a small income from advertising.

The money we had at the end of the semester we used for a Mexican-style lunch, which was in keeping with a unit on early Los Angeles that we were studying in social studies.

By the end of the semester we had written and published twelve issues of the "Room 23 Weekly." We compiled our twelve issues and bound them so we would have a permanent record.

The project achieved several objectives. The children improved in oral and written expression. They improved markedly in spelling. They had excellent motivation for creative writing. They had to improve their handwriting so the printer could read their copy. They improved in social arts, thanks to our many discussions. The newspaper also contributed to improvement in reading because we read each issue after it was published. We analyzed one another's stories and suggested ways of improving them. Finally, the children recognized a real-life use for arithmetic.

The newspaper fulfilled all the purposes I had in mind at the start. We had many difficulties that might not have arisen in a class of older children, but the project did have much interest for the children in this age group. In view of the fact that the reading ability of this class ranged from the preprimer to the fifth-grade level, the children achieved much. Here were thirty-six children of a wide range of ability, yet they were able to write stories independently. Granted that some stories were only one sentence long, every child, even the poorest pupil, participated.

The newspaper was useful for good public relations. It was a medium through which the parents could keep in touch with the activities in the classroom, as indicated by the comments that many parents made to the children and to me.

But a teacher should not handle such a project single-handed. The help I received from one parent was invaluable. If I had the same type of help, I would want to try this sort of project again.

58 *Creative writing: Japanese Haiku*

ALLAIRE STUART

This article describes how a creative teacher developed a psychological "set" for creativity by providing a stimulating classroom environment. Notice the source of her ideas about Haiku.

THE AREA OF creative writing is one of the most challenging and, at the same time, the most disappointing to teachers of upper-elementary children because good results are so difficult to achieve. Children are not apt to produce imaginative, fluent writing without some stimulation and, even then, they are able to express their thoughts and feelings well only if a rich background has been provided for them. To know words is not enough in itself; to know how to use them must also be possible.

A particularly successful unit in creative writing which my class undertook was attempted only at the end of the school year after a year's extensive and intensive reading program. I feel that one of the surest and most effective ways of enriching a child's background and broadening his scope of information is through reading. Supplying the child with a variety of good books so that he may see the many ways words can be used and feel their power is certainly one of the best ways to help him become articulate himself.

Poetry is an area of creative writing which every teacher feels that children should attempt. Each year for many years I have tried to familiarize my sixth-grade class with old favorites in poetry, sometimes going back as far as the nursery rhymes if the background of the children was meager. I made every effort to show children that poetry can be fun, that it is a medium of expression which some writers prefer to prose, and that there is nothing "sissy" about knowing and liking poetry. Having once hurdled the objections which many children have to poetry, we've tried writing some of our own. The results have never been very outstanding because the children have felt frustrated right from the start in trying to find words which rhyme and yet make sense, in keeping a meter, or in trying to maintain some kind of balance in the lines. The poems which the children have produced after much hard work have usually been no better than glorified limericks, artificial and stilted in caliber. How to stimulate children to write with ease in a natural, unaffected, graceful manner in this medium?

Reprinted with the permission of the National Council of Teachers of English and Miss Allaire Stuart from *Elementary English,* 40:35-36, 37, January, 1963.

An answer came one day when the children's librarian in the Boulder Public Library gave me an article to read about Japanese Haiku. The article, by Alfred L. Creager, appeared in a family magazine, *Woman's Day*, and was entitled "You Can Be a Poet, Japanese Style." The children's librarian felt that this form of poetry would be especially suited to children of sixth grade, for children at this age are very perceptive. She felt, as I did, that they have difficulty expressing themselves when burdened with many limiting literary disciplines and the Haiku has the advantage of being very simple in form.

I began the experiment by introducing Haiku, explaining its discipline, meaning, subjects, and even its history and place in Japanese literature. The children were told that the Haiku is made up of only three lines, that instead of having difficult rhyming patterns and meter, it has just seventeen syllables. The first line contains five syllables, the second line seven, and the last, five syllables again. Haiku from the Creager article in *Woman's Day* were read to the children, as well as some from other sources. Then we discussed the subject matter. It was noted that the favorite subjects of Haiku writers are the seasons of the year, and that each Haiku expresses the thoughts, feelings, experiences, and/or observations of the writer. The Haiku does not have to be in the form of a complete thought, but it should have enough suggestiveness so that a picture is conveyed to the reader enabling him to complete it in his own mind.

One full period was spent in reading Haiku and in discussion, and then the children were free to write verses of their own. From the beginning, the reaction of the class was one of enthusiasm and keen interest. The Haiku seemed to afford the children an outlet by which they could express themselves. Although there are subleties in the true Haiku which are far beyond twelve-year-old children, the brevity and simplicity of this Japanese verse form appeals to them and releases amazing and delightful thoughts, as these examples will show:

At dusk the sun's faint
song is heard as the swaying
trees whisper each verse.

The roses soft in
color, dance in the sun by
the tune of the birds.
—Jacqueline Hazzard

When the school days end,
I will roam the fields not to
be scolded by you.
—Karen Pospahala

Is it a flower,
or is it just a bit of
paint, or a white moth?

A swish through the air,
an animal's painful cry,
and the archer's joy.
—Roger Pearson

On and on goes the
comet with its tail waving
back and forth through space.
—Randy Lentell

Red flames leaping up
burn the building to the ground.
Cigarettes flicked down.

The clock's hands creep on,
all day they work endlessly
around the numbers.
                    —Kristina Hansson

Swiftly through the woods
goes the majestic buck. He
wears the name of fame.

I am going to
the beach where the cool water
meets my anxious feet.

The cabin is small
in the vast whiteness. Only
the smoke reveals it.
                    —Carol Bartlett

I'm glad spring is here.
The winds sing a mournful tune,
but the rose has cheer.
                    —Susan Culshaw

The eye of the rain
very high on the mountain
is looking for you.
                    —Debbie Basnett

A hot summer day;
I see no children playing
—just the butterflies.
                    —Chris Zier

Deer go through the woods
swift, but very noiselessly.
Hunter strikes one down.
                    —Stephen Strenge

Three very small elves
took rides on the rainbow slide,
Now, colorful elves!
                    —Bob Lowenbach

Dawn's early sunrise
creeps through the shadowless trees
while the night passes.
                    —Steve Crouch

The children thoroughly enjoyed writing Haiku and did so with astonishing ease and rapidity. Even after the actual project had ended, they wrote verses of their own free will. One boy, whose younger sister was home ill in bed, wrote Haiku for her, pinning them up all over the house wherever he thought she'd see them. Another child had an emergency appendectomy which necessitated his being out of school for a few days. His classmates sent him "get well soon" messages, most of which were in the Haiku form.

It must be apparent that writing cannot be divorced from reading. Writing easily and fluently is a talent which cannot be developed without an intensive program in reading which will broaden the child's background so that he has material upon which he can draw. Creative expression cannot be an isolated subject if it is to thrive at all. It can't *be* at all unless extensive reading is encouraged. Through wide reading and through much creative writing, words will become familiar and useful friends to any child. We feel that the Haiku these children wrote are powerful testimonies to this.

N I T A   M .   W Y A T T

This is an excerpt from an article which reviews research on creative writing. The author states her conclusions in the form of six questions.

1. WOULD THE WRITING abilities of children be improved if teachers and administrators surveyed the language needs and abilities of the children in their particular area before they adopted any textbook or any method of teaching? What is useful to average sixth-grade children over the nation may be of little use to the sixth-grade children in any one school.

2. Would the writing abilities of children be improved if they were helped as individuals to study the mechanics of writing for which they have the greatest need?

3. Would the writing abilities of children be improved if teachers recognized that writing is a complex function and not a series of isolated skills which may be practiced until they are mastered? Children learn to write by writing—not by learning rules and filling out workbook pages.

4. Would the writing abilities of children be improved if they were given more freedom to use imagination in their compositions? The child in the upper-elementary grades writes extensively if the total time he spends with pencil in hand is considered. Much of this writing, however, tends to emphasize reproductive or narrative-descriptive writing* if not actual parroting of the thoughts of others. What would happen if he were allowed to use a greater part of his total writing time in writing the type of material in which he seems to be most interested?

5. Would the writing abilities of children be improved if teachers acted as though children differed in their writing interests and abilities and if they sometimes grouped the children for instruction in writing? Particular atten-

---

Reprinted from *Educational Leadership, 19*:310, February, 1962. Copyright 1962 by the Association for Supervision and Curriculum Development.

* Earlier in this article Wyatt writes: "Schonell studied reproductive, narrative-descriptive, explanatory, and imaginative compositions written by children. He found that children with mental ages of six to eight years experienced some confusion in writing imaginative compositions, but that this type of composition led to a greater variability of expression and greater interest on the part of children having mental ages of nine and ten. The greater interest shown led to automatic improvement of mechanical and structural aspects of writing" (p. 307). Wyatt's footnote on this was: Fred J. Schonell. *Backwardness in the Basic Subjects*, London: Oliver and Boyd, 1942, pp. 399-401.

tion needs to be paid to the child who has already learned to express his ideas rather well, for he is the child who often receives the least help in actually improving his writing. Larom has suggested one procedure which should be of interest to children who are more mature in their writing than are most of their classmates.[1]

6. Would the writing abilities of children be improved if writing were treated as a communicative art from first through sixth grade? Too often children's compositions communicate to no one other than the teacher. Oral sharing of compositions could replace much of the marking done by teachers. The language-experience approach to teaching beginning reading in which the child uses as basic reading material his own compositions seems to hold great promise for the improvement of children's writing abilities if the under-lying philosophy can be implemented through the sixth grade.[2]

60   *Linguistics—but not quite so fast*

L . M . M Y E R S

Grammar has long been a bone in the throats of students and a grim task for teachers. All too often, the rules of grammar are not carried over to the students' writing and speech.

1. WE SHOULD OBSERVE the language directly, and draw our conclusions honestly from what we have observed. It is legitimate to use scholars as guides, to help us see and hear more accurately. It is reasonable to respect their opinions when they have observed more extensively or more precisely than we have been able to. But we should not use their authority to pass on to our students as truth anything that we have not really absorbed and understood

Reprinted with the permission of the National Council of Teachers of English and L. M. Myers from *College English,* 23:29-30, October, 1961.

1. Henry V. Larom. Sixth graders write good short stories. *Elementary English,* 37:20-23; January, 1960.
2. R. Van Allen and Gladys C. Halvorsen. The language-experience approach to reading instruction. *Ginn Contributions to Reading,* No. 27, Boston: Ginn and Company, 1961.

ourselves. We can no longer say, for instance, that there are eight parts of speech just because the book says so. We should discover how many different classes of words we can recognize consistently by their forms or by the positions they can fill in sentence patterns; then we should show (not merely tell) our students about them.

2. We should remember—and bring home to our students—that the spoken form of the language is the primary one, and that the written form never fully reproduces speech. (But we should *not* say that language is speech and speech alone. We already have *speech* to designate speech alone, and we need some word, which might as well be *language*, to cover both forms.) We should teach our students that by bringing their ears as well as their eyes into play they can read more accurately and write more effectively. For example, we can show them how to hint at certain intonation patterns by punctuation. (This will often do more good than thirteen different rules for using commas—and we don't have to mention single-bar junctures.) We can also show them that many sentences that are perfectly clear when spoken are ambiguous in writing and therefore need revision. Since they can't help a reader with intonation, a word order that can be justified is not good enough; they'd better be careful to use one that cannot easily be misunderstood.

3. We should make it clear that a language is composed of dialects, and that it is impossible to speak English at all without using some dialect or mixture of dialects—nondialectal English simply does not exist. (I do know a very nice lady who insists that she talks *with* a Boston *accent* and not *in* a Boston *dialect*—but even she admits that at least a few of the other local varieties of our language are also legitimate.) A teacher who respects the dialects of his students and asks them to aid him in comparing dialectal differences gets over one big hump at once. Instead of filling many of them with resentment, and perhaps arousing discord at home, he at once bolsters their self-respect and encourages them to take an active interest in the language. He is then in a position to show what modifications in a student's dialect will convert it to standard—and he will probably find it easier to make the student believe that such modification is sometimes desirable. Tell a boy that *knowed* and *blowed* may lose him opportunities that he wants and he is quite likely to start practicing *knew* and *blew*. But the minute we tell him that only ignorant and vulgar people use *knowed* and *blowed* his loyalty and judgment may combine to make him stick to the forms. He is quite likely to think of them as typical of people he admires more than he does us.

4. For generations lip service has been paid to the criterion of usage; but the working definition of this, though never quite put into words, has usually turned out to be something like: "The final criterion of our language

is the usage that our best authors would no doubt have observed if they had had the opportunity to read this book and follow all its rules." Obviously we need something better than this circular approach, but the "leave your language alone" attitude won't quite do. Maybe Eskimo is simply what the Eskimos use, especially if you know only a few Eskimos; but standard English turns out to be not only uncomfortably various but complicated by strong emotions. However we select our standard speakers, we shall find that some of them do not accept all the habits of the others as standard, and perhaps even more of them are doubtful about some of their own usage.

We should of course use the best available evidence about standard usage, even when it happens to conflict with our own prejudices; and we should take the time and trouble to examine a good deal of this evidence. We shall then be in the position to give an honest opinion about the status of a given item as well as its structural implications; and we ought to have a pretty fair idea about when to insist on conformity and when to allow free choice.

5. Perhaps most important of all, we should remember Edward Sapir's wonderful statement that "all grammars leak." At best their rules are generalizations of something less than perfect accuracy. A simple statement that is about 98 per cent true can be of great value and comfort to a class. But if we explain it in three minutes, and then spend the next forty-seven dealing with exceptions brought up by brilliant nuisances who don't need the rule anyhow, most of the value and all of the comfort evaporate. And if we try to doctor the rule to make it waterproof we only make it too complicated for any general use—without ever quite stopping all the leaks.

A teacher can do a reasonably good job even with a "traditional grammar" if he realizes its limitations and uses it only for what it is worth. I think he can do a better job with any of several modern grammars because they fit the language better and base their explanations on evidence that the students can more easily understand. But it is a little early to be using any of these as sacred texts.

CHAPTER 13

Communication by Effective Handwriting and Spelling

EFFECTIVE written communication requires accurate spelling and legible handwriting. What curriculum decisions will you make about instruction in these skills? Will you give the same spelling test (using a prescribed list) to all pupils on Monday and Friday, and will the per cent of words spelled correctly on Friday constitute the mark you will record for each pupil? On Tuesday, Wednesday, and Thursday will you have your pupils write each incorrectly spelled word twenty times? Yes? If so, why? If not, what will you have your class do instead?

And what will you do about penmanship? Should you repeat what your teachers did with your classes when you were an elementary-school pupil? Is drill needed? What about manuscript versus cursive writing?

It is clear that before responsible curriculum decisions can be made about these questions, the professional literature on these topics must be investigated. This chapter provides a brief introduction to some of the literature.

61   *Manuscript and cursive writing*

VIRGIL E. HERRICK

In this, one of the author's many authoritative reports of his exten-sive handwriting studies, are discussed some of the factors involved in making the transition from manuscript to cursive handwriting.

MANY TEACHERS and parents are undecided as to the role of manuscript and cursive styles of writing in today's elementary-school programs of hand-writing instruction. All kinds of qualities of virtue and rightness have been attributed to both cursive and manuscript writing styles, and both positions have been supported enthusiastically.

Unfortunately this enthusiasm has crystallized questions in respect to writing symbols not really worth this much excitement. Changes in writing styles in this modern day probably do not shake our educational and social foundations. If a new form of writing which would be comfortable, efficient, and highly legible could be invented, cultural and social sanctions should not be used to prevent its introduction into our schools. Writing by hand is laborious and tension developing at best; any way to make this task easier should be utilized.

Most elementary schools introduced manuscript writing as a form of be-ginning writing between 1935 and 1949. In these same schools, the general practice is to change to cursive writing between the second half of the second grade and the last half of the fourth grade. Thus, most children are taught two kinds of letter symbols and two forms of writing. Fewer than one school in every twenty-five schools teach either one exclusively. On the basis of pre-vailing practice, then, the only instructional problem besides the necessary one of how to teach legible and efficiently produced manuscript and cursive hand-writing is the one of how the transition from manuscript to cursive forms should be made.

Many people, however, do not accept the finality of the prevailing prac-tice of two systems and would like (a) to teach only manuscript, (b) to teach only cursive, or (c) to introduce another writing style such as "italic" handwriting. The major argument used by all groups to support one system

Reprinted by permission of the Association for Childhood Education International, 3615 Wisconsin Avenue, N.W., Washington 25, D.C. Manuscript and cursive writing, by Virgil E. Herrick. From *Childhood Education*, February, 1961, Vol. 37, No. 6, pp. 264-67.

of handwriting is why teach two complex ways of writing when one would serve just as well. On its face, the simple logic of this position is persuasive, especially when we realize that *handwriting is a tool skill which should become routine as rapidly and efficiently as possible in order that it may be used functionally by a person to express and record his thoughts and feelings for himself and others to read.* This is the critical and significant use of written language, not letter and word form. To this argument most people would agree; they would disagree, however, on what would be the best writing style to use.

Fortunately, there is a growing body of comparative data which enables us to form a few judgments.

The arguments for using manuscript writing rest on three propositions:

First, the straight line, the circle, and the spacing forms of manuscript writing are more in line with the motor and eye-arm-hand coordinations of the young child than are the complex movements and letter formations of the cursive system. Empirical evidence shows that five- and six-year-olds learn manuscript letter forms easily. Many schools which have changed to manuscript writing in the primary grades were able to observe a greater freedom and willingness to write stories on the part of children when compared with their previous experience with cursive writing. There is some research to support this.[1]

Second, the manuscript writing (printscript) of the child is like the printed symbols he is learning to read and thus he does not have to learn to read two forms of written language at a time when he is already overwhelmed with the magnitude and complexity of his total learning task. Most people accept the good sense of this proposition.

Third, manuscript writing is generally more legible than cursive writing. This proposition is well supported by research.[2] The distinct clarity of the letters contributes to better spelling.

1. Gertrude Hildreth. Copying manuscript and cursive writing. *Childhood Education, 13*:127-28, 142, November, 1936. Edward A. Townsend. A study of copying ability in children. *Genetic Psychology Monographs, 43*:3-51, 1951. William H. Gray. Experimental comparison of the movements in manuscript writing and cursive writing. *Journal of Educational Psychology, 21*:259-72, April, 1930.
2. Olive G. Turner. The comparative legibility and speed of manuscript and cursive handwriting. *Elementary School Journal, 30*:780-86, June, 1930. Frank N. Freeman. An evaluation of manuscript writing. *Elementary School Journal, 36*:446-55. February, 1936. E. Mildred Templin. A comparative study of the legibility of handwriting of 454 adults trained in three handwriting styles: All manuscript, all cursive, or manuscript-cursive. Unpublished doctor's dissertation, New York University, 1958.

The objections to manuscript revolve around four main arguments:

First, the socially accepted form of handwriting is cursive; therefore, it is wasteful to teach the child something he will have to change anyway.

The first part of this argument is not open to research. People generally like what they do. The second part would argue equally for maintaining manuscript as a single system rather than changing to cursive.

Second, there is a claim that manuscript writing is slower and more cramping (tension producing) than cursive.

The research on comparative speed of the two handwriting styles is inconclusive. One is about as fast as the other. Under extreme increases in speed, the quality of the manuscript writing deteriorates less rapidly than does cursive.

The evidence on cramping and increased tension in handwriting is meager and inadequate. No one has been able to devise a good measure of tension or cramping.

Third, there is the claim that the manuscript signature is not legal. A manuscript signature is legal in most states if it is the usual signature of the individual concerned.

Fourth, manuscript writing has been criticized because of its lack of individuality and character. There are many examples of artistic writing using manuscript symbols both in England and America. Yet it is easier to get consistency and uniformity in manuscript symbols and thus high legibility.

The summing up of these arguments pro and con regarding the relative effectiveness of manuscript and cursive writing styles and the review of the supporting research data tend to support either (a) maintaining manuscript writing throughout the common school or (b) making the transition at a time when it can be efficiently and economically done.

NO AGREEMENT ON FORM

The transition from manuscript writing to cursive is complicated by the lack of uniformity in the formation of both manuscript and cursive symbols. A recent study[3] of practices advocated by commercial systems of teaching handwriting revealed little agreement on form of writing symbols.

3.   Virgil E. Herrick. *Comparison of Practices in Handwriting Advocated by Nineteen Commercial Systems of Handwriting Instruction,* Madison: Department of Education, University of Wisconsin, 1960, pp. 47-50.

For upper case manuscript alphabet, there was agreement only on the letter *P*. Letters *E* and *M* showed the greatest variety of forms (5). For lower case manuscript there was agreement on only two letters, *i* and *o*. Letters showing greatest variety of recommended forms were *g* (5), *p* (5), *q* (7) and *y* (5). There was no agreement as to the form of a single manuscript numeral.

Differences found in manuscript forms are basically (1) in actual form of letter or numeral, (2) order of stroke in forming symbols, (3) stroke direction, and (4) number of times writing instrument is lifted from paper in forming a letter or numeral.

There is no agreement among commercial systems of handwriting on the formation of a single upper case cursive letter. Greatest uniformity is found for letters *A*, *J* and *M* (3 forms each) and *O* (2 forms). Greatest variation in form is found for *B* (7), *F* (10), *I* (7), *P* (8), *R* (10) and *T* (8). For lower case cursive letters general agreement is found for *a*, *i*, *l*, *m*, *n*, *s* and *t*. Showing greatest variation are *c* (6), *g* (5), *r* (6) and *y* (5). Among cursive numerals there is agreement on formation of *1* and *0*. There is greatest variation on numeral forms for *2* (11) and *3* (8).

The differences among cursive forms for the same letter are more subtle for the most part than those found in manuscript form but may be classified generally as (1) inclusion or elimination of loop strokes, (2) use or elimination of end strokes, (3) use or elimination of beginning strokes other than loops, (4) direction and curvature of end strokes, (5) straight versus curved portions, (6) overlapping versus non-overlapping loop strokes, (7) major differences in basic letter structure and (8) length of loop below the base line.

This evidence reveals the need for any teacher of handwriting to know the nature of the differences in letter formation in manuscript and cursive symbols. This knowledge will enable him to identify the help a child needs to move from one form of manuscript to a particular form of cursive letter formation. This evidence suggests also the importance of an elementary-school staff agreeing on a particular form of upper and lower case letter formation for both manuscript and cursive styles.

NATURE OF TRANSITION

An examination of nineteen commercial systems of handwriting instruction reveals that three teach only manuscript or cursive writing. Of the rest who teach both manuscript and cursive, seven companies provide for a transitional program of instruction and nine do not. In the latter programs, the transition is sudden and the cursive writing is taught as a separate process with practices and skills independent of the earlier learned manuscript style. Since most programs of writing instruction are determined by their commercial system, two different procedures are thus used to help children change from manuscript to cursive writing: one to teach cursive writing as independent from manuscript and the other to move from manuscript writing gradually into cursive writing. The latter procedure is characterized first by moving from manuscript forms to joined manuscript writing, then to vertical cursive, and finally to slanted cursive writing.

In making the transition, it is helpful if the teacher and the children realize the following differences between manuscript and cursive writing forms: (1) Some letters are not formed the same—the child will need help in learning how to form these letters; (2) the writing instrument is not lifted after each letter in cursive writing—the child will need help in making the proper connectives between letters in forming a word; (3) cursive writing has slant—the child needs help in moving from vertical writing to the proper slant orientation; and (4) some children may have to learn to read cursive writing. The latter is less true the longer the transition period is postponed because of the increasing practice the child has had in reading script.

Two major factors have been mentioned most frequently as important in the production of good writing: (1) letter formation (poor letter forms—the looped letters cause most of the trouble in making the transition, wavering or angular strike, lack of distinct strokes) and (2) alignment and spacing (improper spacing between letters and words—the making of the connective is important in this respect, lack of uniformity of line, inconsistent slant, cramped or scrawled writing). It is easy to see why the problem of looped and curved letters, connectives and uniform slant loom large in any program of transition. This is why Newland found four types of difficulty in letter formation caused over one-half of all illegibilities: (a) failure to close letters, (b) closing looped letters, (c) looping nonlooped strokes, and (d) straight up strokes rather than rounded strokes.[4]

The illegibilities of only four letters (*a, e, r* and *t*) contribute to about 45 per cent of all error in child and adult writing. Writing *e* like *i* accounts for about 15 per cent of these. Help on these few letters will go a long way toward helping a child deal with his common trouble spots in the task of improving his writing.

Since the writing of most people deteriorates under sharp increases in speed, speed as a factor should not be emphasized during the transition period. The child will need help later in relating and controlling his speed of writing

4. T. Ernest Newland. An analytical study of the development of illegibilities in handwriting from the lower grades to adulthood. *Journal of Educational Research,* 26:249-58, December, 1932.

so that the quality level of his writing is appropriate to the personal-social standards essential to the writing task of the moment.

Most teachers have found that periods of fifteen to twenty minutes per day over a period of four to six weeks are sufficient to help third- and fourth-graders make the transition from manuscript to cursive writing. Helping children to continue their development in handwriting, of course, should not cease after this initial period of specific instruction. The most important resource the teacher can have in insuring improvement is the child himself. Every effort should be made to help the child understand what he is trying to do, how he can practice his writing in all situations of use, how he can evaluate his writing progress, and how he can help plan his own program of improvement. With this kind of help every child can achieve the transition between manuscript and cursive writing easily and rapidly and continue this development of his writing skill to an appropriate level of quality and efficiency.

62 *Suggestions for "lefties"*

HAROLD D. DRUMMOND

The Latin word for left is sinister; *the French word is* gauche. *Notice that both words have negative or derogatory connotations in English. Except in baseball players, left-handedness is often regarded by most people as somehow a little strange. The author discusses some reasons left-handers have writing difficulties and offers specific teaching suggestions.*

LEFT-HANDED CHILDREN often cause teachers real anguish. In spite of encouragement and exhortation, many left-handers gradually adopt the upside-down writing style. What can teachers do to help left-handed children with handwriting?

1. *We need to understand* why the lefty gradually brings his hand

Reprinted from *The National Elementary Principal*, 38:15, February, 1959.

around to the upside-down position. There are at least two good reasons. First, the natural way to draw a horizontal line is from the middle of the body outward. A right-handed person draws a line naturally from left to right. A left-handed person draws a line naturally from right to left. Moreover, the natural way to draw a circle is counterclockwise for the right-handed child; clockwise for the lefty. Since English is written with the left-to-right progression, and since most ovals in cursive writing are made counterclockwise, we must recognize that we are trying to teach something which is unnatural. Secondly, the right-handed child can much more easily see what he has written than can a lefty who writes with his wrist in the natural position. Moreover, the hand of the lefty tends to smear what has been written unless he gets the hand out of the way. If he twists his wrist around and writes upside-down, so to speak, he can see what he is doing. Moreover, if he is using ink, the copy has a chance to dry before his hand rubs across the writing and smears it.

2. *Specific suggestions can be made* to help keep the lefty honest (straight wrist instead of crooked!):

Provide lots of writing on the chalkboard. It is practically impossible to use the upside-down style at the board.

Make sure the paper is properly placed on the desk. For manuscript, paper should be square with the desk. For cursive, the bottom right corner should be pointed at the body. It is hard to write in the upside-down position if paper is placed properly. Also, less hand-smearing occurs.

Permit lefties to continue manuscript writing indefinitely. Their writing is almost always more legible before they learn to write cursive than afterward. As the left-handed children begin to change to cursive, though, watch like a hawk the placement of the paper.

Encourage children to hold pencils or pens so that the top of the writing instrument is pointing over the shoulder of the same arm.

Encourage lefties to develop a writing slant which feels natural and good. The slant will, undoubtedly, be a bit backhand compared to generally accepted handwriting styles because it's natural that way. A *consistent* slant makes writing legible, and a lefty is not likely to be consistent using a slant which is natural for right-handers.

Furnish lefties with pencils which have slightly harder lead than that used by right-handers. Harder lead will not smear as easily, thus providing less reason for twisting the wrist so that the hand is in the upside-down position.

When ink is used, be sure that all lefties have a good nonskip ballpoint pen which has a high-quality nonsmear cartridge.

Encourage lefties to learn to type. Most classrooms should have typewriters to encourage children to write creatively. With lefties, the need for typewriters is even greater.

3. In spite of all our efforts, position for good writing feels wrong for most lefties—and it feels right when they get the wrist in the upside-down position. Many of them will write that way in spite of everything teachers can do—so don't make too big an issue of it. Consistently follow the above suggestions; but if it appears the war has been lost, work to improve better formation and writing style from the upside-down position. Good citizens write *legibly*—and it is better to have a cooperative, enthusiastic, eager lefty who writes legibly upside-down than to have a disgruntled, antagonistic, lethargic lefty, with a properly-placed wrist, who does not choose to write.

63   *Studying spelling independently*

H O W A R D   E .   B L A K E

New teachers often find themselves at a loss for specific things to teach in spelling and reading lessons. To aid teachers in planning individual and group spelling activities, the author presents forty-three aids to correct spelling.

LEARNING how to spell is largely an individual matter. Spelling research for the past half century has shown that few children learn to spell words by the same method. We also know from the field of child development that all children are different and that the older children become the greater the range of differences among the children in a particular group. Our knowledge of spelling and children, then, would indicate that considerable emphasis be placed upon independent spelling study. Yet, in most of today's elementary-school classrooms group instruction in spelling is the prevalent method. Independent study is not encouraged to any significant extent in many classrooms and that which is provided is seldom actively guided by the teacher. What can upper-grade children do during independent spelling time? How can they most efficiently spend the time allotted for independent study? How can the teacher effectively guide this independent study?

Reprinted with the permission of the National Council of Teachers of English and Dr. Howard E. Blake from *Elementary English,* 37:29-32, January, 1960.

There is nothing wrong with group instruction in spelling. In the primary grades, where all the children in a class are very near the same level of development in spelling ability, it has to be the main method of instruction. In the upper grades it is many times the most efficient way to teach a needed skill to the whole class or to a small group within the class. Children in such groups often need to study syllabication of words, learn to identify root words, study prefixes and suffixes, practice dictionary skills, develop spelling generalizations, etc. Whenever children show evidence as a group of needing such instruction, then group instruction by all means must be given. The chief point here is that spelling programs which rely solely upon group instruction for teaching spelling inhibit optimum spelling development for many children. The needs of the class are the determining factors as to whether group instruction should be offered or whether time should be given for independent, individual study.

Both college methods courses and spelling textbooks generally advocate that a spelling chart be placed in every classroom, and consequently, in practically every classroom in our country we find such a chart, which typically says:

Hear the word correctly.
Look at the word.
Say it aloud to yourself.
Close your eyes, look away, try to remember how it looks.
Look at the word and study it again.
Write the word.
Check the spelling.
Write the word three to five times.

The purpose of spelling charts, of course, is to provide a plan for and to give attention to independent study. And it is plain to see from the foregoing chart that if it were followed step by step a teacher would be making a provision for independent study. On this basis the spelling chart per se is a proper technique.

But does the spelling chart realistically provide for thorough independent study? I do not think it does, for these reasons:

1. It assumes that all children learn to spell independently in the same way because every child is asked to do the same thing. It attempts to bring about conformity in the concept of word study rather than encouragement of original, diverse, and truly independent thinking about words. It fails to take into account the fact that there are "private" ways of studying words which might differ completely from those used by any other pupil.

2. It does not afford adequate teacher guidance for beneficial and efficient independent study. In the particular chart given above, the instruction "Look at the word" is given twice. What does it mean? How does one look at a word? This is the chief point at which the chart bogs down. Pupils do not know innately how to look at a word; they must be taught a method. Left on their own, they develop wasteful devices which result in inefficient spelling growth.

Such teaching, and concomitant learning, leads to the criticism so repeatedly cited in our mass media of communication and by critics of education that "kids today are not learning to spell like they used to." These critics may or may not be right. Regardless, we should be teaching spelling in the very best way we know. Teachers agree that from all we have learned about the nature of the spelling process, independent study is an essential feature of a successful program. But reliance upon spelling charts alone as *the* method of teaching spelling is not enough. In fact, this overreliance has obviously led to weaknesses in the way spelling is learned. Tightening our belts on this one point alone might bring about a significant improvement in the quality of spelling among the young people of our country.

Recently, members of my graduate and undergraduate classes in language arts have been giving some of their attention to this problem. In our work we have devised a master list of possible questions which a pupil beyond the primary grades can follow during independent study of a word list. These questions give pupils a guide in the problem of "looking at a word." The questions provide for practice in phonetic, structural, and meaning analysis as well as in usage practice. The questions are intended to be used with a spelling chart and should be considered a supplement to it. It is also assumed in these questions that the test-study plan of spelling instruction is followed in these upper grades.

No child would answer every one of these questions about every word on the list; much of such a practice would be needless drill. Rather, it is intended that from this list, under the teacher's guidance, a pupil will find those questions which provide for more efficient independent study of words of the type habitually missed. With guidance, a pupil will discover those questions which he must apply to every word week after week in order to bring about improvement in spelling ability. He would eliminate those questions which do not contribute to spelling growth.

It is anticipated that as children go about using these questions the teacher would from time to time offer total-group or small-group instruction, depending upon the needs of the class. As a regular part of daily instruction he would provide seat-work in addition to that suggested in the textbook, which would give practice in analyzing the words on the weekly list. Seat-work exercises should give practice in those details suggested by the questions. In this sense these questions can be a helpful guide to the teacher for providing balanced, thorough seat-work. Results would show progress to both pupil and teacher. Teacher analysis of individual's mistakes would provide clues as to what questions particular children should concentrate upon in this and future lists.

Teachers can handle these questions in various ways. The most common method is to duplicate them and have children put them in their spelling note-books where they can serve as a reference during spelling time. Another teacher had children paste their copy in the front of their spelling textbooks. Still another teacher had his children tape their copy to a piece of stiff cardboard, which frequently could be seen in its propped position on various desks during spelling time. The chief point is the necessity of each child having his own personal copy available in some fashion or other.

My experience with these questions points to the fact that when the method is used in the manner described children will improve in their spelling ability, both on spelling tests and on written work. Children taught through this method seem to have been motivated to enjoy spelling more and to have built up a desire to want to improve their spelling, perhaps because of the security they developed from having a rather definite procedure to follow when given time to study words independently. No doubt, the teacher's active guidance of these children's independent study has been a factor in their spelling growth.

The questions are offered here for those teachers who wish to try them out with their own children.

Phonetic analysis

1. What other words can I write that sound like this word?
2. What other words can I write that begin like this word? End like this word?
3. What silent letters are contained in the word?
4. Which syllable is accented?
5. Do the vowels have long or short sounds?
6. Can I pronounce the word correctly?
7. If the consonants *c*, *g*, or *s* appear in the word, do they have a hard or a soft sound?
8. Does the word contain a sound that might be spelled in more than one way? (e.g., phone; near)

Structural analysis

1. Is this a root word for formation of other words? If so, write the new words.
2. Is there a root word in the new word?
3. What is the prefix, if any, in this word? Can other prefixes be added?
4. What is the suffix, if any, in this word? Can other suffixes be added?
5. Can this word be made plural?
6. Are there any small words in this word?
7. Is this a compound word?
8. Is a new word formed by spelling this word backward?
9. Can I arrange these words alphabetically?
10. Can I write this word correctly several times?
11. Does this word begin with a small or with a capital letter?
12. How does this word look in configuration?
13. Does the word contain any double letters?
14. Is this word a contraction?
15. Can I write the syllables for this word?

Meaning

1. What is the dictionary definition for the word? Does the word have more than one meaning?
2. What are some good synonyms for the word?
3. What are some good antonyms for the word?
4. Does the word have a homonym?
5. Is this an action word (verb)?
6. Is this a telling word (noun)?
7. Is this a describing word (adjective)?
8. Can this word be used in more than one of the ways stated above in 5, 6, or 7?
9. Can I find a picture to illustrate the word?
10. Can I find pictures to illustrate the plural of the word?
11. Which of the words appear in current events articles I have recently read or am now reading?
12. Which words appear in my other texts, reference books, and story books I am now studying?
13. If this word can be dramatized, can I do so?
14. Can I illustrate the word through art?

Usage

1. What good article can I write for the class or school newspaper using this word and others on the list?
2. Am I spelling this word correctly in my other schoolwork?
3. Do I understand the word and its synonyms, antonyms, and homonyms well enough to use them in my speech and writing?

4. What story, poem, announcement, report, letter, or instruction can I write using this word and others on the list?

5. Keep a spelling notebook in which examples of the usage of words—stories, sentences, poems, clippings from current events material, etc.—are kept.

6. Can I make a crossword puzzle using this word and others on the list?

It is the responsibility of the elementary school to teach children to spell. Evidence shows that our spelling programs need to be improved to some extent. Toward this end, without a doubt, more attention must be given, particularly in the upper-elementary grades, to the principle that all children learn to spell differently. Adherence to this principle calls for a changed emphasis on group instruction and for increased attention to vigorous teacher guidance during children's independent study. The plan outlined here might help us improve in this kind of spelling teaching.

CHAPTER 14

Learning and Using Mathematics

In the preceding chapters we considered the use of words as symbols for communication. In mathematics, words are still important, but numerical symbols are of primary significance.

In the Preface, I made note of the importance for teachers to keep abreast of professional literature. Important changes are taking place in education. The subjects we learned in school can no longer be passed down to the young in a simple, mechanical, vertical way. Mathematics and the mathematics curriculum are excellent examples of intellectual transition in our era.

> Until recently, the mathematics curriculum in elementary and secondary schools had been relatively unchanged for a century or more. It had been generally uniform across the nation. For the most part, the sequence of topics and their grade placement was determined by tradition rather than by efforts to discover what could be learned most effectively by children at various age levels, although experimental studies of the 1930's had some influence on the elementary-school sequence. Mathematical principles and concepts developed over the last half of a century were treated briefly, or not at all, in the school curriculum. The increasing need on the part of scientists and social scientists for competence in the "new" mathematics as well as increased recognition of the subject's intrinsic importance has given a double impetus to curriculum studies in this field.[1]

The first article in this chapter deals with the "newer" mathematics.

1. Dorothy M. Fraser. *Current Curriculum Studies in Academic Subjects: A Working Paper Prepared for the Project on the Instructional Program in the Public Schools,* Washington, D.C.: National Education Association, 1962, p. 27.

Two articles describe ways to help pupils learn and remember mathematics. Another article deals with a particular kind of teaching resource, the Cuisenaire rods. The final article is a review of research on the teaching of mathematics in elementary schools.

୬✑৩

64   *Including the newer mathematics with the regular program of the primary grades*

E D W I N A   D E A N S

R O S E   K O U R Y

There is controversy among mathematics specialists over how much "newer mathematics" should become part of elementary-school programs. Teachers and citizens should have some knowledge of the subject, which is not as mysterious as some people think. This article provides an excellent introduction to the newer mathematics for teachers who feel unsure of their ability to grasp it.

SCHOOL SYSTEMS today find themselves in the position of making many decisions with regard to the newer mathematics. Few complete courses in the newer mathematics are available for general use at the present time. If a school system decides to venture forth into the new mathematics at the primary level, choice is decidedly limited. Most school systems operate on the basic textbook plan for arithmetic texts which means that book selections are made for a definite period of time. It will be several years before revisions will be made in the currently used textbooks which will incorporate the newer mathematics, or before new series can be prepared. In the interim how can the primary teacher improve the regular program by enriching it with experiences from the newer mathematics? These experiences, of course, must be selected in such a way that they will really enrich and supplement, but not interfere with, or conflict with the regular program. They must be selected with con-

Reprinted from *The Arithmetic Teacher*, 9:90-95, February, 1962.

sideration of a long-range plan so that mistakes will not be made which will be regretted later. It is with these ideas in mind that the experiences presented in this article have been categorized to fit in with certain accepted basic abilities. Among the abilities which are considered important in all primary programs are these: (1) the number system and place value; (2) addition and subtraction of whole numbers; (3) multiplication and division of whole numbers.

As new materials are available and as primary teachers themselves explore the possibilities, separate school staffs may wish to extend the list with this type of study and experimentation. Over the next few years classroom teachers will be performing an important service to education in general, because determining how much of the newer mathematics is appropriate for primary grades is still a question to be answered. However, with a background of valuable experience from which to base decisions of selection of textbooks and other mathematics materials, teachers will have some basis for judging beyond the claims of experts or the pressures of salesmen. They will know if it works, and if so, with what type of child; if not, where the flaws are, and if there is anything that can be done about them. Many of these experiences can be carried out orally as chalkboard or chart exercises before the textbook is used. They may be used in combination with hundred charts, number lines, and other aids normally used in the primary grades. While there is an element of "newness" in each experience, teachers will find that not many are entirely new, since much will already be familiar to them.

Most of these experiences are adapted from some of the ongoing experimental projects related to elementary-school mathematics which are being conducted in many parts of the country. For brochures of available materials, interested persons may write to the following:

Sets and Numbers: an Experimental Program (Primary Grades)

Project director: Prof. Patrick Suppes
Send project inquiries to: Prof. Suppes
Project office address: Serra House, Stanford University, Stanford, California.

Geometry for Primary Grades

Project director: Prof. Newton S. Hawley
Send project inquiries to: Prof. Hawley
Project office address: Applied Mathematics and Statistics Laboratory, Stanford University, Stanford, California. The geometry workbooks and teachers' manuals are now being distributed by Holden Day, Inc., 728 Montgomery St., San Francisco 11, California.

School Mathematics Study Group (SMSG): Project on Elementary Mathematics

Project director: Prof. E. G. Begle

Send project inquiries to: George Roehr, Assistant to the Director

Project office address: School Mathematics Study Group, School of Education, Stanford University, Stanford, California.

University of Illinois Arithmetic Project (Grades K-6)

Project director: Prof. David A. Page

Send project inquiries to: Prof. Page

Project office address: University of Illinois, 1207 W. Stoughton, Urbana, Illinois.

The Syracuse University "Madison Project" (Grades 3-10)

Project director: Prof. Robert B. Davis

Send project inquiries to: Prof. Davis. However, anyone wishing to visit project classes at Weston (Conn.), Tarrytown (N.Y.), or Syracuse (N.Y.) should write to: Mrs. Beryl Cochran, Weston Public Schools, Weston, Conn.; Miss Cynthia Parsons, Tarrytown Public Schools, Tarrytown, N.Y.; Mr. William Bowin, Board of Education Building, West Genesee St., Syracuse, N.Y.

Project office address: Mathematics Department, Syracuse University, Syracuse 10, N.Y.

The Greater Cleveland Mathematics Program (G.C.M.P.) (Grades K-12)

Project Director: Dr. George H. Baird

Send project inquiries to: Dr. Baird

Project office address: Educational Research Council of Greater Cleveland, 75 Public Square, Cleveland 13, Ohio.

THE NUMBER SYSTEM AND PLACE VALUE

(Grade levels are suggestive only.)

1. (Grade 1, 2) Name the next three numbers (greater than) >29: (30, 31, 32).

   (Grade 3) Name the next three numbers >87: (88, 89, 90); >100: (101, 102, 103); >109: (110, 111, 112); >118: (119, 120, 121).

2. (Grade 1, 2) Name the next three numbers (less than) <21: (20, 19, 18).

(Grade 1, 2) <50: (49, 48, 47).
(Grade 2, 3) <100: (99, 98, 97).
(Grade 3) <110: (109, 108, 107); <120: (119, 118, 117).

3. (Grade 2) What set of numbers is (greater than) >15 and (less than) <20? (16, 17, 18, 19); >3 and <7? (4, 5, 6).
   (Grade 2, 3) >24 and <30? (25, 26, 27, 28, 29); >79 and <85? (80, 81, 82, 83, 84); >99 and <than 110? (100, 101, 102, 103, 104, 105, 106, 107, 108, 109).

4. (Grade 3) What even numbers are (greater than) >20 and <36? (22, 24, 26, 28, 30, 32, 34).

5. Name the next three numbers in each set:
   (*a*) (Grade 1, 2)
   2, 4, 6, _____, _____, _____.
   (*b*) (Grade 1, 2)
   3, 4, 5, _____, _____, _____.
   (*c*) (Grade 2, 3)
   13, 16, 19, _____, _____, _____.
   (*d*) (Grade 2, 3)
   47, 49, 51, _____, _____, _____.
   (*e*) (Grade 1, 2)
   17, 16, 15, _____, _____, _____.
   (*f*) (Grade 2, 3)
   39, 37, 35, _____, _____, _____.
   (*g*) (Grade 3)
   59, 56, 53, _____, _____, _____.
   (*h*) (Grade 2, 3)
   44, 46, 48, _____, _____, _____.

6. (Grade 2, 3) Rearrange the boxes so that the numbers will be in order from smallest to largest.
   (*a*) 24   19   68   50   37
   (*b*) 83   39   20   38   77
   (*c*) 99   117   109   120   100

7. (Grade 1, 2, 3) Name the set of numbers on your hundred chart that have tens, but no ones: (10, 20, 30, 40, . . . 90);
   (*a*) (Grade 1, 2, 3) The set of numbers you would need to count by tens starting with 33: (43, 53, . . . 93);
   (*b*) (Grade 1, 2, 3) The set of numbers that have 6 in tens place: (60, 61, 62, . . . 69);

(c) (Grade 1, 2, 3) The set of numbers that have 4 in ones place: (4, 14, 24, 34, . . . 94);

(d) (Grade 2, 3) The set of numbers (larger than) >50 that have 7 in ones place: (57, 67, 77, 87, 97);

(e) (Grade 2, 3) The set of numbers (smaller than) <50 that have 5 in ones place: (45, 35, 25, 15, 5).

8. Group by 3's, 4's, 5's, 6's, 7's, 8's and 9's:

(a) (Grade 2, 3) Group oranges into bags putting 3 oranges in a bag (select numbers representing 1 through 8 oranges);

Oranges	Bags	Single oranges
4	1	1
3	1	0
6	2	0
5	1	2
7	2	1

(b) (Grade 2, 3) Group bananas 4 to a bunch (select numbers representing 1-15 bananas);

Bananas	Bunches	Single bananas
7	1	3
5	1	1
6	1	2
8	2	0
12	3	0
13	3	1

(c) (Grade 3) Group potatoes into bags putting 5 in a bag (select numbers representing 1-24 potatoes);

Potatoes	Bags	Single potatoes
7	1	2
5	1	0
8	1	3
10	2	0
12	2	2
15	3	0
4	—	4
6	1	1
21	4	1
...	...	...

(*d*) (Grade 3) Follow the same procedure for grouping carrots 6 to a bunch (select numbers up to 30); radishes 7 to a bunch (select numbers up to 35); group by 8 (select numbers up to 40); group by 9 (select numbers up to 45).

The pattern for selecting numbers in these illustrations is to select only those numbers which are below the square of the grouping number so that recording will require only two places. In 8 (*d*) above, further limitation is imposed since children may not know multiplication and division facts beyond five times the grouping numbers.

MULTIPLICATION AND DIVISION

1. (Grade 3) Use flannel board discs or chalkboard drawings to present multiplication as arrays of rows and columns of objects.

```
0     0     0     0     4 in each row
0     0     0     0     3 rows
0     0     0     0     3×4 = 12
```

Show how the array can be tipped so that rows become columns and columns become rows.

```
0     0     0     3 in each row
0     0     0     4 rows
0     0     0
0     0     0     4×3 = 12
        4×3 = 3×4
```

2. (Grade 3) Use a number line to have children imagine a cricket or a rabbit or both, hopping along the line in a designated fashion. Give a starting place, indicate the size and number of jumps, and have children determine the landing place.

	Jumps by 4's Starts at	Jumps	Jumps by 3's Lands
Rabbit	0	4	16
Cricket	0	4	12
Rabbit	12	3	24(3×4 = 12+12 = 24)
Cricket	12	4	24
Rabbit	2	5	22(5×4 = 20+2 = 22)
Cricket	6	5	21(5×3 = 15+6 = 21)

Children may plan jumps so that they will start together and land together but will take a different number of jumps in getting there. They may plan jumps that will put the rabbit ahead, or the cricket ahead.

3. (Grade 3) Set up a table of numbers by 3's from 1-30 and a table of 4's from 1-40. Children may use these tables to help them determine starting places, numbers of jumps to be taken by the rabbit, and jumps by the cricket who jumps by 3's.

1	2	3
4	5	6
7	8	9
10	11	12
13	14	15
16	17	18
...	...	...

Illustrations: Cricket starts at 11 and makes 5 jumps. Where is he? (26). He **starts at 10 and makes 6 jumps.** Where is he? (28), etc.

1	2	3	4
5	6	7	8
9	10	11	12
13	14	15	16
17	18	19	20
21	22	23	24
25	26	27	28
...	...	...	...

4. (Grade 3) Teach division as the inverse or "undoing" of multiplication.

If $3 \times 4 = 12$, then $12 \div 4 = 3$ and $12 \div 3 = 4$.
If $6 \times 4 = 24$, then $24 \div 6 = 4$ and $24 \div 4 = 6$.

5. (Grade 3) Explore a multiplication table as a way of discovering relationships.

$1 \times 5 = 5$	$5 \times 1 = 5$
$2 \times 5 = 10$	$5 \times 2 = 10$
$3 \times 5 = 15$	$5 \times 3 = 15$
$4 \times 5 = 20$	$5 \times 4 = 20$
$5 \times 5 = 25$	$5 \times 5 = 25$
$6 \times 5 = 30$	$5 \times 6 = 30$
$7 \times 5 = 35$	$5 \times 7 = 35$
$8 \times 5 = 40$	$5 \times 8 = 40$
$9 \times 5 = 45$	$5 \times 9 = 45$
$10 \times 5 = 50$	$5 \times 10 = 50$

(*a*) All endings are 5 or 0.
(*b*) The answer for 4×5 is twice as large as the answer for 2×5.
(*c*) The answer for 6×5 is twice as large as the answer for 3×5.
(*d*) Each answer is 5 larger than the one just above it.
(*e*) Each fact in the first table has a companion fact in the second table.

6. (Grade 3) Compare two tables to see what relationships can be discovered.

$1 \times 2 = 2$	$1 \times 4 = 4$
$2 \times 2 = 4$	$2 \times 4 = 8$
$3 \times 2 = 6$	$3 \times 4 = 12$
$4 \times 2 = 8$	$4 \times 4 = 16$
$5 \times 2 = 10$	$5 \times 4 = 20$
$6 \times 2 = 12$	$6 \times 4 = 24$
$7 \times 2 = 14$	$7 \times 4 = 28$
$8 \times 2 = 16$	$8 \times 4 = 32$
$9 \times 2 = 18$	$9 \times 4 = 36$
$10 \times 2 = 20$	$10 \times 4 = 40$

(*a*) The first five answers in the 4's table are also in the 2's table.
(*b*) Answers in both are even numbers.
(*c*) If you list the endings of the answers for 2's and for 4's, you have the same number recurring. They occur in a different order in each list.

(*d*) The answers for 2's are like counting by 2's. The answers for 4's are like counting by 4's.

ADDITION AND SUBTRACTION

1. Introduce frames as placeholders for numerals.
   (*a*) (Grade 1, 2) $6 + \square = 9; \; 8 = 3 + \square$
   (*b*) (Grade 2, 3) $15 = \square + \triangle$

$\square$	$\triangle$
7	8
9	6
10	5
...	...

   (*c*) (Grade 2, 3) $\square + \triangle + \triangledown = 12$

$\square$	$\triangle$	$\triangledown$
2	4	6
3	5	4
5	4	3
...	...	...

2. (Grade 1, 2) Introduce *n* as a placeholder for numerals.
   (*a*) $3 + n = 6$
   $n + 3 = 6$
   $6 - n = 3$
   $6 - 3 = n$
   $n = \square$

   (*b*) (Grade 2, 3)
   $11 - 3 = n; \; n = \underline{\quad}$
   $6 + 4 = n; \; n = \underline{\quad}$
   $n + 7 = 13; \; n = \underline{\quad}$
   $10 - n = 7; \; n = \underline{\quad}$
   $n + 8 = 14; \; n = \underline{\quad}$

3. (Grade 1, 2) Stress subtraction as the inverse or the "undoing" of addition.
   If $3+2 = 5$, then $5-2 = \square$ and $5-3 = \square$.
   If $6+8 = 14$, then $14-6 = \square$ and $14-8 = \square$.

4. Help children generalize addition and subtraction to higher decades (a number line to 100 is extremely useful).
   (*a*) (Grade 2, 3) If $4+3 = 7$, $24+3 = 27$, $54+3 = 57$, $64+3 = 67$, etc.;
   (*b*) (Grade 2, 3) If $9-5 = 4$, $19-5 = 14$, $29-5 = 24$, $39-5 = 34$, etc.;
   (*c*) (Grade 3) $67+6 = 60+(7+6)$ or $60+13$ or 73;
   (*d*) (Grade 3) $25-7 = 10+(15-7)$ or $10+8$ or 18;
   (*e*) (Grade 3) If $7+6 = 13$, $67+6 = 60+(7+6)$ or $60+13$ or 73;
   (*f*) (Grade 3) If $15-7 = 8$, $25-7 = 10+(15-7) = 10+8 = 18$,
   $35-7 = 20+(15-7) = 20+8 = 18$, etc.

5. Use any two letters of the alphabet to be replaced by numerals. Provide a numeral for one letter; children work out the other letter.

(*a*) (Grade 2, 3) $a+b = 13$

a	b
3	(10)
4	(9)
5	(8)
6	(7)
7	(6)
......	......

(*b*) (Grade 2, 3) $c+4 = d$

c	d
8	(12)
(6)	10
5	(9)
9	(13)

(*c*) (Grade 3) $15 = r+s$

r	s
6	(9)
2	(13)
(5)	10
(7)	8
4	(11)

6. Provide children with a set of numbers they can use and the total number they must have after combining and separating. They can add or subtract as many times as they wish and use the numbers in any way which will help them. See how many ways they can arrive at the number.

(*a*) (Grade 1, 2) {1, 2, 3} $\boxed{8}$
$3+3 = 6$ $3+2 = 5$
$6+2 = 8$ $5+3 = 8$
$1+1+1+1+1+1+1+1 = 8$
$2+2+2+2 = 8$
$2+2+2+1+1 = 8$
$3+3+3—1 = 8$ (sub.)

(*b*) (Grade 1, 2) {1, 2} $\boxed{7}$
$2+2+2 = 6$ $1+2 = 3$
$6+1 = 7$ $3+2 = 5$
            $5+2 = 7$
$2+2+2+2 = 8$
$8—1 = 7$

(*c*) (Grade 3) {2, 3, 4} $\boxed{14}$
Illustrations:
$4+3 = 7$ $2+3 = 5$
$7+4 = 11$ $5+4 = 9$
$11+3 = 14$ $9+3 = 12$
            $12+2 = 14$

$4+4 = 8$ $3+3 = 6$
$8+4 = 12$ $6+4 = 10$
$12+4 = 16$ $10+4 = 14$
$16—2 = 14$

(*d*) (Grade 3) {3, 4, 5, 6} $\boxed{13}$
Illustrations:
$5+5+5 = 15—2 = 13$
$6+6+4 = 16—3 = 13$
$3+4+6 = 13$

65   *Making primary arithmetic meaningful to children*

ESTHER J. SWENSON

It is a good idea to help students at any level find meaning in the content of what they learn. They remember longer and are more likely to use what they learn. Consider the applications here of the thinking articles in Chapter 2. Do you think there can be creativity in the arithmetic lesson? And with regard to the Jarolimek article on the taxonomy of levels of thinking, what levels can you get into a mathematics lesson?

LIFE IS A SEARCH for meanings. The young child, in a peculiar sense, spends his waking hours trying to find out meanings: What is this? Why are you doing that? What do you call it? May I try it? What will it do? What can I do with it? Where did it come from?

The seemingly endless curiosity of the young child is a search for meanings in his everyday life.

The school has a special role to fulfill in helping children acquire accurate, clear, and rich meanings. Unfortunately, teachers sometimes forget that words which are clear to an adult may not carry the intended meanings into the life of the child.

Consequently, it is important for us to ask ourselves seriously what we mean when we talk about making any school subject meaningful.

The primary teacher needs to ask himself these questions: What is meant by meanings? How are meanings acquired? What particular meanings should be acquired by children during the early elementary-school years?

The arithmetic meanings to be acquired by most children in the primary grades are, briefly, certain mathematical concepts and processes. We often make a serious error in assuming that primary arithmetic consists entirely of a routine counting, reading, and writing of numerals, and routine oral or written repetition of simple arithmetic facts.

Teachers in the primary grades have the responsibility to teach much more than the oral and written forms. They also need to teach the underlying and surrounding meanings of the concepts and processes which are merely signified by the forms.

The concepts and processes which undergird the whole arithmetic curriculum should be introduced and practiced in the primary grades, for the

Reprinted from the *NEA Journal*, 50:43-44, 61, April, 1961.

primary teacher sets the foundation, be it sound or shaky, on which the whole arithmetic structure rests.

These concepts should not be thought of as primary in the sense that they are just easy ideas for immature learners. They should be considered primary in the sense of being *fundamental* or *basic* ideas.

MEANING IS EXPERIENCE

To a child, the meaning of a word or object is only what his experience with it reveals to him.

To the first-grader, the symbol "6" means whatever experiences he has had involving that symbol—how old he is, the numeral painted on the winning racer in the local soapbox derby, the number of pennies he had to pay for a candy bar.

Meanings cannot be transmitted ready-made from one person to another. Real meanings are built within the learner's experience.

An important word meaning for primary-grade children to learn as part of their arithmetic work is the word "group." Let us review some of the experiences Mary, a first-grade child, has with the word—experiences which become not only the basis but also the very substance of her expanding meaning of the word.

1. On the first day of school, Miss Allen, Mary's teacher, asks Mary to bring her chair and join the group. Miss Allen talks with the children about the group. She says they are a nice, quiet group. She asks Mary if she has anything she wants to tell the group.

Mary knows that the teacher means that all the children gathered together are a group.

2. Later in the day, Miss Allen asks Mary to help put away the picture books on the table. She suggests that she should gather them up and put them in a neat group in the middle of the table.

Mary finds out that not only children but also books can be a group.

3. One day Joe sits in a chair away from the other children, pouts, and refuses to join the other children at his table. Mary tells him he belongs in her group. Joe says, "I'm in my own group." Billy laughs and says, "You can't be a group all by yourself. It takes more than one to be a group."

Mary listens and wonders about that. She is learning more about the meaning of group. It means more than one, according to Billy.

4. On the playground, Miss Allen teaches the children a new game. She

helps them form two groups, but Jim stands out in the middle between two groups. Miss Allen asks, "What group are you in?" Jim says, "I'm in Sam's group." The teacher tells him that he should stay with the other children in Sam's group so that everyone will know he belongs in that group.

Mary understands the importance of having all members of a group together.

5. On later occasions, Mary hears her teacher tell the children to group themselves around the tables, to group the books on the shelves of the bookcase, to group the pennies, the nickels, and the dimes when counting the lunch money.

Mary has a chance to extend her meaning of the word "group." "Group" is not only the name of more than one thing put together because of some similarity, but is also something you do to things when you put them together to make a group.

This is by no means a complete story of Mary's learnings through experience about the meaning of the word "group." However, it indicates how she had an opportunity to improve and expand her understanding of the meaning of the word. Her learning came about not by definition but by *experience* with the word applied correctly in situations which were understandable to her.

It may be asked whether or not this is really arithmetic. Yes, it is. The idea of the group which Mary acquired through experience in a variety of situations is one of the basic concepts of arithmetic.

Understanding of numbers rests on understanding of groups in their quantitative aspects. Understanding of addition, subtraction, multiplication, and division is of necessity based on understanding of the verb "to group," for these fundamental processes of arithmetic are themselves processes of grouping and regrouping.

MEANING IS CONTEXT

In a real sense, meaning *is* context. Further, meanings are *derived* from context. Meaning accrues through experiencing a thing, event, or situation in relation to other things, events, or situations. Therefore, the types of meanings and the quality of meanings vary a great deal in terms of the quality of the environment in which they are learned.

The teacher should realize that the preschool child or the primary-grade pupil learns arithmetic meanings in relation to a certain context or to the various contexts in which those meanings are experienced. The richer the learning environment is with respect to the particular meanings, the better are the chances of acquiring accurate and full understandings.

· Consider, for example, the learning of the meaning of standard measures. Too often, children learn in a strictly verbal context that 12 inches = 1 foot, 3 feet = 1 yard, and 5280 feet = 1 mile.

What they learn by reading and repeating those statements is a limited meaning of those measures. How much better it would be if they could learn the meaning of inches, feet, and yards in a context of use in and out of the schoolroom.

Perhaps the children are helping to plan the placement of shelves in a new bookcase. They measure the tallest book to go into the bookcase to find how wide to make the space between shelves. They measure the books and count those of various sizes to see how to space the shelves.

In so doing, they are acquiring meanings of inch and foot in a context which is bound to contribute to better understandings of these measures.

MEANING IS INTENT

Meaning is also intent. *Meaning represents a means to an end.* Meaning indicates purpose or aim.

We may ask, "What did he mean?" We could just as well have said, "What was his intention?"

When arithmetic processes are taught meaningfully, they are taught so that they serve as means to ends. A child who knows the meaning of addition, subtraction, multiplication, and division can use these processes as means for achieving certain aims, intents, or purposes.

At the risk of seeming to accentuate the negative, let us consider not only the absence of meaningful use of arithmetic processes, but also let us recognize the fact that sometimes children are even taught wrong meanings of processes.

Occasionally, for example, they are told that adding is "getting more." In other words, the purpose of adding is to get more. This is not true.

The child who puts a group of four books on the shelf with another group of five books is not using the addition process for the purpose of having more books. He is merely trying to put two groups together to make a new total group.

If he knows the addition fact $4 + 5 = 9$ and understands it, he uses it to mean that putting a group of four books and a group of five books together will result in having a new group of nine books.

The same nine books were there before he added and after he added;

the difference is in the way they are grouped. The equal sign should express *equality* in the child's thinking as well as in oral pronunciation.

MEANING IS ORGANIZATION

Clear meaning results from effective organization, and effective organization results from clear meaning. Children as well as adults need to see how the pieces fit together.

Not only do children need to see each arithmetical process as a means to an end, as serving a peculiar purpose, but they also need to see how the various processes relate to one another. They need to experiment with groups and with grouping of objects, taking groups apart and putting them back together, adding groups to make a new total group, separating that total group into new subgroups.

Two basic arithmetical concepts which must be taught well if arithmetic is to be meaningful are the concepts of *base* and *place value*. Of course, they are not taught completely in the primary grades, but to omit emphasis upon them in the early years of schooling is inexcusable.

The meaning of a "group" has already been emphasized. It is essential as a forerunner of the idea of the basic collection or group which we call the *base* of our number system.

Our number base happens to be ten; possibly an understanding of the base of ten is sufficient for most primary-grade children. That is not enough, however, for their teachers.

A teacher who does not understand the concept of the number base with numbers other than ten probably lacks the clarity of understanding which will make him the best guide in teaching this concept. The good teacher always needs to know more than he teaches in order to teach well that which he expects his pupils to learn.

Our number system is a highly organized pattern of relationships. Its simplicity in representing complex ideas is its beauty.

But young learners can hardly be expected to come to appreciate that beauty of structure and organization except as they are given well-planned sequences of experiences through which they may discover for themselves.

DAVID RAPPAPORT

How would you teach a group to find 3/4 of 5/6? How would you teach so that pupils would remember to apply the methods they learned in doing this algorithm to other problems? How can you be sure that pupils really understand what they are doing? Rappaport asserts: "The teacher will be more effective in his teaching if he recognizes the three levels of learning—operation, generalization, and rationalization. . . ."

TEACHERS who stress learning by discovery, so that children will better understand the basic meanings and concepts in arithmetic, will find it helpful to consider three levels of learning—operation, generalization, and rationalization. An understanding of these levels of learning will help the teacher conduct the class in a way that will stimulate the children to develop according to their abilities and rates of learning.

At the beginning of a unit of study all the children work on the operational level. Most of the children proceed to the generalization, or discovery level. The very bright children proceed to the level of rationalization, or the explanation of why the generalization works.

The three levels of learning can be illustrated by an example with fractions. Many teachers have introduced children to fractions by means of circles. Each child is supplied with a set of circles of the same size. One circle is divided into two equal parts, a second circle into three equal parts, a third circle into four equal parts, and so on. The equal parts of a circle are fractional units. The teacher asks the class which is larger 1/2 or 1/3, 1/4 or 1/6, 1/6 or 1/8. To find the answers the children compare the fractional units by placing one unit over another.

This first level of learning, or the operational level, is learning by manipulating concrete devices. At this level the children resort to concrete or semi-concrete manipulative aids. The child who counts on his fingers when he is adding, or who makes marks on a paper, is on the operational level of learning.

After the children have worked with fractional units on the manipulative

Reprinted from *The Elementary School Journal*, 63:286-90, February, 1963, by permission of The University of Chicago Press. Copyright 1963 by the University of Chicago.

level, the teacher asks them to arrange the units according to size, beginning with the largest unit. They write the series, 1/2, 1/3, 1/4, 1/6, 1/8, 1/12. The children can then discover that the larger the denominator, the smaller the fractional unit. They have reached the generalization level. Once they have made this generalization or discovery, they can use it in deciding that 1/24 is greater than 1/36.

The teacher then encourages the children to find an explanation of why the fractional unit decreases as the denominator increases. At this level a simple explanation should be acceptable. The children may reason that if you cut one pie into a number of equal pieces and a second pie into more equal pieces, the pieces of the second pie are smaller than the pieces of the first pie. Also, if you cut a third pie into fewer pieces than the first pie, the third has larger pieces.

We can illustrate the three levels of learning with another example. The children are asked to express 1/2 as fourths, sixths, eighths, or twelfths. Let us assume that they have the set of circles divided into various fractional units as in the previous example. The children manipulate their paper units. They place fourths over the half unit and find that 1/2 = 2/4. They place sixths over the half unit and find that 1/2 = 3/6. They also find that 1/2 = 4/8 and that 1/2 = 6/12. In like manner they learn that 2/3 = 4/6, 2/3 = 8/12, 3/4 = 6/8, 3/4 = 9/12, 1/6 = 2/12, 5/6 = 10/12, etc. They have found their answers by using concrete devices. At this stage they are on the operational level of learning.

The children are asked to write the equivalent fractions on a sheet of paper. When they have a number of equivalent fractions, the children make the discovery or generalization that if you multiply the numerator and the denominator of a fraction by the same number, you get an equivalent fraction. The children are now on the second level of learning.

The third level is the rationalization level. Why is the size of the fraction unaffected when the numerator and the denominator are multiplied by the same number? The children may reason that if the pieces are smaller, one needs more pieces to have the same amount. If 1/6 is one-third as great as 1/2, it will take three 1/6's to make 1/2. This is one kind of rationalization. Another child may reason that multiplying the numerator and the denominator of a fraction by the same number is, in fact, multiplying the fraction by 1. This does not change the size of the fraction. Thus,

$$1/2 \times 1 = 1/2 \times 3/3 = 3/6; \text{ or}$$
$$3/4 \times 1 = 3/4 \times 3/3 = 9/12.$$

Although all children should be encouraged to rationalize, not all children should be expected to rationalize. Some children reach the rationalization level later than others, while some children seldom or never rationalize. It is a mistake for teachers to expect all children to rationalize all generalizations. In the same classroom some children will be on the operational level of learning, some on the generalization level, and others on the rationalization level.

A third example of the three levels of learning is again taken from work with fractions. The children are learning multiplication of fractions. They have learned that the fraction symbol has several meanings. The symbol 3/4 is a statement of quantity, namely, three one-fourths. The symbol 3/4 is also a symbol of operation. It says that we are to divide a base unit into four equal parts and that we are to take three of them. The exercise 3/4 × 5/6 asks the children to take three one-fourths of each of the five one-sixths. They find the answer by operating with concrete or semi-concrete objects.

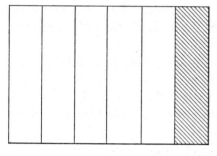

Fig. 1.

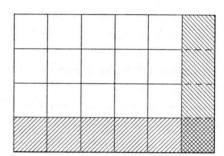

Fig. 2.

This process can be illustrated in the following steps. First, the child takes 5/6 of a base unit, a rectangle. The unshaded portion of the rectangle (Figure 1) represents 5/6. Then the child takes 3/4 of the 5/6. The unshaded portion of the rectangle (Figure 2) shows the results of this operation. The child counts the unshaded rectangles and finds that there are fifteen. To determine the size of the fractional units, he must first find out how many fractional units are required to cover the larger rectangle, the base unit. In this manner he has found that 3/4 × 5/6 = 15/24. Some children will do all the multiplication exercises in this manner. They will work on the operational level.

After the children have done a number of exercises on the operational level, some children will discover that the numerator of the answer is the product of the numerators of the two fractions and that the denominator of the answer is the product of the denominators of the two fractions. Once they have made this generalization, they may apply it in other multiplication exercises.

The question still remains as to why this generalization is true. This is the level of rationalization. Many children may discover the generalization, but few will be able to rationalize it.

When the processes are simple, all the children pass through these three stages or levels of learning. As the processes become more complicated, fewer children reach the rationalization level. It is the teacher's function to help the child develop to the best of his abilities. The teacher can perform this function best when he understands the child as well as the levels of learning. The child who is required to generalize or to rationalize before he is ready will be frustrated. The child who is working only on the operational level when he is capable of generalizing or rationalizing has not been challenged sufficiently. Children should be led to the higher level of learning when they are ready for it.

The examples of the three levels of learning were taken from the work with fractions. The same three levels can be shown in all areas of arithmetic, algebra, and geometry.

Some writers have confused the issues by combining generalization and rationalization and treating them as one process, namely, verbalization. They make no distinction between generalization and rationalization, but they do demand precise verbalization for all generalizations. Gertrude Hendrix writes,

> Then, in the second place, the verbalization attempt at this grade-school level is doomed to frustration. Numerical variables, universal quantifiers, and the zero restrictions on domains are all necessary to a precise formulation of the generalization the child has just discovered. The most that a teacher can do is to accept a garbled verbalization of what was at the beginning a clear, dynamic insight. The more sensitive a child is to precision in use of his mother tongue, the more damaging this process can be to him and to the learning which a moment before was so clear on the nonverbal awareness level.[1]

When a child discovers that to multiply two fractions you multiply the numerators and the denominators, he verbalizes this discovery. Hendrix does not accept the child's simple explanation and calls it "garbled verbalization." There is no reason to call such verbalizations "garbled." The child is thinking, and he expresses his thoughts on his own level. Of course we should encourage more precise verbalization. The kind of verbalization demanded by Hendrix, namely, "precise formulation of the generalization," is really rationalization.

1. Gertrude Hendrix. Learning by discovery. *Mathematics Teacher, 54*:297, May, 1961.

Both generalization and rationalization can be verbalized, but they are still distinct processes. The demand for more precise verbalization too soon leads to frustration because a demand is made on the child to operate on a higher level before he is ready to do so.

The simple verbalization rejected by Hendrix is the verbalization of a generalization in order to use the generalization. The precise verbalization demanded by Hendrix is a proof of the generalization or, in reality, rationalization. Hale warns against premature verbalization, but he makes no distinction between generalization and rationalization. He writes,

> In fact, premature or incorrect verbalization of a generalization may hinder the use of the generalization. Of course, precise verbalization at some time is necessary for purposes of communication and proof, but this verbalization should come only after the individual has become thoroughly familiar with the generalization and has had adequate opportunity to test and refine it.[2]

Premature verbalization is not necessarily inappropriate or unwise. It is a simple statement of the discovery made by the child. The precise verbalization for purpose of proof, as demanded by Hale, is really rationalization. Teachers should be patient with children, accept each child at his own level, and refrain from premature demands for sophistication and precise verbalization.

The teacher will be more effective in his teaching if he recognizes the three levels of learning—operation, generalization, and rationalization—and if he recognizes the need of the child to work on his own level of learning. With such understanding, the teacher can encourage each child to progress, or to develop, to the higher level of learning.

2. William T. Hale. UICM's decade of experimentation. *Mathematics Teacher, 54*: 616, December, 1961.

67   The Cuisenaire rods: a teaching aid in keeping with the new math curriculum

CLARA DAVISON

The Cuisenaire rods, invented by a Belgian schoolmaster, are used in some schools in the United States and Canada, as well as in Europe, Australia, India, and some countries of Africa. Using these rods, pupils discover mathematical principles, rather than merely passively receive their teachers' didactic explanations.

THE CUISENAIRE-GATTEGNO materials are a set of rods that combine color and length to embody algebraic principles and number relationships. The young child learns these basic principles of mathematics by playing with and manipulating the rods. In accordance with major revisions in the mathematics curriculum in Canada and the United States, the Cuisenaire method shifts emphasis to the child's discovery of mathematical principles.

The method can be used from the beginning and throughout the child's schooling. Addition, subtraction, multiplication, division, and fractions are learned simultaneously, because all of these relationships become obvious to the child in his use of the rods. Since these interrelationships are clear from the first, much teaching time is saved.

The Cuisenaire rods (which come 291 in a compartmented box) are brightly colored and accurately made to basic dimensions. Since they are only a centimeter square in cross section, small hands can easily manipulate two, three, or more. Because they are light, a child can carry a full box of them; being compact, they are easily stored.

The color is not random and meaningless; the true significance of the rods cannot be understood in terms of ordinary blocks, toys, counters, machines, and the like. An entirely new principle is involved.

There is a blue-green family (in terms of unity, 3, 6, and 9), a red family (in terms of unity, 2, 4, and 8), a yellow family (5 and 10) and finally the black rod (7) and the white cube (1). In the child's hands, these rods will express a variety of fundamental mathematical properties to the senses—directly and appealingly. For instance, in the blue-green family, the green rod is the base for a group of rational proportions; in the red family, the red rod is the base, and so on.

Reprinted from *Audiovisual Instruction,* 7:144-46, March, 1962.

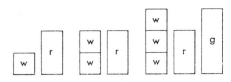

Fig. 1. The white is half of the red. Two halves of the red are as long as the red itself. Three halves of the red are as long as the light green, etc.

Fig. 2. If we place a red and a light green rod end to end we find that together they make a length that is equal to the yellow rod. We can say that the red rod plus the green rod equals the yellow rod and can write, r+g = y. The following relationships, therefore, are all derived from this simple arrangement of three rods:

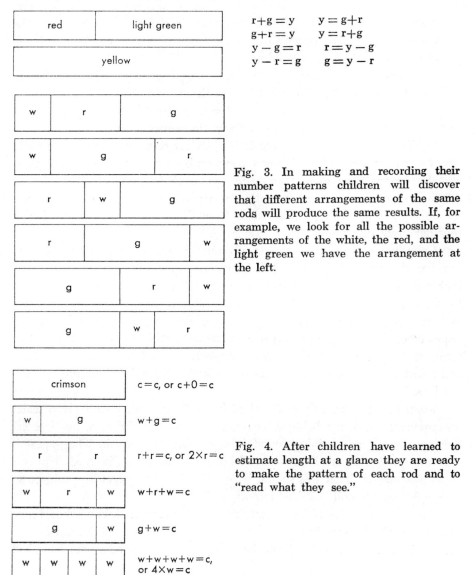

red	light green

yellow

$$r+g = y \qquad y = g+r$$
$$g+r = y \qquad y = r+g$$
$$y - g = r \qquad r = y - g$$
$$y - r = g \qquad g = y - r$$

w	r	g

w	g	r

r	w	g

r	g	w

g	r	w

g	w	r

Fig. 3. In making and recording their number patterns children will discover that different arrangements of the same rods will produce the same results. If, for example, we look for all the possible arrangements of the white, the red, and the light green we have the arrangement at the left.

crimson

$c = c$, or $c+0 = c$

w	g

$w+g = c$

r	r

$r+r = c$, or $2 \times r = c$

w	r	w

$w+r+w = c$

g	w

$g+w = c$

w	w	w	w

$w+w+w+w = c$, or $4 \times w = c$

Fig. 4. After children have learned to estimate length at a glance they are ready to make the pattern of each rod and to "read what they see."

Since the child's mind is not narrowly confined to units of measure, he is, from the start and all the way through, practicing mathematics. This is something much greater than physical measurement. The idea of measurement and of reduction to unity arises naturally as part of the whole enterprise.

The children identify a rod early by using the name of its color. This sustains a flexibility that would be impossible if the rods were marked off in unit measure and called by number names instead of color names. Taken altogether, the rods put the children in the presence of a great variety of properties ranging from multiple proportion to the ordinary unit-measure possibilities. Since these properties are inherent in the design of the rods, the child is really not "playing with the blocks" or "using counters" but is being presented with embodied principles.

The rods provide a free play situation which exploits the child's potential. This is an important psychological key to the matter. The ideal is not regimentation, but the employment of a device so flexible in its combinations that the child's mind is constantly making discoveries.

Studies have shown that at about five, six, or seven years of age, a child passes from the stage of performing concrete operations to one of entertaining abstractions. The mind then begins to work in terms of principles of which it recognizes any one operation as a particular case. The rods permit the child to work with grouped ideas from the beginning. Rote learning is thus definitely discouraged.

Counting, measuring, fractions, proportion, and even multiple proportion are all there to be exercised. It is precisely to maintain this freedom that each rod is not marked off internally in units. Further relations are provided by the color families. The child sees the colors in natural families. This establishes certain relationships as noted above. Thus the blue-green family is a sequence of 3, 6, and 9 in terms of centimeter number but of 1, 2, and 3 in terms of the proportions of the rods. Similarly the red family are both 2, 4, and 8 in terms of the centimeter as unity, and 1, 2, and 4, in terms of proportions.

From the start, therefore, the child is not bound solely to a given scalar measurement. He is not being driven, nor narrowly conditioned, but is exercising a form of self-training found in any enjoyable pursuit. The appeal is that of a sport or an art. One might claim that when reason is freed, it proves to be imagination. That this should be possible in early years in a subject so seemingly logic-bound is indeed important.

The two main difficulties we have met in the Oakville Public Schools may serve to emphasize the difference between this approach and the more conventional ones. The first has been the attitude of the teachers who have had to re-think the subject for themselves, and, instead of instructing the children in the old way, have had to guide them through experiment and questioning to understanding and conviction. The other difficulty has been the reluctance of many children to accept responsibility for their own achievements after having been brought up to expect everything to be done for them.

68   *Research should guide us*

J A M E S   T .   G A N E

The author summarizes the results of investigations into several aspects of the teaching of mathematics (1) teaching for meaning and providing direct experiences; (2) using drill; (3) teaching problem solving and improving pupils' mathematics vocabulary; (4) providing for differences in pupils' abilities; (5) clarifying professional terminology, e.g., the term "mental arithmetic."

AT THE OUTSET it should be stated that not all research findings are valid. Due to faulty techniques and subjective interpretation, the conclusions of many studies are not applicable to the ordinary classroom. In addition, all research is tentative and subject to possible modification by the results of subsequent studies. To a considerable measure, however, the improvement of learning in arithmetic is dependent upon the extent to which the classroom teacher is familiar with the findings of research and the degree to which he utilizes that knowledge.

Perhaps the most important change in recent years in the teaching of arithmetic is the prominence given to the meaning theory. Brownell in his original statement in 1935 defined the meaning theory thus: "The meaning theory conceives of arithemtic as a closely knit system of understandable ideas, principles, and processes—the test of learning is not mere mechanical faculty—the true test is an intelligent grasp of number relations and the ability

Reprinted from *The Arithmetic Teacher,* 9:441-45, December, 1962.

to deal with arithmetical situations with proper comprehension of their mathe-matical as well as their practical significance."[1]

The effectiveness of this approach has been ably demonstrated by nu-merous researchers. Harding's and Bryant's well-administered ninety-day ex-periment with Grade 4 pupils is one of the best examples. The control group followed the arithmetic text, page by page, and stress was placed on individ-ualized drill whereby the pupil attempted to improve his own personal record. In contrast, the experimental group used the texts only occasionally, as a refer-ence or for explanation of processes. Emphasis was given to meaningful and practical learning situations, such as preparing and selling lunches to fellow pupils, weighing and measuring one another for health charts, building kites for a kite-flying contest, making curtains for the classroom windows, selling candy which they bought from wholesalers, and a number of other activities involving the use of arithmetic.

The two groups were comparable both in intelligence and past arithmetic achievement. In addition, the same teacher taught both groups.

The experimental group, as a whole, was better in computational skills at the end of three months; the pupils' reasoning ability clearly surpassed the control group; and they showed a much greater improvement in study habits, grades, and behavior. The experimental group also manifested more desirable social attitudes and emotional stability than did their counterparts.

The experimenters justifiably concluded: "Direct, firsthand experiences with projects and enterprises in which children have a personal interest, proved more effective than vicarious experiences and drill procedures in developing the ability to solve problems as this ability was measured by the 'Arithmetic Reasoning' section of the achievement tests."[2]

Fred and Eleanor Schonell go so far as to state: "If teachers do not oc-casionally use projects, however small, as a supplement to ordinary lessons, they are neglecting one of the most stimulating and effective learning devices of the century."[3]

There are many more studies which clearly indicate the wisdom of guid-ing children to acquire meanings in their study of arithmetic. Brownell, how-ever, injects a sobering thought to those who believe this to be a simple matter. "The teacher, curriculum maker, or textbook writer who knows arithmetic

1. Vincent J. Glennon and C. W. Hunnicutt. *What Does Research Say About Arithmetic,* Washington: Association for Supervision and Curriculum Development, National Education Association, 1955, p. 12.
2. L. W. Harding and I. P. Bryant. An experimental comparison of drill and direct learning in a fourth grade. *Journal of Educational Research,* 37:335, January, 1944.
3. Fred J. and F. Eleanor Schonell. *Diagnosis and Remedial Teaching in Arith-metic,* Edinburgh: Oliver and Boyd, 1958, p. 45.

only as it was taught in the first three decades of this century is in no position either to practice or to expound the subject in its meaningful aspects."[4] In my opinion, there are many schools in which arithmetic is still taught as it was in the first three decades of this century. As a consequence, the teacher who desires to make arithmetic meaningful to his pupils must first be certain that the subject is meaningful to himself.

The fact that the drill method is unsuitable for teaching and learning arithmetic has been taken by some to mean that drill is an undesirable classroom activity. However, as Buckingham has noted, "The most thorough examination of the research concerned with the meaning theory of learning arithmetic will not reveal evidence to suggest that drill be abandoned."[5]

Brownell and Chazel showed that premature drill in the third grade makes little or no contribution to growth in quantitative thinking, does not guarantee immediate recall of number combinations, and has no effect on procedures employed by children. However, they also stated, "This does not imply that drill has no place in arithmetic. Drill is exceedingly valuable for increasing, fixing, maintaining and rehabilitating efficiency otherwise developed."[6] As a major guiding principle they stated that drill must be preceded by a thorough program of instruction aimed at the building of meaning. If a high level of performance in arithmetic is to be sought, then practice, after understanding, is essential.

The nature of repetitive drill is important. Practice material should be interesting to the child, well written, and organized so that the individual pupil can progress at his own rate. In addition, he should be guided to transfer his newly-acquired skills to new materials and situations.

One of the most difficult problems faced by elementary-school teachers is that of helping children to develop proficiency in solving arithmetic problems. In reviewing the research prior to 1944, Johnson has shown that there is much conflicting evidence. Two things did seem apparent however: slow learners seem to derive some benefit from prescribed methods of attacking problems, and providing the learner with some instruction in problem solving is better than no help at all.[7]

4. W. A. Brownell. When is arithmetic meaningful? *Journal of Educational Research*, 38:482, March, 1945.

5. B. R. Buckingham. What becomes of drill? *Arithmetic in General Education*, Washington: National Council of Mathematics Teachers, Sixteenth Yearbook, 1941, p. 197.

6. W. A. Brownell and Charlotte B. Chazel. The effects of premature drill in third grade arithmetic. *Journal of Educational Research*, 39:26, September, 1935.

7. H. C. Johnson. Problem solving in arithmetic: a review of the literature. *Elementary School Journal*, 44:481, May, 1944.

To examine the form that this instruction might take, it is interesting to make a direct examination of some of the studies. Sutherland states that ability to solve the problems used in his investigation appeared to consist of three factors of equal significance: general intelligence, a verbal factor, and a number factor. As number skill and verbal skill are acquired abilities, he claims it should be possible to achieve considerable improvement in the competence of children to solve problems.

One of Sutherland's findings which seem to be verified in several other studies is one which we might expect. Problems set in a familiar setting are easier for the child to solve. The children in Sutherland's study scored 36 per cent higher in problems of this type compared to problems set in an unfamiliar situation, but of the same difficulty. He concluded, "Since the object of education is to equip the child for life, and since only a very small minority will ever find themselves in an unfamiliar situation, it is reasonable to suppose we should concentrate on simple problems dealing with familiar material."[8] In this regard it is interesting to note that in examining the written problems which appeared in arithmetic texts, Dexter found that less than 1 per cent of all these problems could be described as real in the sense that they were pertinent to a child's experience and interest.[9]

One other factor that appears to have a bearing on the ability to solve problems is the extent of the pupil's mathematical vocabulary. Many of the studies concerned with this relationship have concluded that specific training in mathematical vocabulary will result in higher achievement in problem solving. As the result of a recent study at the University of Illinois, Teachers' College, Phillips concluded that, "More attention should be given to ideas and the words that convey them."[10]

In no other school subject is the matter of individual differences so apparent as in arithmetic. In one survey involving 519 eighth-grade pupils, grade-level scores were spread out over ten years. Eleven of the children were as far advanced as the first year of university, while some were still working at the fourth-grade level.[11]

Methods of dealing with individual differences in arithmetic are varied.

8.   John Sutherland. Investigations into some aspects of problem solving. *British Journal of Educational Psychology*, *12*:46, February, 1942.
9.   C. E. Dexter. Analysis of written problems in a recent arithmetic series. *Education*, *65*:489, April, 1945.
10.   C. Phillips. The relationship between arithmetic achievement and vocabulary of elementary mathematics. *The Arithmetic Teacher*, *7*:242, May, 1960.
11.   Stewart Jones and R. E. Pingry. Individual differences. *Instruction in Arithmetic*, Washington: National Council of Teachers of Mathematics, Twenty-fifth Yearbook, 1960, p. 142.

As with reading, grouping has been applied but with less success. Grouping in arithmetic, when used, should be of a periodic nature. It is suggested that the class as a whole should be taught new processes and that grouping should be utilized in the application and practice of what has been learned. Other means of providing for individual differences in the teaching of this subject include differentiating the pace, using concrete materials, reviewing and providing a variety of supplementary teaching aids. Research has shown that utilizing one or more of these devices will alleviate the problem to a worthwhile degree. One study illustrates the superiority of instruction based on individual diagnosis as compared with conventional group instruction.[12] Tilton, as the result of his study, suggests that even a relatively small amount of individualized instruction will produce significant results.[13] At the present time it would appear that the method most favored is the one whereby differentiation in instruction takes place on an individual basis. This together with the provision for different levels of work within the same area makes it possible to retain class unity.

In recent years increasing attention has been directed toward the place of mental arithmetic in the elementary school. The fact that daily living frequently requires a person to compute without the aid of pencil and paper suggests that our instructional practices in this area should be reappraised. One researcher, on examining ten sixth-grade arithmetic texts, failed to find the subject listed in the indices of six of them. The remaining four contained a paucity of information on this phase of the arithmetic program.

Hall has pointed out that mental arithmetic now has a broadened terminology. When he examined the fifth- and sixth-grade textbooks he found the subject listed under such headings as: sight problems, thinking without a pencil, write only the answers, and so on. Teachers should familiarize themselves with this new terminology and make certain their pupils clearly understand the terms used. Even with this broadened terminology taken into account, it is my personal belief that many teachers do not provide their pupils with sufficient instruction and practice. Unfortunately, the number of teachers who follow a prescribed text, page by page, is still considerable. If the text possesses a deficiency such as the omission of any mental arithmetic, the pupils are often deprived of any experience with this most useful skill.

Flournoy's study showed the effects of a fifty-two-day program on 550 pupils in the intermediate grades. The children were given a ten-to-twelve-

12.   Walter S. Guiler and Vernon Edwards. Experimental study of methods in computational arithmetic. *Elementary School Journal, 43*:360, February, 1943.
13.   John W. Tilton. Individual and meaningful instruction in arithmetic. *Journal of Educational Psychology, 38*, February, 1947.

minute lesson each day of the experiment. Not only did their ability to compute and solve problems without pencil and paper improve significantly, but their progress in written arithmetic was also highly satisfactory. In addition, their growth in arithmetic achievement as measured by standardized tests showed a gain of eight months in the fifty-two-day period. Similar results were obtained with teacher-made written tests.[14]

To the classroom teacher contemplating a similar program of mental arithmetic, one important factor should be kept in mind. Provision for practice in this area should be provided at various levels. The range of individual differences in this subject is considerable. When Hall presented fifty carefully selected mental arithmetic problems to 179 sixth-grade pupils, their scores ranged from two to forty-seven. He found that the correlation between achievement in this field and general intelligence was .74 and concluded that there are definite limits in the ability of dull children to solve complicated two- and three-step problems without pencil and paper.[15] Despite this limitation, however, mental arithmetic can and should play an important part in the arithmetic program of the elementary school. Flournoy has clearly demonstrated the value of such a program when it is conducted on a regular and carefully planned basis. The teacher who neglects this phase of arithmetic, or who turns to it only sporadically, is failing to provide his pupils with a worthwhile means of developing their arithmetic ability.

The research studies referred to suggest a number of guides for the teacher of elementary arithmetic. They may be briefly summarized as follows:

1. Desirable classroom practice in the teaching of arithmetic necessitates guiding children to acquire meanings. Meaning facilitates learning, retention, and transfer.
2. There is a place for practice in the arithmetic program. It should always be preceded by understanding.
3. Children's ability to solve problems will improve by (a) providing some definite instruction in problem-solving techniques, (b) setting the problems in meaningful situations, and (c) providing pupils with opportunities to develop their mathematical vocabularies.
4. Individual differences are greater in arithmetic than in any other subject. Utilizing one or more of the methods recommended for dealing with this problem will result in significantly higher achievement for the pupils.
5. A regular and carefully planned program of mental arithmetic provides a realistic preparation for the everyday use of arithmetic which the child encounters out of school. Improvement in mental arithmetic tends to improve ability in all phases of arithmetic.

14. Mary Frances Flournoy. The effectiveness of instruction in mental arithmetic. *Elementary School Journal,* 55:152, November, 1954.
15. Jack V. Hall. Solving verbal arithmetic problems without pencil and paper. *Elementary School Journal,* 48:235, December, 1947.

CHAPTER 15

Learning and Using Science

"In the early years of the decade 1960-70," writes one observer, "teachers of science in the elementary and secondary schools of the United States are witnessing ... 'the Revolution in Science Teaching.' "[1] A statement prepared by a committee for the National Science Teachers Association includes this passage about the intellectual goals of science education:

> The primary goals of science education should be intellectual. What is required is student involvement in an exploration of important ideas of science. The mental stimulation and satisfaction of exploring one's environment, learning about its past and probable future, examining man's role in the scheme of things, discovering one's own talents and interests—these are reasons enough for the study of science, just as they are for the study of most disciplines. Science is one of man's major intellectual accomplishments, a product of the mind which can be enjoyed—not for its material fruits alone but for the sense which it provides of the order in our universe.[2]

Memorization of lists will not help pupils to achieve such goals. How can pupils experience the sense which science provides of the order in our universe? How can they develop the courage and desire to face what is not yet known? How can we equip people intellectually, emotionally, and morally to make competent social and scientific decisions in fields of inquiry which have not been discovered yet?

1. Sidney Rosen. Innovation in science teaching—a historical view. *School Science and Mathematics, 63*:313, April, 1963.
2. The NSTA position on curriculum development in science. *The Science Teacher. 29*:32. December, 1962.

69   Research on the teaching of elementary-school science

PAUL C. BURNS

Before reading this article, ask yourself a few questions. With what kinds of questions will these reports on the teaching of elementary-school science deal? What kind of data will be sought? What conclusions might be drawn from a review of research studies in elementary science? Might any application be made to teaching science in your classroom?

IN THIS ARTICLE a brief review is presented of several studies at the elementary-science level which deal with instructional methods and procedures. It is hoped that many of our readers will be able to discover applications of some of the findings to their own teaching techniques.

A study was made of the effectiveness of two methods of teaching science in fourth, fifth, and sixth grades by Stefaniah to determine whether teachers taught by the lecture method did a more effective job than teachers exposed to the individual laboratory method.[1] Experimental and control groups of in-service teachers participated with the instructions centered around a list of forty principles of science. Pupils were pre- and post-tested to determine gains or losses in interests and content. Results seemed to favor teaching of those instructed by individual laboratory method, although the difference was not marked.

Baker studied the reactions of pupils to science experiments by conducting a series of experiments in grades three through six.[2] No explanation or comment was given during the experiment, but following it the children were asked, "What happened and why?" It was found that many pupils could interpret and generalize without help of the teacher.

An early study reported by Beauchamp sought to determine the relative efficiencies of two different methods of study, semi-directed study and directed study, of science materials. He came to the general conclusion:

Specific training in finding the central thought of a paragraph, determining the question one must be able to answer in order to obtain adequate under-

Reprinted from *The Science Teacher*, 27:48-49, March, 1960.

1. E. Stefaniah. A study of two methods of teaching science in grades 4, 5, 6. Unpublished doctor's dissertation, Boston University, Boston, Mass., 1955.
2. Tunis Baker. Effective uses of science experiments in elementary school. *NEA Addresses and Proceedings*, 79:584-85, 1941.

standing of a topic, and reading an entire block of material through for its general plan, results in a more thorough comprehension of subject matter than undirected study on the same material.[3]

Robertson carried out an experiment to compare the relative effectiveness of a "guidance-outline" method and a "developmental-discussion" method.[4] He selected six units of work and then taught one group by the developmental-discussion method in which discussion was based on the children's interest. He taught the other group by guidance. With guidance, the children worked individually receiving aid when needed. Groups were equated on basis of reading ability and previous science achievement, and other necessary factors were held constant. In addition, the groups rotated during the course of the experiment. The groups were tested for immediate and delayed recall; the developmental-discussion group did slightly better on both tests.

Haupt reported the results of an experimental study in which a philosophy of science education, as set forth in the Thirty-first Yearbook of the National Society for the Study of Education, was applied.[5] He selected one objective of instruction (consideration of energy relationships between sun and green plants) and used it as a basis of teaching. He equated and pretested groups of children in grades one through six, instructing them in respect to the objectives. Then he retested them. He concluded that the same instructional objective could be used at all grade levels; that the same mental activities occur at all levels, differing only in complexity; and that children generalize at all levels.

Should science be integrated with other elementary-school subjects? Mallinson made an analysis of elementary science and geography books to discover what similarities existed in the two subject matter areas.[6] He found that similarity did exist in the areas of agriculture, air, earth as a planet, forest, fishing, and mining. He felt that where similarity exists, the two subjects could be properly integrated.

Integration of science with mathematics at the seventh- and eighth-grade

3.   Wilbur Beauchamp. A preliminary experimental study of techniques in master of subject-matter in elementary physical science. *Studies in Secondary Education I, Supplementary Educational Monographs 24,* The University of Chicago, Chicago, Ill., January, 1923.
4.   Martin Robertson. Study of effectiveness of two methods of teaching elementary science. Unpublished doctor's dissertation. University of Michigan, Ann Arbor, Mich., 1930.
5.   George W. Haupt. An experimental application of a philosophy of science teaching in elementary school. *Science Education, 28:*234-38, December, 1934.
6.   George Mallinson. Relationship between work of elementary science and geography teachers. *Journal of Geography, 44:*206-10, May, 1950.

levels was investigated by Gorman.[7] He selected a science and mathematics text and from them determined common topics of study. For the experimental group, he constructed a workbook consisting of common problems and activities. The control group studied science and mathematics independently but covered the same topics. The groups were equated and the results of the study, based on achievement test scores, indicated no appreciable difference in efficiency of the two methods of instruction.

How effective are various multisensory aids? Greene reported a comparative study of efficiency of dramatic and nondramatic methods in teaching science to fifth-grade children. In the experiment two plays were used as teaching procedures, teacher-written ones and pupil-written ones. The control groups used their usual procedures. He concluded:

> Children learn factual information only slightly, if any, more rapidly when taught by a dramatic rather than by a nondramatic method, but the following desirable learnings developed more strongly: speech arts; poise; group organization; social interplay.[8]

Silano conducted an experiment to test results of using drawings as learning aids. He selected two groups of seventh-graders and tested them and determined their knowledge of airplanes.[9] One group was given instruction about planes in a traditional manner; the other group was given usual instruction and in addition was taught to draw a well-proportioned airplane. The two groups were again tested and the experimental group missed fewer questions. One fault of this study, however, was the failure to equate groups at the beginning of the study.

The value of radio broadcasts has been studied. Carpenter reported two studies.[10] In the first he described the results of an experiment in teaching science by radio in the Rochester School of the Air. The radio broadcast followed a prescribed course of study, twice per week for one semester, thirty minutes in length, followed by twenty minutes of class discussion. Results of final achievement tests administered to "radio" class and "traditional" class indicated that "radio" class did only as well as "traditional" class.

7. Frank Gorman. An experiment in integrating seventh- and eighth-grade science and mathematics. *Science Education, 27*: 130-34, December, 1943.
8. Robert Greene. A comparative study of efficiency of dramatic and nondramatic methods in teaching science to fifth-grade children. Unpublished doctor's dissertation, Cornell University, Ithaca, N.Y., 1937.
9. Alfred Silano. The drawing as a learning aid in science. *Science Education, 34*: 51-55, February, 1950.
10. Harry A. Carpenter. Science on Rochester School of the Air. *Science Education, 21*: 77-81, April, 1937.

On the other hand, Brewer worked with experimental and control groups in New York City in testing radio as an aid to instruction in elementary science.[11] He used five broadcasts on certain concepts of nature. With elaborate statistical techniques he secured the results that radio programs do serve as definite stimulus to further activities. Miles came to the same conclusion when the broadcast had been planned carefully and taught specifically as in the experiment designs procedure.[12]

Recorded science lessons were reported by Carpenter.[13] Forty science lessons, ten minutes in length, were recorded. These were heard by approximately 11,000 children. A science interest test was given at the beginning and end as well as a science achievement test. From the results, records appeared functional in increasing factual knowledge, skills, and interests.

Martin carried on a study to discover relationships of "community resources and use of the tape recorder." The tape recorder was a very satisfactory and successful aid in teaching, he concluded from his study.[14]

What summary, in the form of trends and conclusions, may be made at this time relative to research and its implication in the elementary-school science area?

1. There appears to be of recent date an increased proportion of learning studies as opposed to curricular studies in the field of elementary science.

2. Since the early studies there has been marked progress in the refinement of statistical procedure used in the studies.

3. Studies would appear to indicate that efficient teaching of science demands definitely organized experiences, rather than reliance on incidental methods.

4. Most studies favor organization of science around cores of subject matter, supplementing instruction by means of demonstration, discussion, drawing, and experiments. Data from several studies would appear to strengthen the case for a greater laboratory approach at the elementary level. Availability of material no doubt has some effect upon the type of instruction typically used.

11. Lyle Brewer. Radio as aid to instruction in elementary science. *Science Education, 23*:63-68, February, 1939.
12. Robert J. Miles. Evaluation of broadcasts and recordings for the science classroom. *Science Education, 25*:205-6, April, 1941.
13. Harry A. Carpenter. An experiment with recorded science lessons. *Science Education, 24*:181-86, April, 1940.
14. Evelyn Martin. Community resources and tape recorders. *Teaching Tools,* 111: 68, Spring, 1956.

5. As yet there appears to be no final experimental evidence to indicate the value of integration of science with other elementary subjects.

6. Research seems to indicate that multi-sensory devices are helpful in developing interest and possibly toward increasing pupil factual knowledge of science. An additional value is their help to elementary teachers who may lack subject matter background in the field of science.

7. Major emphases in the past few years in elementary-science research appear to be in the field of audio-visual aids and other such devices to learn more about teachers' ability to gain pupil interest.

8. There appears to be a great deal of research still needed with respect to teaching of scientific attitudes and problem-solving skills. Although these are accepted as major objectives of science instruction, it would appear that most teaching still centers around dissemination of factual information, even where problem or unit approach is mainly used. Another area that needs investigation is that of proper use of laboratory exercises.

9. No significant advantage of any one method over another has been definitely proved. All methods are valuable if properly used. While some procedures are superior in a given situation, in general, they all have value at one time or another. Selective use of many techniques is probably still the most advantageous procedure for the teacher.

70   *Fifth-graders explore the atom*

ROBERT L. SHRIGLEY

A class of fifth-graders, after overcoming their teacher's initial scepticism, sought answers to their own questions about the atom, not those prefabricated for them by adults. Note how the teacher guided their study.

Reprinted from *The Elementary School Journal*, 59:277-81, February, 1959, by permission of The University of Chicago Press. Copyright 1959 by the University of Chicago.

THE TEACHER was skeptical. Study the atom in fifth grade?

Maybe in high school. Maybe in college. But in fifth grade?

The children were not to be dissuaded. They wanted to know about atoms. There was no mistaking their interest and enthusiasm.

With atomic-powered airplanes in blueprint, with atomic electric plants under construction, and atomic submarines a reality, the children's curiosity was aroused. They would be satisfied with nothing less than an introduction to the discoveries that had opened wide the doors of a new age.

The children were well aware of the difficulties ahead.

"You'll have to work without textbooks," the class was told. "Very few textbooks for fifth-graders mention atoms."

The warning did not discourage the young scientists.

"We can go to the library and ask the librarian for help. She'll find books for us."

The children's trust was well placed. The librarian did find material on atomic energy written in language that boys and girls could understand. The young researchers gathered up what books they could from the shelves of the public library and then proceeded to raid the school library and neighboring classrooms. We soon had a proud stockpile of thirty-five books and pamphlets and enough illustrations for a bulletin board.

ATOMIC-AGE QUESTIONS

For several class periods, the children browsed through their collection of reading material. When they came to a passage that puzzled them, they jotted down their question. One day in class we listed all the queries.

How small is an atom? How do scientists know the structure of an atom? What makes electrons spin around the center of the atom? What keeps the atom together? How do atoms of various elements differ? What are man-made elements? What is an isotope? What is a Geiger counter? Why are some elements radioactive? How do scientists split the atom? How do atoms produce heat? How does the X-ray machine in the doctor's office work? How can nuclear energy be used constructively? How can we protect ourselves from atomic attack?

The questions were all the children's, though the teacher had several of his own.

How to find answers? We could have divided the queries and assigned a committee to work on each set. But the class voted against the idea.

Many questions were complex, so complex that they warranted the attention of the whole class, the pupils felt. We agreed that the teacher would decide which questions would be studied by the class as a whole and which would be delegated to individuals or small groups. The difficulty of the question and the amount of reference material on hand entered into his decision.

How do atoms produce heat? How can we protect ourselves from atomic attack? Questions like these, the teacher decided, were too complicated for a small group to tackle.

What is a Geiger counter? What is an isotope? Questions like these—that is, questions that called for short, factual answers—were turned over to individuals or small committees.

The class felt that a bulletin board might be useful and that experiments might be necessary. We decided to assign these activities to committees.

So we set to work. The children read books, pamphlets, and newspapers. They sifted information, took notes, and wrote brief reports. Early in their research they learned to scan an index or a table of contents. The skill proved useful for tracking down facts quickly.

The information gathered from the reading found its way into class discussions. Throughout the unit we had plenty of lively talk as the children discussed their plans, described their findings, or analyzed newspaper items on nuclear energy.

SYMBOLS OF SCIENCE

We wanted the class discussions to be as clear and as vivid as possible. Here simple sketches helped. The children became fairly skilled at explaining blackboard sketches. Before the end of the unit, pupils who were giving reports could turn from the class to the blackboard and illustrate for the audience the theoretical structure of such simple atoms as hydrogen, helium, and oxygen.

During the unit, the children learned something of the art of talking. Each pupil was reminded of his responsibility for being prepared to contribute to the discussions. The children were encouraged not to lean on the teacher for all their information.

During the unit, the class also learned something of the rarer art of listening. Since none of our textbooks had information on atomic energy, the children's reading was scattered. No two pupils read exactly the same material. As a result, the children had different backgrounds of information. The children realized that they could learn much by listening to their classmates.

We came to understand that the atom is very small. It is sometimes compared to a miniature solar system.

Originally the word "atom" meant "indivisible." But today we know that the atom can be divided or split.

We learned that the atom has many parts. We considered the nucleus with the proton, which has a positive charge; the neutron, which is neutral; and the electron, which spins around the nucleus and has a negative charge.

UNLOCKING THE POWER

The energy of the atom may be released by splitting the nucleus. Though we commonly speak of "atomic energy," the expression "nuclear energy" is actually more precise, since the energy we speak of is concerned with the nucleus, or center, of the atom.

In chain reaction, a neutron is fired at a nucleus. When the nucleus splits, part of the matter becomes energy, other elements are formed, and excess neutrons are emitted. They, in turn, bombard other atoms. This action forms more neutrons and liberates more energy. The element used to produce a chain reaction is usually uranium or some other very heavy element that disintegrates easily.

To demonstrate a chain reaction, we arranged a bank of dominos upright in a triangular pattern. When we knocked over the domino at the tip of the triangle, the two dominos in the second row fell. They, in turn, pushed over the three dominos in the next row, and so on until the entire bank had fallen over.

Nuclear energy, we learned, can be controlled in an atomic furnace, or a nuclear reactor, where energy is liberated more slowly than in an atomic blast. One method involves the use of graphite in the atomic pile to slow the chain reaction.

Radioactivity, or the emission of rays or particles from such unstable elements as uranium and radium, captured our interest. We were intrigued by the idea that the rate of radioactivity helps scientists estimate the age of the earth.

Watches with luminous dials were brought to class to show a common example of radioactivity. We were not able to get a Geiger counter. The device would have been useful to demonstrate the reaction of the instrument to the radioactivity of the watch dials.

ATOMIC-AGE QUANDARY

In connection with radioactivity, we talked of the hazards of radioactive materials and the many precautions that people who work with these materials must take. We took up the serious problem of the disposal of "worn-out" uranium, radioactive clothing, and tools. It has been suggested that we dispose of these "leftovers" by hurling them into space.

Throughout the unit we stressed the constructive aspects of nuclear energy. We noted that our knowledge of the atom and nuclear energy is the result of cooperation. It has taken years of study, hard work, and experimentation by scientists of many nations to give us today's knowledge of nuclear energy.

We did discuss the possibility of nuclear attack and protection from the effects of an atomic blast. The children displayed neither fear nor defeatism but faced this world problem in an alert and practical manner.

In our exploration of the atom, we made liberal use of the basic skills. Though the unit offered many opportunities to integrate these skills, lesson plans also provided generously for direct teaching.

We have already described the reading and the class discussions in connection with the study.

WORDS OF A NEW AGE

We used arithmetic to help get an idea of how infinitely small the atom is. In spelling class, the children studied such words as: *atom, nuclear, radiation, civil defense, neutrons, protons, electrons, radioactive, fission, matter, elements, cyclotrons.*

The spelling of these technical words did not get as much attention as common everyday words. Each pupil gave some thought to the technical vocabulary, since the words were often used in written work. The more capable pupils voluntarily learned the spelling of the technical words.

We found it necessary to read maps in connection with the study. The children located the fateful cities of Hiroshima and Nagasaki, the first wartime targets of atom bombs. The class also noted the location of deposits of uranium ore and ores of other elements.

As a language-arts activity, the class wrote and mimeographed a nine-page illustrated booklet on nuclear energy. The pamphlet listed questions raised by the children and presented brief reports they had written on such topics as radiation, chain reaction, civil defense, and the disposal of radioactive waste.

The children took exceptional pride in the pamphlet. Each child designed a cover for his own copy. Extra copies were distributed to interested teachers and curriculum centers.

Two movies from the Atomic Energy Commission proved very informative.

We spent about five weeks on the unit, devoting from fifteen to forty-five minutes a day to the subject. The periods were flexible. The length depended on the activity scheduled. On any one day, we used the time we needed and no more.

VISIT FROM A SPECIALIST

The children asked many puzzling questions—as children in science classes often do—questions for which we could find no answers. Obviously we needed to turn to an expert. We decided to invite a physics teacher to visit the class. The children saved their unanswered questions for the guest specialist.

During his visit, which was set for the last session of the unit, the children poured out their questions. The visitor gave carefully considered replies to each query and cleared up several misconceptions. For example, he drew attention to the fact that we were really studying, not atomic energy, but energy locked in the nucleus of the atom—nuclear energy.

The visit was a high point in the study. The children rated the talk, which closed our study of the atom, as the most interesting activity of all.

Looking back on our unit, I see other ways that I could have handled the material. The study of nuclear energy could have been part of a broader unit on energy, which could have included electrical energy, and other forms of energy.

Our study dealt only with fission or the splitting of the nucleus of the atom. The study might also have included fusion, or the combining of atoms to form more complex atoms.

In a large city, civil defense workers could be invited to demonstrate the Geiger counter.

The fifth-graders in this particular class were intensely interested in this timely subject. The children proved to their teacher that boys and girls in elementary school can understand fairly complex scientific concepts. Still, it is doubtful that the study of this area of science should be required for fifth-graders who have only a passive interest in the subject.

The experience was a thoroughly enjoyable one for the children and for the teacher, who learned along with the children. It should be added that science is by no means a masculine subject. The girls in the class were as interested as the boys and learned as easily.

THE UNANSWERED QUERIES

Some questions that the children raised were not answered for the simple reason that the questions were unanswerable. The circumstance was not without advantages. Perhaps children should know that the world they live in abounds with unanswered questions.

The unit on the atom was not planned as a regular part of the science program. The teacher guided the study, but the children launched it. Perhaps we have here one reason why many pupils rated our exploration of the atom as the year's most successful science adventure.

71   *Quantitative science in the making*

RALPH S. VRANA

This report describes a program in quantitative science—or is it science-centered mathematics? Does it matter what it's called? I'm sure you will agree that the topic, or "content," is important for today's boys and girls.

A CONSIDERABLE proportion of the mathematics training in college is directed toward its application in science. Is it possible to make this connection between science and mathematics and give major emphasis to the teaching of arithmetic in the elementary and junior high school? If this connection is made apparent to the student, will it help him learn the concepts of arithmetic, or will it hinder him? In a search to increase the quantitative aspect of science the conclusion has been drawn that much of the material presented could, with little alteration, be placed in the arithmetic period. On this basis, an experimental program was developed as a *science-centered* arithmetic course. The cooperation of parents and staff at the New Lincoln School, New York City, working together for four years in an effort to strengthen the school's curriculum, has been a contributory factor. The results of this laboratory-centered science program for Grades 3 through 8 are given herein. Other parents and educators thinking along this line, may wish to use this material in developing science or mathematics programs, or may wish to exchange ideas with the author. The steps which follow are suggested:

Reprinted from *The Science Teacher*, 30:37, 41, May, 1963.

1. This is basically arithmetic with science content. The effort will be directed by capitalizing on the interest that students in the upper-elementary grades show in science. Science materials will be used to make clear such mathematical concepts as ratio, percentage, generation of curves, coordinate systems, cyclic phenomena, volume, etc. Currently, all areas of mathematics are being searched, for whatever connections they might have to certain fields of science. Likewise, each field of science is searched for quantitative material which can be introduced into the program. The regular science period may be dropped for those classes getting science-centered arithmetic, or both subjects be organized together such as is now done in social studies which combines history and geography. The basic purpose is to experiment with arithmetic and the schedule may be built around whatever serves this purpose.

2. The arithmetic work is strongly oriented toward individual experimentation. The difficulty of achieving this aim has not been overlooked. But unless laboratory work is well planned and rigorously followed (not that the students need be any more rigorous than their maturity permits them), the program would not be much different than the arithmetic program in schools now. Today, the arithmetic text is used in the basic method of teaching arithmetic. It can be used alone, and the student needs to supply only pencil and paper. It is expected that a new text which cannot be used alone will be developed, inasmuch as the work it includes will have to be done by experiment. The modern science text is beginning to adopt this approach. To make it the central one in arithmetic is the goal. As a boy holds a stethoscope to a white rat's chest, he is discovering that the rat's heart beats rapidly. This is considered science learning. Yet if he measures the number of times the rat's heart beats in one minute and compares this with his own, he is learning arithmetic. There is also a simple means for class viewing of the human heartbeat and of measuring its rate at various times. This is done with a slide or filmstrip projector. A glass U-tube (open type) with colored water in it, is placed between a light source and lens barrel and then focused. One end is connected to a rubber hose, which joins a plastic thistle tube, held against the subject's neck at the jugular. Such learnings should have more impact than a statement of fact that hearts of various animals beat at different rates.

3. Use of simple equipment is a necessity. In order for a class of students to work effectively, the work areas must be fairly small. Some changes in furniture and room design at our school have permitted easier laboratory work in science. The same procedure is of value in planning the arithmetic program. Wherever possible, tables are set against walls so that students working there will be out of the way. Simple, old, flat-topped tables are an asset in keeping materials from sliding off onto the floor. The floor plan of the room used makes it possible to handle twenty-seven students for laboratory work situations with room to spare. If the room is large enough, it is worthwhile to "build in" a nook, by adding a wall which extends a short way into the room, so that more wall and shelf space may be obtained. Such a wall need not extend to the ceiling. Much of the work will not require sinks, or Bunsen burners, etc., but every subtraction of such items reduces the flexibility of the room. Each table is equipped with a "cross rig" of two pipes and a wooden crossbar from which the student can hang springs, pulleys, or pendulums. The cross rigs consist of a one-half-inch iron pipe with reinforced crossbar into which hooks are screwed and apparatus suspended. The pipes are screwed into floor flanges, set *under* the tabletop. They can be readily disassembled by students and stored in a shelf immediately under the tabletop when not in use. Details of construction are shown in the figure.

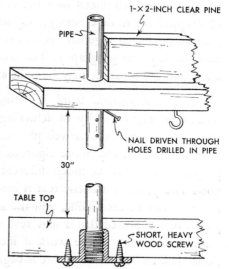

Other simple materials for use in the program include: T squares (a plastic variety satisfactory for this work is obtainable in a variety store), protractors, thermometers, weights, springs, pulleys, wheels, and scales. Even ink is useful. (If two drops of ink are added to varying quantities of water a set of standard concentrations can be made up by the student for measuring the concentration of an unknown ink.)

4. Follow-up work is necessary in this program. Experimentation and drill are both important. If emphasis is placed on experimentation, how will there be time for the student to learn that body of mathematical knowledge which he is expected to learn in the elementary school? In answering this question, there is no denying the need to practice as well as to perform. A series of exercises which are based on the experimental work will have to be developed. If the student has experimented with the appearance of a round surface when it is projected onto a flat one, he has begun to understand the rudiments of map making. (Such experimentation may take a few weeks, and may need to be continued each year.) With such an understanding he should be able to go on to a more complete understanding of maps, which can be done by exercises related to the work he has done in class. These exercises include the construction of several simple maps using the formulae developed in the experimental work. It should be noted also that the "body of knowledge" which comprises elementary-school arithmetic is certainly less comprehensive than that body of knowledge in science which lends itself to measurement by the elementary-school pupil.

Some specific examples of ideas used in developing quantitative relationships follow:

a. Measurement of lung capacity (normal and deep breathing).
b. Chromatography measurements with blotter and ink.
c. Distortion studies by means of lenses, mechanical linkages, and plotting these on graph paper.
d. Use of carpenter levels and other tools in understanding geometrical ideas.
e. Measuring fields of view through various lengths of straws.
f. Use of transparent lined sheets placed over one another to form various grid systems.
g. The study of reflections in hinged mirrors.
h. The study of one-way action in valves.
i. Quantitative measurements in osmotic pressure.
j. Mechanical resonance with stroboscope and measuring of vibrations of a tuning fork.
k. Verniers of two ruled lines on a sheet which are cut and adjusted for measuring small lengths.
l. Micrometers made from bolts.
m. Acoustical tile and pegs for graph plotting.
n. Mobius strips from adding machine paper.
o. A study of latitude and longitude with equatorially mounted "straw" telescopes made with milk cartons and wire.
p. Refraction measurements with prisms.
q. Volume measurements with sugar cubes.

It is helpful to look through the science and mathematics teachers' magazines to locate what another teacher has found successful. Frequently when an article describes a demonstration device, this can be adapted by simplification into something which students can make themselves, or can be made in quantity for them. Since each student experiments, there are problems of space, finances, and simplicity, which have to be solved. Some of the ideas mentioned above can be worked over for unsuspected quantitative aspects. These actually are not hard to find, since everything a person does, he does "to a certain degree." Efforts by staff and parents have brought more quantitative work into the elementary-school science program at our school. Where such work was introduced, the program gained. No attempt was made to prove this gain quantitatively. Moreover, relationships are being sought between science and mathematics and in such an attempt, the teachers themselves are faced with the task of answering in a quantitative way, "How effective *is* arithmetic when it is taught this way?"

☙

72   *Structuring an elementary-school science program*

A L P H O R E T T A   S .   F I S H

The meaning of structure is considered in the articles in Chapter 27; some readers may prefer to read those articles before this one. The author suggests that science be considered a skill subject in the way that reading, arithmetic, or spelling are. From this viewpoint, what skills would you say pupils should gain from an elementary-school science program?

TRADITIONALLY, science curriculums have emphasized subject-matter areas. But science is not a study of areas. Rather it is a process or a method involving a search for environmental relationships and the fundamental principles through which these relationships can be explained and understood.

Science is based on a fundamental structure that embraces all natural phenomena, including the child himself, in a dynamic relationship that involves matter, energy, and change. It seems natural, then, to suggest that the study of science be directed toward developing the child's awareness of this fundamental structure.

Bruner suggests four advantages of emphasizing the fundamental structure of a subject:

1. Understanding fundamentals makes a subject more comprehensible.
2. Unless detail is placed into a structured pattern, it is rapidly forgotten.
3. An understanding of fundamental principles and ideas appears to be the main road to adequate "transfer of training."
4. By constantly reexamining material taught in elementary and secondary

Reprinted from *The Elementary School Journal,* 63:277-80, February, 1963, by permission of The University of Chicago Press. Copyright 1963 by the University of Chicago.

schools for its fundamental character, one is able to narrow the gap between "advanced" knowledge and "elementary" knowledge.[1]

Still another advantage of this approach may be cited. The curriculum that is designed to develop an understanding of, and an insight into, the relationships underlying all natural phenomena, reveals to the learner the past, present, and future dimensions of science. Such insight is basic to an adequate understanding of the self as an entity in the environment and is prerequisite to understanding man's relationship to his total environment.

In the end, however, it is the teaching methods used and the structure of the learning environment that determine whether insight into basic relationships is likely to develop. Furthermore, the teaching methods used depend a great deal on whether the subject matter is thought of as a content subject or a skill subject.

Science has customarily been considered a content subject rather than a skill subject. There seems to be psychological acceptance of the fact that the teacher's primary task in teaching a content subject is to guide the pupils in terms of what to remember. In teaching a skill subject, her primary task is to guide the pupils to discover how to learn and how to function.

Arithmetic and reading have long been considered skill subjects. The child who is attending elementary school is expected to learn how to read and how to do arithmetic by experiencing the reading act and the arithmetical operations. Furthermore, the child learns how to use these skills without being expected to remember every arithmetic problem he has ever worked or every story he has ever read.

Pupils use these skills as a functional part of their everyday living and learning. Furthermore, the skill processes that pupils employ as they read and do arithmetic do not differ markedly from the skill processes that other members of society employ as they read and use arithmetic throughout their lifetime.

Yet in science the child's energies are generally directed not toward skill development but toward remembering facts, principles, and generalizations that he has heard the teacher tell about or that he has read about in a textbook. In addition, in science the child is often expected to remember the name of every living and nonliving thing he has ever studied about.

Is it any wonder that science has not become a functional part of the lives of today's pupils as the other skill subjects have? Is it any wonder that

1.   Jerome S. Bruner. *The Process of Education,* Cambridge, Mass.: Harvard University Press, 1960, pp. 23-26.

the skills and methods pupils use in acquiring a knowledge of science facts, principles, and skills differ sharply from the methods scientists use in their search for new knowledge? If science is to become functional, it must be experienced, and it must be experienced as a skill subject.

The idea of teaching science as an intellectual activity in which the child attempts to explain or "read" environmental phenomena is in complete accord with the manner in which the child learns about his environment naturally. The child can be thought of as an energy system that directs its energies toward solving problems encountered in an ongoing effort to identify himself as an entity.

As the child experiences his environment and then evaluates his experiences, the environment serves as a point of reference—a measuring stick. Gradually and systematically the child formulates a body of generalized truths against which he assesses himself and his actions.

However, as the child—a complex energy system with an ever-changing, ever-expanding base of experience—interacts with his environment—which is, similarly, a complex, ever-changing energy system—his previously formulated truths often develop apparent discontinuities. New ideas are formulated that conflict with present beliefs. It is at this point that the child directs his energies to explaining and clarifying apparent discontinuities and modifies and extends his concepts.

In experiencing problem-solving, the child employs quite naturally, at one time or another, all the skills employed by the scientist: observing, comparing, interpreting, organizing, hypothesizing, analyzing, evaluating, describing, explaining, experimenting, testing, and generalizing. The child's behavior reflects his tested experience; hence learning has occurred.

When the teacher presents science as a skill subject, she is accommodating the child's natural *modus operandi*. What is more, when the teacher structures the learning environment to emphasize the development of skills, she, too, is on familiar ground. For the procedures used in teaching science as a skill subject are consistent with the procedures used in teaching reading, writing, spelling, and arithmetic.

We should remind ourselves also that teachers of skill subjects have discovered that the subject matter of a skill subject can serve as a medium for the development of skills and at the same time provide a rich source for the development of concepts.

As the teacher guides the child, step by step, through the structure of a skill subject, new knowledge and skills are built upon the old in much the same manner that man's knowledge of the subject has developed over the ages. In a sense, the teacher guides the child to relive the structure of subject matter; and in doing so she sees the child's understanding of basic relationships and of science method progress through successively advanced stages. Concomitantly, the teacher sees the child become increasingly independent and effective in his thinking and doing.

Furthermore, the rationale of teaching and learning science can be designed to emphasize structure and skill development, and at the same time provide for the acquisition of scientific knowledge, emotional satisfaction, and insight into how one's learning takes place. But if these goals are to be realized, it is necessary to provide the child with daily opportunities to experience science as a method of bringing meaning to the environment.

Science knowledge and skills are most meaningful to the child when he discovers them for himself. When the child discovers, he is proving to himself that his findings serve to fulfill or to reject a hypothesis. It is this proving to oneself that brings into being an insight that is original and that carries with it all the emotional impact of any original discovery.

The teacher who provides for discovery-learning is aware that she is nurturing pupil self-realization. For she provides opportunity for the pupil to evaluate his learning experience and thus discover that he is learning and that learning is emotionally satisfying. She helps the pupil see a relationship between learning, responsibility, self-discipline, and increased independent action.

In directing science experiences, the teacher of elementary-school science applies techniques used in the other skill subjects. Often she promotes dynamic learning and discovery by guiding the child to organize the data of his past experiences and thus extend and broaden his conceptual base.

For example, the teacher can help the child recall what he knows about environmental change in the weather, in night and day, in the seasons, and in plant and animals. By helping the child recall this information and organize it into a broader pattern, the teacher can plan a science lesson to develop the pupil's awareness of change. Such a lesson can add dimension to the child's concept of change. He may discover, for instance, that change is rhythmic and orderly, that change is universal, that it is a phenomenon that results from the interaction of matter and energy.

The teacher of elementary-school science may plan to guide the child to discovery by prearranging situations that present discontinuities that demand clarification and explanation.

For example, the teacher may assemble two sets of materials to be tested with magnets. One set may include a plastic thimble. Another set may include a steel thimble. Thus the stage is set for the question: "Do magnets attract thimbles?" Obviously a discontinuity will present itself. The ensuing problem-solving activities should be designed to direct the child to discover something about energy and molecular alignment, poles and magnetic fields; to learn the meaning of insufficient evidence and suspended judgment; and to gain some understanding of the difference between the concept of *finding* and the concept of *conclusion.*

Under this approach, the teacher of elementary-school science consistently guides the child to associate the familiar with the unfamiliar. She encourages the child to use this technique to discover new concepts, to extend new concepts to entities not previously identified or categorized, and to understand how learning takes place. For example, by helping the child associate a familiar concept like "copper" with the fact that copper contains only one kind of matter and is an element, the teacher can plan to help the child discover the new concept of "element." She can help him develop the hypothesis that materials such as lead, gold, silver, and iron are also elements. She can help him realize that elements are influenceed by energy in various ways and to varying degrees. She can help him see that learning evolves from reasoned guesses (hypotheses) that must be checked.

Finally, the teacher of elementary-school science who sees science as a skill subject regularly provides appropriate firsthand experiences to insure adequate understanding. She gives the children regular opportunities to observe likenesses, differences, detail, cause-and-effect relationships; to experiment; to classify.

In directing science experiences, the child should be involved in a problem which he has identified and toward which he has chosen to direct his energies. In each instance, it is he who should generalize the discoveries.

It seems reasonable to propose that a content as rich as that of science should function as a medium for the development of skills. This content should, at the same time, be used to guide the child to extend, to clarify, and to refine his concepts concerning the environment by guiding him to systematically examine the significant variables operating in environmental change. Moreover, science experiences should be designed to guide the child to reflect upon and to evaluate various methods of problem-solving in an effort to help him discover and value the precision, objectivity, and relative dependability of scientific thinking and scientific method. Finally, science experiences should guide the child to reflect upon and to evaluate his discoveries about the environment. It is thus that the child learns to value the rhythm, beauty, and challenge in his world.

73 *Women teachers' attitudes toward science in the*

classroom

VIVIAN EDMISTON TODD

Teachers' attitudes and behavior constitute some of the most signif-
icant learning stimuli in elementary-school classrooms. This article
deals with these attitudes and offers suggestions to teachers.

THE ATTITUDES of the woman teacher in the elementary school determine to a considerable extent her effectiveness in teaching science to the boys and girls in her class. The beliefs which underlie, and are expressed in, her behavior are reflected in how and what her pupils learn.

Consider, for instance, what Johnny learns when he comes rushing in one rainy morning with an earthworm dangling from his fist. "Teacher, do you know what? I found this on the sidewalk!" Johnny feels that he is bringing a prize to share with his teacher, but she may feel quite differently about it. "Ugh! A dirty old worm that I don't know anything about," she may say to herself. As she goes after a container for the worm, she says aloud, "So you found a worm on your way to school." She tries to register proper interest, but her tone of voice reveals her feelings, "I hope he won't find any more things to bother me." Johnny might have learned that the worms which come out of the earth when it rains are fascinating to observe. Instead he learned that his teacher does not like him to bring worms to school.

SOURCES OF TEACHER ATTITUDES

Women teachers' attitudes toward science grow out of their training and experience in modern society. Although most women teachers may appreciate the importance of science and its achievements, their experience as members of the feminine segment of society and of what is termed the "middle class" may produce certain attitudes which interfere with their ability and desire to teach science effectively.

For instance, the lack of interest of most women in studying science stems in part from feminine and middle-class mores. The woman teacher who is interested in taking courses in science is the exception rather than the rule. Mallinson describes the situation:

> The vast majority of the studies in this field point to the discouraging fact that most elementary-school teachers have had little or no training in science; the training they do possess is of little value in their work with elementary-school children; and, as a result of their lack of training, they "shy away" from teaching science.[1]

Women teachers who do not know the scope of science feel that it is a masculine activity. They have noted that the leaders in such fields as atomic research, space ships, man-made earth satellites, and the manufacture of explosives are men, and it is men, too, who repair television sets, household appliances, and automobiles. Since these teachers identify science as a field for men, not women, they feel that a woman makes herself conspicuous by showing interest or proficiency in such studies, and they do not want to make themselves conspicuous.

However, the feminine world embraces a great deal of science. Cooking, washing, and house-cleaning are applications of science. Gardening, care of pets, and other outdoor activities of children and grown-ups involve science. The woman teacher who really understands the part that science plays in her daily activities and those of her pupils is well prepared for teaching this subject. The content of science courses for prospective teachers should be reviewed from the standpoint of its usefulness in the daily lives of teachers and pupils, and the courses should be taught so that teachers want more science. Workshops for teachers in service should develop awareness of the place of science in everyday living and encourage favorable attitudes toward this area of learning. It is necessary that the elementary-school teacher want to know more about science, and it is important that an inquiring attitude be developed in training and in service.

As a woman the teacher may find it easy to use feminine "logic" rather than scientific reasoning. When Mary brings her pet kitten to school, the teacher may say: "Oh, what a dear little kitty! You know, I had a black and white kitty when I was a little girl. It . . ."

But the teacher who is looking for an opening for a lesson in science can say: "We'll have fun watching what the kitty does with its tongue when it eats. What food shall we get for it?"

The teacher can learn to drop the traditional feminine reaction to shriek-

1. Jacqueline Buck Mallinson. What research in science education is needed to strengthen the elementary-school science program? *Science Education,* 40:369-71, December, 1956.

ing and jumping on a chair when a mouse appears. Instead she can now show genuine interest in how the mouse carries on its life. But, to make this change, the teacher must first realize what her attitudes are, why she has them, and how they may be changed.

The middle-class teacher has deep admiration for the new and the shiny, an intense appreciation of cleanliness, and a high regard for good housekeeping standards. Science activities in the classroom are often at variance with these values. When a light bulb is brought to school, it is likely to be old and blackened, and the pets that come are "messy." The teacher finds herself torn between her responsibilities in teaching science and the admonitions of her mother: "Keep your dress clean, and don't get your hands dirty!" The teacher needs to recognize and resolve this conflict. If she ignores it, she may be one of those teachers who, somehow or other, never find time to get much science-teaching into the class schedule.

The teacher who realizes that she is avoiding the teaching of science is in a position to do something about it. She can encourage her pupils to develop their science interests, and she can become an enthusiastic learner along with them. When, for example, Johnny brings a jumpy frog to school, she can say frankly, "You know, Johnny, I really don't know much about frogs, but maybe some of the other children do, and probably we can find what people have written about them in books. Our friend, the high-school biology teacher, can help us, too. We'll have fun finding out what the frog eats and how he lives."

TEACHERS' ATTITUDES AND PUPILS' INTERESTS

The way in which a teacher responds to a classroom science situation reveals her attitudes. Let us examine, for example, some possible teacher responses when a child, bringing a sparkling chunk of rock to school, explains: "Look, teacher! Isn't it pretty? I had to crawl under the Smith fence to get it!" The teacher may answer in several ways:

1. By sharing the child's enthusiasm about the object:
"You did! My, look how it sparkles! Tell me where you found it."

2. By enlarging the child's understanding of the object:
"Say, that sparkles like gold. But it isn't. It's what we call iron pyrite. It used to fool the miners, though. They would find a rock like this and think they had found gold. Many people call such rocks 'fool's gold,' even today."

3. By suggesting further activities in connection with the object:
"Would you like to tell the class about your rock? Maybe they will want to have a rock collection, with yours as the first rock in it."

4. By making a tangential response:
"Gracious, you've got dirt all over your clothes! Here, let's get a whisk broom and brush you off."

5. By responding in a manner which postpones discussion of the object:
"Yes, I know. Just wait until I finish taking the roll."

6. By making an unfavorable response:
"Get that dirty rock off the papers on my desk! You've ruined my report! What will the principal think if I hand him a paper like that?"

The child whose science contributions bring responses of the first three types will find his activities satisfying and will be encouraged to make more contributions. The child who usually gets a tangential, or a delayed, response from his teacher will maintain his science interests on his own, if at all. And the child who consistently gets negative responses to his science contributions soon stops making them.

What happens to pupils who year after year have teachers who withdraw from science studies and activities? Their growing disinterest in science has often been reported. For instance, Herbert A. Smith describes how children react:

> One of the fundamental questions that we must face is why students lose interest in science. We are all acquainted with the fact that in preschool and lower primary grades children have a great many interests which might properly be termed scientific. They ask endless questions derived from their observations of their environment. These questions involve plants and animals, the stars and the sky; they involve the processes of reproduction and life and death itself. Why is it then that we see a gradual diminution of these interests as a child progresses through the school? Very frequently by the time the child gets to the junior high school years he seems to have no interests in science at all.[2]

Teacher attitudes are important in answering Smith's question. When the science activities of a child are repeatedly discouraged, he is likely to make other efforts to gain recognition from his teacher. But when his science activities are encouraged by a teacher who also wants to find out more about her environment, his interests are maintained and often enhanced as well.

The explanation of certain findings of research in science education may lie in teachers' attitudes. Studies of pupils' interests have revealed central tendencies which are highly useful in curriculum development, but they have also shown wide variability in pupil interests at each grade or age level. Why are certain first-grade pupils interested in momentum when most children of

2. Herbert A. Smith. Panel statement presented for symposium on "Needed research in science education." *Science Education*, 40:363-69, December, 1956.

the same age are not? An incident like the following may hold the explanation:

> Philip was speeding on his bicycle as fast as his legs could pedal. When he decided to put his brake on hard, both Philip and the bicycle stopped in a heap. The teacher, Miss Finch, gathered the sobbing boy in her arms. "We'll talk about it later," she said to the children gathering around.
>
> After Philip's injuries had been taken care of by the school nurse and the children were back in their room, Miss Finch talked with them about the accident.
>
> "What happened to Philip this morning on the playground?" she asked, with an understanding smile for Philip as well as for the others.
>
> "He fell off his bike," said Tom.
>
> "He went too fast," said Jane.
>
> "He hurt himself," said sympathetic Mary.
>
> "Yes, indeed," said Miss Finch. "Now let me show you what happened. And I'm going to use a great big word. The word is 'momentum.' You watch for it.
>
> Taking a toy bicycle, she put a little doll figure on it. "Here goes Philip on his bicycle. Faster and faster and faster. Now he tries to stop. Well! The bike stopped, but Philip went on the way he was going. The force of *momentum* kept him going ahead."
>
> After a discussion, in which the children absorbed what she had said, Miss Finch continued: "Now let's do it again, but this time Philip goes slowly, slowly. Now he stops, and he is still on his bike. When he went slowly, his *momentum* was not so great and he could stop without falling off."
>
> Again the group discussed and absorbed the new ideas. Miss Finch concluded the discussion by asking, "Who can tell us what *momentum* is?" Philip volunteered, "It's when I put on the brake and don't stop."

Here the teacher was able to make an accident on the playground the basis for a science lesson in which Philip and his classmates grasped the concept of momentum. A few days later, when the class was talking about staying out of the street when an automobile is coming, she again used the word "momentum." The momentum of a fast-moving car, she pointed out, may keep it moving even though its driver has put on his brake. "Keep out of the way of cars. Don't count on the driver stopping," the children concluded.

The teacher who has studied science may know the facts about momentum but may not sense when to teach them. A teacher intent only on imparting scientific facts, for instance, may have tried to give Philip a lesson on momentum the second after he picked himself up from the ground while he was preoccupied with his injuries and his accident. But, if her basic attitudes with the children are those of helpfulness and cooperation, she will time her teaching so that optimum learning will be achieved.

CONCLUDING REMARKS

Women teachers in the elementary school are part of a social order which appreciates science and its contributions to society, but the social groups of which women teachers are a part hold attitudes that interfere with effective science-teaching. As a woman, a teacher may leave to men such chores as home and car repairs and such responsibilities as the study of science. As a woman, a teacher may pride herself on spotless housekeeping and oppose science activities which may interfere with it. As a member of what is termed the "middle class," the woman teacher may be pleased with the shiny and the new and the clean and be displeased with items salvaged from trash cans by children who get dirty in the pursuit of the wonders of nature.

Recognizing her social inheritance, the woman teacher is in a position to do something about modifying her legacy with attitudes more appropriate to science-teaching. Through workshops and other educative experiences, she can study science and acquire attitudes that lead her to encourage her pupils and often to share with them firsthand science activities. As more and more elementary-school teachers revise their attitudes, pupils' interest in science will remain strong throughout the elementary grades, and girls and boys, as well as their teacher, will learn more science.

CHAPTER 16

Learning and Using the Social Studies

WAYS OF teaching the social studies vary markedly from one elementary school to another. The program one observes in some classrooms is this: The children sit in rows. All of them have their history textbooks open to the same page. One pupil stands, reads aloud, sits down. The teacher calls on the next pupil, who stands, reads aloud, sits down. If the pupil encounters a word he cannot pronounce, the teacher supplies the word or calls on another pupil to help the hapless reader. After several pages of the text have been read in this fashion, an assignment to write the answers of the questions listed at the end of the chapter is given. Later in the same day, a textbook on geography is used. The episode described above is repeated with one important exception: The topic is generally different. That is, if the pupils read about the history of one place in the first episode, they often read about the geography of another place in the later lesson.

In other classrooms a quite different pattern exists. Books are used for locating information about questions formulated by the teacher and his pupils. At times the whole class works together. At other times pupils work independently or in small groups. For some events the class joins other classes engaged in similar pursuits. The objectives of this social studies program naturally include acquiring information. But the pupils learn more. They work toward the objectives and use the social sciences in ways noted in the first article. They use maps in ways described in the second article. The features advocated in the third article are used in this program: integration with other subjects, individualized instruction, use of multiple resources.

Underlying this program is a sophisticated theory of the social studies which may be summed up like this:

> A social studies program which is designed to maximize the ability of students to understand and satisfactorily explain human and natural problems should incorporate within itself relevant topics and activities. Fundamental ideas and generalizations about man interacting with the environment coupled with intellectual tools of verification should form the core of the program. In an era characterized by rapid change in so many aspects of life, all students should directly participate in inquiry, invention, and the act of philosophizing. The study of value conflicts in our society and alternative approaches to understanding or resolving them should also have a definite place in the curriculum. A school program which would meet the foregoing criteria would tend to face realistically the challenge of our twentieth-century civilization. A school system operating within such an orientation would provide educational leadership and act as a major reconstructing agent in society.[1]

Important curriculum decisions are required of teachers who teach the social studies in elementary schools. Many times we can define what we do not want to do, but defining our theoretical ideals is difficult. Sometimes we err in trying to make the whole leap all at once. The Muessig article in Chapter 6 shows some valuable ways of bridging the gap.

1. Bryon G. Massialas. Revising the social studies: an inquiry-centered approach. *Social Education,* 27:189, April, 1963.

74 Decision making: the heart of social studies instruction

SHIRLEY H. ENGLE

As citizens in a democracy we constantly make decisions. We vote for political leaders. We express our opinions on public issues. Sometimes we decide to ignore important social problems. Engle says: "If the purpose of the social studies is to be education for citizenship, if its primary concern is to be the quality of the beliefs and convictions which students come to hold on public questions, and if we are to be concerned with the development of skill at decision making, then there are some things which it becomes imperative that we do in teaching the social studies."

If you accept this view of the importance of the social studies, what ways of teaching would you advocate to achieve the goals Engle suggests? Do you think the school actually can have an effect upon pupils' decision-making abilities?

My THEME is a very simple one. It is that, in teaching the social studies, we should emphasive decision making as against mere remembering. We should emphasize decision making at two levels: at the level of deciding what a group of descriptive data means, how these data may be summarized or generalized, what principles they suggest; and also decision making at the level of policy determination, which requires a synthesis of facts, principles, and values usually not all found on one side of any question.

In order to make my case, it is useful to draw certain distinctions between the social sciences and the social studies. The social sciences include all of the scholarly, investigative work of historians, political scientists, economists, anthropologists, psychologists, and sociologists, together with such parts of the work of biologists and geographers as relate primarily to human behavior. Closely related fields include philosophy, literature, linguistics, logistics, and statistics. The social studies, including the content of the textbooks, courses of study, and whatever passes in the school for instruction in civic and social affairs, are based on the social sciences but they clearly involve always a selection of and distillation from the social sciences—they encompass only a minor portion of the social sciences.

Reprinted from *Social Education, 24*:301-4, 306, November, 1960.

Selectivity, therefore, is one of the features which distinguishes the social sciences from the social studies. To social science, knowledge is useful for its own sake; all knowledge is of equal worth; there is no concern for immediate usefulness. To the social studies, a central consideration must always be that of determining what knowledge is of most worth. If all of the knowledge of a field of study is to be boiled down into one textbook, what is to be emphasized? If all of the knowledge of the area is to boiled down into one course of study, what is most important?

There is a more basic distinction to be drawn between the social sciences and the social studies than merely that of selectivity. The impelling purpose of the two is quite different. The orientation of the social scientist is that of research. The more scientific the social scientist, the more specialized becomes his interest, the more consuming becomes his desire to know more and more about less and less, the less concern he shows for broad social problems. He is far more inclined to analyze, dissect, and proliferate than to unite, synthesize, and apply. His absorbing interest is to push back the frontier of dependable knowledge in some limited sector of the social scene.

In marked contrast to the meticulous research orientation of the social sciences, the social studies are centrally concerned with the education of citizens. The mark of the good citizen is the quality of decisions which he reaches on public and private matters of social concern. The social sciences contribute to the process of decision making by supplying reliable facts and principles upon which to base decisions—they do not supply the decisions ready-made. The facts are there for all to see but they do not tell us what to do. Decision making requires more than mere knowledge of facts and principles; it requires a weighing in the balance, a synthesizing of all available information and values. The problems about which citizens must reach decisions are never confronted piecemeal, the facts are seldom clearly all on one side, and values, too, must be taken into consideration. A social problem requires that the citizen put together, from many sources, information and values which the social sciences treat in relative isolation. Thus in the social studies the prevailing motive is synthesis rather than analysis. The social studies begin where the social sciences end. Facts and principles which are the ends in view in the social sciences are merely a means to a further end in the social studies. The goal of the social studies lies not merely in information but in the character of people. The goal is the good citizen.

A good citizen has many facts at his command, but more, he has arrived at some tenable conclusions about public and social affairs. He has achieved a store of sound and socially responsible beliefs and convictions. His beliefs and convictions are sound and responsible because he has had the opportunity to test them against facts and values. In the process of testing his ideas he has greatly increased his fund of factual information and he has become increasingly skillful at intelligent decision making. The development in the mind of students of such a synthesis of facts and values, together with the development of skill in making decisions in the light of numerous and sometimes contrary facts and values, is the special forte of the social studies.

If the purpose of the social studies is to be education for citizenship, if its primary concern is to be the quality of the beliefs and convictions which students come to hold on public questions, and if we are to be concerned with the development of skill at decision making, then there are some things which it becomes imperative that we do in teaching the social studies. I would like to develop briefly some of these imperatives.

We must abandon our use of what I shall call the ground-covering technique, and with it the wholly mistaken notion that to commit information to memory is the same as to gain knowledge. By ground covering I mean the all too familiar technique of learning and holding in memory, enforced by drill, large amounts of more or less isolated descriptive material without pausing in any way, at any time, to speculate as to the meaning or significance of the material, or to consider its relevance and bearing to any general idea, or to consider its applicability to any problem or issue past or present. Even when such material is interesting, and it sometimes is, merely to cover it in this uncritical, matter-of-fact fashion robs the material of its potential for accurate concept formation or generalization which will be useful to students in understanding events and conditions in other times and places in which like data appear. Simply reading and remembering the stories about Indians in our history, no matter how many times repeated, has never insured the development of accurate concepts about Indians or correct generalizations about the relationships between people of divergent cultures and histories. Or, if in our haste to cover ground, we refuse to deal contemplatively and critically with the material we are covering, the student may generalize haphazardly and may, without our help, arrive at totally erroneous conclusions. Thus, it may be said with good reason that the study of Indians frequently does more harm than good, teaching more untruth than truth.

The ground-covering fetish is based on the false notion that remembering is all there is to knowing or the equally false notion that one must be well drilled in the facts before he can begin to think. M. I. Finley, noted British historian, says about ground covering that, "a mere telling of individual events in sequence, no matter how accurately done, is just that and nothing else.

Such knowledge is meaningless, its mere accumulation a waste of time. Instead, knowledge must lead to understanding. In the field of history this means trying to grasp general ideas about human events. The problem is to move from particular events to the universal; from the concrete events to the underlying patterns and generalities."

Equally fallacious is the background theory of learning, or the notion that we must hold the facts in memory before we are ready to draw conclusions from them or to think about their meaning. This theory is at considerable variance with recognized scientific method and the ways in which careful thinkers approach an intellectual problem. The thinker or scientist frequently engages in speculation or theorizing about possible relationships, from which he deduces tests or possible facts which, if observable, verify his theory. (Some of the great break-throughs in knowledge have come about in this way.) To say that a thinker must know all that he needs to know, let alone hold all this in memory, before engaging in thought is to completely hog-tie his intellectual development. And there is no valid reason in this respect for differentiating between a student trying to understand Indians and an Einstein speculating about the meaning of space.

What happens in our classrooms from too strict an adherence to ground covering is that the number of facts committed to memory is reduced to a relatively small number. These are the so-called basic facts which we learn, and just as promptly forget, over and over again. Thus ground covering actually works to reduce and restrict the quantity of factual information treated in our classes. What is needed instead is a vast multiplication of the quantity of factual material with which students are asked to deal in the context of reaching a reasoned conclusion about some intellectual problem. Such an enrichment of factual background will come about when we turn from our preoccupation with remembering to a more fruitful concern for drawing conclusions from facts or for testing our speculations and ideas about human events with all of the relevant data we are able to collect.

For ground covering, or remembering, we should substitute decision making, which is reflective, speculative, thought provoking, and oriented to the process of reaching conclusions. My thesis is simply this, decision making should afford the structure around which social studies instruction should be organized. The central importance of decision making in the social studies has been cited earlier. The point here is that students are not likely to learn to reach better decisions, that is, grounded and reasoned decisions, except as they receive guided and critically oriented exercise in the decision-making process.

Decision-making opportunities in the social studies classroom may run the entire gamut of difficulty, from very simple situations which take the form merely of posing questions for class consideration which require some thought and a synthesis of information supplied in a single descriptive paragraph to very complex social problems involving questions of public policy or individual behavior. Thus, in studying the Plains Indians in the post-Civil War period a low-level decision could be required by asking which of the following sentences accurately, or most accurately, summarizes the difficulty continually experienced in Indian affairs: (1) The Indians were treated by the settlers as trespassers on land which they (the Indians) had inhabited and claimed as their own for centuries; (2) The Plains Indians were wanderers who knew no fixed abodes and recognized no exclusive right of anyone to own the land; (3) Renegade Indians and white outlaws were at the seat of Indian trouble (this is the Hollywood version of Indian affairs); (4) The handling of Indian affairs by the United States government was characterized by wanton disregard of Indian rights, by treachery, and by broken promises; or (5) The different manner of using the land by the Indians and the whites made agreement between the two impossible. At a higher level of difficulty a decision would be required if one asked, "Do you think General George Crook dealt fairly with the Shoshone chief, Washakie, during the military campaigns to pacify the Plains Indians? What are your grounds?" Or at a still higher level of complexity, there is the question of what should be the policy of the United States toward Indians who contest the sovereignty of the United States.

Some decisions involve essentially matters of fact. For example, suppose we are reading about the building of the transcontinental railroads in the 1870's, 1880's, and 1890's and how the government gave large grants of land and money to the railroad companies to encourage them to build the railroads. We read further that subsequently the railroads, or most of them, went into bankruptcy but also that following their construction the country experienced a great expansion of agricultural and industrial wealth whereby our exports of wheat and corn multiplied tenfold in twenty years, and in the same period the value of our manufacturers' products increased 200 per cent, 180 new factories were being built in Philadelphia alone. We have these and many other facts. But the decision rests in concluding what these facts mean. What do they all add up to? Which of the following generalizations accurately summarize these facts? Government subsidization of key industries brings a vast multiplication of other industries under private ownership; private investors will not take the extraordinary risk necessary to start a really new industrial development; one industrial development inevitably leads to other industrial developments; industry in which the government interferes is always inefficient and will fail in the end; private industry can never be expected to provide the transportation facilities needed for an expanding economy; government participation in industry tends to dry up the growth of private industry; industry resulting from government spending is uneconomical and is doomed to fail in the end; if the government had foregone the tax money used to aid the railroads, private individuals would have had money which they would have invested in the railroads. Clearly, the making of decisions among the alternatives listed above is essentially a matter of sorting out and applying facts until a conclusion is reached which honestly and accurately summarizes all facts that are relevant to the problem.

Other decisions, perhaps we should say most decisions, involve values as well as facts. Thus, in dealing with the issue of which of two proposed solutions to the problems of farm surpluses is best, one may conclude, factually, that government support of farm prices leads inevitably to inefficiency in agriculture and to unnecessarily high cost for food and fiber which the farm produces. This much is a factual conclusion. But this does not necessarily get us out of the woods, for one might still prefer government-supported agriculture to an unregulated agriculture because he feared the control of large agricultural corporations (which will almost inevitably follow the removal of governmental restrictions—another factual generalization) more than he fears governmental controls. The latter decision is a value judgment, though one fraught, as are all value decisions, with still further implications which could be grounded factually. For instance, in a hierarchy of values, the *greatest degree of individual freedom* may be the value sought or agreed upon by all involved in the decision. From this premise a factual investigation could be conducted of the relationship between government regulation and individual freedom on the one hand and between corporate control and individual freedom on the other. Thus, though the decision as to value is not in this way resolved, the exact issue over values is clarified by such a factual investigation of the alternatives.

If decision making is to be the focus of social studies instruction, we will need to introduce vastly larger quantities of factual information into our classrooms. Drill to the point of memory on a few basic facts will never suffice. The superficial coverage of one textbook will never be enough. The very moment that a conclusion, such as any of those suggested above, is reached tentatively, the natural demand is for more facts with which to test the conclusion. This means almost surely the introduction of large quantities of supplementary materials, with far too much content to be committed to memory. It means a reversal in the usual attitude on reading habits whereby students will be expected to read larger quantities of materials, to read them more rapidly, and to read them for purposes of getting general ideas or of locating relevant information rather than to read small quantities of material, slowly and laboriously, a few pages each day, for purposes of committing the material to memory. It may mean in the end the abandonment of textbooks and the substitution of numerous, more substantive, more informative, and more exciting books and other materials.

If the quality of decision making is to be the primary concern of social studies instruction, we must take steps to upgrade the quality of intellectual activity in the social studies classroom. Research is demonstrating the disquieting prevalence in many social studies classrooms of what is generously labeled shoddy thinking procedures. In fact, social studies classrooms seem to exhibit a quality of logic far below that exhibited in classrooms in which science, mathematics, or even English is being taught. Admitting the greater difficulty of our content, this is still something about which we cannot be complacent. Among the common errors in logic easily observed in social studies instruction is the acceptance of an assertion as if it were a fact, the confusing of fact with opinion, the validation of the truth of something on authority, the acceptance of a merely plausible explanation for a sufficient explanation, the failure to agree on the meaning of key words (frequently value laden) before engaging in an argument in which the meaning of the word is essential as, for instance, to argue over whether the first Roosevelt was a good or a strong President without first agreeing on a common meaning for "good" and for "strong," and the confusing of questions which must be referred to facts for an answer and those which defer to values for an answer. The persistent practice in our classrooms of errors in logic of the kind mentioned can lead only to intellectual confusion and irresponsibility. If we are really concerned with effective citizenship, we must not only provide the opportunity for decision making but we must see to it that decisions are made in keeping with well-known rules of science and logic and that students get practice in making such decisions.

Lastly, if responsible decision making is the end of social studies instruction, we must recognize value formation as a central concern of social studies instruction. Real-life decisions are ultimately value decisions. To leave a student unaware of the value assumptions in his decision or to leave him untrained in dealing with value questions is literally to lead an innocent lamb to the slaughter. Such a student could, and he frequently does, return to our fold and say, "But you didn't tell me it was this way." Or he may quickly sink into cynicism or disbelief. The question of what values he should hold probably cannot be settled in the classroom, but values can be dealt with intelligently in the classroom. The nature of the values which people hold can be made explicit, the issues over values can be clarified, and the ends to which holding to a particular value will lead can be established factually to some extent. For instance, it is possible to predict with some accuracy the factual results of valuing segregation over integration in the United States with respect to such matters as economic productivity of the American people, the respect with which America is held abroad, the effect on the efficiency of our educational system, the genetic mixing of the races, etc. Thus, it becomes possible to engage in some appraisal of the value in terms of other values held, as, for instance, world peace, Christian brotherhood, economic security and well-being, national unity, the right to choose one's own friends, etc. We can compare and appraise value, to some extent, in an extended hierarchy of values from lower value, such as a preference for having one's hair cut in a segregated barber shop, to higher values, such as the belief that all men should be treated with equal respect.

To duck the question of values is to cut the heart out of decision making. The basic social problem of America today is a problem of value. In simple terms the problem may be stated as to whether we value more the survival of a free America which will require sacrifice for education, for materials of defense, etc., or whether we value more our right as individuals to spend our resources on extra fins for our cars and for all the other gadgets of conspicuous consumptions. It is not impossible to predict the outcome of hewing to either choice. It is not at all certain that our students are being prepared to make the right decision and to make it in time.

My thesis has been a very simple one. It is that quality decision making should be the central concern of social studies instruction. I could cite many renowned people as having essentially supported the position I have here tried to state. Among the ancients these would include Socrates, Plato, and Thucydides, the father of objective history. These would include the great modern philosopher Alfred North Whitehead and such modern critics as the economist Peter Drucker and President Robert F. Goheen of Princeton. But to quote these would continue the discussion overlong, as I suspect I may have done already. So may I quote instead a simple statement from the noted scientist Hans Selye, who has said that "facts from which no conclusions can be drawn are hardly worth knowing."

75 *Introducing maps—a skill*

E D N A   S .   M I T C H E L L

Some teachers employ maps merely to locate places. But maps may also be used to stimulate these kinds of thinking: comparison, analysis, interpretation, the formulation of hypotheses, and the application of facts. This essay contains helpful suggestions for conducting such activities.

INTERNATIONAL EVENTS within recent years have had a serious impact on the life and consciousness of every American. Strange-sounding names of places unknown to us only a short time ago now are commonplace; each day news headlines force us to become aware of other unfamiliar areas. We are realizing, to our bewilderment, how inadequate our knowledge is of simple world geography, to say nothing of the larger aspects of world affairs. Modern communication facilities, increased travel opportunities and worldwide politico-social pressures make it urgent that we abandon provincial attitudes and correct our widespread ignorance regarding other parts of the world. The weight of responsibility falls heavily on our schools which must teach children the skills necessary for interpreting global events.

Maps and globes are the basic skill tools used throughout the entire social studies program. *The ability to use maps and globes is not acquired incidentally or automatically at the fourth grade; it must be taught in a carefully planned sequence beginning in the primary grades and developing slowly, gradually, deliberately, with no point of absolute completion.*

Maps are the beginning of exciting adventures for children, but the spirit and flavor of adventure are too often lost because teaching methods or materials are aimed over the child's head and beyond his experience. The language of maps with its strange symbols, colors, and scales is in reality a foreign language to a child and must be just as carefully introduced.

MAP READINESS

Much difficulty which children have with maps could be avoided if primary map-readiness programs were more widely adopted and deliberately

Reprinted by permission of the Association for Childhood Education International. 3615 Wisconsin Avenue, N.W., Washington, D.C. "Introducing maps—a skill," by Edna S. Mitchell. *Childhood Education*, February, 1961, Vol. 37, No. 6, pp. 279-83.

planned. Map readiness begins as children become acquainted with the landmarks of their neighborhood and push back the boundaries of their world to include a larger community. *The primary child must have an abundant background of direct concrete experiences in observing and analyzing the world about him if he is going to be able later to visualize or "see with his mind's eye" the reality behind symbols on a map.* Examples of foundational experiences which need attention include observing landscapes and seeing the effects of water in tiny rivers, islands, lakes, and floods which form after a rain or with the melting of snow.

Map making is directly approached at the primary level through simple floor layout plans of the school or neighborhood, using movable objects for buildings. Later, symbols such as squares or rectangles can be used. As soon as simple map making is begun attention should be called to cardinal directions by locating places in relation to the classroom. A primary experience in finding cardinal directions is to take children outside at noon and have them stand with their backs to the sun. They will be facing north. If they raise the right arm it will be pointing east. Other directions can easily be noted. Directional concepts, however, must be continually checked at each succeeding grade level because of their abstract nature.

GLOBES—BASIC EQUIPMENT

A large, simplified globe is basic equipment for every primary classroom, including kindergarten. Through informal discussions the children should come to understand that although the world is very large it is round like the globe. They learn that the blue areas are water, the darker areas are land, and there is more water than land. *They should be encouraged to examine the globe and find places which they know about from travel, news reports, stories, and other sources unique to each group.*

As more symbols are introduced in the middle grades additional experiences are necessary which will provide vivid mental descriptions of the area symbolized. Unfortunately, many geography lessons are taught to children who are not visually acquainted with the features being studied. *Pictures, films, descriptions from stories and poems, community resource persons, and other means should be employed when a direct experience is not possible.* An extensive, well-organized picture file is indispensable for clarifying and enriching map interpretations.

DIFFERENT MAPS NEEDED

Maps must be carefully selected so they will not be cluttered with details which are meaningless to the child. Beware of encyclopedic maps crammed with facts! This type of map has a place, but it should not be used as the basic tool for children who are beginning map study any more than an adult-type encyclopedia should be used for basic reading material. Excessive use of all-purpose wall maps makes map study frightful, confusing, and meaningless for children. *No one map can or should give all the important facts about an area, so several different maps of each area to be studied should be available.* Chalk-erasable maps and globes and outline maps allow concentration on a few ideas at a time.

Many common pitfalls of map study can be avoided with a little care and flexibility in teaching. Both children and adults are frequently confused by direction or size and shape of areas distorted by maps. For example, north is commonly thought of as "up" and south as "down." We support this error when we continually hang maps vertically on the wall with north necessarily at the top or when we use the conventional fixed globes with the North Pole appearing on top. "Up" is, of course, a direction away from the earth, while "down" is toward the center of the earth, not toward the South Pole. Placing maps flat on the floor or on a table with directions properly arranged, using a polar projection with the North Pole centered and using a globe in a cradle mounting so it can be turned in any direction will help clarify this misconception. The continuous use of wall maps gives us an east-west orientation to the world which is also misleading. The Soviet Union, for instance, seems to be east of the United States, but by using a globe we can see that it is more nearly north of us.

COMPARE MAPS AND GLOBE

No map can show the curvature of the earth and be completely accurate. Map distortions can be innocently misleading. A child who sees only Mercator projections is sure to think Greenland larger than South America, although it is only about one-eighth as large. *Children should compare several types of map projections and check them with a large globe.* A technical study of these differences is not recommended until much later.

As intermediate children learn about grid work on maps and globes, the foremost concern is to give meaning to the new concepts and terminology. The Equator is used as the beginning of location, noting positions north or south of this great circle. Then placement and use of other east-west lines and north-south lines can be examined. These terms are more descriptive to a child than latitude, longitude or parallels and meridians. Temporary use should also be made of the terms "south sun line" and "north sun line" in place of the abstract names "Tropic of Cancer" and "Tropic of Capricorn." The teaching of beginning grid concepts is made much easier with a markable slated globe.

LIMITATIONS OF MAP MAKING

The making of maps by the children has become a popular method of learning which can be very meaningful and worth-while as well as creative. However, there are serious limitations which need to be recognized before such projects are begun. The time consumed must be justified by the purposes of the map-making experience and by the outcomes. If the mistakes and errors which are made on the map are not openly evaluated, the map becomes meaningless. *If map making is not preceded by research, comparison and selection by the child of facts to be included on the map, the real values of making it are lost.* Merely copying data from other maps does not constitute a worthwhile purpose. Maps made by children can be lovely to look at and they should allow for creativity and the use of artistic abilities, but they are primarily instruments for more complete understanding in the social studies. The emphasis must be placed on accuracy and pupil growth in ability to use and interpret facts, not on the map as a display of art technique.

UP-TO-DATE TOOLS

The importance of an adequate supply of carefully selected materials for each level of maturity cannot be overemphasized! Each classroom should have suitable maps and globes and each school should maintain an additional supply of maps, pictures, charts, models, and other teaching aids which can be shared by several classrooms.

An interested and well-prepared teacher is the most important element in the geography skills program, but even the best teacher needs help. He needs professional help in order to expand and deepen his own understanding of the changing face of the world; he needs the help of an alerted community which recognizes the importance of up-to-date child-geared geography tools in every classroom!

ROSS M. COXE

The author stresses three aspects of a social studies program: (1) *integration with other subjects,* (2) *individualization of instruction, and* (3) *use of multiple resources.*

"WHAT ROME was to the ancient world, what Great Britain has been to the modern world, America is to be to the world of tomorrow. We might wish it otherwise. I do. Every man who was young in the easier America of the pre-war world must long for it at times. But our personal preferences count little in the great movements of history, and when the destiny of a nation is revealed to it, there is no choice but to accept that destiny and to make ready in order to be equal to it."

These words, written by Walter Lippmann in 1939, are as significant now as they were then. The intervening years have brought America to the almost overwhelming responsibilities of world leadership. Prophesy has become reality, and we have no alternative but to exercise our responsibilities with all of the intelligence and vision we can muster.

Today, our nation is in desperate need of a citizenry that is capable of acting responsibly on the host of issues that confront us. We need citizens who possess social literacy and a sense of social responsibility, who can intelligently grasp the complex problems of our social order and wrestle with them productively.[1]

Improvement of the social studies must necessarily come through many approaches and through the efforts of many people. The content of the social studies curriculum must be rigorously evaluated and then planned to serve the social objectives we seek. The ideas of academic scholars and specialists in learning, of classroom teachers and administrators, of parents and community leaders must all be given an audience. But improvement of the social studies cannot be effected unless classroom instruction is strengthened. It is in the

Reprinted from *The National Elementary Principal*, 42:30-34, May, 1963. Copyright 1963, Department of Elementary School Principals, National Educational Association; reprinted with permission.

1. Ralph C. Preston. The role of social studies in elementary education. *Social Studies in the Elementary School,* Fifty-Sixth Yearbook, National Society for the Study of Education, Chicago: University of Chicago Press, 1957, pp. 4-26.

everyday, practical ways a teacher works with children that the social studies are made vital.

Let us look now at three major aspects of social studies instruction and examine some of the ways teaching and learning can be improved.

INTEGRATION WITH OTHER SUBJECTS

If we look at the definition of social studies—the learning experiences drawn from all of the areas concerned with man and his interactions with his environment—it is apparent that every teacher is a teacher of social studies and that every area of the curriculum is related to the social studies. Good teaching does not compartmentalize knowledge or set up artificial divisions between subject-matter fields. And good teaching is based on conscious efforts to relate one idea to another, to generalize and interpret.

Science and social studies, for example, should be closely related in the elementary school. If a group of children were studying a science unit on climate, they would immediately get into an investigation of how climate affects man—how it affects his dress, his home, the food he raises, the occupations he pursues. As they related the study of climate to the social studies, the children would discover some of the reasons why people live in different ways.

As another example, if a class were studying automation as part of their science program, they would very naturally need to consider the effects of automation on man. If an industry in their community were automated and half of the working population were thrown out of jobs, how would this affect their fathers and the community in which they live? This is social studies —and social studies of a very vital kind.

By relating social studies with the basic reading program, a primary teacher might help her group of learners to understand another country and its people better through reading stories of other cultures. This would be an opportunity to use the globe and maps and talk with the children about the country's location. At this level, the children have a very limited understanding of space and direction, but they can begin to learn that the earth is round and the meaning of north and south, east and west.

Consider the relationship between mathematics and the social studies. The teacher has a wonderful opportunity to teach some basic social studies concepts and skills through math. In the first grade, for example, a class might be working on an arithmetic unit on telling time. As part of their study, they can learn something about time zones (geography) and about sundials (history and cultural anthropology).

Of the language arts. If we define the language arts as the communication skills of reading, speaking, writing, and listening, the social studies become an important avenue for instruction. You cannot teach reading in a vacuum. You cannot teach children to listen unless you say something for them to listen to. Drawing upon the content of the social studies, we can develop the communication skills, and these skills, in turn, are important to learning in the social studies.

Good social studies instruction, then, must be related to good instruction in other areas of the curriculum. The study of man and his relationships to his environment should be broadly conceived. And it is precisely because the social studies are so encompassing that they should be central to the elementary-school curriculum.

INDIVIDUALIZING INSTRUCTION

One of the greatest problems we face in the social studies is individualization of instruction. The idea that people are different, and that these differences should be taken into account in education, is not new. Plato, for example, recognized human variability when he said, "For it comes into my mind when you say it that we are not born all exactly alike but different in nature for all sorts of different jobs." Comenius treated individual differences at length. He besought teachers to accept nature, to adjust methods and materials accordingly, and to start instruction at the pupil's level. Rosseau, too, recognized variation both among and within individuals, almost advocating a tutorial system.

We all believe that each human being is unique, that he is different from his fellows. Yet when one looks at school organizations and practices today, he wonders. Generally, the social studies curriculum is planned for the group rather than for the individual. One of our biggest tasks, then, in improving social studies instruction, is to examine our organizational plans and instructional practices and seek better ways to meet individual differences. We need to develop programs that will help each individual to develop his potentialities and achieve his goals.

We should begin by making sure that we understand what we mean by individual differences. Teachers, principals—all educators—need to have a thorough understanding of individual differences in childhood and adolescence. We need to recognize the physical, social, emotional, and intellectual behavior of different children at various stages of development. We need to be aware of the individual differences that exist in reading achievement and reading interest, in hobbies, in extent of travel, in the amount of stimulating conversation at home, in interests and talents, in intellectual curiosity, in study skills, in written and oral expression. Unless we are aware that all of these individual differences exist, how can we truly make instruction fit the pupil?

Let us look now at a number of ways in which instruction can be individualized in the social studies program.

Individualizing units. The unit method of teaching is valuable if we understand and apply two basic concepts. First, a unit does not have to be of any specific duration. One unit might last for a day; another, two weeks; another, three months; yet another, the entire school year. Secondly, a unit does not need to produce uniformity of instruction; all of the children do not have to study the same materials in the same way at the same time. This second point, in particular, merits some explanation.

Let us say that a group of fifth-graders are organizing for a unit of work on the New England states. The program of work can and should be planned to take into account individual differences. The slowest learning youngster in the class might only be capable of studying and making a map of the New England region by tracing from an atlas or by use of an overhead projector. At the same time, the average youngsters are also doing research and practicing their work-study skills of locating, interpreting, organizing, and utilizing information. But in keeping with their particular abilities, the average youngsters are studying the occupations of people in the New England states and the area's geography, history, and resources. The rapid learners in the class will very quickly grasp all of these phases of the unit. They can go into depth and study the role that the New England states play in the nation's economy; they can learn something about the interdependence of New England and other regions of the country. At times, the entire class can work together—for example, viewing a film or taking a field trip.

By organizing a unit in this way, social studies instruction can be individualized. Each child works according to his abilities and interest. Yet, at their own levels of comprehension, all are learning to do research. All are having an opportunity to discover and utilize information. All are learning something about the New England states. The teacher's role is to help each child achieve ever higher levels of competence and understanding—to work with the slow-learning youngster, who at first is only able to make a regional map, so that he can move on to the next higher level of activity.

Invariably when this kind of an approach to unit study is proposed, the question is raised of how you can be sure that the curriculum guide or textbook will be covered. We would do better to attend to the business of making what we do teach valuable. Every teacher has a responsibility to help children uncover material—not to cover it. Content is a means to an end and not an end in itself. There is little merit to covering a voluminous amount of material without understanding it. There is little merit to covering the curriculum guide or textbook if instruction is not individualized to help each child acquire the values, concepts, and skills which the material was designed to develop.

.   .   .   .

Individualizing through classroom organizations. There are many ways to individualize instruction in the classroom—among them, by grouping, by enrichment, by acceleration, and by independent work.

As we pointed out in discussing social studies units, ability grouping offers one means of individualizing instruction. Groups, of course, can be established on the basis of other criteria as well—on the basis of interests, for example. Taking into account the many variables that comprise individual differences, a teacher might divide a class into groups to do specific jobs in relation to a unit of study. If a class were studying their community, one group of youngsters might investigate the community's government. Another group could study local industries. Another might make a mural depicting the history of the town. Another might find out about the cultural resources of the community. Still another could study the town from a sociological standpoint. Each group's findings would be reported back to the total class so that all the children would benefit from each of the studies.

Enrichment is another means of providing individualized instruction. Too many teachers think that enrichment is just more of the same. It isn't. Enrichment provides learning experiences outside of the regular course of study that take children into depth and broaden their understanding and concepts. Properly conceived, enrichment can be used to provide each pupil with experiences beyond the regular classroom fare which are uniquely fitted to his abilities and interests.

Acceleration is a third way to individualize instruction in the classroom. Most of us think of acceleration as skipping a grade. In the context in which it is used here, acceleration refers to the repositioning of content, keeping the youngster with his class and repositioning content as he is ready for it. In this context, acceleration obviously can help to provide individual differences.

A fourth method by which a teacher can individualize the program is through independent study. There are times when every child should have the opportunity to work alone—perhaps in the classroom, perhaps in the library with the guidance of the librarian, or perhaps in the community. This is an excellent technique for individualizing instruction, especially for rapid learners.

In all of these ways—through the organization of units, through school organization—teachers and principals can develop practical ways to accommodate the individual differences in every class group. There is no one best way to individualize. The important thing, if we are to improve the social studies program, is to be sure that we do it.

USE OF MULTIPLE RESOURCES

One of the most important ways in which teachers and principals can practically improve the teaching of social studies is through the use of multiple resources.

The day of the single textbook has passed. A really vital social studies program cannot be taught "by *the* book." Why? First, we cannot rely on any single textbook to give us all of the information we need on a given subject. Secondly, no one textbook can meet the wide reading range in any class of children. Thirdly, if we really want to help children to learn the techniques of research, we must encourage them to use a variety of materials. Fourthly, a textbook usually reflects one person's opinion or, in the social studies, is slanted to geography, or history, or economics, or civics to the exclusion of other social science disciplines.

Three of our major goals in the social studies are to teach critical thinking, to teach children how to solve problems effectively, and to help them generalize and draw their own conclusions. If we are to achieve these goals, we must use multiple-learning materials. Pupils must have resources available which give many points of view on an issue, which discuss a problem from the perspective of several disciplines. Only then do they have a basis from which to analyze, generalize, and come to their own conclusions.

We do, of course, need to use textbooks. They help us organize our teaching. They can serve as a common point of departure from which children can move into supplementary texts and reference books, maps, globes, and charts, films, filmstrips, and records, tradebooks and pamphlets, and community resources—both natural and human. But this kind of use of a textbook is entirely different from the narrow page-by-page approach of previous years.

The creative use of multiple resources is being supported currently by the development of materials learning centers, in which a school system houses all of its instructional materials in a central location. Under this arrangement, teachers can go to the center and select from a large collection those materials which fit the needs of her class. Each teacher has a much wider range of resources available than she would under a classroom-by-classroom or school-by-school allocation of learning materials.

Whether or not there is a central materials center, the important thing is that teachers have available and use a variety of resources in teaching the social studies. When we do this, and do it creatively, we will have taken a major step toward the strengthening of the social studies program in the elementary school.

77   *Merger of social studies and science in sixth grade*

ROLAND WEST

In this article the author takes us behind the scenes to show us how he planned and carried out a unit that combined the social studies and science.

THE TEACHER'S plan book is a handy guide to educational practice. There was a day when a glimpse into almost any plan book showed pages divided into blocks with such headings as history, geography, nature study, science, health, and penmanship. Today several of these subjects are no longer given separate listing. In some schools they have not been listed separately for twenty-five years. Consolidation, one of the most popular movements in education during the last quarter of a century, accounts for the change.

In the last twenty-five years we have seen mergers in the teaching of subject matter. Today geography, history, and civics are commonly blended into a single program. We have seen mergers, too, in the teaching of the basic skills. Today the proficient teacher does not teach these skills in isolation. Rather he presents them as tools to help children solve problems that arise in everyday life in and out of school. Accordingly, reading and writing skills are often taught along with subject matter.

Many state departments of education have merged history and geography into a unified social studies program. Many states have also consolidated health, nature study, and other natural sciences into a unified general science

Reprinted from *The Elementary School Journal, 58*:445-48, by permission of The University of Chicago Press. Copyright 1958 by the University of Chicago.

program. A number of educators doubt whether further consolidation would have any value. However, consolidation has by no means been carried out as far as it might be. Most state and local school authorities still publish separate courses of study for social studies and science, for example.

ORIGIN OF A MERGER

The writer began his teaching career in a sixth grade in the fall of 1956. Social studies and science were scheduled separately, and at first the writer taught them separately. But as the months passed, he became convinced that consolidation of these subjects would prove a boon to teaching as well as to learning.

The observation is hardly original. Others close to the classroom have come to this conclusion. It played a large part in prompting two major changes in the school program: the introduction of social studies units in many elementary schools and the introduction of core curriculums in many junior and senior high schools.

Even the merger the writer had in mind, the consolidation of science and social studies, is not unheard of. The move has been suggested by Ralph C. Preston. Social studies and science, he points out, often compete for the attention of teachers and pupils. Where integration is impractical, he suggests that brief units in science be alternated with slightly longer units in social studies. Apart from being psychologically sound, Preston believes that the change would reduce time needed by the teacher for class preparation. Teachers can be hard pressed to complete background reading, to locate and organize class materials, and to plan activities for several subjects. Consolidation can lighten this load.[1]

MATERIALS FOR MERGING

In the summer of 1957, the writer set out to prepare a program merging social studies and science. As a first step, he reexamined the state courses of study for sixth grade. The science program included the following topics:

Food for growth and energy.
Weather and climate.

1. Ralph C. Preston. *Teaching Social Studies in the Elementary School,* New York: Rinehart & Co., Inc., 1950. See also: Preston. The role of social studies in elementary education. *Social Studies in the Elementary Schools,* Fifty-Sixth Yearbook of the National Society for the Study of Education, Part II, Chicago: University of Chicago Press (distributor), 1957, Chap. 1.

Electricity and its uses.
The world of sound.
The solar system and the universe beyond.
The improvement of plants and animals.
Safeguarding our health.

The social studies syllabus listed the following items:

A survey of Western civilization from ancient and medieval times to the present.
A geographic survey of the Eastern Hemisphere.
The culture and economy of representative nations in present-day Europe, Asia, and Africa.
Techniques of map reading, including the reading of latitude and longitude.
Research skills, including the ability to use encyclopedias and atlases and to read and construct graphs and summary tables.

Even this brief summary suggests several possible correlations. Weather and climate are easily related to latitude and longitude, and all four have a bearing on the economy and the way of life of a country. Agriculture, nutrition, and the improvement of plants and animals are also closely bound together. These relationships are only a few examples. Study will disclose many other relationships on which a unified program of science and social studies can be built.

WE STARTED WITH THE UNIVERSE

Needless to say, no two teachers using these materials will work out exactly the same program. Plans will vary depending on the teacher's starting point or viewpoint. Five units of the program prepared by the writer are summarized here. They are offered as an example of how the classroom teacher can merge science and social studies.

Our world and beyond. We began this unit with a study of the universe, its galaxies, important stars, and constellations. Moving closer to home, we studied our solar system and then our own planet Earth. In this more familiar realm, we explored political geography, mathematical geography, the lands and waters of the globe, and the history of geographical science. In our lessons on weather and climate, we traced the cycle of the seasons; the causes, measurement, and prediction of weather.

Man and his food. This unit included two sections on social studies: farming around the world and the history of agriculture. In history, we covered farming from early times and the Middle Ages to our own day. In our survey of farming across the globe, we studied patterns of agriculture in representative regions: hot and dry lands, hot and moist lands, cold lands, lowlands, and mountain lands. The topics on science worked in easily. We outlined the essentials of human nutrition—from food elements and the seven basic foods to the digestive process and the use the body makes of food. We studied what scientists are doing to improve crops and livestock; we noted new varieties of plants and improvements in farm animals. The stories of Gregor Mendel and Luther Burbank added to the children's information and heightened their interest in experiments with plants.

Western Europe. In the third unit we turned our attention to Europe. Our main emphasis here was on social studies. First, we took an overview of the continent, noting physical features, political divisions, and the vast Eurasian land mass. Next, we surveyed European history. The children had a look at life in Europe from the year 1100, through medieval times and the Renaissance to the present. After this panoramic view, we took a closer look at the modern nations of western Europe: Great Britain, France, Germany, the Scandinavian countries, the Low Countries, and the countries of southwestern Europe. Our last topic in this unit touched on recent developments in western Europe: political movements and parties, economic unions, the North Atlantic Treaty Organization.

Communications, today and yesterday. Man's first words, the origin of the alphabet, early forms of writing—with these topics we launched our study of communication. After tracing early developments, we surveyed major inventions after 1800. Science was very much in the foreground as the children learned about early experiments with magnetism and electricity, the discovery of the electromagnet, and the invention of electrical devices for communication. Still on the subject of science, we considered how each of us keeps in touch with the world around us. The question led to a study of light and sound, the eye, the ear, and the nervous system. In exploring modern media of communication, we considered various forms of publication, television, radio, the essentials of being a selective viewer and listener, systems for classifying facts, and the outlook for communication.

Problems of modern living. This unit centered on social studies. We started with one of man's major problems—war. The class traced the origins and background of World War II, and followed the course of the conflict in Europe and the Pacific. We viewed the aftermath of the war, including the problems of occupation and reconstruction, and went on to the problem of building peace. In this connection we studied the United Nations and its role in world affairs. The children compared democracy and communism and outlined their areas of conflict. As Russia played a prominent part in the discussion, the class gathered information on the people, the land, and the economy of the Soviet Union. After a geographic overview of the nations of Asia and Africa, we surveyed current developments in China, India, and Central Africa. Our survey included the Bandung Conference, and with a report on this important gathering we left the two vast continents of Asia and Africa.

In bringing the unit to a close, we turned to public health, a subject of local and world-wide significance for the present as well as the future. The subject naturally led us to the essentials of personal health. We wound up our study of problems of modern living with a problem pointed to the immediate future of these sixth-graders: getting ready for junior high school.

TIMETABLE FOR STUDY

The writer scheduled about eight school weeks for each unit. While the interval may seem brief considering the scope of the subject matter, it should be remembered that the merging of social studies and science frees large blocks of time in the daily schedule. Often, too, still more time can be freed by correlating the language arts. One example will suffice to suggest the many opportunities along this line: in one well-known set of readers for sixth grade, three out of four stories are directly related to topics in the units summarized in this article.

The program described here has been notably successful in capturing and holding interest in the writer's classes. After a year under the consolidated program, pupils seem to show greater gains in understanding than they do after a year of separate study of science and social studies. Moreover, lessons on the basic skills are more cordially received when they are woven into a unit of study. This observation did not come as a surprise but as a confirmation of a prime educational principle. Children stand to gain when school subjects are taught, not as separate areas with separate goals, but as part of a unified program focused on a central theme. The program then is more likely to be in harmony with children's capacities to understand the concepts presented and their ability to use the skills taught.

SCHOOL, SCIENCE, AND SOCIETY

Links between science and social studies are probably more apparent today than ever before. Now more than ever the problems confronting mankind are inextricably bound up with science and technology. Through science and technology we have speeded the production of goods and achieved an ease of communication undreamed of a few decades ago. Changes such as these have profoundly affected social relations.

We have made long strides in physics, chemistry, and medicine. Now we need to make comparable strides in social relationships. A few years ago John Michaelis wrote:

> We are confronted with such problems as building world unity and preserving peace, conserving world resources, adapting to increasing interdependence, improving community living, educating for international understanding, improving intergroup relationships, and controlling scientific developments for the good of all mankind.[2]

These imperatives of our age, Michaelis asserts, call for a new emphasis in social studies. And the new emphasis, he believes, should take new account of science.[3] It has been alleged that, in a society dominated by technology, widespread scientific illiteracy can be a serious handicap. This shortcoming can be aggravated by our failure to relate social and scientific knowledge.

Today the cry is for more and better science instruction in the schools— a demand that reaches down into the classrooms of the elementary school. Yet how can we find time for an expanded and enriched science program? The vitally necessary subjects—reading, language, arithmetic, and social studies— often crowd out science. From the standpoint of economy, logic, or sound educational psychology, it would seem advantageous to merge science and social studies and to introduce related material in the language arts as well.

Of course, a great deal of study is still needed to determine criteria for the selection of useful, meaningful subject matter in social studies and science. However, in light of the emerging needs of our day and the growing demands on school time, both subjects may well be reexamined seriously with a view of merging them into a single unified program.

2.   John Michaelis. *Social Studies for Children in a Democracy*, New York: Prentice-Hall, Inc., 1950.
3.   *Ibid.*

CHAPTER 17

Learning About Oneself and Others

ROUSSEAU WROTE, "Physical exercise teaches us to use our strength, to perceive the relation between our own and neighboring bodies, to use natural tools which are within our reach and adapted to our senses. . . ." Physical education and play are of vital importance: Children learn things in a kinesthetic way that most adults have forgotten.

Children need to learn a rational strategy of inquiry about, and an emotional acceptance of, themselves and others. The articles in this chapter are directed toward these objectives. The first two articles are about physical education and play. Health and sex education are the concern of the following three. The next two consist of specific suggestions to help pupils view themselves in relation to other people.

Teachers must teach pupils how to function in such important episodes as fire drills, lunchtime playground activity, dismissal time in nice weather, and dismissal time in bad weather. These episodes often involve pupils other than those in one's own class. It is urgent that teachers get together and plan to teach consistent patterns for the safety and well-being of their pupils.

78 *Physical education: why children need it*

VAUGHN L. HALL

Whether or not a physical education specialist conducts the physical education program, the classroom teachers should know the goals and ways of teaching used in the program. After all, the physical education period is a most important time of the day to the pupils.

NEXT TO the instinct to survive, the urge to play is the strongest drive in the life of the elementary school child. When a choice becomes necessary, he will miss meals or sleep, resort to deceit and falsehood, and finally openly rebel to gain the chance to play. When left to himself, the elementary school youngster almost always seeks companions and together they choose to engage in "big muscle activities." *This is physical education.*

Physical education has always existed in some form in all human societies. At different times, in various places, people's motives have influenced this program. Cyrus of Persia and Hitler of Germany used it to enhance the military power and prestige of their countries. Swedish and Danish systems of physical education emphasized health values. The early American programs of physical education were borrowed from Europe, but gradually changed to reflect the American culture. During and after the Industrial Revolution, the problem of leisure time created by the invention of laborsaving devices led to another motive—educating for leisure-time pursuits.

In modern times, the worth of physical education has been enhanced by the acceptance of the proposition that man is a unified organism. It is left almost unfettered by the medieval concepts of asceticism, scholasticism, and puritanism. Today, physical education's greatest value is seen in the contribution it can make to the total growth, development, and adjustment of all children.

BASIC MEANS OF DEVELOPMENT

When children participate in activities, they learn. Running, jumping, skipping, hopping, balancing, hanging, dodging involve not only the "big muscles" but the entire nervous system and all other components of the body, including perceptive organs and the mental processes of reasoning, judgment, etc.

Reprinted from *The National Elementary Principal, 39*:8-11. April, 1960.

Many people think of physical education as being associated with the junior and senior high schools. If this observation be only partially true, it suggests a weakness which is of great concern. Really, it is the early years of the child's life which are the most crucial. These are the important developmental and skill-learning years when children are possessed of the abundant energy, curiosity, and drives which propel them on and on to new experiences and the practice or repetition required for mastery of themselves. Many people are beginning to recognize and understand that one of the greatest untapped sources of education for total development of the elementary school child is physical education.

AN ADDITIONAL NEED AND CHALLENGE

Time was when organized physical education required less attention than it does today. Play was a natural thing in connection with daily living: "Muscle building" chores were the rule. Carrying wood and water, chasing the sheep and cows, or riding a horse or pony—once common occurrences in the life of an American boy or girl—have largely vanished from the scene.

Today, people do less strenuous physical work. Urbanization, technological advances, changed social conditions, and improvement in transportation and communication often leave boys and girls robbed of activities that once were their blessing. Modern-day youngsters are too frequently found riding instead of walking, watching instead of participating, giving more time and interest to sedentary occupations than to those which involve muscular effort, and being enticed to believe that intellectual endeavor is superior to that which involves the total individual. Indeed, our wonderful age of mechanical wizardry, gadgetry, and automation presents a challenge without precedent.

There are many thoughtful persons who sincerely believe that there is a relationship between the lack of consistent "big muscle activity" and the apparent increase in certain degenerative diseases, bad posture, digestive disturbances, cardiovascular difficulties, mental breakdown, endocrine upset, and the lack of bodily strength and endurance. Whatever the actual causes and degree of relationship of physical participation to these problems, there is ample evidence to suggest that elementary schools should plan and organize physical education programs to meet the needs of children. It is no longer a question of "Shall we?" but rather "We must!" Therefore, it is really a question of "How well?"

Much attention has been focused on these problems through the personal interest of the United States. The creation of the President's Council on

Youth Fitness has done much to emphasize the need—the special need—for all agencies and interests in America to promote organized programs to replace and replenish the natural opportunities for physical education so conspicuously missing in our modern society.

OBJECTIVES OF PHYSICAL EDUCATION

The results of activities in relation to the needs of children are the source from which we must choose our objectives in education. It seems entirely safe to say that the more we learn about the growth and development of children, the more apparent it becomes that physical education is an indispensable element in modern-day education.

Seldom, if ever, does anyone question the contributions of physical education to organic fitness, normal growth, and health. Through "big muscle activities," healthy children build organic power. These benefits are noticeably associated with the systems of circulation, respiration, nutrition, heat regulation, and elimination. Few, if any, school situations provide better motivation for implementation of health habits and practices. One of the most important things which we know about "big muscle activity" in relation to its effect upon growth and development of children is that it cannot be made up if missed in early years.

A well-adjusted person is an integrated person. "Physical education is an integrative force in the life of the child and is, therefore, not an adjunct, but is the essence of mental health."[1]

The playground and gymnasium afford the school its greatest opportunity for emotional and social development. It is here that some of the most impressionable and lasting lessons are learned concerning the value of cooperation, the appreciation of others, the value of honest all-out effort, the recognition of the rights of others, the meaning of freedom with responsibility, and the development of a wholesome attitude toward and respect for the opposite sex. In this program, a child may best learn one of the most fundamental lessons of life—that he may play and lose and play again.

One writer has aptly suggested the necessity of acquiring skills, knowledge, and interests in meaningful leisure-time pursuits by describing a challenging phenomenon of our day. He says we live in a great new world of means without ends. We have more time to do as we please, but "What do

1. National Education Association, American Association for Health, Physical Education, and Recreation. *Children in Focus,* 1954 Yearbook, Washington, D.C.: the Association, 1954, p. 288.

we please to do?" is the question. He points out that we "dabble," we "putter," instead of purposefully performing a task. He further suggests that the typical American should always be depicted as sitting down watching someone else perform.

The importance of building skills for leisure through physical education can be pointed up with the fact that today we have more leisure for *Americans* and more Americans for leisure. *Elementary school years are the skill-learning years.* Not only should the physical education program contribute to the development of the children here and now, but it should emphasize activities and outcomes which will aid them in leisure-time pursuits in later life.

Public schools have not always recognized moral and spiritual values as a part of their field of operation. Within the past decade, increased attention has been given to this aspect of the child's life as a legitimate concern of the school and as a vital objective of education. The leader of children in physical education activities must admit of more than a passing interest in these goals, for we have always talked of sportsmanship, fair play, ethics, and morals as they are expressed through games, sports, and dances.

Here, again, experience tells us it is the early years that are most important. Church schools have demonstrated the truth of this principle. All of the moral or spiritual values which are suggested by the Educational Policies Commission can be found and translated into everyday experiences for children in the elementary physical education program.[2]

Every teacher has the challenge and opportunity to put into the teaching of physical education the understanding of moral and spiritual values. Children should constantly be encouraged to apply these values to daily life, both during and away from the physical education program.

To ensure desirable results from participation in physical education activities, good leadership must be provided. The teacher is the most important leader, for it is he whose personality most directly and finally affects children in the program. Good professional preparation is important, to be sure, but what the teacher *is* matters more than what he says or knows.

No one has ever disputed the fact that example is the most powerful force in leading or teaching young people. Emerson says: "That which we are we shall teach, not voluntarily, but involuntarily. Thoughts come into our mind through avenues which we never left open, and thoughts go out of our minds through avenues which we never voluntarily opened."

2. National Education Association and American Association of School Administrators, Educational Policies Commission. *Moral and Spiritual Values in the Public Schools,* Washington, D.C.: the Association. 1951.

ESSENTIALS OF A GOOD PROGRAM

Certain essential characteristics identify a sound elementary school physical education program. Experience over a period of many years shows that when these elements are present the program thrives; but most important, children—all children—in the school reap benefits which meet their needs and propel them onward toward maturity and responsibility. Briefly, these essentials may be listed as follows:

All pupils are enrolled in physical education activities and participate daily. The program includes a large variety of activities.

Natural play-type activities are recognized as superior to formalized drills. By natural activities is meant those which meet the children's current interests and where movement is used in games that involve hunting and fleeing, stunts, rhythm, and mimicking animals, things, or persons.

The instructional program in physical education has adequate time allotment. This should be approximately thirty minutes daily for each child.

The program has balance between the instructional period, free play with guidance, and special events or play days.

The program of activities is adapted to the needs of all pupils—to the superior athlete as well as the physically handicapped.

The program is stressed equally for boys and girls.

The activities are carefully selected as to value and are appropriate to the age, sex, and individual differences of the pupils.

Health records, participation records, and achievement records are kept and used to the advantage of the child. They are referred to often in adapting the program to individual needs.

Competent, exemplary leaders are in charge of the program and keep in mind all of the objectives which they are seeking through physical education.

Adequate facilities, equipment, and supplies are available for conducting the program of activities for all pupils.

The program has and maintains the support of the public.

79 *Dramatic play and cognitive development*

LUCILE C. PERRYMAN

Many adults do not know that children do some important thinking as they play. Observe young children out of school as they measure themselves against their world and integrate and articulate meanings in words, or sounds, or motions. During outdoor periods pupils of capable teachers play through what they learn in school—and learn some more. When your pupils carry your school program into their intimate world of play, you know that you have really reached them.

Play is significant not only for little children; it is part of the cognitive development and emotional growth of everyone.

> Happy hearts and happy faces,
> Happy play in grassy places,
> That is how in ancient ages,
> Children grew to Kings and Sages.

ROBERT LOUIS STEVENSON in this short poem expresses clearly and beautifully, as only a poet can, the main theme of this article—i.e., children learn to understand their world and discover reality through dramatic play.

We as adults need to reexamine our attitudes about play to see if in our hectic, rushed, and harried post-Sputnik lives we have come to distrust play and consider it a waste of precious time. Have we come to use words like testing, exploring, experimenting, or even manipulating, in preference to the word "play"? How easily and honestly are we able to say "I would like to play with this idea or thing so that I can get the feel of it and understand it better"? Or do we feel more comfortable when we say "I'll need to test it out. I want to explore its dimensions and experiment with it so that I can understand it more fully."

We must remember that play is all of these things: testing, exploring, experimenting, and manipulating, with the added dimension of being a self-directed, spontaneous activity which the player does with complete involvement.

None of us will deny that we learn best when we do a task because we want to do it, we choose to do it, and we do it with a wholehearted spirit. This is why children, and adults too, perhaps, learn best through play.

Reprinted from *Journal of Nursery Education,* Vol. 17, No. 4, September, 1962, 185-88.

THEORIES OF PLAY

But what really is play, and more specifically, what is dramatic play? Play is a complex phenomenon composed of many variables. It appears in many guises and a great variety of forms. Its results are so subtle and far-reaching that any one definition or explanation will of necessity be partial and incomplete. The whole truth regarding play is still unknown. It appears to be intimately related to the whole phenomenon of life itself, and only as the complex processes of growth and development are unraveled and understood will a clearer, more accurate theory of play be evolved.

One of the oldest and best known theories of play is the Schiller-Spencer surplus-energy theory. It is the common-sense answer to, "Why do children play?" Shorn of its scientific terminology it says that children play because they have to, in order to work off their surplus energies or tensions. In essence Spencer says that at any time a man or animal finds he does not need all of his energies in the struggle for his survival, he will use his surplus energies in play. Moreover, the form the play takes will be a simulation of those activities which are needed by the player in his survival struggle.[1]

Those of us who work with children see many examples of play that appear to be the result of draining off excess energy. Further, we see many examples of imitative or simulated adult activity which represent basic survival activities such as cooking and marketing and caring for babies or mock fighting and combat. Yet this explanation of play as surplus energy leaves us unsatisfied, and with a desire to go behind the scenes more deeply.

G. T. Patrick, building on the ideas of Morritz Lazarus, proposed a diametrically opposite theory of play in his book, *The Psychology of Relaxation.*[2] Patrick explains play as the demands of the higher cerebral centers for relaxation. Play is the restorer, the conserver of energy, not the drainer of surplus energy.

It is not hard to find examples of recreational play in either children or adults. When we grow fatigued from imposed tasks we turn easily to other activities to which we can give ourselves in wholehearted abandon and emerge refreshed despite what appears to be an enormous expenditure of energy. It is not at all apparent, however, that we can explain this whole phenomenon solely on the central nervous system's demand for relaxation.

Karl Gross also believed that the Schiller-Spencer surplus energy theory

---

1. Herbert Spencer. *The Principles of Psychology,* New York: D. Appleton and Co., 1873, II, 630.
2. P. T. Patrick. *The Psychology of Relaxation,* Boston: The Houghton Mifflin Co., 1916, pp. 33-39.

of play was incomplete and he turned his attention to a more penetrating analysis of play. Gross concluded that play was a basic instinct, or as we would say, a basic need, of all higher forms of life. He described an instinct as a complex act mostly connected with the organism's struggle for life and the preservation of the species. He believed that in lower animals there was no true play, for it was not needed in their struggle for survival. In lower forms of life where the newborn is able to do almost everything the mature member of the species can do within hours or days after its birth, there is no need to practice in simulated play situations the activities the animal will need to perform as an adult. Gross put it into these words, "Children do not play because they are young, but they are young in order that they may play."[3]

Gross also saw play as a safety valve for the expression of pent-up emotions. This doctrine of catharsis was to be picked up and more fully developed by Sigmund Freud. Spencer also hinted at the notion that some forms of play were a type of compensation when he described mimic chase and fighting activities and games as an "ideal satisfaction for the destructive instinct in the absence of any real satisfaction for them."[4]

Sigmund Freud expressed these ideas in his dissertation, *Beyond the Pleasure Principle*. Freud advanced the theory that man's basic desire was "instinct gratification" and that lack of gratification, or frustration of basic instincts, gives rise to numerous substitute activities. These substitute activities occur under the domination of the pleasure principle, i.e., that all organisms seek pleasure and avoid pain. Thus play can in large measure be accounted for as compensatory pleasure-seeking behavior. In Freud's words, "When basic instincts are frustrated, the organism resorts to play as an outlet or substitute."[5]

This explanation of play has proven most heuristic, and although individual writers today may depart from a pure Freudian point of view, they agree that play can be the mirror of the child's inner world. Through his play, a child reveals many of his problems, his satisfactions, his strengths and weaknesses and his individual needs. Further, they agree that play can heal sick minds and bodies, and prevent the buildup of dangerous and destructive emotions.

John Dewey also was concerned with play. He did not agree with Freud's theory that play was basically compensatory behavior tied to the individual's seeking of pleasure and avoidance of pain. Dewey believed play

3. Karl Gross. *The Play of Animals*, New York: D. Appleton and Co., 1915, p. 23.
4. Spencer, *op. cit.*, p. 630.
5. Sigmund Freud, *Beyond the Pleasure Principle*, London: The International Psychoanalytical Press, 1922, p. 11.

was an expression of the natural urge of all living things to be active. He stated, "When the myth of natural quiescence is surrendered with its accompanying myth of the need of a special premium in order to arouse an inert agent, it ceases to be necessary to search for any special object in order to account for play. It is enough to say that action is basic to all living organisms and this need for action gives rise to play."[6] Play from this point of view is a natural part of all normal growth and development and the maturational level of the player will influence the form the play will take.

DRAMATIC PLAY

Let us now turn to dramatic play in particular. This form of play is engaged in spontaneously by children in the early childhood years, roughly between the ages of three and seven. In this kind of play the child imitates and relives various experiences he has had. In his play the child becomes the object or person he is trying to understand. As the child plays at being a mother, father, groceryman, policeman, or even a fire truck, airplane, or boat, he begins to know what these people and objects in his life represent and what his relationships to them are. As he plays he seeks more words to express his growing understandings.

In his dramatic play the child has many opportunities to test out his new-found words and learn their power. From his verbalizations he begins to develop a schematization or frame of reference. As Joseph Church explains in his book, *Language and the Discovery of Reality,*[7] verbal expression helps tie the environment together into a coherent familiar dependable whole, against which the child can test subsequent experiences.

In dramatic play the child sees the need for written symbols as well as verbal ones, and he begins to use them. The child playing motorman or truck driver begins to make and read signs which say "Go," "Stop," "Dead End," "One Way." The child playing grocer or shopper makes and reads labels as he sells and buys merchandise. He begins to count, add and subtract, and make change. The child playing mother or father in the house writes a letter and makes a shopping list. In this way the child grows easily into the use of symbols, which help him in sorting and arranging all his perplexing perceptions of the real world.

6.   John Dewey. *A Cyclopedia of Education,* New York: The Macmillan Co., 1925, IV, 725.
7.   Joseph Church. *Language and the Discovery of Reality,* New York: Random House, 1961.

In his dramatic play the child is unafraid to test out his ideas, knowledge, and feelings. By the manipulation of the symbols he uses in his play he is able to rearrange situations which in reality might resist such reorganization.

Those who have studied children's thinking or cognitive development have recognized the symbolic and social nature of the thinking process as well as the close relationship existing between language and thought. David H. Russell expressed this relation in these words, "There is little disagreement among philosophers or psychologists about the close relationship between language and most thinking—both tend to be directed toward some goal or conclusion, both exhibit symptoms of searching for related materials and both involve some sort of integrative patterning."[8]

Jean Piaget was one of the first to explore the language and thought of the young child. He concluded that language and thought development followed a rather strict chronological serial order, moving from a preverbal sensory-motor stage to an egocentric animistic stage of monologues and collective monologues, and finally to a social, rational, and logical stage.[9] Piaget makes a distinction between the egocentric speech and thought of the child and the social, rational, logical speech and thought of the adult. Some writers have challenged this concept and feel there is no such sharp distinction. Joseph Church expressed it very well when he said, "The most sophisticated adults in their everyday lives, and especially in personal matters, show evidence of egocentrism, of realism, of anthropomorphism and animism, of instability and inconsistency and of failures of symbolization."[10]

It does seem, however, that children's rational thinking is governed somewhat by their maturation level, particularly in the areas of space and time. But one must realize that logical thought does not develop automatically by the sheer passing of time; if it is to develop, it must be nurtured and guided. As we have seen in dramatic play all the necessary ingredients are present for the development of rational thought. There are opportunities for countless firsthand experiences with objects and people where the child can bring all of his senses into play in order to get accurate perceptions. There are opportunities to use words in connection with experiences and to build a verbal frame of reference or schemata, which will help the child organize his past experiences and will mobilize him for future experiences.

8. David H. Russell. *Children's Thinking,* New York: Ginn and Company, 1956, p. 24.
9. Jean Piaget. *The Language and Thought of the Child,* New York: Meridian Books, The Noonday Press, 2nd ed., 1955.
10. Church, *op. cit.,* p. 49.

ROLE OF THE TEACHER

An important difference between spontaneous dramatic play in school and free dramatic play in the home or back yard is in the guidance which the teacher can and should give. The teacher provides the props and environment that will suggest the topic and direction of the play. At appropriate times the teacher should introduce new materials, equipment, and experiences which will move the play toward certain desired educational goals. The teacher knows what new experiences and materials will be needed by keeping alert to all the child says and does as he plays. By providing time after play for questioning, answering, and discussing what has happened, telling and listening to related stories, going on trips to nearby places to gain more concrete experiences, and viewing pictures and films which are visual symbols of those concrete experiences, the teacher provides the child with opportunities to exercise his growing cognitive powers. This helps him to increase his skill in observation, to be more discriminating and to make more logical generalizations. The teacher must also help the child in every way possible to gain greater understanding and confidence in himself and his relationships to his environment. It is this concept of self which will ultimately free the child to revise his immature ideas and move on to more mature and rational thought.

Dramatic play can be a powerful tool for cognitive development when it is guided by an adult who uses critical and creative language and is symbol-minded.

80   *Building an effective health program*

ROBERT S. FLEMING

What occasions lend themselves to the informal teaching of constructive attitudes and facts about mental and physical health? What kind of formal program should be organized?

CURRICULUM LEADERS are concerned at the present time with individual differences, balance in the curriculum, and evaluating growth of pupils. These

Reprinted from *The National Elementary Principal,* 39:10-13, February, 1960.

are thought to be the most basic items for study as a means of improving the school program. Such areas of concern are appropriate in connection with all phases of the modern school. The health program, to be effective, must focus on each individual. Balance, in the area of health, is of great importance in making sure that health is viewed in its broad perspective. Evaluation of progress being made by both the individual and the group is essential.

SCOPE OF HEALTH PROGRAM

Health covers a multitude of things. There is John with a drippy nose. There is Rose who is overweight. There is Sue with a stye. There is Alice with a headache. There is Ralph who runs a temperature. There is Gladys with poison ivy.

These are more or less obvious health problems. There are a variety of other problems children may have that also concern us. There is Fanny who has had seven accidents. There is Clara who is always eating. There is Susan, the first-grader, who gets sick at reading. There is Paul, the shy one. There is Lillian who went to the bathroom twenty-seven times one day. There is Phil who always wants praise. There is Louis who does not participate.

Many health problems confront children daily. Some deal with physical difficulties such as infectious diseases and nutrition, while others deal with emotional problems—children's feelings, relationships with individuals and groups, perceptions of self. But all in all, health problems in any school are interrelated and concern physical and emotional factors. The modern school cannot remain indifferent to health or fail to know individuals as they reflect their own syndromes.

The modern school of the sixties likely does not need to be concerned with its water supply, provision for sewerage disposal, or the control of insects. Pellegra, itch, typhoid, and the like are not the persistent problems today which they were at one time. But our health situation is not good, our problems are not solved, and our curriculum is not in order.

Health is commonly accepted as one of our basic areas of concern in elementary education and most schools list many specific health goals. They recognize that the healthy child tends to learn more, that the well-adjusted child tends to stay in school, that health problems are related to other difficulties, and that problems of growth, development, and adjustment cannot be isolated from health.

The individual with a behavior disorder, the chronic absentee, the individual having a temper tantrum, the child with nutritional difficulties—all must be considered in terms of health. A variety of studies have demonstrated the relationship between physical and emotional problems and learning. If one assumes that the major goal of the elementary school is to promote learning, it follows that he must also concern himself with health. A teacher must begin his work with an individual in terms of health if his major purpose is learning or if his goals are concerned with broad aspects of growth and adjustment.

CURRICULUM DEVELOPMENT

The same basic principles should be employed in the development of a health program as are used in planning any other area of the school program. Actually, curriculum development in health is no different than in any other field. The following principles seem important.

The health program should reflect the health problems of a particular group of children in a particular community setting. In their planning, a faculty might well have in mind two sets of concerns. One would involve certain basic understandings in the field of health which children should develop, and the second would center around the provision of opportunities to solve existing health problems.

The more impressive and important aspects of the health program are those which emerge from local conditions. There is the New Jersey school in which there have been children with encephalitis; there is the Canadian community in which there has been a tragic school bus accident; there is the football team whose players were violently ill with food poisoning; there is the community in which a rat bit a child. These are but illustrative of recent health problems of local importance which should be reflected in the school program.

Not all problems are as dramatic as these. Children have many health questions worthy of active concern. These deal with understanding where babies come from, taking care of a sick dog, avoiding a cold, or understanding what happens to the food we eat.

The teacher must be alert to "set the stage" for children to raise questions. He may do this in a variety of ways. There is the complete openended kind of questioning in which children raise questions about anything, even outside of the field of health. There is the technique in which they raise specific questions about nutrition, about keeping well, about safety. There is the more confining and perhaps less effective technique in which children write specific questions about vitamins or malaria or colds or the room temperature. Questions of concern to the learner are basic forces in planning with children.

As a teacher begins to work with a new group of children, his most important first task is to observe. He is looking for the individual who has trouble seeing the board, or the one who cannot hear, or the person with allergies, or the child who is very thin or the one who is fat. In other words, the teacher opens his eyes to recognize any health factors present. As these are recorded and summarized, he has some basis for planning functional, meaningful curriculum experiences.

This principle of identification of health problems seems basic to the development of any program. It takes time, it is developmental, and it requires insightful teachers.

The health program requires a team approach to program planning, execution, and evaluation. It seems urgent from time to time to provide an opportunity for the teachers of a school to share information about an individual child. This often goes far beyond information to be found on existing school records. One of the most powerful resources of a school is the collective information of a group of teachers who have known a child over a period of time.

The health program often requires additional resources. The teacher obviously cannot be an authority in all fields of health. Cooperation from the school nurse, contacts with the school or family physician, and referrals to specialists in speech, hearing, and other areas are of great importance. As an individual teacher deals with certain emotional problems of children—nausea, headaches, finger sucking, nail biting, anger, fears, and the like, it is essential that the teacher, nurse, parents, and others pool their information, seek advice from medical or mental health specialists, and coordinate their efforts.

The health program should provide opportunities for children to have firsthand experiences in dealing with vital problems. There has been too much teaching "about health" in the past and too little "study or solving of current health problems." There have been too many teachers having children learn certain health rules which are taught as universal. We now see that maximum progress comes as children have opportunity to deal with issues in a firsthand way.

The famous trip to the water supply needs to be reconsidered and greatly extended. There must be many places in any community which children may profitably visit. There is the meat-packing plant, the slaughterhouse, the barbership, the dairy, the hospital, the weather station, the laboratory for testing milk and water, the street-cleaning department, the garbage dump, the potential spots for mosquito and fly breeding, the houses without screens and adequate sewage disposal, the crowded, unattractive homes, the safety hazards, the streets without stop lights, the neighborhoods without playgrounds, the playground with nails, rocks, holes—and on and on it goes. As children visit such places, describing through words and pictures their findings, unlimited learning can occur. Such an active approach to curriculum experience is not an end in itself, for these experiences create additional concerns which children can pursue through their research and further study.

Evaluation is an ongoing dimension of curriculum planning. These curriculum principles have given prominence to evaluation as a way of identifying needs and planning program experiences. No longer does evaluation simply consist of a terminal test for a given unit. Rather, one begins with evaluation as a basis for planning.

The modern school makes continuous use of a variety of evaluation techniques. Many of these techniques are observational, some are projective, some involve cumulative records (anecdotes) of how children feel about what they are doing, and many consist of products of children's work. This is not to rule out tests as important evaluative devices, but it does suggest that the test is but one source of data. Perhaps the child himself should become the most central figure in evaluating his progress in health.

Information should be accumulated about a variety of growth and health factors. Frequent analyses of attendance should be made. Such instruments as the Wetzel-Grid record of growth and development should be cumulative for many, perhaps all, children. Records might also include photographs of children taken at various times, records of friendship patterns, pupils' concerns and behavior problems.

It is interesting that many schools have inconsistent practices. For example, the teacher attempts to help a group understand the nature of infectious diseases. He relates the sneezing, coughing stage of a cold to spread of the disease by droplet infections. As he helps young people understand their social responsibility to avoid contaminating others, one manifestation of accomplishment would be that the child would stay home when he is in such a condition. The irony of this situation is that many schools reward children with a certificate when they have no absence, regardless of their health when present. Perhaps children should be certificated as they apply basic health knowledge in daily living.

Ongoing study of the total health program and of ways for increasing its effectiveness is essential. This is more than evaluation of pupils. It suggests that a variety of action research studies should be undertaken to determine ways of better facilitating the health growth of children. Specific illustrations of professional questions which should be considered include ways of making more valid observations, sharing information, securing information about the health status of children, working with the medical and dental professions, keeping up with research in nutrition and other health areas, and evaluating results.

These are areas which need to be better understood in our schools. It is only as a school faculty attempts to improve the program that it can be improved. In all this, however, care must be taken not to assume that the school is all things to every child. Other individuals and agencies work on important health problems of the community and the school must relate its health instruction and services to their activities.

As the above principles of curriculum development are put into practice, schools will begin to relate more directly to individual, group, and community problems. It would be shortsighted if one attempted to deal with health in isolation from other learning areas. Our history has too long demonstrated the ineffectiveness and shortsightedness of teaching health in isolation from language, science, social studies, physical education. Health can be taught creatively. Perhaps our schools desperately need new, novel, dynamic approaches to the solution of health problems of individuals and groups.

HALLMARKS OF A GOOD PROGRAM

The following hallmarks of the health program are listed as a simple self-evaluative instrument which may be used for study and improvement of current practices. Mark S those qualities you feel most satisfied with and N those you consider need major attention. Those marked N should then be discussed to see how improvements can be made.

Local current health problems are identified.   ———

Children are frequently encouraged to relate their health concerns.   ———

The faculty attempts to summarize and analyze local problems and children's concerns.   ———

The faculty works together, shares ideas and materials, and seeks professional advice.   ———

The school is thought of as a friendly, pleasant place to which children like to go.   ———

Teachers are free to talk about their problems with the principal or other appropriate individuals.   ———

Children have firsthand experiences in studying and solving meaningful problems.   ———

Children use a variety of learning aids.   ———

Evaluation occurs throughout the learning experience, using a variety of procedures.   ———

Effort is made to relate health information to other aspects of the
school program.   ___

A growing complexity of problems is studied by children of various
age levels.   ___

A variety of creative, dynamic practices is used to relate health to
current problems of home, school, and community.   ___

Records summarize a child's development and growth in health
knowledge, including records of attendance, immunization, adjustment, nutrition, growth, relations with others.   ___

Children are helped to apply health principles in daily living, in
dress, temperature control, nutrition, washing, grooming, care of
infections, and playground safety.   ___

Teachers demonstrate good health practices in their nutrition, conduct, dress, attitudes.   ___

The faculty continuously surveys local resources for extending the
effectiveness of their teaching.   ___

The faculty seeks to understand recent developments in research
and their implications.   ___

The faculty systematically studies their problems and carries on action research to improve their program.   ___

The principal gives leadership to the task of planning and improving the health program.   ___

These are qualities which must be maintained in the modern elementary
school at any price. Not all of our practice in the teaching of health in the
past has been bad; not all of it has been good. The profile for the future should
ensure that we use the best that research can give us, that we relate our teaching to the concerns of people, that children have opportunities for dynamic
experiences, and that the resources of the local community be tapped in the
cooperative solution of problems. We must insure that there be a continuing
quest for greater productivity in creative, human values.

WALLACE H. MAW

Do you agree with Maw's contention that "all schools are doing something about sex education"? How was sex education treated in the elementary school you attended? in your present college or university? As a teacher—or a parent—to which idea listed here would you subscribe? Are there other possibilities for elementary and secondary schools?

How is your school handling sex education? To say that sex education is not a function of the school is begging the question. All schools are doing something about sex education. When the subject is avoided, children are learning that sex is a topic which cannot be approached openly and objectively.

IDEAS OF SEX EDUCATION

Just what do we mean by sex education? A study of the ideas expressed regarding this topic fall under the following overlapping rubrics:

1. Silence
2. Moral suasion
3. Fear
4. Factual instruction
5. Ethical understanding
6. Personal development
7. Human relations

Silence. Silence is exemplified actively and passively. It is active when attempts are made to prevent dissemination of information concerning sex or to stop particular programs of sex education. It is passive when information about sex is omitted from textbooks and when writers substitute euphemisms for biological terms.

The idea of silence was more prevalent before World War I than it is today. Yet even now, there are those who believe that the scripture should read, "The truth shall make you free—*except in matters pertaining to sex.*" There are still communities where school personnel may be dismissed for

Reprinted from the January, 1963 issue of *Education*. Copyright 1963 by the Bobbs-Merrill Co., Inc., Indianapolis, Indiana.

teaching about sex and reproduction. A biology textbook used in some schools discusses several tropical diseases, but fails to mention venereal disease.

Moral suasion. One of the earlier methods of sex education was to correlate sex and sin. Children were taught that violation of the accepted pattern of sexual behavior led to eternal punishment, while staying on the "right path" promised eternal reward.

During the 1890's, many books were published that admonished youth to live virtuous lives. In one sense these books were better than some published today. The authors were honest in their aims and did not attempt to cover their moralistic efforts in a cloak of camaraderie or in a slangy give-and-take. However, these books lost much of their effectiveness when stories used to "prove" the case were shown to be false.

Too often the sex-is-sin theme was taught too well. The attitudes learned could not be changed as a result of the marriage vows. Many divorces and other social tragedies are known to result when sex impulses are linked so closely with sin that even accepted sexual behavior falls under its aegis.

Fear. By 1910, the failure of "preachy" methods was apparent. The theme shifted. Fear of dangers in the present life was substituted for fear of consequences after death. No one can deny that there are real dangers of venereal infection, illegitimacy, insanity, sterility, and social ostracism.

It is an obligation of society to alert its members to such dangers. The warnings, however, were often given so as to arouse fears that endangered normal relationships. Sometimes the warnings became dares. The more venturesome put their emphasis on not getting caught.

With the increased availability of knowledge about contraceptives and simple cures for venereal diseases, these fears, together with those involving sterility and social ostracism, faded into the background. Unfortunately, the information was more false than true and the gamblers lost far too frequently. Finally, those who would teach by evoking fear hurt their cause by drawing conclusions which were not tenable.

Factual information. During the twentieth century many writers felt that children and young people should be taught the facts about sex and reproduction. Several approaches were used. The sexual reproduction of lower animals was described and pupils were expected to draw conclusions applicable to human beings.

The "facts" were too often scattered through other material and were approached tangentially. Books for young people to read themselves, or have read to them, became available. These varied from crude, almost pornographic attempts at describing sex to aesthetic, meaningful presentations. Many were so filled with sentimentality that the facts were obscured. Special lectures and films were also used.

Unfortunately, the facts were devastating for many children. The need was not for facts alone; the need was for more understanding and support. By the time most children had the facts presented to them, they were less concerned about anatomical differences and more deeply interested in resolving their anxieties about why life functions as it does. The quest for purpose demanded less biology and more emotion.

Ethical understanding. Recognizing this limitation, many advocates of sex education related their informational presentations to ethical understanding and stressed the development of attitudes. The responsibility of the individual for the human race, monogamic marriage, sanctity of the home, aesthetics of sex, and character became matters of increasing concern.

The trend in sex education toward a broader viewpoint had its counterpart in developments taking place in other parts of the school program and in the community. Expanding the curriculum, interrelating subject matter, and developing guidance programs are a few of these changes. Outside the school, eugenics, woman suffrage, and mental hygiene played prominent roles in emphasizing the ethical aspects of sexual behavior and in de-emphasizing the biological aspects of sexual behavior.

Unfortunately, at times, the de-emphasis went too far. While biological facts do not constitute a program of sex education, facts are important. Denying the anatomy can be as harmful as overemphasizing it. Ethical understanding often became ethical misunderstanding. Efforts were made to mold society into a particular pattern by accepting "facts" that served this purpose and rejecting those that didn't.

Personal development. Those who challenged the espousing of "the ethical point of view" questioned whether schools should not help pupils develop an ethical basis for sexual behavior without prescribing exactly what the attitudes should be. They believed sex instruction should be part of guidance programs designed to help pupils develop wholesome lives. Sex education was identified as part of a broad program, not as a separate phase of education.

The advocates of the idea of personal development pointed out that problems of sexual adjustment were best handled when their existence was recognized, when one tried to solve them himself with help from others, and when feelings and anxieties could be expressed in confidence.

The most effective approaches to sex education as personal development were those that tapered content to the unique needs of a particular pupil. Mass presentations, except in the case of very rudimentary materials, were not used. Many books and materials were available, but more important, there were people who could give needed support and answer questions without shock or censure. Every teacher became a guidance counsellor working not only with pupils in his own classroom but also with other pupils who felt more at ease with him.

It became apparent that if sex education were to become effective in meeting the unique needs of the individual it could not be left entirely to the school. Schools served an auxiliary role in performing this function.

The proponents of the personal-development theme were also aware that turning the problem over to parents did not solve it. It was necessary for schools, PTA's, mental and social health committees working independently and cooperatively to develop programs to help parents.

Human relations. Human beings are gregarious. Programs of sex education based upon personal development fused with those emphasizing socialization activities. At first the program dealt principally with domestic science. Family relationships and responsibilities became the core of instruction. Preparation for future marriage was emphasized.

The need to help pupils solve problems of peer relationships was at first neglected. By World War II, however, more and more books and courses were adapted to problems of boy-girl relationships. Dating, youth organizations, and wholesome activities became their foci.

Terminology also changed. "Sex instruction" and "sex hygiene" gave way to the more descriptive terms of "family-life education" and "human-relations education."

Finally it was perceived that no sex education could be successful until all personalities were respected. One works out adjustment with the opposite sex not only on the basis of sex-membership but more on the basis of a common membership in the human race. A start can be made by helping children appreciate individual differences from the moment they are noticed and by teaching respect for all people regardless of age, race, color, or sex.

CONCLUSION

How is your school handling sex education? Which of these ideas are reflected in your philosophy of education?

In practice, many curriculums are eclectic, employing something from all the ideas. The more effective programs, however, are less restricted to the ideas of silence, sermons, threats, and facts and increasingly focused upon the teaching of ethical understanding, personal development, and human relations.

Is your school pursuing a narrow course or is sex education so much a part of the entire program that your pupils are developing an appreciation of all human beings regardless of sex? An evaluation of what is emphasized in your curriculum in terms of the ideas stressed in this paper should tell you what role your school is playing in the sex education of your pupils.

❧

82 *Sex education in the public schools*

G. G. WETHERILL

A program for sex education in San Diego, California, schools was formulated through the efforts of teachers, school administrators, physicians, nurses, parents' groups, church groups, and social agencies. The excerpt below contains a list of lessons planned for sixth-graders.

1. How WE GROW, differences in the growth patterns of boys and girls, responsibilities of growing up, the importance of caution with strangers, how to choose the right friends, your appearance, glands that are responsible for growth and changes in our bodies, good attitudes, and the right names of the body's organs and functions. Questions and answers.

2. Films on animal reproduction (*The Sunfish, The Snapping Turtle, Snakes Are Interesting*). Questions and answers. This helps boys and girls understand that with all living things a male cell and a female egg must join before a new life can begin. This is a good impersonal introduction to human reproduction.

3. Read a short book or monograph on human reproduction. Questions and answers.

4. (Boys) Discuss glandular changes, growth of sex organs, formation of sperm, seminal emissions, masturbation, reasons for body changes, and use of self-control. Questions and answers.

Reprinted from the *Journal of School Health*, 31:237, September, 1961.

4. (Girls) Review the sex organs, discuss menstruation (you may wish to show a film on menstruation), discuss reasons for body changes, sex relations, and self-control. Some schools show the film *The Story of Menstruation* in the fifth grade when the need is apparent.

5. Show the film *Human Growth* to review and clarify previous lessons and to set the stage for further discussion of such things as strengthening right attitudes toward sex and growing up, correct terminology, cell division, twins, sex determination, heredity, boy-girl relationships, moral and spiritual values. Question and answer periods follow all of the lessons.

83   *School project helps pupils learn about children by contact with preschoolers*

M O R T O N   E D W A R D S

Some educators might call this a project in health education, others, family-life education. These pupils engaged in useful discussion, did a lot of reading, saw films about child development, and studied the social organization and behavior of preschoolers.

TEN- AND ELEVEN-year-olds are given opportunities to see what growing human beings are really like when they serve on the school's Service Squad and help nursery school teachers handle groups of preschool youngsters. This novel project in family-life education enables children to learn about the role of adults in our society by practicing the role, teaches them the dynamics of human nature through observation and later discussion, and shows them that interactions between people constitute a great source of power in our society. The fact that these youngsters are learning to take responsibility, do a job and see a task through is also important, to say nothing of the satisfaction they derive from knowing that they're doing a job needed by their school.

At appointed times during the school day, these ten- and eleven-year-olds

Reprinted from *The 2-to-5-World News* (now *Today's Child*), 5:6, March, 1957.

quietly slip out of their rooms, head for the nursery classes, and set about their clearly outlined tasks in a most businesslike manner. Enthusiastically, they help the little ones with lunch, at story and activity time, and at juice and rest periods.

Their preschool charges look to members of the Service Squad with affection and trust, and this has a profound effect on the older children's attitudes and actions. At periodic seminars, these fifth- and sixth-graders tell faculty members their personal reactions to the program and pass along the generalizations they have formed about the small children they help. In return, they are taught the basic principles of child development. They view films and read material on mental health. They soon get to talk with remarkable insight about the proper ways of achieving discipline, of allowing freedom within limits, and by what means adults can make a child feel secure. They also quickly learn the importance of a quiet voice and manner from watching the reactions of the younger.

Work on the Service Squad frequently represents the only contact some of the older youngsters have with small children. Here is preparation for parenthood which does not interfere with academic work at all, yet may help to eliminate the stereotype of the desperate mother or father who, faced with a normally active preschooler, wails: "But I didn't *realize* children are like *that.*"

84   *How to use sociodrama*

LESLIE D. ZELENY

Sociodrama is one of many ways to help pupils feel as well as think about their world. Do not try to dictate to pupils what they should feel and say in sociodrama. Probably no other activity calls for more careful choreography. (See Teaching classroom routines, *p. 87.)*

Effective sociodrama, in the hands of a skillful teacher, can help pupils express their perceptions of many kinds of personal-social situations. Sometimes this form of expression helps pupils know themselves and others better. But this is no gimmick to be "fooled around with" by anyone but the most serious and steady teacher. One good way to learn to use sociodrama with children is to participate in sociodrama yourself with other adults.

WHAT IS A sociodrama? A sociodrama is the "acting out" of a problem in social relations in which pupils spontaneously play roles in the same manner as persons involved in the real problem. By this means, problems in social relations become objects of study. Students are helped to understand personalities in their human relations and to draw useful lessons from their analysis of a re-created experience.

PRODUCING A SOCIODRAMA

To produce a sociodrama the teacher-director should have in mind some fundamental elements of procedure. His function is to release spontaneous action that leads to the re-creation of life roles in certain social relations, and to the understanding and practice of desirable social roles. As the sociodrama develops, the teacher participates less and less and the students more. However in helping the students to select their problem the teacher knows that it must be one which interests the pupils and which at the same time relates to a major social problem.

The procedure which follows suggests seven steps for development of the sociodrama.

1. Recognition of a problem. By accepting a problem in social relations as worthy of study, the class begins the development of a sociodrama. An

From Pamphlet 20 of the How-to-Do-It Series. Washington, D.C.: National Council for the Social Studies, 1955, pp. 1-3, 7-8.

easy way to accomplish this is to ask the pupils to name problems in social relations which they would like to have solved, then select the one which is of interest to the largest number.[1]

Jennings did this effectively with a fifth-grade class in social studies by asking the children to name situations which bothered them.[2] In this instance, the most common was that of unnecessary errands at home. Many fifth-graders disliked making two successive trips to the store when one would do, but they did not fully understand the problem, nor what to do about it. Under the teacher's direction they were ready to re-create the problem situation, analyze it, and try to find a "solution."

2. Identification of roles. When talking about the problem the class identifies the parts or roles taken by persons in the real life situation. Tensions in social relations are often created because persons do not understand the requirements of their role in a particular situation. Many do not stop to consider such elements as the actions and feelings of others and the effect of one upon the other. If roles in a situation can be identified and described with special reference to personal feelings and consequent actions of others, much can be learned.

Jennings fully realized the importance of the identification, the inter-relationship of roles and associated feelings when she helped her fifth-grade class identify the roles in the errand problem. They were those of the thoughtless mother, annoyed daughter, and irritated father. She guided the class in the identification of the roles and in the description of actions and feelings appropriate to each.

She prepared for action by encouraging the children to imagine what the mother, father, and daughter would actually say and do in their problem situation. Needless to say, the fifth-grade class made a variety of suggestions. The discussion of the possible actions and feelings of the characters in the real situation became the "warm up" for the next step.

1. Charles E. Hendry, Ronald Lippitt, and Alvin Zander. Reality practice as educational method. *Psychodrama Monograph* No. 9, New York: Beacon House, 1947. To this fundamental article the writer owes much, especially for the suggestions for procedure.
2. The sociodrama in a fifth grade referred to here is from Helen Jennings. Sociodrama as an educative process. *Fostering Mental Health in Our Schools,* 1950 Yearbook, Washington, D.C.: Association for Supervision and Curriculum Development, a department of the National Education Association, 1950. Direct quotations are with permission of Helen Jennings and the Association for Supervision and Curriculum Development. Responsibility for interpretation is assumed by the writer and any errors are his.

3. *Selecting role players.* After roles have been identified and characterized, the class is ready for volunteers to enact the problem before the class. It is important not to force pupils to participate, for roles can be played freely only by those who wish to do so. Later, timid students may volunteer.

When teachers divide their classes into small groups of three or four persons, each pupil can take a role in an informal and semi-private "practice." This is a desirable preliminary to the final selection, and has the advantage of encouraging retiring students to test their talents.

Before role playing starts the "actors" confer for a few minutes, without attempting to rehearse what is to be said. The conference serves primarily to permit each role player to make a statement of the position he or she is to take and to agree upon a setting for the action.

After identification of roles in the "errand" problem, Jennings asked for volunteers from which role players were selected.

A brief conference followed in which the players reviewed their roles and planned their setting which was to be the family living room. The drama would open with the daughter seated at a table reading a school book, the mother lazily turning the pages of a picture magazine, and the father buried in the sports page of the local newspaper.

4. *Role playing.* For the role playing itself Jennings selected three fifth-grade volunteers to present a sociodrama of the errand problem before the class. Interest was good because the class had selected the problem, identified the nature of the roles, and noted the feelings associated with the situation. It was necessary only for the teacher to direct attention to the nature of the different roles. A part of what was said follows:

> Mother: I want you to go to the store for a loaf of bread and a bottle of milk.
> Marilyn (looking up from notebook): Can't you wait for a little while?
> Mother: I want you to go right now.
> Marilyn (throwing down pencil): Oh, all right! (Leaves room.)
> Father: I can't stand the way she talks.
> Mother: We'll just have to break her of the habit.
> Marilyn (comes back): Here's your bread and milk.
> Mother: Put them in the kitchen. (Marilyn puts them in the kitchen and starts to work again.)
> Mother: Oh, I forgot, I want some Sunshine cleanser. (Marilyn sighs, goes out in a disgusted manner.)

All the class members saw that the daughter had a problem; that an unnecessary errand was an annoyance and that there was no good reason for it.

5. *Analysis of the role playing.* The sociodrama does not stop with the presentation of roles by the "actors." The whole class makes an analysis of what happened, the effectiveness of the role players as a group and individually, and the possibilities of a more telling portrayal of the problem. They also consider a "solution" presentation.

In this fifth-grade sociodrama there was an opportunity for each child to compare his "picture" of each role with the one portrayed. The teacher took advantage of this interest by asking, "How did the situation come out?" One said, "The mother got her way but nobody was pleased." The class also saw why no one was pleased. The teacher provided for expression of these "whys" by asking, "Can you think of anything that might cause the situation to be the way we saw it?" The class responded immediately with suggestions: "They [mothers] didn't get their memories trained." "Sometimes they feel like bothering you, I guess." "It's to find out if you like them!"

In this analysis the children perceived important aspects of faulty behavior in a life situation. They had acquired new social insights. They saw how people could show more consideration for others.

6. *Replaying of roles.* An analysis of a sociodrama sets the stage for replaying the roles, which can be done two ways: (1) an improved presentation of the problem situation, and (2) the enactment of a "solution." Replaying may be done by the same students in the same or different roles, or by a new cast. In this fifth-grade sociodrama, the analysis readily suggested a combination of roles which could solve the problem of conflict. Among the numerous suggestions was one that "she could ask if her mother needed anything at the store before she started on her homework."

After discussion of the various proposals, the class was ready for a reenactment of the family scene to show reduced conflict over a simple daily problem. Three new volunteers enacted the solution thus:

Mother: I want you to go to the store. (Betty starts to make a list.)
Father: Get some lunch meat.
Betty (looking over mother's shoulder): Do you need some lettuce?
Mother: No, see if they have any salad dressing.
Father: I like Magic Whip mayonnaise if you can get a jar of it.
Betty: Okay. Do you want a cake for your lunch, Dad?
Father: Yes, and get some cigarettes.

The solution is simple indeed! But many children are not aware of it before the enactment of the "solution" sociodrama. They must learn ways of making role taking useful in daily life.

7. *Developing rules for the conduct of life.* Each sociodramatic production develops insight into the meaning of a specific kind of problem. Each class member who faces a simulated dilemma in human relations sees how a conflict of roles produces the dilemma, and endeavors to find a combination of roles which might lessen it. He develops an understanding of a way of behaving or a rule for the conduct of life which is approved by his fellow students. In this way, ethical standards are formed through a meeting of minds. This procedure is of the utmost significance in a democratic society where decisions are made through the adjustment of wills.

After studying their own role playing Jennings' pupils saw that a polite inquiry with respect to parents' needs was a more acceptable way of behaving than hastily accepting first requests knowing an unpleasant extra errand would probably be necessary. A simple rule, indeed, for reducing family tensions!

PURPOSES OF THE SOCIODRAMA

A sociodrama can re-create problems in ordinary daily living. It may also re-create problems of contemporary societies and even vital human issues of the past. The actions and feelings of people in situations near or remote, present or past, may be made real. And the situations can be studied as they are re-created.

The simple daily problems which may be role-played are many. All ages are faced with problems in relations between parents and children and among siblings. Problems in boy-girl relations are legion. Certain personal problems not unique but common to a group lend themselves to sociodramatic treatment—shyness, social isolation, abnormal physical size, speech difficulty. How to choose an occupation, apply for a job, refuse a loan, or meet the difficulties facing an immigrant are also likely subjects.

Moreno, the founder of sociodrama, proposed its use for the study of contemporary conflicts, and it is in this area that role playing has been most successful as an educational instrument for adults. Moreno would apply it to Negro-white, Gentile-Jewish, and capital-labor relations; and to political issues. In the classroom, where sociodramas dealing with simple, personal problems are the most effective, contemporary social problems have proved to be workable when related to the immediate interests of pupils.

Some teachers have tried to extend the sociodramatic method to the more remote issues of contemporary life and of history. Here it becomes difficult because these events are often removed from the experiences and interests of students; consequently, the dilemma does not arouse the desired spontaneity. Experienced teachers, however, have reported some success in these areas, and sufficient information is now available to make the proper adaptation of socio-drama to many issues of modern and past societies.

Role playing is more than an exercise. It can be used to teach social skills and desirable attitudes, and to promote the learning of behavior patterns necessary for good citizenship as well as for individual success in social life. Among values readily developed are social responsibility, loyalty, honesty, fairness, respect for personalities, leadership, followership, and ability to cooperate.

.   .   .   .

SUMMARY

A sociodrama is a re-creation of a dilemma in human relations through spontaneous and faithful enactment of the roles with the accompanying feelings involved in the situation.

To guide pupils through a sociodrama they must be helped to do each of the following:

1. Recognize a problem in human relations which they feel is worthy of study.
2. Identify and describe the human roles which, in their interrelationships, make the situation a problem.
3. Select willing role players.
4. Enact or play the roles in the problem situation.
5. Analyze the roles as played and the situation portrayed.
6. Replay the sociodrama to improve the interpretation of the social situation and/or to suggest a solution to the problem.
7. Build understandings for the conduct of life from the meanings made clear by the sociodrama, its analysis, and its replaying.

The sociodrama has important educational possibilities. It makes possible not only the analysis of life situations of immediate concern in the daily life of children and youth but, when adequate preparation is made, it also makes possible the re-creation for analysis of some of the great social issues of our times and of the past. Over and above this, through the method employed, it enables pupils to gain skill in the way problems are solved in a democratic society. Thus the use of sociodrama contributes directly to citizenship education.

CHAPTER 18

Developing with Art and Music

IN THE INTRODUCTION to Chapter 1 we quote Lawrence Kubie's notion of emotional maturation, "the harmonious coordination and integration of conscious and unconscious levels of personality" (page 2). One would hope that all activities teachers plan, sometimes for and sometimes with pupils, would be conceived with such an objective in mind. Kubie's goal for students is self-knowledge. He writes, "It is this self-knowledge which penetrates below the levels of conscious awareness, which integrates all levels in the make-up of the human being...."[1] All school experiences, all subjects, topics, lessons, and units somehow contribute to this self-knowledge—for better or worse. Possible contributions of the arts in helping students gain self-knowledge and emotional maturation are outlined below:

> Through the ages, the advancement of social cultures has been manifest in art forms. The visual arts, music, dance—even though thousands of years old—speak of love, fear, hope, and frustration as vividly as if they were expressed yesterday. Man has been able to observe himself in a kind of historical perspective through a legacy of his own creative work.
>
> It is known that all perception—all learning—takes place only when light, sound and motion—principally light and sound—impinge upon the individual from some outside source. These act as catalysts to help man build a personal universe. Does this not place a new responsibility on the role of the arts in education?
>
> Unfortunately, most of us have only educational concepts and pre-

1. Lawrence Kubie. The psychiatrist considers curriculum development. *Teachers College Record, 50:*246, January, 1949.

cepts which belong to another time—techniques, tools, and skills—
methods which become alarmingly out-of-date with the passing of
each year. It is natural, then, to retreat to the comfort of familiar
procedures and ideas which have served *us* well.

We often forget that media and materials are *only the means* by
which children can express ideas. We must be reminded that the role
of the arts in the educative process should be to develop sensitivity
to sound, rather than to learn a certain song; to cultivate vision and
and help children see, rather than paint a picture; to develop motor
coordination, rather than learn a particular dance. A child's or a
youth's fulfillment depends on the fact that, quite literally, there is
often no sharp boundary between what he is and what the universe is.
To provide him with the natural tools for finding his individual
uniqueness—this is the reason for art, music, dance, and drama, in the
curriculum. In this way, children and youth come into a sense of their
own reality. Thus they become one with their environment through
self-discovery.[2]

85   *Knowledge, knowing, and the visual arts*

E L L I O T   W .   E I S N E R

*The author writes: "It is my view that the roles the visual arts have
been generally assigned in the schools have been irrelevant to the
distinctive contribution they might make. This has been due in part
to a faulty conception of art and a narrow view of education." Eisner
advocates a deeper and more vibrant conception of art and art
education. This article should cause some teachers to think twice
before saying in an offhand way, "After their work is done, I let my
class do some art."*

WHAT PLACE can the visual arts justly claim in the curriculum? At present
their position is at best tenuous, for although some form of art instruction is

Reprinted from The *Harvard Educational Review, 33:*208-18, Spring, 1963.
2. Mayo Bryce. Identifying the role of the arts in education. *School Arts, 62:*29,
April, 1963. Used with permission of the author and publisher.

available in most schools and has been for many years, art instruction tends to be regarded as more of an embellishment than a necessity.[1] Pleas are often heard that the arts and the humanities generally should be given their proper educational due, yet with the increasing emphasis upon science and the mounting pressures placed upon students to study the "solids" such exhortations pale by comparison. If one considers the position of the visual arts in relation to what is considered central to education, the conclusion that art is a frill is hardly escapable. Empirical evidence for this was obtained in a study completed a few years ago.[2] In this study almost four thousand educators and lay citizens were asked to rank, in order of importance, sixteen tasks traditionally encompassed by the school. Aesthetic development, as one of the tasks, was placed twelfth in the list of sixteen by educators and fourteenth by noneducators, being outranked by physical development, patriotism, citizenship, and the like. Although the rank of aesthetic development increased with the educational level of those interviewed, in no case did it break into the upper half of the list. As much as some might write or speak of their importance, the visual arts have come into their own in American education. What is it that the arts have to contribute? And why is it that one of the most humane areas of human activity should hold such a tenuous place in the schools?

A brief look at the various roles the visual arts have assumed in American education may provide some clues useful for answering the latter question and an examination of the character of art may help us deal with the former.

When the academies arose after the revolution, art instruction was considered important primarily for developing cultured tastes. To develop these tastes and cultural refinements, children were taught how to sew pictures on velvet, to work in wax, and to paint pictures on glass. Competence in art was considered an accomplishment, a mark of refinement, something analogous to good manners, something every well brought up and well schooled child should have. But with the growth of industry in the 1800's a new function of art emerged. When in 1871 Walter Smith left his post in the South Kensington Art School in England to become director of art for Boston, this second role was already under way. In this role art was considered important because it could help children develop skills that would aid them vocationally. In 1874 a U. S. Bureau of Education Bulletin described this new view of art as follows:

In addition to the increased competition arising from steam-carriage, new

1. The visual arts include those art productions within the general categories of painting, graphics, and sculpture.
2. Lawrence Downey. *The Task of Public Education: the Perceptions of People,* Chicago: Midwest Administration Center, University of Chicago, 1960.

and cheaper methods of manufacture, and increased productiveness, another element of value has rapidly pervaded all manufacturers, an element in which the United States has been and is woefully deficient—the art-element. The element of beauty is found to have pecuniary as well as aesthetic value. *The training of the hand and of the eye which is given by drawing is found to be of the greatest advantage to the worker in nearly every branch of industry.* Whatever trade may be chosen, knowledge of drawing is an advantage and in many occupations is rapidly becoming indispensable. This training is of value to all the children and offers to girls as well as boys opportunity for useful and remunerative occupations, for drawing in the public schools is *not to be taught as mere "accomplishment."* The end sought is not to enable the scholar to draw a pretty picture, *but to so train the hand and eye that he may be better fitted to become a breadwinner.* [Italics mine.][3]

With the initiation of the child study movement in the 1880's, a new direction and slow evolution of the role of visual arts emerged. This third view, buttressed by the growth of Freudianism in the 1920's, conceived of art as being important primarily for its therapeutic value. Art expression became a kind of preventive medicine, a way of helping the child express his impulses and anxieties, thus contributing to the development of healthy personalities. Teachers were not to interfere, art instruction could only obstruct, the child was to be left free to express himself. Art was in the service of mental health.

The fourth role for art developed when in 1918 the seven cardinal principles of education were hoisted upon the educational mast. The cardinal principles spoke of educating for worthy home membership and worthy use of leisure time, and schoolmen attempted to justify art's claim to educational time by extolling the virtues of the arts in relation to their ability to provide for worthy home membership and worthy use of leisure. The arts were viewed as contributing no more and no less than the other subjects to a growing list of educational purposes. If school systems desired the schools to produce good citizens, the arts were volunteered for their contribution; after all who could deny that art made for good citizenship? And ethical behavior, to this too the arts were well suited. Art was justified because it was said to contribute to almost any educational aim formulated by the local school boards. Thus the arts, like the other subject areas, could shout "me too" when the agenda of objectives was drawn up and posted.

A fifth role emerged when in the twenties and thirties the project method was popularized. As a modification of a kind of Platonism, art was used pri-

3. The relation of art to education. *Circulars of Information of Bureau of Education,* No. 2, Washington, D.C.: Government Printing Office, 1874, pp. 86-88.

marily to teach ideas. If the teacher wanted a social studies concept firmly embedded in the children's minds, what better means was there to use than to have the children make *papier mâché* maps, houses, boats and the like? Very often this method worked. The children liked it, the teacher could present visible evidence of an activity curriculum and the principals were happy because the trappings of "progressive education" could be displayed. Thus, in this fifth role art was placed in the service of concept formation.

To some extent these conceptions of the function of art still permeate school programs. There are, however, other reasons of perhaps even greater importance that have influenced the role of the visual arts in the schools. These reasons have to do with the way in which education is conceived and the purposes the schools are expected to serve.

Schools are now and have long been concerned with helping children learn how to produce and acquire knowledge. Notwithstanding the few periods in American educational history when other concerns dominated, the belief that schools should pass on to children the knowledge and wisdom of the ages has been pervasive. Helping children acquire knowledge is a reasonable and proper goal for schools to aspire toward, perhaps even a primary one. The difficulty lies in the tendency to limit knowing to a conception of knowledge defined in narrowly linguistic, discoursive, or propositional terms. Such a conception disregards the school's potential capability of developing other, at least equally important ways in which men are capable of comprehending their world.[4] The virtually exclusive use of discoursive language as a vehicle for knowing is obvious from even a cursory view of school curricula. Our schools are essentially language schools: we value high-level language skills, we reward them and if our tests are any indication we act as though we believed that knowing something is synonymous with being able to put it into words.

Our concern with discoursive language is also reflected in the fact that the "three R's" crown the list of school purposes. All three share a common characteristic, all three are embodied in symbols and of necessity are once removed from the immediacy of their referents. Symbols mediate experience and the language systems in which they exist often act as a buffer, a mediator,

---

4. I am not suggesting that discoursive language is not important for students to learn to use with a high degree of precision. I am suggesting that language can be used in nondiscoursive ways such as in poetry, in the construction of metaphor, and in stylistic forms. Such a use of language can provide meanings that may be inaccessible to the discoursive. The visual arts, painting, graphics, sculpture, may be conceived as nondiscoursive modes of apprehension, expression, and communication and thereby can provide an important way of knowing.

a screen for the child's percepts. All too often the child learns to substitute the symbol of the thing experienced for the qualities of it. Instead of seeing it, he learns to symbolize it. Recognition replaces vision.[5] He moves from percept to concept, from the sense of the thing to the idea of it, a process so firmly reinforced that by the time he is nine the child who was once able to generate the poetic image of an oil slick as a dying rainbow is no longer able to do this.[6] The language of the intellect is substituted for poetic vision. And as the use of language becomes more theoretical its power to alienate man from the subtleties of feeling strengthens. Lionel Trilling has put the case this way:

> It is a truism of contemporary thought that the whole nature of man stands in danger of being brutalized by the intellect, or at least by some one of its apparently accredited surrogates. A specter haunts our culture— it is that people will eventually be unable to say, "they fell in love and married," let alone understand the language of Romeo and Juliet, but will, as a matter of course say, "Their libidinal impulses being reciprocal they activated their individual erotic drives and integrated them within the same frame of reference."[7]

The emphasis we have placed on a linguistic conception of knowledge is complimented by our suspicion of the sensibilities. It may seem paradoxical

5.   Both John Dewey in *Art as Experience* and Ernest Schachtel in *Metamorphosis* discuss the distinction between seeing and recognizing. For Dewey "Bare recognition is satisfied when a proper tag or label is attached, 'proper' signifying one that serves a purpose outside the act of recognition.... It involves no stir of the organism, no inner commotion. But an act of perception proceeds by waves that extend serially throughout the entire organism. There is, therefore, no such thing in perception as seeing or hearing *plus* emotion. The perceived object in a scene is emotionally pervaded throughout. When an aroused emotion does not permeate the material that is perceived or thought of, it is either preliminary or pathological." And Schachtel, speaking of how language may function in perception says: "The word, of course, never can take the place of the object or the quality or the activity which it designates or indicates. But most of the time, when we listen to the spoken or read the written word, we neither perceive nor imagine the referent of the word but are in contact only with the words (concepts). We behave as if the word were really all there is to the object which it designates. The label (sign) becomes a substitute for its referent, all thus, in listening or reading we are divorced from any experience of that which the words point to."
6.   Lawrence Kubie, speaking of the iconic character of the preconscious in its role in creative behavior suggests that where the child is tied too firmly to the demands of external reality either through pressures from adults or from a formal system such as logic he is apt to have his preconscious processes impeded and thus his ability to function creatively hampered. See: L. Kubie. *Neurotic Distortions of the Creative Process,* Lawrence, Kan.: The University of Kansas Press, 1958.
7.   Lionel Trilling. *The Liberal Imagination,* Garden City, N.Y.: Doubleday and Company, Inc., 1953, p. 271.

but when it comes to art the sensibilities are not trusted. The public's reaction to nonobjective art is clear evidence of this. Most of us are not quite sure if the modern painter is pulling our leg. If we only had some criteria to use, some yardstick with which to measure the artistic worth of a painting. If we only understood the painting—as if a painting could be understood in the same terms that we apply to logical systems. Our suspicion of purposely arousing the sensibilities may be a remnant of the Puritan belief that art is play and that the emotions are to be controlled and subdued. The emotions lead to the passions, the passions to the pleasures of the flesh, and the pleasures of the flesh—well you know where they lead! Since the arts play upon the emotions, they too are to be controlled. And in addition, they never quite make the grade as work. The arts are not solid.

Our concern with knowledge as it is embedded in discursive language is also evidenced by what we test for in the schools, what we reward, and what we expect of our children.

The school, like no other social institution, is replete with tests and testing. Furthermore, with the continued expansion of research in education the use of tests is likely to increase. This increase in testing is also likely to accelerate because the growing number of students wanting to enter college have forced the colleges to become more selective. Part of this selectivity manifests itself in tests such as the college board and the entrance examinations. The colleges expect high proficiency on these tests and few if any high schools can afford to ignore them. The ripple that had its birth at the university threshold goes right down to the elementary school. What the universities value the high schools learn to value. What the high school values the elementary school prepares for. Thus, the university, by placing high priority on the possession of knowledge defined almost exclusively in narrowly linguistic terms, and by reinforcing this priority by testing for it, is beginning to determine what shall be taught in the high school. The visual arts play a very small role in these tests, mainly because proficiency in the arts is not especially valuable in the college program and partly because we have few good tests of artistic performance or appreciation available. It's not easy to capture the quality of the student's experience of a painting on an IBM card.

The tests that are most widely used deal primarily with items that are easiest to test for, possession and understanding of knowledge. Since test scores have significance for the college bound student, schools tend to emphasize those subject areas which are most likely to enable the student to pass these tests. While we might wax eloquent over the more grandiose purposes of education, our tests give us away. This is not to indict the test makers. The plain fact is that we have not yet learned to construct the kinds of tests that, within the disciplines, assess the higher levels of cognitive behavior.[8] Thus the arts, by virtue of a narrow conception of education and by virtue of their resistance to the testing methods now available, have been placed in the gallery on the American educational scene.

What do the visual arts have to contribute to the education of children and youth? What claim can they justly make upon the school program? Perhaps this can best be answered by examining some of the characteristics of the visual arts in the hope that we may discover and become able to articulate what many of us have intuitively valued.

Perhaps one of the most important characteristics of the visual arts is that they are organizations of qualities. A quality is synonymous with one's experience of anything sensible.[9] In the visual arts the elements of color, line, shape, composition are common. Qualities existing within these classes of elements are capable of eliciting differing reactions as evidenced in the ordinary way we describe certain colors as cool and others as warm, certain compositions as balanced, others as not, and certain lines as active while we describe others as static or placid. It is with these qualities and their combinations that the creative artist constructs in the artistic act. These qualities serve as the raw material for his productions. But these qualities alone and isolated constitute no artistic product; they must be selected, modified, and organized into some coherent whole; the artist must qualify qualities. He must arrange qualities in such a way that their effect taken jointly is coherent as well as sensible. It is in the successful execution of this task that intelligence is exercised, an intelligence that may be called qualitative.[10] Qualitative intelligence may be looked upon, at least partially, as both the ability to conceive of qualitative ends and to formulate the means whereby those ends are realized.[11] This abil-

8. Some recent tests such as the STEP Test display a marked improvement in assessing high-level cognitive behavior, but the vast majority of standardized achievement tests seldom measure more than the student's ability to recall or comprehend information. The higher levels in Bloom's taxonomy, for example, are seldom assessed.
9. Numerals are sensible and can act primarily as qualities *provided* their meanings are disregarded. This holds true for any sensible form that also has theoretical meaning.
10. I am indebted to Francis Villemain of the University of Toledo and to David Ecker of the Ohio State University for valuable discussion on the qualitative aspects of intelligence.
11. The term qualitative intelligence is used here in distinction to aesthetic sensitivity or appreciation since it is meant to connote action designed to resolve a problematic state of affairs. This state of affairs exists in the domain of the qualitative and may be resolved in the physical ordering of qualities as exemplified by the activities of the visual artist or by the viewer who must actively perceive and order qualities residing in artistic works. Aesthetic sensitivity and appreciation are *products* of intelligent inquiry into the domain of the qualitative. It is through qualitative intelligence that such ends are achieved.

ity has been alluded to by Dewey in several sections of *Art as Experience* and suggested in other forms in the writings of Ernst Cassirer and Herbert Read.[12] It will be sufficient at this point if the reader is able to conceive of the artist's problem as largely, but not totally, devoted to the aesthetic ordering of the qualitative, a task requiring the use of qualitative intelligence. In pursuing this task the artist's decisions, selections, and rejections are made through a keenly developed sensitivity to the qualities that flow from his ongoing actions and from his awareness of that subtle order and coherence that marks the completed work.

It would be a mistake to think, however, that the capacity to make these judgments is the sole property of those we call artists. Anyone who has ever faced the problem of making selections in the domain of the qualitative—housewives engaged in setting a handsome table, gardeners planting a flower-bed, amateur furniture builders designing a bookshelf—has, in degree, exercised qualitative intelligence.

The fact that qualitative intelligence is exercised in the construction of qualitative wholes is not meant to imply that it is not used when such elements are already ordered. The appreciative act is no less a qualitative problem and no viewer of great art can experience its aesthetic qualities if he has not developed the intelligence necessary to do so. Thus, what both viewer and artist hold in common is that they both share a qualitative problem: the artist in the physical ordering of disparate elements and the spectator in the intelligent reconstruction of the product's qualities. The importance of developing such intelligence through the schools is probably obvious to anyone who values the distinctive contribution of the arts. Through such development students become able to intelligently control qualities and therefore to be able to experience them artistically.

Treating the production of art as consequence of qualitative intelligence has several assets. First such treatment removes it from the realm of the mystic and makes it at least potentially susceptible to scientific study. It is not inconceivable that tests designed to measure various modes of qualitative intelligence could be developed. Such tests might be constructed on a factorial basis similar to many group intelligence tests. It seems reasonable to expect that individuals differ with respect to their ability to intelligently control different visual elements.[13] Such differences might emerge in a factorial study of qualitative intelligence.

12. See especially Cassirer's chapter on art in *An Essay on Man,* New Haven: Yale University Press, 1944; and Read's *The Forms of Things Unknown,* New York: Horizon Press, 1960.
13. Note the differences among artists in their ability to cope with line, color, composition—differences evidenced in the works of Botticelli, Titian, and Reubens, to mention only a few.

A second advantage of substituting the concept of qualitative intelligence for talent is that it may counter our traditional disposition to view talent as a dichotomously distributed ability or trait. If talent is dichotomously distributed, it would seem reasonable for those who do not possess it to direct their energies elsewhere. If, however, qualitative intelligence is analogous to intelligence as measured by tests now available, then differences among individuals are only a matter of degree. With this view the problem for the teacher shifts; it becomes not so much a problem of finding a substitute study for the untalented, but a matter of helping the student develop whatever qualitative intelligence he may possess.

The development of qualitative intelligence through the visual arts also acts to remind us that a thing may be its own end. In an age when the instrucmental view of life is most pervasive, when people as well as things are used as tools, the arts whisper of another world view. The arts teach us that a full encounter with even the most insignificant thing (notice the attention modern painters give to discarded relics and found objects, things that would have been considered unworthy of artistic attention years ago), has its own reward. A dealer may look at a painting as a piece of merchandise to be sold, a critic as something to write about, an investor as a more or less promising sort of stock. In every case where art is used that way it ceases to act as art, for in such cases the qualitative is made instrumental, art is made a tool and it is in the nature of art that it can be either a tool or art but not both *at the same time*.

The visual arts have a second contribution to make. The artist's view of things is valuable not only because it intelligently perceives the qualities that constitute objects but also because it can see what lies beneath them. The first contribution of the arts, the development of qualitative intelligence through the perception and organization of the qualitative, is supplemented by insight into those qualities which are not visually sensed. If this sounds paradoxical, a few examples of such vision will attest to its credibility. Recall Edward Hopper's view of the quiet loneliness of the corner diner in *Nighthawks,* John Sloan's view of turn of the century tenements, Ben Shahn's perception of the Sacco-Vanzetti trial, Giocometti's concern with the condition of modern man and his estrangement from his fellow. It is obvious that these artists created no mere description of visual qualities. Their constructions penetrated qualities that are simply not circumscribed either by discoursive language or by faithfully imitating the object's visual detail. By his perception of these depth qualities and his ability to transform them into visible form, the artist provides us with a documentation of his experience, an experience derived from his sensitive vision. It is through his ability to make the felt visible that we are able to share with him this new view of the world.

What I have been attempting to describe in language is the contribution artistic vision can make to a view of the world. The fact that sensitive artists perceive aspects of life that are often hidden from others is evidenced in the insight we attribute to great artists. In the field of literature this fact is perhaps even more obvious. The characterizations of Dostoyevsky, of Conrad, of Hemingway penetrate deeply into the life of man. The insight of the great visual artist reaches no less deeply. It seems to me that the preparation needed to obtain this view warrants an important place in the educational program.

A third contribution of the visual arts to education is the one it makes to our subjective world. While the first two contributions of art deal primarily with the organization and depth perception of the outer world, the third contribution of the visual arts resides in its ability to clarify our inner world. The thoughts, phantasies, hopes, and fears which so fleetingly pass through our minds can be grasped and, as it were, pulled upward through the act of artistic creation. The transformation of these evanescent thoughts and phantasies into material form allows one to see them in durable and stable fashion. Through the physical making of the art object we become able to see what we have so evanescently felt and thought. Of course the very act of transforming these feelings and thoughts into visible form changes them, yet this modification differs significantly from the change they would undergo if transformed into discursive language, and because many of our phantasies and most personal visions are visual it may be that a truer view of these inner visions may be obtained through the visual arts than through any other mode of human expression.

The psychological values derived from the making of art have been noted since Pythagoras and anthropologists have found evidence that art production is characteristic of almost all cultures. Franz Boas has pointed out that such activity is prevalent even in societies most desperately struggling for survival.[14] Even when energies may be more "practically" directed, art has held its place. The sacrifice of art to the more "practical" matters in education is bound to exact a heavy price. John Ciardi, the poet, once computed this price for a group of successful business executives. He told them:

> There is no poetry for the practical man. There is poetry only for the mankind of the man who spends a certain amount of his time turning the mechanical wheel. But let him spend too much of his life at the mechanics of practicality and either he must become something less than a man, or his very mechanical efficiency will become impaired by the frustrations stored up in his irrational human personality. An ulcer, gentlemen, is an

14. Franz Boas. *Primitive Art,* Cambridge, Mass.: Harvard University Press, 1927.

unkissed imagination taking his revenge for having been jilted. It is an unwritten poem, a neglected music, an unpainted watercolor, an undanced dance. It is a declaration from the mankind of the man that a clear spring of joy has not been tapped, and that it must break through, muddily on its own.[15]

Finally, making in the visual arts teaches us that a great difference exists between knowing something and having knowledge of it. The knowing that comes through the making of art is produced by the maker's struggle to see qualities and to give these qualities visible life by transforming them into artistic form. Through this process the artist comes to know his experience in a way that can only be realized in the struggle to bring it to the surface as a personal and public form. Thus knowing art, like knowing science, requires an intimate and deep involvement with it. Knowing anything in its deepest sense means knowing how to be creative with it. The studio is to the artist what the laboratory is to the scientist, for it is in the *production* of art and science that knowing is realized.

Consider for a moment what children would miss if they merely learned *about* art rather than learning how to make it. In the making of art children learn how to respond to and order qualities. They learn to use their qualitative intelligence to select and reject the qualities needed to make things beautiful. They learn to see what they look at. And above all, children begin to learn what only art can teach: that to make something beautiful you must first learn to make it beautifully. This is the way of knowing.

It is my view that the roles the visual arts have been generally assigned in the schools have been irrelevant to the distinctive contribution they might make. This has been due in part to a faulty conception of art and a narrow view of education. Art instruction can provide vocational skills, it can make the teaching of ideas more interesting, and it can contribute to worthy use of leisure time. It's not that art instruction is useless for achieving such ends, it's simply that these ends are essentially nonartistic. In emphasizing such ends the distinctive contributions of art tend to be overlooked.

I would hope that as we continue to improve American education, we would recognize the qualitative ways in which men apprehend and comprehend and that we would place art in a position much closer to the heart of education than it now enjoys.

15. John Ciardi. From a speech entitled An ulcer gentlemen is an unwritten poem. Copyright by the author 1955, 1956.

86　*A letter to a social studies teacher*

E D W A R D   G L A N N O N

Asked to write a piece on the relation of the art teacher's work to the social studies, the author chose to present his views in the form of a letter. On art and the social studies he writes, "What is social studies but the story of man—his past and his potential? Art is a physical part of man's body, but is there any better proof or record of his soul?" On art as a way of helping pupils learn concepts, Glannon writes, "If you were only memorizing dates and battle sites, you would not need me."

DEAR RUTH: I am going to write an article and I need your help. This article should be about an art teacher's work and its relation to the social studies. It's a question of how my work relates to yours.

If I may use you as a target and write at you, it will make me think a little straighter. I never could fool you where teaching is concerned and, with you, it concerns just about everything.

I have been asked to answer the question, "Should we have art for art's sake or should art be the handmaiden of the social studies?" Of course, I would reject both of these choices, but it is a choice I've never had to make.

The notion of art for art's sake is too narrow and too confining to permit a man to do a decent job. A healthy art was always strong enough to use its forces in support of the ideas it found worthy. And it always did this without any sense of loss. Only the weakest and most anemic concepts of art must protect themselves from life's contaminations. As to being a handmaiden, that seems a little comic. Art is too old and too big and too masculine and too courageous ever to be much of a handmaiden for anyone or anything.

It seems to me that a curious and futile dualism has persisted in education. I am speaking of that notion that there is a difference in quality between those studies which are purely verbal and those which require physical action and can be embodied in actual physical objects. Neither of these can be less or more than the other. They are one and the same thing. The education of a human being should be, itself, a work of art. It has a body as well as a soul. Burn the body of any work of art and where is the soul?

What is social studies but the story of man—his past and his potential. Art

Reprinted from The *Journal of Educational Sociology, 30*:349-52, April, 1957.

is a physical part of man's story but is there any better proof or record of his soul?

You and I both know that the only part of our teaching work which has any ultimate value is that which actually becomes part of a human being. It has to grow into a child like his own cells and become part of his thinking. It only matters if he can think with it and bring it to bear on all his future learning and all his decisions.

We have tried hard to build a continuing sequence of concepts into each child—and we have always tried to give him a decent chance to affect the reality around him in the light of his new learning. This I think is the essential clue to our relationship. I have invented many ways to make it possible for children to invent ways to embody and to realize the concepts you were building up.

When your children were Indians, we worked within the limitations of the Indian. We learned the sources of the Indian materials and we used the products of nature as they came. We built a lot of strength within these simple and rather rigid patterns.

Then they became Vikings. I changed when they did. It was time for them to learn that man can reshape nature's materials according to his needs and purposes. He could curve planks and melt metals and so cross oceans. The wonderful virility of Viking design was easy to teach them because they knew the Indian concept so well that they could think with it to move beyond. Once they understood how the Vikings could turn a ship upside down on stone walls to make a fortress, it wasn't hard to teach them the meaning of a castle. And when they got that strongly in them and understood the nature of its closed and world-resistant form, we were ready for a look at the open, defenseless design of a cathedral. After that most of them should know enough to discover the United Nations Building for themselves.

Naturally, I want to be in on it when they study Colonial America. For me, the integrity of design in so many of those early American implements is just as important an historical fact as the Whiskey Rebellion. I want the child to know this kind of creative integrity. Whether he gets it under the heading of Social Studies or Art or Science is of no particular concern to me— just so he gets it.

I want to see these youngsters make a creative, constructive approach to reality on every front. I want them to think of art, in its biggest sense, as a way of approaching anything.

I want them to think of art as a way of applying form to human action, as a way of making form and content one. I accept entirely the idea stated by Goethe when he said, "Content without form is chaos. Form without content is a spinning of cobwebs."

The richer the content the greater are the possibilities for form. The content of your social studies is deep and rich and whole. It's at the very center of their learning lives. It's just what I need to do my work.

As I see it, Ruth, my job has two phases. Both of them are vital and are often in competition with each other. I must work with both hands and sometimes I must resist with one hand the job that I am doing with the other.

With one hand I am trying hard to help make these children into social beings. I am trying to teach them the common languages and customs and standards of the society in which they live.

With the other hand, I am trying to save their individual souls. I am trying to protect them from being completely swallowed up in the patterns of society. This is an essential part of my job and I can't relate it directly to social studies or any other program in the school. It has to do with maintaining a sensitive relationship over a period of years with each individual child in the school. It is the effort to foster and encourage a certain inwardness, a certain harmony which the human individual can find only within himself. It is an effort to preserve the unique poetry of childhood so that at least its spirit may survive and someday be a part of a living woman or man.

It's an effort to preserve that sense of wonder, that feeling for spiritual adventure. It's an effort to coax out and to foster the creative responsibilities in each young person. It's an effort to preserve the unique and precious qualities of the individual life against all the inroads and the pressures of a mass-production, mass-communication world.

Working here with, say, a third-grade class, is like standing in a patch of wild flowers. We know that they will grow up and to grow up means to be transplanted into something like a formal garden. Each child is unique now, but soon he will be an adolescent and will be desperately anxious to join the human race. They will be all too anxious to take on the codes and conventions of society. After all, man is a social being.

The trick now is to strengthen and encourage the young wild flower, give it faith in its uniqueness so that it will be able to survive the socializing process, hoping that it will retain something of its wildness, something of its native flavor, something of its individual soul.

I feel a little foolish even saying this to you. You are their teacher. You know the need as well as I do—and you are just as anxious for the same result.

On the other hand, we know that they are going to live in an organized society and we know that they are going to influence or even reshape that society pretty much according to the way that they interpret history, the story of man's past and his potential.

Each new generation must re-interpret history for itself. No teacher can control the way in which the next generation is going to interpret history.

What can we do about it? I think our biggest influence is that we can teach them how to gather the evidence on which they will base their decisions. We can introduce them to stronger, deeper, more meaningful sources of evidence. We can teach them how to evaluate evidence. In other words, we do help to create their standard of judgment.

The more profound and the more humane the sources they explore, the better will be their decisions. I believe strongly in the power of art at its highest level to help them in evaluating and judging human history. I want them to be aware of man as the creative creature which he is. I try to inject artistic concepts into the study of history wherever I can.

Because your social studies program treats of people as whole human beings, I must support it. If you were only memorizing dates and battle sites, you would not need me.

I want all these children to know how to paint and build and carve. I want all of that—but I want more. The functioning of art in society at the biggest level hinges on man's sense of history and his sense of human destiny. It requires the discernment and the highly developed sense of values on the part of many people so that they will accurately distinguish and readily absorb and apply ideas and concepts offered by the best creative minds of their own time. That dimension of insight which can see beyond average, that's what makes art a vital force.

We have worked together many years. I have not been your handmaiden any more than you've been mine. When teachers become entrenched along the lines of subject matter, children pay the bill. I am grateful to you because you could always focus your concern upon a certain group of youngsters. You wanted them to have what they needed and get it where they could. That left me free to do the same. We didn't do all that we wanted to, but we did the very best we could. Many children are better off because we worked to-gether. What else matters?

Thanks,

EDDIE

87　The place of music in our elementary and secondary schools

CHARLES LEONHARD

Music programs must be planned with an aesthetic understanding of music and a professional interest in music education. The author suggests some possibilities for a rich music program.

MUSIC MERITS an important place in the educational system because it represents one of the most significant human achievements, because it is a unique symbolic system which appeals to the life of feeling and of the mind, and because musical competence contributes unique aesthetic richness to the quality of living. Furthermore, the right kind of experience with music can make a powerful contribution to the development of rational powers, and such development is almost universally accepted as the central purpose of education.

Unfortunately, some school music programs provide no more than a casual contact with music, and many more fail to offer their pupils or students meaningful experience with great music. In many elementary schools, for example, children dance, play games, and paint to music; they sometimes listen to recordings but with no purpose beyond that of immediate satisfaction and pleasure.

Teachers often use music for recreational purposes and for a kind of emotional catharsis. When children are tired from concentration on reading and arithmetic, bored, overwrought, or obstreperous, it's time for music. This use of music is appropriate, healthy, and consistent with music's great powers, but it does not represent a valid music education program because it leads nowhere and results in no significant musical learning.

In many schools a limited number of youngsters have experience in musical performance which requires serious and sustained effort on their part. However, limitations in technique frequently preclude performance of great music. Unless they have experience with music other than what they perform, youngsters have little opportunity to develop their esthetic insight beyond the level of their performance skill. Moreover, students who do not perform have progressively fewer opportunities for organized musical experiences of any kind as they advance through the secondary school. As a result, for all students

Reprinted from the *NEA Journal,* 52:40-42, April, 1963.

the influence of the mass media on musical taste and preference is likely to remain dominant.

The objectives and the focus of many current music education programs need realignment if music is to assume its logical role in education for richer living. There is urgent need for administrators, music teachers, elementary classroom teachers, and parents to understand that the purpose of the music program is to develop musical competence, musical understanding, and knowledge of the whole range of music literature in all students.

A music program in the school is justified only when it makes a significant difference in the pupil's conception of music, his understanding of it, and his competence with it. The purposes of music education, therefore, are achieved only when a music program results in musical learning that would not take place without it.

Essential products of musical learning include the musical skills that provide a measure of musical independence—the ability to sing, to play instruments, and to read music. Other essential outcomes include developing the ability to perceive the elements of form; to understand musical structure, musical style, and the notational system; to discern quality in performance and compositions; to listen perceptively and be aware of what happens musically as a composition unfolds; and to understand and use musical terms correctly.

In brief, the purpose of the music program has been served only when the pupil has become well-acquainted with many distinguished examples of the musical heritage and when he has had an opportunity to find in music what he would not have found on his own. Only then is he in a position to control his musical life intelligently and to make its aesthetic quality a matter not of chance but of choice.

The point of view that music is a subject meriting serious study has far-reaching implications that apply equally to music programing and to music instruction in the school.

In the first place, the music educator must differentiate liking and interest from entertainment and pleasure. Immediate liking for a piece of music is not a valid criterion for including it in the music program; many fine pieces of music require repeated hearing and close attention before youngsters like them. Furthermore, not all students can be expected to like a given piece of music, and there is no reason why they should.

What is important in the selection of music is that it provide an avenue for students to explore and discover musical meaning and to develop musical insights. Limiting them to music that is immediately appealing binds both teacher and youngsters to the obvious and trite with which they are already surfeited.

For at least two reasons, the music program should not concern itself with entertaining youngsters: First, music teachers cannot compete successfully with professional entertainers; secondly, the mere titillation of the senses is not a valid function of the school. What the music program should do is provide youngsters with the pleasure and satisfaction that results from authentic musical learning and achievement.

The principal guideline for program planning is the involvement of youngsters in activities concerned with music—music which is worth-while, challenging, and suited to their level of musical and intellectual comprehension. There should be a variety of music representing many styles and periods, many media of performance, and many music forms.

All youngsters should have the experience of performing vocal and instrumental music, both in general music classes and in specialized groups, and they should be expected to attain a significant level of proficiency. Developing technique in musical performance is a demanding task which requires serious study, effort, and application both in the classroom and elsewhere.

All students, furthermore, should have music classes in which they study music intensively. If anything significant is to be achieved, youngsters need to read copious amounts of music on their level, hear and analyze the structure and style of a great deal of music that is beyond their level of performance proficiency, and become acquainted with major composers, conductors, and performing artists.

The work in these classes should be characterized by intellectual comprehension and ability to perceive relationships among composers, musical styles, musical forms, and musical performance media. The students should, in addition, learn to understand the theory of music, not as an end in itself but as a means of clarifying their conception of music.

A music education program in the early elementary school years should be devoted primarily to developing basic singing and listening skills and to introducing fundamental musical concepts. The program in the intermediate grades should concentrate on refinement and extension of listening and singing skills, on clarification of musical concepts, and on development of an understanding of notation.

In the secondary school, increasing emphasis should be placed on cognition. Both music classes and performing groups should seek to develop understanding of the nature of musical expression, musical forms, and musical styles, and of the place music and music literature hold in the cultural heritage.

In addition, the understanding of notation developed in the elementary school should now be used in helping children learn how to read music and to follow scores.

The rhythm of musical learning should be from the obvious musical meaning to the subtle; from casual awareness to intensive involvement; from crude response to precise control. Experience with music must be extensive and intensive—extensive in that the student becomes familiar with as much music literature as possible; intensive in that, especially in the secondary school, he comes to know selected examples of great music intimately, to hear them in their full reality, and to understand them thoroughly.

Achieving all these objectives requires concentration and serious study. To this end, administrators should provide regularly scheduled music classes under musically qualified teachers at all levels. Moreover, they should accord secondary school music classes full academic status and credit.

For their part, teachers should actively involve students in rewarding experiences with significant music and help them overcome the obstacles to their understanding of such music. They should not hesitate to assign such meaningful homework tasks as reading about and reporting on music and musicians, analyzing musical compositions, comparing different recorded versions of the same composition, and evaluating music heard on TV and radio or at local concerts.

Finally, it is essential that music educators, administrators, and parents come to differentiate between the casual pleasure of music for recreation and the significant achievement of music for education. Both are important; both are consistent with the magnificent power of music. The school, the home, the mass media, and other agencies contribute to the former. The school has the crucial role and the primary responsibility for the latter.

88 *Music and the teaching of American history*

JOHN KIMBALL

Although this article was written for the high-school teacher, the excellent recommendations apply to many grades in elementary schools. Possibilities for cooperation between classroom teachers and music teachers are enormous. Some schools are "singing schools" where pupils of many ages know the same songs and enjoy a community of meaning and empathy by singing together.

How CAN HISTORY be made more meaningful?" "Are we giving as much attention to the cultural aspects of our history as we give to the political, economic, and international phases?" "Have our pupils learned how the music, art, architecture, and literature, and even the philosophy of a period reflects or is influenced by the historical developments?"[1] These questions should be examined for a number of reasons, none of which needs to be recounted here, for it is not the intention of this paper to discuss course content, but rather to suggest the introduction of music as a supplementary aid in the teaching of history.

Oftentimes, students can gain a deeper understanding of a particular period and a clearer insight into the events that took place at that time from listening to the songs that have come down to us through the years than they have been able to obtain from any reading they may have done.

There is a wide variety of approaches to the use of songs in the classroom. The suggestions here presented are intended merely as a starting point from which it is hoped both teacher and student may be encouraged to explore the field further.

Either printed songs or recordings may be used. For example, a teacher could introduce a unit on the American Revolution by playing a number of recordings of songs popular at the time of the Revolution. The students might then read the words of "Columbia the Gem of the Ocean" and discuss the thoughts and feelings they believe are expressed in the song.

If a discussion of the lyrics of a song of a particular period is used to introduce a unit, it is interesting to reopen the discussion at the termination of the unit. The students will undoubtedly find new meanings in the lyrics after

---

Reprinted from *Social Education,* 27:23-25, January, 1963.
1. *Senior High History Bulletin,* Baltimore Public Schools, January, 1960.

they have had the opportunity of studying the period in which they were written.

The founders of this country brought songs with them from their old countries. Often they modified the words of these songs to fit their new situations. It is interesting to note here that many songs have a long and varied history, cropping up in many different locations with slight modifications in the words. A student might trace the history of a particular song and show the different ideas it had been used to portray. Negro spirituals, folk songs, work songs, and early church music all reveal insights into the thinking and feelings of the people and the times. Music of this kind will do much to make students aware of what went into the making of America.

Correlation between the teaching of history and music may be accomplished in a number of ways and to varying degrees. The following suggestions, although obvious, may be helpful in pointing the way to further applications.

Songs can be used:

To introduce a unit or the study of a given time period.
To increase the appeal of the study of history.
To provide more associations with an event or period.
To exemplify given events in a time period.
To illustrate what people were doing and thinking in a particular time in our history.
To emphasize an event—Bunker Hill, Independence Day, etc.
To point up similarities and differences in modes of living, occupations, thoughts, etc.
To provide a meaningful feeling for people of the past by developing an understanding of the hopes and fears common to mankind (particularly in folk songs).
To provide a setting or background (e.g. Puritan life, the War between the States, etc.).
To indicate our relationship with other nations and cultures.

Coordinated activities might be worked out between the history and the music departments of the school. For example, students might create a musical setting for a unit or lesson in history under the guidance of the music department.

Although many of the suggestions here listed will be the basis of student work, it may be helpful to list a few activities that may be carried on entirely by the students themselves.

Research projects—tracing thoughts, as they have been expressed in songs, on freedom, justice, the Constitution, national heroes; tracing the history of slavery in song; following through songs the westward expansion and migration; portraying through songs conditions on the frontier; tracing the history of transportation through song (railroads, riverboats, etc.).

Compositions—e.g. The Growth of Industry, from ideas found in songs.

Panel discussions—e.g. The War between the States in song.

Singing—Pupils singing for the class (folk songs, songs of nations, etc.).

These suggestions are of a general nature and allow wide latitude in application. The field of music and song is of such great and diverse dimensions that it is unnecessary to put each suggestion in a specific framework. Each person working with these ideas will wish to fit the suggestions into his own situation according to his needs and available resources.

A great wealth of songs, books, and recordings are available for use by teachers and students. We list here some of the more readily available materials. The first listing suggests songs appropriate to a particular time period, the second, songs appropriate for use during the study of a particular topic. There is some duplication of song titles in these two lists, but this is intentional, for the lists are meant to suggest the many ways the same song may be found useful in different situations. Following the lists is a bibliography of books in which these songs may be found. They may also be found in two inexpensive paperbacks: W. Hille. *The People's Song Book*, New York: Boni and Gaer; B. Ives. *The Burl Ives Song Book*, New York: Ballantine.

Songs Appropriate to Various Time Periods in American History

TIME PERIOD	SONG TITLES
1607-1789	Tobacco's But an Indian Weed
	Confess Jehovah
	The Escape of John Webb
	Old Hundred
	The Dying British Sergeant
	Why Soldier Why
	Free America
	Chester
	Yankee Doodle
1789-1815	Ye Parliaments of England
	The Star-Spangled Banner
	Columbia the Gem of the Ocean
	Perry's Victory
1815-1860	America
	Home Sweet Home
	A Yankee Ship and a Yankee Crew
	Rocked in the Cradle of the Deep
	Erie Canal

1815-1860	Green Grow the Lilacs
	The Sioux Indians
	The Little Sod Shanty
	Old Folks at Home
	Sweet Betsy from Pike
1860-1877	John Brown's Body
	The Battle Hymn of the Republic
	Tenting Tonight
	Go Down, Moses
	Maryland, My Maryland
	Sour Apple Tree
	John Henry
	The Utah Iron Horse
	Acres of Clams
1877-1890	The Farmer Is the Man
	Red River Valley
1900-Present	Goin' Down the Road
	Soup Song
	Oh, Freedom
	We Shall Not Be Moved

Songs Appropriate to Various Topics in American History

TOPIC	SONG TITLES
Freedom	The Star-Spangled Banner
	We Shall Not Be Moved
American Revolution	The Old Lady Who Lived Over the Sea
	What a Court Hath Old England
	The Battle of Trenton
	The Fate of John Burgoyne
	Come Out Ye Continentalers
	To the Commons
	Riflemen of Bennington
Work	Take This Hammer
	Joe Hill
	Tarrier's Song
Railroads	Paddy Works on the Railway
	Track Laying Holler
	Track Calling
	Wake Up Call
	Casey Jones
Machines	Wanderin'

Songs Appropriate to Various Topics in American History, *Continued*

Depression	Beans, Bacon, and Gravy Goin' Down the Road
Unions	Joe Hill Solidarity
Morality-Justice (Badmen and Heroes)	Jesse James Pretty Boy Floyd Captain Kidd Quantrell Jim Fisk Bold Turpin
Coal Mines	Down, Down, Down The Miner's Doom
The Sea	A Roving Heave Away Johnny Boker Blow the Man Down Rollin' Home
Immigrants	Danny Boy
Cotton	Boll Weevil
Chain Gang	Rock Me Momma Cornbread, Meat, and Molasses Pick a Bale of Cotton
The West	Saddle Song Home on the Range Dreary Black Hills Sioux Indians Bury Me Not on the Lone Prairie Chisholm Trail Arkansas Traveler Kansas Boys

BIBLIOGRAPHY

High-school library books on music and songs. The following books are from the standard high-school library catalog. Each book listed has certain features to recommend its use in American history classes. Some are straight histories with relatively few songs; others are just the opposite with the proportion of songs greater and commentary at a minimum.

Barzun, J. *Music in American Life.* Garden City, N.Y.: Doubleday and Company. 1956.

Bauer, M. *How Music Grew.* New York: G. P. Putnam's Sons. 1939.

————. *Music Through the Ages.* New York: G. P. Putnam's Sons. 1946.

Britten, B. *Wonderful World of Music.* Garden City, N.Y.: Garden City Books. 1958.

Carmer, C. *America Sings.* New York: Alfred A. Knopf. 1942.

Ewen, D. *Homebook of Musical Knowledge.* New York: Prentice-Hall. 1954.

————. *Panorama of American Popular Music.* New York: Prentice-Hall. 1957.

Felton, H., *Cowboy Jamboree.* New York: Alfred A. Knopf. 1951.

Howard, J. T., *Our American Music.* New York: Thomas Y. Crowell. 1954.

————. *Short History of American Music.* New York: Thomas Y. Crowell. 1957.

Lomax, J. *American Ballads and Folksongs.* New York: The Macmillan Company. 1934.

Sandburg, C. *American Songbag.* New York: Harcourt, Brace & Company. 1927.

Spaeth, S. *History of Popular Music in America.* New York: Random House. 1948.

Wheeler, O. *Sing for America.* New York: E. P. Dutton. 1944.

Books available from Enoch Pratt Free Library. The Enoch Pratt Free Library (400 Cathedral St., Baltimore 1, Maryland) has an extensive collection of books which will be found useful in studying the role of the song in the history of the United States. The titles listed here are those thought to be most useful to both teacher and pupil.

Andrew, E., *The Gift To Be Simple.* Locust Valley, N.Y.: J. J. Augustin. 1940.

Barnes, E., *American Music from Plymouth Rock to Tin Pan Alley.* Washington, D.C.: Brookland. 1936.

Brand, O., *Singing Holidays.* New York: Alfred A. Knopf. 1957.

Carmer, C. *Songs of the Rivers of America.* New York: Rinehart and Company. 1942.

Downs, O., and Siegmeister, E., *A Treasury of American Song.* New York: Howell. 1940.

Flanders, H. *Ballads Migrant in New England.* New York: Farrar, Strauss and Young. 1953.

Greenway, J., *American Folk Songs of Protest.* Philadelphia, Pa.: University of Pennsylvania Press. 1953.

Haywood, C., *Bibliography of American Folklore and Folksongs.* New York: Greenberg, 1951.

Ives, B. *The Burl Ives Song Book.* New York: Ballantine Books. 1953.

Jackson, G., *Early Songs of Uncle Sam.* Boston: Humphries. 1933.

Lawless, R. *Folksingers and Folksongs in America.* New York: Duell, Sloan and Pierce. 1960.

Lomax, A., *Cowboy Songs and Other Frontier Ballads.* New York: The Macmillan Company. 1938.

Niles, J., *Singing Soldiers.* New York: Charles Scribner's Sons. 1927.

Sonneck and Upton. *Bibliography of Early American Secular Music.* Washington, D.C.: McQueen. 1905.

RECORDS

Pupils and teachers alike will undoubtedly have many fine suggestions for records to be used in teaching history through song. Many schools have record collections in their music departments which could be borrowed for use in history classes. One of the most comprehensive guides to collections of folksong records, readily available, can be found in *Folksingers and Folksongs in America* by R. Lawless (New York: Duell, Sloan and Pierce, 1960).

A fine student project with a high interest rating could be the listing of all the suitable titles of records about a given topic available locally, such as those owned by class members, records in the school collection, items in the local library, or those available in stores.

The records listed here are available from the Department of Audio-Visual Aids, Department of Education, Baltimore, Maryland. The catalogue number appears in parentheses at the end of each listing.

American Song Album. General collection of songs. (RS 14)
California Gold Rush. Story and song. (RS 122)
Daniel Boone Opening of the Wilderness. Songs. (RS 128)
De Glory Road—Negro Spiritual. (RS 65)
Edward. Ballad. (RS 65)
Freedom's People—Contributions to Music. Negroes and song. (RS 74)
John Brown. Music and story. (RS 117)
LaSalle. Music and story. (RS 68)
Lewis and Clarke. Music and story. (RS 68)
Lord Randall. (RS 64)
Maryland, My Maryland. Story and song. (RS 66)
The Star-Spangled Banner. Story of the song (RS 67)

❧

Part Four

THE SCOPE OF EVALUATION

WHEN MANY people hear the word "evaluation," their quick response is "test." Yes, testing is an important aspect of evaluation. Recall my definition of "curriculum," wherein the pupils' perceptions of their experiences formed the crucial ingredient. If pupils perceive a test as a form of diagnosis to help them do better, what a different experience from perceiving a test as a punishment.

Testing is but one part of evaluation. Pupils think they are being evaluated all the time. They think teachers are evaluating them by the way the teachers seem to look at them and the way they respond to pupils or answer questions. They presume teachers judge them as "smart," "good," and "clean," or "dumb," "bad," and "dirty."

Of course, teachers cannot be responsible for all the perceptions of their students. Some students bring to school socially and emotionally predetermined sets which twist anything a teacher does or says into a personal curriculum of reproach and rejection. Teachers can only hope to alter these perceptions eventually. In short, teachers must help pupils learn that teachers are professional workers who evaluate in order to help pupils learn better. Pupils are influenced both by the devices teachers use and the attitudes teachers exhibit.

In this section, Chapter 19 shows the variety of formal and informal methods for evaluating a wide range of educational goals. Chapter 20 deals specifically with tests—the use of standardized tests and the construction of teacher-made texts. Chapter 21 directs our attention to another aspect of evaluation—reporting, conferring, and working with parents.

CHAPTER 19

Variety of Evaluation Methods

OUT OF OUR PROFESSIONAL values come our means of evaluation. The first selection shows the breath of possibilities available to teachers whose professional aspirations determine for them a wide range of classroom goals. The second article is about pupils' self-evaluation; a checklist is presented to help students sharpen their views of their own work. The third article is a research report on the subjectivity of teachers' marks.

89 Evaluating learning

ROBERT S. FLEMING

In this selection Fleming outlines twenty different evaluative procedures, which give us a variety of approaches to evaluating many kinds of goals. This is a useful checklist for a teacher to use in determining whether he is considering a broad enough scope in his evaluation. This list also may serve teachers as they prepare for conferences with parents or get ready to fill out report cards.

Reprinted from *Curriculum for Today's Boys and Girls,* Robert S. Fleming (ed.), Columbus, Ohio: Charles E. Merrill Books, Inc., 1963, pp. 508-16. (Footnotes have been renumbered.)

EVALUATION PROCEDURE	PURPOSE	COMMENTS
1. Achievement Tests in any area of importance, such as: reading, arithmetic, and other subject areas.	To describe status in specific areas assumed important for a particular group and individual as means of comparison with those in other schools.	Tests should be used in manner consistent with *purposes* being sought. Tests should be used early in year as a means of helping to diagnose student's status in specific academic areas. Specific scores in various areas rather than as a composite score are helpful in diagnosing status of learning.
2. Teacher-made tests (any field).	To determine understandings of content thus providing information for the teacher and learner. May be used as means of self-evaluation for both student and teacher.	Tests are carefully prepared by teachers to cover basic content of a topic, unit, or learning experience. Tests may take form of specific questions or problems. Tests usually involve individuals working alone. The test should provide another learning experience for the learner.
3. Observations of pupils by teachers in terms of specific purposes. May include qualities such as: a. Work habits b. Play c. Relationships with other children d. Relationships with adults e. Health status f. Health practices g. Reading habits h. Handwriting i. Use of time	To collect specific information concerning behavior of pupils in various types of situations.	Observations should be made systematically. Specific purposes for observation need to be identified. Records must be kept of specific factors observed. Each observation should be dated. At intervals observations should be summarized and analyzed. Development of an observational guide may be helpful. Observations may be made by teacher, principal, parent, or supervisor.

EVALUATION PROCEDURE	PURPOSE	COMMENTS
4. Collection of products of student's work. These may take form of writing, art work, creative work, special assignments, news, exhibits.	To analyze status of learning, find evidences of improvement in specific areas, discover needs, misconceptions, strengths and weaknesses, discover interests, identify values.	Provide each student with folder. Each item included must be dated. At intervals materials in a given subject field should be examined chronologically, analyzed and summarized. Selection of "typical" samples may be helpful. Emphasis given to help learner raise *his* standards for *his* work. In some cases the "product" is in the form of a project, dance, or group activity which might well be recorded and described.
5. Record of the results of listening to children's discussions, conversations, comments.	To identify speech and discussion needs. To collect leads which enable the teacher to better understand a child's interests, attitudes, anxieties, concerns.	As one hears evidence of growth, expanding interests, improvement in discussion techniques, major growth in understanding of concept and relationships, records should be made. Teachers may listen for a specific purpose such as vocabulary, pronunciation, misconceptions. Teachers may listen to determine concerns, anxieties, fears. Teachers should record major items heard. Often they are taken as questions or hypotheses to be followed up in discussions with individuals or groups. Each record should be dated.

EVALUATION PROCEDURE	PURPOSE	COMMENTS
6. Analysis of reading bibliography.	To describe status of reading activity. To be used in assessing interests. To provide a means of communication with the individual.	Each student might well keep a bibliography of books, magazine articles, papers read. Each item should be dated as recorded. Provides a basis for questioning, conferences, discussions with parents.
7. Provide for free response writing.	To provide an opportunity for a child to express his feelings, beliefs, understandings.	As students have opportunities to write about their ideas and understandings they often reveal interests, values, concerns. Free response writing may portray one's skill in communication and in expression, in handwriting, in sentence construction, in critical thinking.
8. Word lists.	To develop and extend vocabulary. To serve as an indication of understanding and interests.	Individuals may keep lists of new words learned in certain fields. May serve as incentive for new learnings. Provides basis for communication with the teacher. Teacher may find list an index to problems, interests, difficulties.
9. Sociometric data.	To provide a picture of an individual's place in a group and a group's acceptance or rejection of the individual.	Development of a series of sociograms may be helpful. Sociograms must be made in a series of different situations. Each sociogram must be dated. Group relationships may change.

EVALUATION PROCEDURE	PURPOSE	COMMENTS
10. Student's summary of work in a given study, unit, topic.	To provide an opportunity for an individual (or group) to prepare a record of work carried out in given period of time. To assist the student in organizing, summarizing, and reporting.	Time interval may vary from a single class period to several weeks. Individual (or group) describes such items as what was done, purposes, method of work, summary of findings, conclusions, etc. Ability of an individual (or group) to summarize major findings may reflect growth.
11. Record of an interview with a student (or group).	To provide evidence of major understanding, maturity of insight, growth.	An interview guide may be helpful in identifying major emphasis of interview. Record (summary) should be made and dated. Teacher must take findings at face value. Teacher's role is to ask few probing questions and to create a situation for student to talk and to reveal himself.
12. Record of an interview with a parent.	To determine parents' perceptions of work of the child. To secure information about the child's activities, attitudes, concerns. To interpret work underway and to clarify purposes and next steps.	An interview guide may be helpful in identifying major emphasis of interview. Record (summary) should be made and dated. To provide evidence of major understanding and growth. Teacher must take findings at face value.
13. Preparation of a series of newspaper articles on work of school (or group).	To interpret work under way. To provide information of activities and procedures.	Articles on variety of topics may be helpful. Display of articles dated and arranged in systematic means enables one to study balance, variety, participation.

EVALUATION PROCEDURE	PURPOSE	COMMENTS
14. Record of assembly program.	To provide information of progress of children toward certain purposes assumed to be important (assuming responsibility, leadership, creativity expression).	Summary of planning that went into program. Role of individuals in assuming responsibility, creating scenery, improvising, composing music. Degree to which individual became more responsive.
15. Record of exhibits, displays, or demonstration.	To describe evidence of student's accomplishments, understandings, and creative work. To communicate work of the school.	As students become more active in communicating ideas, growth is occurring. Subtle accomplishments may be evident—growth in harmony, resourcefulness. A series of photographs, or descriptions of an exhibit or demonstration of a student or group may provide evidence of cooperation, understandings, knowledge of relationships, creative work, etc.
16. Responses of boys and girls to particular problem situations (emergency, seasonal, etc.)	To study student's behavior in variety of problem situations, as means of describing maturity, balance, poise, ingenuity, resourcefulness. To provide for an application of knowledge and attitudes.	As students can express feelings and attitudes, their growth in human qualities may be described. Observations of reactions of students to a fire, theft, death; to new student, to routine tasks, may reveal values, attitudes, understandings. Learning outcomes are numerous and varied.

EVALUATION PROCEDURE	PURPOSE	COMMENTS
17. Tape recordings of work of an individual (or group) in such activities as 　poetry 　reading 　piano 　chant 　singing	To record actual experiences of children as a source of data from which value judgments can be made.	Tapes recording specific work of individuals can be developed. Dates must be established and conditions under which the tape was developed should be described. Opportunity should be provided for an individual to listen to his tapes and analyze progress, problems, next steps.
18. The development of a film, filmstrip, or series of slides.	To serve as a source of data describing progress. To provide a specific record of work over a period of time.	Planning for a pictorial summary of a project provides a variety of learnings. Useful in interpreting work to parents and community.
19. Record of group discussions of faculty members concerning an individual child and/or class group.	To summarize existing information in a school. To be used in assessing status, needs and progress.	Several teachers in a given school have extensive knowledge about a group (or individual). The pooled information of the faculty group provides extensive information. Progress and problems become evident.
20. Use a variety of commercial tests other than "subject matter" tests.	To be used in studying a group quietly in terms of a general purpose (interest). To establish some general characteristics of the group. To learn more about an individual child.	A variety of tests are available w h i c h help teachers b e t t e r know groups and/or individuals. (See below.) Results used in planning. Results may help individuals know themselves better. Results aid in communication with parents. Results may be taken as hypotheses to be tested.

EVALUATION PROCEDURE	PURPOSE	COMMENTS

Illustrative Tests

A. SRA Junior Inventory.[1]	Grades 4 - 8	To identify student problems.
B. What I Like To Do.[2]	Grades 4 - 7	To identify interests.
C. A Book About Me.[3]	Ages 5 - 7	To better understand a child's home background and maturity.
D. Davis-Eells — Test of General Intelligence or Problem-Solving Skills.[4]	Primary Test, Grades 1 - 2 Elementary Test, Grades 3 - 6	Correlate intelligence to problem-solving ability. Test items deal with realistic problem areas and child responds to variety of verbal material.
E. Ohio Social Acceptance Scale.[5]	Ages 4 - 8	To study social acceptance and relate it to behavior.
F. Van Pit Series— Wishes.[6]	Grades 4 - 8	To aid in identifying unfulfilled emotional needs.

No effort is made to suggest specific techniques for a given teacher or school to use. It is not proposed that any teacher would necessarily use every evaluative procedure listed above. Rather, it is felt that individual teachers must make decisions in terms of their purposes, their facilities, and their situation. Many teachers use some informal, casual, and subjective procedures. Such informal procedures can be used in a manner which increases their reliability. When the total evaluation program is considered, its validity and appropriateness seem evident. The criterion of comprehensiveness must be employed locally in terms of local purposes. The teacher is constantly on the alert for ways of increasing the reliability of procedures used.

1. Science Research Associates, Inc., 259 East Erie Street, Chicago 11, Illinois.
2. *Ibid.*
3. *Ibid.*
4. Harcourt, Brace and World, Inc., Tarrytown-on-Hudson, New York.
5. Bureau Educational Research, Ohio State University, Columbus, Ohio.
6. Modern Education Service, Box 26, Bronxville, New York.

M . S C O T T   N O R T O N

Before reading this article, consider Dewey's view of the goal of self-evaluation: "The child ought to have a positive consciousness of what he is about, and be able to judge and criticize his respective acts from the standpoint of their reference to the work which he has to do. Only in this way does he have a normal and healthy standard, enabling him properly to appreciate his failures and to estimate them at their right value."[1]

This article contains ideas for helping pupils evaluate their own work. Norton stresses that pupils need help in clarifying their performance for themselves rather than being passive recipients of their teachers' views. These ideas may, of course, be applied to other subject-matter areas by creating evaluation guides based upon the objectives of those areas.

IMPROVEMENT IN arithmetic is dependent—dependent upon the individual's awareness of various weaknesses, a desire to improve in this area, and a knowledge of the procedures that possibly may bring about the desired improvement. This idea of self-improvement is carried on in arithmetic classes in our school through the use of our self-evaluation plan. Although rather simple in nature, this self-evaluation technique has proved a valuable device for helping pupils help themselves in arithmetic improvement.

As frequently as it may seem necessary, usually once each six weeks, each pupil is asked to evaluate his progress in the arithmetic class with the use of our self-evaluation checklist. The student is asked to think seriously about his work quality, effort, progress, strengths, weaknesses, and other areas of importance in regard to his arithmetic class. If some weakness is stated by the pupil, he is asked to suggest his own possible solutions which might lead to improvement in these areas. This step of self-appraisal is, in our opinion, the first step in any improvement program. Teachers' suggestions, comments, and recommendations which may be of value to the student in his improvement are listed in the space provided at the end of the self-evaluation checklist. If

Reprinted from *The Arithmetic Teacher*, 7:203-4, April, 1960.
1.   John Dewey, *Educational Essays*. London: Blackie & Sons., Ltd., 1910, p. 36.

the case appears of a serious nature, a private conference between the pupil, teacher, and parent may be held.

In one instance, a pupil of good potential in arithmetic was receiving failing marks in the course. His self-evaluation pointed out that he was spending all of his time out of class on one subject that he was taking. He solved his own problem by suggesting that he set up a time schedule which would budget his study time more adequately. As a result, his work began to improve and he is now one of the top pupils in the class. Without some type of self-examination, this boy might have lost out completely in arithmetic. Another individual wrote at some length about the proper methods of study that should be used for improvement in arithmetic. His improvement indicated that he himself was beginning to follow his own advice. Other cases of pupils' improvement through the use of self-evaluation are too numerous to mention. Citizenship, too, may be improved through the use of this device. One individual listed ten ways in which he could improve his citizenship during the coming term. The result was an improvement not only in this person's citizenship but improvement scholastically as well.

Only by using this technique can one appreciate its real merits. Both pupil and teacher benefit from the evaluations that are made. Guidance teachers in our school have become interested in this technique and have suggested that the checklist be filed in the individual folder of each pupil concerned. The checklist included in this article is the one used at our school, but may not meet the needs of other teachers and other schools. Each school should devise its own evaluation list and adapt it to its own particular situation.

Self-evaluation checklists in arithmetic are not meant to be all-thorough and comprehensive. The important thing appears to be that pupils have an opportunity to evaluate themselves, to appreciate their strengths and their weaknesses, to begin to search for ways to improve, and to profit from their own and their teachers' suggestions. We give this technique of self-evaluation, self-education, and self-appraisal our highest recommendation.

Self-Evaluation Checklist for Arithmetic and Mathematics Pupils

Please be sincere, honest, and thorough in dealing with the questions that follow. It is the purpose of this checklist to help you diagnose and know more about your progress in this class to this date. Think carefully about each question before answering. Your answers will help your teachers to be more able to help you help yourself.

1. I feel my progress in arithmetic (or mathematics) up to this date has been: (a) very good, (b) satisfactory, (c) below average.
2. In general, I have put forth: (a) more effort on my work in arith-

metic since my last evaluation, (b) about the same amount of effort, (c) less effort.

3. I need improvement most in the areas of: (a) daily preparations, (b) preparations for tests, (c) class participation, (d) study habits, (e) citizenship, (f) effort, (g) list any others:

———————————————————————————————————————

4. My best work has been in the areas of: (a) daily preparation, (b) tests, (c) class participation, (d) citizenship improvement, (e) list any other:

———————————————————————————————————————

5. I need more work and help on the areas I have listed below: (a)
    (b)   (c)   (d)   (e)

6. Several ways in which I can improve in each of the areas I checked in Question 3 are as follows:

———————————————————————————————————————

———————————————————————————————————————

———————————————————————————————————————

———————————————————————————————————————

7. I need to spend about _____ more minutes per day on my arithmetic assignments in order to improve next term.

8. In my opinion, I could earn about a (Class Grade) in arithmetic. This term I feel I have earned about a _____ in arithmetic.

9. My citizenship in this class has been: (a) very good, (b) average, (c) below average for this term. I feel I should receive a grade of _____ in citizenship for this term.

10. List other comments, attitudes, and ways you can improve next term in the space provided below. You might comment briefly on your plans for improvement in study habits, class attention, initiative, use of class time, and other areas you feel important to your self-improvement in arithmetic.

The space below is provided for teacher's comments, recommendations, and advice to the pupil concerned.

*An evaluation of subjectivity of elementary-school
teachers in grading handwriting*

ORESTE R. RONDINELLA

*Studies such as this one have also been made with respect to evalua-
tion of other subject-matter areas. Notice the clear, objective way the
author presents the problem, procedure, findings, and conclusions.
This kind of reporting is very much appreciated by readers of research. Evaluation specialists continue to explore ways to reduce
subjectivity in marking.*

LITTLE RESEARCH has been directed to the problem of teacher subjectivity in
grading penmanship. The purpose of this investigation was threefold: (1) to
ascertain if subjectivity on the part of teachers was a significant factor in
grading the handwriting specimens of elementary-school children, (2) to
establish what factors were considered in the subjective grading of penmanship, and (3) to determine the degree to which criteria used in handwriting
scales were employed as standards in grading penmanship papers.

PROCEDURE

A penmanship exercise was administered to 239 children of the fourth,
fifth, and sixth grades in a New York City school. Two teachers and the investigator, all skilled in the use of Freeman's *Chart for Diagnosing Faults in
Handwriting* and the *Ayres' Handwriting Scale*, independently graded the 239
exercises on three successive days. On the fourth day they jointly reevaluated
the 239 papers. Seventy-two samples, 24 from each grade level, were selected.

In February, 1960, the investigator initiated meetings with 210 inter-
mediate-grade teachers of 37 participating elementary schools in New York
City and Rockville Centre, Long Island. Rating forms were distributed, and
the specimens were rated by the teachers. They were instructed to use their
normal handwriting rating standards.

The investigator tallied the teacher ratings of specimens at the three grade
levels and found the mean of 70 grades for each sample. The standard devia-

Reprinted with the permission of the National Council of Teachers of English and
Dr. Oreste R. Rondinella from *Elementary English,* 40:531-34, May, 1963.

tion for each teacher's rating form was computed. Standard scores z were determined and inspected to ascertain variability of ratings assigned by different teachers to the same specimen.

FINDINGS

1. The spread of verbal values, varying mean scores, distribution of standard deviations, and variability of the standard scores z indicated inconsistencies in ratings among 24 specimens for each grade level by 70 teachers at each grade level.

2. Fourteen characteristics of writing were mentioned by the 210 teachers. Only five of their criteria are used in the Freeman scale. Further analysis indicated that 12 teachers made no mention of scale criteria, 89 teachers considered no more than three scale factors, 66 teachers noted four scale criteria, and 43 mentioned five norms of the Freeman scale.

3. Letter formation, the most important criterion of Freeman's scale, was considered of major importance.

4. Stroke was considered the least important of the Freeman criteria.

5. Neatness, not included in the Freeman or Ayres' scales, was noted by 77 teachers.

6. Quality and speed were mentioned once each by teachers.

7. A majority of the teachers mentioned legibility, height, slant, and space as factors which influenced their judgments of writing specimens.

8. The coefficient of correlation between the means of seventy ratings for each teacher at each grade level and those assigned each sample by experts was greater than the tabled value of .413 at the 5 per cent level. This indicated that the agreement between the mean average of 70 teachers at each grade level and experts was so close that it could not be easily attributed to chance.

9. The differences between the correlations of grades four and five, four and six, and five and six were not significant.

10. The mean and standard deviation scores of 70 teacher rating forms, at each grade level, indicated that only slight differences existed in rating writing samples among the teachers at each grade level on the basis of teaching experience.

CONCLUSIONS

1. Subjectivity exists among teachers in rating handwriting specimens of elementary-school children.

2. Many teachers are insufficiently aware of the major criteria for grading writing specimens.

3. Teachers consider letter formation as the single dominant criterion in the rating of penmanship.

4. Neatness of a writing exercise affects teacher ratings, although it is not a specific criterion of either scale used.

5. A teacher majority is influenced by writing which can be easily and quickly read.

6. Teachers do not consider general quality as a factor in the rating of penmanship.

7. The correlation between grades assigned to handwriting specimens and those assigned by experts indicates that substantial agreement exists between the two.

8. Teaching experience has little or no effect on subjectivity in grading handwriting.

An instructional program in handwriting functions less effectively when teachers are grading subjectively. The penmanship program from the fourth to the sixth grade should be redesigned to improve objectivity in rating of handwriting. Teacher in-service courses in the use of objective handwriting scales should improve the rating of penmanship by experienced and inexperienced teachers. Teachers who are unfamiliar with the use of writing scales cannot conduct diagnostic and remedial handwriting instruction effectively.

CHAPTER 20

Ways of Testing

TEACHERS' CURRICULUM decisions about testing give clear indications of their philosophies and theories of education. Some teachers test to diagnose pupils' difficulties and strengths. Others believe test results stand for the entirety of what pupils know. These teachers feel comfortable about assigning marks based upon test scores, forgetting that tests are only samplings.

A specialist explains the nature of testing:

> Testing may be viewed as a systematic sampling of an individual's characteristics at a given time under specified conditions. The responses of an individual to given problems, tasks, and questions are summarized to yield one or more index values intended to describe the specified characteristics.[1]

The three articles in this chapter show ways in which teachers may, by using the positive qualities of tests, avoid mistakes and do this sampling in a professional way.

1. Benjamin S. Bloom. Testing cognitive ability and achievement. *The Handbook of Research on Teaching,* N. L. Gage (ed.), Chicago: Rand McNally & Company, 1963, p. 380.

92　*A psychometrician views human ability*

HENRY S. DYER

The "back to normalcy" era of the 1920's placed great faith in the practice of putting all tests scores into a "normal curve". Psychometricians of that era often believed that tests could yield certain absolute information. There are some who still cling to this view of measurement today. However, many leaders in the field of testing continue to strive to perfect tests while maintaining a healthy awareness of what tests cannot do. Notice that the author of this article cares more for people than for tests. Many of us who teach would be wise to share his "healthy skepticism toward all gimmicks."

IN THE NEWSPAPERS and popular magazines there has recently been a rash of articles on tests and testing. Many of these articles are profoundly disturbing to a professional tester like me. It is not that the writers occasionally lambaste testing and all its works. Some of the criticism is cogent and healthy, and may serve a useful purpose in deflating the wild claims of wrongheaded optimists who have lately wandered into the testing business. What does worry the conscientious psychometrician (psychometrician is simply the $64 word for a person who puts the most serious part of his mind on the making of tests and all the paraphernalia that goes with them) is that the typical hostile critic of testing berates the tester for ideas he (the tester) does not hold and for a point of view he regards as fanciful if not fallacious. What worries him even more is that his very defenders have a curious habit of unwittingly ascribing to him opinions and attitudes that he himself regards as intellectually impossible.

I believe this predicament comes about, at least in part, from the fact that the psychometrician's view of human ability is basically different from the ordinary view held by people in general, including most teachers, guidance counselors, and other educators. Accordingly, I shall try to tell you how I, as one psychometrician, look at human ability in the hope that we may approach a meeting of minds.

SUPERSTITIONS ABOUT APTITUDE

First I shall comment on a few widely held superstitions about mental

Reprinted from *Teachers College Record, 61*:394-403, April, 1960.

ability as measured by aptitude tests, and these include IQ tests. One of the most persistent superstitions is that an aptitude test measures something called "native ability." When people speak of native ability they usually seem to mean something fixed and immutable inside the human being, some constant quantity of something that is born in the individual and that determines how well he does on tests and ought to do in school or college or in a career.

The notion that such an inherent entity exists is not unreasonable, although nobody has ever seen it under a microscope. Studies in genetics support the idea, and so do certain psychological studies, especially those tracing the development of twins reared separately under different conditions. But (and this is a big but) even though native ability may be a reasonable concept—or rather a construct growing out of a multitude of observations, just as the gene itself is a construct—it is certainly not reasonable to suppose that any test of mental ability measures the construct in any meaningful way. In itself a score on an aptitude test tells you literally nothing about a particular child's native ability.

What an aptitude test does measure is the quality of a pupil's performance on a number of mental tasks. It tells how well he can cope with tasks like those on the test at the time he takes the test, and it tells nothing more. Everything beyond this datum is pure inference. And the inference of "native ability" is a particularly shaky one. It is shaky because the tasks that appear in aptitude tests are invariably of a sort that a child (or an adult) has had to *learn* to perform as a result of his experience in the world around him—experience at home, at school, on the playground, on the job, in front of a TV set, at the movies, and elsewhere.

The amount of learning that has taken place by the time the child meets the questions on a test depends on a number of things that can vary enormously from one individual to another—the vividness of his experiences, the contexts within which they have occurred, the frequency with which a given experience has been encountered, the receptiveness of the child to what is going on in the world, and so on. With all this variability in experience between the time of birth and the time of taking the test, it is absurd to suppose that an aptitude score measures some fixed entity that the child was born with.

Let me cite a small but revealing example. At an early age my son was interested in fishing and was particularly intrigued at the sight of fish leaping out of the water to catch flies. One of the questions in a standard intelligence test for children is this:

> Birds fly; fish————.

The correct answer, of course, is "swim." My son's answer was "jump." A good answer, perhaps, but atypical and therefore wrong—wrong not because he is innately stupid but because his experience with fish differed from that of the general run of children. This incident is not intended to suggest that all intelligence tests are a snare and a delusion but merely to emphasize that aptitude test scores are inevitably determined in considerable measure by what the child has seen and heard done.

Let me reemphasize that the psychometrician thinks of ability not as a constant entity inside the individual but simply as the quality of his behavior with respect to any set of tasks that may confront him at the moment. If these tasks constitute a test, then the individual's score on the test *is* his ability with respect to the kinds of tasks the test contains. The ability is always a construct derived from the test score. We don't measure the construct; we arrive at it through the measurement of behavior. Under this definition, which I suppose you might call an operational definition, an individual's ability may vary with time and with the kinds of tasks that make up the test. He may get one score on Text X one day and a different score on the same test another day. To the psychometrician this means that the individual's ability as defined by the tasks on Test X has *changed* from one time to another.

This point of view, as contrasted with the ordinary point of view about human ability, has important consequences in the way one interprets test scores.

THE FALLACY OF THE "UNDERACHIEVER"

To think that an aptitude test measures something fixed in the pupil's internal mechanism, something unaffected by his learning and experience, can, in the psychometrician's view, lead to confused thinking about the student himself. One fallacious notion that comes out of such thinking is that a student with high ability scores and low marks in school is an underachiever— one who is not working up to capacity. The reasoning implicit in such a statement goes something like this: (1) Johnny's ability score, and therefore his ability, is high; (2) this means that Johnny is equipped by nature with ability to do good school work; (3) he is not doing it; (4) therefore he is not using the ability with which nature endowed him. The fallacy in this reasoning occurs in the assumption that a high ability score means that Johnny is equipped by nature with ability to do good schoolwork. It may mean nothing of the sort. What it does mean is that Johnny has done well on the kinds of questions that the test poses. The fact that Johnny does not also do well on the kinds of questions his teachers pose may be merely an indication that the questions in the two situations are different—that his teachers are expecting one kind of performance (or ability) from him and the test expects a different kind of performance (or ability).

In building a scholastic aptitude test, of course, the psychometrician puts into it a series of tasks that he hopes will correlate high with the kinds of tasks a student is expected to perform in school. But the correlation is never perfect because schools vary and teachers vary in their demands on pupils, and because pupils vary in their perceptions of the tasks required of them.

Nevertheless, the notion of the underachiever—the child who is not working up to ability—has taken deep roots in spite of the efforts of some psychometricians to kill it. We thought we had it buried back in the 1930's, but in the past few years it has again raised its ugly head. The customary, and ordinarily fallacious, diagnosis is that the student with a high ability score and low marks in school is *ipso facto* unmotivated or lazy or suffering from some emotional disturbance traceable perhaps to faulty toilet training. Granted that these are possibilities, nevertheless it is a vast mistake to assume that they can be inferred solely from the discrepancy between the scores and the marks. The first question to ask is, Why has Johnny learned how to answer the test questions? Perhaps the trouble is not in Johnny at all but in the kinds of questions on the test, or in the kinds of questions the teacher asks, or even in the teacher's skill as a teacher.

"CULTURE FREE" TESTS?

Some people are wedded to the idea that ability tests *ought* to measure an unchanging native ability and that failiure to do this represents a serious weakness in the tests. This point of view leads to the frequent demand that such tests should be "culture free"; that is, unaffected by the cultural milieu in which a child has been brought up. It is plainly impossible to satisfy such a demand. Consider what any test essentially is. It is made up of a series of pieces of the environment to which the pupil is expected to react in one way or another. These pieces of the environment are questions, problems, situations which, no matter how cute or original or apparently novel, are inevitably drawn from the culture. In selecting pieces of the environment for a test, the test-maker tries to sample the common culture as broadly as possible, but even so he cannot make his test equally appropriate to all the subcultures in American life. There are too many differences between the environment of the city and that of the farm child or between the environment of the child of foreign-born parents and that of the child of native-born parents. If the tester, on the other hand, attempts to eliminate from his test all elements which are not perfectly common (or perfectly uncommon) for all groups—and this has been tried—he is likely to find himself with a test whose scores may not be very helpful in predicting school success, for most schools and colleges reflect the dominant culture in the society of which they are a part.

If a child does poorly on an aptitude test because he comes from the wrong side of the tracks, it isn't the test that is being "unfair"; it is the hard facts of social circumstance that are unfair. Anyone who is seriously interested in improving the lot of the culturally underprivileged, should direct his attention not to changing the tests—which would accomplish literally nothing—but to improving the quality of educational opportunity for all children.

WOBBLY TEST SCORES

Another unreasonable demand that people seem to make of tests—whether they are aptitude tests or any other kind—is that the scores they yield should be absolutely accurate measures of whatever it is they purport to measure. Take an intelligence test for example. Some people are shocked to discover that a pupil's IQ—his score on the test—can change with time and with the test. He can get an IQ of 100 this year and one of 120 next year. If he takes two different brands of an intelligence test on the same day, he may score an IQ of 110 on one and an IQ of 95 on the other.

Teachers, guidance counselors, parents, and others find this wobbly quality of the IQ disconcerting. It destroys the notion that the IQ is an unchanging personal possession; that you can decide once and for all what a child's IQ is; or that if a child at age twelve turns up with an IQ of 115 or better he ought to be steered toward college, but if his IQ is less than that, any college plans he or his parents may be toying with should be permanently discouraged. Test scores are slippery things, and anyone who uses them without realizing how slippery they are can make serious errors in judgment and do considerable damage to a child's education.

Wobbliness in test scores is no news to the tester. It is something that he accepts as inevitable for all tests of every description: aptitude tests or achievement tests, interest tests or personality tests, paper-and-pencil tests or performance tests, objective tests or essay tests. No test ever devised or given is more than a *sample* of a pupil's reactions. If you give a pupil a spelling test of 100 words drawn from among the thousands he has encountered in his studies and he gets 75 out of a 100 correct, what do you have? You have an *estimate*, based on a sample, of how he would do on all the words to which he has been exposed. If you draw another sample of 100 from the same pool of words, the number of words the pupil spells correctly on this second test will in all probability be different. He may get 63 right, he may get 92 right, or anything in between or outside of these limits. You now have a different estimate of his ability to spell all the words he is supposed to know.

But the difficulty does not end here. Suppose that, without allowing the pupil any opportunity for study in between you ask him to spell the *same* sample of 100 words two days in succession. Would he get the same number correct each time? Probably not, because his response to any given word can change. Today he spells *irresistible* correctly; tomorrow he leaves out one of the *r*'s or uses *a* instead of *i* in *ible*. Today he spells *scissors* incorrectly by omitting the *c;* tomorrow he gets it right. What a pupil does with a particular word on one occasion is thus only a sample of what he would do with the same word on other occasions. What a pupil does in any test situation—a word to spell, an arithmetic problem to solve, a story to write, a cake to bake—is never more than a sample of all the possible responses he might make to the situation if given the opportunity.

TESTS AS SAMPLES

In a nutshell this means that every test is two kinds of sample—a sample of the situations to which a student is expected to respond and a sample of the kinds of responses he is likely to make to each situation. Taken together, this double sampling inevitably makes for uncertainty in test results, uncertainty rooted in the fact that whenever we deal with a sample we have to cope with errors of sampling.

The brutal fact about errors of sampling is that they are not the kinds of errors you can rectify. You cannot "correct" for errors of sampling. The sampling error in a pupil's test score does not mean that the score is "off" by some ascertainable amount; it simply means that we have to face the fact that it is clouded with uncertainty, that it could have been different, that if we use it to estimate a pupil's ability we run the risk of making the wrong estimate. If Johnny gets a mark of 70 on a history examination and Joe gets a mark of 55, we cannot be dead sure that Johnny passes and Joe does not. If we had given them a different sample of history questions, Joe might have got 70 and Johnny 55.

Many people, probably most, find this uncertainty hard to take. Too many of them close their eyes to it, and among those who do are many teachers, guidance counselors, college admissions officers, and others who make frequent use of test results. They seem to feel that the professional test-maker has let them down by allowing sampling error to creep into his tests. Every year after the results of the College Board examinations come out, I receive a rash of telephone calls from dismayed school officials or parents or college admissions officers who say, in effect, "Johnny took your Scholastic Aptitude Test last May and got a score of 550. He took it again this January and his score dropped to 475. What's happened to your crazy test?"

Under the circumstances it is a little difficult to persuade the party at the other end of the line that nothing has happened to the test, that nobody has made a terrible mistake, that Johnny, bless his soul, is merely a victim of sampling error—as are all the other Johnnies and Marys who submit to *any* kind of test whatsoever. To an anxious parent or a harried admissions officer this sort of answer is hardly comforting. Uncertainty is always uncomfortable despite the fact that in the assessment of human ability it can never be avoided.

INEVITABILITY OF THE SAMPLING ERROR

In defense of the test-maker, be it said that if he is worth his professional salt he is acutely aware of the sampling error in his tests, and although he knows he can never get rid of it (and wishes everybody could understand this fact), he also knows how to do something about it. He knows how to get a good estimate of the amount of sampling error (that is, the amount of uncertainty) in any test, and he knows what to do to reduce the size of this error.

Professional ethics requires him to make known to his customers how much sampling error a given test contains. If he fails to report this and other matters faithfully, there are professional associations that may call him to account for unethical practice. In other words, testers take very seriously the matter of knowing, and letting the public know, how much sampling error a test contains. They only wish the public would pay more attention to this information and not go on being surprised every time the sampling error in a test becomes painfully apparent.

In the test-making business one of the aims is to make the uncertainty of measurement as small as possible. Other things being equal, the sampling error in a test becomes smaller as the size of the sample becomes larger. Obviously a 100-word spelling test will surpass a 10-word test as an estimate of a pupil's ability to spell. But the size of the sample, though of prime importance, is not the only consideration. One has to worry also about the composition of the sample: Is it truly representative of all the different kinds of tasks a student could meet in a particular field—hard ones, easy ones, simple ones, complex ones? The sampling error in a test can also be affected by the manner in which the test is presented. How nearly uniform are the conditions of testing from sample to sample? If a child takes a test while a pile driver is pounding in the next block, the sampling of his responses may not be typical. All such matters the tester does his utmost to control, and the result is that the best of his tests if properly used provide as reliable a sample of pupil performance as can be found anywhere. Even so, looked at critically, a highly reliable test still has a lot of uncertainty in it.

IMPRECISION IN CASUAL OBSERVATION

People who have been generally aware of the wobbliness in test scores are often surprised, even shocked, to realize the extent of the wobbliness. If this is the best that the best of ability tests can do, they say, why not go back to the old-fashioned tried-and-true ways of sizing up students? Why not rely on teachers' judgments and direct observation in face-to-face contact? Well, these old ways have long been tried, but their results are far less precise than those of a well-made test. When it is possible to check upon unfettered observation and judgment, one wonders whether the old methods can be relied upon at all.

I once witnessed such a checking up which occurred more or less by accident. A youngster was applying for a scholarship at a well-known university. He had been interviewed by three people independently—an alumnus and two assistant deans. The alumnus rated him "satisfactory," one of the assistant deans rated him "topnotch," and the other rated him "impossible." As for teachers' judgments, there is the instance of a student who had one English teacher during the first semester and another the second semester. The first one gave him an F, the second one gave him an A. As instances like these multiply, one cannot escape the impression that good tests, for all their lack of precision, give vastly less wobbly results than do the "old-fashioned" ways of assessing human performance.

TESTS AS PREDICATORS

The principle of uncertainty in testing extends to matters beyond the wobbliness in the scores themselves. It applies also to the use of tests for predicting how well students are likely to do in school and college. Among the most important purposes that tests can serve is that of helping the guidance counselor or the college admissions officer predict what kind of marks Johnny is going to get if he takes a certain course or enrolls in a certain college. Such predictions are the stuff of which vital educational decisions are made.

But some people seem to have funny ideas about prediction. Johnny's mathematical aptitude score suggests that Johnny will get a B in advanced algebra. Johnny takes the course and turns up with a C. "You see," they say, "the test was wrong! You can't trust it." This attitude strikes the tester not only as unreasonable but as one that grows out of the mistaken idea that prediction must always be an all-or-none, right-or-wrong business. It would be fairer to the test and would contribute to better decision-making if prediction were thought of as a matter of calculating the chances; of figuring the risks rather than of asserting an on-the-nose expectation. We should not say the aptitude score predicts an A for Johnny; we should say it shows that Johnny has 6 chances in 10 of making an A in algebra, 8 chances in 10 of making a B or better, 9 chances in 10 of making a C or better, only 1 chance in 10 of flunking the course. This approach underlies the uncertainty that is always involved in the prediction of events. It also provides information about the amount of uncertainty with which the interested parties will have to cope when making up their minds whether Johnny should take advanced algebra.

To recapitulate briefly, I have said that an individual's ability is the quality of his performance on a series of tasks which we may call a test. I have said that our estimate of an individual's ability from any particular test is always clouded with uncertainty because of the inevitable sampling error in any test. I have suggested that in attempting to predict an individual's ability to cope with some situation in the future, there is also an unavoidable amount of uncertainty. This is because the kinds of tasks we can reasonably expect an individual to perform at one point in time may be, and usually are, to some extent different from the kinds of tasks we may reasonably expect him to perform at a later time, after he has had new learning experiences. That is, the kinds of tasks with which you test a student's mathematical ability before he takes algebra cannot be the same as those with which you would test his mathematical ability after he has taken algebra. He has learned and his ability has changed, and the remarkable thing is that in a given field we can predict future performance from past performance as well as we do.

DIVERSE ABILITIES

Let us now look at another aspect of the matter, namely, the different *kinds* of human ability. To say of an individual that he has a large amount of ability is essentially meaningless to the psychometrician. He will counter with the question, "Ability in doing what?" A person may have a large amount of ability in spelling (that is, he may get high scores on spelling tests), but he may have only a small amount of ability to solve problems in arithmetic (meaning he may score low on an arithmetic test).

During the past forty years psychometricians have devoted a good deal of effort to identifying different kinds of ability through the technique known as factor analysis. Factor analysis is essentially a form of experiment in which the psychometrician tries to discover how all the different kinds of mental tasks tend to cluster. As might be expected, psychometricians have found that tasks having to do with words, their meanings, and their combinations tend to form one homogeneous cluster; tasks having to do with numbers and their manipulation form another homogeneous cluster. A homogeneous cluster of tasks is defined empirically as one in which the performance of students on any task in the cluster is highly correlated with their performance on all other tasks in the cluster. Thus, students who test high on vocabulary knowledge tend to test high also in reading comprehension, in grammatical usage, in theme writing, and so on. Such a cluster of tasks is called the verbal factor, and students who test high on the tasks constituting this factor are said to have high verbal ability. Similarly, the cluster of tasks dealing with numbers is called the mathematical or quantitative factor, and students who test high on this factor are said to have high mathematical ability. Other clusters of tasks define such things as the mechanical factor, the memory factor, and the perceptual factor. And the correlatives of these factors are mechanical ability, memory ability, perceptual ability, and so on.

Factor analysis is a fascinating and powerful technique that has done much to tease out the dimensions of human ability, but we must not make the mistake of supposing that it has somehow penetrated the mystery of mind and uncovered hidden determiners of human performance. It has, however, made possible the classification of human performance into various categories of ability. It is nevertheless culture bound in the sense that the categories it defines might appear quite different if the rewards accorded by society to various kinds of performance were radically changed and if such changes were reflected in a fundamental reorganization of school curriculum. It is conceivable, for instance, that verbal ability and mathematical ability, which now appear so different, might merge into a single new ability if reading and arithmetic in the elementary schools were taught not as two separate subjects but as a single subject called, let us say, logical analysis.

PITFALLS IN PROFILES

The availability of tests for several different kinds of ability has led, as you probably well know, to the development of what are known as multi-aptitude test batteries for use in guidance. These test batteries have within them rich possibilities, but they have not been an unmixed blessing. For one thing, they have encouraged the oversimplified notion that a profile of ability scores summarizes clearly and efficiently a large amount of reliable information about most of the important abilities of an individual. Psychometricians have been worrying about this problem for a long time. They have inveighed repeatedly against the overconfident use of profile charts, on the ground that such charts are often grossly misleading; that the differences in ability they depict—even when they appear large—may be, and usually are, unreliable; that the score scales used for the several tests in the profile may not be comparable; that the several measures which show on the profile may appear to be highly independent measures when, in fact, many of them may be highly correlated—in short, that the apparent clarity and efficiency of an ability profile are really illusions covering up all sorts of pitfalls in score interpretation which even the most wary can scarcely avoid. Yet the profile chart is still in wide use, primarily I suppose because it is extraordinarily convenient.

Within the past few years there have been several attempts by psychometricians to develop data on which a more or less foolproof type of profile chart could be based. This research falls into the category of what are known as differential prediction studies. We have one such study going on at ETS. The studies in connection with the General Aptitude Test Battery of the USES are another example. But probably the largest and best known is the differential prediction study being conducted at the University of Washington under the direction of Paul Horst. The goal of all these studies is to provide a profile of probable success in each of several educational or vocational fields rather than a profile showing simply where a student stands on a series of tests whose predictive validity is unknown or at least unstated in the profile itself. That is, the elements in the probability profile are *fields*, not tests, and probability that a student will succeed in a given field is based on test scores and other data.

PROBLEMS IN DIFFERENTIAL PREDICTION

The probability profile chart, as contrasted with the ability profile chart, would, I take it, be very helpful in guidance if it could actually be produced. But the differential prediction studies that must underlie such a chart are surrounded by a number of difficult problems. In the first place, such studies are extraordinarily expensive. In the second place, since they require a follow-up of student performance over several years, they take a long time. In the third place, since it is obviously impossible for every student in the study sample to try himself out in each of the fields open to him, it is difficult, though not methodologically impossible, to get data *across* fields which are meaningful and comparable. In the fourth place, the probability data obtained in such studies are interpretable only for a particular setting, that is, only for the school or college or specific occupational group for which the original data were developed.

All these problems, difficult though they may be, are surmountable if the money and time are forthcoming to surmount them. But it is still, in my judgment, an open question whether we shall ever in the nature of things be able to get test score data or any other kind of data that will permit us to draw the kind of probability profile the differential prediction studies are aiming at. To me, the University of Washington results as well as our own are discouraging. They provide reasonably good over-all prediction, but so far they do not provide much *differential* prediction. That is, the probability that a given student will succeed in any one field is not so greatly different from the probability that he will succeed in most other fields, and one wonders whether such differences as there are can be considered real and reliable. The hope is, of course, that by introducing better and more sharply differentiated tests, more sharply differentiated probability statements will become possible. But this is still only a hope, and it is a moot question, it seems to me, whether *any* tests can ever be found that will separate very far in advance the student more likely to succeed in biology from the one more likely to succeed in history. Despite all the work of the factor analysts over the past forty years, I think it is possible that human abilities are sufficiently fluid over time so that, if circumstances are right, the person who today looks like a good biologist and a poor historian may undergo experiences which will convert him into a good historian and a poor biologist. You see, the trouble with the well-known square-peg-in-round-hole analogy is that it is completely static. It assumes that neither the peg nor the hole can ever change shape, when we know perfectly well that the patterns of people's abilities change as they adapt to circumstances, and circumstances change as people adapt to them. In other words, I suspect that there are dynamic elements in the relation of an individual to his changing environment which are not being taken into account in the differential prediction studies and which may, indeed, prevent them from ever arriving at any very fruitful results. But in any case, the question is still open, the problems are enormous, and the need for vast quantities of research is dire.

I suppose my basic worry about the use of profile charts, whether they are ability profiles or probability profiles, is that they tend to conceal the very great and complex problems of human functioning about which we actually know so little, and make them seem so much simpler than they really are. I doubt that we are likely to get very far in improving the guidance process or any other educational process by adopting devices which lure us into thinking we know more about human ability than is at the present knowable.

IMPORTANCE OF DOUBT

I realize that this discussion has been appallingly negative. I have suggested that the concept of native ability has little if any practical utility. I have suggested that any ability as defined by the tasks on which a student performs can be highly variable and elusive. I have pointed to the unreliability of measures of ability and to the uncertainties involved in using them for prediction purposes. I have tried to show that the categories of performance which constitute different kinds of ability are subject to change as the dominant elements in our culture and in the educational process change. I have cast doubt on the utilty of ability profiles as used in guidance and have questioned whether the differential prediction studies as at present constituted may not be based upon a false assumption about the ways in which human abilities develop under training.

If I have plunged you into unrelieved doubt, I am not sorry, really, for I believe that if we are ever going to get anywhere in trying to understand human behavior, we must always realize that it comprises the most complicated phenomena on the face of the earth. And we must approach it with a healthy skepticism toward all gimmicks and with a humility that encourages caution but never gives up hope.

ELIZABETH HAGEN

*There are thousands of published standardized tests.[1] Which ones
would you use? Why? How?*

*This article packs into a few pages much technical information
needed by any teacher who makes use of standardized tests. Hagen
contends that although grade norms are most widely used, they are
most widely abused: A teacher or parent may say, "Johnny is at the
6.5 grade level in reading," with little understanding of what that
statement means and does not mean. Haven't you also heard people
talk about the "class's average achievement level" or worse yet, the
"class's average IQ"? See what the author says about average scores.
Also be sure to see the ways standardized tests can be of real assistance in helping a teacher make plans for his class. This is not easy
reading for the uninitiated, but it is clear and it is very important.*

STANDARDIZED TESTS are given to obtain information about students. The information they provide must be used and used constructively to improve the
teaching-learning situation or else should not be given. The classroom teacher
is the critical person in the constructive use of test results. He must be able
to analyze the test results for a group or an individual and interpret the scores
in terms of what they mean for teaching the group or the individual.

In order to interpret the scores from a test or series of tests, the teacher
must know what the tests measure. This point may seem obvious, but many
classroom teachers do not know specifically what the tests they use are measuring. One cannot depend upon the title to tell what is being measured by the
test. For example, reading comprehension tests differ markedly from each
other both in the range of reading skills which they measure and the emphasis they give to the different reading skills.

The first thing that a classroom teacher should do is to analyze each test
carefully both for the content being measured and to the mental processes
required of the examinee to answer the items. Many of the tests published

Reprinted from The *National Elementary Principal,* 41:11-17, November, 1961.

1. See Oscar K. Burros (ed.). *The Fifth Mental Measurements Yearbook,* New
Brunswick, New Jersey: Gryphon Press, 1959.

since 1955 provide an analysis of the content in the manuals written for the classroom teacher. For example, the Iowa Test of Basic Skills and the Sequential Test of Educational Progress (STEP) provide an item by item analysis of the skills being measured and classify and categorize the items for easy analysis. However, the classroom teacher should check the test publisher's analysis by taking the test himself. He should make a note of any items that are inappropriate for his students. He should also note the kinds of skills or content not being tested so he will be aware of the limitations that must be put on his interpretation of the scores.

Only when the classroom teacher knows thoroughly the tests that his class has taken is he prepared to work with the test results. However, before he can organize the scores in some systematic way as a basis for analysis, the teacher must know what kind of scores he has.

NORMS

Since the raw score (the number of correct answers) on a test has no direct meaning in and of itself, the raw scores on a standardized test are given meaning by comparing them to the performance of a standard reference group. This standard reference group is called a norm group and the score obtained by such a comparison is called a norm.

A norm is *merely a description* of the performance of a certain group such as a sample of fifth-grade students throughout the United States; it is *not* a standard of achievement. For example, on the arithmetic computation subtest of the Stanford Achievement Test, the norm for students at the beginning of the fifth grade is 21 items correct out of a total of 45 items. However, the standard of achievement that one would like to reach is 100 per cent accuracy in computation. One cannot even say that the norm, particularly a national norm, represents a desirable level of achievement. A national norm group is made up of bright, average, and dull students drawn from outstanding, average, and poor schools, subjected to good, poor, and indifferent teaching. With such a heterogeneous group, one can scarcely be satisfied with the performance of the norm group when he knows that improvements in curriculum and teaching could vastly improve performance.

Three kinds of norms are usually provided for standardized tests at the elementary-school level. These are age norms, grade norms, and percentile norms.

Age norms. Strictly speaking, age norms are not relevant to achievement test results because progress in school achievement does *not* depend upon chronological age, but upon exposure to the learning situation in the class-room. For this reason, age norms should not be used for achievement tests.

Grade norms. The grade norm is the most widely abused type of norm at the elementary-school level. Although it is useful, the grade norm is so frequently misinterpreted that one wishes it had never been used. A grade norm merely describes the typical performance of a specified grade group. For example, on the paragraph meaning subtest of the Stanford Achievement Test, Intermediate Battery, the median score for students in the fifth month of the fifth grade in the normative sample was 30 items right; therefore, a score of 30 items right was assigned a grade equivalent score of 5.5. This means that one-half of the students in the normative sample who were in grade 5.5 scored higher than 30 and one-half scored lower than 30. Since the norm is usually defined as a median, in an unselected sample of students, one-half must fall above the norm and one-half must fall below. One can see, then, the ridiculousness of the statement that everyone in a class should be "up to the norm."

Another kind of misinterpretation of grade norms occurs with grade-equivalent scores that deviate markedly from the grade placement of the in-dividual student. For example, consider the student in the fifth month of the fifth grade who obtains a grade-equivalent score of 11.7 on the paragraph meaning subtest of the Stanford Achievement Test, Intermediate Battery. One frequently hears classroom teachers say that this student is reading at a high eleventh-grade level. This is nonsense. Eleventh-grade students have never taken this particular test. An extreme score such as this means only that this particular student is a very outstanding reader in comparison to the typical student in the fifth month of the fifth grade.

There is one other basic defect in grade norms that causes trouble in in-terpretation—grade norms on different tests do *not* have the same meaning. Look at the following scores for a student who took the Stanford Achieve-ment Test in the second month of the fifth grade:

Test	*Grade-Equivalent Score*
Paragraph Meaning	7.4
Word Meaning	7.0
Spelling	6.5
Language	7.7
Arithmetic Reasoning	6.6
Arithmetic Computation	6.1

Looking at the set of grade-equivalent scores, one would say that the student had performed best in language and poorest in arithmetic computation. However, every one of these scores equals or exceeds the performance of 90 per cent of the norm sample at that particular grade level. In other words, the student performed equally well on all the tests in spite of the fact that the grade-equivalent scores are *not* the same. This phenomenon is *not* caused by a defect in this particular test or a defect in norming; it is due to the differences in variability of performance of students on the tests. There is a much greater spread of scores among students in the same class in reading and language than there is in arithmetic and spelling because these last two are more closely tied to the curriculum of the school than is reading.

Percentile norms. The lack of equivalence in meaning of grade scores from test to test is serious when one is trying to compare scores for a group or an individual on different tests. For this reason, percentile norms are preferable in most cases. A percentile tells the percentage of a group that falls at or below a particular score. For example, if a student obtains a raw score of 15 on a test and this is equivalent to a percentile rank of 20, it means that 20 per cent of the norm group scored lower than 15 and 80 per cent obtained scores higher than 15. The percentile norm has the additional advantage of keeping the reference point where it belongs—in a group of which the individual can be considered to be a member. That is, a fifth-grade student is compared with other fifth-grade students, not with sixth-grade or fourth-grade students.

The percentile norm would be an ideal norm except for one defect: It does not have equal units all along the scale. An increase of five percentile points from the 50th percentile to the 55th percentile does *not* represent the same increment in score as an increase in five percentile points from the 90th to the 95th percentile. This defect in percentile norms is most troublesome when one wants to measure growth or increase in achievement from year to year.

STANDARD ERROR

Up to this point, we have been concerned with two kinds of things that the classroom teacher should thoroughly understand before he attempts to analyze and interpret test scores: (1) the test itself; and (2) the kind of score that is being used to report test results. There is one additional point that the classroom teacher should keep in mind as he analyzes and interprets test scores. He should remember that when we give a test to an individual or a group of individuals we are getting an estimate of the student's performance on the items on that particular test. From this estimate, we then make an inference about the ability of the student in the area being measured by the test.

For example, suppose we had given a fourth-grade class the Otis Quick-Scoring Mental Ability Test, Beta. Each of the students taking the test would mark his answers in the appropriate place; then, the number of right answers that the student had marked would be counted. The number of right answers would be the individual's score, which we would call his mental ability. But the score itself is *not* the mental ability. It is a *record* of a *sample* of behavior. Any judgment regarding mental ability is an inference based on the evidence provided by the number of correct answers on this particular *sample* of behavior. In other words, we have an estimate of his performance on a series of items purportedly measuring mental ability. This estimate is *not* absolutely accurate; it contains a certain amount of error called the error of measurement.

When a classroom teacher is looking at a set of scores for an individual, he must always allow for this error of measurement. He can never consider a score obtained by a student as an unvarying point on a scale but must, instead, always think of it as a band. Suppose for example, that on the Otis test mentioned previously, an individual obtained a score that yielded him an IQ of 115 for his performance on that test at that particular time. The manual for the Otis test states that the standard error of measurement is 4 IQ points. The classroom teacher should multiply the standard error by two, which would give 8 IQ points, and think of that individual as most probably having an IQ on that test of somewhere between 107 and 123. And this is as accurate as he can be in estimating that individual's mental ability on the Otis test.

The standard error of measurement varies from test to test. The manuals for the test usually give the standard error but, as a rough rule-of-thumb, it would be well for the teacher to estimate intelligence test score bands by adding 10 to the obtained intelligence quotient and subtracting 10 from the obtained intelligence quotient. For example, a student obtains an IQ of 103 on X intelligence test. The teacher should think of the student as having a score most probably between 93 and 113 on X intelligence test. On an achievement test when using grade-equivalent scores, a rough guide is to allow a full grade below and above the obtained score. If a student had been given a reading comprehension test and had obtained a grade score of 4.7, the teacher should think of the score as being most probably somewhere between 3.7 and 5.7. This should make the teacher very wary of interpreting small differences between scores on different tests for an individual student.

When a classroom teacher is working with average scores for a group of individuals, the error of measurement is smaller than for an individual. The reason for this is that the errors in measurement are due to chance factors; in some instances, the error of measurement will make a score for an individual higher than it should be and in other instances, it will make the score lower than it should be. When scores are averaged over a large number of individuals, these chance effects cancel each other so that the average score for a group has a smaller standard error than does the score for an individual. How much error there is in an average score for a group depends upon the number of people in the group and other factors.

Now let us suppose that the classroom teacher understands thoroughly all of the things previously mentioned. How does he organize the test data so he can obtain a better understanding of the students as a group and as individuals? The kinds of tabulations and analyses of data that the teacher makes are, of course, dependent upon the kinds of questions he is trying to answer. Although one probably cannot foresee all of the questions a classroom teacher is likely to ask about a set of test data, there are certain questions that are commonly asked and these will be discussed here.

AVERAGE SCORES MISLEADING

Let us assume that the classroom teacher has been given for the 30 students in his class an alphabetical listing of scores on a verbal group intelligence test and an achievement battery that includes tests of reading comprehension, vocabulary, spelling, language usage, arithmetic computation, arithmetic reasoning, and study skills. If the list also contains average battery scores for all tests combined or average scores obtained by averaging two or more tests—for example, an average arithmetic score obtained by combining the arithmetic computation score and arithmetic reasoning score—the teacher can ignore them since this type of score can be misleading. Consider the following students in grade 4.3 who obtained a composite average grade-equivalent score of 4.6 on the battery of achievement tests:

Test	Student 1	Student 2	Student 3
Reading Comprehension	2.9	6.1	4.8
Vocabulary	3.1	6.5	4.6
Language Usage	4.5	5.8	4.5
Spelling	4.8	5.1	4.3
Arithmetic Computation	6.0	3.2	4.4
Arithmetic Reasoning	6.5	2.0	4.9
Study Skills	4.4	3.5	4.7
Composite Battery Score	4.6	4.6	4.6

On the basis of the composite average battery score, the three students appear to be achieving at the same level and appear to be very much alike. However, a look at the scores for each student on the separate tests shows that these students are quite different and need quite different instructional programs. Student 1 shows a definite weakness in reading and vocabulary and definite strengths in arithmetic computation and arithmetic reasoning. On the other hand, student 2 shows quite definite strengths in the verbal areas of reading, vocabulary, language usage, and spelling and very definite weaknesses in the quantiative areas of arithmetic computation and arithmetic reasoning. Student 3 shows no outstanding strengths or weaknesses but is an even performer on all of the tests. The use of an average score for all the tests obscures these differences among students; therefore, it is advisable for routine classroom use to ignore the average scores and use only the scores on the individual tests.

SCANNING FOR INCONSISTENCIES

When a classroom teacher receives a list of scores for students in his class, the first thing he should do is scan the scores for each individual pupil to see if they are internally consistent and check the scores of each individual pupil against previous test scores or other information about the student. This scanning will avoid the necessity of trying to find explanations for test performances that are internally inconsistent or are inconsistent with other data on the individual when the inconsistency may very well be due to clerical errors in scoring the test, errors in using a table to convert scores, or errors in recording the results. Test papers scored by teachers contain a large number of errors in scoring—some quite substantial. Test papers scored by outside agencies or by electronic machines can also contain errors.

To illustrate what is meant by internal inconsistencies or inconsistencies with other data, let us consider an example. Suppose you are a sixth-grade teacher and have received the following scores for an individual student in the third month of the sixth grade (6.3):

Test	Score
Verbal IQ	85
Reading Comprehension	10.6
Vocabulary	10.7
Language Usage	6.6
Spelling	6.8
Arithmetic Computation	10.4

Test	Score
Arithmetic Reasoning	11.7
Study Skills	10.5

Before you blithely label the student as an "overachiever," it would be well to check the intelligence test to determine whether the test has been scored accurately and the intelligence quotient has been computed accurately. The intelligence test score is singled out for attention in this case because the achievement test scores are consistently high. If you can find no error in the scoring of the intelligence test or in the computation of the intelligence quotient, check against previous test data on the student. Suppose this student had been given the same intelligence test when he was in the fourth grade and had obtained an intelligence quotient of 120. The difference of 35 points between the fourth-grade testing and the sixth-grade testing is too large to attribute to error of measurement and the student should be retested. Test scores that are inconsistent or out-of-line with other evidence on the individual should *never* be entered on a permanent record card until their accuracy has been established.

ANALYZING THE TOTAL CLASS: USE OF MEDIANS

After eliminating the inconsistent cases from consideration in the analysis, the classroom teacher is ready to organize the class data in order to obtain answers to his questions. The first question to be answered is usually, "How did the class on the whole perform on each of these tests?" To answer this question, the teacher should tabulate or list the scores on each test from the highest score to the lowest score. Then for each set of scores, he should determine the median score—the score which divides the class in half.

Having computed the median for each of the tests, the teacher is ready to look at the pattern of the medians in order to obtain an answer to the question, "What are the strong and weak points of the class as a whole?" In looking for patterns of performance, the classroom teacher should group median scores for related areas. For the achievement battery that we are using as an example, the medians for reading comprehension and vocabulary should be examined together; the medians for spelling and language usage should be looked at as a unit; the medians for arithmetic computation and arithmetic reasoning should be looked at as a unit; then, the medians for study skills. This type of pattern analysis needs to be done in order to differentiate a class disability from an individual disability. To illustrate, let us look at the following example showing medians for a fourth-grade class tested in November (4.3):

Test	Class Median
Verbal IQ	105
Reading Comprehension	5.1
Vocabulary	4.8
Language Usage	4.5
Spelling	4.2
Arithmetic Computation	3.0
Arithmetic Reasoning	2.7
Study Skills	2.7

This particular class shows strength in the verbal-language areas and weaknesses in the quantitative and study skills areas. Since the class shows a very marked weakness in the quantitative and study skills tests, the teacher might well ask the question, "Why are these students performing so poorly in these areas?" To obtain more specific information about what the class does and does not know in these areas, the teacher should make a sample item analysis of the arithmetic and study skills tests.

ITEM ANALYSIS

In order to make an item analysis of the tests, the teacher needs the answer sheets of the students. With the answer sheets at hand, the teacher can make a tally of the number of correct answers, the number of wrong answers, and the number of omitted answers to each test question. Then, he should look at the items that have been marked correct and incorrect by a large proportion of the class.

In the school from which these data were taken, such an item analysis was made and showed three things: (1) the students on the whole were slow workers; a large proportion of students had never reached the last twenty items on the test; (2) the students tended to make mistakes on simple addition or subtraction items that were written on a line instead of under each other; most of the students missed items involving the use of decimals unless they were problems dealing with money. The teacher investigated the previous educational experiences of the students in arithmetic and found that accuracy had been emphasized; that the students had always been given their addition and subtraction problems in the same form; and that problems involving decimals other than money were a part of the curriculum for the last half of the fourth grade. With this information, the teacher could do better planning for the class in arithmetic than he could with just the scores alone.

PERFORMANCE AND EXPECTANCY

When the teacher is looking at the median scores for his class, he frequently asks, "Are these scores what they should be in light of the ability level of the class?" This question deals with the relationship between obtained scores and expected scores and poses a sticky problem. Too frequently, the classroom teacher tries to make a direct comparison between intelligence test scores and achievement test scores. However, both scores have errors in them and the correlation between intelligence and achievement is not perfect.

The level of achievement in a group depends not only upon the scholastic ability level of the group but also upon the educational experiences to which it has been exposed and the cultural backgrounds of the individuals making up the group. The judgment of whether a group is performing at the expected level can be made only if median scores for groups of like-level of ability are available for comparison. If the median level of scholastic ability for the group is average, if the median socioeconomic level is about at the average for the nation as a whole, and if the curricular emphasis in the school is like schools in the United States as a whole, then and only then can the national norm be used as a reference point for judging whether the group is performing at expectancy. If the classroom group deviates from the national group on *any one* of these points, then the national norm cannot be used to judge whether a particular group is performing at expectancy, and local expectancy charts must be set up for this purpose.

IDENTIFYING NUMBER OF ACHIEVEMENT LEVELS

The last question that a teacher is likely to ask about the group as a whole is, "How many distinct levels of achievement do I have in each of the areas covered by the tests?" Again, it is better if the classroom teacher looks at patterns of scores.

If the teacher has arranged the scores for each test from high to low and computed medians for each test, he can then compute the 25th percentile and 75th percentile on each test. These three score points will divide the scores on each test into four parts: the lowest quarter, those falling below the 25th percentile; the second quarter, those falling between the 25th percentile and the median; the third quarter, those falling between the median and the 75th percentile; and the fourth quarter, those falling above the 75th percentile. He can use some simple designation for each quarter such as L (low) for lowest quarter; LA (low average) for second quarter; HA (high average) for the third quarter; and H (high) for the fourth quarter. The teacher can then list the students alphabetically, and rule off columns for each test and enter the appropriate symbol for each student for each test. The record would look something like this:

Stu-dent	Int.	Read. Comp.	Voc.	Lang. Usage	Spell.	Arith. Comp.	Arith. Reas.
John A	H	LA	LA	HA	LA	H	H
Anne B	LA	LA	LA	LA	HA	L	L

A record such as this not only helps the teacher to see how many groups he needs, but also helps him see the pattern of scores for the individual students and locate students who need enriched programs, remedial work, or a modified program.

INTERPRETING THE INDIVIDUAL'S SCORES

The analyses that have been proposed not only will give the teacher a picture of the group as a whole, but also will serve as a point of reference for interpreting the scores of an individual student. There are two questions concerning individual students that are frequently asked: (1) Is the student performing at expectancy according to his ability level? and (2) How much growth or progress has the student made since the last testing? Both of these questions are difficult for the classroom teacher to answer because they involve rather sophisticated statistical procedures. In both instances, we are dealing with scores that are highly related to each other and have a certain amount of error of measurement. When we make these comparisons, we are dealing with the difference between two scores and these differences are less reliable than either of the individual scores.

Let us consider the question of how well a student's performance conforms to the level of performance expected of him. The classroom teacher needs outside help in order to determine levels of expectancy of different ability levels. In large systems, the school as a whole can help the teacher by preparing expectancy charts. To do this, one needs the intelligence test scores and the achievement test scores for each individual. A large number of students is also required in order for the expectancy chart to be stable. For each achievement test, a bivariate or two-way distribution of the achievement test scores against intelligence test scores should be made. An example of a basic expectancy chart is shown in the table on the next page.

EXPECTANCY TABLE FOR END OF 3RD GRADE ON
METROPOLITAN READING TEST ACCORDING TO OTIS IQ

Reading Grade Score on Metropolitan Reading Test

Otis IQ	1.5 to 1.9	2.0 to 2.4	2.5 to 2.9	3.0 to 3.4	3.5 to 3.9	4.0 to 4.4	4.5 to 4.9	5.0 to 5.4	5.5 to 5.9	6.0 to 6.4	6.5 to 6.9	7.0 to 7.4	7.5 to 7.9	8.0 to 8.4	8.5 to 8.9	9.0 to 9.4	Ttl.
120 & above	0	1	4	4	10	19	14	7	4	3	2	0	1	1	1	2	73
110-119	0	2	5	23	19	27	21	8	7	4	3	0	2	1	0	0	122
100-109	0	2	19	21	39	26	21	21	5	5	0	1	2	0	0	0	162
90 - 99	1	5	25	25	26	24	12	6	5	1							130
89 & below	1	5	19	17	10	4	2	2									60

The basic chart is made up with intelligence test scores (in broad groupings) on one axis and the achievement test scores on the other axis. Each student is tallied in the box that correctly identifies him as to intelligence test score and achievement test score. For example, a student who obtained an Otis IQ of 105 and a reading grade score of 4.7 would be tallied in row three (IQ grouping 100-109), column seven (reading grade score 4.5-4.9).

Once the basic expectancy chart has been prepared, one can compute the 25th percentile, the median, and 75th percentile for each row of intelligence test scores. The decision about what represents the expected level of achievement is a somewhat arbitrary one. For this example, expectancy for any intelligence level was set as the middle 50 per cent, below expectancy was set as the lowest 25 per cent, and above expectancy was set as the highest 25 per cent.

The teachers in the school where this expectancy chart was made were given the following summary table to use in interpreting individual cases:

SUMMARY TABLE

Summary	IQ's 120+	IQ's 110-119	IQ'S 100-109	IQ's 90-99	IQ's 89 & below
Below Expectancy	3.9 & below	3.4 & below	3.4 & below	3.0 & below	2.6 & below
At Expectancy	4.0–5.1	3.5-4.8	3.5-4.8	3.1—4.3	2.7—3.6
Above Expectancy	5.2 & above	4.9 & above	4.9 & above	4.4 & above	3.7 & above

The question of how much growth an individual student has made since the last testing cannot be answered by simply subtracting the two scores.

About the best judgment a teacher can make is in terms of whether a student is maintaining his relative position in the group. If he is, his progress is satisfactory. If he has improved his relative position, he has made more progress than the average child. If his relative position is lower, he has made less progress.

The analyses suggested in this article may seem to be involved and time-consuming, but they represent a wise use of time. If the classroom teacher, with the help of others in the school, will do them, he will have information about teaching problems of the coming year, about areas in which emphasis is needed, and about individuals who need special kinds of attention. With these types of information, the classroom teacher will be better able to provide appropriate learning experiences for both the total class and individual children.

94   *The ABC's of test construction*

JULIAN C. STANLEY

This article distills many technical aspects of the job of constructing teacher-made tests. It is unlikely that proficiency can be developed by reading this one article; practice is essential. There are many excellent sources which contain suggestions for creating tests.

CONSTRUCTING a good test is one of the teacher's most difficult duties. Good tests do not just happen. Actual test construction, therefore, requires much thought and careful planning.

PLANNING THE TEST

A well-planned test will provide the means for evaluating progress toward the expected outcomes of instruction, as expressed in the educational philosophy of the particular school and as defined in the objectives of the particular course.

If the school hopes to produce "good citizens" with "integrated personalities," for example, tests must measure the development of good social attitudes and a widening range of significant interests.

For any given course, instructional objectives must be expressed in terms of the specific changes in pupil behavior or growth which the teacher hopes to bring about.

A teacher, for instance, should be conscious that such an objective as the development of an appreciation of literature may express itself in various forms of student reaction. He sets out then to phrase test questions which will determine whether a particular piece of writing gave individual students a sense of satisfaction and enthusiasm, made them want to read more by the same author, stimulated their own creative expression.

The well-planned test will reflect the relative amount of emphasis each objective has received in the actual teaching of the course. The same test might not be equally valid for two teachers of general science if one has emphasized the memorizing of isolated facts, while the other was more concerned with the interrelation of facts. Each teacher would be helped by drawing up in outline form a kind of table of specifications to indicate not only

Reprinted from the *NEA Journal,* 47:224-26, April, 1958.

the objectives of the course, but also the relative amount of time spent on each.

The content of the test should show a similar proportion in regard to the *number* of items to be included but not the *type*, for the type of item depends upon the nature of the objective to be measured.

The well-planned test must be designed to accomplish the purpose it is to serve. If the purpose is to give the basis for school marks or classification, it will attempt to rank the pupils in order of their total achievement. But if the purpose is diagnosis, its value will depend upon its ability to reveal specific weaknesses in the achievement of individual pupils.

Diagnostic tests would cover a limited scope, but in much greater detail than a test of general achievement, and would be arranged to give scores on the separate parts. The range of difficulty of items is relatively less important, also, in diagnostic tests. This is true, too, of mastery tests administered at the end of a teaching unit to see whether minimum essentials have been achieved.

The well-planned test will also fit the conditions under which it is to be administered, such as the time available for testing, facilities for duplicating the test copies, and cost of materials, as well as the age and experience of the pupils being tested.

PREPARING THE TEST

In actual construction of a test, these suggestions have helped:

1. Prepare a rough draft of the test as soon as possible. Many teachers jot down items day by day for possible inclusion to help insure that no important points will be omitted, particularly those appearing in supplementary material that might be overlooked if the textbook itself is the chief basis of the test.

2. Do not make the test items too easy. Many teacher-constructed tests fail to make the items difficult enough. This, no doubt, is due in part to the influence of the "70 per cent should be the passing grade" tradition. However, the test that is too easy is not an efficient instrument for measuring pupil progress.

3. Include more items in the first draft than will be needed in the final form. This will permit culling out of weak items and those not needed to produce proper balance.

4. Subject the test to critical revision some time after it is drafted by checking items against the table of specifications to see if they show the desired emphasis on various topics. If tests are submitted for criticism to other

teachers of the subject, points of doubtful importance can be weeded out and ambiguous wording corrected.

5. Include more than one type of item in the test. A variety of test types is more interesting to students. The test situation may also require that three or four forms of objective items be used, or that these be combined with discussion or essay-type questions.

6. Place all items of one kind together in the test. Sometimes completion, true-false, and multiple-choice questions are thrown together in random order. This arrangement is rarely, if ever, desirable. When like items are grouped, the pupil can take full advantage of the mind-set imposed by a particular form, and the teacher will find scoring and interpretation of scores easier.

7. Arrange test items in an ascending order of difficulty. The placing of very difficult items at the beginning is likely to produce needless discouragement for the average or below-average student.

8. Avoid a regular sequence in the pattern of responses. If items are arranged alternately true and false, or two true and two false, pupils are likely to catch on and answer correctly without considering the content of the item at all.

9. Make directions to the pupil clear, concise, and complete. Instructions should be so clear that the weakest pupil knows what he is expected to do, though he may be unable to do it.

It is better to tell young children to "draw a line under" than to "underline." In lower grades, teachers find it helpful to read instructions aloud while the class follows silently the written instructions. If the form of the test is unfamiliar or complicated, a generous use of samples correctly marked, or practice tests, is recommended.

Regardless of how carefully a test is planned and edited, it is impossible to know solely by inspection exactly how good it is, or which are the weak items. If possible, therefore, the test should be given some advance tryout which will approximate the conditions under which the real test will be given, show the actual length of time it will require, and indicate what scoring difficulties may result.

Because various studies have shown that a majority of teachers, especially at the high-school level, use a combination of essay and objective questions, the uses and limitations of both will be briefly examined here.

THE ESSAY TEST

The essay test has both unique advantages and serious disadvantages. Some authorities claim that it calls forth less than half the knowledge the average pupil possesses on a subject, compared with results from an objective test, and takes twice the time to do it; that it overrates the importance of knowing how to say a thing and underrates the importance of having something to say; and that the score resulting from an essay test depends more upon *who* reads it and *when* than upon the student who wrote it.

Offsetting the serious scoring difficulties connected with essay tests and their frequently low degrees of validity, there is much to indicate that such tests have a legitimate place in the modern school.

Specifically, they are useful for measuring functional information, certain aspects of thinking, study skill and work habits, and an active social philosophy. These are educational objectives which emphasize the *functioning* of knowledge rather than its mere possession.

Such tests are especially valuable in courses in English composition and journalism, where the student's ability to express himself is a major instructional objective, and in advanced courses in other subjects where critical evaluation and the ability to assimilate and organize large amounts of material are important.

Essay tests have at least one other general merit: When pupils expect the test to be of that type, in whole or in part, they seem more likely to employ such desirable study techniques as outlining and summarizing, and to make a greater effort to recognize trends and relationships.

Despite popular opinion to the contrary, a high-quality essay test is more difficult to construct than is a good objective test. These three rules, however, should be helpful in improving the construction and use of essay tests:

1. Restrict such a test to those functions for which it is best adapted.

2. Increase the number of questions asked and decrease the amount of discussion required for each.

3. Make definite provisions for teaching pupils how to take such examinations.

TYPES OF OBJECTIVE

The simple *recall test* item employs a direct question, a stimulus word or phrase, or a specific direction to elicit from the pupil a response based on his previous experience. The typical response is short—hence its other name, the short-answer question.

The main problem is to phrase these test items so that they will call forth responses from a higher level than mere memory, and so that they can be readily scored.

Example: Eight is what per cent of 64?

The *completion test* consists of a series of sentences in which certain important words or phrases have been replaced by blanks to be filled in by the students. This test has wide applicability, but unless very carefully prepared, it is likely to measure rote memory rather than real understanding, or to measure general intelligence or linguistic aptitude rather than school achievement.

Scoring is also more subjective, and complicated by the fact that the missing words are written in blanks scattered all over the page, rather than in a column. This difficulty can be avoided by a form such as this:

1. The man who headed the first expedition to circum-
   navigate the globe was
                                                        ————.
2. The Articles of Confederation were in force from 1781 to————.

An *alternative-response test* is made of items each of which permits only two possible responses. The usual form is the familiar true-false item and its cousins, the right-wrong, yes-no, and same-opposite.

While the true-false type of question is popularly considered easy to prepare, experienced test-makers point out that this type of test requires great skill, and care must be taken in wording so that the *content* rather than the *form* of the statement will determine the response. The following suggestions may be useful in constructing such tests.

1. Avoid specific determiners, that is, strongly worded statements containing words such as "always," "all," or "none," which may indicate to pupils that the statement is likely to be false.

2. Avoid using the exact language of the textbook, with only minor changes to give the true-false pattern, because this puts too great a premium on rote memory.

3. Avoid trick statements which appear to be true but which are really false because of some inconspicuous word or phrase, such as "The Battle of Hastings was fought in 1066 B.C."

4. Avoid "double-headed" statements, especially if partly true and partly false, as in this sentence: "Poe wrote 'The Gold Bug' and *The Scarlet Letter.*"

5. Avoid double negatives lest pupils versed in grammar conclude that two negatives equal an affirmative, while others think such statements are emphatic negatives.

6. Avoid unfamiliar, figurative, or literary language and long statements with complex sentence structure—for reasons which should be obvious.

7. Avoid words that may have different meanings for different students. "Often" may mean once a week to one child; three times a year to another.

A *multiple-choice* test is composed of items which require the student to select a correct or definitely better response from two or more alternatives (at least four whenever possible). This is one of the most useful test forms. It may be used to ascertain the ability to give definitions, identify purposes and causes, similarities and differences, or to ask many other varieties of questions.

In phrasing multiple-choice questions, it is essential to avoid giving irrelevant or superficial clues, and to assure that the question measures more than memory. The diagnostic value of this type of item depends as much on the skillful wording of the incorrect choices presented as upon correct statement of the right choice.

Scoring may be facilitated by arranging the items in groups, putting together all items with the same number of choices, and requiring the simplest possible method of recording the response.

Other useful rules are:

1. Make all responses grammatically consistent. For example, if the verb is singular, avoid plural responses.

2. Use direct questions rather than incomplete statements whenever possible. This helps eliminate irrelevant clues.

3. Arrange the responses so that the correct choice occurs about equally in all positions, and do not consistently make the correct answer longer or shorter than the others.

4. Make all the responses plausible, and when testing at higher levels, increase the similarity in the choices under each item in order to better test the powers of discrimination.

A *matching test* involves the association of two things in the mind of the learner by requiring him to pair the items in two columns: events and dates, events and persons, terms and definitions, laws and illustrations, and the like. Matching exercises are well adapted to testing in *who, what, where,* and *when* areas but not to measuring understanding as distinguished from mere memory.

Since most of the tests used in classrooms are teacher-made, it is highly important that teachers develop proficiency in the building of tests by discriminating use of what is now known, by keeping themselves informed on new studies of testing techniques and methods, and by careful evaluation of their own testing, day by day.

CHAPTER 21

Reporting to and Working with Parents

THE ARTICLES IN this chapter touch on some of the responsibilities of teachers in reporting to, conferring with, and working with parents. The first article emphasizes dilemmas facing teachers as they make decisions about marks. The second article describes a program in which parents are permitted to choose between report cards and conferences with teachers. The third article presents research evidence on ways in which teachers communicate with parents in conferences. The final article describes a teacher-parent project designed to help children do better work in school.

95   *Reporting to parents—why? what? how?*

WILLIAM M. ALEXANDER

The complexities involved in adequate reporting to parents are discussed in this article. Reporting is a topic some educators would rather ignore than face. For teachers, and for parents and citizens, there are significant professional and social issues involved.

Reprinted from the *NEA Journal*, *48*:15-18, December, 1959.

FOR SOME twenty-five years now, there has been widespread experimentation with newer types of reports. Reporting to parents has changed in many respects, mostly to the good. More information than percentage marks in the subjects is now commonly given in reports. Much effort is devoted to exchange of information and advice between parents and teachers. Many teachers try very hard to use the whole marking and reporting system as a means of helping their pupils to carry on self-appraisal and improvement.

But have those who are zealous to improve reporting sometimes confused parents, pupils, and even some teachers? In trying to communicate better with parents, are teachers sometimes making it more difficult for parents to understand later on when their children encounter other reporting practices? Have some fine efforts to aid pupil progress made it more difficult for pupils to judge their progress?

I would answer yes to these questions, because some teachers and interested parents have frequently overlooked two relevant if unfortunate facts:

1. Differences in reporting practices from level to level and school to school are not easily understood by pupils and their parents.

2. Try as many teachers and parents may to guide learning for learning's sake, there has been far more guidance of learning for the sake of grades and good reports.

Perhaps further improvement in reporting would be aided by more common understanding of the logical answers to three questions: Why report? What to report? How report?

WHY REPORT?

Any boy or girl can tell us why schools send reports home: so that parents may know how their children are getting along in school.

The newer practices have not reduced parents' basic interest in their children's progress. Indeed, informative reports may have whetted the interest of many mothers and fathers. Reporting systems that fail to convey to parents information they understand about their children's progress (or, perhaps more factually, their class standing) invite trouble.

Reports become the signposts of passing or failing. Although retardation has been drastically reduced in the past half century marks still separate pupils by achievement in those schools in which a pupil's previous record determines his assignment to homogeneous groups or tracks.

In recent years, school people, pressed by many needs for better public support of the schools, have awakened to the public-relations aspects of reporting. Here is one place, it was realized, where teachers and parents have a common interest and a reason for getting together. Therefore, reporting systems have been geared in many communities to their potential for interpreting the school and its needs to parents.

However, reports to parents were and are so widely used by both parents and teachers as clubs over the heads of children as to make the report card—and school in general—hateful to many. Are today's parents, whose own parents granted or withheld privileges on the basis of marks on the report card, likely to perceive their child's report as a happy symbol of the parent-teacher partnership?

Undoubtedly, one purpose of reports to parents has been to provide pupils with the incentive to do schoolwork that neither parent nor teacher knew how else to supply. However, indiscriminate clubbing through marks is known to have quite different results from those which well-meaning parents and teachers seek for children.

Of these various and frequently conflicting purposes of reporting systems, two seem clear-cut and justifiable:

1. Parents should have information about their children's progress and standing in school. If this information can be given in a way that promotes understanding of home and school, all the better. But the information needs to be sufficiently factual, even if disappointing, so that the mother and father can use it to understand and help their child. Certainly such information at the high-school level should also be available to college-admission officials and prospective employers.

2. Ultimately, it is even more important that boys and girls have the best information available in understandable form about their own progress. To understand themselves, to capitalize on their strong points, and to remedy, if possible, their weaker ones, they need to know what these strengths and weaknesses are. Many types of evaluative data are needed for this purpose in addition to a six- or twelve-weeks' set of marks, but the accumulation and summary of facts at reporting time may be very useful in the pupil's own plan for continued, improved progress.

WHAT TO REPORT?

Differences of opinion and practice about the purposes of reporting seem almost minor as compared to those which exist about the content of reports. Great variations occur in the items on which information is reported and in the marking symbols. These variations are both vertical, from level to level, and horizontal, from school to school at the same level.

The educational philosophy in a school or system and especially in the classrooms concerned would be expected to control the nature of the instructional program and the content of the report.

If achievement in subject matter is a central goal, the report card would report pupils' standing in knowledge of subjects of the curriculum. If behavior according to stated criteria of growth and development is a goal, then a description of relevant behavior would be reported. If progress in various work skills and habits is desired, then the report would indicate pupils' status or progress in specific skills and habits.

Since the instructional program typically serves more than one of these goals, the report may give a mark in the subjects and a check on various behavior traits and work habits. Sometimes, however, the philosophy is not clearly stated in the report or understood by either parent or teachers, and what the report is trying to report on is not really defined.

The dominant philosophy relates also to the basis on which standing and progress are determined:

Does an A, for example, mean that the pupil is doing top work with respect to his own potential or to the norm of the class? And if the latter, is the norm determined as an average of the distribution of marks in the class, or by the teacher's expectation of some standard of achievement, or by the norms of some standardized test? And does it describe the pupil's present standing or his progress since some previous time?

An A may mean any of these things in different communities, in different schools in the same community, or perhaps even in different classrooms of the same school.

Confusion arises, at least among some pupils and parents, when the items and underlying philosophies vary from level to level. The transition from elementary to secondary schools in many communities includes introduction to the use of letter marks for achievement and perhaps elimination of reports on behavior characteristics and work habits.

Even at the same level teachers may, and sometimes do, disregard in written forms the check lists or other spaces for reporting on items other than subject achievement. In oral reporting there may be even less uniformity in the items about which teachers and parents converse.

Lack of parent understanding may be increased by varieties in the symbols used in written reports and records. Elementary schools may use S and U and perhaps also an E (excellent) or O (outstanding), or other symbols; and secondary schools, the traditional A's, B's, and C's. Or 1, 2, 3, 4 may replace A, B, C, D.

Ability grouping introduces still another problem: Does an A in the low section mean the same as in the high? Indeed, can A's be given in the low section? Actually, these are problems only if the report is focused on relative standing rather than individual progress.

I am not alarmed by these variations or even by the confusions they create for parents and pupils. Instead I see them as encouraging signs of genuine concern by American teachers for finding better ways of reporting to parents in the interest of helping individual pupils.

Although further experimentation with what to report is critically needed, would it not be well, meanwhile, to stick to the two central purposes for reporting mentioned earlier?

Should not the school faculty be certain, first, that parents understand what their children's reports are intended to tell, and secondly, that the reports summarize data which pupils can use, and indeed have already used, in self-appraisal and improvement? If so, should not the report clearly distinguish between marks and comments related to present standing and those related to recent progress, and also among goals such as subject-matter achievement, work habits, and behavior traits?

HOW REPORT?

Where teachers are certain of the purposes of reporting and of what to report, the form of reporting seems to follow logically. Perhaps the great differences in reporting procedures are created by varying degrees of understanding by school faculties on the *why* and *what* of reports.

Certainly our knowledge of communication methods brings into real question the use of written reports alone, especially when these consist of letter symbols and check marks only. Face-to-face communication seems to be as effective in reporting to parents as in other matters. My belief—which has been strengthened by many comments from parents and others—is that the single most effective reporting medium is the teacher-parent conference.

But whatever the method of reporting, there is still the question of how to express that which is to be reported. Marks and checks are simple to write but hard to explain.

The single hardest question to answer—and the one for which most parents would probably settle—is, "How is my child doing?" The complete record, plus samples of work, helps the teacher to explain Johnny's progress but may still fail to answer this question. The teacher, therefore, needs to explain two things to parents: First, how Johnny is doing in relation to his potential, as best it can be estimated (and teachers estimate it very freely among themselves), and secondly how he is doing in relation to the class norm.

A satisfactory answer to the basic question in which parents are interested really means a two-way or dual marking system. In the elementary school, this system may be fairly simple. It may be enough, for example, to explain that Johnny is doing as well as he is expected to, although he is below the class average in arithmetic. But in the secondary school, marks are generally needed, and Johnny's status will probably have to be expressed by two sets of letter grades—one for progress or effort, the other for relative standing or achievement.

THE DILEMMA OF REPORTING

This overview of practices and problems in reporting may suggest that the situation has become hopelessly confused. To the contrary, I see it as having been hopefully experimental. However, we do need more widespread understanding of present variations in the *why*, *what*, and *how* of reports.

The perplexity of parents and others caused by varied reporting systems is real and must be recognized. Just as real and to be recognized, however, is the teacher's desire for better ways of helping individual learners.

This is the dilemma we face in reporting systems: A uniform system of reporting throughout the nation might eventually be more easily understood by everyone, but it might also greatly inhibit effective provisions for individual differences among both pupils and communities. In fact, providing for individual differences has already been adversely affected to some degree by greater uniformity of marking and reporting practices in high schools.

I believe that the following items are essential to improve the reporting system throughout the country: agreement among the teachers in each school as to the purposes of reporting and as to what is to be reported; careful explanation to each parent, both on the entrance of his child to school and repeatedly thereafter, of the reporting system used (and of its relationship to any previous systems the parent has known) and careful planning with parent groups as to the method of reporting most useful and convenient for both parents and teachers.

In addition, more systematic publication of relevant research findings, of results of experimentation with different reporting procedures, and of surveys of practices by local, state, and national educational agencies might help to bring about the understanding and spread of good practices.

96   *Glencoe parents can choose cards or conferences*

MARGARET CARLSON

*Here is a novel idea. Which would you prefer as a parent? as a teacher?
If you were a pupil in elementary school, which would you wish your
parents to choose?*

STUDENT PROGRESS reporting at Glencoe, Ill., helps cement teacher-parent cooperation. In this Chicago suburb, most teachers and parents agree that the
personal conference is the best single way to report student progress in elementary grades.

Teachers and parents confer five to ten weeks after school begins in the
fall. After the first session, held usually at school, parents are given the following options for winter and spring reports:

1. Conference.
2. Letter.
3. Report card.
4. Other (parents are requested to specify type of report desired).

Both parent and teacher understand that these choices are subject to
change depending on the child's development. It also is understood that a conference may be called at any time during the year when circumstances suggest that it would be of benefit to the child.

Teachers get at least three days of released time during the year to make
out reports, conduct conferences, or scout for field trips. Teachers may use
the time as they see fit; most of this time, however, is devoted to fall conferences with parents.

Teacher-parent conferences aren't impromptu get-togethers at Glencoe.
Because the success of the conference rests mainly with teachers, they make
advance preparations in one of two ways: writing a summary or marking a
report card. In both cases, two major areas are considered: effort as well as
achievement. Attitudes, work habits, and all academic and special classes are
graded for *effort* in relation to the child's individual abilities. The child's
achievement in relation to his classmates is also weighed in the same areas.
Teachers refer to these notes and summaries when talking with parents. In

some cases, parents ask for, and are sent, copies of the profile a teacher has prepared of their child's effort and achievement.

Although no accurate records are kept, we have found that most parents like the conference because of these advantages:

—Personalizes the child's education and guidance.

—Helps parents develop a positive attitude toward their child and his school.

—Influences and helps child improve impression of himself as results of chats often held, separately by both teacher and parents, with the child concerning points covered at teacher-parent conference.

❧

97   *Contrasting levels of performance in parent-teacher conferences*

HAROLD J. MAVES

This article describes a study of parent-teacher conferences. It should help prospective teachers to consider their own relationships with parents.

PARENT-TEACHER conferences are increasingly used today for pupil evaluation. Report cards are criticized for the unreliability of the marks given by teachers as well as for the unreliability of the interpretation of marks by parents. Furthermore, the effect of marks on a child's efforts is likely to be temporary. The parent-teacher conference makes possible the pooling of significant information about a child and allows for the planning of his future development by two persons vitally concerned—the parent and the teacher.

In Richmond, California, where parent-teacher conferences have been a part of the instructional program in the elementary schools for over five years, an extensive study of the conferences was recently completed. The

Reprinted from *The Elementary School Journal*, 58:219-24, January, 1958, by permission of The University of Chicago Press. Copyright 1958 by the University of Chicago.

analysis was based on tape recordings of sixty actual conferences held during one of the regularly scheduled semiannual conference periods. Attending these conferences were parents and teachers of a representative sampling of children enrolled in the fifth grade.

During the research it became clear that the performances of parents and teachers in the conferences could be separated into two groups. One group consisted of "high-level" performances, the other of "low-level" performances. Performances were judged in relation to sets of items in six categories, namely, "Teachers' aims for conferences," "Parents' aims for conferences," "Outcomes of conferences for teachers," "Outcomes of conferences for parents," "Topics occurring in conferences," and "Topics stressed in conferences." Once these criteria had been determined, it was possible for the analyst to separate the protocols into two contrasting groups.

The reliability of the judgments involved was determined by obtaining the extent of agreement between the judgments of two accredited judges and the judgments of the analyst on the six sets of categories. The per cent of agreement was high, ranging from 88.9 to 96.5, and indicated a high level of reliability in the analysis of the semantic content.[1]

This article gives a résumé of the factors which primarily contribute to the contrasting levels of performance in conferences and presents illustrative excerpts from each group of conferences.

ESTABLISHMENT OF RAPPORT

The establishment of rapport appears to be the main factor contributing toward achievement of a high level of performance by the participants of parent-teacher conferences. Rapport is generally established early in the conference and is maintained throughout. In the successful conference characterized by good rapport there is free exchange of information. Although the initiative is generally assumed by the teacher, a comfortable working relationship exists, and contributions are freely made by both participants.

After an exchange of introductory conversation, the teacher generally starts the conference by selecting one of the child's strong points and then continues to focus attention on the child throughout the conference. Although there may be some general conversation and personal visiting, the conference is basically purposeful. Even though a child has a marked academic or behavior problem, discussion of the problem does not prohibit a high level

1. Bernard Berelson. *Content Analysis in Communication Research,* Glencoe, Ill.: Free Press, 1952.

of conference performance once rapport has been established and is maintained.

The opening of one high-level conference on school progress is eased by the mother's statement, "Mike met me at the door and said that I should see his arithmetic paper for today because that was at least one paper that was all right." After mutual laughter, the teacher follows the cue offered by the parent and shows other examples of work in arithmetic and in other subject areas which are "all right." The teacher frequently interjects incidents about the child with an introductory phrase such as, "One of the things I wanted to tell you which is so nice about Mike . . ."

In another conference stressing child behavior, there is some general conversation about the mother's employment. This introductory conversation was prompted by the teacher's remarks of appreciation for the mother's arranging to get time off from her work. The teacher then mentions that the child's improvement in relation to others in the class stands out above all else. The teacher states, "Norma used to take too much care of the children in the room, and they didn't like it. She now has several good friends in the room and that, in itself, is an improvement. Last year Norma was umpire for all differences of opinion on the playground and in the classroom, but now she gets her attention in better ways."

The mother wishes to know how the teacher achieved this and is told that it is because the child has earned the respect of her peers. The teacher relates how the child has been given extra duties, such as keeping records and acting as classroom librarian, and thereby has obtained the attention she desires. The mother reciprocates by relating that Norma is having tennis and swimming lessons to aid in developing poise and grace. When the mother elaborates on the child's reaction to the lessons, the teacher, with an occasional interjection, encourages the recounting of considerable background information. The conference closes with a summary of the child's progress in social growth. At the end, when the mother questions, "In other words, you think she'll be all right?" the teacher says, "Oh, yes, she's doing nicely, and she's such an attractive girl."

In a conference depicting a low level of performance, where it is evident that rapport has not been established, the participants do not engage in introductory conversation upon meeting. The teacher introduces himself to the mother and asks her to be seated. He presents the mother with a guide sheet of the checklist type and, without allowing her any time to go over it, opens the conference by reading the items aloud and indicating how he has checked them. Once during the report the teacher abruptly says, "Now, I don't want to do all the talking. You do some."

"Dave seems to be doing all right," responded the mother.

The teacher continues reading the list and, at the end, says, "I shouldn't do all the talking, you know. Do you have any questions?"

The mother replies, "No, I guess not. The same things are checked as last year."

Although the teacher had indicated that the child was shy and was retarded in his reading and arithmetic, there was no specific planning for improvement. The teacher gained no insight from parental reactions or contributions. The teacher's final statement was, "I believe our plan for the year should be to bring him out of his reticence."

DOMINATION IN LOW-LEVEL CONFERENCES

In conferences of low-level performance the discussion is frequently dominated by one of the participants. The free, comfortable working relationship manifested in high-level conferences is not evident.

These conferences are most frequently dominated by teachers. This condition stems from the belief of the participants that it is the teacher's responsibility to give a report to parents. As part of the total study of conferences, parents and teachers were asked to state their aims prior to the conferences. These statements indicated that teachers considered their primary function was to make a report to parents. Parents indicated that the primary aim was to obtain a report from the teachers.

The domination by one of the participants occasionally results when one or the other participant is put on the defensive. Direct, inept questioning by the teacher often fails to elicit a response from the parent and leaves the teacher in the dominant role. Frequently the low-performing teacher adheres rigidly to a conference guide sheet, gives a report, and fails to engage the parent in discussion, as in the last conference reported above. While a guide sheet is employed in conferences of both levels, its use is more flexible in the high-level conference. Domination by the parent may give the teacher an insight into home relations and the history of the child, but it usually gives little or no direction to the conference.

One parent-dominated conference begins with a discussion about a note which the parent had sent to the teacher some time previously and which the teacher had misplaced. The mother engages in a long discourse regarding an illness in the family, and the attendant hardships, which had been explained in the note, and it is some time before attention is turned to the child. The teacher listens but makes little attempt to direct the discussion. The mother places herself on the defensive and dominates the conference throughout. Her lengthy accounts of the home background and the child's problems offer insight for the teacher but give no helpful direction to the conference. Many areas related to sibling and peer relations are considered, but there is no common planning for cooperation in the correction of the child's behavior problem.

On several occasions the parent states, "If you have any suggestions, I'll be glad to go along with you." In response to this the teacher cites instances of the child's behavior at school or agrees with the mother that the child's difficulty with her peers is a tit-for-tat situation. There is no reference to obtaining help from specialists. The conversation appears to leave the participants with a feeling of hopelessness. The teacher tells the parent that the child needs to learn the multiplication tables, and the mother defends her child by saying that the tables were not taught to the girl while she attended another school. There is a similarly ineffectual discussion about the need for improvement in spelling. The conference concludes with the parent's request that the teacher write her a note if she has any suggestions.

A teacher dominates another conference by adhering rigidly to the checklist type of guide sheet. In opening the conference, the teacher explains the checklist and says that, by using it, he will certainly cover everything. In the beginning, when he mentions that he feels the child's health is good, the mother agrees and says, "That's all right, and I feel that her school work is better now than at the beginning of the year, but she needs to practice the multiplication tables." The teacher says, "I've got something down here on that" (obviously pointing to the place on the checklist), and returns to the earlier point of discussion. Thirty-nine specific items are classified under four headings of adjustment and growth on this checklist, and the teacher indicates how he has evaluated the child's performance for each of the items on a three-point scale. Occasionally he gives an illustration to emphasize a point, but he allows for virtually no interjection by the parent and encourages none. After running the gamut in fourteen minutes, he asks the parent if there are any questions or comments. There are none. The parent is given a copy of the checklist, and the conference is closed.

USE OF ILLUSTRATIONS AND PLANS FOR FUTURE DEVELOPMENT

High-level performing parents and teachers give more specific illustrative incidents in reference to a point of discussion than do low-level performing parents and teachers. High-performing teachers use more samples of the children's work to illustrate past achievement and to aid in planning for improvement in a specific area.

In conferences having a high level of performance, there usually is evidence of the interpretation of some phases of the school program in light of the child's present status or grade level. There is usually evidence of planning for the child's future development. The teacher may describe his plans for the individual or the class, or teacher and parent may work out an agreement for concentrated teamwork in some area.

In one conference of high-level performance, the mother furnishes insight into family life by telling how the father aided the pupil to learn the multiplication tables by inventing a game using casino rules; how the boy voluntarily reads since he has been selected chairman of a social-studies committee; how this reading has led to discussions at home, including one on religious freedom in the New England colonies; and how the mother and her son got an "excellent" mark in spelling one year. There is a discussion of the child's writing and arithmetic, which are in need of improvement, followed by the making of a plan for improvement. The teacher gives the mother a folder of work but does not discuss all the papers in it. She refers only to items pertinent to the discussion and thereby makes them meaningful.

Another mother is interested in knowing the place of oral reading in the school. The teacher gives examples of its use in the classroom, such as reading phrases which answer questions, reading sections to prove a point, and reading for audience situations. At this point the teacher volunteers the information that the child is near grade level in reading achievement. A discussion of the child's need for reading and also for studying spelling at home closes the conference.

One teacher begins a high-level conference by telling the mother that her son has considerable ability and by showing her samples of the child's work. Although the teacher begins rather abruptly by telling the mother that the boy is immature in his work habits, he gives her a frank account and qualifies it with evidence. For example, the teacher shows a test paper in which the child did poorly and states, "I really jumped all over Bob that day." He then presents the next test paper, pointing to the marked improvement. Because the child failed to assume the responsibility for completing work while having been on traffic-patrol duty, he was removed from the patrol. When he mentioned to his mother that he had quit, his younger sister said, "You mean you got fired." His reply was, "No, but I knew I was going to be!" It was agreed that he should be reinstated on the patrol if his work continued to improve. When the mother had told her son that he would have to begin to do better work so he would be successful in college, he had said he might go to reform school and that "wouldn't cost her anything." The mother and the teacher agree to attempt to interest the child in current school projects and to place renewed emphasis on participation in those sports in which he excels.

Low-level performing parents give few specific illustrative incidents, and the teachers use few or no samples of children's work. These conferences give less evidence of interpretation of the school program and less evidence of planning for the child. In the main, the low-level conferences are mere verbalizations of a report, as evidenced in the inflexible illustrative excerpts noted previously.

USE OF COMMENDATION

In the high-level conferences teachers more frequently commend the children and express pleasure with having them in their classes. In these conferences, parents more readily extol the teachers, and both groups of participants make voluntary commendation of the conferences themselves.

Commendation of children or of conferences is not evident in the low-level performances. In the latter type there is some criticism of the conferences by parents and teachers. During one low-level conference a parent volunteers, "I think the parent-teacher conference is too time-consuming to be regularly scheduled. I prefer a report card, and, if a conference is necessary, it will be asked for anyway." Although teachers do not openly criticize the conferences during the participation, the brisk manner of one teacher during a low-level conference is apparent. In stating his purpose, he remarks, "A conference is expected of me by my superiors, so I give one. There is no point in this one at all."

In the course of the conferences, high-level performing teachers extol children and conferences with such remarks as:

Thank you for coming. I think these conferences are wonderful opportunities for both of us, don't you?

Mark is a champ in my book.

Raymond is a fine boy, and so considerate.

She's an excellent student.

Marcia and I have become close friends.

I get nothing from a report card, but the conference is as much for the child and for me as it is for you.

High-level performing parents make these remarks:

Sharon finds school interesting and stimulating because of you.

It takes a lot more than just nature. The teacher next year won't have as much trouble because Frank had you this year.

She likes you, and that's important. Teachers are so important to her.

I admire you teachers. I don't know how you can wrestle with so many children at one time.

The PTA is fine and it's nice to visit with you there, but the conference is so much beyond that. I feel it is just for me.

During these four years that I've come for conferences, I've never been in doubt as to just where my daughter stood in school. I didn't feel that way when we only had report cards.

CONCLUSION

When criticisms of parent-teacher conferences are based on the characteristics of conferences representing a low level of performance, it is clear that the criticisms are justified. The lack of communication between the participants and the failure of common planning for the child are all too apparent.

Conferences which are representative of a low level of performance can be improved with freer exchanges of information by the participants. The teacher must avoid direct, inept questioning which fails to elicit responses from the parents and leaves the teacher in the dominant role. The items on a guide sheet should be limited in number and should not be adhered to rigidly. Only a few points should be discussed, but these should be stressed. Specific illustrations and examples of work should be used to make the discussions meaningful, and purposeful planning should be done jointly by the teacher and the parent.

It is evident from the characteristics of parent-teacher conferences representing a high level of performance that the conference is more than a pupil-progress report. It is an experience in cooperative human relationships. It offers an opportunity for communication between two persons vitally responsible for guiding a growing child in meeting his needs and the demands of democracy.

Advocates of improved public relations for schools state that even the most casual contacts tend to influence the public attitudes toward schools, favorably or unfavorably. The parent-teacher conference, which can be used in any community, is a dynamic potentiality for continuous publicity, educational interpretation, and cooperative endeavor. The conference must, however, reach a high level of performance if it is to be of the most value.

98 *Focus on achievement*

MILDRED B. SMITH

CARL I. BRAHCE

This article goes beyond mere reporting. It shows how parents and teachers can work together to support school programs of so-called culturally deprived pupils.

THE IDEA that parents can be enthusiastic about elementary curriculum to the extent of improving academic achievement may seem to be a misty dream. Yet, unlike the illusory apparition that plagued Hamlet, such a vision appears to have practical benefits for elementary educators.

An experimental program designed to raise the achievement level of culturally deprived elementary children has brought illuminating evidence. This program has proved that parents and teachers, with cooperative support of administrators, can kindle in children a fresh interest in learning. Statistical evaluation subsequently showed marked gains in academic achievement.

This experimental program was designated, "School and home: focus on achievement." It was started following a decision by the teachers in an elementary school and a curriculum consultant to "quit talking and do something" about raising the students' levels of achievement and of interest in the classrooms.

The hypothesis of the program, though not academically new by any means, centered around an idea that many teachers long have held—that children will achieve more if they learn early to develop sound work habits and attitudes. Underlying this thought is a corollary, that to perform such an educational awakening, the cooperative support of parents is important.

The school principal, teachers, and administrative staff offered their services. This resulted in a meeting with students' parents at the school. At this discussion meeting, pertinent facts were presented. If the parents wanted their children to finish school, they had an obligation to begin now to help prepare their youngsters. The current industrial picture was studied. The fact that automation is cutting off many young, unskilled workers from many jobs was explained. Parents learned of the teachers' and administrators' concern and interest in giving their children an education that would prepare them to be useful, responsible citizens.

The cooperative program that grew out of this session stimulated much enthusiasm among parents. The program also created interest on the part of students, and a concerted effort by teachers, principals and administrators to work together on this team objective.

SETTING OF THE PROGRAM

The experiment was undertaken in one elementary school, and later was started in a second school during the 1961-62 school year. The program involved children enrolled in kindergarten through the sixth grade. These youngsters were primarily from the low-income families living in the industrial hub of Flint, Michigan. With few exceptions, the parents had moved to the city from the rural South to seek employment in local industrial plants. A majority represented limited educational backgrounds. Approximately one thousand one hundred children were included in the program.

A control group was established in another Flint public elementary school. These children represented similar socioeconomic backgrounds.

It should be noted that the Flint public schools are community centers, having gained national recognition as working-action examples of the community education concept. These schools, open after regular hours for all neighborhood persons, are regularly used by thousands of youngsters and adults in a variety of educational, recreational and cultural programs. Such a program gives the teachers and staffs a ready acceptance for new ideas from the standpoint of parental interest, since many of the parents previously had been involved in some school functions. The Charles Stewart Mott Foundation, operating in partnership with the Flint Board of Education as the Mott Program, had provided opportunities for educational advancement and achievement for students in the study and for other students also.

This favorable "climate" doubtless provided a shortcut for gaining public and parental acceptance of an experimental program that would require more planning and graduated involvement in other schools where such programs are not in operation.

FRAME OF REFERENCE

The theoretical frame of reference for the study is based on the action theorists' postulations[1] that the group in which the individual is socialized influences his motivation to achieve in school.

1. See: George H. Mead. *Mind, Self and Society,* Chicago: University of Chicago Press, 1934; and W. B. Brookover. Some social psychological conceptions of classroom learning. *School and Society, 87:*84-87, 1959.

It seemed that a program designed to raise the achievement of children who lacked the necessary motivation to achieve adequately must involve working with these children's "significant others"[2] for the purpose of getting them to expect more of these children. The students were expected to "internalize" the expectations of these "significant others" and, therefore, to expect more of themselves. It was predicted that this change in their attitudes and values would take place as they learned their values from "significant others."

ROLE OF PARENTS

The "significant others" for elementary-school children were assumed to be parents and teachers. In the parent-teacher meetings, mothers and fathers learned that their attitudes and values greatly influenced those of their children. The parents were made to understand that without awareness and intent, they were not setting the kind of example that brings about desirable attitudes and habits toward schoolwork.

Parents were: (a) impressed that they must do more than *tell* their children that they need to achieve in school. They were frequently reminded that they must *show* the children that their schoolwork is important; (b) given suggestions of activities and behavior which would provide at home a climate conducive to academic achievement.

The interest evidenced by parents was heartwarming to the teachers and administrators. The parents not only agreed to carry out the suggestions, but for the most part were highly supportive. The reason, so the program planners believe, was that the parents realized that school officials cared enough about their children to seek help from them.

Another facet of parental involvement was that of getting parents themselves to call on other parents. Some of the mothers, anxious to do a little extra, took the initiative in getting all parents involved. These community leaders made numerous home calls, followed up with telephone reminders. The school communities were divided into blocks, so that every section was contacted. The stimulating result was that parents heeded the message and supported the experimental program in greater participation than imagined by the program's initiators.

ROLE OF TEACHERS

It has already been shown that the teachers had a real interest and concern in the achievement of their students. This interest stimulated their own

2. "Significant others" is defined as those people who are important to an individual.

group meetings, discussions involving principals and curriculum consultants. The interest shown by parents in the open meetings whetted the teachers' appetites for upgrading instruction in the classrooms. Ideas were freely shared and explored, as were materials and teaching techniques.

The teachers at both schools placed primary emphasis on reading comprehension and vocabulary development. The students took books home frequently for individual as well as family reading. The teachers saw that each primary child was given an inexpensive metal file box and word cards to aid in improving sight vocabulary. These word cards frequently were sent home for study.

In all these activities, the teachers worked closely with parents. The teachers: (a) sent books home with students, (b) sent study assignments home, and (c) called parent conferences as needed. Parental contacts included home visits, inviting parents to the schools for discussion-information conferences and special problems. The staff developed a reading incentives program for students in second through sixth grades. Called The Bookworm Club, this special project appealed to young imaginative minds offering incentives to progress in reading skills. Parents assisted teachers in the preparation of small booklets designed to stimulate interest.

Teachers came up with creative hints for parents. Students arrived home wearing tags that read: "Please read to me," "May I read to you?" and "Please help me study my spelling." Students, too, took an active part in their own study assignments. Under direction of teachers, each class developed a checklist for doing assigned work. The students did their own self-checking, adding to the fun atmosphere of learning at school and home.

Getting the support of the parents meant continuing their interest in the program. To help accomplish this over an extensive period of time, parents were given these suggestions which sum up basic objectives:

1. Read daily to your children—preschoolers included. Fathers also are encouraged to take turns reading to their youngsters.

2. Listen to your children read.

3. Provide a quiet period in the home each day for reading and study. This should be at a regular time so that it becomes a part of the family's routine. (Research indicates that low-income families lack routine and regularity in the home.)[3]

4. See that children have pencils, paper, a notebook and a dictionary for

3. See: Martha Ericson. Child rearing and social status. *American Journal of Sociology, 52*: 190-92, 1946; and Allison Davis and Robert J. Havighurst. *Father of the Man,* Boston: Houghton Mifflin Company, 1947.

home study. (Observation indicates that children of low income families often lack proper tools for schoolwork. These same children may have an abundance of gum, candy, and gadgets, indicating the problem to be one of values rather than a problem of money.)

5. Parents were reminded that if they show that they value school achievement, their children likewise will value it.

To supplement these suggestions, teachers gave booklets to the parents, explaining techniques of reading aloud to their children; ways that parents can help their children improve their study habits; and ways to develop favorable attitudes toward school. Again, the handbooks were discussed with parents.

During the summer vacation, the program was continued through use of summer materials. Parents asked that they be provided with a list of summer activities to help them in maintaining the attitudes and habits their children had acquired during the school year. Each child also was given a summer Reading Record Booklet. The child was expected to keep a record of books read during the summer and to return this record to his teacher when fall classes resumed.

Forms 1 and 2 of the Gates Revised Reading Tests were administered in pre- and post-test situations to all children in the two experimental schools. The same test was administered simultaneously to all second- and fifth-grade students in the control school. Their reading gains were compared with gains made by second- and fifth-year children in the two experimental schools.

EVALUATION OF THE PROGRAM

Children in the two experimental schools showed over-all gains of 5.4 months in reading during the five-month period between pre- and post-tests. Children in the control school showed an over-all gain of 2.7 months in reading during the same period.

The evaluation showed that gains made by Experimental School C generally were greater than those made by Experimental School B. One factor which may contribute to this finding is that Experimental School B entered the program somewhat later than did the Experimental School C, with some problems in getting total staff involvement in School B. Children in all schools showed greater gains in reading vocabulary than in reading comprehension. Since reading comprehension encompasses a broader base than vocabulary, equivalent progress in comprehension can be expected with time.

The second-grade children in the two experimental schools made greater mean gains in vocabulary and comprehension than did children in the control school. The mean gain differences are highly significant[4] for vocabulary for Experimental Schools B and C, compared with Control School A. The mean difference for comprehension is highly significant for Experimental School C, but is not significant for Experimental School B.

Fifth-grade children in the two experimental schools also made significantly greater gains in vocabulary than did children in the control school. Gains made in comprehension are moderately significantly greater for children in Experimental School C but not significantly greater in Experimental School B.

A questionnaire was sent to each family in the two experimental schools to determine what opinions parents held about the Focus on Achievement Program. Approximately two-thirds of all questionnaires were returned. Of these, 85 per cent contained written-in comments and suggestions. The questionnaire contained three check-type questions and three open-ended questions. Parents indicated that they felt the program helped the children with schoolwork. They also said they would like to have the program continued. As a side benefit, the parents indicated that their involvement had helped them to improve their own academic skills.

The teachers conducted a home-study survey to see if parents had set aside the quiet time for study and reading. Parents indicated the daily study time, with not one reporting that the home study was not helpful. Results of this survey showed that 90 per cent of the children in the experimental schools returned their completed questionnaires, another indication of parental interest in the program.

The experimental study has definitely resulted in improved student work habits and attitudes toward schoolwork, teachers report. The experiment is continuing at the two schools. In addition, the administrators and teachers are cooperating in establishing the program in a third school following a request by parents.

The Flint Community School administrative staff and teachers have obtained as complete statistical evidence as possible. This corroborates findings that, as good practicing educators, they believe to be true.

In summary, they believe these findings offer sound evidence to educators in the elementary field, and perhaps higher levels as well, that education today is and must be a cooperative home-school project. Educators need not be afraid to go to parents with their educational problems. Indeed, as shown by the Flint experimentation, parents, when approached with forthright honesty, will return a thousandfold creative efforts of their own.

4. A probability of .05 is interpreted as moderately significant. A probability of .01 is interpreted as highly significant.

Part Five

༄

SOME CURRICULUM ISSUES

IN ALL PROFESSIONAL fields of endeavor, members of the calling differ on fundamental philosophical issues. Politicians, scientists, artists, and attorneys often differ from their colleagues on certain basic assumptions and essential methods. This is no less true in education. At times we educators rigidly attach ourselves to ideas on an issue and stick to them through thick and thin, sometimes flying in the face of facts. Many citizens, often intelligent and open-minded about other issues, thoughtlessly parrot opinions about educational issues which they have picked up from newspapers and popular magazines. Frequently, little consideration is given to the competence of the writers who deal with these issues.

There is a clear and urgent need in many communities for teachers and citizens with enlightened views on educational issues. But to deal intelligently with fundamental issues is hard work. Our experiences and prejudices shape our beliefs, and these beliefs often tag along with us whenever we talk about schools. One commentator, observing our refusal to accept the necessary changes, remarks that above all "we have our own selves to contend with." He suggests a possible reason why so many people urge that we go back to the good old days:

Most of us were reared in an autocratic tradition, and ourselves lack skill in democratic techniques of living with others. We have inherited a curriculum which no longer serves us in meeting our new demands, but we are habituated to it, and feel insecure out of it. This all adds up to an arthritic condition above the neck, which hampers and reduces our mobility in the face of changing needs and conditions.[1]

Accepting, as we must, the intellectual and personal difficulties involved in considering educational issues, let us turn to a few of these issues in the final part of this volume. The first three chapters deal with related topics that are very much in the news and that demand responsible curriculum decisions from educators: Chapter 22 reviews literature on the problems involved in grouping; Chapter 23 deals with the question of whether there should be special programs for pupils who appear to have high or low academic abilities; Chapter 24 offers an introduction to professional literature on two possible patterns of organizing elementary-school classrooms. These alternate patterns differ from the typical, graded, "self-contained" classroom pattern with which most of us are familiar. The role of elementary-school teachers with regard to prejudice, intergroup education, and integration is discussed in Chapter 25. The three final chapters raise at once highly practical and profoundly philosophical questions. The issues are programed instructional materials, the concept of structure, and the use of lesson plans.

---

1.   Kelley, Earl C. Foreword. *The Journal of Educational Sociology, 23:*498-99, May, 1950.

CHAPTER 22

How Should Pupils Be Grouped?

OBJECTIVE TESTS became popular in the 1920's. "Individual differences" was a popular catchphrase, and "homogeneous grouping" (ability grouping) was thought to be an appropriate curricular implementation of educational theories. When educators began to consider the totality of students' school experience, homogeneous grouping lost popularity. In recent years we have witnessed a resurgence of interest in this way of grouping students. You are sure to witness, as teachers, parents, and citizens, many an academic brawl with regard to this topic. The two selections in this chapter contain essential professional background knowledge. The first article describes a wide range of ways to group and reviews selected research and discussion on these ways to group. The second selection contains reports of research on ability grouping.

H A R O L D   G .   S H A N E

Shane observes that "grouping has been one of the most persistent of the problems enlivening and complicating elementary education." He notes some problems involved in making decisions about how classes of pupils should be formed and goes on to list thirty-two plans which have been tried from time to time. The next time someone tells you about the latest grouping scheme at his school, first ask him what research evidence supports his enthusiasm, then check the plan's novelty against this list.

WHILE GROUPING in both elementary and secondary schools is a topic of perennial interest in this country, current demands for improved instructional quality and for greater individual attention, among other factors, make it of particular concern today. The résumé offered here consists of a brief statement of problems involved in grouping; a commentary on types of approaches to grouping developed over a long period of years in the U. S.; and a summary of selected research and recent miscellaneous writings on the topic.

SOME PROBLEMS INVOLVED IN GROUPING

Along with the reporting of pupil progress and the dilemmas created by promotion policies, grouping has been one of the most persistent of the problems enlivening and complicating elementary education. The following are examples of the difficulties encountered in establishing sound grouping practices:

1. Lack of explicit and reliable data pertaining to individual children. Many schools lack information with respect to intelligence, achievement, social adjustment, etc., at a given time, hence have little reliable evidence on which to base grouping schemes (assuming that agreement can be reached as to what constitues sound grouping practice).

2. Pupil turnover, at least in some schools, makes grouping difficult because information on new entrants is fragmentary.

3. The uneven growth patterns of individual children make grouping

Reprinted from the *Phi Delta Kappan*, 41:313-18, April, 1960.

hazardous. One is never completely certain that a particular child will long retain the personal and academic attributes governing his placement in a group.

4. The uneven social and academic profiles of most individual children complicate grouping, at least insofar as any type of ability grouping is concerned. Many children vary in achievement by as much as a year from one subject area to another. (E.g., a child's arithmetic computation score at the time he is in Grade Four, seventh month, may be 3.9 years, while his reading comprehension may be 5.8 years.)

5. Differences in the philosophy, experience, and competence existing among teachers in the same school building may place any *arbitrary* or *uniform* grouping policy in a precarious position.

6. Grouping is influenced by the maturity and competence of administrative leadership. No plan is superior to the effectiveness with which it is executed, and even grouping schemes of dubious value required by central administrative directives may be *"made* to work well" by an able principal and staff.

7. The nature of the curriculum—i.e., the locally-developed design for the experiences children share in school—may facilitate or preclude effective grouping.

8. The nature of teaching aids, such as adopted textbooks, and policies governing their use can have a positive or negative influence on grouping.

9. The size of the elementary school unit bears, at least indirectly, on grouping practices. Certain plans are feasible only in schools enrolling five hundred or more children; others are workable only in schools with appreciably fewer.

10. Personnel resources may "make or break" grouping plans. Some plans are feasible, for example, only when there is a principal with no teaching duties to absorb his time and/or when there are available such persons as school psychologists, a guidance corps, special teachers, personnel in the public health field, and so forth.

HISTORICALLY INTERESTING AND EDUCATIONALLY PROMISING PLANS

For over a century of U. S. education, diverse grouping plans have been initiated, discarded, modified, or gradually accepted on a widespread scale. Here is an overview, with annotations, of some plans and programs that have both cross-fertilized elementary education and given variety to the pedaguese of elementary teachers.

1. Ungraded groups. In an earlier day, children in small schools in Grades 1-8 were taught by one teacher who handled all subjects (*and* janitorial duties), especially in nineteenth-century U. S. These were the original ungraded schools. One-teacher schools are still common, but much less so, even, than in the 1940's.

2. Primary-intermediate groups. Introduced when the one-room school grew too large for one teacher to handle, this plan often resulted in a 1-4 and 5-8 "two-room" or "two-teacher" school.

3. Grade grouping. This term simply refers to an arrangement whereby one teacher works with a given grade group. Such a grade group is usually a part of an elementary school organized on a K-6 or K-8 plan. This is also, in effect, *chronological age grouping* or *heterogeneous grouping*.

4. Heterogeneous grouping. This is essentially the absence of a structured grouping plan, i.e., children enter the kindergarten or Grade One at age five or six and are taught by the teacher to whom they are assigned irrespective of intelligence, achievement, etc. Individual differences may be met by program enrichment, acceleration ("skipping"), and/or interclassroom grouping as in primary reading.

5. Homogeneous grouping. Also known as *ability grouping*, this plan frequently makes intelligence, readiness, and achievement test data the determinants of classroom placement.

6. X Y Z grouping. This is a form of ability grouping in which the X, Y, and Z labels refer to three levels of intelligence or to three levels of assumed potential performance in academic areas such as arithmetic.

7. Intra-subject-field grouping. This plan is most often used at the junior-high and especially senior-high (or 9-12) levels. E.g., at the New Trier Township High School (Winnetka, Illinois) a student may be in an "advanced ability" group in mathematics and in a "middle ability" group in English. As many as five labels have been used for such grouping.

8. "Vestibule" groups. The label here suggests the idea of an anteroom or small entrance room or hall which one enters before actually going into a house. For example, in some schools (e.g., Chicago at present) there are "1-c" groups in which less mature children are enrolled prior to progressing through "1-b" and "1-a" in first grade. Thus, certain children, without "failing" or repeating, spend one and one-half semesters in Grade One. "Vestibule" groups or classifications have also been used at the threshold of high school to help slow learners and children with cultural flaws increase their prospects of success in the secondary school. That is, students may spend four and one-half or five years in progressing from the eighth grade to the high-school diploma.

9. Cooperative group plan. Originally conceived by James F. Hosic in the 1920's, this plan calls for *teachers* to work in small cooperative groups under a group chairman. It is a novel twist, since all other plans involve grouping *children*. Under it, staff members were in charge of special rooms (e.g., a literature, composition, story-telling, reading, spelling center) but were not so much "subject specialists" as specialists in teaching children. Work for a given group of children was planned at frequent intervals by the "cooperating group" of teachers, who sought to extract from their special area rooms the contributions that each center might make to a unified learning experience.

10. Winnetka Plan grouping. Pupil progress in Winnetka has been influenced for many years by self-instructional materials and what might be called an "individual-within-the-group" approach to instruction. The basic classroom unit in Grades 1-6 in Winnetka is heterogeneous, but *individual* progress continues to be personalized by the use of record forms or "goal cards," which encourage optimum academic growth by each child. Thus, in a sense, individual progress within the group constitutes a grouping device which has many of the merits of ability grouping without some of the problems of so-called homogeneous grouping.

11. Dalton Plan grouping. The classic Dalton Plan was based upon individual progress, group interaction, and a time-budgeting "contract plan" to facilitate individual achievement. Subject matter was grouped in two component parts, the academic and the physical-social. The former was presented predominantly by individualized instruction, the latter by the whole-class method. The work for each grade was laid out in the form of "contracts," which described work to be done over a period of weeks.

12. Multiple-track grouping. This is a type of ability grouping in which children of varied ability complete a given number of units or topics at different rates of speed contingent upon individual ability. An historically important multiple-track plan was developed late in the nineteenth century by Preston W. Search in Pueblo, Colorado. In brief, the multiple-track plan permitted some children to finish eight years of elementary school in seven years, while others (on a slower track) might take up to nine years to complete the same tasks. Thus three ability groups were involved, and the *amount*, not the *nature*, of requirement was "scaled down" for slower learning children in a given year, though all children presumably completed the basic requirements before leaving the elementary school.

13. Platoon grouping. Platoon grouping goes back to 1900, when it was devised by William A. Wirt for use in Bluffton, Indiana. In broad terms, this plan sectioned children into two groups (platoons) so scheduled as to have one group studying fundamental subjects in classrooms while the second group used special rooms for activities. As originally conceived, the plan was designed to encourage efficient use of the school plant and to achieve balance between academic and social activity or creative work. The platoon plan also was known as the Gary Plan (since it was best known for its application in Gary), and the "Work-Study-Play" plan.

14. The Woodring Plan. A plan for reorganizing the American school system advocated by Paul Woodring in 1957 has certain features which involve grouping. In brief, Woodring envisioned grouping aimed at helping both the slower and faster pupils in a manner somewhat reminiscent of the multiple-track and other historically interesting proposals. Woodring suggested that the K-8 organization be divided between an ungraded primary school and a middle elementary school. The more able children would spend as little as two years in the primary, moving to the middle school as early as age seven. The less able might remain in the ungraded primary through age nine. He envisioned the bright children leaving elementary school at age 11, the dull leaving at, perhaps, age 13. Woodring created no entirely new plan, but developed a synthesis of the ungraded, multiple-track, homogeneous, and individualized concepts.

15. Social maturity grouping. A rather loosely defined concept, this one suggests that grouping be heterogeneous but that children be grouped when they leave kindergarten, for example, into three first grades on the basis of social development and friendship patterns rather than on the basis of ability or sheer chance. This plan implies the exercise of professional judgment and the use of available test data in assigning boys and girls to "well balanced" groups, with the most mature and the least mature assigned to separate classrooms.

16. Developmental grouping. Another term used loosely, this one apparently connotes an approach to grouping roughly comparable to "social maturity" grouping.

17. Organismic age grouping. Also a loosely used term, organismic age grouping was apparently coined by persons attempting to apply Willard Olson's concept of organismic age to the grouping of children at varied levels of maturity. In practice, the term probably implies policies similar to those associated with "social maturity" grouping, plus study of various indices of organismic age as determinants of group structure.

18. Social maturity-teacher personality grouping. This refers to "social maturity" grouping coupled or linked to a consideration of teacher personality in the assignment of children to a given classroom. It recognizes that *teachers* as well as *children* vary as individuals and implies recognition of the assumption that some teachers are more effective with less mature children and that some are most effective with the more mature children in an ungraded primary or "social maturity" grouping situation.

19. Ungraded primary groups. This term may be used to describe a situation in which grade levels as such are abandoned at the primary level and where children work together in an environment conducive both to individual and to group progress without reference to precise grade-level standards or norms. The teacher in the ungraded primary may work with the same group for two and occasionally three years. It is her purpose to help children progress as far and as fast as they can with less regard for conventional minimum essentials than for total human development.

20. Ungraded intermediate plan. Not widely used, the ungraded intermediate approach to grouping involves assigning a group of children in, say, Grades 3-5 or 4-5 to one teacher. The program or curricular design is appreciably influenced by teacher-pupil planning. As distinct from the split or "hyphenated" group (see #21 below), the ungraded intermediate grouping is intended to enrich and to improve learning rather than merely to compensate for uneven distribution of pupil enrollment.

21. Split grade or "hyphenated" groups. The "hyphenated" or split group is one enrolling children from two and occasionally three grade levels. As a rule, groups are split in the smaller schools when, for instance, there are too many children in the fourth and fifth grades for efficient instruction, yet too few to justify dividing both grades. When this situation occurs, a division may be made as follows:

1959-60	1960-61
3rd grade—40 pupils	4th grade—30 pupils
4th grade—40 pupils	4-5 grade—20 pupils
	5th grade—30 pupils
Total 80	Total 80

The "hyphenated" grouping plan is obviously an administrative-organizational device for securing smaller classes while adding one rather than two new teachers.

22. Departmental grouping. Rarely used below the intermediate level, a departmental program is one in which children move from one classroom to another for instruction in the several subject fields by different teachers. The departmental program is the antithesis of the unit classroom program in which one teacher handles all (or most) subject areas for one group of children.

23. Intraclassroom grouping. A number of teachers make use of various schemes for grouping within the classroom. This is especially true of primary teachers, who create two or more groups when teaching reading. As a rule, intraclassroom grouping is "part-time ability grouping," designed to permit the teacher to work with youngsters of roughly comparable ability. (See also #26, "grouping through teacher-pupil planning.")

24. Interclassroom grouping. Some schools have developed the idea of grouping children not within the classroom but within a given grade or grade range for instruction in a particular subject field (commonly reading), presumably to allow for individual differences. This type of grouping requires that all three teachers in Grade Five, for instance, schedule reading at the same hour. Then each of the three fifth-grade teachers works with the children who remain in or come to her room (on the basis of reading ability) for instruction in reading. Frequently several grade levels are involved in this temporary interclassroom grouping. For example, *all* children may, at a given time, exchange rooms for reading activities, the children going to the classrooms which presumably correspond to the level of their reading ability. E.g., the fourth-grade child reading at the third-grade level would report to the third-grade room.

25. Intergrade ability grouping. This is very similar to interclassroom grouping (described in #24 above) and to departmentalized grouping, but is limited exclusively to shifts made within a single grade. For example, three fifth-grade teachers may schedule their mathematics period for a given hour daily, then shuffle their enrollment according to ability so that one teacher works with the children in the top-achieving group, one with the middle-, and one with the slow-achieving section.

26. Grouping within the classroom through teacher-pupil planning. Such grouping involves the creative or emergent planning of experiences with children in such ways as will eventuate in the selection of various pupil activities to be developed and pupil responsibilities to be carried out. Once a topic, project, or unit has been selected, the teacher and children discuss: (a) What do we already know about this topic? (b) What do we want to find out? (c) How shall we go about it? At point (c) various class committees or groups are formed, each of which assumes certain responsibilities for assembling information, for construction work, etc. Teacher guidance is essential to insure that the children volunteering for or assigned to these temporary groupings are challenged by the work on the one hand, yet are not frustrated by a too-difficult task on the other.

27. *Self-selection grouping.* This term is rather closely related to #26 above. It implies the creation of a rich environment which is also diversified so as to provide a variety of activities or projects from among which children can "self-select" work in which they will engage (individually and/or in groups) in conjunction with a topic or subject which promises to be a sound "center of interest" or "group interest" compatible with the developmental levels in the group.

28. *Extracurricular activity grouping.* Especially in the upper grades, many children may be involved in such activities as band, orchestra, or sports. This type of grouping is designed to group children (especially in semide-partmental or departmental programs) so that those in, say, the orchestra can be free to rehearse or practice at the same hours during the week. To serve this purpose, children in the school orchestra, for instance, have their programs or groupings so designed as to free them for rehearsal at the same hour of the day.

29. *Special grouping for the gifted.* In schools with large enough enrollments to permit it, there may be special groupings for high IQ children which go beyond the provisions of mere ability grouping and which segregate these high IQ pupils in special programs or even in special schools or centers.

30. *"Opportunity Room" grouping for the slow learning or mentally handicapped.* For many years, the educable mentally handicapped or trainable mentally handicapped child has, in some schools, been placed in special un-graded groups with small teacher-pupil ratios. Special instruction and training are provided, usually for children with IQ's of 70 or below.

31. *"Self-Realization Room" grouping for the gifted.* The S-R room is the reverse or antithesis of the so-called opportunity room for the slow learner and, indeed, is a "grouping" plan only in a very broad sense. In brief, the S-R room is one presided over by a highly capable teacher, well-equipped with study and research aids, and open during the day for gifted children in Grades 1-6 or 1-8 to use as they see fit. This plan is based on the assumption that the gifted will be placed in the regular classroom but will also be free to supplement their personal-intellectual development under expert guidance when they have completed basic work with their peers or age-mates. In a school of five hundred or six hundred pupils, perhaps twenty to thirty would have S-R room privileges and responsibilities. That is, only from one to three youngsters would be likely to come from each grade level.

32. *Ungraded four- and five-year-old kindergarten grouping.* A few places

have introduced "ungraded" kindergarten programs for four- and five-year-olds. Depending on his social and intellectual maturity, the child may spend from one to three years at the kindergarten level. This approach to grouping is designed to reduce the range of individual difference.

SELECTED RESEARCH AND WRITING

This brief summary of research data and writings on grouping which follows focuses on the 1950's, ending with 1958; hence many significant items of an earlier period are omitted.[1]

Research of recent date dealing with grouping is quite extensive. Shane, following a survey of nationally recognized suburban elementary schools, reported that there is a trend away from chronological age grouping and toward grouping on the basis of social maturity in the early 1950's. Ability grouping was the least common in his selected sample, which probably reflected liberal administrative thinking.

Among writers expressing enthusiasm for ungraded primary grouping are Anderson, Kelly, and Polkinghorne. Anderson, after some years of experience with the plan in Park Forest, Illinois, concluded that it stimulates improved instruction and improves mental health of children. Kelly reviewed ten years of an ungraded primary program in Milwaukee. He concludes that it is psychologically desirable, enhances individualized teaching, and facilitates good curricular practices. Polkinghorne ascertained by questioning 130 primary-group parents that the ungraded approach is popular with both parents and children. Parents believe that the children are helped significantly in making adjustments to the third grade. Two articles by Goodlad provide background for understanding the merits of ungraded plan, and his recent book, written in collaboration with Anderson[2] is an excellent and complete statement of the program and of strategy for achieving it. Austin obtained information on the over-all status of the ungraded primary and ascertained that developmental values were sought by the schools using this grouping or organizational plan.

Sociometric grouping as a device for enhancing group morale when children are placed in the next higher grade was used with some success, according to Alt, in a Pueblo, Colorado, school. Dineen and Gerry experimented with 170 children at the sixth-grade level to ascertain whether sociometric procedures can be used to improve human relations. Socioeconomic classroom

1. The writer drew upon a section he wrote for the 1960 edition of the *Encyclopedia of Educational Research* in preparing this résumé of educational writings.
2. John I. Goodlad and Robert H. Anderson. *The Nongraded Elementary School,* New York: Harcourt, Brace & Co., 1959.

cleavages, they state, were reduced or weakened but not eliminated by sociometric grouping.

Blumenthal, in a New York City study, attempted to gauge the influence of heterogeneous groupings by correlating chronological age and achievement, a relationship which proved, unexpectedly, to be negative. He concluded that mental rather than chronological age is the better guide to grade grouping. Edmiston and Benfer examined the relation between group achievement and range in ability within the group, using sixteen fifth and sixth grades in Hamilton, Ohio. With respect to the academic skill of reading, they concluded that a wide IQ range within a classroom eventuates in greater individual progress than when the IQ's are comparable. The Blumenthal and Edmiston-Benfer researches, while not parallel, illustrate the difficulty of generalizing with respect to grouping. The Blumenthal data suggest the importance of the M.A. in relation to grouping, while the latter study indicates that a heterogeneous group facilitates success, at least in reading. Such findings dramatize the fact that many variables determine outcomes in experiments in this area.

Further examples of recent conflicting evidence were provided by Roberts, Houston, and Lawson, who were encouraged by the results of ability grouping, while Russell reported that interclass ability grouping for reading resulted in no significant gains for children thus grouped. Of course, no two of these studies were exactly comparable, a fact which further confuses the situation. An extensive and definite study of ability grouping remains to be done, and this constitutes an important challenge to the profession.

Jones' study of 288 children, divided so as to provide a control group, suggests a possible solution to the heterogeneous vs. homogeneous controversy. Jones concerned himself with the nature of instruction rather than with grouping per se, and compared the outcomes of individually planned teaching with a prescribed curricular program. Children in the flexible-programs group, whether bright, normal, or dull, made more academic gains than those in the formal program. Perhaps an able teacher, given freedom to work creatively, is more important by far than any mechanical scheme, however ingenious. Not only Jones' inquiry but that of Holmes and Harvey supports this comfortable conclusion. Holmes and Harvey compared permanent and flexible arithmetic groupings at the intermediate level and ultimately concluded that an effective teacher, one sensitive to pupils' individuality, was a more influential factor than the grouping scheme they devised.

Speaking of homogeneous grouping, two investigators, the Luchinses, explored 190 children's attitudes toward being sectioned in terms of ability. Interviews with these youngsters showed that they felt their parents wanted them to be in a top ability group. Moreover, if they were in a "bright" group they preferred to be there even if they disliked the teacher. Children in two low ability groups were consistently willing to have a poor teacher if only they could be in a "bright" group. The Luchinses felt that their interviews clearly show that children classed as "dull" feel stigmatized and that the "bright" ones are snobbish with respect to their top-group status.

SOME CONCLUSIONS

The matter of grouping children continues to be characterized by: (1) problems of terminology, including overlapping terminology and conflicting interpretations of terminology, (2) insufficient comprehensive research data and conflicting data, and (3) appreciable differences in both practice and opinion.

It seems reasonable to conclude that the "best" grouping procedures are likely to differ from one school to another, the most desirable practice often being dependent upon such factors as: (1) the competence and maturity of the local staff; (2) the nature of the physical plant, (3) school size, (4) class size, (5) the local curriculum or design of instruction, and (6) a highly intangible quality—the intensity of the desire of a teacher or a group of teachers to make a particular plan work effectively.

The philosophy and ability of the able teacher are undoubtedly more important than any grouping plan, however ingenious it may be, with respect to creating a good environment for teaching and learning.

100 *Propositions on grouping*

INDIANA ASSOCIATION FOR SUPERVISION AND CURRICULUM

DEVELOPMENT RESEARCH COMMITTEE

Although the Committee asserts that research evidence on grouping is not conclusive, it does note that "there is a more substantial body of research findings available than is generally used."

Reprinted from *Grouping: Nine Propositions,* Indiana Association for Supervision and Curriculum Development, pp. 2-11. n.d.

1. Ability grouping of elementary children by classrooms as a device for the improvement of instruction does not in itself produce improved achievement. A common assumption underlying this practice of ability grouping has been that bright students would learn more if they were unfettered from their slower peers. However, the evidence would seem to indicate that improved achievement seems, rather, to result from the manipulation of other variables: varied curriculums, wider variety of teaching methods, broader range of materials, and the ability of the teacher to relate to children.

A recent study involving several thousand students in New York City concluded that grouping elementary children by ability as a device to secure major improvement in achievement is a waste of time. Achievement gains were influenced more by teacher differences and group differences than they were by ability range or intellectual ability of the class.

There is some evidence that this finding may also hold true in the secondary school. A study was done on matched secondary-school students who had been grouped in four different instructional patterns in high schools: a highly selective special high school, a high school where the bright students were grouped in honors classes, a high school where students received part of their work in honors classes, and a high school where the pupils were grouped heterogeneously. In a follow-up of these students during the first two years of college no significant difference was found in the achievement of the students who were exposed to the different instructional patterns.

2. Ability grouping of elementary children by classroom as a device for the improvement of instruction may be detrimental to the children who are placed in the middle and lower groups. Although the learning climate of a classroom is influenced by a multitude of factors, one which is believed to be of considerable importance is what children learn from each other. Also, the teacher's attitude toward the children as a class seems to influence their self-perception as students. In a study comparing achievement among three groups, the middle and low group suffered when compared with matched peers who were in heterogeneously grouped classes. These researchers hypothesized that removing the more academically talented students may deprive the children in the middle and lower groups from the intellectual stimulation that is provided by the brighter children. Moreover, children grouped into three different ranges are more likely to be acutely aware of the differences in grouping and to stereotype their groups as bright, average and dull.

3. Ability grouping of elementary children by classroom as a device does not appear to greatly influence the achievement of brighter children. One extensive study found that the brighter children seem to do as well when left in the average and slower sections. In their discussion of this finding, the researchers hypothesized that the brighter children may be receiving as much intellectual challenge and stimulation as they can handle outside the school environment. Consequently, they were not benefiting from the increased academic diet which was provided the advanced group.

4. *Ability grouping of children by classrooms using conventional methods, group intelligence test scores and achievement test scores, appears to favor unduly the placement of children from the higher socioeconomic class in the higher ability groups.* Children from the lower socioeconomic classes do not do as well on the tests which are commonly used to group students. Consequently, grouping using standardized test scores as a basis will, to a certain extent, follow socioeconomic lines. However, in one study the children who appeared to profit most from the stimulation of the higher ability groups were students from the more impoverished cultural backgrounds; ironically, these are the children most unlikely to be in the higher ability groups.

5. *Ability grouping of children by classrooms may militate against the development of general education skills, those skills which are required of all citizens.* Many of the general education skills and attitudes which are necessary for the maintenance of the "social cement" of the society are best taught through contact in groups which contain the diverse subcultures of our society. Grouping practices, which separate students on the basis of some standardized measurement, reduce the likelihood that students will be directly exposed to the range of ethnic and cultural differences in our society. Although it is granted that the performance of the classroom teacher is the most single significant classroom factor in developing attitudes, nevertheless, the structural arrangements of groups may assist the teacher and promote more meaningful learning of the skills and attitudes of democracy.

The available research seems to indicate that in the secondary-school children's needs and interests develop a range which requires grouping for instruction in special interest areas. Nevertheless, despite the growth of special interests in the secondary school there appears to be a core of general education experiences which all students can profitably pursue as an undifferentiated class.

6. *Ability grouping of children by classrooms as a device to promote improved academic achievement may establish a milieu which emphasizes the attainment of academic goals at the expense of broader behavioral outcomes.* One study found that ability grouping emphasized the attainment of narrow

academic goals at the expense of attitudes of cooperation and responsible group conduct. Some practices on personal and social development indicate that grouping practices can develop social situations containing inherent attitudes which children accept as part of the social structure to which they are exposed. This social structure is influential in determining the student's perception of self, his sense of dignity and worth, and his attitudes toward other children and groups. The heightened awareness of a student's membership in a specific group by vivid reminders of this membership can produce attitudes. Apparently this factor which social psychologists call salience is functioning in some grouping arrangements.

7. *Ability grouping of elementary children by classrooms reduces differences to a very limited degree.* Research done in Detroit several years ago demonstrated that it was difficult to narrow the differences more than four years in any one subject. If grouped in one subject, the differences remained in other subjects for the variations are nearly as great within the individual as among individuals. However, ability grouping may reduce the social-attitudinal differences which exist among children in some groups, thus, developing groups which are quite docile and teacher-oriented and other groups which are hostile and antagonistic toward the teacher as an authority figure. Some further evidence suggests that a teacher's own personality, feeling of security, classroom poise will play a major role in her ability to accept and relate to different individual children and groups of children.

8. *Ability grouping of children by classrooms utilizing mainly group intelligence test scores, standardized achievement test scores, and teacher judgments may penalize students who are quite creative.* Creative potential as judged by proved performance at this time is not accurately measured or detected on commonly used standard instruments of measurement. Other recent research seems to indicate that the creative student may be relegated to lower ability groups or be encouraged to suppress his creativity as a condition for admission into the higher ability groups. These creative students, it has been found, do not, in many cases, relate well to teachers or instruction and are penalized for their attitudes.

9. *It is quite unlikely that any type of grouping of children by classrooms will obviate the need for use of flexible grouping in the classroom.* As the purposes and focus of instruction changes, the abilities of children will necessitate a shift in the grouping within a classroom. Flexible grouping (characterized by shifting group membership and development of groups in accordance with the instructional needs and abilities of students) does enable

a teacher to provide more individualization of assignments. One study found when attempts were made to increase the range of differences in a classroom by grouping several grades together, improved achievement resulted. Under these conditions much of the instruction had to be individualized. Other research supports the contention that classroom procedures which encourage individualization of instruction stimulate student achievement.

BIBLIOGRAPHY

Abrahamson, David. The effectiveness of grouping for students of high ability. *Education Research Bulletin*. *38*:169-82. October 14, 1959.

Argyrus, Chris. *Personality and Organization*. New York: Harper & Brothers. 1958, p. 291.

Bettleheim, Bruno. The ignored lesson of Anne Frank. *Harpers*. *221*:45-50. November, 1960.

———. Segregation: new style. *School Review*. *66*:251-72. Autumn, 1958.

Clark, Kenneth. Disadvantaged students and discrimination. *The Search for Talent*. Bulletin 7 on College Admissions, College Entrance Examination Board. Princeton, N.J.: Educational Testing Service. 1960, pp. 12-19.

Cook, W. W. The gifted and the retarded in historical perspective. *Phi Delta Kappan*. *39*:249-55. March, 1958.

Eckstrom, Ruth. *Experimental Studies of Homogeneous Grouping: A Review of the Literature*. Princeton, N.J.: Educational Testing Service. April, 1959.

Getzels, Jacob, and Jackson, P. W. *Creativity and Intelligence: Explorations With Gifted Children*. New York: John Wiley & Sons. 1962.

———. The meaning of "giftedness": an examination of an expanding concept. *Phi Delta Kappan*. *40*:75-77. November, 1958.

Grouping without instructional changes questionable. *Educational Summary*. *14*:5. April 12, 1962.

Harrison, Emma. Negro curbs cited by psychiatrists. *New York Times*. February 28, 1960, p. 18.

Jules, Henry. Attitude organization in elementary classrooms. *American Journal of Orthopsychiatry*. *27*:117-33. January, 1957.

Holmes, Darrell, and Harvey, Lois. An evaluation of two methods of grouping. *Educational Research Bulletin*. *35*:213-22. November 14, 1956.

Hull, C. L. Variability in amount of different traits possessed by the individual. *Journal of Educational Psychology*. *18*:97-104. February, 1927.

Husen, Tortsen. Loss of talent in selective school systems: the case of Sweden. *Comparative Education Review*. *4*:70-74. October, 1960.

———, and Sevson, Nils-Eric. Pedagogic milieu and development of intellectual skills. *The School Review*. *68*:36-51. Spring, 1960.

Jones, Daisy M. Experiment in adaptation to individual differences. *Journal of Educational Psychology*. *29*:257-72. May, 1948.

Katz, Robert L. Toward a more effective enterprise. *Harvard Business Review*. *38*: 80-102. September-October, 1960.

Lawrence, William E. Brainy machines. *New York Times*. July 17, 1960. Part IV, p. 7.

Luchins, Abraham, and Luchins, Edith. Children's attitudes toward homogeneous grouping. *Journal of Genetic Psychology*. *72*:3-9. March, 1948.

MacKinnon, Donald W. What do we mean by talent and how do we test for it? *The Search for Talent.* Bulletin 7 on College Admissions, College Entrance Examination Board. Princeton, N.J.: Educational Testing Service. 1960, pp. 20-29.

Mann, Maxine. What does ability grouping do to the self-concept? *Childhood Education.* 36:357-60. April, 1960.

National Society for the Study of Education. *The Dynamics of Instructional Groups: Sociopsychological Aspects of Teaching and Learning.* Fifty-Ninth Yearbook, Part II. Chicago: University of Chicago Press. 1960, p. 286.

Newcombe, Theodore M. The prediction of interpersonal attraction. *American Psychologist.* 11:575-86. November, 1956.

Northy, Arwood S. Classification of pupils. *Encyclopedia of Educational Research.* Walter S. Monroe (ed.). New York: The Macmillan Company. 1950, p. 1168.

Otto, Henry. Classification of pupils. *Encyclopedia of Educational Research.* Walter S. Monroe (ed.). New York: The Macmillan Company. 1950, pp. 376-78.

Passow, Harry A. The maze of the research on ability grouping. *The Educational Forum.* 26:281-86. March, 1962.

Rudd, W. G. A. The psychological effect of streaming by attainment. *British Journal of Educational Psychology.* 28:47-60. February, 1958.

Shane, Harold G. Grouping in the elementary school. *Phi Delta Kappan.* 41:313-19.

———. Organization of the elementary school. *Encyclopedia of Educational Research.* Chester Harris (ed.). New York: The Macmillan Company, 1960, p. 427.

Southern schooling—the Negro pupil. *Newsweek.* Part II. 50:71. September 2, 1957.

Staines, J. W. Self picture as a factor in the classroom. *British Journal of Educational Psychology.* 28:97-111. June, 1958.

Thelen, Herbert A. Classroom grouping of students. *School Review.* 67:60-78. September, 1959.

Torrance, E. Paul. *Guiding Creative Talent.* Englewood Cliffs, N.J.: Prentice-Hall. 1962, p. 278.

CHAPTER 23

Should There Be Special Programs for Some Children?

MANY LAYMEN and educators, unaware of the existence of the professional literature presented in the previous chapter, staunchly advocate special programs for exceptional children. The term "gifted" is tossed about irresponsibly by polemicists who neglect evidence such as that presented in the Givens article in Chapter 2.

Many of the curriculum questions involved in this issue have already been discussed in this book—questions of objectives, ways of teaching, subjects and topics used, and evaluation. Some educators urge, "Stimulate the best minds." Others insist, "Find the gift in every child." This is a complex issue, one which splits many communities into warring factions.

In this chapter the first article describes one kind of program for pupils who appear to have the capacity to succeed in school work, the second article presents an enrichment program for everyone, and the final article deals with children who are not meeting with much success in school.

101   *Gifted children in an enriched program*

JAMES M. DUNLAP

Newspapers and popular magazines show a steady concern about excellence. Some parents' groups exert pressure for the creation of programs designed for the "gifted." This article describes one possible approach.

MOST ELEMENTARY school children who test in ability in the top 4 or 5 per cent of the general population, IQ 125 or higher, also achieve at least one or two years above their grade level. However, this is not always true of the brightest of this gifted group. One fifth-grade boy, for example, having a Stanford-Binet IQ of 150, never rated better than average in achievement. When asked what trouble he was having with his schoolwork, he replied, "None at all. If you are referring to my achievement test scores, I do poorly so my teacher won't expect too much of me. Then I can fool around and have fun." Teachers are often baffled and concerned by the mediocre achievement of supposedly capable students. "They do such poor work for me I can't believe they are gifted," said one teacher referring to two eleven-year-olds with Stanford-Binet IQ's of 181 and 199, "They don't even write legibly."

Perhaps these instances are exceptional but, when a teacher has thirty or forty pupils in her class, it is difficult in a crowded schedule to provide for the individual needs of children at the extremes. Because positive motivation can be overlooked so easily, gifted children often need a definite program which is enriched specifically to stimulate their interests and to challenge their dormant abilities.

University City, like many residential suburbs, has a high proportion of brilliant children. The program which has been developed there, however, is one which could be organized in any school district, large or small, even where only eight or ten gifted children have been located. Organized three years ago with fifty gifted pupils in six elementary schools, the program reached an enrollment of 197 the following year. In the first two years, a total of 239 different pupils participated in enrichment. At the present time, 275 children in eight elementary schools receive special instruction from two and one-half full-time teachers in thirty different groups.

Reprinted from *Exceptional Children, 21*:135-37, January, 1955.

WHO ARE THESE GIFTED CHILDREN?

Pupils are selected from Grades 2-6 on the basis of a review of all previous school marks, standardized tests of ability and achievement, teachers' recommendations, a group screening test, and finally an individual intelligence test. This variety of methods must be used because all gifted children do not make good marks on standardized tests or in the classroom, and teachers, without special help, often fail to recognize many of their brightest pupils. Generally, a Stanford-Binet IQ of 140 at least is required, but this IQ is not always the minimum. Depending upon the number of qualified candidates found, this figure may be higher in some schools and also may vary from grade to grade within a school.

WHAT IS THE ENRICHMENT PROGRAM?

Pupils meet with their enrichment teacher in groups of eight to ten for periods of forty or fifty minutes twice each week during regular school hours. For the most part, they explore topics not generally included in the prescribed curriculum or, if prescribed, not studied intensively. These topics emphasize language, social studies, and science. They are given such titles as The History of the Wheel, Children in Other Lands, Prehistoric Times, St. Louis Industry, Mythology, Great Inventions, Sky Pictures, and many others. The children themselves, with the help of their teacher, usually choose their own topics.

In these study units, reading, discussions, and written and oral reports are supplemented by lectures given by outside authorities, by experiments, by trips to make firsthand observations, by construction of models or equipment, and by preparation of charts, graphs, maps, and pictorial representations which the children need to illustrate their projects. The original plan was to study two or three different units each year. The pupils, however, in every instance, since the beginning of the program have insisted on continuing their initial topic. Such sustained interest not only indicates gifted children's ability to concentrate on a subject for a long time but also suggests their eager acceptance of the special opportunities offered by an enrichment program.

Sixth-grade enrichment pupils, in addition to their usual studies, plan and carry out projects for the week-long school camp program which all sixth-graders attend each spring. Last year, one group constructed a weather station which was used by pupils of every school. Predictions compared favorably with the United States Weather Bureau forecasts. Other groups prepared aluminum signs identifying flora and fauna of the camp area and formulated provocative questions for campers on nature hikes.

These unit studies are not the only means of enrichment. Parts of some periods are devoted to discussions of current happenings using such references as newspapers and periodicals or the map, *World News of the Week.* At other times, a series of questions stimulates lively discussion. Provision is made for creative writing, for the study of good human relations, for the examination of current popular magazines, and for games, puzzles, and the like. Typing was introduced recently not as a skill but as a new adventure and as an additional means of communication.

These activities in themselves are not of major importance. It is the attitudes, study habits, and ways of getting along with people that are the objectives of the enrichment studies. The variety of challenging activities that can be introduced in an enrichment program by an imaginative teacher is surprising, particularly in view of the limited amount of time devoted to the special program. Forty- or fifty-minute periods twice a week are a total of only two or two and one-half weeks out of the entire school year.

DO GIFTED CHILDREN BENEFIT FROM ENRICHMENT?

Gifted children evaluate their own programs. They *know* when school work is fun, when their teacher requires their best effort and when their activities have real meaning for them. Recently, when all sixth-grade pupils were sent home while their classroom teachers had regular, scheduled conferences with parents, the entire enrichment group came back to school *in the middle of the afternoon.* They explained, "We have enrichment only twice a week and didn't want to miss half of it."

A principal who was showing his school to out-of-town educators finally conducted his guests to the enrichment room during the noon hour. There they found six children quietly at work when they could have been out playing. "Of course," the principal explained, "these children are perfectly capable of working without supervision." A classroom teacher reported to the enrichment teacher, "I want you to know how much you are doing for these children. John has gained so in self-confidence and Mary has just blossomed since being in enrichment." A parent explained, "My boy describes enrichment as 'the icing on the cake.'" A father acknowledged, "It keeps the old man on his toes too." A mother reported, "Enrichment isn't just for the children. It is an experience for the whole family and the whole family enjoys it."

However, these comments do not imply that all reactions are positive. In two and one-half years, questions have arisen concerning twenty-five out of the 340 children who are or have been in enrichment. In thirteen instances the program did not meet their needs. These children were not temperamentally suited to the extra work or the extra responsibility. Occasionally, a teacher complains that the wrong child is in the program. "Why," she asks, "is Dick in enrichment when he takes no interest in his class work while Jane is not in the program and she is my best student?" Seldom has a parent objected that enrichment is not beneficial to his child. Occasionally, a mother asks why her child is *not* in enrichment but not a single parent has further questioned the school's decision after an explanation has been made. Enrichment has always been an integral part of the whole school program just as are music, art, school patrol, remedial teaching, speech correction, and similar activities which take children from the classroom. Enrichment is just another way of meeting an individual need.

A follow-up study of the first twenty-three enrichment students to enter junior high school also gave an opportunity for evaluation. The pupils were matched for intelligence as measured by a group test (the Henmon-Nelson Test of Mental Ability, Grades 7-12) administered to all entering seventh-grade students and also for sex in order to make up a control group. These groups were compared with the Honor Roll pupils, with the entire seventh grade and with each other. The data are shown in the accompanying table. Although the number of cases is small, it represents all of the available enrichment students.

The seventh-grade Honor Roll at the end of the first nine weeks marking period was made up of 62 pupils out of a total of approximately 440. To this group, enrichment students contributed 14 as contrasted with only 4 from the control group. This is a ratio of three and one-half to one. The medians of the enrichment and control groups, each 23 in number, were 10 IQ points higher than that of the Honor Roll as a whole. If the enrichment and control honor pupils were omitted from the entire Honor Roll, the median of the enrichment and control groups as a whole would be 13 and 18 IQ points higher respectively than that for the remaining Honor Roll pupils. The median of the total Honor Roll group itself exceeded that of the entire seventh grade by 11 IQ points.

Factors other than the enrichment experience which might have influenced the three and one-half to one ratio were carefully considered. Age, previous school attended, section assigned in junior high school, and the number and kind of extracurricular activities chosen were substantially the same for both groups of children. They also were almost identical to comparable data for the Honor Roll group. The findings remained the same throughout the school year.

INTELLIGENCE (GROUP IQ'S) OF SEVENTH-GRADE PUPILS

Group	No.	Low Score	Lower Quartile	Median	Upper Quartile	High Score
Enrichment						
All pupils	23	127	140	145	154	169
Honor roll	14	133	140	146	154	169
Control						
All pupils	23	127	140	145	154	165
Honor pupils	4	133	143	150	156	164
Honor Roll						
All pupils excluding enrichment and control honor pupils	62	111	129	135	144	169
honor pupils	44	111	125	132	136	154
All 7th-grade candidates	440	73	112	124	133	169

That the honor pupils of the enrichment group were representative of the enrichment group as a whole is shown by the fact that the median and quartiles were identical or varied only one IQ point. For the control group, the honor pupils rated from two to five IQ points higher, and in view of the limited number of cases seem to be representative of the entire control group.

IMPLICATIONS

Evidence from spontaneous comments of children, principals, teachers, and parents indicates that the enrichment program fosters certain desirable outcomes for a large majority of gifted children. Statistical data, within the limits of this small study, point to the fact that the bright but not the brightest pupils are frequently the best students. However, more important is the evidence that the enrichment program helps to motivate a substantially greater number of the *most* able pupils to make more effective use of their abilities.

Whatever the provisions may be for gifted children, their effectiveness and success as adults in a democracy depends not only upon their general intelligence but also upon their motivation, drive, personal adjustment, and desire to serve their community and nation in ways for which they are best qualified. To help direct their adjustment and to stimulate their desire to put forth their best effort, appropriate provisions must be made for gifted individuals while they are still children. From the beginning, they must learn to *want* to direct their abilities toward solving the important problems of living together whether their interests be business, industry, education, science, religion, or human relations.

102   *Enrichment for everyone*

ROSE REMAVICH

PIETER ZILINSKY

In this report the writers describe an enrichment program for all pupils. Children choose from a wide variety of activities; teachers have a chance to teach in fields they most enjoy. The writers are enthusiastic about their program but discourage blind imitation of it.

THE SPECIAL AREAS program at Oakwood School was launched to provide wider and more specialized experiences for our pupils, to stimulate them to greater achievement, and to give them opportunities to develop their abilities and talents.

Through the program we also hoped to make greater use of the resources of the faculty. Any school staff has individuals who have special interests and unusual backgrounds that unfortunately are often neglected in the classroom.

In selecting teachers for our staff, we gave serious consideration to the contribution that a candidate could make to the program, which requires teachers who have a wide range of interests or an extensive knowledge of a specialized area. It is worth noting, too, that the program offers incentive to the applicant who has special ability that he wants to use.

In any school group, the rate and the quality of achievement vary from child to child. Our program allows pupils who have similar abilities to study

Reprinted from *The Elementary School Journal,* 63:317-23, March, 1963, by permission of The University of Chicago Press. Copyright 1963 by the University of Chicago.

under similar conditions. Children who have limited abilities work with their peers in suitable learning situations. Children who have wide interests are offered new experiences that help enrich their classroom learning. Thus, the program offers remedial work as well as advanced instruction.

We gave much thought to selecting areas that would satisfy children's interests and provide experiences that are important to children's social and emotional development. A sense of security is established with others who have similar capabilities. But a child need not spend an entire year in the group to which he is assigned. Self-confidence is generated by allowing children to work toward a minimum standard and by allowing them an opportunity to see their own growth.

Guided by these considerations, the staff of the Oakwood Elementary School launched the special areas program in the fifth and sixth grades. The faculty felt that the program would be more effective in these grades than in earlier grades.

We allowed each fifth- and sixth-grader to indicate his preference of areas, for we believe that the children in this age group have the maturity to benefit from and enjoy studies they have elected.

The child's need for diversity at this stage of development requires a broad range of teaching approaches. This need provided a framework for our program, which exposes the child to more of his peers and to more teachers in direct, stimulating learning situations than the usual program of the self-contained classroom does.

The awareness of the needs of the gifted and the realization that these needs can be met by making the elementary-school program more flexible are sources of inspiration to the teacher who works in such a program.

The cooperation of the faculty is the heart of the program. The role of the classroom teacher is extremely important. Each teacher has a fourfold task: to plan the study areas in terms of his own ability; to select and place children in suitable groups; to teach his areas; and to evaluate his part of the program.

Teachers with special preparation in language, in history and sociology, in science and mathematics, or in English and dramatics work in areas that require their special skills.

Each teacher in the program handles two subjects for two periods a week each. For such subjects as Russian and reading, however, four periods a week are considered necessary.

The classroom teacher has the responsibility of placing each child in her home-room into appropriate groups. Each teacher decides the content to be covered in her special group and assembles the materials to be used.

Among those who are called on to develop the work of the group are the classroom teacher, community resource persons, and the curriculum coordinator. Each teacher keeps a record of the children's response in terms of interest, understanding, and skill improvement, and discusses his observations with his colleagues. The records and the discussions help the teacher guide his area with greater effectiveness.

The administrator has a vital role in planning the program, but it is also important for him to become an active participant. His role in supervising and in teaching in the program helps establish a new kind of relationship to the children. Because of this association between principal and pupil, the administrator is no longer isolated from the people he directs. His primary responsibility of providing leadership is supplemented by his equally important responsibility of providing good learning experiences in his school.

Consultants also have an important role in our program. Music and art consultants welcome the opportunity to work with keen, talented children. We believe that the consultants can best help a group if the children are taught in their own classroom. The program provides the basis for a good relationship between the special teacher and the pupil—a relationship like that between the pupil and his classroom teacher.

Our first step was to survey the background and the abilities of each member of the staff. We found that three of our teachers were qualified to teach languages—French, Spanish, and Russian. One staff member who had been a jet pilot was able to introduce a new area—the theories of flight.

After we had a clear picture of the available resources of the staff, we prepared tentative lists of areas for the program. The lists were drawn up by the fifth- and sixth-grade teachers, the administrator, the consultants, and the fourth-grade teachers. The fourth-grade teachers are included in the planning because they know the work of the children who will be entering the program.

Next, the staff assigned each child to an area. The main factor in a child's placement is the classroom teacher's recommendation, although a consultant may request that a child be placed in a particular area. The decision on placement is made after careful observation of the child and his classroom work, and a study of the cumulative records.

Before any final assignments are made it is important that the classroom teacher work with his class for at least a month so that the decisions can be made after the teacher has had an opportunity for direct personal observation of his pupils. Final placement is made by all personnel directly involved. This phase of the planning may take several meetings.

Since two periods a week are scheduled for each area, in two years the average pupil can have special study in as many as four different areas. Most children are exposed to three areas.

Some pupils express a strong desire to go on in an area in which they have shown unusual interest and have had exceptional success. It is possible to build an effective program by having some of the highly successful children continue a second year. Children in our foreign-language groups often follow a course for two years.

The program usually begins in early or mid-October and ends in May. The weekly schedule for special areas has four periods, two for each area, except for languages, which are scheduled for four periods a week.

The periods are forty minutes long. A period of less than thirty minutes would be impractical. A period of more than forty minutes would be possible but not advisable for children of this age.

The content of the program depends on the community in which the school is located. Obviously the areas chosen for study differ greatly from school to school. Once the needs of the participating children are clearly stated, the areas generally follow a given pattern.

The pupils' backgrounds and interests reflect the occupational composition of their community. By careful study the faculty can discover gaps in the children's experience that the program can take account of and facets of the children's background that the program can profitably strengthen.

Our school community suggested one possible direction: more enrichment areas. Parents who are interested in enrichment and attempt to involve their children in worth-while cultural experiences have supported this emphasis. A balance between enrichment and developmental work is desirable but not always feasible.

We gave considerable thought to class size. The ideal class size depends on the activity. For areas that require definite individual performance, such as public speaking and foreign languages, the number of pupils should not exceed twenty.

The content of our enrichment areas changes only moderately from year to year. At present we are offering depth studies in world affairs, science, advanced mathematics, and public speaking. We are also offering creative art and music appreciation for children who have special interests and abilities in these fields. Remedial areas in the program include developmental mathematics and developmental reading. For our abler students, we offer Russian, Spanish, and theory of flight.

In world affairs, children who have an active interest in the workings of nations, in new developments in science and the arts, and in the study of the past as it relates to the present, have a chance to discuss these subjects together.

Various projects grow out of the discussions. Children write letters to men and women who are prominent in politics. They make detailed studies of a particular area in the news and prepare reports. And they debate current issues. The newspaper becomes an important tool in understanding our world. The knowledge of major current events that these children gain helps them contribute to their regular class activities.

In science enrichment, the children work on individual projects, exploring more thoroughly areas covered in the classroom. The high school is one of our important resources for this program. Children engage in advanced scientific activities such as dissections and long-term experiments. In the experiments, the use of the scientific method is promoted.

In advanced mathematics, the children work complicated problems; they use mathematics in related subjects and get a brief introduction to algebra and geometry. In this course, pupils discover many of the possibilities that arithmetic offers after the basic fundamentals are thoroughly understood.

Public speaking affords children an opportunity to work in various situations with various media. The primary objective is communication through speech and disciplined listening. The pupils are offered many experiences in speaking and listening. They have a chance to give formal speeches, to make introductions, to tell stories, to present reports, to conduct interviews, and to take part in choral speech. Media of communication used include the tape recorder and recordings made by pupils. Class discussions are scheduled on subjects selected by the teacher or the pupils. In these discussions, respect for the ideas of others and freedom to express one's individual judgment lead to sound conclusions based on group cooperation and consideration.

In reading enrichment, the children study material that relates to and extends the formal reading program. The librarian works with the children and introduces them to various forms of literature, including biographies, plays, and poems. The primary goal is reading for pleasure. As the children find pleasure and enjoyment in books, the library becomes a new world.

For children who have special interests and abilities in art and music, the program includes creative art and music appreciation. In creative art, the children try new media and new techniques. They paint with oils, they design mosaics, and they go to art exhibits.

In music appreciation the children attend demonstrations and go on trips to attend musical events in famous concert halls. The program encourages students who are musically inclined, develops their taste for music, and provides new ways of using leisure time.

The enrichment phase of the program has resulted in more classroom activity, more self-direction, greater curiosity and self-reliance, and a closer relationship between achievement and ability.

The remedial aspects of the program include developmental mathematics, which is taught by the administrator. Children who have serious difficulty in arithmetic are recommended for this class, where they can work in a small group. The additional time and individual attention that slow learners require are provided. Techniques of problem-solving form the basis for most of the work. The class is not merely a drill period, but a time for building arithmetic learning in meaningful situations. Diagnostic and achievement tests are a regular part of the class. Results are relayed to the classroom teacher. Several useful devices for strengthening the arithmetic program have come from this area.

In the developmental reading class the reading consultant and a classroom teacher work together. The children in this group are below grade level in achievement. The program is built around the children's needs. Reports on results of diagnostic tests and on work progress are regularly referred to the classroom teacher, along with recommendations. One advantage of the class is that the child can see and appreciate his progress. Several pupils have so improved their work that they have left the group and entered other areas in the schedule.

Experimentation has an important part in our program. We are doing new work in foreign languages and in theory of flight, areas that require teachers who have special training.

In the Russian class, which meets four times a week, new ideas and new methods of foreign-language teaching are being tested. The main activities of the course are oral and written exercises, music and poetry, and the study of basic cultural background.

In the Spanish class, the method of direct conversation is used. The fifth- or sixth-grader learns to speak and to converse; his pronunciation and inflection are not hampered by the self-consciousness that can hinder the older pupil.

Information about the level of achievement and the benefits of early language-learning is valuable in curriculum-planning. New techniques that confirm or disprove current ideas about language-learning are tried in these classes more readily than at higher levels.

In the class on theory of flight, children learn about the fundamentals of flight and the history and development of aviation. The children discuss the many problems of putting a man in space, including physiological reactions at high altitudes. They review airfield operations, and their trips to airfields and to military aviation facilities bring to life topics discussed in class. The instructor of the course is an aviator who for many years was a fighter pilot for the U.S. Marine Corps and is now a member of our staff.

We have found that the children, the school, and the staff profit greatly from the special areas program. It demands additional work and time, particularly at the beginning of the school year, for planning and for individual attention to children. Whether this effort is justified is a question that must be answered in terms of the goals set up by the school.

Of necessity, the teachers' judgment of the results is of major value. Our staff has found that the program diversifies teachers' efforts while bringing the teachers themselves closer together in the search for better ways of achieving effective teaching. The program has allowed the teacher who is not a specialist but is proficient or talented in certain areas to find expression for those skills. Our experience has shown that our teachers must be persons of wide interests.

We have observed that children find learning more interesting and more exciting. We have come to know our pupils better, and they have shown greater confidence in their teachers.

The program has given children who have special talent and ability the opportunity to demonstrate and test their skills with greater enjoyment than under a normal program. This result has been achieved without removing the children from regular classes. One particularly rewarding example was an exhibit of our pupils' work in a local art show.

New subjects have been added to the curriculum. Our pupils have learned that there are fields of learning and activity other than school subjects.

Much has been done to prepare children for future school experiences. Our pupils have been introduced to some of the subjects and study conditions they will meet later on in school. We have begun to exchange personnel and ideas with the high school and the junior high school.

We have been trying to improve class placement of our pupils. Through our program we have been able to study the children more closely in a wider range of activities than we have previously. We believe that we now have a better basis for placement than we have had in the past.

The methods of selection for an area have made us more sensitive to needs and talents in the school population. We have used our experience to develop a questionnaire concerning the emotional, social, and academic development of each pupil. At the end of the year, the fourth-grade teacher fills out a questionnaire for each child. In this way we have not only improved our selection of areas for the program, but have secured information about the children that can be useful to their classroom teachers.

Our program is dynamic. We have made changes based on increasingly careful evaluation. We have found it necessary and advantageous to modify or replace certain areas each year to relate activities more closely to the children's capacities. New talent on the staff also influences our plans and offerings.

What new approaches have resulted from direct teaching experiences? We realized that in our class on developmental mathematics, a new approach was needed for greater effectiveness. Our principal, who teaches this area, is examining the importance of vocabulary in the teaching of arithmetic. The results of the inquiry will be used to revise next year's presentation. Observation of the hearing-speaking-writing sequence used in the Russian class has helped accelerate the drive for greater stress on conversation in foreign-language instruction and on the installation and expansion of language-laboratory facilities in our junior and senior high schools. Experience of this kind has helped us improve certain parts of our regular curriculum.

The community has shown enthusiasm for the program. The public has a standing invitation to observe, and at an annual assembly visitors are offered a sample of the work in each area. Not only can visitors see some of the direct results of the year's work, but they can study copies of outlines of goals set up for a given area.

We welcome the comments of visitors who may have suggestions based on their own experiments. We feel that our staff is now better able to evaluate other programs and to identify features that may be helpful for us.

Our program is not based on some ideal model. We strongly caution against imitation without investigation. Our program is an instrument designed to mesh with the specific needs and opportunities of a particular school situation. To evaluate the merits of any enrichment program, a clear understanding of the goals of the school is essential.

In our program we provide for individual differences by effective use of a good professional staff. The program has been a rewarding experience for all who have cooperated to make it part of elementary education.

103   *Teaching slow-learning children in elementary school*

RUTH STRANG

"Slow-learning children are not a homogeneous group." To support this statement, Strang shows that analyses of test performances and informal evaluations provide more useful diagnostic help than do mere test scores. Strang cites specific examples of how teachers may affect "an atmosphere of learning and growing." Notice the optimism with which she writes. She gives one the impression that slow-learning children are temporarily slow-learning. Many experienced teachers can testify to the validity of this view. Perhaps the faith of these teachers is the greatest power in bringing about improved learning.

WHETHER TO PLACE slow-learning children in special or in regular classes is still a disputed question. Both plans have advantages. Having the slow learners in a special class is easier for teachers. They have smaller numbers of pupils, more special materials and equipment, and less responsibility for meeting the needs of a wide range of interests and abilities.

Being in a special class has been found to increase the slow learner's self-confidence and self-esteem; he is not constantly made aware of his brighter classmates. He is given more individual attention. As one youngster said, "In the small class we can learn what we need to know, not what everyone else needs to know."

On the other hand, being in a regular class may stimulate the slow-learning child to do his best to keep up with some of the more able learners. And, of course, it removes whatever stigma may be attached to being in a special class.

The conflicting results of research on this issue are due in part to differences in teachers' personalities and skills in both forms of organization. In either type of grouping, understanding the individual pupils, creating a classroom atmosphere conducive to learning, and skill in helping children to learn without unnecessary failure are essential.

KNOWING THE PUPILS

Slow-learning children are not a homogeneous group. Among those who score between 70 and 90 IQ on the Stanford-Binet or the Wechsler intelligence tests, there are individual differences in learning rate, reading ability, interests, emotional stability, motivation, and home influences.

Analysis of a child's low mental age score on the Wechsler scale often makes a teacher less fatalistic about it. Such an analysis may show emotional factors, such as uncontrolled anxiety or lack of drive, that may be an important part of the child's low performance. It will also often show unevenness on different parts of the scale, as, for example, a higher score on the performance as compared with the verbal part of the scale.

If a child diagnosed as a slow learner makes a relatively high score on the similarities test, which indicates general reasoning and abstract ability, one would hope that under favorable conditions the child would rise above the slow-learner classification. It is interpretations of this kind that the teacher should expect the psychologist to give. Merely reporting the IQ or the mental age may be quite misleading.

Similarly, standardized reading test scores may be misleading. On a multiple-choice type of test, a child may mark each exercise at random and obtain a grade score of two to three years. But when given a second-grade book, he cannot read it.

More effective is an informal method of appraising the reading ability of slow learners. To prevent initial embarrassment at not being able to read, the teacher may ask the child to read something she is sure he knows, for example, his name, his address, and some of the common signs such as "Stop," "Go," "Boys," "Girls," "Exit," "Left Turn," "School—Go Slow."

When the child has gained some confidence through being able to read these familiar words, the teacher may ask him to choose a book from several that she has placed on the table. These range from the simplest beginning books to whatever grade level she thinks the child may be capable of reading. She will also try to select for older children books on their levels of interest, which are simple in vocabulary and sentence structure.

The child selects one of these books and reads part of it aloud. Meanwhile the teacher notes difficulties in word recognition and later tests his comprehension. To obtain a more systematic appraisal the teacher might learn to give a diagnostic test such as the *Durell Analysis of Reading Difficulty* or ask a psychologist or reading specialist, if one is available, to give it.

In her day-by-day contacts with these children the teacher may learn more about their functioning intelligence and reading and number abilities than any test can tell. It was sound practice in England and Scotland not to place a child in a special school for the mentally retarded on the basis of tests alone. Instead, he was observed for a year in a regular school before the decision was made.

In a school for exceptional children in this country, the children, in an atmosphere of affection and encouragement, often achieve beyond test expectation. A sound rule for all teachers of slow-learning children is to provide the best possible learning opportunities for each child and to note the progress he makes regardless of the test IQ.

From daily observation, too, the teacher may gain insight into the child's interests and motivation, and into home conditions that may be helping or interfering with his learning. One child's interest in reading stemmed from her love of a pet dog. She made a scrapbook on dogs, and comprehended a leaflet on the care of dogs which the teacher thought was above her reading level. An older boy, who had a good singing voice, was motivated to learn to read the titles of his records and the words of songs he wanted to sing.

CLASSROOM ATMOSPHERE

An atmosphere of learning and growing is very important for slow-learning children. In one class of boys from nine to twelve years of age, everyone was unusually happy. The teacher had printed on large cards a number of personalized directions. As she held each direction in front of the class, every boy was intent on reading it to see whether it applied to him.

One card, "The boy with red hair will sing a song," was quickly recognized by all, and the boy with red hair, who had special singing ability, took the card and sang a song.

In this period all the children had the experience of giving wholehearted attention, putting forth the optimum of effort, and having a thoroughly happy experience. In such an atmosphere, learning flourished.

In a regular class the teacher is concerned with the attitude of other children toward the slow learner. He does not want sympathy; that might increase his sense of inferiority. What he wants is respect. By her courteous, considerate treatment of each child, the teacher evokes similar attitudes toward one another from the children.

In such an atmosphere, one child who stuttered was feeling sad because he could not be in the play. But one of the other children said, "Oh, we need you for the stage manager." When another slow-learning child was discouraged by his score on an arithmetic test, a bright youngster said to him, "But see how much better your mark was today than last time." Friendship means much to these children.

A teacher sometimes has time to help a slow-learning child acquire a skill or do a simple experiment which he can demonstrate to the class. She makes sure he knows the answers to certain questions and then calls upon him for the answers. In a group project, he can read the simplest material available on the subject, learn a few simple lines in a play, help paint the scenery, or otherwise contribute to the success of the performance.

TEACHING SKILLFULLY

In the last analysis, the teacher's greatest contribution to the best development of slow-learning children is her skill in teaching. Too often, a well-meaning teacher will recognize some ability in a child, such as drawing or woodworking, and let him do this to the neglect of other learning.

The success of the learning machines recently invented by Dr. Fred Skinner depends on two conditions: (1) a careful analysis of the learning process and (2) the rewarding of progress at each step in the process, rather than waiting until the child has achieved the final result. A skillful teacher does not need machines to fulfill these conditions.

Another aspect of skillful teaching is that of taking advantage of "teachable moments" and using the child's real interests and drives. One mentally retarded, emotionally disturbed ten-year-old girl who had encouraged the teacher by learning a number of words the day before, seemed to have forgotten them all the next day; she did not respond to any of them.

At this point the teacher said, "Let's play you are the teacher." The child began asking the teacher the meanings of the same words. When the teacher made mistakes, the child corrected her instantly.

An older boy, deeply concerned about his vocational future, had begun to do part-time work in a filling station. When the teacher provided him with a reading workbook about gas stations, he put forth his maximum of effort in learning to read the words and sentences in it.

Teaching slow learners, whether in special classes or regular classes, requires understanding of and faith in them as persons. It requires respect for their good qualities, approval at each successful step in their learning progress, and skill in finding and using the trigger that releases their effort to learn.

CHAPTER 24

What Are Some Different Ways of Organizing Classrooms?

IN THE MIDDLE of the nineteenth century there was a shift from individualized, interage instruction to group teaching of classes organized by grades. Although this change was not universal when most of us went to school, I suspect that we never contemplated the possibility of any scheme other than organization by grades with one teacher per class. Nor, I suspect, did most of our teachers envision any other possibilities for organization.

Within the past decade, some educators have been considering other ways to organize classes. Some big foundations have underwritten programs to study and disseminate information about team teaching. The first article in this chapter deals with this subject. The second and third articles present ideas about nongraded classes. Team teaching and nongraded classes are the two major ways of organizing classrooms, but you will discover others in the course of your career.

104   Team teaching: fundamental change or passing fancy?

MALCOLM P. DOUGLASS

In Part One I indicated that while the self-contained classroom is the most common type of arrangement, there are other ways to organize a classroom. Team teaching is one of them. It is hard to find an article that deals with the question of team teaching in an objective, professional way. Enthusiasts and detractors generally present their views without regard for evidence. Douglass is a notable exception.

WHAT WILL BE the future of team teaching? Judging from its present attractiveness to a large segment of the public and the profession, it appears that it will soon be given a trial of one kind or another in virtually every school district in California.

What evidence is there to support such an enthusiastic response? Do the organizational arrangements for teaching and learning provoked by the team-teaching concept bring about fundamental changes which will benefit children and society? Or will they, in a few years, merely leave vestigial remains to remind us of our folly—of one more venture into the land of fad?

As we look at team teaching today, it should be clear that it can only be provided for, not guaranteed. And it can only be provided *for* when three organizational elements are brought into existence within a school; i.e., when (1) there is an identifiable group of students taught by (2) a small faculty group with complementary talents assisted by (3) certain additional persons, including teacher aides, talented citizens, and others. In a very real sense, the team of students, teachers, and others, comprises a school within a school. How they work together in this setting is properly termed "team teaching."

It is the responsibility of the teachers on the team to plan and teach the student group in one or more areas of the school curriculum. At the elementary level this usually means that the team of teachers will be responsible for the total program for one or more grades in the school. At the secondary level, the team may be composed of teachers from only one subject matter area; or it may deal with two, three, or more. Those people who assist the student-teacher team are the teacher aides, talented citizens, and others in the school and community who may be available for some special purpose.

Reprinted from the *CTA Journal*, 54:26-29, 55-56, March, 1963. Permission granted by the *CTA Journal*. Copyright by the California Teachers Association, March, 1963.

In the daily operation of the team, modern instructional devices and flexible grouping will be employed. In most team-teaching programs, therefore, we see considerable experimentation with educational television, teaching machines, "new" mathematics programs, and the like. Similarly, we notice such practices as small and large group instruction, situations in which two teachers instruct a group or one teacher will conduct large group sessions in a particular subject area, and frequent regrouping according to ability or special interests.

SOME START WITHOUT PREPARATION

During the past two or three years, the concept of team teaching has become increasingly attractive throughout the profession. Today, we are witnessing such a surge of interest that many school people are embarking upon their own programs—sans outside financing and often with little, if any, assistance from others who have had experience with team teaching. To these people, the ideas associated with the team-teaching concept are so "right" and the desire to improve educational opportunities so strong that they literally cannot be stopped.

Many of the team-teaching programs thus being developed are soundly conceived and will be well executed. However, it is quite apparent, as one looks about our own state, and indeed across the nation, that the bandwagon is rolling and many people are too anxious to get aboard. In their eagerness, they are lumping virtually any departure from the conventional school pattern under the term "team teaching." A simple cooperative teaching plan between two or three teachers, for example, becomes team teaching. A nongraded or a continuous progress plan for an elementary school becomes team teaching. Departmental meetings—hardly new at the secondary level—suddenly become team teaching. And so on.

What, then, does team teaching look like in action? What are its presumed advantages over typically organized elementary and secondary schools? What evidence do we have of its successes and failures? And what should school people consider as they contemplate the values of team teaching for their own school and, indeed, for their own teaching?

The teaching team, as we have indicated, consists of (1) a distinct student group, (2) a small faculty group with complementary talents responsible for teaching the student group, and (3) certain persons who assist the teachers and students. The manner in which these elements in a teaching team interact can vary widely, of course. Hence, it is impossible to describe a "package" arrangement which can be applied anywhere and everywhere. In the project sponsored by the Claremont Graduate School, with which the writer is most familiar, there have been, over the last four years, twenty-one secondary teams and twelve elementary ones. Each has been somewhat different. Multiply the extent of these differences by all of the team-teaching projects under way around the country, probably several thousand, and one can readily understand why there is confusion over what is really meant by the term team teaching.

Speaking in quite general terms, then, the teaching teams associated with the Claremont project are comprised of from 120 to 180 pupils at the elementary level and from 90 to 180 students at the secondary level. Teacher-pupil ratio is the same as is found in conventionally organized classrooms—thirty or thirty-five to one. Therefore, elementary teams are composed of from four to six teachers; secondary teams from three to six teachers. Each team of teachers elects or has chosen for it by its administration a team leader. Some of the teams include intern teachers, but in the main, team membership as far as professional people are concerned is made up of fully certificated teachers. The third element in the structure of the team, those who assist students and teachers, consists of the teacher aide, auxiliary teacher (at the elementary level only), and various talented citizens selected by the team for their ability to make specialized contributions to the instructional program planned by the team. The teacher aide is a noncertificated person drawn from the community who works at the direction of the team in a part-time capacity. The auxiliary teacher is a certificated person who provides twenty days of released time for members of the elementary teams for planning, research, visitations, and other activities deemed worthwhile by the team.

Both elementary and secondary teams draw extensively upon talented members of the school community at various times during the year. Local citizens may assist with some specific aspect of the instructional program, such as delivering a talk, or giving a demonstration; they may lead student study groups during or after regular school hours; or they may assist in remedial work over an extended period of time where individual attention is the prime need of the student. Talents represented in the community have been found to be more varied, useful to the school, and freely given than even the most optimistic planners of team-teaching programs anticipated.

In way of contrast, mention might be made of different types of team organization as they are seen over the United States. In the program being conducted jointly by the University of Wisconsin and nearby school districts, for example, teams consist of from sixty to eighty children at the elementary level. Two regularly certificated teachers and two intern teachers, in addition to the teacher aide, make up the team. Community resources are also employed extensively. In team programs sponsored jointly by school districts and Harvard University under way in the greater Boston area, teams consist of about the same number of students and teachers as there are at Claremont. However, there are supplementary personnel, such as special subject teachers at the elementary level, who provide opportunities for regrouping, especially in small groups, and released time for teachers for planning and research. In secondary teams, more large group instruction is planned than is presently true in most programs seen in the western part of the United States.

Since team teaching itself is nothing more than the total pattern of educational experiences planned for the students on the team, the quality of those experiences obviously cannot exceed the talents, collectively and individually deployed, which exist among the team teachers and their nonprofessional associates. It is, therefore, in large measure true that there is nothing in conventionally organized schools which precludes teaching students in those ways which have been associated with the concept of team teaching, for example, large and small group instruction, the use of modern instructional tools, flexible groupings, and use of talented citizens. The fact is, for whatever reasons one wishes to assign, that these kinds of educational experiences appear more often to develop from the teaching-team arrangement than in the conventionally organized school. However, when this is said, immediate qualification is necessary in at least two important respects. First, do they result directly from teaching, or are there other elements at work, such as the fact the program is "experimental," and motivation for teaching and learning somewhat artificial? In other words, how important is the Hawthorne Effect in team teaching? And secondly, do these educational experiences actually provide superior learning? We do not really have an answer to the first question. But one may be coming shortly from those school districts which are striking out on their own with the idea. As for the second question, too little is known, but there are some research straws in the wind which are commented upon below.

SOME PRESUMED ADVANTAGES OF TEAM TEACHING

Since team teaching seeks to improve education across a broad front, the hypothetical advantages attributed to it are global in nature. It is hypothesized, therefore, that the education of the child or young adult will be enhanced because the teaching-team organization will encourage, to a greater degree than usual, the following:[1]

Practical and effective in-service education through frequent team meetings.

Marked success in inducting new teachers into school systems by using interns as team teachers.

The use of aides to release teachers from routine duties.

Teacher involvement in planning and developing curriculum because of team structure.

Recognition for outstanding teachers through selection of team teachers and election of leaders.

Because of team structure, the ability to group and regroup frequently by achievement, ability, or interest levels.

Because of team structure, the ability of the team to form large and small groups for instruction, from one teacher for one student, to one teacher for two hundred students.

At the elementary level, the ability to develop exchange teaching opportunities among the team teachers in order to exploit teachers' special talents, knowledge, and training.

Improved guidance from the planned exchange of information about students and the atmosphere of fellowship within the team.

Improved correlation of subject matter because of cooperative planning in team meetings.

Through team leaders and team meetings, the identification and use of talented citizens and other educational resources of the community.

The planning of field trips for team students in team meetings and the reduction of interference from field trips with other teachers' classes.

Because of their children's common experiences, increased interest and involvement of parents.

Because teams can be kept together for more than one school year, the organization to develop sequences of content and intellectual process.

Improved climate of motivation because of the accent upon individual identity and team spirit.

Because of the team structure, the best use of teacher talent which should yield the highest quality of instruction.

Because of varied groupings and presentations, greater student interest.

1. Annual report of the teaching-team program, 1961-62 (John A. Brownell, ed.). Claremont Graduate School, Claremont, California, 1963.

No simple means exist for confirming these hypotheses. To make matters worse, most of the projects in team teaching supported out of foundation grants have provided for a minimal evaluation program. Rather than formal research, experience derived from field trials has been deemed a sufficiently satisfactory indicator of success—or failure. Such evidence should not be depreciated entirely—just taken with a grain of salt. And the condition itself suggests the need for more controlled research before hasty judgments are entered vis-à-vis the future and worth of team teaching.

SOME EVALUATIVE STRAWS IN THE WIND

Even within these restrictions, some pieces of reasonably objective evidence are becoming available. For example, studies of the Claremont project have involved attitudes and opinions of people in team teaching and those who have close knowledge of team operation but not direct participation. Comparative analyses have been conducted in school achievement. Attitudes of elementary and secondary students toward team teaching have been probed, and several other of the assumptions listed above have been or are presently being subjected to some sort of systematic scrutiny. Like other team-teaching programs around the country, more substantial data will be forthcoming in a year or two—team teaching is still too young to provide the framework for any large quantity of data. Within these limitations, the following information gathered at Claremont over the past four years may be helpful:

With respect to the opinions and attitudes of people concerning the desirability of team teaching and its personal attractiveness to them, a three-year study involving about 7000 students, 450 teachers, 1200 parents, and 50 administrators is yielding useful information. Generally speaking, those who have participated directly in the program support the concept enthusiastically and wish to continue their team-teaching program. Teachers who have observed but not participated in team teaching are not at all sure they wish to get involved themselves. This tendency to wish to remain out of the program has been a constant factor over the extent of the study. Parents of children in teams and administrators of teams have shown the strongest desire to continue the program, followed by team teachers and then by team students.

The question is constantly raised whether a team-teaching program can survive without outside financial assistance—as through a foundation grant. Whereas early in the Claremont project there was a strong feeling that the program could not continue without such assistance, there is now a feeling that the additional support needed for team operation can and should be provided at the local level. Since foundation support will cease in the field at the end of the current school year, this question will not be an academic one much longer.

When teachers who are participating in team teaching are asked what they consider the most important effects of team teaching on various key aspects of the school curriculum, their comments are consistently positive. The one area most considerably affected, however, has been the team teacher's own pleasure and satisfaction in teaching. The impact upon curriculum development, guidance functions, student motivation, etc., while positive, is not as important an effect in their minds.

TESTING THE TEAM-TEACHING IDEA

When teachers were asked what factors they felt indispensable for an adequate test of the team-teaching idea, a majority responded with: (1) time for teacher planning, (2) active administrative support, (3) agreement among team teachers on standards, (4) teachers with enthusiasm for team work, (5) the help of a team leader, (6) clerical assistance for team teachers. Those factors believed unimportant or undesirable in any test of the team-teaching idea included: (1) students with above average ability, (2) time for conferences with individual students, (3) continuation of the same group of students for at least two years, (4) students with seriousness of purpose, (5) class size smaller than average, (6) frequent meetings with parents, (7) students enrolled with team teachers for at least four of their classes.

Teacher members of teams had a variety of responses when asked which experiences they particularly liked. In this sample, at least 80 per cent appreciated being in an experimental program, working on common problems with team teachers, sharing responsibilities with team teachers for students' progress, using different methods of teaching in team classes, feeling rapport with members of the teaching team, having an opportunity to make significant contributions to education, being on a team rather than working alone, working closely with students who need help on personal problems, being challenged to do a better job in the classroom, learning to work together as a team, having new ideas to work on in the Teaching Team Program, exchanging ideas about classroom problems with team teachers, feeling zest for new ways of working, exchanging information about students with team members, planning with team teachers how to put new ideas into use, doing something different from regular teaching, trying out new ideas in the classroom, getting better acquainted with team teachers, having team students know the teacher better.

Results on all aspects of this opinion and attitude survey have been remarkably consistent over the past three years.

To date, four studies using standardized tests of achievement have been conducted at the high-school level. Each of the studies compared a control group with the experimental (team) group. In every study, the differences between groups on total scores and sub-scores were not found to be statistically significant. At this date, therefore, we are concluding that, "to the extent the standardized tests measured the important aspects of achievement in the subjects comprising the teams involved, the teaching team produced no significant superiority in subject achievement over conventional classroom organization nor, more forcefully, any deficiency in subject matter achievement." It may reasonably be argued that standard tests measure a very limited range of desirable achievement. When one examines the types of curricular innovation introduced by the teams associated with the Claremont project, it becomes apparent that available standard tests provide an inadequate basis for judgment in those areas and that new instruments capable of discriminating among such matters are needed.

The nature and significance of students' attitudes toward team-teaching are currently being explored through depth interviews and the development of case studies. From these well-springs of information has come a wide range of responses—from delight with team teaching to utter boredom. The smallness of the sample and the range of responses precludes generalizing until more data are obtained. However, the nature of the responses at the uppermost levels has led to a re-examination of the kinds of team models most appropriate for that age.

In process is a study at the junior and senior high-school level which seeks answers to the question, "Do team teachers know their students better than regular classroom teachers?" Preliminary analysis of the data fails to show that team teachers in the three schools included in the study have more knowledge of their students than teachers in typical school situations. Further analysis may yet yield differences worthy of notice.

These are merely representative samples of the type of research being conducted at one center for the study of team teaching. Other centers are producing information, at an increasing tempo, which will be useful in making judgments about the worth of team teaching for a particular school setting. It is important for us to realize that we do not yet have enough information to say yea or nay to team teaching with sufficient authority to make it stick.

But we can glean from the experiences of those who have participated in the Claremont project and in other teaching-team programs around the country these guides for those who find the concept so intriguing they wish to start on their own:

1. Read what people have to say who have had experience with various kinds of teaching programs. Talk with them personally if possible.

2. Select only those teachers for the team who really want to be on it. Then provide the additional indispensable elements for successful team operation: (a) time for teacher planning, (b) active administrative support, (c) agreement among team teachers on standards, (d) the help of a team leader, (e) clerical assistance for team teachers.

3. Approach the whole idea of team teaching with an experimental attitude: be willing and able to judge the quality of what is happening within and to the team. Cultivate imaginative ways to solve old problems in curriculum, guidance, and all other aspects of the school's work.

4. Keep parents and others who have a stake in the experiment reasonably well informed.

5. Provide some formal means of evaluating the experiment. Employ creative approaches to evaluation; do not rely exclusively upon existing standard tests.

In other words, study the situation first. Approach team teaching with a plan and with an experimental frame of mind. Resource the idea adequately—do not cut important corners. Evaluate frequently, creatively, and as objectively as possible. Remember that parents tend to be more enthusiastic about team teaching than teachers. And finally, if these criteria cannot be met, it is probably better to leave experimentation in team teaching to others who are in a better position to give it a fair try.

J O H N   I .   G O O D L A D

Goodlad is one of the leading advocates of the nongraded school. He cites facts and discusses values that should guide educators in devising school programs. Pointing out his reasons for believing that the traditional graded structure is inadequate, he presents grouping methods, activities, materials, and evaluation methods used in nongraded programs.

SOME VALUES AND REALITIES TO GUIDE EDUCATIONAL PRACTICE

In EXAMINING educational practice, each of us looks through a screen of values which imposes pleasing or displeasing colors upon what we see. At the head of my list of criteria for judging the adequacy of school structure are three which I apply as questions. *First, does the structure encourage continuous progress for each child?* There should be no undue pauses, no damaging gaps, and no meaningless duplications—just steady progress geared to the irregular development of the child himself. *Secondly, what alternatives exist for placing children who do not appear to be profiting as they should in their present educational environment?* Most schools provide only for repetition or skipping vertically, with little or no provision for horizontal replacement of the child. In other words, if the child does not "fit" where he now is, only some kind of extralegal provision is available for his readjustment. *Thirdly, does the structure encourage a reasonable balance of success and failure?* It is estimated that approximately 25 per cent of children in the grades experience from 70 to 80 per cent of the failure. This situation does not appear to provide a wholesome balance of success and failure.

Twentieth-century education at all levels must take into account at least two major kinds of realities. *First, knowledge is expanding at an explosive rate.* This fact has been stated many times and in many ways. Robert Oppenheimer has said that most of the knowledge worth learning today was not in the textbooks when today's adults were in school. Others have said that the

Reprinted by permission of the Association for Childhood Education International, 3615 Wisconsin Avenue, N.W., Washington 16, D.C. Inadequacy of graded organization, by John I. Goodlad. From *Childhood Education*, February, 1963, Vol. 39, No. 6, pp. 274-77.

knowledge accumulated since 1900 is equivalent to the total of all knowledge that had accumulated prior to the beginning of this century. A perhaps more dramatic statement is that 95 per cent of the scientists ever born are still living. *The second inescapable reality is that human beings are profoundly different from one another.* There are biochemical differences; that is, differences in under-the-skin composition. Several hundred such differences have now been identified and classified. There are physiological differences in energy patterns, causing children to be quite different in their readiness for the activities school provides. And there are academic individual differences. In the fourth grade only 15 per cent of the children are at grade level—that is, range from 4.0 to 4.9 in all subjects—at the middle of the year. At the fourth grade there is a four-year spread in over-all average achievement; at the fifth grade, five years; at the sixth grade there is a six-year range; and so on. These individual differences simply cannot be accounted for within the conventional graded structure of school organization.

At least two major proposals now before us on the educational scene seem to support the values and the realities enunciated above. The first of these proposes a longitudinal curriculum organized around basic concepts, principles and methods of inquiry in the various fields of knowledge. The second, closely related and designed to account for such a curriculum, proposes elimination of the stratified, lock-step grade system and the substitution of a nongraded plan.

INADEQUACY OF GRADED SYSTEM

When the graded school was established as the pattern for American education in the middle of the nineteenth century, the prevailing view of individual differences was quite different from the picture drawn above. Children apparently were regarded as fundamentally alike, major differences lying in areas of determination, application, hard work, and so on. "If at first you don't succeed, try, try, try again" was the slogan. Such a perception leads to reward and punishment as the major stimulants to and perhaps differentiators of progress. At that time, too, with knowledge expanding at a much slower rate, it may have been possible to define something called an elementary education. Today, the packaging of a few bits of knowledge considered to be of most worth is impossible. However, it is important to remember that the view of individual differences and the rate of expansion of knowledge current in 1850 were not in any way antithetical to the graded structure that was rapidly emerging and crystallizing.

Once the graded structure was established, it became necessary to fit the child to the structure. Nonpromotion was a natural concomitant. If the child doesn't succeed you simply have him do over again what he failed to do in the first place. But we now have a substantial body of research indicating that nonpromoted children do not learn as well as do their promoted counterparts; nonpromoted children are less well adjusted personally and socially than are youngsters of equal ability who are promoted; nonpromoted children, more than promoted children, dislike school and wish to discontinue their formal learning as soon as possible.

It is possible for creative teachers to "beat the graded system," so to speak. But in so doing they must run counter to prevailing practices, proposing and initiating adjustments that deviate markedly from existing practices. Often they become nuisances to administrators and other teachers who prefer that things remain as they are and have been. To remedy this situation I would legalize the deviation of creative teachers in order that what they do may become accepted as standard practice.

NONGRADING

In the nongraded school, grade demarcations are swept away. Some schools eliminate grade designations at the outset. Others move toward this step slowly, perhaps first experimenting with multiple-age or multiple-grade groups and in various ways deliberately expanding provision for individual differences within a given class. One of the major goals is to eliminate the grade-mindedness often firmly established in the thinking of teachers.

Essentially, nongrading seeks to recognize and deliberately plan for the range of pupil realities actually present in a given class. This means accepting the fact that there are children working at levels below grade designation, varying widely from subject to subject. At the top end of the scale, it is necessary to provide activities that would be classified at several grades above usual pupil grade placement. In so doing there is no fear of encroaching on the work of the next grade; there is no need to stop because the work of the grade has been completed or because the teacher above expects children to be neither above nor below grade assignment.

It is absolutely essential that there be a thoroughgoing redistribution of materials. Instead of a single set of textbooks for a class, for example, there should be five copies of this, four copies of that, seven copies of something else. Materials should be selected in anticipation of the range of accomplishments now present and to be present within the group as learning progresses.

Above all, there is no attempt to account for several years of pupil progress through an arbitrary and necessarily incorrect grade classification. Energy is devoted to providing for the range of individual differences that exists. By a system of overlapping the accomplishments present in any one group with the accomplishments present in lower and higher groups, it is possible to provide several placement alternatives for any given child at any given time. Thus, in an elementary school with six classes encompassing the first three grades—two classes per grade—there would be a spread of accomplishment ranging from less than kindergarten to above the fifth grade, depending upon the field of study in question. In the conventional graded plan, this pair of classes would be approximately alike in the individual differences recognized and in the instructional arrangements provided. Classes would be viewed in an end-to-end relationship, the conclusion of the second leading directly to the beginning of the third, and so on.

In a nongraded plan one might arrange for a pair of classes, X_1 and X_2, with an anticipated spread of individual differences from kindergarten to the usual second grade. Y_1 and Y_2 would anticipate a spread of from at least the conventional first to the conventional third grade. Z_1 and Z_2 would provide for a spread of accomplishment ranging from the second to the fifth grade. Now, it may be seen that one pair of classes overlaps another pair of classes. In fact, each pair overlaps each of the other two pairs, thus providing several alternative placements for any child at any given time. (See figure.)

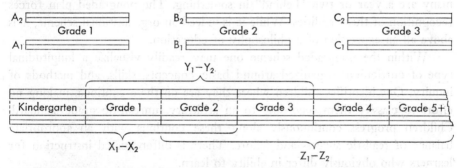

This chart illustrates several differences about the graded concept as contrasted with the nongraded concept. The graded school normally provides for a single year of expectations in each class. Thus each class at subsequent grade levels is in an end-to-end relationship. The child leaves off in A_1, for example, and moves directly to B_1 as though he had precisely finished the work of A_1. We know that this is not the way children are, and school organization should accompany reality rather than fiction. The first section of the chart shows a progression with each graded class picking up where the previous graded class left off.

The second part of the diagram shows two essential differences in nongraded structure. First, the spread of expectations for a single class encompasses more than one year. Thus X_1 begins well below the first grade (where many children are) and continues well beyond the conventional first grade for children who are capable of so progressing. However, the next class does not expect all children to come up to an equivalent standard; and so it begins a good deal back of where children left off the previous year but provides for a considerable extension beyond the year's work in order to take care of youngsters at different rates of progression. Thus each pair of classes overlaps each other pair of classes. You will note that the "Z" pair overlaps not only the "Y" pair but also the tip of the "X" pair. Such a gross overlap is not necessary, but it does indicate the variety of alternative placements possible for a child when the overlapping nongraded structure is used.

In the nongraded scheme there is continuous progress for each child; there are several alternatives for placing children who do not appear to be profiting from their present environment; and there is improved opportunity for a reasonable balance of success and failure because the classroom environment is designed to legalize several levels of accomplishments at any given time. Some children may be moved more quickly through the years of the primary unit. Some may take a year longer. In no case does a child skip; nor is he failed. Most children are a year or two "ahead" in some field or other; many are a year or two "behind" in something. The nongraded plan forces recognition of these realities. While it is indeed an organizational scheme, it is above all an expression of a philosophy of education.

Within the nongraded scheme one may readily visualize a longitudinal type of curriculum organized around basic concepts, skills, and methods of inquiry. One identifies children where they are on these continua, making no effort to classify them according to an arbitrary, unrealistic grade standard. Children progress continuously along these continua with an appropriate balance of realistic success and failure. There is differentiated instruction for learners who obviously differ in ability to learn.

At present the nongraded scheme is most prevalent at the primary level. A few plans extend into the upper elementary grades. In an isolated community or two, consideration is now being given to the possibility of nongraded junior and senior high schools. There is no reason why the nongraded concept cannot be extended from kindergarten through the entire twelve- or thirteen-year structure of education. In fact, the very logic of nongrading leads to a continuous stream of elementary and secondary education. Logically, then, the nongraded plan leads to reduced discontinuity among elementary, junior high and secondary units of the school system as well as to elimination of the lock-step inherent in the traditional graded plan.

L I L L I A N   G O R E

The following is part of the School Life *editor's introduction to Dr. Gore's article: "In this article Dr. Gore reports on the nongraded primary unit as it is practiced in ten school systems she has visited and in twenty-eight systems whose material she has studied. Her study includes material from well-established programs, such as the one in Milwaukee, and new ones, such as the one in Fairfax County, Va."*

THE NONGRADED primary unit is one that follows a design or plan of organization which disregards grade-level designations and expectations. Such a plan places children in flexible groups and allows each child to progress at his own optimum rate. It avoids gaps in learning and unnecessary repetition. Some educators believe that its object is to make possible a broader scope of education by providing a framework within which to "cultivate the higher mental processes, develop the unique potentialities of the individual, [and] stimulate creative inquiry."[1] In the mind of many educators it has much value for mental health practices.

The ungraded primary unit usually works in this way: Children beyond kindergarten age but below fourth grade are grouped together in classes without the use of the labels "first grade," "second grade," or "third grade." The words "Miss Jones, Primary" appear on the teacher's door, and "Billy Smith, Primary" on the pupil's record. A child remains in a group for two or three years—possibly longer—where he has, in the main, the same kinds of experiences and lessons he would have in a regular first-, second-, and third-grade class where provisions are made for individual differences. He masters skills and gains understanding, appreciation, and attitudes appropriate to his age at his own rate, with time for satisfaction and thoroughness in his work before moving on to other tasks. In some instances the same teacher teaches a group over the two- or three-year period, with the advantage that she gets to know her pupils and can offer them more guidance and help. In others, the teacher works with a different group each year. The administrative organization of the unit does not change, however, when the teacher changes.

Reprinted from *School Life,* 44:9-12, March, 1962.
1.   John I. Goodlad. *The Encyclopedia of Educational Research,* New York: The Macmillan Co., 1960, p. 222.

Though most nongrading is in the primary grades, a few schools are extending nongrading to the middle years.

According to its proponents, the philosophy which underlies the primary unit encourages the maximum development and accomplishment of every child. Both the child and the teacher work best and accomplish most, they say, when tensions arising from unrealistic pressures and the threat of failure are removed. They believe the plan to be based on sound research which does show wide differences among children—differences in potentials, achievement, personality, motivation, and rates of growth—differences that defy the efforts of teachers to apply grade standards to any group of children at a given time. For them flexible grouping allows the child to progress in accordance with his potentials, assets, and rate of growth. He may be grouped within his class according to his achievement in a subject, his interests in a problem, or his need for a skill; or he may work individually in a subject like reading.

Though the plan is a way of putting into practice a philosophy that values progress and success for the individual child, "it is not an attempt to sell the public on an easy school."[2] Nor does it ignore the essential place of challenging solid work. Goodlad and Anderson take the position that the school they advocate, though adapted to the needs and tempo of children, must provide for trial and error since each pupil needs the opportunity "to encounter failure at little more than the price he would pay for success."[3] They add that failure at something the child might achieve under different circumstances, rather than at something impossible for him, may serve as a healthy stimulant. It may lead him to a realistic idea of himself and a wholesome attitude toward work.

Whatever term a school system uses to refer to the unit—whether primary unit, nongraded primary school, continuous progress plan, primary cycle, or another—all plans tend to embody these basic features:

1. They put into practice a philosophy that values each child as a person in his own right.
2. They eliminate grade names and all they stand for.
3. They facilitate the continuous progress of a child and attempt to offer him appropriate sequences of learning at his own rate.
4. They eliminate nonpromotion.
5. They place children in flexible groupings to promote their development in the best way.
6. They require the understanding and support of both teachers and parents.

2. Albert Brinkman. Now it's the ungraded school. *The PTA,* No. 10, 55:24-26, June, 1961.
3. John I. Goodlad and Robert H. Anderson. *The Nongraded Elementary School,* New York: Harcourt, Brace & Co., 1959, p. 158.

Although a few schools experimented with the nongraded primary unit as early as the 1920's, its major development has taken place since 1940. Milwaukee, the first major city to establish a successful ungraded primary organization, began using the plan in 1942. Appleton, Wis., changed in 1947; Coffee County, Ga., in 1950. The plan has continued to spread in the last decade. Goodlad concludes that there were several hundred nongraded schools in 40 to 50 communities during the school year 1957-58;[4] he estimates that in 1961 at least 500 schools had eliminated grade labels, "most frequently at primary levels, but occasionally throughout the entire elementary unit,"[5] and that in 1962 there may be 1,000 nongraded schools in the United States.[6] Dean found that the nongraded primary unit had been adopted by 18 per cent of the more than 4,000 schools in urban places (population 2,500 or more) he studied in October 1958—January 1959 and that it was in use in all sections of the country and in all population groups studied.[7] Downs (1962) says that only a small percentage of elementary schools were experimenting with it in 1955, but "now the movement is spreading widely."[8]

Reports from school systems using the ungraded primary unit indicate that they were strongly influenced by two things to change from conventional organization to the unit. One is the extensive research on the effects of nonpromotion, particularly its incidence and ineffectiveness in stimulating achievement. The other is the growing realization among educators of the meaning of individual differences among children.

Some schools have based their decision to change on research within the school system itself. In Appleton, for instance, professional groups and parents decided to adopt the "continuous progress plan" because they had studied the effects of nonpromotion in the local schools.

Once the school system decides to adopt the nongraded unit, one of the most important problems facing it is how to group the children. As we have seen, the usual practice is to place children beyond kindergarten age but below fourth grade in class groups without grade labels; but practice varies

4. Goodlad, *op. cit.,* p. 55.
5. John I. Goodlad. Promising practices in nongraded schools. *Education Digest,* No. 2, Vol. 27, October, 1961.
6. John I. Goodlad. Individual differences and vertical organization of the school. *Individualizing Instruction,* Sixty-first Yearbook of the National Society for the Study of Education, Chicago: University of Chicago Press, 1962, p. 228.
7. Stuart E. Dean. *Elementary School Administration and Organization,* U.S. Office of Education, Washington, D.C.: U.S. Government Printing Office, 1960, pp. 24-27 (OE-23006).
8. Miley E. Downs. The ungraded primary school. *School and Community,* No. 6, 46:22, February, 1962.

among school systems. Milwaukee sees the unit as a plan whereby children of similar chronological ages and social-emotional maturity are kept together when administratively feasible.[9] In Appleton, school officials point out that one of the richest possibilities for better education is found in groupings that bring children of varied ages together in the same room. "When Appleton completely solves this problem [how to mix children of different ages], it will have broken the chronological lockstep completely."[10] The nongraded primary unit of the Englewood Elementary School in Sarasota County, Fla., has evolved from a single grade to a multigrade class-grouping pattern; from a multigrade pattern to a multiage.

Some school systems rely in varying degrees on reading achievement, expressed by a series of reading levels, as an important basis for assigning children to class groups. In one, reading readiness is the main basis of assignment, though groups are otherwise fairly heterogeneous.

On the other hand, schools in Lincoln County (Ky.), Coffee County (Ga.), and Appleton are among those that do not rely primarily on reading achievement as the basis for assigning children to class groups. By broadening the base they have avoided the danger of equating reading levels with grade-level hurdles. Lincoln County groups its pupils on the basis of social and learning maturity. No child is placed in a group he is too old or too young for; thus no child can feel either superior or inferior on this score and no teacher has too wide a range of abilities to cope with.[11]

One of the characteristics of flexible grouping is the practice of changing a child to a different primary-class group when necessary. Some schools transfer pupils at irregular intervals. Appleton, for example, emphasizes the point that a child may be shifted to a different class at any time, except at the end of the year, when shifting might be associated with promotion and non-promotion.[12] Some, however, transfer pupils at the end of the year.

Another characteristic of the nongraded primary unit is its effect on the curriculum. Although nongrading is essentially an administrative plan, to put it into practice necessitates viewing the curriculum as an unbroken though irregular continuum of learning for the child. What the nongraded unit does over and above graded classes is to emphasize continuity and bring freedom

9. Conference with Florence Kelly, director, primary education, Milwaukee schools, March, 1959.

10. Arthur D. Morse. *Schools of Tomorrow—Today,* New York: Doubleday and Co., Inc., 1960, p. 38.

11. Continuous growth plan comes to Lincoln County. Mimeo. Lincoln County (Ky.) schools, 1960.

12. Conference with Martha Sorensen, director, elementary education, Appleton schools, March, 1959.

to the teacher to work creatively. She and her pupils are free to use books and other materials regardless of the grade levels indicated on them. The teacher can, for instance, in developing the idea *that people communicate in various ways,* use subject matter appropriate for a given group of children according to their maturity, interests, and the resources available to her and to the children. Nongrading presents the teacher with opportunities for developing a curriculum program suited to the needs and interests of the children she is teaching. It does not hold her to a rigid plan or a rigid time schedule, but rather it may help her make a program with ever-increasing depth and scope. More then would be provided through nongrading than mere variations in rates of pupil progress.

Since progress is an essential aspect of the plan, to evaluate the child's achievement the teacher compares it with his former record. One school system maintains a four-page folder skill card on each child which charts his academic progress. The card lists skills to be mastered during the six years of primary and intermediate school, but indicates no target dates. The teacher enters the date a skill is introduced and the date the child masters it. The card is passed from teacher to teacher as a record of the pupil's progress.[13] At the end of the year the child takes home a report of his attainments that makes no mention of a grade assignment for the next year. At the end of his year in kindergarten and at the end of each subsequent year until he is ready for the fourth grade, the Park Forest child receives a slip assigning him to "primary school."[14] Schools use somewhat different ways of reporting pupil progress to parents, although they have moved from report cards focused on the expectancies of single grade levels expressed by figures and letters. Many hold conferences with parents or issue comment or checklist types of written reports.

An important part of the changeover from graded classes to a primary unit is the transition from report cards focused on what is expected in a single grade to other forms of reporting, such as parent conferences. Accomplishing this changeover may bring into focus not only methods of reporting progress to parents, but the whole issue of school-home relations by involving study groups and parent participation. In some instances the process of ungrading has brought groups of teachers and parents together to work on problems of grouping, curriculum development, uses of materials and community resources, human development, and evaluation of learning.

It is not easy to adopt and operate a nongraded unit. School officials have

---

13. Morse, *op. cit.,* p. 33.
14. Goodlad and Anderson, *op. cit.,* p. 72.

found it wise to make the change slowly—only after a year or more of professional study on the part of the staff and after parents have been brought into a study of the possibilities. Some administrators have begun with a few teachers in a school, who, believing in its philosophy, have tried the program on an experimental basis. In one school system the elementary principals who were studying the plan divided themselves into three groups, one composed of those who had already adopted the plan, one of those planning to try it the following year, and the third of those who were not planning to try it immediately.[15] In another school system, the committee studying the plan includes representation from the high school and PTA groups, as well as the elementary-school staff. Frequently, only one school in a district will try it to start with, usually beginning with the year beyond the kindergarten only. The second year it will add an additional unit, the third year another, and so on. If the plan proves successful, other schools may start a unit.

Some administrators suggest initiating the plan only after a reasonable variety of trade books and reference materials, in addition to textbooks, are available to the staff. It appears, however, that once nongrading has been accomplished, it brings about a demand from teachers for more materials to enrich and advance the education of children to meet their individual needs.

Certain warnings have been sounded about the primary unit. Stendler observes that level standards can be as rigid as those of grade standards, and she questions "whether substituting three levels a grade for the old single grade is much of an improvement."[16] Similarly, Frazier, in commenting on some of the plans for individualizing teaching, notes that the ungraded school becomes a school of many levels and warns that the criterion of "how much can be covered how quickly" carries "the old conception of the curriculum to a new point of impoverishment."[17] Goodlad notes also that many plans are "more graded than the graded schemes they presumably replaced" and warns against equating coverage with education.[18] Perkins finds that in most nongraded schools instruction is individualized only in reading and suggests that pacing of instruction in other areas is overdue.[19]

15. Conference with Virginia Benson, director, elementary education, Fairfax County (Va.) schools, July, 1961.
16. Celia Stendler. Grouping practices, those first school years. *National Elementary School Principal*, No. 1, *40*:158, September, 1960.
17. Alexander Frazier. Needed: a new vocabulary for individual differences. *Elementary School Journal*, No. 5, *61*:260-63, February, 1961.
18. John I. Goodlad. Individual differences and vertical organization of the school. *Individualized Instruction*, Sixty-first Yearbook of the National Society for the Study of Education, Chicago: University of Chicago Press, 1962, p. 235.
19. Hugh V. Perkins. Nongraded programs: what progress? *Educational Leadership*, No. 3, *19*:169. December, 1961.

A teacher in Milwaukee who works with children in a nongraded school summarizes some of the advantages and problems that result from the use of the unit:

> The ungraded primary is made for children. Its flexibility allows the child to progress at his own rate. The child competes with himself. It is possible for all children to have the satisfaction of continuous progress.
>
> The hurdles of arbitrary grade and achievement levels are removed. The child can relax and grow, free of the psychological upsets caused by a too rigid grade structure. Since there is a great variety in the rate and time of development of children at this age level, this flexibility is very important.
>
> The pitfalls . . . seem to arise out of misunderstandings, most of which result in an attempt to bring all the evils of the traditional graded primary school into the ungraded.[20]

The primary unit, in short, is an administrative device which some educators are using to put into practice a democratic philosophy that values the individual child. So used, it may prove to be a means of improving guidance, learning opportunities, and parent participation.

Before we can say much about the merits of the nongraded primary unit we need research that will furnish us the facts on which to assess the outcome of nongrading. Studies of organizational patterns and practices, of the reactions of pupils, teachers, and parents are generally favorable to the practice. Some local school systems—Flint, Milwaukee, and Appleton among others—have found from tests that children's achievement definitely favors the nongraded school. But a number of questions must be answered before we can evaluate the unit:

1. How does nongrading in the primary unit affect the curriculum and the nature of the learning environment; the ideas, behavior, and skills the child is acquiring; the use of materials and other resources; evaluate techniques used; parent participation?

2. How does nongrading affect the teachers concerned—their relations with children and parents; their skill in grouping, regrouping, and working with individual children; their professional relations with their peers; their satisfaction in teaching?

3. How does nongrading affect the child—his academic progress; his relations with his peers; his self-concept; his thinking, inquiry, work habits, values, and creative efforts?

20. Alan T. Wilson. The ungraded primary school. *American Teacher,* No. 3, *43:*5-6, February, 1959.

Administrators and their staffs should carefully consider the meaning of individual differences among children for the total school program and policies before changing from a graded to a nongraded structure. Such study requires time, it requires the cooperation of parents. A change to the non-graded unit should only follow a growing dissatisfaction with the old organization and a belief that the old way is a hindrance to the progress of children. When dissatisfaction does exist, teachers should make penetrating studies on grouping children, planning more appropriate curriculum sequences, working with parents, and learning better ways of appraising the learning and behavior of children. Effort should focus not on a narrow curriculum through which children move at differing paces, but on the broadest and most significant program possible.

CHAPTER 25

What Can Schools Do About Prejudice, Intergroup Education, and Integration?

SOCIAL SCIENTISTS tell us of the many ways culture shapes the individual personality. Before children come to school they have been taught many of the values of their families and of other groups in society. The children have caught a whiff of general cultural values. They have learned whom to revere and whom it is permissible to hate.

In the 1960's we face the issue of equal educational opportunities for all American children. What role does each of us play as a citizen with regard to the problem of prejudice? What role does each of us play as a teacher? Realizing that our own feelings are involved in prejudice, we must be intellectually informed about the nature of prejudice and constructive educational programs to combat it.

107 *Intergroup education in the public schools*

ROLF MUUSS

CELIA BURNS STENDLER

This article presents data on cultural and personality factors influencing the development of prejudice in children. The authors conclude by discussing how some of the practical implications of their findings can be applied to the school program.

AWARENESS of the existence of prejudice in children is not a new phenomenon among educators. Over thirty-five years ago Lasker published an extensive collection of anecdotal records showing children's awareness of group differences.[1] Subsequently many more research reports have clearly indicated that prejudice does not spring full-blown into being in adulthood but that intergroup attitudes are shaped during the childhood years. Furthermore, it has also been clearly demonstrated by research that the process of attitude-formation can be studied scientifically and that knowledge concerning attitude change can be used to replace negative attitudes with positive ones.

American public schools hold as one of their goals the training of citizens for a democracy. Educators generally accept the position that our schools should give students an education that will equip them to live, not in a fascist society, not in a police state, not in an anarchy, not in an elite society, but in a society founded upon democratic principles. Basic to this position is the belief in the supreme worth of the individual and the right of that individual to achieve the richest fullest life regardless of race, religion, nationality background, or social class membership.

During the past quarter of a century research findings have indicated the existence of prejudice toward minority groups which runs counter to our democratic principle. Not only prejudiced attitudes but prejudiced actions exist, which keep people from living in decent housing, having a decent education, holding a decent job, enjoying equal opportunity in respect to recreational facilities and having proper medical care. All of these are in direct contradiction to our belief in the supreme worth of every individual.

Reprinted from *The Educational Forum, 20:*151-64, January, 1956. Used by permission of Kappa Delta Pi, owners of the copyright.

1. Bruno Lasker. *Race Attitudes in Children,* New York: Henry Holt & Co., Inc., 1929.

By no means have all teachers been persuaded that building desirable intergroup attitudes should be their professional responsibility. Perhaps teachers might be roughly grouped as follows:

1. Teachers who themselves are prejudiced. It is unfortunate but true that many teachers share the prejudiced attitudes that exist in our society. In our midwestern community—ironically enough the larger of two communities where one of the biggest state universities in the country is located—a powerful group of teachers succeeded in blocking a move to hire a Negro teacher to teach in white schools. Such teachers we hope are in the minority but they do exist.

2. Teachers who believe the community doesn't need intergroup education. Some teachers equate the need for intergroup education with the existence of group tensions in the community. Mr. X, for example, who teaches in a bedroom community of Chicago doesn't see why intergroup education is necessary for his upper-middle-class pupils; they never come in contact with children from minority groups. Intergroup education is all right for places where there are race riots or bad feelings, says he, but not for his school. Mr. X's pupils, however, are Americans, not inhabitants of a desert isle, and as Americans should be concerned with the problem of squaring our practices with democratic ideals.

3. Teachers who think the community is not ready for intergroup education. Mr. Y has expressed himself in favor of intergroup education but only when the community "is ready." He is loathe to mention Hanukkah and Passover at Christmas and Easter, for example, because some parents might object. He does not see that teachers can be a force in making a community "ready" for intergroup education.

4. Teachers who are men of good will but who lack knowledge of how attitudes are formed and changed and so use inefficient techniques. These are teachers who think that if only pupils of different races could attend the same schools, we would have no problems. Or they may try having their eighth-grade boys play the parochial school team in order to build better attitudes. Such teachers have hearts in the right place but they lack knowledge of the research in this area.

5. Teachers who are cognizant of what has been tried in intergroup education and who utilize the best of present knowledge. These are teachers with a sound grasp of how attitudes are formed and changed, insofar as this knowledge is available to us.

6. Teachers who are in the forefront of intergroup education and who

are interested in experimenting with new ways of building desirable attitudes.

Primarily this paper is beamed at readers in Groups 4 and 5. Those in Groups 1, 2, and 3 probably are not readers of this journal and for those in Group 6 it will serve only as reinforcement of what they already know. To those in education who might benefit by a review of research related to the formation and changing of attitudes we direct our efforts.

I. THE ORIGIN OF ATTITUDES (PREJUDICES)

Since attitudes in general as well as attitudes toward racial and religious groups in particular are not innate but acquired, they can be influenced and shaped. This means that they can be influenced in both directions, toward inequality, hatred, and destruction as well as toward equality, understanding, and co-operation. One of the basic principles on which this study is based is that attitudes are complex psychological phenomena and cannot be explained or understood by one single factor. It will be shown that they must be considered as the product of multiple causation.

Many recent investigations have dealt with such questions as: "Why does a person become prejudiced?" "How does prejudice develop?" "What needs do prejudiced attitudes serve?" One of the dramatic changes that these investigations have brought about in regard to the traditional concept of group prejudice is that group prejudice is no longer considered as an objective manifestation of the qualities which Negroes, Jews, Indians, or Mexicans have but that the reason for a prejudiced attitude has to be found either in the prejudiced person himself or in environmental factors that influence the prejudiced person. Bettelheim and Janowitz conclude that intolerance is less a function of the object social situation than of one's personal evaluation of that situation.[2] Horowitz says that attitudes are chiefly determined not by contact with Negroes, but by contact with the prevalent attitude toward Negroes.[3] Minorities or out-groups develop certain characteristics and prejudices as a defense against discrimination or because of the limitations imposed upon them. However we will be concerned in this study with the prejudices of the majority or in-group, with the factors that cause these prejudices, and with the variables related to prejudice and its development.

There are two general theories by which the origin of prejudice can be explained: first, learning theory and secondly, scapegoat theory.

2. Bruno Bettelheim and Morris Janowitz. *Dynamics of Prejudice,* New York: Harper & Brothers, 1950.
3. Eugene L. Horowitz. Development of attitudes toward Negroes. *Readings in Social Psychology,* Newcomb & Hartley (eds.), New York: Henry Holt & Co., 1947.

1. Learning theory

There is little doubt that the child while growing up, accepts, imitates and adopts the attitudes, values, ideas, and the behavior of his parents. From early childhood, social facts, particularly the feelings of belongingness to certain groups, are among the most fundamental constituents of this growing world, and determine what the individual considers right or wrong, his wishes and goals.[4] The acquisition of prejudice is usually gradual and closely related to the total socialization process. The child incorporates his ethnic value schemes and his race attitudes in much the same way in which he learns his other social lessons—from significant adults, such as his parents, from his peers, and from the incontestable facts of life itself.[5] The separation of the living quarters in some towns, the segregation in schools, and the distinction in seating in buses and trains are all learning situations that do not need further interpretation.

Other media such as propaganda, indoctrination and habituation operate also under the principle of the learning theory and are of importance for children as well as for adults. Skillfully directed propaganda can "educate" prejudice, but even "harmless" movies can—more or less purposefully—influence people in their attitude because of the high degree of ego-involvement.

2. Scapegoat theory

The scapegoat theory has been used to explain a subconscious psychological process. It is based on the assumption that being prejudiced fulfills underlying personality needs. Group prejudice, like any other hostility, is a reaction not to an external stimulus, but to an internal process—frustration.[6] The sources of frustration can be manifold, such as tensions, insecurities, economic difficulties, dominating parents, or an autocratic group which needs the scapegoat as a means of distracting the masses.[7] The accumulation of frustrating experiences generates aggression and hostility. Since society does not permit an open expression of aggression and hostility against parents and other authorities, these feelings have to be repressed. Therefore the latent aggression is directed against minority or out-groups in the form of culturally accepted

4.   Daniel J. Levinson. An approach to the theory and measurement of ethnocentric ideology. *Journal of Psychology, 28*:19-39, July, 1949.
5.   Marc Vosk. Correlates of prejudice. *Review of Educational Research, 23*:353-64, 1953.
6.   Nancy C. Morse and Floyd H. Allport. The causation of anti-semitism: an investigation of seven hypotheses. *Journal of Psychology, 34*:197-233, October, 1952.
7.   Kurt Lewin. *Resolving Social Conflicts,* New York: Harper & Brothers, 1948.

prejudices toward these groups.[8] Minority groups are a preferable outlet for aggression because they are weak, defenseless, and sometimes even dependent on the majority group. The unacceptable hostility which could not be expressed finds a definite object through the process of displacement. In order to justify the hostility toward the minority group convincing negative attributes which show that the minority group deserves hatred and hostility have to be found. This is done by projecting anxiety, feelings of guilt, aggression, and other unacceptable traits of the majority group into the minority group. This irrational behavior is rationalized through the use of stereotypes. Stereotyping allows the prejudiced one to treat all members of the minority group alike and ascribe to them irrational qualities such as "Negroes are aggressive," "Indians are lazy," "Germans are stubborn," "Jews are shrewd," and "Americans are sloppy." The choice of the scapegoat can be explained partly by historical factors, partly by cultural traditions, and partly by religious differences.

There seems to be sufficient evidence that both theories apply to practical situations and have to be regarded as sources that create prejudice against minority groups. Because learned prejudices are not deeply rooted they can be changed easily, while prejudices that fulfill psychological needs in a frustrated person are deep-seated and are therefore difficult to change.

II. VARIABLES THAT INFLUENCE THE FORMULATION OF ATTITUDES

Ethnic attitudes do not exist in isolation; they are an integrated part of attitudes in general and are interrelated to the whole personality and its environment. The knowledge of these variables that are found to be related to prejudice will be valuable if we intend to change ethnic attitudes. We will be concerned here with the influence of these variables and will postpone consideration of methods of change to the latter part of this article.

1. The child accepts adult attitudes toward the group

While we have already said that attitudes are learned, we have to add here that the child also absorbs "unconscious" teaching from adults because in many families racial problems are "taboo," and no verbal teaching takes place. Even in that case the child would absorb the attitudes of the parents; for example, the expression on a mother's face when she encounters a member of a minority group, especially if it is a repeated experience, will affect the child. Adult values and interpretations of the social world play a considerably

8.   Paul H. Mussen. Some personality and social factors related to children's attitudes toward Negroes. *Journal of Abnormal and Social Psychology*, 45:423-41, July, 1950.

more prominent role than do interpersonal experiences of the child with members of any of the out-groups.[9]

2. *Authoritarian climate at home creates prejudice in children*

While the theory is generally accepted that children learn their ethnic attitudes from their parents, there is no one-to-one relationship between parents' and children's attitudes, as Harris, Gough and Martin have shown.[10] They found that the ethnic attitude of the child is significantly related to the practice of the mother in child rearing and her attitude toward children. The authoritarian parents who believe in rigid discipline raise prejudiced children even if they themselves are not prejudiced. It would seem that prejudice in children is not so much a result of imitation as it is a reaction to a complex of parental attitudes which are involved in authoritarian child rearing but in which prejudice may or may not be present.[11]

3. *Socioeconomic status*

Socioeconomic status has been considered as one variable that is related to prejudice. It is generally believed that Protestants with lower socioeconomic status are highly prejudiced. Nevertheless there is no complete agreement among researchers on this fact. Watson found that economic difficulties are related to prejudice against the out-group.[12] Bettelheim and Janowitz say that the socioeconomic status per se is not related to prejudice, but that downward social mobility is correlated with increase in prejudice.[13] A study made by Campbell showed that dissatisfaction with personal economic circumstances is highly correlated with hostility toward Jews.[14] Lewin claims that need of the majority for a scapegoat grows out of an economic depression.[15] It has also been shown that the social distance between colored and white people both with low socioeconomic status is much larger than that between people of high socioeconomic status.

9.   Marian J. Radke *et al.* Social perceptions and attitudes of children. *Genetic Psychology Monographs, 40:*327-447, 1949.
10.   Dale B. Harris *et al.* Children's ethnic attitudes: II. Relation to certain personality factors. *Child Development, 21:*169-81, 1950.
11.   *Ibid.*
12.   Jeanne Watson. Some social and psychological situations related to change in attitude. *Human Relations, 3:*15-56, 1950.
13.   Bettelheim and Janowitz, *op. cit.*
14.   Angus A. Campbell. Factors associated with attitudes toward Jews. *Readings in Social Psychology,* Newcomb & Hartley (eds.), New York: Henry Holt & Co., 1947.
15.   Lewin, *op. cit.*

4. Education

Education, which is, generally speaking, related to income, is also related to prejudice. Levinson reported a low but significant negative relationship between education, intelligence level, and prejudice.[16] The evidence of national opinion polls indicates that a higher education level is generally associated with lower prejudice, according to Rose.[17] Campbell on the contrary claims that unfriendliness toward Jews is positively related to the extent of education but his study is limited to Jews only.[18]

The evidence points to the fact that both low income and low education are associated with greater prejudice.

5. Contact with out-group

The influence of contact with the out-group as a factor in the formation of prejudice has been studied extensively. The findings show that the contact itself is not as important as the circumstances under which it occurs and the socioeconomic status of the out-group with whom contact takes place. Favorable or frequent contact or experience with members of minority groups, especially in childhood, as well as contact with equal or higher status level individuals acts as a barrier to the development of prejudice.[19] The study of the opinion about Negro infantry platoons in white companies by the U.S. War Department shows that positive attitudes toward minority groups are held by those people who had close contact on an equal basis with Negroes.[20] However, contact alone does not determine whether prejudice will exist. Campbell's study, which was mentioned before, says that people who had no contact with Jews seldom expressed hostility toward them. People who had considerable contact were no more apt to indicate dislike of Jews than people who had occasional contact.[21] The study by Rosenblith shows on the contrary that students in South Dakota who had little or no contact with Jews and Negroes had a higher prejudice score than those obtained by Allport and Kramer at Harvard, Radcliffe, and Dartmouth.[22]

16. Levinson, *op. cit.*
17. Arnold Rose. *Studies in Reeducation of Prejudice,* 2nd ed.; Chicago: American Council on Race Relations, 1948.
18. Campbell, *op. cit.*
19. Vosk, *op. cit.*
20. U.S. War Department Information and Education Division. Opinions about Negro infantry platoons in white companies of seven divisions. *Readings in Social Psychology,* 1947.
21. Campbell, *op. cit.*
22. Judy F. Rosenblith. A replication of some roots of prejudice. *Journal of Abnormal and Social Psychology, 44:*470-89, 1949.

There is far-reaching agreement among researchers that situations involving cooperation on equal status will reduce prejudice. While contact with the out-group definitely has an influence on the formation of attitudes, the amount and the direction is determined by other variables such as socioeconomic status, whether both groups have equal status, whether experience is favorable or unfavorable, degree of intimacy and the personality structure of the involved person.

6. Group and family factors

Group membership has a definite influence on ethnic values and attitudes because it is related to the child's basic need for acceptance.[23] Lewin and Grabbe termed group-belongingness the outstanding way through which an individual accepts new systems of values and beliefs.[24] The labor union in general has operated against discrimination while the Ku Klux Klan has encouraged and practiced rather severe forms of discrimination. Since certain groups and organizations have taken a definite stand in favor or in opposition to discrimination most of their members will have quite similar attitudes. This can even be extended to a nation as a group, since it can be observed in history that extreme nationalism is usually accompanied by strong prejudices that might even lead to persecution. Morse and Allport found that the individual's sense of national involvement (nationalism) is by far the most important factor associated with anti-semitism.[25]

The most important group for a child is the family. Research has stressed again and again the importance of a wholesome family atmosphere at home, which reduces tension and provides security and love. It has also been shown that many of the prejudiced children come from broken homes, or from families where conflicts and tension between the parents are common. Few extreme ethnocentric children have had sufficient love and affection in their childhood. In a study of forty cases of anti-semitism not a single person was found whose parents had had a permanently well-adjusted marital relationship.[26]

7. Regional differences

Regional differences are generally well known to be related to prejudice. The Mason and Dixon Line is considered the dividing line between the South

23. Radke *et al., op. cit.*
24. Kurt Lewin and Paul Grabbe. Conduct, knowledge and acceptance of new values. *Journal of Social Issues, 1*:53-64, 1945.
25. Morse and Allport, *op. cit.*
26. William Van Til and George Denemark. Intercultural education. *Review of Educational Research, 21*:274-86, 1950.

and the North and such expressions as "the deep South" have connotations of prejudice. However, the studies that have been made, even though they are not so comprehensive that they allow a general conclusion, showed that boys tested in regard to their attitudes toward Negroes in Tennessee and Georgia showed no more prejudice than those tested in New York.[27] Rosenblith found a high total score of prejudice in South Dakota.

8. Historical factors

Historical factors and regional differences are closely interwoven. The facts that the Negroes were brought as slaves to this country and that the end of slavery was one of the issues in the Civil War do influence attitudes of many people.

III. PERSONALITY FACTORS ASSOCIATED WITH PREJUDICE

In studying prejudiced persons a number of related attitudes and values have been found, which permit us to talk about a prejudiced personality. The archetype of the prejudiced person is the "authoritarian personality." A number of recent studies have dealt with the authoritarian personality. Even though authoritarianism is an ideological concept it has been found to stand in close relationship to personality. The correlation between ethnocentrism and authoritarianism was found to be $r = 0.73$, which is very high. The more authoritarian the personality structure, the greater the acceptance of ethnocentrism.[28]

Authoritarians are often rigid conformists who dislike differences from socially approved norms but favor discipline. They divide the social world into in-groups and out-groups of which the first are "good" while the latter are perceived as "bad" and they appear to be puritanical moralists for whom sex roles are distinctly defined; they worship strength and power but despise intellectualism and weakness; they lack insight into their own inner life and motivation and perceive the world as a threat.

Mussen reports that boys who were high in prejudice have more aggressive and dominance needs, more hostility toward their parents, than boys who were low in prejudice.[29]

Other terms, such as fundamental conservative, distrustful, hostile, resentful, nationalistic, suspicious, cynical, fearful, submissive, less confident,

27. Horowitz, *op. cit.*
28. Richard Christie and John Garcia. Subcultural variation in authoritarian personality. *Journal of Abnormal and Social Psychology,* 46:457-69, October, 1951.
29. Mussen, *op. cit.*

insecure, more complaining, more pessimistic, more prone to feelings of victimization, and tendencies to conformity have been used in recent studies to describe the prejudiced personality.[30]

Nevertheless, it must be emphasized that personality factors alone are not sufficient to explain why people discriminate against certain minority groups nor why prejudices are stronger against one group than against another.[31] While most authoritarians are prejudiced, not all are prejudiced; on the other hand there are some nonauthoritarians who are prejudiced. It is also reported that adult authoritarians breed (socially speaking) child authoritarians.[32]

The study on the characteristics of the prejudiced personality has been extended to children by Frenkel-Brunswik because origin and development of these attitudes should be found in children.[33] The goal of her study was to show what factors influence and what factors can be found together with racial or ethnic prejudice and similar forms of undemocratic attitudes in children. In her study of 120 children from ages 11 to 16 the following factors were found to be associated with prejudiced children:

1. Ethnocentric children tend to show a stereotyped, rigid, and glorified concept of the self and the in-group to the extent of national chauvinism and a rejection of minority and out-groups to the extent of open aggression and hostility; e.g., they often would disagree with the following statement: "Different races and religions would get along better if they visited each other and shared things."

2. The liberal child can more easily remove himself from immediate needs and think in terms of far-reaching social and national good, while the prejudiced child is more concerned with himself and his surroundings; e.g., for the liberal child the biggest problem today is "The atomic bomb"; for the prejudiced child, "Taxes on everything" or "The cost of living is too high."

3. The ethnocentric child rejects all that is weak or different; e.g., they frequently agree with the following statement: "The world would be perfect if we put on a desert island all of the weak, crooked, and feeble-minded people."

4. The rejection of the weak is related to the admiration of the strong,

30. Dale B. Harris *et al.* Children's ethnic attitudes: I. Relationship to certain personality factors. *Child Development,* 21:169-81, 1950. Christie and Garcia, *op. cit.;* Vosk, *op. cit.*
31. Vosk, *op. cit.*
32. M. Radke and J. Sutherland. Children's concepts and attitudes about minority and majority groups. *Journal of Educational Psychology, 40:*449-68, 1949.
33. Else Frenkel-Brunswik. A study of prejudice in children. *Human Relations, 1:* 295-306, 1948.

tough, and powerful, as well as to money, which is admired as something important but also feared as something evil. They often agree with the following statements: "Might makes right; the strong win out in the end," or "A person who wants to be a man should seek power."

5. There is an emphasis on the dichotomy of sex roles in the ethnocentric child; the opposite sex is perceived as an out-group. They tend to agree with the statement: "Girls should only learn things that are useful in the house."

6. Admiration for success, power, and prestige may be assumed to result from submission to authority based on fear of punishment and retaliation; e.g., the ethnocentric agrees more frequently than the liberal child with the statement: "Teachers should tell children what to do and not try to find out what the children want."

7. The parents of the prejudiced child show an exaggerated concern with social status, they favor rigid rules and discipline, while the liberal child is brought up on an equalitarian basis.

8. The ethnocentric child expects—and gives—social approval on the basis of external moral values, including cleanliness and politeness. He has a strong urge to conformity and dislikes nonconformists, as expressed in the statement, "There is only one right way to do anything."

9. The prejudiced child is intolerant, inflexible, rigid, and incapable of facing ambiguous situations.
10. He has a more fearful and catastrophic conception of the world and is more superstitious than the liberal child.

Frenkel-Brunswik concludes that the personality structure of the ethnocentric child is quite similar to that of the ethnocentric adult, the difference essentially being that the ethnocentric child is still more flexible and changeable than the adult who has become quite rigid and inflexible.

In general, children react more like the ethnocentric adult than like the liberal adult. Therefore, the ethnocentric adult might be considered more infantile than the liberal adult. The difference between the ethnocentric child and the liberal child increases with age. There is some indication that ethnocentrism is a natural stage of development which should be overcome if maturity is to be reached.

IV. THE DEVELOPMENT OF CHILDREN'S ATTITUDES

The development of ethnic attitudes is, as has been said before, a continuous, gradual process. Before a child is able to have an attitude he must have learned to distinguish in the first place between one person and another person such as his mother and his father and later between one group and another group, such as Negroes and Whites. The child develops the ability to differentiate as his age increases. In the Philadelphia Study, all the children were able to distinguish between Negroes and Whites.[34] But a fifth of the white and half of the Negro children were unable to identify "Catholic" and "Jew." Sixty per cent of the white and 90 per cent of the Negro children did not know what "Protestant" meant.

Negative attitudes toward minority groups increase as the child grows older, so that it is generally true to say the lower the school grade the lower the percentage of children who have developed definite prejudices. Nevertheless, there is fairly general agreement that many children develop very early some preference for the in-group. Some few attempts at testing special cases at three and four years of age elicited such comments as (from a three-year-old) "I don't like black boys," and (from a four-year-old) "I don't like colored boys."[35] Twenty-four per cent of Goodman's 103 four-year-olds manifested "high awareness" of race.[36]

The progressive increase of negative attitudes toward minority groups with age was also observed by Radke and Sutherland.[37] The proportion of negative attitudes toward one or both minority groups by grade level was: Grades 5-6, 46 per cent; Grades 7-8, 53 per cent; Grades 9-10, 68 per cent; Grades 11-12, 68 per cent. Rejecting both minorities at the same level were 17 per cent, 33 per cent, 48 per cent and 60 per cent.

Ammons showed in another study with younger children to what extent they were able to differentiate skin color and facial features in a projective situation.[38] He worked with preschool children from the age of two up with ten children of each age group. The results showed that 60 per cent of the whole group were able to identify skin color and facial differences between the white, brown, and black dolls, including two of the two-year-olds and five of the three-year-olds. One of the ten four-year-olds and four of the ten five-year-olds made responses definitely evidencing negative feeling toward the Negro doll. The four- and five-year-olds showed scapegoating reactions toward the Negro doll.

Therefore, we can conclude that many children can and do discriminate

---

34. Radke *et al., op. cit.*
35. Horowitz, *op. cit.*
36. Vosk, *op. cit.*
37. Radke and Sutherland, *op. cit.*
38. Robert B. Ammons. Reactions in a projective doll-play interview of white males two to six years of age to differences in skin color and facial features. *Journal of Genetic Psychology,* 76:323-41, June, 1950.

between white and black skin color, some of them as early as two years of age. To the extent that they are insecure they will be ready for negative acts against children that are "different." Prejudice will probably always develop where some individuals in a group are perceptibly different from others and where there is some insecurity or tension.

Dr. Kenneth Clark, who prepared the White House Conference Report on the effects of prejudice and discrimination, made a similar statement to the effect that children are aware of racial differences as early as the age of three.

It is proposed that the young white child acquires first of all a generally unfavorable attitude toward the Negro, which makes him unwilling to attribute to the Negro any "good" traits. With increased age and experience, the child gradually learns to apply the adult stereotypes. Among the sixty terms employed the earliest ones to be applied with a high degree of agreement are "clean," "neat" and "good manners" which are applied to the white group. The opposite of these terms were not employed on the opinion test form, but they would doubtlessly have been attributed to the Negro.[39]

V. CHANGING ETHNIC ATTITUDES

Having looked at the causes of prejudice, we now turn our attention to the problem of how antidemocratic attitudes can be changed. Here the situation is much more complicated; research results abound in confusion and conflicting results.[40] Out of the confusion, however, certain basic principles with respect to changing attitudes seem to be clear. We present these to the reader as a guide to the social engineering job in which he is engaged:

1. Other things being equal, the younger the school child the more susceptible he is to change. This generalization is derived not so much from experimental work involving a comparison of change of attitude between primary-school and secondary-school children as it does from the field of human development. Studies in this area indicate that early childhood experiences are much more powerful in shaping human behavior than later ones. The reason for the importance of early experiences would seem to be this: that the child's later perceptions are likely to reinforce his earlier learnings. The first experiences of the child set up a frame of reference in terms of

39. Robert Blake and Dennis Wayne. The development of stereotypes concerning the Negro. *Journal of Abnormal and Social Psychology, 38*:525-31, April, 1943.
40. Eugene L. Hartley and Ruth E. Hartley. *Fundamentals of Social Psychology,* New York: Alfred A. Knopf, 1952.

which he evaluates subsequent experiences.[41] The child who learns early in life that Pogo-Pogans are dirty is likely to look at Pogo-Pogans with a much more critical eye than otherwise. A spot on a Pogo-Pogan's shirt will be noticed whereas a really soiled shirt on a white child will escape observation. Furthermore, finding the spot will strengthen the child's belief that all Pogo-Pogans are dirty. There is a constancy about our perceptions which arises out of the fact that we see what we are looking for. Positive attitudes can be built in children while they are still young; these are likely to grow increasingly strong as the child matures.

2. Whenever and wherever possible, a multidimensional approach using several different methods of attitude change is better than the single approach.[42] Movies, literature, contact with various ethnic groups, direct study, psychotherapeutic methods, each of these techniques may be effective with some pupils under certain conditions; a combination will reach more students. Reading about Jewish holidays may help the pupil who is merely misinformed in this area, but it may not change the attitude of his more basically prejudiced classmate. Having contact with Negro children in a summer boy's camp made some boys less prejudiced, but it strengthened the prejudices of others.[43] Because the effectiveness of any one technique is difficult to predict, a sounder approach is the multidimensional one.

Where the prejudice is deeply rooted in personality, psychotherapeutic techniques in addition to informational ones would seem to be necessary. Play therapy, role-playing, and various other procedures have been helpful in getting pupils to first express their prejudices openly and then adopt more democratic attitudes.[44]

3. On the whole, greater success is obtained when groups work on problems of common interest rather than on problems directly concerned with intergroup relations.[45] Units of work on "Negro Spirituals," "Famous Jews and Their Contribution to America" are not so effective as units on "Housing in Our Community," or "Earning a Living in Our Community" in which information relating to ethnic groups is discovered. Indeed, the special units on intergroup education may actually intensify prejudice in some children who feel themselves in competition with a minority group

41.   David C. McClelland. *Personality*, New York: William Sloan Associates, 1952.
42.   Otto Klineberg. *Tensions Affecting International Understanding*, A Survey of Research (Bulletin 62), New York: Social Science Research Council, 1950.
43.   Mussen, *op. cit.*
44.   Hartley and Hartley, *op. cit.*
45.   Klineberg, *op. cit.*

for status and who may react more negatively than before after studying "Famous Negroes in Our Society." The teacher who is convinced of the importance of intergroup education should use every opportunity and every school subject to encourage intergroup understanding. Here is an incident where a teacher used as completely unrelated a field as health to build demo-cratic attitudes:

> Miss Novak has discovered that many of her first-graders are very much afraid of visits to the doctor which involve "shots." As part of her health teaching, she plans to take some time to let the children talk out their fears and to discuss the different kinds of shots and what these do for us. She suggests that the children might like to invite a real doctor to come to class to tell them more about injections. The name she suggests is that of a Negro doctor with whom she has already been in touch. When he comes, the doctor shows the children the contents of his bag, talks with them about various injections, and answers their questions. This visit provides an opportunity for her upper-middle-class children to become acquainted with a Negro who is in a profession. Miss Novak does not tell the children in advance that the doctor is of a different race, but when this is mentioned in the discussion following Doctor Howe's visit she wel-comes the opportunity to help the children understand (1) that Negroes can, and do, work in many different occupations, and (2) that it is more difficult for Negroes than for whites to find certain kinds of work.[46]

4. Changing the group norm with respect to ethnic groups will affect the attitudes of individual members of that group. Prejudice can be made either popular or unpopular in a particular group. Where the group norm is in the direction of excluding lower-class children from some school activities, more pupils are likely to be prejudiced against lower-class children. But where it is unfashionable to snub such children, prejudiced attitudes may be changed. The junior-high-school middle-class child who holds a lower-class student's shabby gym suit high in the air and with a smirk and a holding of the nose says "Peeee——u" may be encouraged to make fun of her classmate by the delighted laughter of her peers. But if someone says "Cut it out" or "That's not funny" she is not so likely to repeat the behavior.

An important corollary of this principle has to do with the group status of the initiator of a behavior. As some investigators have pointed out, a particu-lar behavior be it good or bad is more likely to be imitated if it originates with a person who has high group status.[47] This means that teachers must give particular attention to reaching individuals who have prestige in the group.

46. Celia Burns Stendler and William E. Martin. *Intergroup Education in the Kindergarten—Primary Grades,* New York: The Macmillan Company, 1953.
47. Norman Polansky *et al.* An investigation of behavioral contagion in groups. *Human Relations,* 3:319-48, 1950.

5. The climate of the classroom will have some effect upon the strength of prejudiced and unprejudiced attitudes. Since the presence of prejudice appears to be related to the general adjustment of the individual, it is important to have the kind of atmosphere in the classroom that will help each child feel most secure. In such a climate there is not so much need to find a scapegoat. While increased feelings of security alone will not eradicate prejudice, to the extent that each child has his social needs satisfied, the tendency to find a scapegoat is lessened. In a classroom where the atmosphere is highly competitive, prejudiced attitudes may be strengthened in pupils, particularly those of low status.[48]

6. The teacher is the key person in intergroup education. Whether the classroom is on a first-grade or college level, it is the teacher who can play a large role in modifying group attitudes. Unfortunately, teachers sometimes exert an influence in a negative direction. Witness the following account of an observation of one teacher at work with children:

Teacher showing Y club pictures of "children of other lands." Teacher asks who are these children? (They are photographs of Dutch children in costume.) Y club guesses—"Russian," "German." One child says timidly "Merican?" Teacher, amused, says, "No, Americans don't look like that" (meaning costume). Quickly, another suggests, "Chinese?" Teacher shakes head "No," and prompts by suggesting, "Look at their shoes." Child goes up close to picture, holds head in hands, wags head, mocks shoes. Teacher asks, "Why would they wear such shoes?" (trying to relate geographic conditions to clothes, etc.). Children, following on "not American" theme—"I wouldn't want to wear such shoes!" one says scornfully. Another following the same vein, "Holy God! You can't even lift your feet!" Then stands up and walks around clumsily to show how silly, awkward it would be. The group laughs with glee at his ridicule. Teacher pursues the subject matter. Shows other pictures where Dutch are eating. Teacher interprets the picture, "They eat cheese and drink goat's milk." Several children make disgusted grimaces. Others quickly follow with disgusted noises. By the end of the session children had repeatedly made invidious comparisons between how "they" look or do things and how "we" do. In every instance, "we" was said proudly and "they" scornfully and with rejection.[49]

A teacher more sensitive to the area of intergroup education will pick his materials more carefully. He will also direct the discussion in such a way that

48.   Muzafer Sherif. A preliminary experimental study of inter-group relationships. *Social Psychology at the Crossroads,* John H. Rohrer and Muzafer Sherif (eds.). New York: Harper & Brothers, 1951. pp. 388-424.
49.   Helen G. Trager and Marion Yarrow. *They Learn What They Live,* New York: Harper & Brothers, 1952.

acceptance of differences is encouraged, rather than ridicule of differences. Democratic attitudes can be taught but only by a teacher who is convinced of them. It is important, then, for those people engaged in teacher-education to devote some time and study to the problem of how such attitudes can be built in those training to be teachers in our schools.

CHAPTER 26

What Are Some Fundamental Questions About Programed Instructional Materials?

PROGRAMED instructional materials were recently reintroduced by B. F. Skinner.[1] Some irresponsible people have since made fantastic claims for the powers of teaching machines and programed texts, and some newspapers and magazines, picking up these claims, have inflated them and proclaimed as fact the machines' alleged—and unproven—virtues. On the other hand, most responsible educators and psychologists have given sober professional attention to this interesting field. The two articles in this chapter represent the latter type of effort.

---

1. B. F. Skinner. The science of learning and the art of teaching. *Harvard Educational Review, 24*:87-97, Spring, 1954.
———. Teaching machines. *Science, 128*:969-77, October 24, 1958.
———. Why we need teaching machines. *Harvard Educational Review, 31*:377-98. Fall, 1961.

HERBERT J. KLAUSMEIER

PHILIP LAMBERT

In this discussion of teaching machines, the authors define some of the theoretical bases of (1) learning theory related to teaching machines, (2) some possible learning outcomes, and (3) the construction of these machines. The need for research is stressed.

SOME SCHOOL PEOPLE are ignoring the existence of teaching machines. Some are probably waiting impatiently for communication experts, psychologists, philanthropists, and others to design and install perfectly operating machine instruction in their schools. However, most educational leaders are demanding thorough study first and much subsequent research in school settings to ascertain the best uses of teaching machines. The leaders themselves must initiate the needed research and evaluation in their schools in order to make wise decisions.

The teaching machine under consideration in this article presents a programed series of questions or other information to the student, provides a means for and requires the student to respond to each item in the program, and indicates the correct response to each item after the student has responded.[1] This article is further limited to mechanical and electromechanical machines, devised primarily for facilitating verbal or symbolic learning, rather than psychomotor or affective.

Eliminated from the present discussion are TV and radio, electronic equipment including tape recorders, sound movie films, and similar material, typewriters and similar equipment, computers of all types, simulators used in flight and driver education, and all forms of books. Though not discussed further, TV in many subject-matter areas and electronic equipment in foreign language, speech, and shorthand show considerable promise for improving instruction. Combinations of these, of course, may be successfully incorporated into complex machines.

Reprinted from *Educational Leadership, 18*:278-83, February, 1961. Copyright by the Association for Supervision and Curriculum Development.

1. J. D. Finn. Teaching machines. *NEA Journal, 49*:41-44, November, 1960. [This article gives verbal and pictorial descriptions of five machines.]

THEORETICAL BASIS

The teaching machine is based upon three widely discussed conditions of learning—operant conditioning, contiguity, and repetition.[2]

Pavlov demonstrated that hungry or thirsty animals, under control of the experimenter, could be conditioned to make a response to a new stimulus that previously had not elicited the response. Skinner bypassed this traditional approach to conditioning and proposed operant or response conditioning. He demonstrated that hungry or thirsty animals, under the control of the experimenter, could be conditioned to make a specific response or a series of responses rapidly when rewarded by the experimenter directly or by a mechanical arrangement. His ideas concerning conditioning have resulted in dramatic improvement in training animals, and have led directly to the recent high interest in machine instruction in the schools.

The teaching machine being discussed is thus firmly based upon principles of conditioning that imply controlling the student and what he learns and rewarding the student, reinforcing, or confirming the correct response as soon as it is made. The proper incidence and spacing of reinforcements in a complete program and the proper amount of repetition can be ascertained and controlled through study and use of the program.

At this point four significant questions for educational practice emerge: (a) Which outcomes of learning are adaptable to machine instruction? (b) Which outcomes of learning can be programed successfully? (c) Can a student acquire the outcomes more efficiently when using a machine than when participating as a member of a larger classroom group in listening to the teacher, discussing with the teacher and classmates, studying independently, reading books, and the like? (d) To what extent will the responses learned by use of the machine transfer to nonmachine situations?

OUTCOMES ADAPTABLE TO MACHINE INSTRUCTION

Factual information is more readily adaptable to machine instruction than are other outcomes of learning such as attitudes and values, concepts, skills, problem-solving techniques, creative expression, and personality integration.[3] Facts, of course, are important in all the latter outcomes, including concept

2. E. R. Hilgard. *Theories of Learning,* 2nd. ed.; New York: Appleton-Century-Crofts, Inc., 1956. [Hilgard interprets various theories; the present authors make the applications to teaching machines.]
3. H. J. Klausmeier. *Learning and Human Abilities: Educational Psychology,* New York: Harper & Brothers, 1961. [Principles applying to efficient learning of each outcome are presented.]

attainment. Consider now the nature of factual information and concepts in relation to teaching machines.

A fact is something that has happened, an event, an actual state of affairs which is widely accepted as correct or true. The correct pronunciation and spelling of each word; the names given to the symbols in mathematics, music, and science; the foreign-language equivalent of each English word; the location and names of geographical places; the time, place, and occurrence of historical events—all of these exemplify factual information. Much of the factual information possessed by mankind can be put in question or other form and the responses the learner makes can be judged as correct or incorrect. Further, the correct response can be supplied in a machine program, thus serving as a reinforcement or reinforcing stimulus if the response is correct and serving as an immediate correction if the response is wrong.

A concept depends partly upon factual information but is more than an addition or integration of many facts in symbol form. For example, what man knows about birds can be put in words and other symbols. Yet, though a nine-year-old child has all of the information he can verbalize about birds, his concept of bird will be far poorer than if he has the information but also has seen, heard, and touched a number of different birds. The teaching machine cannot provide the realistic experiences which are necessary for the full attainment of many concepts.

PROGRAMING THE MATERIAL

Developing excellent programs to elicit the student's response is more complex than writing a series of textbooks, courses of study, or curriculum guides. The programer must decide all the responses to be made by the machine user, the best sequence of material to elicit the desired responses, and the proper amount of repetition and related reinforcements to assure permanent learning. Assuming that the machine instruction is to be self-contained, with the teacher providing no new or supplementary information, the programer must start with readiness material and gradually, bit by bit, lead up to each final desired response or sequence of responses.

Programs are being developed first in instructional areas such as spelling, in which the factual information is self-contained, and in symbols, most systematically organized, and least subject to more than one interpretation. The correct spellings of all words are already incorporated in dictionaries and considerable research is already completed on difficulty and frequency of use of English words. If one accepts the idea that learning to read is simply learning to pronounce words correctly, reading instruction can also be programed but with more difficulty than spelling since a verbal rather than a written response is required. There is no reason to believe, however, that an audio device cannot be incorporated in a more complex machine to give correct pronunciations and thereby permit reinforcement of correct verbal responses, as is the case with the electronic equipment widely used in foreign-language instruction.

Now follows a sample of Porter's program in spelling:[4]

1. Underline these words: *thunder, steady, soaked, frightened*
I hadn't gone halfway when thunder rolled and rain came down in a steady pour. I was soaked. I made a dash for an old horse shed. And there was Wolf. Crouching in the shadow, he looked so like a wolf that for a moment he frightened me.
frigthened   steady   thunder   soaked
2. Circle the word that rhymes with *ready?*
thunder steady pour soaked
          steady
3. Circle the word that means firm, regular, or not shaking:
steady thunder umbrella southern sweeping
steady
4. Write the missing letters:
Then rain came down in a s—ea—y pour.
                steady
5. Write the missing letters; they are all the same:
Ragged clouds were sw—ping the south—rn sky.
             sweeping   southern
6. Write the missing letters:
Without thinking of an umbre—a, I set out.
                umbrella,
7. Write the missing letters:
Halfway to the store thu—er rolled.
                thunder
8. Write the missing letters:
Then rain came down in a s—ea—y pour.
                steady
9. Write the missing letters:
Brushing, moving quickly, s—ee—ing.
                sweeping.

Notice that a relatively high level of reading is required for use of this part of a program in learning to spell. The italicized word or words under

4. D. Porter: Some effects of year-long teaching machine instruction. In E. Galanter (ed.), *Automatic Teaching: The State of the Art*, New York: John Wiley & Sons, Inc., 1959, pp. 86, 87.

each item are presented in a box immediately after the student responds and serves to inform him of the correctness of response or to provide the correct form if he has not responded correctly.

EFFICIENCY OF MACHINE INSTRUCTION

Few educators deny that learning factual information as defined previously is and should be required in many instructional fields, primary through graduate school, and that much of the factual information must be memorized originally and then reviewed. Yet the amount of repetition and subsequent memorizing of the same factual material at successive school levels is a serious indictment against the instructional procedures currently employed. The principal problem here is that many teachers are presenting the same material to all individuals within the class but the students are neither acquiring nor remembering it efficiently. The original learning is inefficient in part because students cannot learn at the same rate and in part because one teacher working with a classroom group of twenty-five to thirty-five cannot provide either the proper amount of reinforcement or confirmation at the right time for each student nor can he help each student to identify and overcome errors immediately.

Permanent learning of factual material is facilitated when the learner wants to acquire, retain, and use the facts; the facts are organized into appropriate learning units; the learner makes the correct response on the first try; correct responses are reinforced and errors are corrected immediately; distributed practice is carried out until the facts are firmly established; and each individual proceeds at a rate appropriate for him. It is entirely possible that these conditions can be incorporated into machine instruction for individuals within a class better than any teacher can incorporate them into daily activities with a group of students in a classroom.

However, for machine learning of factual material to be efficient, an approach to curriculum and instruction different from that in many schools must be accepted; namely, each student must be encouraged to proceed at a rate suitable for him. In some schools today, the highly proficient fourth-grade children are not being permitted to study the fifth- and sixth-grade spelling lists; and the less proficient are held to the fourth-grade list even though the second-grade list is better suited to them. The same is true in many other instructional fields, particularly in high school and college, where teachers expect students to somehow acquire identical amounts of factual material in the same amount of time.

Final answers as to which outcomes, besides facts, might be acquired more efficiently by children and youth of varying characteristics through machine than nonmachine instruction wait upon further research. The authors believe that machine instruction as currently conceived promises greatest effectiveness for the type of factual information previously illustrated.

TRANSFER

What are the possibilities for transfer of machine-acquired responses to other situations? Four generalizations about transfer of learning must be considered. First, general information, principles, methods of study, attitudes and values, and methods of adjustment transfer more readily from one situation to another than do technical information, isolated facts, and specific skills or responses. Secondly, outcomes acquired with meaning transfer more readily than do those acquired without meaning by rote memory and repetition. Thirdly, outcomes which are learned well originally, and therefore are not forgotten, transfer more readily than do those not learned well. Fourthly, the learner must perceive how present learnings apply to other situations.

The main possibility for better transfer from machine instruction is in connection with the third generalization. Machine instruction may lead to more thorough learning originally. Also, some programed material may be more meaningful than the same material which is currently presented in textbooks, workbooks, and orally by the teacher. We may expect verbal learnings acquired by machine use to transfer to other situations in a fashion similar to that between learning to spell correctly in school and then spelling correctly the same words outside the teaching-learning situation.

Research on rigidity and set in problem solving shows conclusively that when an individual experiences repeated success in solving problems with a certain method or instrument, he clings to that method or instrument even though it is inappropriate for solving new problems he encounters for which other methods and/or instruments are appropriate. Thus, through widespread and repeated use of machines and the method of learning incorporated therein, students may become highly dependent upon someone else to decide for them what to learn, how, why, when, and how well to learn it. This could lead to negative transfer to nonmachine learning situations and to lack of sensitivity to problems, of originality, and of flexibility. Also on the negative side with respect to transfer from machine learning is the possibility that many outcomes cannot be acquired with meaning; further only verbal applications of new learning can be presented in the teaching machine.

Here enters a critical value judgment about education. What is education? Drawing out by the teacher and seeking by the student, or putting into the student correct responses and satiating him? Machine instruction, as indicated in the previous discussion of theoretical bases, is designed to encourage the learner to respond correctly or appropriately, as determined by the programer. The better and more widespread the machine instruction, the more fully must the learner come to rely upon it as the most efficient way for him to learn.

RESEARCH, NOT REJECTION OR FAITH

The above extreme viewpoints about education are not as black and white as described. However, the possibility of negative transfer should not be ignored. At present, little or no research has been reported about the extent to which machine instruction of any outcomes may produce positive, negative, or no transfer to nonmachine situations.

The previous discussion presents some of the strengths and limitations of machine instruction. The two authors do not agree completely on the emphasis given to various points, but they agree fully that educational leaders responsible for learning in school situations must somehow mobilize efforts and monies to conduct essential research and evaluation concerning machine instruction. The schools cannot afford to introduce new practices and equipment on good will, faith, and salesmanship in the absence of research; nor should they prevent more efficient pupil learning because of traditions, institutionalized impediments, or apathy.

Educators employed by the schools, with assistance in research design and evaluation procedures from others as necessary, should seek answers to the questions previously raised and these:

1. Which human abilities can be nurtured effectively through machine use? For example, can the ability to communicate orally in a foreign language, the ability to spell correctly, the ability to work well with others, the ability to identify and solve problems, be nurtured equally well with machines?

2. Is machine instruction equally efficient with all age groups? For example, will first-graders learn as well as high-school seniors?

3. How long will students of any age respond with high motivation to machines? For example, if half the instruction is incorporated in machines, will students use the machine without teacher forcing for a week? month? year? six years? twelve years? Will they want to learn from machines throughout life, as many now do from books and other printed material?

4. Can a program of instruction be arranged in the school system which

encourages each student to proceed at a rate appropriate for him, kindergarten through twelfth grade? Though this idea is accepted by many at the verbal level, the authors are unaware of any school system that actually accomplishes it well. And there is no point in introducing machine instruction unless it is accepted in practice. Children can be denied the opportunity for using appropriate levels of programed material, as, for example, many of the more proficient sixth-graders are now being denied use of any of the required textbooks or other instructional material used in the seventh grade.

Little doubt exists that relatively inexpensive machines and programs in such fields as spelling and arithmetic throughout the elementary-school level will soon be available. If the producers and manufacturers cannot sell them to the schools directly, they will sell them to parents, just as encyclopedias, dictionaries, and nontextbook materials are now sold.

109   *Teaching machines and philosophy of education*

JAMES A. JORDAN, JR.

The writer insists that the choice of a teaching device depends upon one's educational philosophy. What do you think?

RECENTLY, in what might be regarded as the house organ of the Center for Programed Instruction, the following question appeared: "Does the utilization of teaching machines and/or programs necessarily commit a school to a particular philosophy of education?"[1] Two distinguished professors answered the question with a firm "no."

B. F. Skinner, in not uncharacteristic fashion, asserted: "All philosophies of education are directed toward efficient learning."[2] He added that teaching machines could certainly be used for part of the task of education; and expanding slightly, he continued, "The processes utilized by teaching machines

Reprinted from *The School Review*, 71:151-57, Summer, 1963, by permission of The University of Chicago Press. Copyright 1963 by the University of Chicago.

1. Programed Instruction, *1*:1, May, 1961.
2. *Ibid.*

are present whenever the student studies. . . . These are age-old processes; the machines simply permit the student to engage in them more efficiently."[3]

Who could argue against the use of a machine that simply permits the student to do more efficiently what he has been wanting to do all along? How could one argue that he had a philosophy of education that is opposed to efficient learning? And even if one did argue so, he could certainly not oppose the use of a machine that enabled the student to carry out efficiently processes that are present "whenever the student studies." There could be no philosophy of education that does not command studying. Since teaching machines add to the efficiency of processes that are necessarily present when students study, all philosophies of education must endorse these machines.

If a teacher or principal had doubts about what he was committing himself to when he used teaching machines or programed instruction, how could he doubt any longer? One of the country's leading psychologists of learning has now assured us that using teaching machines is just part of being efficient. Everybody wants to be efficient. Everybody interested in teaching must want to use teaching machines. Clearly, a teacher or a principal who can resist such assurances is not thinking, not up with the times, not even willing to bet on a sure thing. But perhaps the intuitive foot-dragging of the reluctant teacher or principal deserves support.

No one can dispute Skinner's assertion that all philosophies of education are directed toward efficient learning. After all, no one deliberately adopts inefficient means to achieve his ends, because to do so would be self-defeating. One cannot be rational and try to achieve a goal and also try not to achieve it. Trying to achieve a goal inefficiently is tantamount to trying to achieve a different goal; thus it makes no sense to conceive of a philosophy of education that is not directed toward efficient learning.

But that philosophies of education are directed toward efficient learning recommends no particular tool. A learning process cannot be efficient except in achieving goals. A tool guaranteed to accord with all philosophies of education would have to be one that is guaranteed to be efficient in reaching all goals. No tool of learning is efficient in reaching all goals, because goals are extremely diverse in nature. A tool efficient in reaching certain kinds of goals accords with those philosophies of education that endorse these goals. If one commits himself to a tool, he commits himself to the kind of goal for which the tool is efficient. If a tool is efficient in reaching only some goals, then it accords with all philosophies of education only if these goals can be guaranteed not to conflict with any others.

3. *Ibid.*

Clearly no tool is efficient in reaching all goals, and one is not irrational if he adopts a goal that is in conflict with one efficiently reached through teaching machines. One may or may not adopt such a goal. I suspect that he very likely may. In any case, a proper question to ask before adopting a means is whether it will efficiently achieve some goals without frustrating or hampering the achievement of others.

The question to be answered, then, is not whether the use of teaching machines necessarily commits one to a particular philosophy of education, but what goals one necessarily adopts when he uses teaching machines. Surely there are some. They may be goals that everyone accepts willingly. They may even be goals that it is irrational to reject, though I do not see how this could be so. But surely there are some goals of learning that teaching machines are uniquely fitted to achieve. The question, then, is whether one wants to achieve these goals. If one does, a serious question arises concerning the effect that the achievement of these goals will have on the possibility of achieving other goals that are not to be reached through the use of teaching machines. One's most cherished aim may not be among those to be achieved through teaching machines. Conceivably even, the possibility of realizing that goal may be frustrated by the use of teaching machines, no matter how efficient these machines are in reaching other goals. Should one then use teaching machines? In such a case, does the use of teaching machines accord with one's philosophy of education?

In developing a philosophy of education, one tries to determine what the proper goals of education are. The effect of adopting a particular means for the realization of some goals is an empirical matter to be determined by appropriate empirical investigation. Once the effect of adopting a particular means is known, then whether to adopt this means is again a question to be settled by one's philosophy of education because the question concerns the proper relationship of the various goals of education. It is silly for a teacher or principal to adopt a means for the achievement of unknown ends or even for known ends unless he feels confident about the effect this means will have on the achievement of his other ends. Thus it is certainly not clear that the use of teaching machines accords with all philosophies of education simply because philosophies of education are directed toward efficient learning.

The second answer to the question quoted at the beginning of this paper was given by James McClellan, well-known philosopher of education. McClellan answers:

> It depends, of course, on how you interpret the expression "philosophy of education." Suppose one holds that the only worth-while learning is that

which comes from a student's efforts to deal with his own immediate problems, i.e., those problems that arise outside his school experience. Suppose this same person holds that every student's problems are unique to him. If one held that sort of philosophy of education, he would find little use for teaching machines or programs. Imagine, at the other extreme, a teacher who holds that worth-while learning is always painful, that without suffering there is no real teaching or learning: such a person might find teaching machines far too humane for his philosophy of education.

In both these hypothetical instances, we have interpreted "philosophy of education" to mean a kind of irrational dogmatism, and it is clear that people can have dogmatic objections to the kind of instruction given by teaching machines. If, however, one means by "philosophy of education" a reasoned system of basic beliefs about the purpose and content of education, then surely teaching machines are perfectly neutral. They can be used for good educational purposes or poor. One can develop programs for teaching important concepts or trivialities.[4]

Who wants to hold a philosophy of education that can be branded as "irrational dogmatism"? Who wants to be dogmatic? Since neither irrationality nor dogmatism is desirable, it is clear that nobody will deliberately oppose the use of teaching machines. Who does not wish to regard his philosophy of education as a "reasoned system of basic beliefs about the purpose and content of education"? Since any philosophy of education that is so must see teaching machines as "perfectly neutral," one is forced to conclude about his philosophy of education either that it recognizes teaching machines as perfectly neutral or that it is undesirable. Naturally one must conclude that his philosophy of education is perfectly neutral about teaching machines since no one wishes to regard his philosophy of education as undesirable. Thus again the way is paved for the cautious teacher or principal to embrace teaching machines.

My objection to all this is that we are being led to embrace teaching machines for the wrong reasons. If teaching machines are to be endorsed, it should be because they enable us to achieve efficiently goals that arise from our philosophy of education and because they do not seriously hamper the achievement of goals for which they are not efficient. What we want from people like Skinner and McClellan is not a whopping endorsement of teaching machines and programing—we get enough of these from lesser folk—but (1) a careful analysis of the goals that are efficiently achievable by teaching machines, and (2) empirical evidence about the effect of this achievement on other goals. None of us wants his goals circumscribed by a tool he has uncritically accepted. None of us is willing to give up the goals imbedded in

4. *Ibid.,* pp. 1-2.

his philosophy of education on the basis of recommendations that may or may not take account of these goals.

When McClellan says that teaching machines are perfectly neutral, does he mean they are neutral as an ax is nuetral? With an ax we can cut down large trees or small trees, oak trees or pine trees; and the choice of which trees to cut is surely ours. Then how can one, without dogmatism, object to teaching machines or even suggest that he might object if he understood them and their functions better? There is nothing prejudicing about an ax. The user can in fact still choose his goals. He can even kill people with it, but this fact surely does not mean that anyone who chooses to use an ax is committed to killing people. If one wants trees cut down, it is certainly dogmatic or irrational to object to the use of axes because somebody might use them to hurt people. It is not obviously irrational to point out that some other means of cutting trees down might be more efficient, but whether this is true could be settled empirically. What kind of objection is it to say that one does not want to cut down trees? It is surely no objection to axes. One might even confess that he would like some trees cut down, but that the damage done by falling trees is so great he would prefer not to cut them.

Certainly an ax is neutral regarding the uses to which it is put. But clearly an ax is efficient only for some purposes. If one commits himself to the use of axes, he seems to commit himself to the accomplishment of some task for which an ax can be used efficiently, whether this be cutting trees or cutting heads. An ax is not efficient for driving nails or removing bolts or drilling holes. Although teaching machines may be efficient for all the tasks of learning, it is not clear that they are; and I do not think Skinner or McClellan wish to claim that they are. But what are the learning tasks that teaching machines accomplish more efficiently than any other way of teaching? What is the effect on the realization of all our goals of using teaching machines to accomplish some? Can we just assume that the effect is negligible or even beneficial?

The goals of education are as multifarious as the ideals of men. It is difficult to tell which goals are rational and which are not, which are worthy and which are not, which are necessary and which are not. Deciding on a hierarchy of goals is one of the tasks involved in developing a philosophy of education, at least it is one of the tasks that a developed philosophy of education should not make possible.

It is conceivable to me that a "reasoned system of basic beliefs about the purpose and content of education," to use McClellan's fine phrase, might contain a hierarchy of goals in which those reached efficiently through teaching machines lie at or close to the bottom. At the risk of dogmatism, I must confess that it is even conceivable to me that goals might be so arranged that the use of teaching machines would be clearly prohibited, although I confess also that this seems unlikely.

"Does the utilization of teaching machines and/or programs necessarily commit a school to a particular philosophy of education?" The answer is not a firm no. The answer is "Perhaps not." But clearly the use of teaching machines commits one to goals that can be efficiently reached by using teaching machines. The effect on other goals is uncertain. It is not clear what kinds of goals can be reached along with those that are efficiently reached through teaching machines. Surely, if one uses teaching machines he commits himself to a philosophy of education that endorses goals compatible with the use of these machines. There seems something backward about adjusting one's goals to fit his tools rather than devising tools to fit his goals. It may be that one is dogmatic or irrational if he has goals that clash with the potentialities of teaching machines. Somehow it seems more irrational to decide to use a new and exciting tool before one is sure that it will help accomplish, in the long run, what he wants to accomplish.

CHAPTER 27

What Is Meant by Structure?

THE TERM "structure" is used in many ways. Early in the 1960's, the structure of subject matter was widely discussed. To some educators, structure became a veritable shibboleth, but other educators sought soberly to review their ideas about it.

The emphasis upon structure was strongly influenced by Jerome Bruner's writings and by his many addresses at educational conventions. In 1959, Bruner said, "The object of learning is to gain facts in a context of connectivity. . . ."[1] In his book *The Process of Education* (1960), which was an immediate best seller among books in the field, Bruner states his views on structure. Asking first how students' exposure to materials "can be made to count in [the students'] thinking for the rest of their lives," he asserts that "the answer to this question lies in giving students an understanding of the fundamental structure of whatever subjects we choose to teach."[2]

Two English writers use the word "structure" as a verb:

The representations which the child constructs enable him to perceive sensations arising from various sources, to organize, and structure them in a meaningful way. We know that perception is an *active* process by means of which the ego transforms raw sensory data into meaningful percepts. From this it follows that the child

1. Jerome S. Bruner. Learning and thinking. *Harvard Educational Review, 29*: 189, Summer, 1959.
2. Jerome S. Bruner. *The Process of Education,* Cambridge, Mass.: Harvard University Press, 1960, p. 11.

creates, within his perceptual or *representational* world, images and organizations of his internal as well as external environment.[3]

The concept of structure is a profoundly significant issue for philosophers, psychologists, educators, and all citizens. When we state our views of structure, we are really stating our views on metaphysics and epistemology.

⁊⁊

110   *Structures in learning*

J E R O M E   S.   B R U N E R

In this article Bruner asserts that "every subject has a structure, a rightness, a beauty." He then points out some practical implications of his views on structure.

EVERY SUBJECT has a structure, a rightness, a beauty. It is this structure that provides the underlying simplicity of things, and it is by learning its nature that we come to appreciate the intrinsic meaning of a subject.

Let me illustrate by reference to geography. Children in the fifth grade of a suburban school were about to study the geography of the Central states as part of a social studies unit. Previous units on the Southeastern states, taught by rote, had proved a bore. Could geography be taught as a rational discipline? Determined to find out, the teachers devised a unit in which students would have to figure out not only where things are located, but why they are there. This involves a sense of the structure of geography.

The children were given a map of the Central states in which only rivers, large bodies of water, agricultural products, and natural resources were shown. They were not allowed to consult their books. Their task was to find Chicago, "the largest city in the North Central states."

Reprinted from the *NEA Journal, 52*:26-27, March, 1963.

3. Joseph Sandler and Bernard Rosenblatt. The concept of the representational world. *The Psychoanalytical Study of the Child, 17*:131-32, New York: International Universities Press, Inc., 1962.

The argument got under way immediately. One child came up with the idea that Chicago must be on the junction of the three large lakes. No matter that at this point he did not know the names of the lakes—Huron, Superior, and Michigan—his theory was well-reasoned. A big city produced a lot of products, and the easiest and most logical way to ship these products is by water.

But a second child rose immediately to the opposition. A big city needed lots of food, and he placed Chicago where there are corn and hogs—right in the middle of Iowa.

A third child saw the issue more broadly—recognizing virtues in both previous arguments. He pointed out that large quantities of food can be grown in river valleys. Whether he had learned this from a previous social studies unit or from raising carrot seeds, we shall never know. If you had a river, he reasoned, you had not only food but transportation. He pointed to a spot on the map not far from St. Louis. "There is where Chicago *ought* to be." Would that graduate students would always do so well!

Not all the answers were so closely reasoned, though even the wild ones had about them a sense of the necessity involved in a city's location.

One argued, for example, that all American cities have skyscrapers, which require steel, so he placed Chicago in the middle of the Mesabi Range. At least he was thinking on his own, with a sense of the constraints imposed on the location of cities.

After forty-five minutes, the children were told they could pull down the "real" wall map (the one with names) and see where Chicago really is. After the map was down, each of the contending parties pointed out how close they had come to being right. Chicago had not been located. But the location of cities was no longer a matter of unthinking chance for this group of children.

What had the children learned? A way of thinking about geography, a way of dealing with its raw data. They had learned that there is some relationship between the requirements of living and man's habitat. If that is all they got out of their geography lesson, that is plenty. Did they remember which is Lake Huron? Lake Superior? Lake Michigan? Do you?

Teachers have asked me about "the new curriculums" as though they were some special magic potion. They are nothing of the sort. The new curriculums, like our little exercise in geography, are based on the fact that knowledge has an internal connectedness, a meaningfulness, and that for facts to be appreciated and understood and remembered, they must be fitted into that internal meaningful context.

The set of prime numbers is not some arbitrary nonsense. What can be said about quantities that cannot be arranged into multiple columns and rows? Discussing that will get you on to the structure of primes and factorability.

It often takes the deepest minds to discern the simplest structure in knowledge. For this reason if for no other, the great scholar and the great scientist and the greatly compassionate man are needed in the building of new curriculums.

There is one other point. Our geographical example made much of discovery. What difference does discovery make in the learning of the young? First, let it be clear what the act of discovery entails. It is only rarely on the frontier of knowledge that new facts are "discovered" in the sense of being encountered, as Newton suggested, as "islands of truth in an unchartered sea of ignorance." Discovery, whether by a schoolboy going it on his own or by a scientist, is most often a matter of rearranging or transforming evidence in such a way that one is now enabled to go beyond the evidence to new insights. Discovery involves the finding of the right structure, the meaningfulness.

Consider now what benefits the child might derive from the experience of learning through his own discoveries. These benefits can be discussed in terms of increased intellectual potency, intrinsic rewards, useful learning techniques, and better memory processes.

For the child to develop *intellectual potency*, he must be encouraged to search out and find regularities and relationships in his environment. To do this, he needs to be armed with the expectancy that there is something for him to find and, once aroused by this expectancy, he must devise his own ways of searching and finding.

Emphasis on discovery in learning has the effect upon the learner of leading him to be a constructionist—to organize what he encounters in such a manner that he not only discovers regularity and relatedness, but also avoids the kind of information drift that fails to keep account of how the information will be used.

In speaking of *intrinsic motives* for learning (as opposed to extrinsic motives), it must be recognized that much of the problem in leading a child to effective cognitive activity is to free him from the immediate control of environmental punishments and rewards.

For example, studies show that children who seem to be early overachievers in school are likely to be seekers after the "right way to do it" and that their capacity for transforming their learning into useful thought structures tends to be less than that of children merely achieving at levels predicted by intelligence tests.

The hypothesis drawn from these studies is that if a child is able to approach learning as a task of discovering something rather than "learning about it" he will tend to find a more personally meaningful reward in his own competency and self-achievement in the subject than he will find in the approval of others.

There are many ways of coming to the *techniques of inquiry,* or the heuristics of discovery. One of them is by careful study of the formalization of these techniques in logic, statistics, mathematics, and the like. If a child is going to pursue inquiry as an eventual way of life, particularly in the sciences, formal study is essential. Yet, whoever has taught kindergarten and the early primary grades (periods of intense inquiry) knows that an understanding of the formal aspects of inquiry is not sufficient or always possible.

Children appear to have a series of attitudes and activities they associate with inquiry. Rather than a formal approach to the relevance of variables in their search, they depend on their sense of what things among an ensemble of things "smell right" as being of the proper order of magnitude or scope of severity.

It is evident then that if children are to learn the working techniques of discovery, they must be afforded the opportunities of problem solving. The more they practice problem solving, the more likely they are to generalize what they learn into a style of inquiry that serves for any kind of task they may encounter. It is doubtful that anyone ever improves in the art and technique of inquiry by any other means than engaging in inquiry, or problem solving.

The first premise in a theory concerning the *improvement of memory processes* is that the principal problem of human memory is not storage, but retrieval. The premise may be inferred from the fact that recognition (i.e., recall with the aid of maximum prompts) is extraordinarily good in human beings—particularly in comparison to spontaneous recall when information must be recalled without external aids or prompts. The key to retrieval is organization.

There are myriad findings to indicate that any organization of information that reduces the collective complexity of material by imbedding it into a mental structure the child has constructed will make that material more accessible for retrieval. In sum, the child's very attitudes and activities that characterize "figuring out" or "discovering" things for himself also seem to have the effect of making material easier to remember.

If man's intellectual excellence is the most important among his perfections (as Maimonides, the great Hispanic-Judaic philosopher once said), then it is also the case that the most uniquely personal of all that man knows is that which he discovers for himself. What difference does it make when we encourage discovery in the young? It creates, as Maimonides would put it, a special and unique relation between knowledge possessed and the possessor.

~⧉~

III   *The concept of the structure of a discipline*

JOSEPH J. SCHWAB

In this discussion of conceptual structure and the syntactical structure of disciplines, the author shows how swiftly changes occur in our fund of knowledge and presents his concept of structure.

IN 1941, my colleagues and I offered for the first time a course in the structure of the disciplines. We had devoted an entire year to developing its plan and content. But we had spent no time at all on the problem of how to teach it. The first few weeks, in consequence, were a severe trial of our students' patience. Finally, one of them cornered me.

"Tell me," she said, "what this course is about."

I did so—in twelve minutes. I was impressed by my clarity as much as by my brevity. So, apparently, was my student. For she eyed me a moment and then said, "Thank you. Now I understand. And if the truth is that complicated, I am not interested."

The young lady was right on two of three counts. First, the concept of a structure of a discipline is concerned in a highly important sense with truth, not with truth in some vaguely poetic sense, but with answerable, material questions of the extent to which, and the sense in which, the content of a discipline is warranted and meaningful. Secondly, study of the structures of the disciplines is complicated—at least by contrast to the simple assumptions about truth and meaning which we have used in the past in determining the content and the organization of the school curriculum.

On the third count, however, the young lady was wrong. We cannot

Reprinted from *Educational Record,* 43:197-205, July, 1962.

afford to be uninterested in the structures of the disciplines. We cannot so afford because they pose problems with which we in education must deal. The structures of the modern disciplines are complex and diverse. Only occasionally do we now find among them a highly esteemed body of knowledge which consists simply of collections of literal statements standing in one-for-one relation to corresponding facts. Instead of collections, we find organizations in which each member-statement depends on the other for its meaning. And the verifying relations of such organizations to their facts are convoluted and diverse. This complexity of modern structures means that problems of comprehension and understanding of modern knowledge now exist which we in education have barely recognized. The diversity of modern structures means that we must look, not for a simple theory of learning leading to a one best learning-teaching structure for our schools, but for a complex theory leading to a number of different structures, each appropriate or "best" for a given discipline or group of disciplines.

In brief, the structures of the disciplines are twice important to education. First, they are necessary to teachers and educators: they must be taken into account as we plan curriculum and prepare our teaching materials; otherwise, our plans are likely to miscarry and our materials, to misteach. Secondly, they are necessary in some part and degree *within* the curriculum, as elements of what we teach. Otherwise, there will be failure of learning or gross mislearning by our students.

Let us turn now to examination of a structure, using the sciences as the example.

Forty years ago it was possible for many scientists and most educators to nurse the illusion that science was a matter of patiently seeking the facts of nature and accurately reporting them. The conclusions of science were supposed to be nothing more than summaries of these facts.

This *was* an illusion, and it was revealed as such by events in the science of physics that began in the late 1890's. The discovery of radioactivity suddenly revealed a world within the world then thought to be the only world. The study of that world and of its relations to the world already known led to a revolution in the goals and the structures of physics. By the mid-twenties, this revolution in physics had gone so far that we were faced with the fact that some of the oldest and least questioned of our ideas could no longer be treated as literally true—or literally false. Classical space had been a homogeneous, neutral stage on which the dramas of motion and existence were acted out. The flow of classical time was always and everywhere the same. The mass and length of bodies were each elementary properties independent of other properties. Bodies occupied a definite location and a definite amount of space.

The new physics changed these notions. In its knowledge structure, space was something which could be distorted and its distortions affected bodies in it. The magnitude and position of sub-atomic particles could not be described as we describe the magnitude and position of a one-inch cube here-now.

But these new assertions did *not* come about because direct observations of space, place, time, and magnitude disclosed that our past views about them were merely mistaken. Rather, our old assertions about these matters were changed because physicists had found it fruitful to treat them in a new way—neither as self-evident truths nor as matters for immediate empirical verification. They were to be treated, instead, as principles of inquiry—conceptual structures which could be revised when necessary, in directions dictated by large complexes of theory, diverse bodies of data, and numerous criteria of progress in science.

Today, almost all parts of the subject-matter sciences proceed in this way. A fresh line of scientific research has its origin not in objective facts alone, but in a conception, a deliberate construction of the mind. On this conception, all else depends. It tells us what facts to look for in the research. It tells us what meaning to assign these facts.

A moment's thought is enough to show us how this process operates. That we propose to investigate a chosen subject is to say, of course, that we are, in large part, ignorant of it. We may have some knowledege, based on common experience or on data garnered in preliminary study. But this preliminary knowledge is only a nibbling at the edges. We barely know the superficial exterior of our subject, much less its inner chartcter. Hence, we do not *know* with certainty what further facts to look for, what facts will tell us the significant story of the subject in hand. We can only *guess*.

In physiology, for example, we did not know, but only supposed, that the functioning of the human organism is carried out by distinct parts, that each part has a character and a fixed function in the economy of the whole. Hence, we did not *know* that the facts we ought to seek in physiological research should be facts about the structure of each organ and what happens when each organ is removed. On the contrary, the conceptions of organ and of function were developed prior to sure knowledge of these matters and were developed precisely to make such knowledge possible through research. The conceptions are guiding principles of inquiry, not its immediate fruits.

In physics, similarly, we did not *know* from the beginning that the properties of particles of matter are fundamental and determine the behavior of these particles, their relations to one another. It was not verified knowledge but a heuristic principle, needed to structure inquiry, that led us to investigate mass and charge and, later, spin.

It may, indeed, be the case that the particles of matter are social particles, that their most significant properties are not properties of their very own but properties which accrue to them from association with other particles, properties that change as the associations change. Therefore, it may be that the more significant facts to seek in physical inquiry are not facts about the properties of particles but facts about kinds of associations and the consequences of associations.

Similar alternatives exist for physiology. There are conceptions of the organism that yield, when pursued in inquiry, a more profound knowledge than that afforded by the notions of organ and function.

In short, what facts to seek in the long course of an inquiry and what meaning to assign them are decisions that are made before the fact. The scientific knowledge of any given time rests not on *the* facts but on *selected* facts—and the selection rests on the conceptual principles of the inquiry.

Moreover, scientific knowledge—the knowledge won through inquiry—is not knowledge merely of the facts. It is of the facts *interpreted*. This interpretation, too, depends on the conceptual principles of the inquiry. The structure-function physiologist does not report merely the numerous changes displayed by an experimental animal from which an organ has been removed. He interprets these changes as indicative of the lost function once performed by the organ removed. It is this interpretation of the facts that is the conclusion drawn from the experiment and reported as a piece of scientific knowledge, and its meaning and validity depend on the conception of organ and function as much as they depend on the selected facts.

Here, then, is a first approximation of what is meant by the structure of a discipline. The structure of a discipline consists, in part, of the body of imposed conceptions which define the investigated subject matter of that discipline and control its inquiries.

The significance to education of these guiding conceptions becomes clearer if we repeat once more the way in which they act as guides. First, they severly restrict the range of data which the scientist seeks in inquiry. He does *not* study the whole of his subject, but only some aspect of it, an aspect which his then-current principles of inquiry lead him to treat as the significant aspect. The conclusions of that line of inquiry may be true, but most certainly they are not the whole truth about that subject matter. They are not about some aspect of nature taken in its pristine state but about something which the principles of the inquiry have made, altered, or restricted.

Furthermore, what the scientist makes of these data, what he takes them to mean, is also determined not by full knowledge of their significance, but by the tentative principles of the inquiry.

Now the subject matter may be—in fact, almost always is—far richer and more complex than the limited model of it embodied in the conclusions of the restricted inquiry. Thus, the first significance to education of the structure of a discipline: we cannot, with impunity, teach the conclusions of a discipline as if they were about the whole subject matter and were the whole truth about it. For the intelligent student will discover in time—unless we have thoroughly blinded him by our teaching—that any subject behaves in ways which do not conform to what he has been told about it. His bodily illnesses, for example, are often not reducible to the malfunctioning of specific organs or the presence of a specific bacterium. His automobile does not appear to obey the "laws" of the particular science of mechanics which he was taught. Legislatures and executives do not behave as a dogmatic political science says they do.

It is the case, however, that a structure-function physiology, a Newtonian mechanics, or some particular reading of political behavior throws *some* light on the behavior of our bodies, our automobiles, or our democracy. Or it would if the body of knowledge were understood in the light of the restricted circumstances in which it is valid and known in connection with the restricted range of data which it subsumes. In short, the bodies of knowledge *would* have defensible and valuable meaning to those who learn them had they been learned, not in a context of dogma, but in a context of the conceptions and data that determine their limited meaning and confer their limited validity. This is one significance of the structure of the disciplines to education.

A second significance becomes visible if we look at a further consequence of the operation of a conceptual structure in inquiry. It renders scientific knowledge fragile and subject to change; research does not proceed indefinitely on the basis of the principles that guided its first inquiries. On the contrary, the same inquiries that accumulate limited knowledge by the aid of assumed principles of inquiry also test these principles. As the selected principles are used, two consequences ensue. Knowledge of the subject unfolds; experimental techniques are refined and invented. The new knowledge lets us envisage new, more adequate, more telling conceptions of the subject matter. The growth of technique permits us to put the new conceptions into practice as guiding principles of a renewed inquiry.

The effect of these perennial renewals of inquiry is perennial revision of scientific knowledge. With each change in conceptual system, the older knowledge gained through use of the older principles sinks into limbo. The *facts* embodied are salvaged, reordered, and reused, but the *knowledge* which formerly embodied these facts is replaced. There is, then, a continuing and pervasive revision of scientific knowledge as principles of inquiry are used, tested, and supplanted.

Furthermore, our scientific and scholarly establishment is now so large, so many men are now engaged in inquiry, that the rate of this revision is exceedingly rapid. We can expect radical reorganization of a given body of scientific knowledge, not once in the coming century but several times, at intervals of five to fifteen years. This means, of course, that our students—if they continue to receive all their learning in a dogmatic context, outside the structure of the disciplines—will confront at least once in their lives what appears to be a flat contradiction of much that they were taught about some subject. The effect of this lie-direct to teaching in the schools can only be exacerbation, to an intolerable degree, of the confusion, uncertainty, and cynicism which our young people already exhibit with respect to *expertise*, to schooling, and to bodies of organized knowledge.

Our students and our nation could be protected from the consequences of such misunderstanding, if, again, our students learned what they learned not as a body of literal and irrevocable truths but as what it is: one embodiment of one attack on something less than the whole of the matter under investigation. This is a second significance of the conceptual structure of the disciplines to education.

Whereas the second significance to education arises from the existence of a process of revision, the third and fourth significances emerge from the outcomes of this process—from the advances which it has made possible. In the process of revision, improvement of principle is sought in two different directions. On the one hand, more *valid* principles are sought, principles which embrace more and more of the richness and complexity of the subject under investigation. On the other hand, principles of wider *scope* are sought, principles which will embrace a wider and wider range of subject matters, which will reduce what were before considered as separate and different phenomena to related aspects of a common kind or source. (Thus, Newtonian mechanics united the movements of the heavenly bodies with the behavior of objects thrown and dropped by man on earth, rendering these formerly diverse phenomena but varying expressions of a common law. Similarly, the physics of the century just past found new principles that united the formerly separated phenomena of light, electricity, and magnetism.)

The successful search for more *valid* principles—for more adequate models of investigated phenomena—has led to scientific knowledge of a new "shape" or character, in sharp contrast to older knowledge. Older knowledge tended toward the shape of the catalogue. Old descriptive biology, for example, was ncessarily a catalogue: of the organs, tissues, or kinds of cells which made up the body. Another part of descriptive biology was a catalogue of the species, genera, classes, and so on of the living organisms that populated the earth. Even the experimental physiology of years only recently past tended toward a similarly encyclopedic character—for example, lists of parts of bodies with their functions, meticulous itemizing of hereditary units and their consequent traits. Chemistry, in similar fashion, tended to be a classificatory scheme of elements and of the more complex substances that arose from their combination.

Modern scientific inquiry, conversely, tends to look for patterns—patterns of change and patterns of relations—as their explanatory principles. When such patterns are found, they throw a new and more complex light on the items of our old catalogues. The items lose their primary significance and lose their independence. On the side of significance, an item ceases to be something which simply is, and becomes, instead, one of possibly many "somethings" that fulfill conditions required by the pattern. On the side of dependence-independence, an item ceases to be something which can be understood by itself; it becomes, instead, something which can be understood only by knowing the relations it bears to the other items that fill out the pattern or blueprint.

Thus, it was once possible to teach something about the significance of glucose to the living body by reciting a formula for it—naming the three elements which compose it, indicating the number of each—and naming it as an energy source. Today, it is necessary to talk about the basic pattern of a carbohydrate molecule, how the elements are connected to one another, what happens when connections are made or broken, and so on. This story of pattern is imbedded, in turn, in a still larger pattern—the pattern of processes by which energy is captured, stored, transferred, and utilized in the body. The educational significance of this emphasis on pattern in the sciences is more clearly indicated by the further point that, a few years ago, we could tell the story of energy sources merely by cataloguing glucose and two or three other substances as the common energy sources of the body. Today, the story must be the story of where and when and under what circumstances each of these substances functions as an energy source, and how, in a sense, they function as *interchangeable* parts to fulfill the conditions of the determining pattern.

This shift from catalogues to patterns in the disciplines means, in turn, that teaching and learning take on a new dimension. Instead of focusing on one thing or idea at a time, clarifying each and going on to the next, teaching becomes a process of focusing on points of contact and connection among things and ideas, of clarifying the effect of each thing on the others, of conveying the way in which each connection modifies the participants in the connection—in brief, the task of portraying phenomena and ideas not as things in themselves but as fulfillments of a pattern.

The successful search for principles of greater scope has led to developments of a parallel kind. As the scope of a set of principles enlarges, so does the coherence of the body of knowledge which develops from it, the interdependence of its component statements, a fifth significance. Thus, in a theory which embraces electricity and magnetism as well as light, an assertion about the nature of light borrows part of its meaning and part of its warrant from statements about electricity and magnetism. The significance of the assertion about light cannot be grasped by understanding only its terms and the light phenomena to which it applies. For these terms are defined in part by terms in other statements about other phenomena.

This kind of coherence in scientific knowledge means that our most common way of applying the old query "What knowledge is of most worth?" is no longer entirely defensible. We can no longer safely select from the conclusions of the disciplines the separate and different bits and pieces that we think would be most useful to the clients of the schools. We cannot because the separation of these bits, their removal from the structure of other statements which confer on them their meaning, alters or curtails that meaning. The statements will no longer convey the warranted and valid knowledge they convey in context, but something else or something less.

For students of some ages or of very limited learning competence, such bits and pieces may be appropriate as limited guides to limited actions, limited understanding, and a limited role in society. For many children at many ages, however, we need to face the fact that such a disintegrated content is not only a distorted image of scientific knowledge but a distorted image of the physical world it purports to represent; it will betray itself.

This means, in turn, that teaching and learning, as we have suggested above, need an added dimension. As patterns replace lists and catalogues, learning and remembering of parts remain necessary conditions of learning but cease to be sufficient conditions. A new flexibility is required, a capacity to deal with the roles of things, as well as with things as such, and to understand the relations among roles. The following crude metaphor may suggest the nature of this flexibility. Natural phenomena as now conceived by the sciences must be understood as a dynamic, a drama. The drama unfolds as the outcome of many interacting roles. Therefore, the relation of each role to others must be understood. Secondly, each role may be played by more than one actor; different "actors," despite their apparent diversities, must be recognized as potential players of the same role. Thirdly, each potential player of a role modifies somewhat the role he plays and, through this effect, also modifies the roles, played by other actors. Hence, the unfolding, the climax, and outcome of the drama are flexible, not one rigid pattern, but variations on a theme.

A sixth significance of conceptual principle to education is quickly told.

Different disciplines have widely different conceptual structures. Despite the passionate concern of some philosophers and some scientists for a unity of the sciences, biologists and physicists, for example, continue to ask widely different questions in their inquiries, seek different kinds of data, and formulate their respective bodies of knowledge in widely different forms. It is not quite obsolete in biology, for instance, to ask what system of classes will best organize our knowledge of living things and to seek data primarily in terms of similarities and differences. The physicist, however, continues to find it most rewarding to ask what relations among what varying quantities will best organize our knowledge of the behavior of matter; consequently, he seeks data which consist primarily of measurements of such changing quantities.

Such differences among sciences are so persistent and so rewarding that it is hard to avoid the conviction that there are real and genuine differences among different bodies of phenomena, that differences in questions put and data sought are not merely the products of historical habits among the different disciplines but also reflect some stubbornnesses of the subjects. Some subject matters answer when one set of questions is put. Another answers to another set. And neither will answer the questions to which the other responds.

Among these differences of conceptual structure, there are some which deserve special attention from educators because of the confusion they create if ignored. These are the specific differences among conceptions which two or more disciplines apparently hold in common. Two large-scale examples occur to me: the concept of *time* and the concept of *class*.

Time is deeply imbedded in the conceptual structure of both physics and biology. In many respects, the concept of time is the same in both sciences. In one respect it is radically different. Time for the biologist is unavoidably vectorial and has direction from past to future, like the time of common sense. It cannot, in any sense, be considered reversible. Time, as it appears in most physical equations, in contrast, has no notion of past and future attached to it; it permits, in a certain sense, reversibility.

The concept of class is, perhaps, a more telling instance of difference for the purposes of education. The class of biology is a loose and messy affair compared to the class with which traditional logic (and much of mathematics) is concerned. The logical class consists of members which are all alike in some defining respect. The biologists' class, however, consists of members of which it can be said, at best, that most of them have most of *many* properties which, together, define the class.

The special problem posed by such differences as these is easily seen. The *logical* class, consisting of members alike in some defining respect, permits us to infer with confidence knowledge about members of the class from knowledge of the class. The *biological* class permits no such confident inference. What is true for the class may or may not be true of some member or subclass. Obviously, instruction which permitted this crucially instrumental conceptual difference to go unnoted by teachers and students would lead to all sorts of later confusion and error.

I remarked earlier that a body of concepts—commitments about the nature of a subject matter, functioning as a guide to inquiry—was *one* component of the structure of a discipline. Let us turn briefly to another which I shall call the syntactical structure of the disciplines. By the syntax of a discipline, I mean the pattern of its procedure, its method, how it goes about using its conceptions to attain its goals.

Most of us were taught a schoolbook version of a syntax under the guise of "scientific method." Though oversimple, full of error, and by no means the universal method of the sciences, it will suffice as an example. This schoolbook story (borrowed, incidentally, from an early work of Dewey) tells us that science proceeds through four steps. There is, first, the noting of data relevant to our problem. Secondly, there is the conceiving of a hypothesis. Thirdly, the hypothesis is tested by determining whether consequences expected if the hypothesis were true are, in fact, found to occur. Finally, a conclusion is stated, asserting the verification or nonverification of the hypothesis.

So we are given the impression that the goal of all the sciences is a congeries of well-verified hypotheses. We are left with the impression that verification is of only one kind—the discovery that expected consequences occur in fact.

If this were all there were to the syntax of the disciplines, it would be of little importance to teaching, learning, and the curriculum. Unfortunately, this is not all there is. For different disciplines have different starting points and different goals. That is, their subject matters may be conceived in vastly different ways, so also may what they conceive to be sound knowledge or fruits of the inquiry. Consequently, the path, the syntax, the process of discovery and verification is also different.

Such differences in method of verification and discovery hold even for the similar disciplines called the sciences. They hold, *a fortiori*, between the sciences on one count, mathematics on another, and history on a third.

Among the sciences, let us contrast, once more, biology and physics. Biology, until very recently, has been the science that comes closest to fulfilling the schoolbook version of science. It has consisted, in large part, of a congeries of tested hypotheses. Its inquiries have turned from the verification of one to the verification of another with little twinge of conscience. Biologists have rarely hesitated to formulate hypotheses for different problems that differed widely from one another, that had little, indeed, of a common body of conceptions. Thus, verification for biology was largely a matter of chasing down, one by one, many and various expected consequences of many and various hypotheses.

Physics, on the other hand, has for centuries held as its goal not a congeries of almost independent hypotheses but a coherent and closely knit body of knowledge. It has sought to impose on its diverse formulations of diverse phenomena a body of conceptions which would relate them to one another and make of them one body, inferable from the conceptions which bound them together. Hence, for physics, verification has often meant something far otherwise than its meaning in biology. It has meant, in many cases, that expected consequences had been observed. In a few cases, however, the first reason for accepting a certain hypothetical had nothing to do with observed consequences. Rather, the hypothetical in question was accepted in order to save another conception, one which lay deep in the structure of physical knowledge and had ramifications extending over most of its conclusion. Thus, the "verifying" circumstance had to do with the structure of existing things. (In one such case, the hypothetical in question—the neutrino—was verified some years later by the discovery of expected consequences, to the great relief of many physicists. In still another case—that of the parity principle—the principle itself was discarded and replaced.)

Where physics and biology differ in their goals, science and mathematics differ primarily in their starting points, that is, their subject matters. The consequent differences in their syntax are vast. Let us take algebra as our example and agree for the moment that the subject matter of algebra is number. Now, whatever number may be, one thing is certain: it does not consist of a body of material things, of events accessible to our senses. The idea of testing for the presence of materially existential consequences is meaningless in algebra. The algebraist may conceivably use something called data, but if he does, it is something vastly different from what is meant by data in a science which studies a material, sense-accessible subject matter. Yet, there can be error as well as truth in algebra, hence, some means of discovery and of test. Clearly, then, the means, the syntax of mathematics, must be vastly different from the syntax which has a material subject matter.

A similar great difference holds between most history and the sciences. Few historians would hold that their goal, like the goal of science, is discovery of general laws. They do not take as their starting points things and events which they think of as repeated instances of a *kind* of thing or event. On the contrary, most historians take as their goal the recovery or the reconstruction of some selected, time-limited or space-limited group of past and unique events. But again, there are such things as better history and worse history— the more and the less well verified. Yet, only by the wildest of equivocations can we assert that the historian discovers and verfies in the same way as does the investigator of living things, of falling bodies, or of numbers.

In brief, truth is a complicated matter. The conceptual structure of a discipline determines what we shall seek the truth about and in what terms that truth shall be couched. The syntactical structure of a discipline is concerned with the operations that distinguish the true, the verified, and the warranted in that discipline from the unverified and unwarranted. Both of these—the conceptual and the syntactical—are different in different disciplines. The significance for education of these diverse structures lies precisely in the extent to which we want to teach what is true and have it understood.

CHAPTER 28

Should Teachers Write Lesson Plans?

SOME EDUCATORS may not agree that lesson plans constitute a significant issue. But ask any young teacher about lesson plans and he is sure to tell you that they take up a good deal of discussion time in the teachers' lounge. Furthermore, philosophers who wonder about concepts such as those discussed in the previous chapter also will testify to the significance of this topic.

ROBERT E. CHASNOFF

"WILL WE HAVE to write lesson plans?" Student teachers and beginning teachers frequently ask their supervisors this question. Supervisors' answers differ. Some insist upon detailed written plans. Others believe that a few notes are sufficient. A third group contends that planning is an individual matter and that the results in the classrooms are the most crucial thing. A fourth group holds that lesson plans may inhibit teachers' inspiration during lessons, and that lesson plans interfere with teachers' creative responses to pupils' reactions. These differences have existed for twenty-four centuries or more. From the ancient Sophists, through the followers of Johann Herbart, up to the present, advocates of planning have attempted to analyze, stylize, and conceptualize the ingredients of lessons. The goal has been to find a "preparatory procedure that will be both motivationally and cognitively effective."[1]

My thesis is this: Teachers must plan in a rational way the kinds of experiences that are appropriate for the schools of a society dedicated to democracy. Teachers must plan for pupils to think actively, to find out meanings for themselves, and to interrelate groups of ideas.

At best, it is a tricky thing to write about lesson plans. Some readers may infer that I hope to repopularize the five famous steps revered by the followers of Herbart, or that I am advocating a return to stylized "object lessons." Such inferences would be incorrect. Some readers may suspect that I feel effective learning takes place only when the teacher stands in the front of the room and emits prefabricated and predigested information. These suspicions would also be incorrect. Children learn more than teachers can plan. (Some unplanned lessons seem to grow into brilliant educational episodes.) Rousseau suggested, "The lessons the scholars give one another on the playground are worth a hundredfold more than those they learn in the classroom." Pupils also reconstruct meanings in quiet musing, in solitary reading, in writing a story, or in unplanned conversation. Yet, I submit, teachers must often teach prepared lessons in formal ways. Indeed, a teacher must plan for teacher-pupil

---

This essay was prepared for this volume.

1. Harry S. Broudy. Historic exemplars of the teaching method. *The Handbook of Research on Teaching*, N. L. Gage (ed.), Chicago: Rand McNally Company, 1963, p. 37.

planning, and for the teaching-learning episodes that teachers can anticipate, lesson plans can help.

It is clear that there are many possible ways to write a lesson plan. The scheme on pages 646-48 makes sense to me. You will note that the categories —Objectives, Ways of Teaching, and Evaluation—repeat three parts of the conceptual framework of this book. I have combined the subjects with the objectives.

I suggest, too, that we may think of three phases of a lesson representing three general acts pupils should experience:

A. Attending

B. Understanding

C. Remembering

A. By *attending* pupils relinquish attention to other stimuli and focus attention on the teacher or something the teacher wants the pupils to look at. In this introductory part of a lesson, pupils' attention may be conducted to learning episodes that happened earlier that day or are to happen later. Sometimes pupils are directed to think back to the previous day's lesson on the topic at hand. A lesson may begin with questions raised by pupils or by the teacher.

B. *Understanding* may be gained in many ways. Pupils may learn by being told or by formulating hypotheses and checking them against data. Pupils may build understanding by working with art media, by reading silently, or by discussing what they are studying. The many suggestions given in Parts Two and Three of this book are some ways of helping pupils build understanding and meaning.

C. *Remembering* is essential. Why waste time teaching if pupils do not remember? Pupils remember better when they formulate generalizations out of the experiences of a lesson. They remember better if they can integrate the various intellectual stimuli of a lesson. Finally, the positive memory of a lesson will be more lasting if the lesson was a pleasant one, where pupils were pleased with themselves, where they felt they "belonged" and were not embarrassed, where, in short, the conscious and unconscious recollections of the lesson caused pupils to feel they are good learners.

Sometimes these three phases may be equal in length; at other times, when a group is clear on its objectives, the first phase will be covered quickly. You can readily see that these three thinking phases relate to articles found in Chapter 2 of this book. These phases also relate to the concept of psychological integration.[2] Important for student learning through integration are the following: gaining the desire or set to abstract relationships between two or more phenomena or ideas, forming generalizations, and acquiring the self-concept of themselves as daring and successful explorers into new ideational relationships.

The sample lesson beginning on page 646 might technically be called a social studies lesson, although a great deal of language is involved. (It might come after a lesson in which students learned that during the Colonial Era in America British flags were the official flags of the colonies. One flag was often familiarly called the "Union Jack." The pupils learned that the symbols on this flag were two crosses: a white cross, representing the patron saint of Scotland, St. Andrew, and a red cross, representing the patron saint of England, St. George. Finally, the class discussed the generalization that when countries unite, they often combine symbols.)

The lesson shown here emphasizes objectives that were discussed in Part One of this book. Notice that the plan includes ways for helping pupils to seek out knowledge and to interrelate information. Pay special attention to the kinds of thinking noted in the objectives. Notice how many levels of the taxonomy described in Jarolimek's article are included. Also notice the introductions, the transitions, the summings-up, and the variety of ways of teaching used in one lesson. Study the evaluation methods suggested in Fleming's article on evaluation, and review the combined provisions for total group instruction and for individual group work which were suggested throughout this book.

In preparing a lesson plan for actual class use, a teacher would not need to write down all the details given in this lesson plan. Some teachers might list merely the ways of teaching, using only key words as reminders. Other teachers might want to discipline themselves by being sure to state the objectives in terms of the learners' behavior. Some teachers concentrate first upon the ways of evaluation and work backward. These are all valid approaches. However, as I suggested earlier in my essay on teaching routines, the teacher who plans is prepared to be a flexible teacher. He can react to ideas and change plans when the need arises.

In conclusion, remember that the curriculum is more than the lesson plan, the curriculum guide, or the textbook. The curriculum is what the pupils perceive.

---

2. See: David R. Krathwohl. The psychological bases of integration. *The Integration of Educational Experiences.* The Fifty-seventh Yearbook of the National Society for the Study of Education. Part III. Chicago: University of Chicago Press, 1958, pp. 43-65.

ATTENDING

Objectives	Ways of Teaching	Evaluation
1. Pupils gain proper mood and set for learning.	Get everyone's attention. Be sure everyone can see flags.	Observe how pupils respond to directions.
2. Pupils integrate current lesson with previous lesson, review lesson that when groups unite, they often unite symbols.	Focus lesson by recalling previous lesson on flags: (a) Ask what pupils remember. (b) Ask what the main point in the lesson was. (c) Repeat the main point of yesterday's lesson (if necessary).	See if pupils remember details. See if pupils remember the main generalization from yesterday's lesson. See who gives what responses. This checks comprehension.
3. Pupils focus on flag.	Say: "Today we shall study one of the flags used by the Revolutionists." Uncover "Colonial Colors" and "Union Jack."	

UNDERSTANDING

4. Pupils analyze flags and find likenesses exist because the "Continental Colors" contains a field composed of "Union Jack."	Ask: "In what ways are these two alike?"	Observe which pupils see organizational principles.
5. Pupils learn to see differences by seeing that the "Continental Colors" flag has thirteen stars and stripes.	Ask: "In what ways are these two different?"	On a later test present other pairs of flags, ask pupils to discuss differences.

UNDERSTANDING, *Continued*

Objectives	*Ways of Teaching*	*Evaluation*
6. Pupils interpret from given set of data, find that the thirteen stripes stand for the thirteen British colonies, and learn that the "Union Jack" indicated that colonists considered themselves British.	Ask: "What do you think this one ("Continental Colors") means or symbolizes?" See what they figure out—tell rest.	Check for interpretation and comprehension. Check at later date with an essay question on test.

REMEMBERING

7. Pupils form generalizations based upon the two lessons. They remember from yesterday's lessons that when groups unite, they unite symbols; in today's lesson, they see that when a group becomes disaffected with its "mother country" it may create new symbols to portray its identity.	Help pupils form generalizations.	Check which children form generalizations. See how pupils relate the main points of one lesson to the main points of another.
8. Pupils plan (or receive assignments) for follow-up experiences with work differentiated according to interests and abilities (individualized goals for particular pupils).	Plan with pupils (or give assignments) for future lessons. Differentiate work according to interest and abilities.	Evaluate or have pupils evaluate how they planned.

REMEMBERING, *Continued*

Possible individual or small-group goals	Possible ways of teaching individuals or small groups	Possible evaluation of individuals or small groups
Some pupils create own graphic ideas of new flags using information and concepts learned.	Create pictures of possible flags if two present political units were to unite. Create possible flag for our city or town if it were to secede from our state. Draw flags for our classroom.	Check products for application of information to "new" ideas. Observe pupils for free flow of creation or inhibited, restricted copying.
Some pupils write accounts of possible scenes in which flags were created.	Write imaginative account of the events and dialogue at the creation of a new flag.	The above, plus ability at synthesis.
Some pupils engage in independent research about other flags.	Do research on other political combinations and dissolutions w i t h special emphasis of how flags changed.	Observe pupils' research techniques. Hear or read reports to check knowledge and comprehension.
Some pupils display various flags with their stories.	Make a display of various flags of the American Revolution with their stories.	Have pupils evaluate the displays and how the class worked together.
9. Pupils enjoy reading.	Pupils read widely about flags.	Discuss with individual pupils what they are reading.

Summary and conclusion

LET US LOOK at the lesson plan presented in the last article in the light of the concepts developed in this book. As defined in the Preface, the *curriculum* is considered in terms of pupils' experiences. The curriculum lesson plan, then, is an outline of opportunities or possibilities for certain kinds of experiences we want pupils to have. The selections in Part One provided some guidelines for suggested school experiences. *Educational objectives* were discussed with respect to the kinds of cognitive, affective, social experiences which might help young people take their places as able citizens in a pluralistic nation, in a world of transcience, in a world of political change. Accordingly, this lesson plan provides possibilities for such thinking experiences as: comparing, making judgments, connecting ideas, and in addition provides for intellectual and social contact. The underlying goal is the class as a total group working productively on the topics at hand while the individuals achieve personal and intellectual challenge and satisfaction.

Part Two dealt with *ways of teaching*, which are fundamentally viewed as pupils' experiences with the methods and materials used in classrooms. In the lesson plan you see a variety of ways of teaching. It is unlikely that a teacher would use all the suggested activities noted in the plan in a single classroom episode. However, a teacher might well over-plan, that is, think of some additional learning possibilities in the event that some of his most cherished plans "just won't take" with his particular class on a particular day. Of course, this kind of emergency planning is needed less and less as a teacher learns how to create plans *with* his pupils. Part Two contained many ideas for creating plans for lessons and units. Remember the excellent sources for curriculum ideas suggested in many selections: curriculum guides, syllabi, textbooks, teachers' manuals, free materials, other teachers, and pupils.

Part Three was a brief review of possible pupil experiences, with emphasis upon the various so-called *subjects* generally used as a focus for these learning experiences. As you look at the lesson plan presented here, you may certainly think of many other language experiences which might have been planned. Similarly, you may readily see how many of the other concepts discussed in Part Three might also have been appropriate. Excellent professional books are devoted to each of the subject matter areas discussed in Part Three. Be sure to have a look at some of them. I hope, too, that you become better acquainted with some of the fine professional journals specializing in the areas of study which were introduced in Part Three.

Underlying my planning for Part Four was the following notion: As we seem to evaluate whether we intend to or not, why not design a scheme to do it in an orderly, professional way? Of course, we should not try to compress the many methods of *evaluation* into the plan for a single lesson. But we should recognize that the way we evaluate reflects what we value, and certainly we should value more than mere parroting of prefabricated information. In this lesson plan we see some formal and some informal ways to evaluate knowledge, attitudes, social behavior, and scholarship skills.

The *issues* presented in Part Five represent but a few of the important issues which we citizens and educators must face. These issues are being intelligently discussed in some communities and rather brutally fought over in others, and they absorb much of educators' time, talents, and efforts. School systems in the communities where you live or work will do one or more of the following: devise different ways to group pupils, create special programs, experiment with different organizational patterns, or try to integrate different racial and ethnic groups. These final chapters are intended to help you make wise decisions when these issues and problems come up in your community. It seems to me that a teacher who is well informed about social and professional issues is better able to help pupils study about groups in the past and try to understand something of the behavior of man today.

Regardless of what administrative scheme follows the resolution (or avoidance) of some of these issues, a teacher in his classroom is responsible for literally hundreds of curriculum decisions. As we start to plan a lesson, we must remember that our decisions may turn pupils toward or away from scholarship and influence their feelings of respect for themselves and other people. (It is a wiser course for example, to help pupils understand that the British and the colonists were neither devils nor angels but men and women of their time, reacting in ways which were valid for them.) We can fill pupils' lives with trivia or we can try to help pupils encounter intellectually and personally significant learning episodes in their studies. While it is true that many other forces influence pupils' experiences, it is also true that what we decide to do in our own classrooms is a fundamental influence on pupils.

From the decisions we make and the ways we make them, children learn to see an image of themselves. I would hope that from our plans, from our curriculum decisions, young people might learn to see their own worth, their own humanity—what Goethe called *personalitait*—and help to build a world where everyone might live with dignity and hope.

Selected Bibliography

Part I

Association for Supervision and Curriculum Development. *Perceiving, Behaving, Becoming: a New Focus for Education.* Washington: National Education Association. 1962.

Bennis, W. G., Benne, K., and Chin, R. (eds.). *The Planning of Change: Readings in the Applied Behavioral Sciences.* New York: Holt, Rinehart and Winston. 1961.

Bronowski, J. *Science and Human Values.* New York: Harper & Brothers. 1956.

Haan, A. *Education for the Open Society.* Boston: Allyn and Bacon, Inc. 1962.

Kelley, E. C. *Education for What Is Real.* New York: Harper & Brothers. 1947.

Murphy, G. *Freeing Intelligence Through Teaching.* John Dewey Lectureship Series. New York: Harper & Brothers. 1961.

Sexton, F. *Education and Income: Inequalities of Opportunity in Our Public Schools.* New York: Viking Press. 1961.

Sheviakov, G. V., and Redl, F. *Discipline for Today's Children and Youth.* Washington: Association for Supervision and Curriculum Development, N.E.A. 1956.

Stiles, L. J. (ed.). *The Teacher's Role in American Society.* Fourteenth Yearbook of the John Dewey Society. New York: Harper & Brothers. 1957.

Part II

Arbuthnot, M. H. *Children and Books.* Chicago: Scott, Foresman & Co. 1957.

Baker, E. V. *Children's Questions and Their Implications for Planning the Curriculum.* New York: Bureau of Publications, Teachers College, Columbia University. 1945.

Bingham, A. *Improving Children's Facility in Problem Solving.* New York: Bureau of Publications, Teachers College, Columbia University. 1963.

Darrow, H. F., and Van Allen, R. *Independent Activities for Creative Learning.* New York: Bureau of Publications, Teachers College, Columbia University. 1961.

Davis, D. C. *Patterns of Primary Education.* New York: Harper & Row. 1963.

Educational Policies Commission. *Education for All American Children.* Washington: National Education Association. 1948.

Elam, S. (ed.). *New Dimensions for Educational Progress: a Phi Delta Kappa Symposium Report.* Bloomington, Ind.: Phi Delta Kappa. 1963.

Gwynn, J. M. *Curriculum Principles and Social Trends.* New York: The Macmillan Company. 1960.

Hullfish, H. G., and Smith, P. G. *Reflective Thinking: the Method of Education.* New York: Dodd, Mead & Co., Inc. 1961.

Larrick, N. *Teacher's Guide to Children's Books.* Columbus, Ohio: Charles E. Merrill Books, Inc. 1960.

Leonard, E. M., Van Deman, D. D., and Miles, L. E. A philosophy toward selective homework. *Foundations of Learning in Childhood Education.* Columbus, Ohio: Charles E. Merrill Books, Inc. 1963. Part 10.

Miel, A. (ed.). *Creativity in Teaching: Invitations and Instances.* Belmont, Calif.: Wadsworth Publishing Company. 1961.

National Education Association. *Schools of the Sixties.* A report of the project on instruction. New York: McGraw-Hill Book Company, Inc. 1963.

National Society for the Study of Education. *Individualizing Instruction.* Sixty-first Yearbook. Part I. Chicago: the Society. 1962.

Nelson, L. W. *Instructional Aids: How to Make and Use Them.* Dubuque, Iowa: Wm. C. Brown Company, Publishers. 1958.

Smith, B. O., Stanley, W. O., and Shores, J. H. *Fundamentals of Curriculum Development.* Yonkers-on-Hudson, N.Y.: World Book Company. 1957.

Taba, H. *Curriculum Development: Theory and Practice.* New York: Harcourt, Brace & World. 1963.

Wann, K. D., Dorn, M. S., and Liddle, E. A. *Fostering Intellectual Development in Young Children.* New York: Bureau of Publications, Teachers College, Columbia University. 1962.

Wittich, W. A., and Schuller, C. F. *Audiovisual Materials: Their Nature and Use.* New York: Harper & Brothers. 1962.

Part III

Benezet, L. P. Story of an experiment. *NEA Journal.* 24:241-44, November, 1935; 24:301-3, December, 1935; 25:6-7, January, 1936.

Blough, G. O., and Schwartz, J. *Elementary School Science and How to Teach It.* New York: Holt, Rinehart & Winston, Inc. 1964.

Brogan, P., and Fox, L. *Helping Children Read.* New York: Holt, Rinehart & Winston, Inc. 1961.

Bryce, M. J., and Green, H. B. *Teacher's Craft Manual: a Handbook for Teachers.* San Francisco: Fearon Publishers. 1955.

Center for School Experimentation. *Developing the Language of Children from Poor Backgrounds.* Talent Development Project, Bulletin No. Two, 1961. Columbus: College of Education, Ohio State University.

Cole, N. R. *The Arts in the Classroom.* New York: The John Day Company, 1940.

Dawson, M. A., Zollinger, M., and Elwell, A. *Guiding Language Learning.* New York: Harcourt, Brace & World, Inc. 1963.

Deighton, L. C. *Vocabulary Development in the Classroom.* New York: Bureau of Publications, Teachers College, Columbia University. 1959.

Downing, J. *The Initial Teaching Alphabet.* New York: The Macmillan Company. 1964.

Erdt, M. H. *Teaching Art in the Elementary School.* New York: Holt, Rinehart & Winston. 1962.

Gillham, H. L. *Helping Children Accept Themselves and Others.* New York: Bureau of Publications, Teachers College, Columbia University. 1959.

Gross, R. E. *How To Handle Controversial Issues.* How-To-Do-It Series, No. 14. National Council for the Social Studies. Washington: the Council, N.E.A.

Haan, A. *Elementary School Curriculum: Theory and Research.* Boston: Allyn and Bacon, Inc. 1961.

Harris, A. J. *Effective Teaching of Reading.* New York: David McKay, Inc. 1962.

Hartley, R. E., Frank, L. K., and Goldenson, R. *Understanding Children's Play.* New York: Columbia University Press. 1952.

Humphrey, J. H., Johnson, W. R., and Moore, V. D. *Elementary School Health Education.* New York: Harper & Brothers. 1962.

Jarolimek, J. *Social Studies in Elementary Education.* New York: The Macmillan Company. 1963.

Lowenfeld, V. *Creative and Mental Growth.* New York: The Macmillan Company. 1964.

Mearns, H. *Creative Youth: How a School Environment Sets Free the Creative Spirit.* Garden City, N.Y.: Doubleday, Page & Company. 1925.

——. *Creative Power.* New York: Dover Publications. 1958.

Miel, A., and Brogan, P. *More Than Social Studies: a View of Social Learning in the Elementary School.* Englewood Cliffs, N. J.: Prentice-Hall, Inc. 1957.

National Council for the Social Studies. *Citizenship in a Free Society.* Thirtieth Yearbook. Washington: the Council. 1960.

——. *Skill Development in Social Studies.* Thirty-third Yearbook. Washington: The Council. 1963.

National Council of Teachers of Mathematics. *Enrichment Mathematics for the Grades.* Twenty-seventh Yearbook. Washington: The Council. 1963.

National Society for the Study of Education. *Social Studies in the Elementary School.* Fifty-sixth Yearbook. Part II. Chicago: The Society. 1957.

——. *Basic Concepts in Music Education.* Fifty-seventh Yearbook. Part I. Chicago: The Society. 1958.

Parker, W. R. *The National Interest and Foreign Languages.* Washington: U. S. National Commission for UNESCO. 1957.

Pearson, C. E. *A Classroom Teacher's Guide to Physical Education.* New York: Bureau of Publications, Teachers College, Columbia University. 1962.

Peck, R. F., and Mitchell, J. V., Jr. *Mental Health.* Washington: National Educational Association. 1962.

Polya, G. *Mathematical Discovery on Understanding: Learning and Teaching Problem Solving.* New York: John Wiley and Sons, Inc. 1962.

Pronovost, W. *The Teaching of Speaking and Listening in the Elementary School.* New York: Longmans, Green & Co. 1959.

Salem, D. *Science Experiments for New Elementary School Teachers.* Valley Stream, N.Y.: Teachers Practical Press, Inc. 1961.

Smith, N. B. *Graded Selections for Informal Reading Diagnosis: Grades Four Through Six.* New York: New York University Press. 1963.

Spache, G. D. *Good Reading for Poor Readers.* Champaign, Ill.: Garrand Press. 1962.

Tooze, R. *Story Telling.* Englewood Cliffs, N. J.: Prentice-Hall, Inc. 1959.

——, and Krone, B. P. *Literature and Music as Resources for Social Studies.* Englewood Cliffs, N. J.: Prentice-Hall, Inc. 1955.

UNESCO. *700 Science Experiments for Everyone.* New York: Doubleday & Co. 1958.

Ward, W. *Drama with and for Children.* Washington: U. S. Department of Health, Education, and Welfare. Bulletin No. 30. 1960.

Part IV

Austin, M. C., Bush, C. L., and Huebner, M. H. *Reading Evaluation: Appraisal Techniques for School and Classroom*. New York: The Ronald Press. 1961.

Cohen, D., and Stern, V. *Observing and Recording the Behavior of Young Children*. New York: Bureau of Publications, Teachers College, Columbia University. 1962.

D'Evelyn, K. E. *Individual Parent-Teacher Conferences: a Manual for Teachers of Young Children*. New York: Bureau of Publications, Teachers College, Columbia University. 1963.

Driscoll, G. *How to Study the Behavior of Children*. New York: Bureau of Publications, Teachers College, Columbia University. 1956.

Green, J. A., Jr. *Teacher-Made Tests*. New York: Harper & Row. 1963.

National Council of Teachers of Mathematics. *Selected Items for the Testing of Study Skills and Critical Thinking*. Washington: The Council. 1959.

National Society for the Study of Education. *The Measurement of Understanding*. Forty-fifth Yearbook. Part I. Chicago: The Society. 1946.

————. *The Impact and Improvement of School Teaching Programs*. Sixty-second Yearbook. Part II. Chicago: The Society. 1963.

Thorndike, R. L., and Hagen, E. P. *Measurement and Evaluation in Psychology and Education*. New York: John Wiley & Sons, Inc. 1961.

Part V

Brown, S. *They See for Themselves*. New York: Harper & Brothers. 1945.

Criteria for assessing programed instructional materials. *Audiovisual Instruction*. 8:84-89. February, 1963.

Crow, L. D., and Crow, A. (eds.). *Educating the Academically Able*. New York: David McKay Company, Inc. 1963.

Davis, A. *Social Class Influence upon Learning*. Cambridge, Mass.: Harvard University Press. 1949.

Deterline, W. A. *An Introduction to Programed Instruction*. Englewood Cliffs, N.J.: Prentice-Hall, Inc. 1962.

Dewey, J. *Logic: The Theory of Inquiry*. New York: Henry Holt & Co. 1938.

Dunn, R. (ed.). *Exceptional Children in the Schools*. New York: Holt, Rinehart & Winston. 1963.

Eash, M. J. Grouping: what have we learned? *Educational Leadership*. 18:429-34. April, 1961.

Education of exceptional children. *Review of Educational Research*. 33:1-138. February, 1963.

Fen, Sing-Nan. The learning of social relations in school. *Journal of Negro Education*. 32:87-91. Winter, 1963.

Hosic, J. F. *The Cooperative Group Plan: Working Principles for the Organization of Elementary Schools*. New York: Bureau of Publications, Teachers College, Columbia University. 1929.

Nagel, E. *The Structure of Science: Problems in the Logic of Scientific Explanation*. New York: Harcourt, Brace & World. 1961.

Scheifele, M. *The Gifted Child in the Regular Classroom*. New York: Bureau of Publications, Teachers College, Columbia University. 1953.

Taba, H., and Elkins, D. *With Focus on Human Relations: the Story of an Eighth Grade*. Washington: American Council of Education. 1950.

Index